The Duke Ellington Reader

The
Duke Ellington
Reader

Edited by Mark Tucker

OXFORD UNIVERSITY PRESS

New York   Oxford

Oxford University Press

Oxford   New York
Athens   Auckland   Bangkok   Bombay
Calcutta   Cape Town   Dar es Salaam   Delhi
Florence   Hong Kong   Istanbul   Karachi
Kuala Lumpur   Madras   Madrid   Melbourne
Mexico City   Nairobi   Paris   Singapore
Taipei   Tokyo   Toronto

and associated companies in
Berlin   Ibadan

First published in 1993 by Oxford University Press, Inc.,
198 Madison Avenue, New York, New York 10016-4314

First issued as an Oxford University Press paperback, 1995

Oxford is a registered trademark of Oxford University Press

Library of Congress Cataloging-in-Publication Data
The Duke Ellington reader / edited by Mark Tucker.
p.   cm.   Includes bibliographical references and index.
ISBN 0-19-505410-5
ISBN 0-19-509391-7 (pbk.)
1. Ellington, Duke, 1899–1974—Criticism and interpretation.
2. Jazz—History and criticism.   I. Tucker, Mark, 1954–
II. Ellington, Duke, 1899–1974.
ML410.E44D84   1992   781.65′092—dc20   92-37233   MN

The following pages are considered an extension of the copyright page.

4   6   8   10   9   7   5

Printed in the United States of America
on acid-free paper

For Helen and Stanley Dance

Contents

Introduction   *xvii*

I. Early Years (1899–1927)   3

1. Ellington on Washington, D.C. (1973)   *5*
2. The Washingtonians: First New York Review (1923)   *21*
3. Reviews from the Kentucky Club (1925)   *22*
4. The Washingtonians "Set New England Dance Crazy" (1927)   *24*

II. Cotton Club Bandleader (1927–1932)   29

5. First Cotton Club Review (1927)   *31*
6. R. D. Darrell: Criticism in the *Phonograph
   Monthly Review* (1927–1931)   *33*
7. Abbé Niles on Ellington (1929)   *40*
8. Two Early Interviews (1930)   *41*
   Janet Mabie in the *Christian Science Monitor*   *42*
   Florence Zunser in the *New York Evening Graphic*   *44*
9. Ellington's First Article: "The Duke Steps Out" (1931)   *46*
10. The Ellington Orchestra in Cleveland (1931)   *50*
11. Ellington Crowned "King of Jazz" by
    the *Pittsburgh Courier* (1931)   *54*
12. A Landmark in Ellington Criticism:
    R. D. Darrell's "Black Beauty" (1932)   *57*

III. First Trip Abroad (1933)   67

13. Spike Hughes: Impressions of Ellington in New York (1933)   *69*
14. Spike Hughes: "Meet the Duke!" (1933)   *72*
15. Ellington at the Palladium (1933)   *75*
16. On the Air in London (1933)   *78*
17. Ellington Defends His Music (1933)   *80*
18. Hugues Panassié: "Duke Ellington at the Salle Pleyel" (1946)   *81*
19. Ellington: "My Hunt for Song Titles" (1933)   *87*

IV. Into the Swing Era (1933–1942)   91

20. Wilder Hobson: "Introducing Duke Ellington" (1933)   *93*
21. The "Secret" of the Ellington Orchestra (1933)   *98*

22. Warren W. Scholl: Profile of Ellington in
the *Music Lovers' Guide* (1934)   *102*
23. Roger Pryor Dodge on *Black and Tan Fantasy,* from "Harpsichords
and Jazz Trumpets" (1934)   *105*
24. Constant Lambert on Ellington (1934)   *110*
25. Ellington's Response to Lambert (1935)   *112*
26. Ellington on Gershwin's *Porgy and Bess*—and a Response from the
Office of Irving Mills (1935/1936)   *114*
27. John Hammond: "The Tragedy of Duke Ellington" (1935)   *118*
28. Enzo Archetti: "In Defense of Ellington and His
'Reminiscing in Tempo'" (1936)   *121*
29. Helen Oakley (Dance): The Ellington Orchestra at
the Apollo (1936)   *125*
30. R. D. Darrell: Ellington in an Encyclopedia (1936)   *127*
31. "Ellington Refutes Cry That Swing Started
Sex Crimes!" (1937)   *128*
32. Aaron Copland on Ellington (1938)   *130*
33. Ellington: "From Where I Lie" (1938)   *131*
34. Ellington in *Down Beat:* On Swing and Its Critics (1939)   *132*
35. The Parting of Ellington and Irving Mills (1939)   *140*
36. Wilder Hobson on Ellington, from *Jazzmen* (1939)   *141*
37. A Celebrity Interview (1941)   *143*
38. Ellington: "We, Too, Sing 'America'" (1941)   *146*
39. Interview in Los Angeles: On *Jump for Joy,* Opera, and
Dissonance as a "Way of Life" (1941)   *148*

V. *Black, Brown and Beige* (1943)   *153*

40. Previews of the First Carnegie Hall Concert (1943)   *155*
Helen Oakley (Dance) in *Down Beat*   *155*
Howard Taubman in the *New York Times Magazine*   *158*
41. Program for the First Carnegie Hall Concert
(23 January 1943)   *160*
42. Two Reviews (1943)   *165*
Paul Bowles in the *New York Herald-Tribune*   *165*
Mike Levin in *Down Beat*   *166*
43. The Debate in *Jazz* (1943)   *170*
John Hammond: "Is the Duke Deserting Jazz?"   *171*
Leonard Feather: Leonard Feather Rebuts Hammond   *173*
Bob Thiele: "The Case of Jazz Music"   *175*
44. *Black, Brown and Beige* in a List of
"Classical Records" (1946)   *178*
45. Robert D. Crowley: "*Black, Brown and Beige*
After 16 Years" (1959)   *179*
46. Brian Priestley and Alan Cohen:
"Black, Brown & Beige" (1974–1975)   *185*

VI. The Hot Bach (1943–1949)   *205*

47. Ellington's "Defense of Jazz" (1943/1944)   *207*
48. Carnegie Revisited (1943/1944)   *209*
49. Richard O. Boyer: "The Hot Bach" (1944)   *214*
50. Ellington: "Certainly It's Music!" (1944)   *246*
51. Ellington: "Swing Is My Beat!" (1944)   *248*
52. An Ellington Solo Piano Transcription in *Down Beat* (1944)   *250*
53. "Why Duke Ellington Avoided Music Schools" (1945)   *252*
54. "Interpretations in Jazz:
        A Conference with Duke Ellington" (1947)   *255*
55. Alec Wilder on Ellington (1948)   *258*

VII. The Fifties   *263*

56. Ellington's Silver Jubilee in *Down Beat* (1952)   *265*
    Ellington on Career Highlights   *265*
    Lists of Favorites   *268*
    Billy Strayhorn: "The Ellington Effect"   *269*
    Ned Williams on "Early Ellingtonia"   *271*
    Irving Mills: "I Split with Duke When
        Music Began Sidetracking"   *274*
57. André Hodeir: "A Masterpiece: *Concerto for Cootie*" (1954)   *276*
58. An African View of Ellington (1955)   *289*
59. George Avakian: Ellington at Newport (1956)   *290*
60. Ellington: "The Race for Space" (*ca.* late 1957)   *293*
61. André Hodeir: "Why Did Ellington 'Remake'
        His Masterpiece?" (1958)   *297*
62. Selections from *The Jazz Review* (1959)   *302*
    Mimi Clar: "The Style of Duke Ellington"   *303*
    Quincy Jones on *Newport 1958*   *311*
    Max Harrison on *Anatomy of a Murder*   *313*

VIII. The Late Years (1960–1974)   *317*

63. Irving Townsend: "When Duke Records" (1960)   *319*
64. Ellington: "Where Is Jazz Going?" (1962)   *324*
65. Pete Welding: "On the Road with
        the Duke Ellington Orchestra" (1962)   *326*
66. Ellington with Stanley Dance:
        "The Art Is in the Cooking" (1962)   *332*
67. Ellington on the Air in Vancouver (1962)   *338*
68. Eddie Lambert: "Duke Ellington—1963" (1963)   *342*
69. A. J. Bishop: "Duke's *Creole Rhapsody*" (1963)   *347*
70. Dan Morgenstern on *The Ellington Era* (1963)   *350*

71. A. J. Bishop: "'Reminiscing in Tempo':
     A Landmark in Jazz Composition" (1964)   *355*
72. Ellington: "Reminiscing in Tempo" (1964)   *358*
73. Nat Hentoff: "This Cat Needs No Pulitzer Prize" (1965)   *362*
74. Ellington: "The Most Essential Instrument" (1965)   *368*
75. Ellington: Program Note for "A Concert of
     Sacred Music" (1965)   *371*
76. Rex Stewart at a Recording Session for the First
     Sacred Concert (1966)   *373*
77. Gary Giddins on the Sacred Concerts (1975)   *375*
78. Gary Giddins on *The Afro-Eurasian Eclipse* (1976)   *379*
79. Stanley Dance: "The Funeral Address" (1974)   *381*

IX. **Selected Commentary and Criticism (1964–1993)**   *385*

80. Max Harrison: "Some Reflections on Ellington's Longer Works"
     (1964; revised 1991)   *387*
81. Ralph Ellison: "Homage to Duke Ellington on
     His Birthday" (1969)   *394*
82. Martin Williams: "Form Beyond Form"
     (1970; revised 1983, 1993)   *400*
83. Albert Murray: From *The Hero and the Blues* (1973)   *412*
84. Gunther Schuller: "Ellington in the Pantheon" (1974)   *414*
85. Gunther Schuller: "The Case for Ellington's Music as
     Living Repertory" (1974)   *418*
86. Lawrence Gushee: "Duke Ellington 1940" (1978)   *421*
87. Stanley Crouch on *Such Sweet Thunder, Suite Thursday,*
     and *Anatomy of a Murder* (1988)   *439*

X. **Ellingtonians**   *447*

88. Helen Oakley (Dance):
     "Impressions of Johnny Hodges" (1936)   *449*
89. "The Duke Ellingtons—Cotton Clubbers En Masse" (1937)   *451*
90. Roger Pryor Dodge on Bubber Miley (1940)   *454*
91. Ivie Anderson (1942)   *458*
92. Reactions of a Newcomer: Al Sears Interviewed by
     George T. Simon (1944)   *460*
93. Inez M. Cavanaugh: Three Interviews (1945)   *462*
     Otto Hardwick   *462*
     "Tricky Sam" Nanton   *465*
     Rex Stewart   *468*
94. Double Play: Harry Carney and Johnny Hodges Interviewed
     by Don DeMichael (1962)   *471*
95. Rex Stewart: "Illustrious Barney Bigard" (1966)   *476*
96. Guitarist Freddy Guy Interviewed by
     John McDonough (1969)   *481*

97. Sonny Greer Interviewed by Whitney Balliett (1974)   486
98. Gary Giddins on Paul Gonsalves (1985)   491
99. Stanley Crouch on Ben Webster (1986)   493
100. Billy Strayhorn Interviewed by Bill Coss (1962)   498
101. Ellington: "Eulogy for Swee' Pea" (1967)   504

     Topical Index of Selections   505
     General Index   509

Introduction

Among twentieth-century musicians, Edward Kennedy "Duke" Ellington (1899–1974) is a figure well known and highly regarded. Today, nearly twenty years after his death, his compositions remain popular, enjoyed by listeners throughout the world, championed by performers, and acclaimed by critics. Many of his recordings are still available, with companies in the United States and abroad steadily reissuing old collections and coming out with previously unreleased material. College and conservatory students, meanwhile, increasingly encounter Ellington in their classes and textbooks, and they are learning to play the music on the bandstand, often from scores painstakingly transcribed from recordings. Enthusiasts in North America and Europe belong to societies, receive newsletters, and attend annual conferences devoted to Ellington. And since 1988 scholars have begun exploring the rich collection of Ellington manuscripts, sketches, full scores, and orchestral parts housed in the Archives Center of the Smithsonian's National Museum of American History in Washington, D.C.

While interest in Ellington has accelerated in recent years, it has a long history. In the late twenties and early thirties, some critics and composers recognized the unique qualities of his music and praised his ensemble. As Ellington traveled with his orchestra across the globe and as his records reached ever-greater numbers of listeners, a vast literature grew up around the man and his music—from biographies, critical essays, feature articles, and reviews to memoirs and oral histories, even fiction and poetry. This literature has steadily expanded over the past two decades, reflecting both a higher regard for Ellington's compositional achievements and a stronger commitment—especially on the part of scholars—to studying African American musical traditions.

This volume arose from the need for a source book of writings on Ellington. Appearing over a span of seventy years and in widely scattered publications—many out of print or long forgotten—the selections included here give first-hand accounts of Ellington's life and art, drawing upon the words of those who knew the man, heard the orchestra in person, or simply admired the music from afar. Taken together they trace the contours of Ellington's career, touching on important events and works whenever possible, seeking to give a balanced overview of his life as composer and performer, as public personality and private individual.

Mixed in with the writings of others are roughly a dozen articles by Ellington himself. The earliest, "The Duke Steps Out," appeared in 1931 in the British periodical *Rhythm*. The latest is Ellington's account of growing up in

Washington, D.C., taken from *Music Is My Mistress,* his memoirs published in 1973.[1] With Ellington's prose it is sometimes difficult to gauge how much he wrote himself or how much an editor or collaborator may have supplied. *Music Is My Mistress* seems to have been entirely his own work; at least portions of the manuscript now among his papers at the Smithsonian Institution support his authorship. Yet Ellington was also known to call upon others for literary assistance, two examples being Helen Oakley Dance in the thirties and early forties and Patricia Willard in the fifties. Even if some of the articles under Ellington's byline were co-written or heavily edited by others, they still hold interest as biographical documents, revealing the image he shaped for the public.

The selections included here have been chosen for different reasons. Some have great historic importance, such as R. D. Darrell's "Black Beauty" (1932), the first significant critical essay on Ellington's music. Well-known writers on jazz are represented—among them Hugues Panassié, André Hodeir, Stanley Dance, Max Harrison, Gunther Schuller, Martin Williams, Gary Giddins, and Stanley Crouch—together with such composer-critics as Aaron Copland, Constant Lambert, and Alec Wilder. There are a number of hard-to-locate curiosities, such as Ellington's remarks on Gershwin's *Porgy and Bess* in 1935 and impressions of the Ellington orchestra in 1950 from a novel by the Senegalese author Ousmane Socé. While reviews of performances and recordings are scattered throughout, no attempt has been made to give a thorough chronicle of criticism about Ellington. Instead, I have tried to suggest highlights from each decade, a task made challenging both by the size and quality of Ellington's output. As a result, the volume is highly selective, and certain worthy articles simply could not be accommodated. Above all, though, I have looked for examples of expressive writing that illuminate Ellington's work and reveal the profound impact his music has made on listeners over the years.

Those who read the selections in sequence will note the shift in tone that occurs over the decades, as later writers begin to take Ellington—and jazz in general—much more seriously than their predecessors had done in the twenties and thirties. The flip, frothy style of the early reviews, for example, and the patronizing praise of the composer Constant Lambert gradually give way to veneration and judicious evaluation in the writings of Ralph Ellison, Albert Murray, and Lawrence Gushee. Readers will also discover that, with few exceptions, Ellington's works do not begin to receive extensive analytical treatment until the fifties and sixties, with the appearance of essays by André Hodeir, A. J. Bishop, and Max Harrison, among others. It took American musicologists even longer to enter the field of Ellington studies, owing to the slow process of integrating jazz into the curriculum and validating it as a field of inquiry.

If a single theme resurfaces in this book, it is the struggle Ellington waged against those bent on categorizing him and his music. Writings from the thir-

---

[1] Complete bibliographic information for standard sources on Ellington appears at the end of the introduction.

ties point to the beginning of this conflict, when certain of his works exceeded the length of most recorded jazz and popular music—roughly three minutes, or the length of one side of a 78-rpm recording. Attacks came from both classical-music critics and jazz writers: the former claimed he did not measure up to standards set by European composers, the latter accused him of forsaking his musical roots and abandoning his function as a dance-band leader. But most of the controversy centered around *Reminiscing in Tempo* (1935) and *Black, Brown and Beige* (1943). Articles on the reception of these works show the recurring predicament faced by jazz and popular musicians who seek to push beyond the conventions of their art.

The book falls into three sections: Parts I to VIII survey Ellington's life and music, from the early years in Washington, D.C., to the seventies; Part IX, "Selected Commentary and Criticism," features statements by important writers on Ellington from the last three decades; Part X, "Ellingtonians," focuses on some of the orchestra's notable performers and personalities. Within each of these divisions, selections usually appear in chronological order, according to publication date. The chronology is broken occasionally, however, either to fill gaps in the literature or to broaden the view of a piece or period (for example, Part V on *Black, Brown and Beige* goes beyond 1943 to consider later evaluations of the work).

Brief introductions to each part provide biographical and historical background for the sections that follow. Similarly, each selection is preceded by comments on the circumstances of publication and available information about the author.

Some selections have been abridged to avoid either redundancy or inaccuracy. Newspaper and magazine feature pieces, for example, routinely included summaries of Ellington's life and career. Often cribbed from publicity materials, many of these contained factual errors and have been omitted here (indicated by ellipses in the text). Biographical descriptions have been left intact, however, if they formed an essential component of a piece or revealed contemporary perceptions of Ellington.

Most of the footnotes in the volume have been supplied by the editor, with the aim of clarifying or correcting information in the text; these are always designated by Arabic numerals. In the relatively few cases when footnotes appeared in the original source, these are indicated by asterisks or daggers.

Dates for compositions and recordings mentioned in the selections have been supplied only when necessary for clarifying the context. If further information is desired, readers should consult the comprehensive discography by W. E. Timner, *Ellingtonia: The Recorded Music of Duke Ellington and His Sidemen,* 3rd ed. (1988),[2] also the work lists in *Music Is My Mistress* and in

---

[2] A more detailed discography for collectors is the multi-volume *Duke Ellington's Story on Records,* 1–16 (Milan, 1966–83), by Luciano Massagli, Liborio Pusateri, and Giovanni M. Volontè, while Jerry Valburn's *The Directory of Duke Ellington's Recordings* (Hicksville, N.Y.: Marlor Productions, 1986) gives issue numbers for Ellington records released throughout the world.

Mercer Ellington with Stanley Dance, *Duke Ellington in Person: An Intimate Memoir* (1978).[3]

Although this is the first historical anthology of writings on Ellington, two earlier volumes of related interest should be mentioned. The first, *Duke Ellington: His Life and Music* (1958), edited by Peter Gammond, contains essays and appreciations by a number of British writers, among them Stanley Dance, Charles Fox, Raymond Horricks, and Burnett James. It also includes an abridged version of Richard O. Boyer's 1944 *New Yorker* profile, "The Hot Bach" (the complete text appears in the present volume). Of special interest in Gammond's book is a section by Jeff Aldam, "The Ellington Sidemen," which discusses outstanding band members and lists recordings featuring them. A selective discography surveys Ellington's recordings from the mid-twenties to 1957.

While Gammond's book offers primarily British perspectives on Ellington from the fifties, Stanley Dance's *The World of Duke Ellington* (1970) lets musicians speak in their own words. It features more than two dozen interviews with orchestra members and alumni, among them Billy Strayhorn, Mercer Ellington, Johnny Hodges, Sonny Greer, Barney Bigard, Cootie Williams, Lawrence Brown, and Ellington himself. Toward the end of the volume Dance adds a handful of his own articles on Ellington from the sixties, together with a selective discography and a chronology to 1970.

Most of the articles in this volume have not been reprinted before. Those appearing in previously published collections have been included, often with new annotations, to round out the coverage of topics. While some of the most incisive discussion of Ellington's music can be found in Gunther Schuller's *Early Jazz: Its Roots and Musical Development* (1968) and *The Swing Era: The Development of Jazz, 1930–1945* (1989), both the length of these selections and availability of these studies have made reprinting here unnecessary.

American and British authors dominate this collection, although half a dozen pieces originated in France and Canada. I regret not representing other countries where Ellington performed and where interest in his music runs high—especially Italy, Japan, Australia, parts of Scandinavia and Latin America. But that would have yielded another volume, one that might be compiled from Ellington commentary published in different languages around the globe. Perhaps one day it will appear.

Because readers may want to consult different types of selections—whether general commentary, musical analysis, reviews, biographical profiles, or interviews—a Topical Index of Selections is provided.

In preparing this volume I received good advice and valuable assistance from many people, among them Ed Berger and Dan Morgenstern at the Institute of Jazz Studies at Rutgers University-Newark, Helen and Stanley Dance, Pryor Dodge, Alan Dutka, Gary Giddins, Max Harrison, H. Wiley Hitchcock at the

---

[3] See also Erik Wiedemann's informative article, which corrects and adds to information in these two sources, "Duke Ellington: The Composer," in *Annual Review of Jazz Studies 5*, ed. by Edward Berger, David Cayer, Dan Morgenstern, and Lewis Porter (Metuchen, N.J., and London: Institute of Jazz Studies and the Scarecrow Press, 1991), 37–64.

Institute for Studies in American Music at Brooklyn College, Sjef Hoefsmit, Brooks Kerr, Greg Leet, Kip Lornell, James T. Maher, Carol Oja, Art Pilkington, Brian Priestley, Jerry Valburn, and the late Martin Williams. I am especially indebted to Andrew Homzy and Steven Lasker for making many helpful suggestions and for generously sharing the results of their intensive research on Ellington's life and music. Nancy Pardo, Linda Morgan, and Brian Harker helped with manuscript preparation, while grants from Columbia University's Councils for Research in the Humanities and Social Sciences, the National Endowment for the Humanities, and the National Humanities Center (Research Triangle Park, North Carolina) made completion of the project possible. Thanks to Sheldon Meyer and Scott Lenz at Oxford University Press for their support and editorial savvy.

Finally, I am grateful to all the authors and individuals who answered queries and gave permission to reprint material in this volume.

The following sources are recommended for those interested in Ellington, with abbreviations appearing next to titles frequently cited in this volume:

Barney Bigard. *With Louis and the Duke,* edited by Barry Martyn. New York: Oxford University Press, 1986.

WDE   Stanley Dance. *The World of Duke Ellington.* 1970; rpt., New York: Da Capo, [1981].

MM   Duke Ellington. *Music Is My Mistress.* 1973; rpt., New York: Da Capo, 1976.

DEP   Mercer Ellington with Stanley Dance. *Duke Ellington in Person: An Intimate Memoir.* 1978: rpt., New York: Da Capo, 1979.

Peter Gammond. *Duke Ellington: His Life and Music.* 1958; rpt., New York: Da Capo, 1977.

Gunther Schuller. *Early Jazz: Its Roots and Musical Development.* New York: Oxford University Press, 1968.

———. *The Swing Era: The Development of Jazz, 1930–1945.* New York: Oxford University Press, 1989.

Rex Stewart. *Boy Meets Horn.* Ann Arbor: University of Michigan Press, 1991.

———. *Jazz Masters of the Thirties.* 1972; rpt., New York: Da Capo, [1982].

Klaus Stratemann. *Duke Ellington Day by Day and Film by Film.* Copenhagen: JazzMedia Aps, 1992.

ERMDE   W. E. Timner. *Ellingtonia: The Recorded Music of Duke Ellington and His Sidemen,* 3rd ed. Metuchen, N.J., and London: Institute of Jazz Studies and the Scarecrow Press, 1988.

ETEY   Mark Tucker. *Ellington: The Early Years.* Urbana and Chicago: University of Illinois Press, 1991.

DE   Barry Ulanov. *Duke Ellington.* 1946, 1947; rpt., New York: Da Capo, 1975.

The Duke Ellington Reader

I. Early Years (1899–1927)

uke Ellington spent much of his professional career in motion—traveling with his orchestra from one performance to the next, composing aboard trains and planes and in automobiles, and living out of suitcases in an endless series of hotel rooms as he took his music to audiences across the globe. This nomadic existence differed remarkably from what he had known as a child. For his first twenty-four years, Edward Kennedy Ellington stayed in one place: Washington, D.C. There he was born on 29 April 1899, delivered by a midwife named Eliza Jane Johnson at 2129 Ward Place, N.W., the home of his paternal grandparents. And there, surrounded by a tight-knit family and shaped by the strong individuals and institutions of the city's large African American community, his essential character took root.

Ellington's musical interests were slow to develop. As a teenager he first became serious about the piano and sought to emulate local ragtime pianists. Although poor music-reading skills led to dismissal from at least two large ensembles, he was able to play with small groups and eventually started booking jobs, sending out units under the name of Duke Ellington's Serenaders. By 1920, at the age of twenty-one, he earned enough as a musician to support his wife Edna (whom he had married in 1918) and son Mercer (b. 1919), although he also painted signs on the side.

But Ellington was hardly an advanced musician, much less a promising composer, when he moved to New York in 1923. He would spend the next several years honing his skills as a bandleader, songwriter, and pianist, learning how to function within New York's competitive musical scene, and seeking professional opportunities with publishers and record companies. During much of this time he led a band, the Washingtonians, at a Times Square nightspot called the Kentucky Club (earlier the Hollywood), and in the summers toured a circuit of New England ballrooms and dance halls.

On their first recordings, Ellington's Washingtonians sounded like many other New York dance bands of the mid-twenties. By 1926 and 1927, though, distinctive qualities appeared in such pieces as *East St. Louis Toodle-O, Immigration Blues, Black and Tan Fantasy,* and *Creole Love Call.* After a decade of study and apprenticeship, Ellington emerged an original.

1. Ellington
on Washington, D.C. (1973)

I n the opening section of his memoirs, *Music Is My Mistress* (1973), Ellington pays tribute to his family, discusses boyhood interests, and charts his progress as ragtime pianist—or "plunker"—and fledgling bandleader. Written near the end of his career, these recollections show a famous musician and public figure looking back at the past with gentle humor, nostalgia, and perhaps some idealization.

In describing Washington, Ellington stresses values inherited from his parents and absorbed in a black community that had produced many men and women of achievement. He also documents black Washington's rich musical life and profiles some of its leading figures, among them Louis Brown, Doc Perry, and Henry Grant.

The main family members in Ellington's account are his mother, Daisy Kennedy Ellington (1879–1935), his father, James Edward (J. E.) Ellington (1879–1937), and his sister, Ruth Dorothea Ellington (b. 1915). His maternal grandparents were Alice and James William Kennedy, his paternal grandparents Emma and James Ellington.

Because of the fact that no one else but my sister Ruth had a mother as great and as beautiful as mine, it is difficult to put into understandable words an accurate description of my mother, Daisy. My cousins called her Aunt Daisy, and that became the name by which everyone knew her. She called my father, Edd, although he was really James Edward Ellington. The kids in the family called him Uncle Ed, but to his closest friends and cronies he was always J. E.

When my parents were first married, they lived with my mother's mother, Mrs. [Alice] Kennedy. She was the wife of a District of Columbia policeman, a captain. I only remember him by his pictures, but Mamma, which is what we called my mother's mother, and my grandfather had ten children, five boys and five girls. Grandma was always surrounded by this flock of young girls, who, even after they were married, still came back to visit as though they lived there. It was a wonderfully warm family, and whatever one owned, they all felt they too owned a part of it—and that included me.

So I was pampered and pampered, and spoiled rotten by all the women in the family, aunts and cousins, but my mother never took her eyes off precious little me, her jewel, until I was four years old, when I proceeded to the front lawn with some authority to examine the rosebushes, stumbled over the lawn-mower, fell on a piece of broken milk bottle, and cut the fourth finger of my left hand. This, of course, was a major emergency that called for the whole

Source: "Washington," from *MM*, 6–36.

family to decide what should be done. The mark is still there, and I think I got pneumonia in the same year. My first awareness of how serious that was was when they called *two* doctors. There may have been more, because I know my mother wanted every doctor in Washington to come and work the miracle of saving her little child. She stayed at my bedside night and day until the fever broke. I couldn't speak, but I can still see her, kneeling, sitting, standing to lean over the bed, praying, and crying, "My own child doesn't even recognize me!" Obviously, her prayers brought me through, and back I raced to my grandmother's backyard, to the grape arbor that surrounded four pear trees, to play with her two dogs and my five little girl cousins. Since I had been sick, they allowed me to take complete charge of all situations and discussions. We used to climb the trees and have all kinds of adventures, imaginary and otherwise. Everybody called me Edward then.

When I was five years old my mother put my age up to six so that I could get into first grade at school.[1] She dressed me, and sent me off to school just a few blocks away. She didn't think I saw her, but I did, and every day she followed me, all the way to that school. After school, she was waiting for me at the front door of our home, if she wasn't waiting in front of the school door.

School went all right, I suppose, because I made my grades in spite of my enthusiasm for baseball. One day, a boy was demonstrating his skill at batting, and I turned around for some reason or other, and got hit with that bat— bam!—right in the back of the head. My mother saw it happen. She rushed into the street and rushed me off to the doctor's. It hurt at the moment, and I suppose the mark is still there, but I soon got over it. With this, however, my mother decided I should take piano lessons.

My piano teacher, Mrs. [Marietta] Clinkscales (that was really her name), got paid several times a week for many weeks for these lessons, but I missed more than I took, because of my enthusiasm for playing ball, and running and racing through the street. That I remember very well, because when she had her piano recital with all her pupils in the church, I was the only one who could not play his part. So Mrs. Clinkscales had to play the treble and I just played the umpy-dump bottom! The umpy-dump bottom was, of course, the foundation and understanding of that part of piano-playing I later learned to like. I would like to have learned it, too, because of its strong relationship with what the really outstanding pianists of that day were doing with their left hands. So later for that!

At this point, piano was not my recognized talent. Why, I thought, take it so seriously? After all, baseball, football, track, and athletics were what the real he-men were identified with, and so they were naturally the most impor- tant to me. Washington was in the American League and every day I had to see the game. The only way for me to do that was to get a job at the baseball park [Griffith Stadium]. I succeeded in getting one and had my first experience of stage fright. I had to walk around, in and out and in front of all those

[1] Ellington attended the Garnet Public School, on U Street between Vermont Avenue and 10th Street, N.W., from 1905 to 1908.

people, yelling, "Peanuts, popcorn, chewing gum, candy, cigars, cigarettes, and score cards!" I soon got over my nervousness, although the first day I missed a lot of the game hiding behind the stands. By the end of the season, I had been promoted to yelling, "Cold drinks, gents! Get 'em ice cold!" I was so crazy about baseball, it's a wonder I ever sold anything. The opportunity to walk around there, looking at all those baseball heroes, whose pictures were a premium in the cigarette packages, meant a lot to me.

There were many open lots around Washington then, and we used to play baseball at an old tennis court on Sixteenth Street. President Roosevelt would come by on his horse sometimes, and stop and watch us play. When he got ready to go, he would wave and we would wave at him. That was Teddy Roosevelt—just him and his horse, nobody guarding him.

My father had a job working as a butler for Dr. Cuthbert at 1462 on the south side of Rhode Island Avenue. I believe the house is still there.[2] The cook and the maid were under him, and he was the fellow who made the decisions around the house. The doctor was rather prominent socially, and he probably recommended my father for social functions, because my father also belonged to what you might call a circle of caterers. When he or one of his cronies got a gig, all the others would act as waiters. They hired good cooks and gave impeccable service. They even had a page, I remember, because one day something happened to the page and I had to stand in for him.

My father kept our house loaded with the best food obtainable, and because he was a caterer we had the primest steaks and the finest terrapin. But he insisted on baked chicken, macaroni and cheese on Sunday; baked beans and greens and cornbread on Wednesday; and on the other days there were special dishes that I've forgotten.

During World War I, he quit the butler job and rented a big house on K Street, in the fashionable area where all the suffragettes were. He rented out rooms, and continued as a caterer until he went to work on blueprints in the Navy Yard. He kept at that till he had trouble with arthritis in his knee.

J. E. always acted as though he had money, whether he had it or not. He spent and lived like a man who had money, and he raised his family as though he were a millionaire. The best had to be carefully examined to make sure it was good enough for my mother. Maybe he was richer than a millionaire? I'm not sure that he wasn't.

My mother came to New York first. She came to see me at the Ziegfeld Theatre in 1929, and came back to live in 1930. We finally got J. E. to come the following year. All the standing he had to do while making blueprints was not good for his arthritis, but he kept insisting he had to work. "What am I going to do?" he kept asking. "There's nothing up there for me to do." So when he finally arrived, I told him I had a job for him. I handed him a fountain pen, and said, "You're my social secretary."

My mother, as I said before, was beautiful, but my father was only handsome. While my mother had graduated from high school, I don't think my

[2] J. E. worked for Dr. Middleton F. Cuthbert from about 1897 to 1917. The house on Rhode Island Avenue is no longer there.

father even finished eighth grade. Yet his vocabulary was what I always hoped mine would be. In fact, I have always wanted to be able to be and talk like my pappy. He was a party man, a great dancer (ballroom, that is), a connoisseur of vintages, and unsurpassed in creating an aura of conviviality. When I first went to Europe on the *Olympic* in 1933, I felt so *au fait* with all that silverware on the table. He had told me a gentleman never had any problem selecting the proper fork, spoon, or knife, and he had made sure I knew which to use.

He was also a wonderful wit, and he knew exactly what to say to a lady—high-toned or honey-homey. I wrote a song later with a title suggested by one of those sayings he would address to a lady worth telling she was pretty. "Gee, you make that hat look pretty," he would say. He was very sensitive to beauty, and he respected it with proper gentility, never overdoing or underdoing it. He would never scratch a lady's charisma or injure her image. "Pretty," he used to say, "can only get prettier, but beauty compounds itself."

Whatever place he was in, he had appropriate lines. "The millions of beautiful snowflakes are a celebration in honor of your beauty," he declared in Canada. Complexions were compared to the soft and glorious sunsets in California. In the Midwest, he saw the Mississippi as a swift messenger rushing to the sea to announce the existence of a wave of unbelievably compelling force caused by the rebirth of Venus. In New York and on the East Coast, he spoke about "pretty being pretty, but not that pretty." Sometimes he would attempt to sing a song of praise, and then apologize for the emotion that destroyed the control of his voice.

My mother started telling me about God when I was very young. There was never any talk about red people, brown people, black people, or yellow people, or about the differences that existed between them. I don't remember exactly when, but I was quite grown when I first heard about all that. I am sure my mother felt that God took some rich black soil, some red clay, and some white sand, and mixed them all together to make the first man, so that forever after no man would feel he was better than another.

She was mainly interested in knowing and understanding about God, and she painted the most wonderful word pictures of God. Every Sunday, she took me to at least two churches, usually to the Nineteenth Street Baptist, the church of her family, and to John Wesley A.M.E. Zion, my father's family church. It was never made clear to me that they were of different denominations, and to her, I'm sure, it did not matter. They both preached God, Jesus Christ, and that was the most important thing.

When I was old enough, I was sent off to Sunday School as well. I didn't understand it so much then in spite of the fact that it gave me a wonderful feeling of security. Believing gave me that. As though I were some very, very special child, my mother would say, "Edward, you are blessed. You don't have anything to worry about. Edward, you are blessed!"

Do I believe that I am blessed? Of course, I do! In the first place, my mother told me so, many, many times, and when she did it was always quietly, confidently. She was very soft-spoken, and I knew that anything she told me was true. No matter where I was, or what the conditions, my subconscious seemed very much aware of it. So until this day I really don't have any fears, beyond what I might do to hurt or offend someone else. There have been so many extraordinary and inexplicable circumstances in my life. I have always seemed to encounter the right people in the right places at the right time, and doing the right thing to give me the kind of instruction and guidance I needed.

My mother eventually began to trust me out of her sight with Sonny Ellington as my protector. His real name was William, and he was the son of my father's brother, John. Several years older than I, he was cousin, companion, advisor, bodyguard, and confidant. When we were kids, he used to give me a complete account of everything that was happening according to the sports magazines and *Police Gazette*. Sonny was a very good athlete. His baseball and track prowess were acknowledged by all the guys in the neighborhood, and the way things were going, I should have turned out to be a very good athlete too. Walking is, of course, very good training for athletes, and after church every Sunday he would take me for a little tour that meant walking to all extremes of the District of Columbia, to visit our relatives (like twenty-four aunts and uncles), who just happened to be the greatest bakers of cakes and freezers of ice cream. Aunt Laura was at Fifteenth and H, N.E., Aunt Ella in S.W., Aunt Emma in Georgetown, and so on.

I have never figured how far we walked, but as I look back on it now the distances were actually impossible. One day, out at the Chesapeake and the District line, I got carried away with enthusiasm or desire for some sort of confection, and spent the money that was to be for my carfare home. So we had to walk all the way back to Twelfth and T Streets, N.W. Several times he took me to Rock Creek Park to teach me to swim, but I never got around to taking off my clothes, and I never learned to swim. I just chased rabbits and squirrels, and expected to be a good athlete.

Sonny used to buy all the Western pulp magazines he could find. Uncle John and Aunt Hannah, his father and mother, forbade his reading them, but he'd take them into the bathroom and lock the door, or go into the woodshed, or into the park—anywhere where he could have isolation with the good and bad guys of those mighty Westerns, out of sight of all the objectors. When he finished reading them, he would hand them down to me, and I would go through the same procedure.

By the time I was eleven or twelve years old, I had read Sherlock Holmes, Cleek of Scotland Yard, and Arsène Lupin, and I knew all the literary burglar's theories as well as the murder devices. I knew how to mark cards, deal seconds, and recognize the proper hand position and decoy of pickpockets. Someone once said I'd have made a very good criminal lawyer, but I worry more about how well I would *not* have done as a criminal. What kind of music would I have written while locked up in those dingy old prison cells?

All through grade school, I had a genuine interest in drawing and painting, and I realized I had a sort of talent for them. My mother and father both encouraged me, and the piano was allowed to fade into the background. Our studies became a bit more serious in the eighth grade.[3] In addition to arithmetic, algebra, history, and English, which were taught as the most vital things in the world, my teacher—Miss Boston, the principal of the school—would explain the importance of proper speech. It would be most important in our lives to come. When we went out into the world, we would have the grave responsibility of being practically always on stage, for every time people saw a Negro they would go into a reappraisal of the race. She taught us that proper speech and good manners were our first obligations, because as representatives of the Negro race we were to command respect for our people. This being an all-colored school, Negro history was crammed into the curriculum, so that we would know our people all the way back. They had pride there, the greatest race pride, and at that time there was some sort of movement to desegregate the schools in Washington, D.C. Who do you think were the first to object? Nobody but the proud Negroes of Washington, who felt that the kind of white kids we would be thrown in with were not good enough. I don't know how many castes of Negroes there were in the city at that time, but I do know that if you decided to mix carelessly with another you would be told that one just did not do that sort of thing. It might be wonderful for somebody, but not for me and my cousins. There was a demonstration of how all levels could and should mix at Frank Holliday's poolroom, about which I'll have more to say later.

Every summer, my father would send my mother and me on our vacation, to visit his sister Carrie in Atlantic City, or my mother's brother, John Kennedy, in Philadelphia. We'd travel by Pullman parlor car, and they were wonderful times, but one year she decided to go to Asbury Park. I was about ready for high school then and, although it was a vacation for her, I went out looking for a job.[4]

There was the big Atlantic Ocean and all those big hotels, but it was a rainy season and bellhop jobs were hard to get. A lot of us kids were all crowded around a hotel one day, hoping something would turn up, when the man came out and said, "Well, we don't have any need of a bellhop, because business is so bad, but over on First Avenue they need a dishwasher." So then there was a race of all the kids to First Avenue to get the dishwashing job, and I got there first.

"I hear you have a dishwashing job open," I said, when the housekeeper came to the door.

"Yes, we need a dishwasher," she said, "but you don't look like no dishwasher to me. You ain't nothin' but a child." Then she took another look at me and said, "But come on in!"

She sat me down at the kitchen table and put a great heap of biscuits, cornbread, muffins, pancakes, butter, jam, and milk in front of me.

"I'll go see the madam," she said, "and see what she says."

---

[3] Ellington began attending Garrison Public School, 1714 12th Street, N.W., in 1908, probably continuing there until 1913.

[4] Ellington attended Armstrong Manual Training High School, on P Street between 1st and 3rd streets, N.W., from 1913 until early 1917.

She left me there with that food, and when she came back with the madam the plates were all empty.

"Here he is," she said. "He says he's a dishwasher and he looks like a child, but he eats like a man."

I got the job and entered another world. There was a guy there by the name of Bowser, who had been the dishwasher the year before and was now the headwaiter.

"Boy, I can tell you don't know nothin' 'bout dishwashin'," he said, the very first day. "Let me see what you do."

So I started to wash the dishes.

"No, not like that," he said. "What you do, you take all the dishes, stack them up in this big tank, sprinkle the powder on them, and fill it up with scalding hot water."

He did it, went through the whole thing, and showed me how to dip down to the bottom and pull out a plate.

"That's easy," I said, and I stuck my arm down, but that water nearly burned it off, and I came up *so* quick, with nothing.

"Uh-huh," he said. "I knew you weren't nothin' but a child."

He was a nice guy though, and he did nearly all my dishwashing the whole season, although he had become headwaiter. We used to talk together, and I told him I had been listening to the piano players around Washington.

"Man, in Philadelphia they've got a young piano player called Harvey Brooks," he said. "He's just about your age. You ought to hear him play. He's terrific."

We stayed in Asbury Park the whole summer, but my mother went home before me. On the way back to Washington, Bowser and I stopped off in Philadelphia, where I heard this young kid, Harvey Brooks.[5] He was swinging, and he had a tremendous left hand, and when I got home I had a real yearning to play. I hadn't been able to get off the ground before, but after hearing him I said to myself, "Man, you're just going to *have* to do it." I went around to a couple of piano players, but I couldn't learn anything they were trying to teach me.

My mother used to play piano, pretty things like "Meditation," so pretty they'd make me cry.[6] My father used to play too, but by ear, and all operatic stuff. When I was confined to the house for a couple of weeks with a cold, I started fiddling around on the piano, using what was left over from my piano lessons — mostly the fingering — and I came up with a piece I called "Soda Fountain Rag," because I had been working as a soda jerk at the Poodle Dog Cafe. I started playing this around, and it attracted quite a lot of attention.[7]

About this time, too, just before I went to high school, and before my voice broke, I got my nickname, Duke. I had a chum, Edgar McEntree (he preferred

[5] Harvey Brooks (1899–1968) later toured with Mamie Smith and settled in California, where he performed in bands led by Paul Howard, Les Hite, Kid Ory, and others.

[6] The pianist Brooks Kerr once played C. S. Morrison's *Meditation* (1896) for Ellington, who remembered hearing the piece as a child.

[7] Ellington never made a commercial recording of *Soda Fountain Rag* but played it a number of times over the years in various contexts. For a discussion, see *ETEY*, 33–41.

the accent on the "en"), a rather fancy guy who liked to dress well. He was socially uphill and a pretty good, popular fellow around, with parties and that sort of thing. I think he felt that in order for me to be eligible for his constant companionship I should have a title. So he named me Duke.

One day, soon after I went to high school, the seniors had a party in the gym. Edgar McEntree, my friend, crony, and buddy, pushed into the party, pulling me with him. His friend "The Duke," he announced, was a pianist who wouldn't object if asked to play. With this, I was invited, and I played. It was probably "What You Gonna Do When the Bed Breaks Down?" my second composition, and a pretty good "hug-and-rubbin'" crawl.[8] "Encore, encore!" they cried when I finished. Then the senior boys came over and took me to the grocery store, where they told me they were going to make me a senior right away. They ordered some gin and blackberry wine, mixed them together, passed it on to me and told me it was "Top and Bottom."

The next morning, three of the prettiest little girls you ever saw in your life stood out in front of my house looking up at the second story. "Mrs. Ellington, is Edward ready?" one of them called. "Yes, honey," she answered, "he'll be right down." When I came down, we turned the corner in the direction of the school, but in the middle of the block the girls told me, "We're not going to school today. We are going over to Ina Fowler's house and have a hop. Gertie Wells is going to be there. So are Roscoe Lee, Earl Hyman, Shrimp Brauner, and Claude Hopkins. They're all cutting school." (Gertie Wells was a great piano player, but she never did anything professionally outside Washington.)

Well, that's what we did, and it was quite a success. From then on, I was invited to many parties, where I learned that when you were playing piano there was always a pretty girl standing down at the bass clef end of the piano. I ain't been no athlete since. But if at that time I had ever thought I was learning to play piano to make a living, I would never have made it!

During World War I, I worked at the Navy Department as a messenger. Then they switched me over to the State Department. This was pre-Pentagon, and the State, War, and Navy departments were all in one building to the west of the White House; the Treasury was to the east. I found myself in a newly created section called the State, War, and Navy Transportation Division, and what we did was to make reservations for the brass. My boss welcomed me to my little messenger's desk. Guys in his position were rich, dollar-a-year men, and he, of course, sat at the big desk.

"Now, Edward," he said on the very first morning, "I'm going out to lunch, and I'd like you to watch the telephone."

When he came back, he said I had done very well, and a little later in the afternoon he had to leave again.

"I'm going over to the club for cocktails, and I'm going to ask you to watch the phone again. If anyone calls up and wants a reservation, call up the Pullman Company and have the tickets sent here. Then you personally deliver them wherever they are required."

I did that, and when he came back in the evening he said I had done a

---

[8] This was another piece not recorded commercially by Ellington. See *ETEY*, 41–43.

splendid job. From that day on, I moved over to the big desk, and I remained there until the war was over. I think I knew the schedule of every big train in the country, and that came in useful later.

My man got to like me, and one day he told me how to get rich.

"All you have to do is get the first thousand dollars. When you get that, you will want another thousand. When you get to ten thousand, you will want another ten. And when you get to a hundred thousand, it's just on and on to the million."

So I know exactly what to tell any budding young man who wants to get rich, but putting the plan into operation is something else again. As Django Reinhardt used to say, "Tomorrow, maybe." Of course, I was born rich.

Some of my other extracurricular activities also deserve mention here. Boys under sixteen were not allowed to go to burlesque shows, but at twelve our high-school crowd decided it was time for us either to be or to act like sixteen. So down we went to the Gaiety [Gayety] Theatre, and bought tickets, and got away with it. We found it very interesting, and went back many other times. There were a lot of jokes, and if you had a tendency toward instruction as well as entertainment, as I had, you could begin to understand the foundation, and how these things were built. The shows were very good and I made a lot of observations, on show business techniques, on the great craftsmanship involved, and on the rather gorgeous girls, who looked good in anything they wore. They also looked good, I should say, in *everything* they took off! And then, at about fourteen, I started going to the poolroom, and boys, of course, were not allowed in there either until they were sixteen.

There was one great poolroom on T Street, between Sixth and Seventh N.W., Frank Holliday's poolroom, next to the Howard Theatre. It was not a normal, neighborhood-type poolroom. It was the highspot of billiard parlors, where all the kids from all neighborhoods came, and the great pool sharks from all over town. Some would come from out of town, too, and there would be championship matches. Guys from all walks of life seemed to converge there: school kids over and under sixteen; college students and graduates, some starting out in law and medicine and science; and lots of Pullman porters and dining-car waiters. These last had much to say about the places they'd been. The names of the cities would be very impressive. You would hear them say, "I just left Chicago," or "Last night I was in Cleveland." You do a lot of listening in a poolroom, and all this sounded very big.

Then there were the professional *and* amateur gamblers. One whose name, I think, was Strappy Manning, was regarded as a champ. Freddy Woods was a man who could run the scale on the dice, on the regular straight dice, on an ordinary pool table, and run it from two up to twelve and back to two. He used to do all sorts of demonstrations. Cats would come in there, too, who would take a deck of cards and demonstrate dealing seconds and all other kinds of cheats. When a dealer is dealing with marked cards at Black Jack, and he sees you need five or seven to make twenty-one, and the top card is the card you need, he has to be able to put it back and pull the second one out.

Interns used to come in, who could cure colds. And handwriting experts who would enjoy copying somebody's signature on a check, go out and *cash* it, and bring back the money to show the cats in the poolroom what *artists* they were. They didn't need the money. They did it for the kicks. There were also a couple of pickpockets around, so smooth that when they went to New York they were not allowed in the subway. At heart, they were all great artists.

Among the professional men was Dr. Charles Drew, who was the first to make blood plasma work. Then there were the Curtis brothers. One eventually became an eye specialist, the other a heart specialist. Bub Boller and George Hayes were lawyers. Frank Holliday's very tight buddy was Clarence Cabiness, whose nickname was "Snake." He was the ideal picture of cool—Mr. Cool. His family was rather social, but then he got mixed up and became involved with race horses and that sort of thing.

Of course, all the piano players used to hang out there, too. There was Ralph Green, who never really became a professional piano player. Claude Hopkins was there. Shrimp Bronner was another. Phil Word, who used to play piano at the Howard Theatre, was a good song writer, too. Roscoe Lee, who became a dentist, would be there. He and Claude Hopkins were reader piano players, like Doc Perry, Louis Brown, and Louis Thomas, who came by from time to time. Les Dishman was the *great* left hand. Then there were Clarence Bowser, Sticky Mack, and Blind Johnny. These cats couldn't read, but there was a wonderful thing, an exchange, which went on between them and the guys who did. And I mustn't forget the great drummers who later on used to drive me. Men like Bill Jones and Bill Beasley would go into three-four and five-four, and that kind of thing, and try to throw me.

I used to spend nights listening to Doc Perry, Louis Brown, and Louis Thomas. They were schooled musicians who had been to the conservatory. But I listened to the unschooled, too. There was a fusion, a borrowing of ideas, and they helped one another right in front of where I was standing, leaning over the piano, listening. Oh, I was a great listener!

Louis Brown [ca. 1889–1974] had unbelievable technique. He played chromatic thirds faster than most of the greats of that time could play chromatic singles (his left hand could play an eleventh in any key). The others could only marvel at this, but not with envy, for they enjoyed another piano player's sterling performance. They applauded with wonder and appreciation, laughed and slapped each other on the back when he finished, and then each would take his turn and display his own unique devices. Doc Perry and Louis were the Conservatory Boys but they had also a profound respect for the cats who played by ear, and in spite of the fact that their techniques were as foreign to each other as Chinese, they lauded them, praised them, and there was the most wonderful exchange. Everybody seemed to get something out of the other's playing—the ear cats loved what the schooled guys did, and the schooled guys, with fascination, would try what the ear cats were doing. It was a wonderful, healthy climate for everybody. Even the listeners were enchanted and never had enough. When Doc Perry first heard me play, he obviously heard some talent and I was invited to his home for refreshments, and one by one he showed me things, some of which I still use as guidance out of a cramp. For all he taught me, he never asked a fee: he just somehow liked me, I guess. I was rather a nice kid, of course, but I respected him more than he could ever know.

Doc Perry [1885?–1954] wore glasses and looked very much like the kids try to look today. He was intelligent, had beautiful posture at all times — sitting, walking, in a poolroom, or playing the piano — and talked with a sort of semi-continental finesse. He was extremely dignified, clean, neat, and had impeccably manicured nails and hands. When playing the piano he had that form athletes have. He was respected by musicians, show people, and the laymen as well. Doc was an impressive sight no matter what he was doing, and in spite of his own masterly digital dexterity, he respected any musician, school or ear. It was all a matter of taste. He felt that if the composer wrote it that way, then that's the way the composer would like it played.

I met him like all the other kids who went to dances, and when he heard me play, I think he saw possibilities for me in piano playing. As my drawing and painting teacher at high school, Mr. Dodson, used to say, "You have the ability, now all you have to do is apply yourself." What they meant was, "Apply yourself and learn everything you can about music." I used to go up to Doc Perry's house almost every day, sit there in a glow of enchantment, until he'd pause and explain some passage. Being an educated man of intelligence and tolerance, he had the patience to share with me his theories and observations. He also could switch from his own precise, clean style to that of any other piano player he heard. He was absolutely the most perfect combination of assets I could have encountered at that time. He first taught me what I called a system of reading the lead and recognizing the chords, so that I could have a choice in the development of my ornamentation. He was my piano parent and nothing was too good for me to try. Even if I didn't learn to play it, I knew how it was done. Doc Perry was probably the first in the parade where I found the right person in the right frame of mind to do all that he could for me and my advancement.

He never charged me five cents, and he served food and drink throughout the whole thing. How does one pay off this type of indebtedness? Back in those days, if you were a constant listener and hanger-on like I was, any piano player in D.C. was wide open and approachable. If you were to ask any one of them something like, "How did you do that, that you just played?," they would stop doing whatever they were doing and play it again, while I watched and listened to it and its explanation. Great people like Lester Dishman, top ear-man Clarence Bowser, Sticky Mack, Louis Brown, Louis Thomas, Caroline Thornton, Roscoe Lee, Gertie Wells, The Man with a Million Fingers, all of whom had their own individual style. Like Joe Rochester from Baltimore, but he was not so easily accessible. In his case, I could ask any one of the D.C. guys, mainly Doc Perry, and he would show me, and he knew what he was doing. Everyone else there too. I absorbed everybody and when I found that something I wanted to do was a little too difficult for the yearling that I was then, I would cop-out with something appropriate to my limitations. Naturally and eventually, sooner than I expected, I found my own musical self breaking through with fitting substitutions, some of which were good enough to attract the attention of my superiors. They all encouraged me, and soon it got around that I was a pretty good piano player, and by that time Henry Grant [1886–1954], who taught music in our high school, heard about me and invited me to come to his house to study harmony. It ended up a hidden course in harmony that lighted the direction to more highly developed composition. It was a music foundation, and I jumped at the opportunity because most of the advanced musicians had taken harmony from Henry Grant. All of my teachers, with the exception of Mrs. Clinkscales, had given me instructions orally. There was no question of writing music, but just talk, and I suppose that was the birth of my primitive system of memorizing, which is more or less what I still depend upon.

The main thing about the poolroom, too, besides all the extraordinary talent, was the *talk*. Frank Holliday's poolroom sounded as though the prime authorities on *every* subject had been assembled there. Baseball, football, basketball, boxing, wrestling, racing, medicine, law, politics—everything was discussed with authority. Frank Holliday's poolroom was a great place.

One of my first professional jobs as a musician was playing for a man who traveled and did an act that was half magic and half fortunetelling. I can remember now only his first name, which was Joe. To begin with, I was completely at a loss as to what I was to play on the piano. He told me to ad lib and try to match the mood of what he was doing. I did that, and was rather amazed at my ability to fall into the spirit of the very serious and sometimes mystic moods. I wish it had been recorded, because I think it would have revealed another facet of my character. What happened to Joe afterwards, I never did hear. But I hope that he is still alive and telling of the heavenly future paradise through the grace of God.

I became not only the relief piano player to Doc Perry, Louis Brown, Lester Dishman, and Sticky Mack, but I also worked in about the Number Five band for people like Louis Thomas and Russell Wooding, who had the class work. We moved out into the society world, and I remember playing at Mrs. Dyer's, a dance hall where all the nice young society kids used to go. Louis Thomas furnished the music for it all the time, and I was lucky to go in there. That was where I started throwing my hands up in the air, trying to look like Luckey Roberts, whom I had seen at the Howard Theatre, and they all said, "Oh, yes, Duke's a great pianist. Send him back again!" This, although I still knew only about four numbers. One was "The Siren Song."[9] I never forgot that. Louis Thomas' musicians were all good readers, and the first time I went in there they had been stuck for a piano player. "The big number this week," they told me, "is 'The Siren Song,' and you're going to have to learn it." I took the music home and wrestled with it all afternoon. That night, I took the music to work, put it up on the piano, and everybody thought I was really reading with the music sitting up there!

After I had been playing for him a couple of years, Louis Thomas sent me on another job I can never forget. It was out at the Ashland Country Club— nothing but millionaires—and there was nobody to play but me. I sat there

[9] *The Siren's Song,* by Jerome Kern and P. G. Wodehouse, from the 1917 musical, *Leave It to Jane.*

and played the whole length of the gig without a drummer or even a banjo player. "You're playing by yourself tonight," Thomas had told me. "It'll be mostly atmosphere, just under-conversation music. Collect a hundred dollars and bring me ninety." He was paying me ten dollars a night at that time, but I thought to myself, "What, a *hundred* dollars a night!"

I gave him his ninety dollars, but the very next day I went down to the telephone office and arranged for a Music-for-All-Occasions ad in the telephone book. It was during the war, and there were a lot of people from out of town, war workers, who didn't know Meyer Davis and Louis Thomas from Duke Ellington. My ad looked just like theirs, and I began to get work. And give it. It got so that I would sometimes send out four or five bands a night, and work in them, too. I had real good business sense then. I bought a car and a house, and lived up on Sherman Avenue at 2728. In partnership with Ewell Conway, I was also operating a sign-painting business on T Street between Sixth and Seventh, N.W. When customers came for posters to advertise a dance, I would ask them what they were doing about their music. When they wanted to hire a band, I would ask them who's painting their signs.

Before I left high school, I had won an art scholarship to Pratt Institute. I had talent as an artist and was supposed to make use of it. What I was getting out of music then seemed like a gift or a bonus, and I didn't realize that that was where my future lay. But I never took up the scholarship to Pratt, because by playing piano, and by booking bands for dances, I was making a lot of money.

One of the unique things about being in the band business was that you never knew what would be required when the telephone rang. One time a fellow called from Orange, Virginia.

"We're going to give a barn dance, Duke," he said. "But I want to make sure that *you* will be coming your*self*. I want the Number One band."

"Why, certainly," I said. It was very important, you see, to have me there. This was a special barn dance! But about the night before it was due to take place, he called me again.

"Oh, my goodness . . ." he began.

"What's wrong?" I asked.

"Well, you know, we put a hardwood floor upstairs in the barn," he said, "and we forgot to leave a hole, or a window, big enough to take the piano in!"

"Don't worry about that," I said. "I also play guitar."

So that night I sat up there and played guitar with Bill Miller, and Bill played so loud, of course, that it didn't make any difference whether I was right or not. I had a good personality, but that night I could have been a statue.

Those were the days when I was a champion drinker. I was eighteen, nineteen, or twenty, and it was customary then to put a gallon of corn whiskey on the piano when the musicians began to play. There were four of us in the group, and one hour later the jug was empty. At the end of every hour the butler would replace the empty jug with another full gallon of twenty-one-year-old corn.

The personnel changed from day to day, because sometimes we'd have to split up and put a strong man in another group that was going out. Usually, it was the three Miller brothers with me. Bill played guitar, banjo, and banjorine; Felix played drums; and Brother played saxophone. That was before Toby Hardwick was old enough to go out and play, and before Sonny Greer came to town.

Chauncey Brown was originally a drummer with good contacts in Virginia society. He worked with us, and sometimes we worked with him—a case of one hand washing the other. Since those days he has married, raised a family, and found enough time to play guitar and sing. He is *the* society musician right there in the middle of that society swirl in Warrenton, Virginia. I wonder if I would have been that lucky if I had stayed in Washington?

We used to play the dances that followed horse shows quite often, but one day somebody heard us and decided he wanted us to play the horse show itself. We were getting to have such a good reputation. Normally, they would have a thirty-piece brass band, but I think with only four pieces we went out and played louder than they did.

In Washington there were always a lot of dances, some given by clubs on special occasions, and others on a regular weekly basis. There was an afternoon dance every Wednesday run by a kid named Shrimp Collins. That was a popular affair, and Doc Perry always used to play it. I would take over the last set when Doc had to go to the Ebbett [Ebbitt] House, where he played dinner. I would play "What You Gonna Do When the Bed Breaks Down?" there, too, and it got to the point where it was a pretty fair song. Nothing happened with it, but sometimes now I think I should sing it with a rock 'n' roll group.

I was beginning to catch on around Washington, and I finally built up so much of a reputation that I had to study music seriously to protect it. Doc Perry had really taught me to read, and he showed me a lot of things on the piano. Then when I wanted to study some harmony, I went to Henry Grant. We moved along real quickly, until I was learning the difference between a G-flat and an F-sharp. The whole thing suddenly became very clear to me, just like that. I went on studying, of course, but I could also hear people whistling, and I got all the Negro music that way. You can't learn that in any school. And there were things I wanted to do that were not in books, and I had to ask a lot of questions. I was always lucky enough to run into people who had the answers.

Percy Johnson was a drummer and a buddy of mine. His nickname was "Brushes." One day he invited me over to his house just across from that sign shop on T Street.

"You've got to listen to this," he said when we got there.

He had a player-piano and he put on a roll by James P. Johnson. This was, of course, an entirely new avenue of adventure for me, and I went back there every day and listened. Percy slowed the mechanism down so that I could see which keys on the piano were going down as I digested Johnson's wonderful sounds. I played with it until I had his "Carolina Shout" down pat, and then

Percy would go out on the town with me and show me off. I really had it perfect, so that when James P. Johnson himself came to Washington to play at Convention Hall my cheering section and pals waited until he played "Carolina Shout" and then insisted that I get up on the stand and cut him![10]

I was scared stiff, but James P. was not only a master, he was also a great man for encouraging youngsters. He went along with the whole scene, and when I finished "Carolina Shout" he applauded too. I didn't play any more that night but just leaned over the piano and listened to the one and only. What I absorbed on that occasion might, I think, have constituted a whole semester in a conservatory. Afterwards, he elected me his guide for a tour of all the Washington joints, and I stayed up until 10 A.M. The friendship that began then was important to me later when we got to New York. And all of that was thanks to my good buddy Percy Johnson, to whom I shall always be indebted. God bless him.

The nucleus of the early band was the Miller brothers. Then Otto Hardwick, who later became "Toby," joined us. He was playing bass fiddle, and he was so small his father used to carry the instrument to work for him. When he got a C-melody saxophone, I began to send him out on other jobs, and he was soon known as one of the best saxophone players in town. Artie Whetsol, the trumpet player, used to work with us too, and for years he was one of the band's most indispensable members. Elmer Snowden came in with his banjo, and around this time I met Juan Tizol, the trombonist who came to the Howard Theatre with a band from Puerto Rico led by Marie Lucas. This group impressed us very much, because all the musicians doubled on different instruments, something that was extraordinary in those days. Tizol enters the story again a few years later, but the year before, in 1919, Sonny Greer had come to Washington after playing drums in a trio with Fats Waller at Asbury Park.

He was in the poolroom next door to the Howard when there was an urgent need for a drummer in the pit band. The show was due to go on in half an hour and Sonny didn't hesitate to volunteer. That was how he got the job at the Howard. He struck up an acquaintance with Toby Hardwick, who introduced him to me.

Although Sonny was from Long Branch, New Jersey, he had been to New York, and anybody who had been to New York had the edge on us. We watched him in the pit, and he used a lot of flash tricks. We decided to find out what kind of guy he was, so we stood on the street corner, waited for him, and greeted him. He answered our questions with a line of jive that laid us low. Not long after that, he quit the Howard and joined us.

A place musicians used to gather in after work was the Industrial Cafe, and there every guy used to try to tell a taller tale than anybody else. That's where Sonny showed what he was made of, because he always carried off the honors. He was also a major help to me in band contests, when we needed to employ

[10] The date was probably 25 November 1921, at an event billed as "The 20th Century Jazz Revue."

psychology. One I remember was between Elmer Snowden with eight pieces, and Sonny, Sterling Conway (on banjorine), and myself. We worked out a lot of tricks on piano and drums, and walked away with the cup. The next time, when we were up against Blind Johnny's band—and Johnny played a lot of piano—we were not so lucky. So Sonny organized a cheering section for me, and he soon became the nearest thing I ever had to a brother.

When Leroy Smith's band came to Washington and played at the Belasco Theatre, it made a big impression on me. It was well dressed and well rehearsed, and all the musicians doubled on different instruments. This created an effect of legerdemain or magic that caused an explosion in my desire to explore the further reaches of music's possibilities. Later on, I heard Leroy Smith at Connie's Inn in New York.

There was a period when we were all crazy about automobiles. Claude Hopkins had a Hudson limousine, and I had a Chandler. Toby Hardwick bought a Pullman from a dealer we knew only as Dear-Me. Toby's car was named the "Dupadilly," and it used to stall at the most awkward places. In fact, it was so refractory that one day they all got out and just left it standing on the street.

While we were still in Washington, we were fascinated by the descriptions of players and singers in other cities that visiting musicians gave us. We heard about Joe Rochester, Pike Davis, Reggie Haymer, Cliff Dorsey, and Ike Dixon in Baltimore, but it was New York that filled our imagination. We were awed by the never-ending roll of great talents there, talents in so many fields, in society music and blues, in vaudeville and songwriting, in jazz and theatre, in dancing and comedy.

We heard of Florence Mills, Edith Wilson, Gladys Bentley, Ethel Waters, Gertrude Saunders, Bessie Smith, Monette Moore, Lucille Hegamin, Mamie Smith, Andy Razaf, Spencer Williams, Alberta Hunter, Garvin Bushell, Barron's, Joe Smith, Johnny Dunn, Charlie Johnson, June Clark, Clara Smith, Clarence Williams, Connor's, Ford Dabney, George Tynes (Boston), Jim Europe, Cricket Smith, Leroy's, Bert Williams, J. Rosamond Johnson, Allie Ross, W. C. Handy, Vernon and Irene Castle, Gold Grabben's, Flo Ziegfeld, Sissle and Blake, Smalls' [Paradise], Bob Cole, Jerry Preston, Porter Grainger, Miller and Lyles, Bill Robinson, Bob Gillette, Johnny Powell, Casper Holstein, Madame Walker (Indianapolis), Addington Major, The Beetle, Mattie Hite, Lizzie Miles, Tommy Morris, Broadway Jones, Mal Frazier, Johnny Cobb, Tim Brymm [Brymn], Rudolf Brown, and many, many more.

Harlem, to our minds, did indeed have the world's most glamorous atmosphere. We had to go there.

Then Sonny Greer came up with the opportunity to work for Wilbur Sweatman, who was playing three clarinets at once in a vaudeville show. He had been making records for a long time, and I think he was famous for "The Barnyard Blues." We joined him in New York and played some split weeks in theatres. It was another world to us, and we'd sit on the stage and keep a straight face. I began to realize that all cities had different personalities, which were modified by the people you met in them. I also learned a lot about show business from Sweatman. He was a good musician, and he was in vaudeville because that was where the money was then, but I think things were beginning to cool off for him, and soon we were not doing so well.

Fortunately, Sonny Greer had a lot of face. He would walk in any place, see someone he knew, and go over to him. "Hey, So-and-so, remember me?" he'd say. "Sonny Greer. Jersey kid. Remember?" And we'd be in. He and I hustled around playing pool. We might start with a quarter. The minute we got two dollars, we'd quit, go home, dress up, order two steak dinners, give the girl a quarter, and have a quarter left for tomorrow. We'd be pretty, clean, and neat, and we'd go cabareting, visit Willie "The Lion" Smith, or James P. Johnson, or Fats Waller. You could never want for anything around them, and The Lion was always very encouraging. "I like you kids, you're nice, clean kids," he would say, "and I want you to do well." One day he came up to me and said, "Gee, you need a haircut! Here's fifty cents. Go get one." A beautiful man.

We would never send home for any money, because we knew that would scare our people to death, and stories about our splitting a hot dog five ways were more of a gag than anything else. We were getting more bored with our situation than desperate, until one day I had the luck to find fifteen dollars on the street. Then we had a square meal, got on the train, and went back to Washington to get ourselves together before we tried it again.

2. The Washingtonians: First New York Review (1923)

D espite his professional successes in and around Washington, Ellington decided in 1923 to seek his fortunes in New York. He went there first in March to play in the vaudeville act of clarinetist Wilbur Sweatman, returned to Washington for a bit, then made a second visit in June to join a five-piece band accompanying dancer Clarence Robinson. The latter job never materialized, but the quintet, made up of musicians who had known each other in Washington, stayed together through the summer, playing at Barron Wilkins' Cafe in Harlem, the Music Box in Atlantic City, and occasionally the Winter Garden building in Times Square. This band, soon known as the Washingtonians, contained the nucleus of the future Duke Ellington orchestra. Led by Elmer Snowden on banjo, it included trumpeter Arthur Whetsol, saxophonist Otto Hardwick, drummer Sonny Greer, and Ellington as pianist.

The Washingtonians' first long-term engagement began on 1 September 1923 in a basement cabaret called the Hollywood Cafe, on 49th Street between Broadway and Seventh Avenue. A few months later Abel Green gave the band its first review in the *Clipper*.

In 1923 the *Clipper* was one of New York's principal trade publications for the entertainment industry. Reviews of bands, especially white bands playing in the Times Square area, appeared frequently. Many were written by Abel Green, an astute observer who later served as editor of *Variety*. Green's opinions carried weight. In February 1924 the Washing-

Source: *Clipper* (23 November 1923), 12.

tonians placed an ad in the *Clipper* that reprinted part of the November 1923 review and used the caption, "Here's What ABEL Says About Us."

In his review, Green singled out for special praise a recent addition to the Washingtonians, trumpeter James "Bubber" (or "Bub") Miley. Green's reference to saxophonist Otto Hardwick doubling on violin is curious, since Hardwick is not known to have played the instrument (although earlier he had played bass in Washington).

This colored band is plenty torrid and includes a trumpet player who never need doff his chapeau to any cornetist in the business. He exacts the eeriest sort of modulations and "singing" notes heard.

The Hollywood, a comparatively new Times Square basement cabaret (it opened 1 September last), is on West 49th Street. The band is the sole feature up to midnight, when Harper's Dixie Revue goes on, repeating again at 2 a.m.[1]

The boys can seemingly satisfy without exerting themselves, but for the benefit of the Clipper reviewer they brought out a variety of instruments upon which each demonstrated his versatility. And how!

Elmer Snowden is the leader and banjoist, also doubling with soprano sax. "Bub" Miley is the "hot" cornetist, doubling with the melophone [*sic*]. John Anderson doubles trombone and trumpet; Sonny Greer specializes in the vocal interludes when not at the traps; Otto Hardwick, sax and violin; Roland Smith, sax and bassoon; and Duke Ellington, piano-arranger.

The boys look neat in dress suits and labor hard but not in vain at their music. They disclose painstaking rehearsal, playing without music. They are well known in several southern places and were at the Music Box, Atlantic City, the past summer. They also broadcast every Wednesday at 3:45 from WHN (Loew State building) radio station.

3. Reviews
from the Kentucky Club (1925)

Early in 1924 banjo-player Elmer Snowden, who had been leading the Washingtonians at the Hollywood since the previous September, left the band and Ellington took over. Through the spring of 1927, the Washingtonians were based at the 49th Street nightspot, which in March 1925 changed its name to the Club Kentucky. (Ellington and other musicians always called it the Kentucky Club.)

Occasional reviews of Kentucky Club shows appeared in the entertainment weeklies *Variety* and *Billboard*. These notices tended to focus more on the club's changing roster of

---

[1] Leonard Harper was a well-known black dancer and producer of floor shows in the twenties. Ellington stayed in his Harlem apartment when he first came to New York.

Source: *Variety* (1 April 1925), 44.
Source: *Billboard* (5 December 1925), 22.

singers, dancers, and comedians than on its resident musicians. The two below, however, suggest the favorable reactions the Washingtonians were beginning to draw.

28 March 1925

Probably the "hottest" band this side of the equator is the dance feature at this basement cabaret formerly the Hollywood. It is Duke Ellington's Washingtonians, a colored combo, that plays "blues" as nobody can. The jazz boys who drop in at the place, which runs well into the morning and past dawn, take much delight in sitting around and drinking in their indigo modulations. Similarly, the patrons are just as apt to sit it out for quite a spell in addition as not.

The show itself is headed by Bert Lewis, who sings rag numbers in telling style and clowns all over the place to his and the mob's delight. With him are the Crane Sisters, harmony songsters; Jessie Alcova, rag vocalist; Myrtle Bonnie, prima, and Doris Jackson, "Charleston" specialist. Doris is the sister and image of Bee Jackson at the Club Richman, and it's a toss-up between the two as to the "Charleston" proficiency.

The informality of the place and the free-for-all funning is the feature of the works. Lewis carries the idea through with a vengeance.

November–December 1925

If you must stay up until sunrise, we can't think, offhand, of a better place to while away the small hours than at the Club Kentucky. Here no one wears a high hat—there is no bid for pretentiousness. Bert Lewis, master of "carahmoanies," would probably tell you that "this ain't the place for puttin' on the dawg—we leave that to Park avenoo."

The place, appropriately, is in a cellar, with the music and show correspondingly low down. Lewis is an adept clown, politely offensive at times, and yet the kind one finds easy to forgive. His songs are strictly of the sawdust variety, with gestures equally "blue," but it is this very hotsy-totsiness of material that sells the pudgy little fat man.

Peggy English warbles rag songs like few can. Her Vocalion records, for the exclusive canning of which she signed recently, should outsell other similar discs in another year. Bernice Petkere, too, carols deliciously, while Jane Laurence, a hefty prima donna, is a good vocalist and an efficient check builder. Gypsy Byrne and Margaret Edwards are a pair of capable hoofers. Harry Harris and Sid Clark, also billed, didn't "show" when reviewed.

No "names" here, but with this show they aren't necessary. And now for the band! If anybody can tell us where a hotter aggregation than Duke Ellington and His Club Kentucky Serenaders can be found we'll buy for the mob. Possessing a sense of rhythm that is almost uncanny, the boys in this dusky organization dispense a type of melody that stamps the outfit as the most torrid in town.

Duke Ellington, director, pounds the baby grand, and while he chow-meins in an adjacent eatery Thomas "Fats" Waller understudies. Both lads are deserving of all the available superlatives in the English language, while it is necessary to borrow a few from the Latin to adequately extol the performance of the latter. Sunny [sic] Greer is the third best drum showman in the country, with Vic Berton, of the Roger Wolfe Kahn Orchestra, and Willie Creeger [Creager], now a phonograph arranger, entitled, respectively, to first and second honors. Henry [Bass] Edwards' tuba is all bent from the heat its owner gives it and "Bub" Miley "kills" 'em with his trumpet. Fred Guy plays banjo, Charley Irvis trombones, and Otto Hardwick supervises the sax. section. The couvert at the Kentucky is $1.50, which is right for this place. Easily the best of the "kennel clubs" in town.

4. The Washingtonians "Set New England Dance Crazy" (1927)

Several factors boosted the Washingtonians' popularity in 1926 and 1927. Summer touring in New England gave the band valuable road experience and exposure outside New York City. Recording activity stepped up in the fall of 1926, beginning with the Vocalion sides in November (which yielded the first version of *East St. Louis Toodle-O*). Around the same time, Irving Mills began working as Ellington's manager, helping to secure playing, recording, and publishing opportunities.

In his 27 August 1927 column for the *Chicago Defender,* one of the country's leading black newspapers, Dave Peyton took note of Ellington's rising fortunes, reproducing an article by one "W.E.B." that supposedly appeared in the *New York Tribune.*[1] W.E.B.'s generous praise for the Washingtonians suggests the growing reputation of Ellington's band some months before it entered the Cotton Club on 4 December 1927. Especially striking is W.E.B.'s favorable comparison of the Washingtonians to some of the leading white orchestras of the day. As a black bandleader, Ellington was moving into the position of pre-eminence that a year or two earlier had been occupied by Fletcher Henderson.

In addition to writing for the *Defender,* and earlier the Chicago *Whip,* Dave Peyton (ca. 1885–1956) was an active member of Chicago's black musical community who worked as a bandleader, musicians' contractor, and union official.

The following article consistently misspelled bandleader Mal Hallett's name as "Hallet"; it has been corrected here.

This week this writer is pleased to let the Musical Bunch throughout the country know about Duke Ellington and his band, who have invaded the New England territory and stormed it with their great orchestral ability. Isn't it nice to read good things about the musicians. When I learn of these good

Source: *Chicago Defender*, 27 August 1927.

[1] The original source for this article has not been located.

things, it makes me feel good. The New England papers say all sorts of nice things about Duke and his boys and incidentally, I might state that Rudy Jackson, a Chicago musician, is a member of this bunch. Read the following about Duke Ellington's bunch, clipped from *The New York Tribune* of Aug. 7:

"New York City—This is not an ordinary story about an ordinary orchestra. It relates to you the remarkable rise of a musical organization that within the past two months has set the entire New England states dance crazy: Duke Ellington and his Washingtonians from the Kentucky club, New York, the high spot in Broadway's night life.

"To tell all about this famous band we must first go back some five years when Mal Hallett and his crack outfit made their initial appearance in this territory.

"When Mal and his boys first came to these parts, a travelling orchestra was something of a novelty and a New York band was a treat. From the very start Hallett was a knockout. He brought with him that Broadway atmosphere—the brilliancy of its bright lights—real New York showmanship, a different and better brand of music than the dancers had ever heard before—and they liked it.

"The news of Hallett's success had hardly reached New York, it seemed, before the New England states were flooded with New York orchestras—the best that Broadway had to offer.

"Paul Whiteman, Vincent Lopez, George Olsen, Ross Gorman, Coon-Sanders, and other nationally known musical celebrities cancelled every engagement and headed east with but one thought in mind, to conquer the New England dancer and remove Mal Hallett from his throne.

"Each night, it seemed, brought a new attraction into our midst. Their entertainment was fine and we enjoyed it. They rendered exceptional dance programs and the dancers applauded them—but they did not conquer.

"And with bowed heads, in token of defeat, they packed their grips and returned to Broadway—a success to be sure, but not a riot.

"But out of this princely gathering there is one organization that now holds its head high in the air, proud and mighty Duke Ellington and his Washingtonians. They, too, answered the call of the eastern dance bands and appeared before us three years ago.

"Unlike the others—who came and failed—their entertainment was marvelous. They pounded out number after number that left the dancer standing firm on the floor, applauding, refusing to move, stamping their feet, screaming, practically demanding an encore, then another—and then—just one more. It required but one booking for the manager to ascertain that the dancers craved their music. And what the dancer wants, the promoter books. So when the other orchestras returned—Duke Ellington and his Washingtonians remained—for they had conquered.

"The New England tour of Duke and his boys in 1925 came to an abrupt end after four weeks of triumph when they were obliged to return and fulfill an overdue contract at the Hollywood Inn, what was then New York's most fashionable and exclusive night club, located in the heart of Broadway.

"The proprietors of the Inn soon learned that they had made no mistake by engaging the Washingtonians to entertain their patrons. For on the premier night at the club Duke and his boys gave Broadway a new thrill in dance music and from then on Hollywood Inn was the mecca for Broadway's after-the-theater dance set.

"The Washingtonians held forth at the Hollywood from October in 1926 [*recte* 1925], till June 1926, and this brief period was perhaps the brightest in the career of the orchestra, for during these eight months the band practically monopolized the headlines of the New York papers. If they weren't scheduled to play at some mammoth society charity affair they were billed as headliners at Shubert's select Sunday evening concerts at the Winter Garden or entertaining some select group of Earl Carroll's friends—not the wine bath type—at the Earl Carroll theater.

"These were just in-between engagements, and every night from 11 till 5 in the morning they could be found seated on their cozy little platform at the Inn.

"All through this long engagement there was hardly a night that you could find an empty table at the night club. And if a party did vacate their table there was always another waiting patiently to take their place.

"Some mornings, along towards 2 or 3 o'clock, when all the ballrooms and smaller clubs had closed their doors, [the] Hollywood resembled a musicians' convention. Musicians from every corner of New York would flock to Hollywood Inn and sit till daylight, all eyes and ears, listening to the weird sounds and harmonious strains that sort of glistened from the instruments of the Washingtonians on the platform before them. And if you were to glance around the [room] you would notice the greatest musical leaders of the world seated at this table or that one. Paul Whiteman and Vincent Lopez spent many an hour at Hollywood Inn and not a moment was wasted. They were learning something every minute.

"One evening in particular this writer sat in the night club and saw Paul Whiteman offer the Washingtonians $100 to play "I Love You" in their inimitable way. When Paul Whiteman recognizes another orchestra's superiority they must be very good. It is very unusual for Paul to seek musical information. He usually gives it.

"And all the while Duke and the boys were thrilling Broadway's night life and brother musicians, their New England manager, Charles Shribman, was besieged with calls from promoters who wanted to know when and how soon the Washingtonians would be available for summer engagements. No encouragement was forthcoming, however, until the last of June, when the Hollywood Inn was destroyed by fire. Then the band returned East in all their glory.

"And don't think that the dancers and promoters didn't welcome them with open arms. Their 1926 New England tour was just one triumphant appearance after another. They packed the ballrooms nightly, as they continue to do now.

"Late in September last fall, they returned to carry out an eight months' contract at the Kentucky club, located on the same site as the destroyed Hollywood Inn. Paul Whiteman paid his nightly visits, so did Mr. Lopez. To their way of thinking the Washingtonians were better than ever. In fact their fame had become so far-reaching that they received a flattering offer, which they accepted, to flash their music over the entire world by making records for the Brunswick and Vocalion recording company. Their first record was a huge success and those that followed proved to be leading sellers on the music market. Only last week a New York Brunswick dealer received an order of 100 Washingtonian records for Australia.

"The present N[ew] E[ngland] tour of the Washingtonians opened last month after they had terminated their engagement at the Kentucky club. As in 1926 they are taking the territory by storm. On every appearance they are greeted with a capacity gathering of dancers, young and old.

"Apparently there is nothing unusual about this orchestra, yet, when you start dancing you don't want to stop. When you waltz you sort of wander off into a dream, the music is so soothing. Their slow fox trot, ala Southern style, brings out that soft, weird, entrancing effect that sends you sort of creeping over the floor, and when they play a fast one for contrast, they simply sweep you off your feet.

"Mountains of credit for the success of the band must be given to Duke Ellington, owner, leader, and pianist. He called the Washingtonians together some eight years ago for the first rehearsal and with one or two exceptions has kept the personnel intact ever since. Duke's work is never finished. He must direct rehearsals in the afternoon, lead the band at night and quite frequently sit up till the wee hours of the morning writing new arrangements or thinking of something different to please the dancer and promoter. Duke is aiming for the top of the ladder and that day is not far off.

"The star role in the band is shared by 'Bub' Miley, trumpeter, and 'Sonny' Greer, the drummer.

"Around these two Duke has built his orchestra. 'Bub' is responsible for all that slow, weird music and it is Bub also who plays those hot choruses that send you flying over the floor. Mr. Whiteman says he is the 'hottest' trumpet player that ever set foot on Broadway, and Paul should know his onions. 'Sonny' is the life and pep of the band. His drumming beats are precise and many in number; he is very pleasing as a songster and his funny tactics call for many a laugh from the onlooker. These two men Duke could never replace.

"The Washingtonians are now on the sixth week of their tour. Just when they will return to New York is a mystery. The band is booked solid till September and Manager Shribman has enough requests to book them till the New Year. Duke and the boys are slowly and surely becoming New England's favorite dance orchestra. Hundreds of dancers all over New England drop notes in the ballroom suggestion box naming the Washingtonians as their favorite band. One proprietor in Maine had 68 phone calls in a week inquiring when the Washingtonians were making their next appearance in that town. The promoters now speak of the band as a 'choice attraction' and spend hours planning their advertising to make the next appearance of the band more successful than the last one.

"The band has appeared in every prominent ballroom from Old Orchard,

Me., to Providence, R.I., and on every engagement they meet with so much success that they play return dates almost weekly. The dancers are just beginning to appreciate them. The only bad feature of bringing them east is the knowledge that sooner or later they must leave us. But when they do go they will leave behind them an enviable record for all other orchestras to shoot at and with the thought that when next summer rolls around all New England will be waiting to greet them again with open arms. The Washingtonians are slowly working their way to the top of the musical world. Eventually they will be the leaders, the knights of jazz and harmony.

"The Washingtonians have set N[ew] E[ngland] dance crazy. If you don't think so, ask the dancers and promoters who are clamoring for their services."

II. Cotton Club Bandleader (1927–1932)

new phase of Ellington's career began late in 1927 when his orchestra landed a job at the Cotton Club, one of New York's premier nightspots, located in Harlem at 142nd Street and Lenox Avenue. Operated by the gangster Owney Madden, patronized by wealthy whites, and staffed by blacks, the Cotton Club put on high-powered music revues featuring sultry chorus girls, sensual choreography, exotic production numbers, and plenty of hot jazz. Ellington's orchestra had played for revues at the Kentucky Club in Times Square, but there the scale had been smaller and the stakes lower. At the Cotton Club, some of New York's top black performers joined forces with such talented white songwriters as Jimmy McHugh, Dorothy Fields, Harold Arlen, and Ted Koehler. While celebrities and socialites flocked there to soak up African-American entertainment and Prohibition liquor, listeners around the nation could tune into the sounds of Duke Ellington's orchestra via broadcasts on NBC. As composer and bandleader, Ellington flourished in this environment.

The Ellington orchestra remained at the Cotton Club, with periodic interruptions, until early February 1931. During this time it expanded to twelve pieces: three reeds, three trumpets, two trombones, and four in the rhythm section (piano, banjo or guitar, bass, drums). Trumpeter Arthur Whetsol, who had left the Washingtonians in 1923, returned in 1928, joining other newcomers who would figure prominently in the coming years: reed-players Johnny Hodges and Barney Bigard, trumpeter Freddie Jenkins, and in 1929, trumpeter Cootie Williams and valve trombonist Juan Tizol. Challenged by his job and stimulated by the vivid musical personalities in his band, Ellington began to compose and record prolifically, turning out over 180 sides between December 1927 and February 1931 (compared with the 31 his band had made in nearly four years at the Kentucky Club). Although principally under contract to Victor, the Ellington orchestra regularly recorded for other labels under various pseudonyms, among them The Jungle Band, The Whoopee Makers, and Mills Ten Blackberries.

Ellington's intense creative activity, together with the exposure afforded by the Cotton Club, brought him important notices in a variety of national publications. And the achievements of this period inspired the young Boston critic R. D. Darrell to write "Black Beauty" (1932), the first serious essay on Ellington's music to be published.

5. First Cotton Club Review (1927)

T he Ellington orchestra made its Cotton Club debut on 4 December 1927, per-forming for a new revue with music by Jimmy McHugh and Dorothy Fields. Cov-ering this event for *Variety,* Abel Green devoted most of his article to the danc-ers, singers, and stage production, mentioning the music only in passing. Such a balance suggests the way Cotton Club patrons may have responded to the evening's entertain-ment—at least initially, before Ellington's reputation as the house bandleader started to soar.
For a biographical note on Green, see §2.

The Cotton Club is the Club Richman of Harlem.[1] It is the foremost black and tan cafe featuring a whale of a colored revue that matches any of the preceding editions, all of which have been noteworthy for their artistry and talent.

As in the past, the undressed thing goes double. The almost Caucasian-hued high yaller gals look swell and uncork the meanest kind of cooching ever exhibited to a conglomerate mixed audience. One coocher, boyish bobbed hoyden, said to be especially imported from Chicago for her Annapolis pro-clivities who does the Harlem River Quiver like no self-respecting body of water.[2] The teasin'est torso tossing yet, and how!

The show otherwise is a pretentious affair for a night club, colored or ofay [i.e., white], and cleverly routined by the astute Danny Healy who rates as one of our foremost floor show entrepreneurs. Healy is now of the Ziegfeld "Follies," but his extensive Silver Slipper and other night club training evi-dences itself in the manner of show routining.

Jimmy McHugh is solely programmed-credited for the restricted music, but Dorothy Fields, daughter of Lew Fields, was orally introduced as the authoress of the lyrics. Miss Fields, like her brother Herb, who is now an established musical comedy book author, is turning to the stage for her creative outlet. Even in a night club revue her words to music are impressive. So much for the creative credits, although some of the costumes (by Mme. Bertha) are strikingly noteworthy for their ingenious design.

Aida Ward, who reminds of a Florence Mills in her song delivery, is a charming song saleswoman and the particular luminary of the proceedings. Miss Ward seems to be the nearest approach to the sainted blackbird-looking-

---

Source: *Variety* (7 December 1927), 54, 56.

[1] The Club Richman was a swank nightspot on West 56th Street owned by entertainer and musician Harry Richman (1895–1972).

[2] Ellington's orchestra recorded *Harlem River Quiver* for Victor on 19 December 1927.

for-a-bluebird. Her own "Broken Hearted Black Bird" will become a standard for Miss Ward like other ditties did for Miss Mills.[3]

The 15 numbers take more than an hour to unloose, but it's a type of entertainment that defies lackadaiscal [sic] interest. It compels attention and any over-length is only the result of audience demand.

In the Berry Brothers, a pair of youngsters, who as "the Kalifornia Kids" are sub-billed as "the greatest team since Williams and Walker," more than live up to expectations, without ever having seen [Bert] Williams and [George] Walker. It's hardly possible the ancient team possessed the complete self-assurance, floor presence and showmanship of the young Berrys.

Edith Wilson and Jimmy Ferguson were liked in a comedy skit, although Miss Wilson's build does not brook abbreviated costuming and knockabout comedy. She led "Doin' the Frog" in the second stanza.[4]

Henri and La Perl are a novelty among colored performers, ballroom dancers of fetching appearance and unusual ability. Some astute showmanship could sell them to any mixed audience. Possibly a little ballyhoo on the Afri-castillian hoke might do the trick, as their Spanish stuff is made doubly interesting by the subconscious native syncopation.

Leonard Ruffin, standard colored stepper, is also a feature when not stage managing. Then there is Mae Alix, another Chi[cago] importation, jazzy, hot and a fool for splits.

The big attraction, of course, are the gals, 10 of 'em, the majority of whom in white company could pass for Caucasians. Possessed of the native jazz heritage, their hotsy-totsy performance if working sans wraps could never be parred by a white gal. The brownskins' shiveree is worth the $2 couvert alone.

In Duke Ellington's dance band, Harlem has reclaimed its own after Times Square accepted them for several seasons at the Club Kentucky. Ellington's jazzique is just too bad.

Harry Block with Ben Marden, et al., somewhat interested, continues in control (white management) with a colored service staff.

A trend at the club that Block should curb is the psychological reaction of the service corps to the ofay invaders who, not content to dictate to the blacks downtown, enter the very heart of the so-called Black Belt (Cotton Club is at 142nd street and Lenox avenue) and essay to do likewise. The staff seems to take the attitude that for once it can assert itself in native territory with the morale and service dubious at times. Several instances were noticeable at neighboring tables, possibly complicated through poor distribution of patrons so that one waiter was over-worked and another was churly, because of the captain's slighting him and his section of tables.

But, otherwise, for a "hot" show and something different from the general nocturnal fare, get a load of the Cotton Club.

[3] The famous black entertainer Florence Mills—who was closely associated with the 1924 song, I'm a Little Blackbird Looking for a Bluebird—had died on 1 November 1927.
[4] Recorded by Ellington for Vocalion on 29 December 1927.

6. R. D. Darrell: Criticism
in the *Phonograph Monthly*
Review (1927–1931)

R. D. Darrell was among the earliest writers to grasp the significance of Duke Ellington's music. While his 1932 essay "Black Beauty" (§12) represents his most comprehensive statement on the subject, it was preceded by a regular "Dance Records"—or simply "Dance"—column he wrote for the *Phonograph Monthly Review* between 1927 and 1931. There the shaping of Darrell's views can be traced. The column appeared in a section of the magazine called "Analytical Notes and Reviews by Our Staff Critics," and for it Darrell used the byline "Rufus." These brief notices revealed how frequently new Ellington discs reached the record-buying public and how powerfully they affected one discerning listener.

Born in Newton, Massachusetts, Robert Donaldson Darrell (1903–1988) began reviewing records while attending the New England Conservatory. Over the years he wrote on music for many publications, among them the *Music Lovers' Guide, Saturday Review,* and *High Fidelity.* In 1936 he compiled a pioneering discography, *The Gramophone Shop Encyclopedia of Recorded Music* (see §30).

In a 1980 letter to the scholar Ron Welburn, Darrell described his approach to reviewing popular music and dance records in the twenties: "I operated in those days (in the realms of jazz as everywhere else) almost entirely without advice, supervision, or formed intentions . . . almost exclusively in instinctive reaction to what I heard . . . I had no real jazz knowledge or background or experience when I began."[1] In light of this disclaimer, Darrell's youthful insights seem all the more remarkable.

All of the following selections are excerpts from longer columns by Darrell.

June 1927

With [Columbia] 953-D we come to another real winner, Duke Ellington and his Washington[ian]s playing the *East St. Louis Toodle*[-]*O* and *Hop Head;* they are a new Columbia band and they make a very creditable debut.

July 1927

Two unusually interesting records lead the Brunswick list, indeed are right in the forefront of the releases from all companies. The *Black and Tan Fantasy* (coupled with *Soliloquy* on Brunswick 3526) deserves perhaps the first prize; in it The Washingtonians combine sonority and fine tonal qualities with some amazing eccentric instrumental effects. This record differs from similar ones

---

Source: R. D. Darrell in the *Phonograph Monthly Review,* 1927–1931.

[1] Letter to Ronald G. Welburn, 23 June 1980, reproduced in Welburn, "American Jazz Criticism, 1914–1940" (Ph.D. diss., New York University, 1983), 185.

by avoiding extremes, for while the "stunts" are exceptionally original and striking, they are performed musically, even artistically. A piece no one should miss! The snatch of the Chopin Funeral March at the end deserves special mention as a stroke of genius.

September 1927

Red Nichols's *Delirium* this month, coupled with Ellington's *Down* [*in*] *Our Alley Blues* (Columbia 1076-D) . . . is perhaps the best "buy" of the month, combining as it does the pick of white and colored "hot" jazz orchestras. . . . Going on to Duke Ellington's Washingtonians, besides the Columbia record above, they are to be heard under the Vocalion label with two of the finest jazz couplings perhaps ever released: *East St. Louis Toodle-O* (also available by Columbia) and *Birmingham Breakdown*, and *New Orleans Low Down* and *Song of the Cotton Fields*, with the latter record perhaps first choice, on account of the almost Russian-folksong spirit of the *Song of the Cotton Fields* and the inspired ending of Ellington's own composition on the reverse.

January 1928

The Okeh dance records might well have been taken first, for they contain the largest number of good performances of the month. First by all means is a new performance of *Black and Tan Fantasy* by Duke Ellington that eclipses even the startling Brunswick record of this remarkable piece and even more remarkable performance. If one wishes to hear "effects" that are effects, here is the disk! *What Can a Poor Fellow Do?* on the other side, has a very interesting beginning, but for the rest is not up to Ellington's best. May this 8521 be the first of many Okeh records by this unusual orchestra.

June 1928

If last month's dance releases seldom rose above the mediocre, the disks this month offer full atonement. From the smoothest symphonic dance pieces to the most highly seasoned jazzical eccentricities runs the range; there is a spiced variety of good things for every taste. Victor leads the field with the strongest stable in many months, although the individual prize goes to Duke Ellington with his Okeh coupling of *Jubilee Stomp* and *Take It Easy* (41013). The former piece has a most arresting beginning and a development that sustains its first promise; it can be ranked very nearly with his great *Parlor Social Stomp* (and by the way, when will one of the major companies record that masterpiece?).[2] *Take It Easy* is in the style of the memorable *Black and Tan Fantasy*; hardly as good, it is still miles above the best imitative efforts of any other orchestra.

[2] *Parlor Social Stomp* had been recorded by the Washingtonians for Pathé in March of 1926.

July 1928

July brings us more worthy candidates for the jazzical Hall of Fame than any single month in the last year and a quarter. I find eight truly first class dance disks, records of originality and distinction, and of those eight no less than six bear the Victor label. Profound salaams are in order. I hesitate to assign a definite ranking to the leaders, so various and so contrasted are their characteristics, but there can be no possibility of error in leading off with Duke Ellington's first Victor Race Series release (21284), coupling a furious *Washington Wabble* and a *Harlem River Quiver* of sinewy construction and abundant pace and momentum. Both feature some pianny playing "as is," as well as all the throaty sonority and symphonic ingenuity which have made Ellington the most significant—if not the best known—figure in hot jazz.

August 1928

Leadership this month is divided (as it so often used to be) between the best of white and colored orchestras specializing in hot jazz, Red Nichols' Five Pennies and Duke Ellington's Cotton Club Orchestra. . . . Ellington's Vocalion disk of *Doin' the Frog* and *Red Hot Band* is characteristic of his best work, particularly in the former piece; the latter contains several remarkable effects, notably the furious banjo solo, but is a trifle too noisy. *Doin' the Frog*, however, is altogether admirable, with special mention going to the arresting beginning—a not uncommon feature of Ellington's arrangements, the first few bars of which are usually worth several complete pieces by less inspired directors.

September 1928

Again Ellington and [Red] Nichols contest honors in the realm of hot jazz, while Coon-Sanders and Waring's Pennsylvanians lead the field of smoother dance disks. . . .

Ellington quite surpasses himself on Vocalion 15704 in *Black Beauty* and *Take It Easy*, both his own compositions. Both rank with his finest efforts: the curiously twisted and wry trumpet passages, the amazing piano solo in *Black Beauty*, the splendid melodic urge that animates even the most eccentric measures, are all characteristic of his unique genius for the expression of an overwhelming nostalgia and bitterness in a new idiom, and one entirely his own. *Take It Easy* is superior in this version to those recorded for Victor and Perfect.

December 1928

Victor, with a long list of first-rate dance music, takes the group prize this month, but Okeh boasts the individual stars. Again Duke Ellington bursts forth with two of his inimitable masterpieces: *The Mooche*, a mighty lament that is as expressive and sinewly constructed as anything Ellington has ever written, and *Hot and Bothered,* a piece of fury and intensity that lives quite up to its title (Okeh 8623).

January 1929

Victor, however, boasts the individual winner of the month: Duke Ellington (again!) in a disk which rivals even last month's *The Mooche* from Okeh. The *East St. Louis Toodle-Oo* has been out before from Brunswick, but this version (Victor 21703) is vastly superior—a remarkable piece of deep-throated playing and sonorous recording. The coupling is *Got Everything But You,* a work which can compare with *Black Beauty* for sheer melodic beauty. For anyone unacquainted with Ellington's records, I can recommend no more effective introductory disk than this one.

Ellington heads the Brunswick as well as the Victor lists. His *Awful Sad* and *Louisiana* on Brunswick 4110 are but a shade below his superlative *Toodle-Oo* and *Got Everything.*[3]

May 1929

Turning to the hot records, among which Victor releases have lately begun to figure prominently, we have no less than three magnificent disks from Duke Ellington of Cotton Club fame. On V-38036 he plays *High Life* and *Saturday Night Function,* both of which live fully up to their titles; on V-38035 he has a jaunty *Doin' the Voom Voom* (with a brief pianny interlude of his own) and a more songful *Flaming Youth.* And on V-38034 he has one side devoted to his famous *The Mooche,* while on the other King Oliver plays the *West End Blues.* All Ellington's pieces are of his own composition and all are in his characteristic vein. None of these—good as they are—quite manage to rank with his superb master disks, however. But one of the latter has just come to my attention. It was issued sometime ago, but was never reviewed in these pages: Victor 21137, whereon Duke plays a *Creole Love Call* and the never-to-be-forgotten *Black and Tan Fantasy* that first won him phonographic renown. The performance of the fantasy here is perhaps a shade below that on the Okeh record, on account of the regular beat receiving somewhat undue prominence, but the *Creole Love Call* is a veritable masterpiece of its genre! Now may Ellington re-record some of his early successes, such as the *Parlor Social Stomp, New Orleans Low-Down,* and *Birmingham Breakdown.*

[3] Darrell's different spellings of *East St. Louis Toodle-O* reflect inconsistencies on the original record labels, which printed the last word as "Toodle-O," "Toodle-Oo," and "Toddle-O." Ellington pronounced the word as "Todalo" and claimed the word was misspelled on early recordings of his piece. For more on the title, see *ETEY,* 250–51.

April 1930

The Brunswick miscellany remains, always a fertile field for the dance music connoisseur. Top honors go to the Jungle Band (Duke Ellington's orchestra) in a coupling of *Jolly Wog* and *Jazz Convulsions* that ranks well up among this master's best efforts. *Jolly Wog* features some fine, free, eloquent declamatory hot solos, while *Jazz Convulsions*—not very appropriately named—is a very fetching piece distinguished by a singing melodic phrase that is something of a masterpiece in itself, altogether apart from the characteristic Ellington sonorities and klang tints [i.e., tone colors] with which it is treated (4705).

June 1930

For Brunswick the Jungle Band can be heard on three double-sided disks, the fine *Double Check Stomp* mentioned earlier; *Maori* (a Samoan dance!) and *Admiration* on 4776; *Sweet Mama* and *When You're Smiling* on 4760. For the most part the playing is much more conventional than was Ellington's wont a year or two ago. There are still many flashes, however, in both the arrangements and the playing that are characteristic of Ellington and that serve to make even his minor records noteworthy.

July 1930

A special gold medal goes to the Victor Race list of June 20th, containing some six dance discs, all of them wows. Duke Ellington leads off with a fine performance of his *Double Check Stomp* with great double bass work, and a highly characteristic *Jazz Lips* (V-38129). His *I Was Made to Love You* and *My Gal Is Good for Nothing But Love* (V-38130) is also good, boasting a fine surging tunes [*sic*], but the treatment is more conventionalized and I miss the inimitable singing that helped to rank such early Ellington works as *Blues I Love to Sing* and *Creole Love Call* among the greatest hot performances of all time.

November 1930

The Victor race list is a fertile source of sizzling dance tunes, but the hot orchestral medal of the month goes to Duke Ellington's record of *Check and Double Check* hits, issued in the regular supplement.[4] Victor-22528 is the number, and *Three Little Words* and *Ring Dem Bells* are the pieces. The former is a soulfully chanted number, and except for the Duke's piano intro-

---

[4] Ellington and his orchestra had gone to Hollywood in the summer of 1930 to appear in the Amos 'n' Andy film *Check and Double Check*. Among the pieces they performed in the film were *The Mystery Song*, *East St. Louis Toodle-Oo*, and *Old Man Blues*.

duction and an occasional happy instrumental touch, fairly conventional. But *Ring Dem Bells* will strike joy to the heart of the hot jazzist, an incredibly skillful and lightfooted performance, embellished by natty wa-wa dialogue and joyous rhythmic bell work, altogether fit to rank with the best Ellington recordings of the past—which is lively praise indeed.

December 1930

The Harlem Footwarmers turn in a good piece of slow blues playing in *Rocky Mountain Blues*, but their *Big House Blues* possesses unusual qualities (Okeh 8836).[5] The resilient, swooping melodic line and the singular nostalgic atmosphere of the piece make for music to play with that of Earl Hines in attracting the attention of students of the more celebrated modern composers to the oftentimes quite astounding work of the best of the jazzists.

January 1931

For all the fact that Ellington has become too popular and too busy to do his best work at all times, the Duke still has an occasional disc up his sleeve that is not only quite unbeatable, but is a genuine musical (not mere jazzical) achievement. His Jungle Band's coupling of *Dreamy Blues* and *Runnin' Wild*, on Brunswick 4952, is one of these works. *Runnin' Wild* [by A. Harrington Gibbs] is one of the finest dance tunes ever written (as Gilbert Seldes and many another has testified) and Ellington's version is done with an abandon as magnificent as that of the music itself. But the *Dreamy Blues*, one of Ellington's own compositions, is the real musical achievement. It is a poignantly restrained and nostalgic piece with glorious melodic endowment and scoring that even Ravel and Strawinski might envy. Indeed it actually recalls those hushed muted trumpets of the beginning of the second part of the *Rite of Spring*. The very same piece is played again under the name *Mood Indigo* by the Harlem Footwarmers on Okeh 8840. Despite the change of name in both title and orchestra, the performance sounds exactly the same, although the Okeh recording is less brilliant, departing somewhat from the splendid authenticity of tone color reproduction in the Brunswick disc, but possibly adding a little to the restrained atmospheric qualities of the piece. The coupling here [*Sweet Chariot*] is a lugubrious, slow, bewailing piece of considerable interest (it is also by Ellington), but by no means as striking as the *Mood Indigo* alias

[5] Ellington adopted the "Harlem Footwarmers" pseudonym when recording for the OKeh label in the period 1928–31. For this record date of 14 October 1930, the Footwarmers were seven musicians drawn from Ellington's twelve-piece Cotton Club orchestra: Arthur Whetsol, trumpet; Joe "Tricky Sam" Nanton, trombone; Barney Bigard, clarinet; Ellington, piano; Fred Guy, banjo; Wellman Braud, bass; Sonny Greer, drums.

Dreamy Blues. Is Ellington's band also the Harlem Music Masters?[6] Their performance of *Ring Dem Bells* (Okeh 41468) is very closely akin to that of Ellington in his splendid Victor version of the same piece. Again the jaunty flow, fine coloring and wa-wa work calls for emphatic [praise]. . . . Ellington's current Victor disc (23022) is one of his virtuoso feats. *Old Man Blues* is a grand rollicking tune, played to a standstill by the entire band, with the Duke's piano well ahead. *Jungle Nights in Harlem* contains some more amazing piano and orchestral effects (Rimsky-Korsakow would rub his ears on hearing some of the tone colors here!) Note the parabolic flights in particular. Fantastic music, astoundingly played.

February 1931

Ellington refuses to rest a single month on his laurels. His extensive work of last time is matched by a new series of magnificent recordings, led by a third version of *Mood Indigo* (reviewed last month in the Brunswick and Okeh recordings). Now it is done for Victor in almost exactly the same performance as before, and coupled with a good blues with a fine moaning chorus— *When a Black Man's Blue* (Victor 22587). Ellington's other Victor release (22586) demonstrates that even in more conventional fare than his own compositions his orchestra is still supreme. His versions of *Nine Little Miles* [*from Ten-Ten-Tennessee*] and *What Good Am I Without You*—both grand tunes—are handled with piquant coloristic and coloratura touches that make them hard to beat by any orchestra. Hotter, but no less attractive in ingenious tonal effects are the Jungle Band's performances of *Home Again Blues* and a fascinating *Wang Wang Blues* (Brunswick 6003), in which a sweet vocal chorus [by Dick Robertson] is amusing contrasting with hot, semi wa-wa interjections from Ellington's own vocalist—the versatile drummer of the band—Sonny Greer.[7]

April 1931

Can no one contest Duke Ellington's and Red Nichols' monthly claim for top honors? They're at the top again, the former with his Jungle Band and some magnificent pianny playing of his own in an original *Rockin' in Rhythm* (note the masterly use of ostinatos) and *12th St. Rag* (Brunswick 6038), and under his own name in a fascinating accompaniment to a competent rendition of Gershwin's grand ballad of *Sam and Delilah*. . . . Ellington also appears in the regular Victor lists with *Keep a Song in Your Soul* and *The River and Me* (22614). The treatment is not too hot, nor yet too conventionalized, although

[6] This was a pseudonym for Ellington's regular Cotton Club orchestra at the time: Cootie Williams, Arthur Whetsol, Freddie Jenkins, trumpets; Joe "Tricky Sam" Nanton, Juan Tizol, trombones; Barney Bigard, Johnny Hodges, Harry Carney, reeds; Ellington, piano; Fred Guy, banjo; Wellman Braud, bass; Sonny Greer, drums.
[7] In fact the interjections are by Bennie Payne.

both pieces sag after notably fine beginnings; note especially the fine rhapsodic melodic line of the latter.

June 1931

Ellington comes next, first with a re-issue of his adept performance of the Gershwins' *Sam and Delila[h]* . . . and for Brunswick (alias the Jungle Band) with an original two-part *Creole Rhapsody,* which is good—notably by virtue of the Duke's own work on the keyboard—but not in the finest Ellington tradition (Brunswick 6093).

September 1931

Ellington is at his best in *Limehouse Blues* and *Echoes of the Jungle* (Victor 23283), a disc that will amaze even those who are familiar with the Duke's achievements in the past. The elaborate texture and diabolically ingenious arrangements will astound even the student of such modern orchestrators as Ravel and Strawinski.

7. Abbé Niles on Ellington (1929)

I n surveying jazz recordings from 1928 for the small magazine *The Bookman,* Abbé Niles placed Ellington's releases at the top of the list, above those by Paul Whiteman, Red Nichols, Joe Venuti, Frankie Trumbauer, and others.

Edward Abbé Niles (1894–1963) was a writer, sheet-music collector, and historian of American vernacular music who collaborated with W. C. Handy on *Blues: An Anthology* (1926). He wrote a monthly music column, "Ballads, Songs and Snatches," for *The Bookman* from February 1928 to January 1929.

. . . During the year 1928, I have, for *The Bookman,* listened to a substantial proportion of the current "popular" records of five leading phonograph companies. I have heard and taken notes upon the dance-music, not only of the more polished orchestras that lurk, Tuxedo-clad, beneath the potted palms, but of *Boyd Senter and his Senterpedes; Jelly-Roll Morton's Red Hot Peppers; The Dixieland Jug Blowers; Curtis Mosby's Dixieland Blue Blowers; Wilson's Catfish String Band; Gid Tanner's Skillet-Lickers; Joe Foss's Hungry Sand Lappers; Frank Blevin's Tar Heel Rattlers; Peg Leg Howell and his Gang; Clarence Williams's Washboard Five; Creath's Jazz-O-Maniacs; The Whoopee Makers; The New Orleans Bootblacks; Dad Blackard's Moonshin-*

Source: Abbé Niles, "Ballads, Songs and Snatches," *The Bookman* (January 1929), 570–71.

ers; and The Goofus Five. From the mass of American music, or something, that has been thus passed through my ears, I select a few examples as the richest in the strangeness, the bitter, salty wit and humor, and the flashes of defiant, unwilling beauty which characterize good jazz; examples, in short, by hearing which anyone who will take the trouble may learn whether he likes jazz or not. They are presented, not as great music, nor as *the* American music, but as good jazz. Some are harsh, raucous and unrefined. Only two might be said to have individual importance.[1] But they have ideas and vitality, of a peculiarly American flavor; and on the proposition that that flavor is worth knowing, I rest their case. . . .

Duke Ellington's Orchestra (also known as *The Washingtonians*), especially when playing its leader's own dance-tunes, is dogmatically pronounced to be supreme in this field. I should say that anyone who could not enjoy the savage and mournful Ellington records of "Take It Easy" (*Okeh* 41013), "Black Beauty" (*Br.* 4009, *Vo.* 15704), "Black and Tan Fantasy" (*Ok.* 40955), or "East St. Louis Toodle-Oo" (*Br.* 3480) could not enjoy jazz; save for the fact that from an orthodox atmosphere to Ellington is a formidable jump. There is more and better melody in one of the dances of this astounding Negro than in ten of the pallid tunes of the average operetta, but this fact would be obscured for a beginner by the hair-raising arabesques of the Ellington trumpet and clarinet—even, in the extraordinary record of "The Mooche" and the break-neck "Hot and Bothered" (*Ok.* 8623), by sounds from a human throat which most listeners would swear issued from some tortured instrument. Yet on many hearings, there is not a note that should be changed—and what power, what attack!

8. Two Early Interviews (1930)

In 1930 Ellington and his orchestra drew considerable attention as a result of appearing with Maurice Chevalier at the Fulton Theater in New York, taking part in the Hollywood film *Check and Double Check*, and releasing such records as *Ring Dem Bells, Old Man Blues,* and especially *Mood Indigo.* Toward the end of the year, a profile of the thirty-one-year-old composer and bandleader in the *Christian Science Monitor* attested to Ellington's growing prominence in the musical world.

This article—incorporating one of Ellington's first documented interviews—revealed two concerns that would stay with him for a lifetime: his aversion to the word "jazz" and his commitment to the ideals of "Negro music."

[1] These two were Ellington and the trumpeter and bandleader Red Nichols.

Source: Janet Mabie, "Ellington's 'Mood in Indigo': Harlem's 'Duke' Seeks to Express His Race," *Christian Science Monitor,* 13 December 1930.

Janet Mabie in the *Christian Science Monitor*

His name is Edward Kennedy Ellington. Too heavy and somber a name for a dance-band conductor to tote about with him. But that has been taken care of. Somewhere along the road people began to call him "Duke" and the name has stuck. I shouldn't wonder if it is connected somehow with what is quite apparently Ellington's great gift for understanding and his capacity for a very simple kind of friendliness. You would know he had those gifts if you watched him come into the Harlem restaurant [Cotton Club] whence he broadcasts late at night. People take quite appreciable pleasure when he comes in. They smile, and pat their hands together, and say among themselves, "And now we shall hear something."

Duke Ellington's musical career has something very naïve about it. He started out in the most modest fashion you can think of. Born in Washington, he took common school education through high school. Yes, his father played, and his mother played. "Played with music," Duke Ellington says, and you perceive that he has made a very subtle distinction indeed. They played, evidently, so that the playing, lacking the hard brilliance of technically experienced players, stuck in the boy's thought and helped him.

"When I was very young I took piano." An immemorial phrase, to conjure the picture of a child led protestingly to a piano and told there to school himself in an art. "But I couldn't get interested. Not in Czerny and the little things of Bach. Still, I drifted back into it; I played 'stomps' when I was 14. Then a pianist in Washington, Oliver Perry, very kindly took an interest in me when he chanced somewhere to hear me. He had a dance band and since he could get more work if he had more men, he broke me in to a sort of apprenticeship. It didn't cost him much and it was an advantage to me too. I was drawing and painting some, and I got a scholarship somehow for more instruction in art; but somewhere, inside of me, something said that was not the thing for me either. So I stayed with Perry.

"Then there was a man named Grant. Henry Grant. He was supervisor of music in the Washington schools. He said he would teach me harmony. I had a kind of harmony inside me, which is part of my race, but I needed the kind of harmony which has no race at all but is universal. So you see, from both those men I received, freely and generously, more than I could ever have paid for. I repaid them as I could; by playing for Mr. Perry, and by learning all I could from Mr. Grant.

"Then I came across a stumbling block. I really couldn't play very well the things white people played. So I decided that, since I must play, I should have to write something I could play myself. I suppose that is the beginning of my compositions. When you are doing things they don't seem milestones to you, but I guess having to write some things I myself could play properly was a milestone for me."

Ellington had a certain conscience about the scholarship in those early fine arts days. "I did all I could, though I knew I couldn't make a career of it. I studied hard at illustration, modeling, and wood carving. Well, it is something to put away in your knowledge, that sort of thing."

The war [World War I] came and in Washington there were parties for charity and war chests. A man named [Louis] Thomas practically controlled the music for the parties and Ellington went to work for him. But, he said ingenuously, "We seemed to have a little trouble about money, so I just took some men, and what music I had managed to get together and, by a lot of us looking over the few sheets of music and picking out the orchestration rather as we went along, we made the music do until we had earned enough money to buy some more music and get together some more instruments. And, if you will believe it, we began to make money."

In 1922 [*recte* 1923] there was a man named [Wilbur] Sweatman who wanted Ellington to come to New York, where there was an opportunity for such work. At first he made records for Brunswick; two years ago he went under exclusive contract to Victor.

There is a point of similarity between Duke Ellington and Paul Robeson. Both believe that in the heart of the Africa a man can travel into today there lies a great secret of music. Both want to go there and find it. I should think it was possible that one day both of them will do it.

Ellington's music is very interesting; sometimes too preponderantly brass; sometimes surprising in its velvety dusk of tone. It is a little hard to get precisely at what he means when he says he wants to "develop legitimate humor" because wailing and moaning and the hollow laughter of brass instruments is debatable humor. From jazz, as a subject, he shies as if he had suddenly touched something red hot. I can't say that I blame him. One way and another you cannot try to dissect jazz, as a phase of music. Too many people have pawed it over and changed it from a simple question for leisurely discussion into something that, at times, I have seen transformed into all the making of a nice brisk little war. "I get very confused," Ellington said, "if people ask me about jazz," and very wisely let it go at that.

Something was said about Ellington's own "Mood in Indigo" ["Mood Indigo"]. I got him to play it for me. I had heard it just once before, on the radio. It had seemed to me, of its kind, a sort of thing just a little too pungently lovely to be quite sure you've actually heard it.

"But it is very simple," he said, when he had finished playing it. "It is just one of those very simple little things that you throw together. Of course, the arrangement makes it. But it really isn't anything; the melody isn't. It's funny, I threw that together, and it has caught on. I've worked desperately over things, and then they haven't come out at all. Isn't it queer, not to have anything for a great deal of work, and something for no work at all?"

Yes, I suppose the "Mood in Indigo" is simple. Very simple indeed if you know how to do it.

"I am just getting a chance to work out some of my own ideas of Negro music. I stick to that. We as a race have a good deal to pay our way with in a white world. The tragedy is that so few records have been kept of the Negro music of the past. It has to be pieced together so slowly. But it pleases me to have a chance to work at it."

Two weeks after the preceding article appeared, a headline in the *New York Evening Graphic* displayed the name of a great operatic diva: " 'Opera Must Die,' Says Galli-Curci!

Long Live the Blues!" The article was dominated, however, not by Amelita Galli-Curci (1882 or 1889–1963) but by Edward Kennedy Ellington, the subject of eleven of the fifteen paragraphs. As in the *Christian Science Monitor* interview, Ellington sounded a theme he would champion throughout his career: an interest in composing music that embodied the experience of black Americans. To this end, Ellington told his interviewer that he was working on a large-scale piece called "The History of the Negro." Later in the decade Ellington would refer to this work as an opera. Eventually it emerged as *Black, Brown and Beige,* the three-part instrumental "tone parallel" premiered by his orchestra at Carnegie Hall in 1943 (see Part V).

The section on Galli-Curci has been omitted.

Florence Zunser in the *New York Evening Graphic*

From the extreme corners of the world of music two leaders in their chosen fields of expression step forward to tell what, in their minds, is the future and the fate of music. Though these two artists reign in altogether different kingdoms of music, they have both devoted their lives to the study and interpretations of melody and the muses.

With a blare of trumpets and the echo of the blues threading its way through his songs, Edward Kennedy Ellington, "The Duke of Modern Music," enters the scene. He and his band have introduced a new type of orchestra, a new interpretation of song, and a new understanding of popular music. He has been playing that which is not only "jazz," but which is a totally new type of modern music, and which, he believes, is to take the place of our present-day symphonies, concertos and opera. Music that will be the truest expression of the people; music that will be a mirror reflecting the real spirit of humanity!

"The future of music," said Mr. Ellington, "lies in the hands of those writers of Tin Pan Alley who see in popular songs and melodies of today the embodiment of the voice of the people."

The Duke believes that the real music of a country is not what is written by the inspired pen of a genius, but is the plain, simple folk songs that are hummed while men are at work and at play, and that are handed down from generation to generation. There have been, in the entire history of the world, but a handful of men who have written music that has been the true expression of the people of their countries, but there are countless folk songs that hold all the sorrow and joy of a nation in their simple melodies. . . .

The white man has never been able to throw himself into song and feeling the way the Negro does. Perhaps that is why Dvořák, in his "New World Symphony," turned to the Negro song "Goin' Home," for pure, simple beauty, and why George Gershwin uses the real black man's "Blues" throughout his "Rhapsody in Blue," and why Wilbur Dan Hanly [*recte* William Christopher Handy], sometimes called "The Father of the Blues," took a Negro melody

Source: Florence Zunser, " 'Opera Must Die,' Says Galli-Curci! Long Live the Blues!" *New York Evening Graphic Magazine,* 27 December 1930.

for his world-famous "St. Louis Blues," and why, perhaps, it will take a man like Duke Ellington, a full blooded Negro himself, to lead the way to music that is pure, unadulterated and unrestrained. The music of the future, the spontaneous song of the people!

Duke Ellington goes on to say: "You have only to watch a dance floor full of dancing couples to realize that music is the most vital thing in swaying the emotions of a multitude. You play real mournful blue music, and you will see the effect on the crowd. The next moment you turn to something "hot" — some "shout" or "stomp," as it used to be called, and you can watch the immediate, remarkable effect all about you.

"I am not playing jazz. I am trying to play the natural feelings of a people. I believe that music, popular music of the day, is the real reflector of the nation's feelings. Some of the music which has been written will always be beautiful and immortal. Beethoven, Wagner and Bach are geniuses; no one can rob their work of the merit that is due it, but these men have not portrayed the people who are about us today, and the interpretation of these people is our future music. . . ."

Besides being the leader of an orchestra which has revolutionized all jazz bands, Duke Ellington is a composer of note. "The Black and Tan Fantasy," "The Mooch," "Mood Indigo," "I'm So in Love with You," "Ring Dem Bells," "Old Man Blues," "Black Beauty" are just some of his many compositions. At present he is at work on a tremendous task, the writing, in music, of "The History of the Negro," taking the Negro from Egypt, going with him to savage Africa, and from there to the sorrow and slavery of Dixie, and finally "home to Harlem."

From the time he was 14 he has been composing, studying the piano and the music of his race. In Washington, the city where he was born, he played in several orchestras, and about eight years ago came north to New York. This was before the vogue for Harlem night clubs, and Ellington discovered that the city, contrary to expectations, was not paved with gold.

Four years ago Irving Mills became interested in him after hearing him playing in a night club [Kentucky Club]. The Duke's orchestra then consisted of five pieces. Mills was so impressed with the striking new note in Ellington's music that he became his backer. The orchestra was enlarged to twelve pieces, and they entered the Cotton Club, there to reign supreme as "the aristocrats of Harlem." His methods and orchestration in playing the "Tiger Rag," "St. Louis Blues" and countless other numbers have been copied the world over. People have flocked from every corner to hear him. His song sources, variations, and improvisations are unlimited, because, as he says, "The Negro is the blues. Blues is the rage in popular music. And popular music is the good music of tomorrow!"

9. Ellington's First Article:
"The Duke Steps Out" (1931)

E llington's first published article appeared in *Rhythm,* a British magazine aimed at dance-band musicians that ran from 1927 to 1939. In the early thirties *Rhythm* often commissioned essays from well-known bandleaders and musicians; Cab Calloway, for example, contributed a piece to the October 1931 issue.

The editors at *Rhythm* may have worked over these articles fairly thoroughly. The syntax and diction of the following phrase, for example, sound uncharacteristic of Ellington: "that modern dance music of the best type is completely rhythmic is only in accordance with the natural law." Yet the views expressed seem to be Ellington's—at least similar ones had surfaced earlier in newspaper interviews and would reappear with frequency later.[1]

Although keeping his musical discussion basic, Ellington offered trenchant comments on the process of arranging and gave an eloquent evaluation of black American music and his own role in its development.

My first thought when I began to write this article was one of admiration for whoever chose the name of this magazine. Our very lives are dependent on rhythm, for everything we do is governed by ordered rhythmic sequences: that modern dance music of the best type is completely rhythmic is only in accordance with the natural law.

Much has been said of the show part of the band—the melody instruments—and I have grown a little tired of this perpetual eulogy, because everyone who really understands the dance band of to-day knows that it is the rhythm section which is by far the most important; without a solid basis of impeccable rhythm, no matter how brilliant the melody section, the band can never be successful.

In many bands the soulless nature of this continual churning out of four-in-a-bar rhythm has developed apathy in the section, the players losing interest until their performance becomes stodgy and mechanical. In my view, much of the mechanical nature of playing in the rhythm section can be avoided, and in this article I propose to show how it can be done.

Undoubtedly the most important member of the rhythm section is the pianist. His job is to feed the band with rhythm; florid arpeggios and rapid chromatic runs are taboo until he plays solo. Then he can allow his imagi-

---

Source: Duke Ellington, "The Duke Steps Out," *Rhythm* (March 1931), 20–22.

[1] Much more severe editorial tampering appeared in various profiles of American musicians published in the British periodical *Melody Maker* in the early thirties. In one of a series of articles offering technical advice by members of Ellington's orchestra, for example, the effervescent, smooth-talking drummer Sonny Greer is credited with such turgid statements as: "It is a well-known psychological fact that pianists experience a peculiar sense of satisfaction when playing with the hands close together, or even overlapping, and I maintain that the percussive equivalent of this idiosyncrasy is the combination of manual and pedal action on a single pair of cymbals" ("Paradoxical Percussionism: Drummers Must Have Unerring Sense of 'Rightness' Says Sonny Greer," *Melody Maker* (24 June 1933), 13).

Ex. 1

Ex. 2

Ex. 3

nation free rein, utilising all the devices within his technique to impart the utmost rhythm to his rendition.

This avoidance of the sometimes overwhelming urge for the pianist to play or extemporise on the melody cannot be emphasised too strongly, for once he begins to neglect his immobile rhythm the whole section, which is dependent on him, immediately loses its essential snap and becomes ragged.

Long association between players should result in their being able almost to anticipate each other's thoughts, so that the first desideratum, viz., that they should play as one man, is not hard to attain. The first step to this end is to stabilise the rhythms played by the section.

One of the most important of rhythms is that generally known as the "after beat." This rhythm is ubiquitously played, but unless it is played as Example 1 it is seldom effective. This accenting of the bass is most important. An effective use of the after-beat rhythm is afforded in choruses where the section plays softly against a solo instrument or the melody instruments. In Example 2 a four-in-a-bar rhythm is shown with the first and third beats of the bar accented. This rhythm may be applied to a chorus where the band is playing *forte*. Here we have the accents on the first and third beats of the bar.

A problem which must have worried many pianists is, what to play during the last ensemble chorus. Amongst the pell mell of the other instruments the tendency to roam over the keyboard is again very ominous, but once more I say: Don't do it! In Example 3 I give you a rhythm which is eminently suited to ensemble choruses. I call it a "Walking Bass." It will be found to give depth and solidity to the last chorus, while retaining a rhythmic swing, and it has the further excellent quality of inspiring the rest of the section to give their best.

We do not use any printed orchestrations. These are much too stereotyped. For a band to keep in the top flight to-day it must be original. I therefore make all my own arrangements, and my first care when doing this is the rhythm section. Piano, banjo, bass and drums all play the same rhythms simultaneously; this is essential. I never write out a drum part, however, and to explain this apparent paradox I must say that my drummer, Sonny Greer, seems instinctively to know what rhythm I am going to play, and long association has shown me that his intuition in this direction is so uncanny that I can safely leave the percussion entirely in his capable hands.

What little fame I have achieved is the result of my special orchestrations, and especially of the cooperation of the boys in the band. I cannot speak too highly of their loyalty and initiative. During the past three years we have made the band our work and our hobby; all our creative powers have been put into its success, and the fact that our engagement at the Cotton Club, New York City, is now extending into its fourth year is an excellent testimonial and a pleasant reminder that we have been appreciated. Readers in England will be interested in the players, I know, so I am giving you the personnel.

Meet the boys: Harry Carney, Johnny Hodges and Barney Bigard are the saxophone section; trumpets are three, Arty Whetsol, Charlie [Cootie] Williams and Fred Jenkins. Perhaps you will think that three trumpets is one too many, and indeed I seem to be one of the very few leaders who have three, but I can only refer you to my records and ask you if you don't agree that the brass sounds much fuller in this way. Then on the trombone there are Joe Nanton and Juan Tizol. So you will see that my melody section is eight strong and we are able to get a full harmony that has depth without being in any way sluggish. In the rhythm section Wellman Braud plays bass, Fred Guy is on the banjo, Sonny Greer is the drummer, and I am at the piano. There they are, and you can guess how proud I am of them.

I am always being asked how I write the trick phrases and rhythms that my band plays, and I can only say that I get an inspiration in the most unconnected way, and out of it a new phrase or rhythm is born. In much the same way I write my tunes. About five years ago I wrote a tune called "Birmingham Breakdown" [1926], and this introduced a phrase shown in Example 4. This phrase I used for over twenty bars. Apparently it was before its time, and the phrase did not catch on, so that you can imagine how I felt when Jimmy McHugh came along with "The New Low Down" [1928], which was entirely dependent on this phrase and made a great hit. Everyone will remember "Crazy Rhythm" [1928], which also contained this old phrase of mine long forgotten in "Birmingham Breakdown."

The numbers I write are never, I think you will agree, of the "corn-fed" type. Always I try to be original in my harmonies and rhythms. I am not trying to suggest that my tunes are superior to those of other writers. Because I think

Ex. 4

that the music of my race is something which is going to live, something which posterity will honour in a higher sense than merely that of the music of the ballroom to-day, I put my best musical thoughts forward into my tunes, and not hackneyed harmonies and rhythms which are almost too banal to publish.

The involved nature of my numbers prevents them being great popular successes, but their popularity amongst musicians has meant a lot more to me than monetary gain, although, of course, I have to consider the financial side.

But I am not content with just fox-trots. One is necessarily limited with a canvas of only thirty-two bars and with a strict tempo to keep up. I have already said that it is my firm belief that what is still known as "jazz" is going to play a considerable part in the serious music of the future. I am proud of that part my race is playing in the artistic life of the world. Paul Robeson, Roland Hayes, your own [Samuel] Coleridge-Taylor, are names already high in the lists of serious music; that from the welter of negro dance musicians now before the public will come something lasting and noble I am convinced.

The music of my race is something more than the "American idiom." It is the result of our transplantation to American soil, and was our reaction in the plantation days to the tyranny we endured. What we could not say openly we expressed in music, and what we know as "jazz" is something more than just dance music. When we dance it is not a mere diversion or social accomplishment. It expresses our personality, and, right down in us, our souls react to the elemental but eternal rhythm, and the dance is timeless and unhampered by any lineal form.

You, as musicians, have your innate sense of rhythm, and will understand what I have written above: there is no necessity to apologise for attributing aims other than terpsichore to our music and for showing how the characteristic melancholy music of my race has been forged from the very white heat of our sorrows and from our gropings after something tangible in the primitiveness of our lives in the early days of our American occupation.

To-day we are an important and intrinsic part of the population of the great United States of America. In Harlem we have what is practically our own city; we have our own newspapers and social services, and although not segregated, we have almost achieved our own civilisation. The history of my people is one of great achievements over fearful odds; it is a history of a people hindered, handicapped and often sorely oppressed, and what is being done by Countee Cullen and others in literature is overdue in our music.

I am therefore now engaged on a rhapsody unhampered by any musical form in which I intend to portray the experiences of the coloured races in

America in the syncopated idiom. This composition will consist of four or five movements, and I am putting all I have learned into it in the hope that I shall have achieved something really worth while in the literature of music, and that an authentic record of my race *written by a member of it* shall be placed on record.

This is the first time I have written for any musical paper, but I feel that my ideas will be appreciated in a country which has accorded such a welcome to many of our distinguished artists. To you all I send the greetings of myself and my band, and the sincere hope that you find the records we make interesting. Remember that your most important asset is your rhythm—but I can hardly imagine you not doing that when your magazine has it for a title!

10. The Ellington Orchestra in Cleveland (1931)

During its Cotton Club engagement the Ellington orchestra would occasionally perform in other venues around New York and out of town. Beginning in February of 1931 it began to stay on the road for longer stretches, leaving Harlem to appear at dances and vaudeville theaters throughout the country.

A July engagement at the R-K-O Palace in Cleveland, Ohio, prompted three articles by critic Archie Bell in the *Cleveland News*: a short preview ("Duke Ellington Opens Here Tomorrow," Saturday, 4 July), a review ("Ellington Orchestra and Singer Make Hit," Monday, 6 July), and a lengthy feature piece with excerpts from an interview with Ellington ("Duke Ellington's Orchestra Draws Big Crowds," Wednesday, 8 July 1931). While the first of these pieces is routine, the latter two show Bell's unusual receptiveness to Ellington's art and appear below.

In his 6 July review of Ellington's opening at the Palace the day before, Bell singled out Ivie Anderson for special praise; the vocalist had joined the orchestra in February 1931 and was to remain until 1942 (see §91). Interviewed by Bell for the 8 July article, Ellington contrasted the experience of playing for dancers versus theater audiences and discussed his "rule-breaking" approach to composition.

A longtime journalist based in Cleveland, Archie Bell (1877–1943) wrote on theater and music for the *Cleveland News* from 1917 until his retirement in the mid-thirties.

Source: Archie Bell, "Ellington Orchestra and Singer Make Hit," *Cleveland News*, 6 July 1931; Archie Bell, "Duke Ellington's Orchestra Draws Big Crowds," *Cleveland News*, 8 July 1931.

6 July 1931

. . . The program at the R-K-O Palace . . . strikes me as being one of the best hot or cold weather programs that I have seen at that or any other house for a long time. Both for variety of acts and their quality. Duke Ellington and his Cotton club orchestra are star-lined and they bring along a remarkable new-comer (to this pair of eyes and ears), Ivie Anderson. The program offered by this sepia ensemble is well worth the price of admission to the Palace, and everything else seems added for good measure.[1] As I have said many times, these chocolate-tinted folk have something distinctly artistic and fine to offer, when they adhere to their own idiom. In the present instance, that is done. No effort to imitate a Ziegfeld Follies, White's Scandals or Carroll's Vanities, which is too frequently the case. The Duke is a wise showman. He is fully aware of the value of his offering and the means by which it should be pre-sented. And with Miss Anderson added, there's entertainment equal to most of the darktown musicals for which other prices are charged.

Here again we have another exceptionally entertaining comedienne, in no way that I could detect copying any of the styles or mannerisms of other brown singers. She doesn't need to do so, because she has a great individual style of shouting her songs that carries them across the footlights with the skill of a song recitalist who aims to tell a complete story and establish a distinct mood by each selection.

And one of the required qualities of the genuine comedienne, she has a note of pathos in her voice, used with effectiveness in her closing "I'm Going to Get Even with You"—whatever its formal title may be.

Here's an artist who takes her place with Ethel Waters, Adelaide Hall and a small group of her race.

The Duke offers several selections, some of which are familiar and others in rhythmic arrangements that make them appear to be something new. Throughout his program, there is the effort to afford ample opportunity to various instrumental virtuosi, who give good accounts of themselves, for instance, the trombonist [Joe Nanton], who tells a tearful story in something so like a human voice that it is almost uncanny, as well as amusing.

The chief number is the "Black and Tan Fantasy," which introduces some extraordinary instrumentation. Yes, it's played in vaudeville by a Negro orchestra noted for its rhythm and syncopation; but I'll wager the guess that there's more originality and worthy experimentation in it than in half of the "new" music that is offered in a season by the Cleveland orchestra.

On this score, I would venture the opinion that it is worth more than, for example, [Charles Martin] Loeffler's "Evocation," which was composed for the opening of Severance hall [on 5 February 1931]. It has more in it that will serve as an example in orchestral effects of modern composers than any amount of the newer stuff that is coming out of Russia. . . .

[1] Also on the bill with Ellington were singer May Usher, comedian Joe Herbert, dancers Lee, Lee, Lee, and Lee, the film "Ex-Bad Boy" (starring Robert Armstrong and Jean Arthur), and clips of the recent heavyweight bout between Max Schmeling and Young Stribling.

8 July 1931

They're all talking, along theater row, about the phenomenal business at the R-K-O Palace this week. Most of them are explaining it. "Cooler weather, for one thing," is heard. "The pictures of the big fight," is another explanation. But, of course, everybody knows that it's Duke Ellington and his Cotton Club Orchestra that's drawing the crowds. They'd do the same thing if the weather were blistering hot like last week. They'd do it if the streets were piled with snow. Everywhere they go it's the same thing. And the crowds not only follow this dispensation of jazz and syncopation, they demand more and more of it. "Never had so many requests for numbers since I've been in the theater," said a house attache yesterday. "Everybody has a favorite and the list has become so long that Duke says he'll devote his program next Friday night to request numbers, so presumably everybody will be satisfied." But don't believe it. Even the long list of "requests" will bring encores galore. Why, those sepia-tinted artists could give a "continuous" show, I imagine, and the crowds would still surge in and out of the theater. What does it mean? That jazz is taking another spurt, after having gone to its deathbed several months ago? That people are music-hungry? That they want stage orchestras again, after the vogue was supposed to have passed? (Several orchestras are booked for the near future at both the Palace and the State theaters and it looks like a revival of interest in them.)

But none of these things explains the popularity of Duke Ellington and his instrumentalists, also not forgetting Ivie Anderson, the singing comedienne, an important member of the aggregation.

The fact is that Duke has the best band of its kind to be heard anywhere. Also, he's new in Cleveland. He tells me that he has played here for a dance, but never before in a local theater.

You know, it's the smartest thing to have him as the chief merry-maker at a fashionable ball. He was selected, for example, to entertain the Prince of Wales, when that personage was the guest of honor at a country breakfast on Long Island.

Since then, if you want to give your guests the last word in entertainment, you engage Duke and his crowd to play—and then let your guests "express themselves" in terpsichore.

He has so many of these ultra engagements in the residences of the wealthy and so many calls from fashionable clubs that he finds it impracticable to make bookings for long tours over the theatrical circuits. So he plays "spot" engagements, this week with one circuit in a key city, next week with another, or perhaps devoting all his evenings to playing for society to kick up its heels.

"There's method in my apparent madness," he told me yesterday. "Of course, it's more satisfactory to me and to the boys to appear in a theater like the Cleveland Palace, where we are received as artists by the large audiences that come to see a vaudeville program. When we play for dances, we're just there as hired entertainers and we know it. But, do you know, it's a mighty good thing for the boys, this playing for dances, it keeps them on their mettle.

"I haven't had a wide experience in vaudeville, but I have observed that if we play the same old program four or five times a day in one theater after another, week after week, we are likely to let down a bit and become careless. Not that there's a conscious desire to slump, but from the very nature of the routine. My boys don't cheat, so far as work is concerned; I think anyone will admit to that who has heard them and seen them. But when we break into the routine and go to the ballroom, where we must offer new numbers and where we must keep our energies at fever heat—well, it's a good thing for all of us; and we go back to the theater the next week with a new gusto and vim." . . .

The Duke told me: "When I'm making my arrangements or composing something new, I try to think of something that will make my hearers feel like dancing. It's a primitive instinct, this dancing business, perhaps; but it also signifies happiness and the desire to step around a little means that people are not bothering very much about the cares of the world, at least for the moment. And I like to see happy people. I like to think that I'm contributing something that promotes at least temporary happiness."

This orchestra leader, who has forged to the front to an amazing degree of popularity in recent months, was born in Washington. "Yes, I was what they called 'musical' from the start as a boy," he related. "And, mind you that while I move my lips and pretend to sing today, although I'm not much of a songbird, I was considered a baritone with a worthwhile voice, when I was a member of a glee club.

"Truth is, however, that music and baseball had a mighty struggle in me, each endeavoring to make a decision in regard to my future. I studied music, devoting myself first of all to the piano; but I was glad when the practice hours were over and I was out on the field playing ball.

"Music won out, I guess, because I went along to harmony and composition. The joke of it was, however, that when I became what might be called an active musician, I discarded most of the rules I had learned and found greatest success in doing the things that my harmony instructors had warned me against; but that was in the air then, just as it is in the air today. Composers and arrangers decline to be held down by a set of rules and don'ts—and if you ask me, I'll say that's one of the things that is putting new life into music."

When he is composing he doesn't ask himself whether he is putting down notes that will be admired and praised by conservatory professors of theory, harmony and composition: "Will that musical phrase give 'em a kick?" or "will they feel like hopping around a bit when they hear that?"

Very wisely, as I have commented before, Ellington doesn't try to imitate or adapt himself to what might be called "white folks' compositions," that is, he doesn't attempt to follow the ancient formula that originated in Europe.

Rather, he thinks Africano, knowing that there's a fertile field there that thus far has only been tapped. Spanish music, as it is known today, came from Africa, brought across by the Moors. It's easy to trace even the now popular "Cuban rhythm" to the same source. "Whatever they attempt to prove," says Ellington, "jazz had its origin in Africa. It's something distinct and well worth the cultivation and development that it is now receiving; and its reception by the entire world within the last few years proves that it's something impossible to dismiss with a gesture of contempt."

11. Ellington Crowned "King of Jazz" by the *Pittsburgh Courier* (1931)

B oth white and black publications celebrated Ellington's growing fame in 1930–1931. After winning a "Most Popular Orchestra" contest sponsored by the *Pittsburgh Courier*, one of the major black newspapers, Ellington was described by reporter Floyd G. Snelson as "a source of inspiration to every striving musician of the race."

Snelson identified the second part of his article as a reprint of something called "Harlem Limited Broadway Sound." Its biographical section—probably derived from publicity material supplied by Irving Mills, or perhaps an actual press release—contained minor inaccuracies, as in stating that Ellington studied with Henry Grant before going on to Mrs. (Marietta) Clinkscales. Yet it is included here to illustrate one way Ellington was presented to the public at this stage in his career—as the "typical American boy" whose musical talent had taken him to the top of his profession.

During the past year or more the name of Duke Ellington has lingered upon the lips of radio fans, dance lovers, theatregoers and the amusement public of the Nation in general. The colorful career and sudden rise to fame of this young man reads like fiction, and is beyond doubt a source of inspiration to every striving musician of the race.

Crowned "King of Jazz" last week in the National "Most Popular Orchestra" Contest conducted by the *Pittsburgh Courier,* reigning supreme and having polled 50,000 votes, the largest amount, competing with over 50 orchestras and bands all over the United States, Duke Ellington has proved that he is the most popular orchestra leader today.

Moreover, the *Orchestra World,* a white publication, published at 1674 Broadway, New York City, printed in the April (1931) issue: "Ellington Takes Lead in Popularity Contest." First returns show hot players favored for individual honors. Here's the leaders in order named: Duke Ellington; Gordon Kibbler; Leo Hannon, Abe Dyman [Lyman], Rudy Vallee tie for third honors; Mal Hallett; Smith Ballew; Guy Lombardo; Fred Waring; and Paul Tremaine. These leaders represent the big ten. Incidentally the Duke also led in the contest for the best individual player: Sonny Greer, drummer in Duke's orchestra standing second.

He is declared to be the "King of Jazz" in America today. Long live the Duke and may he reign upon the throne for many moons.

"The Hottest Band On Earth," which is the description given to Duke Ellington and His Famous Orchestra, and won by unanimous vote of the music

Source: Floyd G. Snelson, "Story of Duke Ellington's Rise to Kingship of Jazz Reads Like Fiction . . . ," *Pittsburgh Courier,* 19 December 1931.

loving public that reaches from New York to Los Angeles. And now he is the "King of Jazz."

The record of achievement and heights of fame is the usual barometer by which an artist is judged in the arts and professions. If this be the case, it goes without saying that the Duke has inherited this enviable position in the music world. He has toured the country during the past 10 weeks, playing the Paramount and Warner Brothers' largest cities of the east and middle west. These playhouses concede with high appreciation, that Ellington has broken their attendance and box office records for the season, and in most instances has added new life and vigor to the institutions.

At the Oriental Theater, the foremost Paramount in Chicago, the Duke made his sixth appearance a few weeks ago within a year, and the receipts totaled over $19,000, breaking all former records of the house for the year. Managers and promoters all agree that he is the biggest hit of all time, regardless of race or color.

(Editor's Note: The succeeding part of this story is a reproduction of "Harlem Limited Broadway Sound" printed last February.)

Broadway has been agog with the name of Duke Ellington—having completed an engagement of 70 performances at the New York Paramount Theater, the world's cinema center, having reached the pinnacle of success along with Rudy Vallee, Paul Ash, Vincent Lopez, Paul Whiteman and others. The first time a Negro orchestra has played in this favored spot, sharing honors with Maurice Chevalier.

The Duke and his boys were billed at the Paramount like Barnum and Bailey, with mammoth [sic] signs, gigantic posters of every description, fleeting flags that heralded them blocks away. This was positively the greatest ovation ever extended an artist of the Negro race in history.

In addition to this vast achievement, Duke was featured attraction in Amos 'n' Andy's radio talking picture "Check and Double Check" which has its premiere across the street at the new Mayfair Theater. It was Duke Ellington on both sides of Broadway—up and down the gay white way. The music shops were "grinding" away the Duke Ellington Victor records—pianos "plunking" his fascinating music. Still more the stations WEAF and WJZ of the NBC nightly were thrilling its millions of fans over the air with his glorious syncopation. His jungle rhythm and barbaric interpretations are in the heydey [sic] of delight and fascination.

Long after the radio stations had ceased, Broadway itself had taken on an air of sophistication, theater crowds had retired in quietude. Duke and his boys were back at the Cotton Club in Harlem, making the whoopee for the aristocratic night-club revellers and the millionaire class of the Bradstreet variety.

It takes iron nerve, valiant courage and unceasing vigilance, as well as confidence and reliability, that these lads gave the best that is within them. They received a million hands of applause and I know dear readers you will join hands in giving them millions more.

Born and reared in the District of Columbia, April 29, 1900 [*recte* 1899], and was christened Edward Kennedy Ellington, and lived most of his early life at 2129 Ward Place, northwest, attending Garrison and Garnett [Garnet] schools and was graduated from Armstrong High. There he completed courses in art, painting, designing, etching, etc. Was an all-round athlete and his six feet of brawny manhood made him an ideal football, baseball, basketball, cinder path, or broad-jump candidate—anywhere a virile ability was required. The Duke loved them all. It was in his school days that he gained the nomenclature as the Duke. His smart appearance and popularity among the classman [sic] merited him the title, which he has made famous.

Began his studies of pianoforte at the age of eight years under the tutelage of Prof. [Henry] Grant and later with Mrs. [Marietta] Clinkscales. He proved to be quite apt and displayed his remarkable gifts of music. Making brilliant strides in his scholastic work as well as a most unique talent at the piano, it was a quandary to his parents which one he would major [in]. Many occasions his mother hailed young Edward from a good baseball game to his music lessons. His hobby for sports created him a typical American boy.

He is a son of Mr. and Mrs. James Edward Ellington, long residents of the capital. His father retired after many years' service as a blue-printer for the United States Navy Yard. His mother was formerly employed in the Government departments. Has a younger sister, Dorothea Ruth [recte Ruth Dorothea], a pretty sub-deb, now a student at Wadleigh High. Some months ago Duke removed his parents and sister to New York, and they now reside with him in their spacious apartment, at 381 Edgecombe Avenue. He is a handsome provider for his family, a most dutiful son, generous brother, and recently presented his . . . [line missing in original source—probably intended to be, "mother with a new automobile"] and maintains a chauffeur for her convenience.

Duke and his wife, Mrs. Edna Ellington, have lived apart for some time—however he grants her every wish and they are true platonic friends. They have a 12-year-old son, Mercer, who lives with the family, when not in the care of his mother.

It is interesting to note that Duke Ellington began his professional career at the age of 16 years, during his school days in Washington, with Louis Thomas, w[ell] k[nown] musician who supplied orchestras for D.C.'s wealthy society and diplomatic circles. They played in all sections of the surrounding territory of Virginia and Maryland. He later organized his own band, which he called the Washingtonians.

He came to New York in 1923 and played for dances, etc. and his first job was at the Hollywood Cafe on Broadway. While there he made quite a name for himself, and later worked at summer resorts, clubs, hotels, and the like. Finally, he was engaged at the Cotton Club, where he started upon his road to fame. His music became the sensation of New York and his radio programs were the peer of the air. During this time he was featured in Ziegfeld's "Show Girl" and played many important engagements at the Hotels Astor, Biltmore, Plaza and other places of aristocracy, which leads up to his triumphant tour that has made him the nation's favorite and "The King of Jazz."

12. A Landmark in Ellington Criticism: R. D. Darrell's "Black Beauty" (1932)

P ublished in *disques*, a magazine usually devoted to new classical recordings, R. D. Darrell's "Black Beauty" was the first major critical statement on Duke Ellington's music. Provocative, insightful, in many ways prophetic, it remains one of the most important articles ever written about Ellington.

In the essay, titled after a 1928 Ellington composition, Darrell both recapitulated observations he had made earlier in the *Phonograph Monthly Review* (see §6) and expanded on them. Steeped in European music, both classical and modern, the twenty-eight-year-old critic identified traits that distinguished Ellington as a composer and that set him apart from others, such as Aaron Copland and George Gershwin, who had attempted to write serious works employing the jazz idiom.

At the end of the article Darrell appended a discography of Ellington's works from 1927 to 1932. This has been omitted below, since more accurate information can be found in such standard sources as Brian Rust's *Jazz Records 1897–1942*, 5th ed. (1983) and *ERMDE*. Darrell's selective guide to important releases—"A Note on the Ellington Records"—has been included as an example of his preferences in 1932.

For a biographical note on Darrell, see §6.

"Nothing is lost that's wrought with tears," said Blake; and since every personal revelation of life through art, so long as it is authentic and communicative, is infinitely precious, there can be no question of the value of such disclosure of temperament and experience . . . —*Lawrence Gilman.*[1]

Gilman's words were applied by him to Loeffler, but they are no less applicable to others who write directly from the heart and sensibilities, and whose works—a small but golden core of the musical repertory—strike home to us with an intensity of feeling, an evocative magic, that is more intimately moving than the great dramatic, passionate, fantastic utterances of music's *Uebermenschen* [supermen].

In the last century music has immeasurably enlarged its scope and enriched its texture, but there has been an increasing preoccupation with sheer rhetoric and gaudy sound splashes, the vehemence of whose statement disguises their essential incoherence and unassimilation of true feeling. Decadence sets in with its emphasis on detail at the expense of the whole. The tendency to *schrecklichkeit* [frightfulness], the striving for greater dynamic extremes, is not yet curbed. The urge to originality defeats itself, forcing into the background organic principles: economy of means, satisfying proportion of detail, and the

---

Source: R. D. Darrell, "Black Beauty," *disques* (Philadelphia: H. Royer Smith, June 1932), 152–61.

[1] From "A Musical Cosmopolite," Gilman's chapter on Charles Martin Loeffler in *Nature in Music and Other Studies in the Tone-Poetry of Today* (New York: John Lane, 1914), 204. Lawrence Gilman (1878–1939) was an influential music critic, author of books on Edward MacDowell and opera, and program annotator for the New York Philharmonic and the Philadelphia Orchestra.

sense of inevitability—of anticipation and *revelatory* fulfillment—that are the decisive qualifications of musical forms.

The "personal revelation," the "authentic and communicative" grow even rarer than the mighty dramatic peaks. The always small audience for personal revelation grows still scantier, and where some hear it in the latter works of Strawinski, others hear only barrenness. The Teutonically romantic-minded find an experience in Bruckner and Mahler that is shoddy and over-blown to those who find their rarest musical revelation in the pure serenity and under-statement of Delius. One searches far afield, and having found, discovers the fruit to be sweet to oneself alone, an experience that cannot be shared, scarcely comprehended by others.

So when I upturn treasure in what others consider the very muck of music, I cannot be surprised or disappointed if my neighbor sees only mud where I see gold, ludicrous eccentricity where I find an expressive expansion of the tonal palette, tawdry tunes instead of deep song, "nigger music" instead of "black beauty."

II

The way was paved for me by a few of the early "blues," before the blues singers made money and acquired sophistication. The artless, tender singing of Lena Wilson in *I Need You to Drive My Blues Away* and *I'm a Good Gal But I'm a Long Ways from Home* struck me as the unworked stuff of pure folk music.[2] I had a glimpse of how such material might be worked by a musician who had the mind as well as the heart, the skilled hand as well as the natural voice—a musician who would compose as tenderly as Lena Wilson sang, as simply and richly as Paul Robeson, as intensely as Roland Hayes. But Lena Wilson came of age with the rest of the blues singers and toyed as slyly with delicate obscenity; Robeson and Hayes brought to flower their matchless interpretative technique: the creative spirit was lacking.

With the majority I did not recognize it when it first came to my ears in the form of the "hottest, funniest record you ever heard." It was a Brunswick disc by a dance band named the Washingtonians, and I laughed like everyone else over its instrumental wa-waing and gargling and gobbling, the piteous whinnying of a very ancient horse, the lugubrious reminiscence of the Chopin funeral march. But as I continued to play the record for the amusement of my friends I laughed less heartily and with less zest. In my ears the whinnies and wa-was began to resolve into new tone colors, distorted and tortured, but agonizingly expressive. The piece took on a surprising individuality and entity as well as an intensity of feeling that was totally incongruous in popular dance music. Beneath all its oddity and perverseness there was a twisted beauty that grew on me more and more and could not be shaken off.

A work like this was alien to all my notions of jazz. It had nothing of the sprightly gusto of Gershwin or Kern, nothing of the polite polish of the White-

[2] Lena Wilson, sister-in-law of singer Edith Wilson, appeared in black theatrical productions of the twenties and recorded a number of sides between 1922 and 1931.

man school, nothing of the raucous exuberance of the Negro jazz I had known. Nor was it in the heavily worked "spiritual" tradition, except in that it sounded an equal depth of poignance. For all its fluidity and rhapsodic freedom it was no improvisation, tossed off by a group of talented virtuosi who would never be able to play it twice in the same way. It bore the indelible stamp of one mind, resourcefully inventive, yet primarily occupied not with the projection of effects or syncopated rhythms, but the concern of great music—tapping the inner world of feeling and experience, "realizing a temperament without describing it, with the mobility of the soul, with the swiftness of consecutive moments . . . seizing the human heart with that intensity which is independent of the 'idea.'"

III

That the *Black and Tan Fantasy* was no haphazard lighting of a spark in the dark I was soon to discover when I heard and studied the new works that flowed from the pen and orchestra of its composer. Out of the vast bulk of his work, thrown off in his cabaret-dance-hall-vaudeville-recording routine, I found a goodly residue of music that was of the same or superior calibre as the fantasy; and disregarding all that was merely conventional, noisy, and cheap, there was still a quintessence of precious quality for which one has no apter term than genius. At last I had found the answer to Clive Bell's accusation that jazz had a childish horror of the noble and the beautiful; the answer to his demand for "thought rather than spirits, quality rather than color, knowledge rather than irreticence, intellect rather than singularity, wit rather than romps, precision rather than surprise, dignity rather than impudence, and lucidity above all things."[3]

The answer was—and almost alone still is—Duke Ellington, a young Negro pianist, composer, and orchestra leader, gifted with a seemingly inexhaustible well of melodic invention, possessor of a keenly developed craftsmanship in composition and orchestration. A man with a burly athlete's body like Robeson, the sensitive face and hands of a Roland Hayes. A man who knows exactly what he is doing: exercising his intelligence, stretching to new limits his musicianship, while he remains securely rooted in the fertile artistic soil of his race. A man who has evolved a unique pianistic technique, orchestral rather than solo, and who out of a group of some ten men has built his own orchestra, one of remarkable attainments in whatever it plays, but in his own creations a superb and personal instrument. And the man has stated in unmistakable words his own credo,* no press agent's blurb of a talented but ungrounded

[3] From the conclusion of Bell's polemical article, "Plus De Jazz," *New Republic* (21 September 1921), 92–96, reprinted in *Since Cézanne* (1922).

* The music of my race is something more than the "American idiom." It is the result of our transplantation to American soil, and was our reaction in the plantation days to the tyranny we endured. What we could not say openly we expressed in music, and what we know as "Jazz" is something more than just dance music . . . There is no necessity to apologize for attributing aims other than terpsichorean to our music, and for showing how the characteristic, melancholy music of my race has been forged from the very white heat of our sorrows, and from our gropings after

black, but the staunch ideal of a new Negro[4]—evolution of the Southern darky and Harlem buck—an artist who has the right to claim, "I put my best thoughts into my tunes, and not hackneyed harmonies and rhythms which are almost too banal to publish."

IV

As a purveyor and composer of music that must be danced to (if he is to earn his living), Ellington's composition is narrowly limited by dance exigencies while he is allowed a wide range of experimentation in the way of instrumentation and performance. It is hardly remarkable that the latter experimentation has borne fruit; what is remarkable is that working within constricted walls he has yet been able to give free rein to his creative imagination and racial urge for expression. Perhaps the very handicaps, permitting no high-flown excursions into Negro Rhapsodies and tone poems, allowing no escape from the fundamental beat of dance rhythm, have enabled Ellington to concentrate his musical virility, draw out its full juice, dissipating none of his forces in vain heaven-storming. He finds his subjects close at hand and the very titles reveal the essential unity of his music-making with the life of his people in deep South or darkest Harlem: *Black Beauty, Awful Sad, Saturday Night Function, Parlor Social Stomp, Rent Party Blues, Song of the Cotton Field, Jungle Nights in Harlem, Swampy River . . .*[5]

Ellington writes naturally for instruments alone, unlike the tunesters of Tin Pan Alley who can never divorce themselves from "words and music." Words may sometimes be added to his pieces, but always unhappily, and the only piece of his that falls into ordinary song classification—*I'm So in Love with You*—is the only one I know that is utterly devoid of character and interest. The human voice is not disdained, but in his works it operates only in an instrumental technique, wordlessly, one might say inarticulately if it were not for the definite articulation of its expressiveness. Once or twice actual words appear, but merely in the nature of a motto or catch-phrase—"Play me the blues, boy, it's the blues I love to sing." The larger works of Gershwin, the experiments of Copland and other "serious" composers are attempts with new symphonic forms stemming from jazz, but not of it. Not forgetting a few virtuoso or improvisatory solos (by Zez Confrey, [Joe] Venuti and [Eddie] Lang, Jimmie [James P.] Johnson, or others), one can say truthfully that a purely instrumental school of jazz has never grown beyond the embryonic stage. Ellington has emancipated American popular music from text for the first time since the Colonial days of reels and breakdowns.

---

something tangible in the primitiveness of our lives in the early days of our American occupation . . . I think the music of my race is something which is going to live, something which posterity will honor in a higher sense than merely that of the music of the ball-room of today. *Rhythm*, March, 1931 [see §9].

[4] The "New Negro" is a phrase that gained currency around 1925 and was applied to younger writers, artists, intellectuals, and political activists whose work was seen as challenging older conceptions of black identity and culture. See, for example, educator Alain Locke's *The New Negro* (1925).

[5] All of these compositions are by Ellington except for Porter Grainger's *Song of the Cotton Field*.

V

Ellington's compositions gravitate naturally toward two types, the strongly rhythmed pure dance pieces (*Birmingham Breakdown, Jubilee Stomp, New Orleans Low Down, Stevedore Stomp,* etc.), or the slower paced lyrical pieces with a less forcefully rhythmed dance bass (*Mood Indigo, Take It Easy, Awful Sad, Mystery Song,* etc.). Occasionally the two are combined with tremendous effectiveness, as in the *East St. Louis Toodle-O, Old Man Blues,* or *Rocking in Rhythm.*

The most striking characteristic of all his works, and the one which stamps them ineradicably as his own, is the individuality and unity of style that weld composition, orchestration, and performance into one inseparable whole. Ellington's arrangements of other composers' pieces reveal the same mastery with which he scores his own (indeed at times he comes close to creating an entirely new composition, as in *Got Everything But You*); his performance of even banal pieces like *Nine Little Miles from [Ten-Ten-] Tennessee* or *Three Little Words* are brilliant in the extreme; his own pieces retain many of their distinctive qualities when played by others. But all these variants present only scattering facets of his talents. To be observed completely and in their full expression they must be heard fused into one.

Except in certain solo works the balance and unity between content and form, written notes and sounded performance, has become something of a lost art since the Elizabethan madrigals and instrumental fantasies. A few composers, like Debussy and Delius, find the happy identity between material and medium, but they are not so lucky as Ellington in possessing the instrument and ability to play their scores as ideally as they are written. The rise of virtuosity broke the golden nexus between creative and executive artist. Music has become too complex. Few modern works can be heard ideally except mentally, poring over the written score. Popular music sounds the lowest depths with one man writing a tune, another harmonizing it, a third scoring it, and a fourth called in for the actual performance. And one's ears cannot be deceived as to the barbarous conglomeration of individualities, blurring or burying whatever fragrance or delicacy any one talent may have contributed. Ellington is of course the rare exception, but his work—composed, scored, and played under one sure hand—gives a glimpse of an Utopian age in music that seemed forever lost.*

VI

In stylistic individuality alone Ellington is outstanding in popular music, for while Tin Pan Alley boasts many personalities, their color is seldom blended

---

* The individual touch is carried even further into recording, and an occasional record, made with a keen understanding of microphone technique, reveals Ellington's work better than even a performance in the flesh. Hear such bits of matchless recording as the prominent bass saxophone melody in *Got Everything But You* with a trumpet counterpoint above, amazingly distant, pianissimo, and yet perfectly distinct; or the beginning of the *Mystery Song,* a similarly successful experiment in tonal perspective, with piano, string bass, and banjo fairly close to the microphone, while the brass, carrying the theme, are far back, sounding as ethereal as the "horns of Elfland, faintly blowing."

inextricably with their music. Whiteman was individual only when he alone had mastered a polished style; today he is a second- or third-rater. Gershwin, better The Gershwins, have developed a marked individuality; several others to a lesser degree. There are of course many highly individual soloists, but even when the finest are collected together, as they were in the hey-days of Red Nichols' Pennies, one gets marvellous but hardly homogeneous performances. It is as if one put Gieseking, Szigeti, Tertis, and Beatrice Harrison to playing chamber music together; whereas Ellington's band has achieved a homogeneity comparable only with that of the Flonzaleys.[6] Imagine if you can that the Flonzaleys composed and scored as one man even as they played as one man, and that the style was not a perfect blend of four individualities but an entity, and you have some idea of the fusion of content, form, and medium in Ellington's work.

Within an Ellington composition there is a similar unity of style among the essential musical qualities of melody, rhythm, harmony, color, and form. Unlike most jazz writers Ellington never concentrates undue attention on rhythm alone. It is always vital, the exuberant life blood of his work, but its use is never synecdochical. Delightful and tricky rhythmic effects are never introduced for sheer sensational purposes, rather they are developed and combined with others as logical part and parcel of a whole work. There is a high degree of subtlety in treating the inexorable fundamental dance beat. It is never disguised, indeed often stressed, but it is combined with the flowing bass so adroitly that it provides the sturdy substructure on which Ellington rears his luxuriant structure of moving parts, forgotten except in that it provides the measure by which to appreciate the boldly declamatory freedom of the upper voices.

Harmonically Ellington is apt and subtle rather than obvious or striking. Except for sheerly declamatory lines, his melodies are clothed in the harmonies they themselves suggest. He thinks not in chordal blocks but in moving parts, and the resulting harmony (complex as it may be upon analysis) derives simply, inevitably from the fluent weaving of contrapuntal lines, each in itself melodically interesting.

In the exploitation of new tonal coloring, as has already been suggested, Ellington has proceeded further than any composer—popular or serious—of today. His command of color contrast and blend approaches at times an art of poly-timbres. Beauty of quality is the prime consideration, even although Ellington's beauty may be distorted, lean, and spare to unaccustomed ears. But he has liberated the saxophone from its usual oily blandness, expanded the tonal palette of the clarinet (particularly in the *chalumeau* register), and given the brass a range of kaleidoscopic tonal nuances that opens up a new world of enchanting tonal loveliness and poignancy.

Formally Ellington has not gone as far, although he has mastered the small

---

[6] Darrell's hypothetical example of a heterogenous chamber group includes the German pianist Walter Gieseking (1895–1956), American-Hungarian violinist Joseph Szigeti (1892–1973), English violist Lionel Tertis (1876–1975), and English cellist Beatrice Harrison (1892–1965). The Flonzaley Quartet, active from 1902 to 1928, was one of the most celebrated American string quartets in the first quarter of the century, notable for its elegant and polished ensemble style.

form as thoroughly as Gershwin, and even *The Man I Love* is no more completely *durchkomponiert* [through-composed] than the *Creole Love Call* or *East St. Louis Toodle-O* with their perfectly sustained moods through even the contrasting episodes. The one attempt at a larger form, the two-part *Creole Rhapsody* (Brunswick), is not wholly successful, although it does develop and interweave a larger number of themes than is common in his work. Expanded to fill both sides of a twelve-inch disc (Victor) it becomes less integrated and the various episodes tend to fall apart. It is here that Ellington has most to learn and his present talents can find their best scope for further development.

Ellington achieves homogeneity in his compositions by the simple but natural development of rhythm, harmony, color, and form—even as they evolved in the history of music—from melody. The intoxicating rhythmic and coloristic multiplicity of his pieces springs from the fertility of his melodic invention. Since Brahms (except perhaps for Sibelius and Elgar) noble, spontaneous, unforced melodies have seldom been written. Melodies tend to become more and more short-breathed and unvocal, whereas Ellington's finest tunes spring into rhapsodic being as simply, as naturally as those of Mozart or Schubert. Characteristic of even the lesser tunes is their astounding fluidity and resilience of line, a return to the true rhapsody and freedom of earlier music, first scotched by the tyranny of the bar-line and eight bar phrase dogmas. Over the straining, strongly pulling bass and the fundamental beat, the true melody, or more often two or more melodies dip, curvet, swoop, and spiral in the untrammelled, ecstatic freedom of soaring gulls. And in addition to the Elizabethan buoyancy and flexibility of line, Ellington often captures something of the intensity of meaning attached to certain notes or phrases that Wagner was perhaps the first to give, making any note in the scale sound as though it were a "leading tone." In the melodies of *Black Beauty* and *Take It Easy* the looping line returns again and again to points of incredibly sharpened poignance.

VII

Analysis of Ellington's best compositions would be futile without lengthy illustrations in full-score notation. Even then the score could be fully appreciated only with the aid of a recorded performance. I can only analyze some of my own impressions of the works, beg the alert listener to hear and study the records, and leave it to his own sensibilities. To me the hushed trumpets, "far away and long ago," in *Mood Indigo* and the *Mystery Song,* sing of as enchanted a Spring as Strawinski's trumpets at the beginning of the second half of the *Sacre [du Printemps]*. To me the most daring experiments of the modernists rarely approach the imaginative originality, mated to pure musicianship, of a dozen arresting moments in Ellington's works. To me the most brilliant flights of Rimsky's or Strauss' orchestral fancy are equalled if not surpassed by many passages in the Ellington records—a blazing parabolic trajectory, tail-spin and swoop, of clarinet, saxophone, or whole woodwind choir; a delicate birdlike fluttering or vigorous statement of the piano; a monkey-like chatter and stutter of the trumpets; a pattern, half-melodic, half-rhythmic, used *ostinato* fashion on the tubular bells, cymbals, or suddenly percussive piano.

To me again there is absolutely nothing in popular music, all too little in any music, that touches the uncannily twisted beauty, the acrid pungence of nostalgia which Ellington in his great moments achieves. I can compare it only with the tortured rapture of Roland Hayes' face and hands as he sings certain spirituals, an agonized ecstasy too profound, too piercing to be glimpsed without a sense of sacrilege that so naked a baring of the soul should be witnessed by others.

Ellington may betray his uniqueness for popularity, be brought down entirely to the levels of orthodox dance music, lose his secure footing and intellectual grasp in the delusion of grandeur. Much of his commercial work evidences just such lapses. But he has given us and I am confident will give us again more than a few moments of the purest, the most sensitive and ineluctable revelation of feeling in music today. And where the music of his race has heretofore been a communal, anonymous creation, he breaks the way to the individuals who are coming to sum it up in one voice, creating personally and consciously out of the measureless store of racial urge for expression.

These are lofty statements, but I have not set them down without weighing them carefully and finding their justification in an absorbed study of Ellington's work during the past five years. I feel it no blasphemy to say of him as [George] Dyson says of the composer [Frederick Delius] whom I revere above all others of the last century: "He does not distil his thought into a single line, nor into a striking passage. He is concerned primarily with texture, just as Bach was. It is sustained atmosphere he seeks, and texture is his approach to it . . . So homogeneous he is that it is sometimes hard to tell where folk song ends and Delius begins."[7] Ellington's scope is vastly smaller, his atmosphere is sustained only over small canvasses, but to me intensity and not size is the true measure of musical worth. Working within his small but wholly personal range Ellington to me is one of Proust's great artists "who do us the service, when they awaken in us the emotion corresponding to the theme they have found, of showing us what richness, what variety lies hidden, unknown to us, in that great black impenetrable night, discouraging exploration, of our soul, which we have been content to regard as valueless and waste and void."

• • •

A Note on the Ellington Recordings

Duke Ellington and his orchestra have recorded at various times for all the major American recording companies and for several of the minor companies. For Victor they have recorded some seventy pieces, and there are others still to be released. For Brunswick some forty-five pieces (many of which are performed under the alias of the "Jungle Band"). Ellington is now under contract to Brunswick for twenty-four new record sides, to be released under his own name. For OKeh some twenty-four pieces (some of which are performed under the aliases of the "Harlem Foot-

[7] George Dyson, *The New Music* (London: Oxford University Press, 1924), 146.

warmers" or "Harlem Music Masters"). Ellington recorded his only disc of piano solos for OKeh. For Columbia he and his orchestra have recorded seven pieces (some under the aliases of "Joe Turner's Memphis Men" or "Sonny Greer's Memphis Men").

A brief list of the best and most characteristic Ellington recordings should include the following (and might be extended considerably further):

East St. Louis Toodle-O and *Got Everything But You*	Victor 21703
Black Beauty and *Take It Easy*	Brunswick 4009
Creole Love Call and *Black and Tan Fantasy*	Victor 21137
The Mooche and *Hot and Bothered*	OKeh 8623
Black and Tan Fantasy and *What Can a Poor Fellow Do?*	OKeh 40955
Blues I Love to Sing and *Blue Bubbles*	Victor 22985
Old Man Blues and *Jungle Nights in Harlem*	Victor 23022
Creole Rhapsody (two sides)	Brunswick 6093
The Mystery Song (one side)	Victor 22800
Rockin' in Rhythm and *Twelfth St. Rag*	Brunswick 6038
Dreamy Blues (*Mood Indigo*) and *Runnin' Wild*	Brunswick 4952
Sweet Dreams of Love and *Sweet Jazz O' Mine*	Victor V38143
Awful Sad and *Louisiana*	Brunswick 4110
Limehouse Blues and *Echoes of the Jungle*	Victor 22743
It Don't Mean a Thing and *Rose Room*	Brunswick 6265
Haunted Nights and *The Duke Steps Out*	Victor V38092

I should add *Parlor Social Stomp* and *Georgia Grind* (Perfect 104), *Song of the Cotton Field* and *New Orleans Low Down* (Vocalion 1086), but these are no longer obtainable, as I found to my dismay in trying to replace my own lost or broken copies.

III. First Trip Abroad
(1933)

lthough Ellington eventually toured Europe many times, his first visit in the summer of 1933 stands out as exceptional. Brought over in early June by the English bandleader Jack Hylton, the Ellington orchestra performed for nearly six weeks in Britain before traveling to the continent for appearances in Holland and France.[1] Its reception in England was especially warm, with large audiences turning out for concerts and critics providing extensive coverage in newspapers and the trade press.

In 1932 the return of saxophonist Otto Hardwick and the addition of trombonist Lawrence Brown had brought the orchestra to a total of fourteen players. Joining these musicians on the trip abroad were the singer Ivie Anderson and the dancers Bessie Dudley, Bill Bailey, and Derby Wilson. Performances took place in movie houses, concert halls, and variety theaters, beginning with two weeks at London's famous Palladium. At one private party the Duke of Kent asked Ellington to play *Swampy River,* and the Prince of Wales briefly took Sonny Greer's place at the drums. While in London, the orchestra recorded for Decca and broadcast over the BBC.

For Europeans this was their first glimpse of Ellington after first encountering his work through recordings and the 1930 film *Check and Double Check.* Many were impressed, even overwhelmed by the impact of hearing the orchestra live. Others remained untouched: "Duke Ellington I suffered for 15 min. and then switched off," wrote a reporter for the Yorkshire *Observer.*[2] Still others, like the *Melody Maker* correspondent Patrick "Spike" Hughes, changed their minds as a result of the visit. Initially a rabid fan, Hughes became disillusioned after a 25 June concert (sponsored by *Melody Maker*) when Ellington programmed such numbers as *Trees* (featuring Lawrence Brown), *Some of These Days,* and *In the Shade of the Old Apple Tree:* "Is Duke Ellington losing faith in his own music and turning commercial through lack of appreciation, or does he honestly underestimate the English musical public to such an extent that a concert *for musicians* does not include *The Mooche, Mood Indigo, Lazy Rhapsody, Blue Ramble, Rockin' in Rhythm, Creole Love Call, Old Man Blues, Baby, When You Ain't There,* or *Black Beauty?*"[3]

While some of the criticism may have stung Ellington, overall the trip seems to have proven invigorating. As he wrote later in his memoirs: "The atmosphere in Europe, the friendship, and the serious interest in our music shown by critics and musicians of all kinds put new spirit into us."[4]

[1] The orchestra left New York on the S.S. *Olympic* on 2 June 1933, arriving in Southampton on 9 June. Coming back, it boarded the S.S. *Majestic* in Southampton on 2 August and reached New York on 8 August.
[2] Quoted in *DE*, 139.
[3] [Spike Hughes], "Mike's Report," *Melody Maker* (1 July 1933), 2.
[4] *MM*, 85.

13. Spike Hughes: Impressions of Ellington in New York (1933)

I n 1933 the twenty-five-year-old composer and bassist Patrick C. "Spike" Hughes (1908–1987) was a regular contributor to the *Melody Maker*, England's trade magazine for dance-band musicians. For this publication he wrote exhaustively on Ellington's first trip abroad, sometimes under the byline "Mike."

Visiting New York in April and May, where he stayed with the critic John Hammond and recorded some of his own compositions with an all-black ensemble (including Coleman Hawkins and Benny Carter), Hughes had met Ellington and heard his orchestra both at the Cotton Club and over the radio. Following is his account of that experience for readers of the *Melody Maker*, perhaps intended as a preview of Ellington's impending arrival.

Hughes's criticism of trombonist Lawrence Brown, newest member of the brass section, and his strong preference for Ellington's "hot" originals over the band's more popular fare were soon to be echoed by other British critics responding to Ellington's performances in their country.

. . . It has recently been on my mind that America does not honestly know or appreciate the real treasure she possesses in Duke Ellington. It must be the old, old story of the prophet being without honour in his own country when Duke is billed as "The King of Symphonic Jazz" (Whiteman is now "The Dean"!) — oh, the vulgarity of Broadway advertising!

So many times I have thanked my stars to have been born a European, proud in the knowledge that our dear old bankrupt continent has the sense to appreciate good music when it hears it without having to wade through a mass of tasteless hokum first.

To illustrate exactly what goes on in this remarkable city — of which I am inordinately fond, let me assure you — I cannot do better than try to describe Duke's opening night at the Cotton Club.[1]

The band *did* play, but I will return to that later. Most of the time was taken up by a very professional floor show ("fastest show in the world") which is, I suppose, more than three times too long. The dancing is remarkable, it is true, but every turn consists of at least three routines too many, and one gets to a stage when one would cheerfully die rather than watch any more tap-dancing or listen to any more bawdy songs.

Source: Spike Hughes, "The Duke—In Person," *Melody Maker* (May 1933), 353, 355.

[1] Although Ellington's orchestra had not been based at the Cotton Club since early February 1931, it returned there periodically for brief engagements.

Noel Coward went up one evening, was bored to tears, heard Duke play a couple of numbers and remarked that he could not understand why the singers did not say what everybody knew they meant and have done with it.

For my own part, I walked out of the opening night proceedings in disgust. I was more than infuriated at having to pay an immense sum for the privilege of hearing Duke play chords of G, to introduce the spotlit celebrities that were present. The "celebrities" consisted of (rightly) out-of-work film stars, two members of the British Peerage (what a thrill!) and a few obscure Broadway columnists and song-writers.

And the Cotton Club is New York's conception of Harlem! A place where no Negroes are admitted, though as a special concession the more distinguished members of the race, like Paul Robeson and Ethel Waters, are allowed, rather apologetically, to sit away in the corner.

Why they do not move the Cotton Club down to the Forties I cannot imagine.[2] It would save many an expensive taxi-fare. On the other hand, the unimaginative American business man and his peroxide stenographer might not feel that they were being "wicked" if it were located in the mid-town section.

What most outrages me is that Duke is playing at the Cotton Club.

I have been there since the opening night, but I took good care to find myself in especially charming company, and as she—I mean, they—had already seen the show, we ignored it altogether and talked. Eventually, Duke came over to our table and we persuaded him to play all our pet "Lazy Rhapsodies" and "Blue Tunes." That was more like . . .

But for the rest, I make a point nowadays of being home every night at two, to hear his half-hour broadcast. (Twice a week he also broadcasts for half-an-hour at midnight as well.)

I may say that I look forward to these periods so much that I have almost completely neglected to visit my respected mother at Philadelphia on account of her radio not being able to pick up WMCA, which is a local New York station and not powerful.

The Ellington band is all, and more, than I expected.

Each individual member of the orchestra (with one exception) is completely and utterly a mouthpiece for Duke's own ideas. There is not a note which comes from that remarkable brass section, or from the rich tone of the saxes, that is not directly an expression of Duke's genius. One can conceive of nobody to replace [Barney] Bigard, or [Harry] Carney, or [Johnny] Hodges, or [Otto] Hardwick; "Cooty" [Williams] or Freddy Jenkins or Art Whetsol, or that superb trombone-blower, "Tricky Sam" [Nanton].

The one person, to my mind, who is definitely out of place is Lawrence Brown. This artist is a grand player of the trombone, and would be a tremendous asset to any other band on account of his original style, but his solo work is altogether too "smart," or "sophisticated," if you will, to be anything

---

[2] In fact this happened in 1936, when the uptown Cotton Club closed in February and re-located in September to 200 West 48th Street.

but out of place in Duke's essentially direct and simple music. Brown is as much use to that band as Kreisler would be playing first fiddle in the New York Philharmonic. It is not that his individuality is too strong; just misplaced.

This is, of course, only my personal opinion. I have nothing but admiration for Lawrence Brown's talent, as such, but by its very nature it seems to me to belong elsewhere.

After all, can you imagine Hawkins or Armstrong in Duke's band?

I can't.

Duke and his band are the only two things, apart from Toscanini, which have exceeded my wildest hopes of New York.

For one thing, Duke plays almost entirely his own music, and the very best of that. ("Sophisticated Lady" turns up a little too often for my liking, but one can forgive this commercial lapse from grace. Even Dukes have to live these days.)

Even when an Ellington radio programme includes one or two of the more trashy current popular songs, these are treated with so much contempt as to be most pleasantly unrecognisable. "Echo in the Valley," for instance, is taken at a fast swinging tempo, and we are spared the tune altogether.

"Cooty" opens the proceedings with the dirtiest solo imaginable, and from that moment the fun begins. (It is encouraging to note, by the way, for the benefit of "Mike," that nearly every radio announcer makes a point of giving the name of the composers of the better tunes. "Mood Indigo" is never played by any band without our being told that Ellington wrote it. Rodgers and Hart, Kern, Youmans, Berlin and Co., all come in for what credit they deserve when their tunes are played.)

I cannot begin to describe some of the sounds the Ellington aggregation produces. The use of the full muted brass section, close to the microphone, results in a sound which is not of this world at all; another very exciting noise comes from Duke's scoring for the saxes, with much use made of Johnny Hodges' soprano as the lead.

I will not give away any secrets concerning the mutes used for the brass; let it be said that the bands here have a mute which is not to be found in England, as far as I know.

Anyway, I am keeping the knowledge very much to myself—for obvious reasons.

I was pleasantly surprised to find that Sonny Greer, who is surrounded by the most imposing array of percussion instruments ever seen, makes very good use of timpani in some numbers. A nicely timed roll adds a terrific emphasis to some passages of "Echo[es] of the Jungle," for example. It is little touches like this, in themselves so simple, which make Duke's band so really thrilling.

If your mouths, or ears, are not already watering I might add here some of the pieces I have heard Duke play: — "East St. Louis Toodle-Oo" (his signature), "The Mooche," "Blue Tune," "Lazy Rhapsody," "Blue Ramble," "Double Check Stomp," "The Duke Steps Out," "Black and Tan Fantasy," "Mood Indigo," "St. Louis Blues," "Limehouse Blues," "The Mystery Song," "Baby, When You Ain't There," "The Whispering Tiger" ("Tiger Rag" played *pianissimo* throughout, a favourite trick which Duke applies to other numbers) and a host of other and new things like "Jive Stomp," "King of Spades," "Ev'ry Tub" (?), "Drop Me Off At Harlem," and "Slippery Horn"—all of which we shall probably hear on records shortly.[3]

My own modest contributions to Duke's repertoire have been those two pieces which are most nearly his "cup of tea": "Sirocco" and "Siesta."[4]

The former opus we tried over at Columbia one day—and was my face red? It really seemed as if I were hearing it for the first time in my life. I think my pride was pardonable when Duke, after playing it through, commented: "Gee, I go for that!"

I must confess that I could go on writing from now until the Judgment Day on the topic of Duke as a person and an artist, of the way he starts his numbers by rippling away at the piano until the band is set to go, of how he accompanies tap-dancers, of how his personality, as he sits in front of the band, expresses every mood of his own glorious music, and of the thousand and one other things that go to make him one of the most delightful and vivid characters of our time.

14. Spike Hughes: "Meet the Duke!" (1933)

T he following article appeared in London's *Daily Herald* on the eve of Ellington's arrival in England. In it, Spike Hughes asserted that while Americans viewed Ellington as "just the successful leader of a successful band," Europeans had discovered him as "the first genuine composer of Jazz." Earlier selections in this volume by R. D. Darrell, Abbé Niles, and Janet Mabie counter that claim. Yet Hughes's effort to separate Ellington's importance as a composer from his popularity as a performer—as though the two were mutually exclusive—underlines a recurring theme in Ellington criticism.

Tomorrow, Duke Ellington, the Aristocrat of Harlem, and his "hot" dance band will broadcast to all British stations. Here is a pen portrait of this amazing musician.

"Beat it out, boy! Beat it out!"

With these words ringing in his ears, a young Negro sat down at the piano of a Harlem speakeasy.

Prohibition was only three years old then; alcohol in these up-town "gin mills" was neither so good nor so cheap as it is to-day.

---

[3] *Jive Stomp, Ev'ry Tub* (or *Hyde Park*), and *Drop Me Off at Harlem* were all recorded in 1933, as was *King of Spades* under the title *Merry-Go-Round*. *Slippery Horn* dates from 1932.
[4] To what extent these two numbers became part of "Duke's repertoire" is not clear; Ellington did not record them. (Hughes's own orchestra had recorded them in England in 1932.)

Source: Spike Hughes, "Meet the Duke!" *Daily Herald*, 13 June 1933.

But the pianist did not touch the glass of corn-liquor at his elbow. His hands were occupied; his mind was absorbed in the music he played. He hummed quietly to himself—in a different key.

And as he played the white-coated waiter trod more lightly between the tables, swaying rhythmically under a heavy tray.

The singing and laughter suddenly died down in every corner of the dim-lit basement.

Duke Ellington was playing. . . .

That was ten years ago.

To-day, at thirty-one [*recte* thirty-four], Duke Ellington is, thanks to Jack Hylton, paying his first visit to London—with the orchestra that he has made world-famous.

To meet Edward Kennedy Ellington for the first time is to know a tall, splendidly built young man with a slow, infectious smile and a quick sense of humour. Why he is called "Duke" it is easy to understand, for he possesses rare dignity and personal charm. His modesty is as attractive as it is unusual among American musicians; and he has about him an air of quiet confidence that convinces all who know him that here indeed is one of the few real artists America has produced.

Yet, curiously, he is a prophet almost without honour in his own country. To most Americans he is just the successful leader of a successful band which specialises in what are vaguely termed "voodoo harmonies" and "jungle rhythms."

It has remained for us in Europe to discover, if not at first hand, at least through the medium of gramophone records, that Duke Ellington is something more than a band-leader; that he is, in fact, the first genuine composer of Jazz.

This may come as a shock to many who, like most music critics, inevitably associate Jazz with the "Rhapsody in Blue," or who consider Jazz to be any noise made by any dance band as a background to conversation, or as an excuse for those ungraceful, hiking movements which pass for modern "dancing."

If Jazz were really a matter of trite, unoriginal melodies wedded to semi-illiterate lyrics, then it should not only now be dying ("Jazz on its last legs" was announced fifteen years ago at least), but it should never have been born in the first place.

But fortunately Jazz is not, and never has been, a brain-child of Tin Pan Alley. It is the music of Harlem gin mills, Georgia backyards and New Orleans street-corners—the music of a race that plays, sings and dances because music is its most direct medium of expression and escape.

Duke Ellington alone has brought this music out of the semi-twilight of small night-clubs into the broad daylight of the outside world.

But he has added something of his own in the process.

As a boy, in his native Washington, he took elementary lessons in piano playing and harmony, but firmly declined to "study" composition.

"I have seen too many folk spoiled that way," Duke will tell you. "I am a Negro; I am American; I have something to express which can only be expressed one way—the way of our Race."

The music of the American Negro has much in common with the folk-music of Hungary, of Ireland and Russia. Under the superficial gaiety of its tunes runs a peculiar strain of melancholy: the simple, sincere utterance of an oppressed people.

In Duke Ellington's music we find this mixture of grave and gay, elation and despair. A cheerful, carefree tune will suddenly give way to a mournful, elegiac outburst—something as moving and powerful as anything in music. Nowhere is there any trace of that vulgarity and conscious "sophistication" (the most misapplied word in the American vocabulary) with which Jazz is associated in the popular mind.

In common with many other musicians, I have long been bewildered by the almost universal and distressing acceptance of the "Rhapsody in Blue" as the apotheosis of Jazz. George Gershwin is surely first and foremost a composer of "light" music that can be, and is, "arranged" for performance by anything from male quartets to harmonica bands. The mere fact that a Gershwin "number" is incidentally used for dancing does not mean that it is Jazz.

Ellington's music, on the other hand, cannot be sung in revues or cabarets. It needs no Broadway love lyrics. It is not "about" anything—except Duke himself.

Unlike many less fortunate composers in the past, Duke Ellington carries around with him the ideal instrument upon which to play his music—his own orchestra.

Developed from the modest four-piece affair of the early Harlem days to the superbly drilled combination of fourteen men now in London, this orchestra is indisputably the finest of its type in the world.

But it is a band to be seen as well as heard. It is not a "show" band; its members do not wear funny hats, nor do they attempt any "comedy." It is a band content to play music for its own sake, but with such energy and obvious enjoyment that the listener who is also spectator cannot but be affected by this joy and verve which the Negro puts into his playing.

As a spectacle alone the band is an impressive sight. On the stage it appears as a human pyramid, its apex the drummer surrounded by an unusual array of drums, cymbals, tom-toms and bells.

The arrival of Duke Ellington and his orchestra to these shores means that, at long last, the British public will have an opportunity to hear what Jazz is really all about.

And England will hear music it has never heard before. Music that is alive and beautiful; the music of a race which has suffered, and still suffers, untold hardship and injustice; the music of a race which, when faced by lynchings and "framed" death sentences can sing as those nine Scottsboro boys sang in an Alabama jail;[1] the music of a race which, alone of all the races in America, has remained aloof from the depression—content to sing and dance and make music.

[1] The Scottsboro boys were nine black youths who had been arrested in Alabama in 1931 and charged with the rape of a white woman. Their case became a focal point for civil rights activists in the early 1930s and led to two important Supreme Court rulings in 1932 and 1935.

Nowhere in Harlem did I see the sullen, depression-conscious faces that haunt Broadway.

Duke Ellington, one of America's great gentlemen, is bringing a little of that coloured heaven to London.

"Beat it up, boy! Beat it up!"

15. Ellington at the Palladium (1933)

The Ellington orchestra opened its stay in England with two weeks at the Palladium, described by Ellington in *Music Is My Mistress* as "the number one variety theatre in the world." A front-page story in the 17 June *Melody Maker* by an unidentified "Special Representative"—possibly Spike Hughes again—reviewed Ellington's 12 June premiere there, reporting on the pieces performed and describing the vaudeville format common for the period. In it the author noted that Ellington's longer composition *Creole Rhapsody* (1931) did not turn up on this program intended for a "popular audience"; two days later, however, it was performed on a radio broadcast (see §16).

The article's tone gives a sense of the Ellington fever that swept the jazz press following the bandleader's arrival in England on 9 June. The same issue of the *Melody Maker* featured an Ellington record review, details of the upcoming tour, and ads for both Conn and Selmer instruments with endorsements by Ellington's musicians.

A section describing some of the welcoming ceremonies for Ellington and a reception for him at the home of bandleader Jack Hylton has been omitted.

Well! he's here! We have been reading about the Duke this last four or five years; he has become an almost legendary figure; it seemed impossible that we should ever see him in the flesh, or hear those amazing sounds other than via a gramophone. Yet, unbelievably, he is here.

A handful of us have been fortunate enough to be with, or not far from, the Duke ever since he docked in English waters. I am glad to say that I have been one of them, and I am very much aware that there are tens of thousands of Ellington fans round the country who would have given anything to come into such close contact with the Duke as I have been, so therefore, since it is hardly practicable for ten thousand people to follow Ellington wherever he goes, perhaps if I relate in detail all that has happened, my readers may in some measure share my personal excitement and experiences.

The S.S. *Olympic* sailed from New York on Friday, June 2nd, it docked at Southampton at 12:30 Friday, June 9th. I was there with a crowd of others to welcome the Duke.

We went aboard the *Olympic* and sought him out. He was not difficult to find, for his light suit made him a conspicuous figure even from the quayside.

Source: "Special Representative," "The Duke at the Palladium," *Melody Maker* (17 June 1933), 1–2.

With Irving Mills we renewed our acquaintance of a few months ago. Irving, looking tanned and healthy, was wreathed in smiles, and wore a proprietary air of pride as he said "Meet the Duke!"

There he was! In person! In the flesh! The Duke! Himself!

Tall—over 6 ft.—broad, with the shoulders, and build of an athlete, slightly plump in a way that seemed in accord with his obvious good temper.

A broad smile that had nothing artificial or forced about it. A firm handshake. A pleasant cultured voice.

Behind him were "the boys." There they were, all of them—Bigard, Hodges, Brown, Greer and the rest. Also in the party were two attractive coloured girls—Ivie Anderson, the blues singer, and Bessie Dudley, the dancer.

There was, of course, great to-do's. I think that the Duke's arm must have ached with the hundreds of handshakes! A constant procession of people passed in front of him: "Meet the Duke—this is Mr. So and So!" Poor Duke! All through all of it his smile never faltered and his good humour never cracked under the strain for an instant. The boys seemed a little overwhelmed.

Through the wizardry of Jack Hylton, the usually tedious Customs formalities passed with lightning speed, and before very long Ellington was entrained, en route for London. . . .

As 6:30 p.m. approached on Monday [June 12], I must confess that my excitement rose to fever heat. Although Ellington's band was not on until nearly eight o'clock, I felt as though I shouldn't miss a bit of the whole bill at the Palladium. As a matter of fact I could have done so without serious loss, for with the exception of Max Miller,[1] the supporting acts were very poor. One supposes that the terrific cost of booking the band somewhat tied the hands of the bookers. . . .

The preceding acts went by all too slowly. Ellington was the last turn on the programme—No. 13. It seemed to me, when I discovered this, that it was bad placing, and the fact that the Duke's final curtains were cut short by people getting up and going out in order to avoid the rush, appeared to justify my conclusions. In my opinion, he should either have closed the first half or been last turn but one.

As No. 13 went up on the board the applause grew into a roar, the pit orchestra faded out, and we heard—for the first time in England—the magic sound of "Duke Ellington and his Famous Orchestra."

The curtain went up and there they were! Even the six brass were inaudible in the thunders of applause. Duke, sitting in the centre of the band down stage at the piano, with his back half-turned to the audience, looked over his shoulder and smiled and bowed to the tumultuous reception.

The band was dressed in pearl-grey tail suits, the Duke himself in a double-breasted lounge suit of the same colour and a bright orange tie. On Duke's left were the three trumpets, on his right four saxophones; behind the trumpets, on a higher rostrum, were the three trombones; behind the saxes were the bass and banjo; and high up at the back was Sonny Greer.

---

[1] A bawdy comedian known as "Cheeky Chappie."

There they all were, the names we have met so often in the *Gramophone Review:* (Saxes) Barney Bigard, Johnny Hodges, Harry Carney, Otto Hardwick (misspelt on the programme "Ottox"!); (trumpets) Arty Whetsel (misspelt on the programme "Whetsol"[2]), Charlie [Cootie] Williams, Fred Jenkins; (trombones) Lawrence Brown, Juan Tizol, Joe Nanton; (bass) William [*recte* Wellman] Braud (so that's how they spell it!); (banjo) Fred Guy; and (drums) Sonny Greer.

When the applause subsided a little I discovered that the band was playing "Ring Dem Bells," mostly as the record.

They finished with a sudden and unexpected coda; Duke jumped up from his seat and walked to the footlights. It was minutes before he could make himself heard. He and the boys seemed overwhelmed by the reception.

Then they played "Three Little Words." Then "Stormy Weather," which Ivie Anderson sang. Then followed an encore by Miss Anderson, "Give Me a Man Like That" [*recte* "I Want A Man Like That"]. Then "an old favourite" — "Bugle Call Rag."

It is useless for me to attempt to describe each number separately. You all know how Ellington's band plays through listening to his records, and I can only say that, in the flesh, it is like that, only a thousand times more so. It literally lifts one out of one's seat.

Next came Bessie Dudley, "The Original Snake-Hips Girl," who danced to the familiar "Rockin' in Rhythm." She has a tremendous personality, this girl, and puts over every step of her dance with terrific rhythm.

"The Whispering Tiger" was the next number, which of course, is our old friend "Tiger Rag" played pianissimo throughout. Then "Black and Tan Fantasy."

First encore, "Some of These Days," in which Fred Jenkins created a sensation.

Second encore, "Mood Indigo."

That was the programme, and although the audience was electrified, and wildly applauding, and although the band was perfection in every note it played, it seemed to me that it could have been better chosen.

In the first place, there has been a lot of Press publicity about Ellington as a sponsor of a new kind of music, and all the lay critics, musical and otherwise, were waiting to hear it. Yet "Mood Indigo" was all they got. What about "Blue Tune," "Blue Ramble," "Rose Room," "Creole Rhapsody" and the rest of those numbers which Ellington has made peculiarly his own?

Another fault I have to find is in the interpolated acts. Not that they were not first-class, but they seemed to me to be so unnecessary. When the whole house was fanatically anxious to hear the band, Bailey and Derby tap-danced for four minutes, whilst the band played stop-accompaniment very quietly.

Ivie Anderson, too, although she sang her two numbers admirably, seemed to interfere with the band. Bessie Dudley with her dance, seemed to be more a part of the show, if only because the band was in full blast the whole time.

The answer to this criticism is obvious — and it is wrong. The answer is that

---

[2] "Whetsol," in fact, was a common alternate spelling of the surname "Whetsel."

Ellington is playing in a public hall to a "popular audience," and therefore must intersperse his playing with items of interest to the non-fans.

In normal circumstances this would be a good answer, but with the Palladium full to the roof of enthusiasts who had travelled from all over the country expressly to hear Ellington's band, the argument does not hold water. This attitude seemed to me to be clearly reflected in the audience's reception of the interpolated items. It is true that Ivie Anderson sang an encore to her number, but it is also true that it was omitted in the second house.

I hate to seem hard on the Misses Anderson and Dudley and Messrs. Bailey and Derby—they are all brilliant artists, and undoubtedly would cause a sensation on any variety programme, but it should be clearly understood by whomever is responsible that the Palladium is going to be filled for the whole of Duke's stay with Ellington fans, whose one desire is to hear the Duke play his record numbers.

Perhaps, on second thoughts, it is just as well that the programme was thus arranged, for it will throw into sharp contrast *The Melody Maker* Concert.[3]

16. On the Air in London (1933)

Beginning at the Cotton Club in the late twenties, radio played a crucial role in disseminating Ellington's music. Yet few "air checks"—recordings of broadcasts made by listeners with home disc cutters—survive from before the forties.[1] The following description of the Ellington orchestra's BBC broadcast on 14 June 1933, then, relates the kind of musical program listeners in the early thirties may have heard.

The review is by "Detector," an unidentified writer for the *Melody Maker* who seems well acquainted with Ellington's recordings.

The biggest thrill we have had for ages has come and gone! I refer, of course, to Duke Ellington's broadcast from the studio on June 14th. The band's precision and polish was even more marked on the air than it is on the records, and on the whole the programme was well chosen, comprising most of the numbers we wanted to hear at the Palladium, but didn't.

But with all that it was a disappointment. The arrangements seemed too heavy and complicated for the air, there was so much going on at once that

---

[3] A concert sponsored by the magazine and held at the Trocadero Cinema on 25 June. In the *Melody Maker* issue of 24 June, it was described as a chance for Ellington "to feature some of those quieter and more individual compositions of his which have not been hitherto played in London."

Source: "Detector," "Radio Reports," *Melody Maker* (24 June 1933), 7.

[1] Several broadcasts from the downtown Cotton Club were captured on disc in 1937–38, and as of this writing, one excerpt (still unissued) from an early thirties performance has surfaced and circulated among collectors.

it was difficult to sort it all out. The only other fault I have to find was that the transmission was not at its best, and made the band sound a little blurred at times.

The band opened with a few bars of its signature tune, "East St. Louis [Toodle-O]," and then went straight into the first number, "Lightnin'," which was appropriate enough, for there was not a moment wasted between numbers—an annoying fault with most studio broadcasts . . .

The next number was "Creole Love Call," with three excellent solos from Art Whetsel, trumpet, Barney Bigard, clarinet, and "Tricky Sam" [Nanton], trombone. . . .

"Old Man Blues" came next, and opened with a lovely clarinet solo and trumpet obbligato. I particularly noticed the solidity of the rhythm in this number, and the baritone solo by Harry Carney. The Armstrong style trumpet solo was strong on the top notes, but there is only one Louis.

The announcement of the next number evoked a cheer from me—"Rose Room," one of my favourite records. It was practically the same, except for a different introduction and the piano solo by the Duke. Lawrence Brown added to the record arrangement a trombone solo with a wonderful glissando lead-in and the sweetest tone I have heard.

The next, "Limehouse Blues," opened with clarinet and piano, and continued into a terrific swing arrangement, in which the trombone almost spoke Chinese!

The next number was "Best Wishes," specially composed [in 1932] and dedicated to Great Britain, which Henry Hall's band broadcast for the first time earlier in the week. Ivie Anderson, who came over with the band, and is appearing with them, sang a chorus, and so did the drummer, Sonny Greer. But it is not a very inspiring tune, and the words are inappropriate to the point of absurdity. A nice gesture, though.

Then followed a selection from "Blackbirds of 1930 [recte 1928]," including "I Can't Give You Anything But Love, Baby," which contained a good straight trumpet solo, "I Must Have That Man," with Tricky Sam doing his stuff; "Dig-a-Dig-a-Doo," with some very neat clarinet and sax team work; "Doing the [New] Low Down," chiefly noticeable for Barney Bigard's wizard technique; "Porgy," a straight alto solo by Otto Hardwick; "Dixie," a muted trumpet solo with a tremendous lilt, and then back to "I Can't Give You Anything But Love"—the real Armstrong version this time.

The next number drew another cheer from me—Ellington's latest composition, "Sophisticated Lady," then "It Don't Mean a Thing." These were the two best items of the broadcast, in my opinion. I liked Ivie Anderson's vocal in the latter number, but not in "I've Got the World on a String," in the selection of popular tunes that came next. The peculiar vibrato at the end of each word was not a pleasing effect.

And then, all too soon, came the finale, "Mood Indigo," which was used as a "fade-out" number for the programme. I could have done with a lot more of it. This tune was the only number played from the stage show, in which it was also used as a finale.

17. Ellington Defends His Music (1933)

L ater in Ellington's career, when his orchestra toured the globe, he often displayed a keen curiosity about the indigenous musical traditions of the places he visited.[1] That same curiosity, coupled with his formidable powers of charm, emerged in an interview Ellington gave a Scottish newspaper journalist prior to a 1933 appearance in Glasgow.

Seeking to strike a sympathetic chord with readers of the interview, Ellington drew a parallel between Scottish folk music and his own. He also alluded to criticism he had received in England and predicted that Scottish audiences would react more appreciatively, given what he called the "definite relationship between the rhythms of reels and the Highland fling and the music I play." While it is hard to gauge how seriously Ellington offered such remarks, he handled the press adroitly.

"Some people say that my music is uncouth and without form—a weird conglomeration of blatant discords which never has, and never will mean anything at all."

"But"—and here Duke Ellington, the negro composer-conductor, looked at me with twinkling eyes—"What, may I ask you as a Scotsman, do the same people think about bagpipe music? It is quite as weird, quite as 'tuneless.' But it is recognised as the music of a nation, as folk music."

Thus Duke opened his argument.

"My contention about the music we play is that it also is folk music, the result of our transplantation to American soil, and the expression of a people's soul just as much as the wild skirling of bagpipes denotes a heroic race that has never known the yoke of foreign dictatorship."

That was the defence he put up for himself and his music when I saw him in Liverpool last night.

"I am looking forward to my visit to Scotland—to Glasgow—particularly," said this smiling "Duke," who is not to be found among Debrett's list of the peerage, but who is being presented by Jack Hylton at the Glasgow Empire tomorrow night.

"I want to hear a full bagpipe band, if there are such things. I want to hear Scots folk music played by Scotsmen, I want to see them dance the Highland fling, and I want to learn something about Scottish clans.

"It is my honest belief that in Scotland I shall find an appreciation of my music not to be found south of the border line. There is an inherent feeling for wild music in Scottish nature, and there is a definite relationship between the rhythms of reels and the Highland fling and the music I play."

Duke warmed up to his argument.

Source: "Duke Ellington Defends His Music," *Sunday Post,* July 1933.

[1] See, for example, Ellington's remarks on visiting the Middle East and India in 1963, in *WDE*, 16–26.

"You have no idea of the fury with which people have attacked me through the press and by personal letters," he continued.

"One man wrote saying that as my music is at present it is an insult to the word.

"He said that if the broadcast programme had been called a programme of effects representing the sounds of a coal cart's brakes being screwed on tightly, of train smashes, and of animals in pain, it could, no doubt, have been termed clever. But not unless.

"The same gentleman wanted to know why it is called 'hot' music, but, then, so do I. Mine isn't 'hot' music.

"It is essentially negro music, and the elaborations self-expression."

Tall, suave, and stylishly-dressed in brown suit, wearing brown suede shoes and bright yellow tie, this handsome negro smiled charmingly.

He had been smiling ever since I first met him. His handshake was firm, his manners of the public school quality—or better.

On the stage Ellington hums to himself all the time, shouts to his musicians perched in a picturesque pyramid behind. He is a happy man.

"I shall go sailing on the Clyde to the Kyles of Bute," he declared. "I shall try and visit the great ship yards, and go to Greenock.

"I shall do everything possible to get to know Glasgow, its people, their customs, and their music. I have a great admiration for Scotland and Scotsmen.

"And another very good reason for wanting to go to Scotland," he whispered.

"No, not whisky—but I have promised to take back to Harlem at least one haggis."

18. Hugues Panassié:
"Duke Ellington at the Salle Pleyel" (1946)

When the Ellington orchestra reached Paris in late July 1933, on hand was the twenty-one-year-old Hugues Panassié, a writer, jazz enthusiast, and founding member of the Hot Club of France. Panassié not only heard Ellington in concert at the Salle Pleyel but spoke with several band members offstage. His accounts of conversations with trumpeter Cootie Williams and reed-player Barney Bigard are among the earliest recorded interviews with these figures. Bigard's comments on clarinetists and the concept of "swing" are of particular interest.

Panassié (1912–1974) went on to become one of jazz's most important and influential critics. He edited the journal *Jazz Hot* from 1935 to 1946 and produced a series of historical, biographical, and discographical studies, among them *Le jazz hot* (1934), *The Real Jazz* (1942), *Jazz Panorama* (1950), and *Louis Armstrong* (1969).

The following excerpt is from Chapter 12 of *Douze Années De Jazz* (1946), a memoir

Source: Hugues Panassié, "Duke Ellington a la Salle Pleyel," from *Douze Années De Jazz, 1927–1938: Souvenirs* (Paris: Editions Correa et Cie, 1946), 107–19. Translated by Stanley Dance, 1991.

of Panassié's encounters with jazz in the twenties and thirties. Stanley Dance, the English-born critic and Ellington authority (see §§66 and 79) generously provided the translation.

During the following month, July, I learned that Duke Ellington's orchestra, after a triumphant tour of England, Holland, and other European countries, was going to play in Paris. So finally I would be able to hear "in flesh and blood" the group that I considered the best jazz orchestra in the world!

The concerts were announced for 27 and 29 July in the Salle Pleyel. I was in Paris on the morning of the 26th and was getting ready to go to the station to look for Duke and his musicians when I learned from one of the concert organizers that the orchestra would not arrive that day, its manager Irving Mills having fallen ill in Holland. There was even talk of postponing the concerts till a later date. That didn't stop the evening papers from announcing the arrival of Duke Ellington, of reporting his so-called remarks on leaving the train, and his first impressions of Paris. Photographs illustrated these articles; they were probably taken when the orchestra arrived in neighboring countries.

Finally, Duke's arrival was announced as definite about 6 o'clock the next day. While on my way to the station, I studied the posters advertising the concerts. They were worded in a rather strange manner: "On the occasion of the Davis Cup [which was taking place at this time], Jack Hylton presents in Paris Duke Ellington and his orchestra composed solely of colored men." Nobody ever understood why the Davis Cup got in there. As for Jack Hylton, he must have arranged with Irving Mills in England to gain some extra publicity in France by presenting himself the person he comically called his "rival."

At the Gare du Nord, I found myself among people I knew. There were several black musicians, among them Freddie Johnson,[1] the directors of the Hot Club, and also Canetti, who had contrived to participate in the organization of the concert and had been entrusted with writing the program.

The train arrived. I didn't have long to wait: after two or three minutes I saw Duke's musicians making their way to the exit. I had seen them so often in photographs that I recognized almost all of them without the least effort, as though they were old acquaintances. Duke arrived among the last. Freddie Johnson introduced me. In the course of a short conversation, I asked Duke if he would have total liberty to play as he wished or if any "commercial" concessions had been imposed upon him. I was much afraid that Jack Hylton would have strongly urged Duke and his manager not to play too "hot," in order to have more success. Duke replied that he would play as he intended, and there would in fact be almost no commercial concessions during these concerts.

I had dinner at Freddie's, in company with two of Duke's musicians to whom Freddie was closest: bassist Wellman Braud and one of the trumpets,

[1] American pianist Freddie or Freddy Johnson (1904–1961) had come to Europe in 1928 with Sam Wooding. In the early thirties he played solo in Bricktop's club and in bands with trumpeters Arthur Briggs and Freddy Taylor.

Freddy Jenkins. We had scarcely finished dinner when it was necessary to rush off to the Salle Pleyel, where the concert was to begin about 9 o'clock. Backstage, I met a musician I was sure I had often seen in photographs, but to whose face I could not put a name. Someone introduced us: it was Cootie [Williams], the most important of Duke's trumpets. I was often to discover later that his expression changed constantly in so strange a fashion that it was difficult to recognize him. This peculiarity can very well be seen in photographs of the orchestra. While everybody can easily recognize [Johnny] Hodges, [Harry] Carney, [Barney] Bigard, [Otto] Hardwick, Tricky Sam [Nanton], etc., whenever there is a face hard to identify, you can be sure that it is Cootie's. He changes so much from one photo to another that, even forewarned, one finds it hard to believe it is the same man. What is more astonishing is the fact that this "changeable" face is basically full of character.

I questioned Cootie eagerly, for I wanted to know which were the solos played by him on the [orchestra's] records, never having been able to be certain on this subject. At this time, it was supposed that only Cootie was responsible for the wa-wa growl solos and that he did not play many without mute. "Is it you or Freddy Jenkins," I asked him, "who is the trumpet in the second chorus of *Ducky Wucky*?" Cootie looked at me vacantly; there was nothing on his face to show that he had understood or even heard my question. After a few seconds of silence, however, he said to me in as neutral a tone as possible, "It's me." Curious person, I thought to myself. I asked again: "But it is Freddy Jenkins who plays the short trumpet passage in the last chorus?" And I looked at him intently to try to be quite sure that he clearly understood my question. His face remained as inexpressive as before, the same silence prevailed, and then Cootie said: "No, it's still me," as if he were pulling out the words with difficulty. I put several more questions to him about other trumpet solos on various records of Duke's. The reply was always the same: "It's me." And Cootie's expression—dull, vague, half-dazed—never changed as he rolled between his fingers a cigarette from which he occasionally took a nonchalant puff. "He is completely stupid," I said to myself, "and I have wasted my time with these questions; the fact that he has always replied 'it's me' is proof enough that he has not even paid attention to what I was asking." But I did not have long to wait to recognize my error: in the course of the concerts, I saw Cootie execute all the passages in question, even those I had always attributed to Freddy Jenkins. And still later I had the opportunity to verify that Cootie's sleepy manner did not prevent him from realizing very well what one was saying to him, and to reply with a precision one seldom encountered among the other musicians.

A few minutes later, I was seated in the hall near the stage, waiting impatiently for the concert to begin. Knowing by heart all the numbers Duke had recorded, I was extremely curious to see what effect these would have on me in direct, live performance, and to what extent the solos would resemble those the musicians had improvised when recording.

Duke began with the excellent *It's a Glory,* and the first bars of it will always echo in my ears. The sound of the band, as was to be expected, was much richer than on the records. But the solos of the less powerful instruments—I mean the saxophones and clarinet relative to the brass—were more or less overshadowed by the accompaniments of counter-melodies. Thus I had much difficulty in hearing most of Johnny Hodges's solos during the concert. In this regard, it is obvious that on records the microphone can overcome such disadvantages. In the same way, the saxophone section, as heard at the Salle Pleyel, seemed rather feeble in comparison with the brass section, while on records the saxophones are placed near enough to the mike to adjust the balance. Last, the bass, which seemed so powerful on the records, could scarcely be heard in this concert hall.

That said, the live sound proved itself much superior. Thus, for me, Cootie's playing was a veritable revelation. I am not speaking so much of his wa-wa solos as of those played without a mute: records gave no idea of the fullness and beauty of tone they revealed. Not only his tone but the power of his playing was astounding, and his inspiration seemed to me in general much higher than on records, while the playing of the other musicians was simply what I had expected. I will always remember the trumpet solos Cootie played that night on *Ducky Wucky*, full of moving flights and vehement ascents to the upper register which literally transported me. They were quite different from the solos, no matter how beautiful, on the records. In general, the solos didn't much resemble the recorded ones; some, however, were identical (or almost), the musicians presumably having judged their recorded improvisations to be successful, and that there was no need to try to do better.

What struck me strongly was the discovery that the arrangements themselves sometimes differed from those used on the records. I understood that some had been done over, improved, enriched over the years by new ideas that came to Duke or his men. For others, I realized with astonishment at the second concert, several quite different arrangements existed which Duke used alternatively—sometimes one, sometimes another. Thus the *Mood Indigo* of the first concert scarcely resembled that of the second, where the melody was stated *pianissimo* by an extraordinary brass sextet.

Duke directed his orchestra in lordly fashion. At the piano, with a quick, elegant gesture, he would lift an arm from time to time to indicate a nuance to his musicians. The ease and nobility of his manner, notably when he got up and came to the front of the stage to announce the next number, were indescribable.

Each of the musicians carried himself onstage in a quite different manner, according to his temperament. Among the saxophonists, whereas Johnny Hodges, Hardwick, and Barney Bigard seemed phlegmatic and even inattentive, Harry Carney stamped around his huge baritone sax, violently beating time with both feet. But Barney Bigard was astonishing when he got up to take a solo; he would throw his head back, point his clarinet straight into the hall, and execute the most difficult phrases while remaining almost totally motionless, whereas from the records I had imagined him to be a nervous, restless individual.

Among the brass, Tricky Sam and Cootie made a real show. When he had a long solo to play, Tricky Sam would come to the front of the stage, bring his heels and legs together, and play his solo without changing position for an instant. With his "noble-rustic" appearance (everything round—his body, his cheeks, his goggle-eyes) he did not lack personality, but, together with the "wah-wahs" of his act, above all it had the effect of stirring the audience's laughter.

Cootie's behavior surprised me much more. When he is taking a solo his movements are indescribable. His expression becomes ferocious. He fixes his eyes on his trumpet and raises his eyebrows; his body falls prey to strange contortions. One has the impression that he is struggling with his trumpet and that, at times, in his rage he would like to devour it. As Jean Van Heeckeren justly wrote in the magazine *Orbes*, "one could truly say that he wanted to eat it white hot."

If the first part of the evening was a concert in the proper sense, the second was not. We saw different black dancers—excellent, by the way, especially Bill Bailey—and heard the singer and "comedienne" Ivie Anderson several times. These artists received well-deserved applause, but much more sustained than that awarded the orchestra, which dismayed me, for it proved that the public had not on the whole responded very much to Duke's music and was alive only to the visual part. The enthusiasm certain young people made a show of was even very troublesome when it took the form of cries and cheers right in the middle of performances—ostensibly to salute a soloist's merits but in reality for the pleasure of making noise, of a sort that made it impossible to hear the following passage. As for those people who laughed loudly during the trumpet and trombone solos of Cootie and Tricky Sam, and spoiled the pleasure of other listeners, they are the same ones who give you furious looks and treat you as a lout if you are caught laughing, however quietly, at the howling and the pouting mouth of a big-bellied tenor puffing away at the big aria in *Tosca*.

The day after this concert, I went to find Barney Bigard at his hotel to get better acquainted and ask him some questions; for he was one of my favorite musicians and I was curious about his ideas on jazz.

I found him in bed and rather tired. He nevertheless received me with great kindness. He said he was formerly known as a tenor saxophonist, but that he didn't like the instrument much and preferred the clarinet. In fact, after he joined Duke he had taken almost all his solos on clarinet. Of his numerous recorded solos, he considered that on *Take It Easy* the best—the very first record he made with Duke.[2]

I asked him which were his favorite clarinetists. "Jimmie Noone and Buster Bailey," he said without hesitation. "And among the white clarinetists?" I asked. "Pee Wee Russell is probably my favorite," he answered. "I liked Don Murray a lot, but he is dead.[3] As for Benny Goodman, he is an excellent musician, but his style is not much to my taste." Noting that he had cited

[2] Bigard's first sides with Ellington were *Sweet Mama, Stack O'Lee Blues,* and *Bugle Call Rag,* made for the Harmony label on 9 January 1928. He recorded *Take It Easy* at an OKeh session ten days later.

[3] Murray (1904–1929) played with a number of prominent white musicians in the twenties, among them Bix Beiderbecke, Ted Lewis, the New Orleans Rhythm Kings, and the Jean Goldkette orchestra.

neither [Frank] Teschemacher nor Mesirow [Mezz Mezzrow], who were my two favorites, I questioned him about them. As for Mesirow, he liked him very much. "Mesirow," he told me, "is less well-known than the others by the American public, which is only superficially interested in jazz, because he doesn't play in the famous big bands and doesn't seek commercial success. But the people who are really aware know he is a great clarinetist, and isn't that, after all, more important?"

I also asked Barney about "swing." I had noticed for some time that black musicians were using this word more freely than the word "hot"—and with a nuance that to me seemed slightly different, which I was not sure I properly grasped—and I had set out to conduct a regular poll. Barney confirmed my opinion that "to play with swing" was quite simply to execute phrases that irresistibly drove one to dance. He even gave me a little vocal demonstration, singing the same phrase first without, and then with, swing. It was clear enough, but how to define this manner of playing? Barney said to me, "Swing is indefinable. Each musician has his own way of producing swing, very different from the musician beside him, and you can't justly say that one is more right than another." In sum, that was accurate.

Next I showed Barney some articles in *Jazz-Tango* where I sang his praises. Finally, I spoke of my book on jazz that I hoped to succeed in getting published before long. When I mentioned the chosen title, *Le Jazz Hot,* Barney made a face and declared that in his opinion it was not a good title. He took a sheet of paper and wrote "Gettin' off with a swing" on it, and strongly recommended me to adopt it as my title. There was nothing amiss with this except that it was untranslatable into French.

The next day was marked by the arrival in Paris of John Hammond, the young American jazz critic with whom I had corresponded. He had been sending "News from America" regularly to the British magazine *The Melody Maker,* and was the only American, to my knowledge, who wrote competently about jazz. We went together to see Duke at the Hotel George V, but the great bandleader was surrounded by too many people to make possible an interesting conversation. Also, after a few minutes, he declared that he had to go out. This occasioned a very comic incident. Preceding us, Duke crossed an antechamber of fantastic dimensions and tried to open the door, without success. Realizing his error, he went towards another door, which opened to reveal a clothes closet. Completely lost, Duke dashed all about the antechamber and the adjoining rooms, while John Hammond and I opened at random all the doors that might give access to the hotel lobby, but which actually opened on other rooms or huge empty closets. It took nearly five minutes of such searching before Duke, laughing uncontrollably, found the way out. This apartment at the Hotel George V was so huge and so bizarrely arranged that he had not yet managed to find the entrance.

The second concert took place the same evening. It was better than the first. The musicians had recovered from the effects of their travels and were somewhat accustomed to the hall's strange acoustics. Cootie made an even stronger impression on me than at the first concert. Beside me, Freddie Johnson, who is never able to repress his feelings, was jumping in his seat, tossing his handkerchief in the air, and then sitting bent in two like someone who has been tickled too much and has the strength neither to laugh nor defend himself. The hall was as full and the success as considerable as on the first evening.

After the concert, the musicians went to Bricktop's, a cabaret in the Rue Pigalle, where Freddie Johnson, Arthur Briggs, and some other musicians were playing. John Hammond and I went, too. I hoped some of the orchestra's musicians would take their instruments and improvise alongside Freddie and the others. Johnny Hodges, in fact, wanted badly to do so. But I learned that Jack Hylton had specifically forbidden Duke's men to play outside the concerts or they would be fined fifty dollars. That was a ridiculous pretext, because no one could have guessed that Duke's musicians would be at Bricktop's, since they went there simply to eat and were not announced by any form of publicity.

In fact, Jack Hylton was there, too. Flabby and pot-bellied like an English pork butcher, he was rocking grotesquely in his chair. Overwhelmed by heat and liquor, he had a red, congested face and was splattering food on his neighbors and wiping it off mechanically when it fell on his jacket. Alongside him, Duke gave the impression of a prince of the blood, on whom had been imposed the company of a stupid upstart.

I was able to chat with Duke for a moment. He told me of his immense admiration for Louis Armstrong, in his opinion the greatest figure in jazz. I asked him about swing. He said that by its very nature it defied definition: "It is something you have or you don't have, something you feel or you don't feel; but in any case, it is there in all jazz music."

A third concert took place in the Salle Pleyel on 1 August, but I was not present because I had gone back to Aveyron.

19. Ellington: "My Hunt for Song Titles" (1933)

 sequel to Ellington's 1931 article in the British periodical *Rhythm* (see §9) appeared in August 1933, shortly after his trip to England. Ellington once again used the opportunity to explain his music and artistic goals to a foreign audience. But this time he did so by showing how the titles of his pieces reflected aspects of the black-American experience, especially "the life of Harlem."

The question is always being asked whether jazz music will ever be accepted seriously. I think so; and it has to be accepted as serious music because it is the only type which describes this age. As an illustration of what I mean, I must repeat what I said on the radio on the Friday I arrived in England [9 June]. If an artist wanted to paint a picture of a sunset, he would have to use some tone of red to describe it. Similarly, if serious music is supposed to be

Source: Duke Ellington, "My Hunt for Song Titles," *Rhythm* (August 1933), 22–23.

descriptive of a period, then jazz will have to be used to describe this, the jazz age. Since I think jazz is a serious thing, I must be serious in my choice of song titles.

But originality in this matter is always difficult, particularly in these times when the trite sentimental caption is a popular way of naming dance tunes. Our aim as a dance orchestra is not so much to reproduce "hot" or "jazz" music as to describe emotions, moods, and activities which have a wide range, leading from the very gay to the sombre. It will not, therefore, surprise the public to know that every one of my song titles is taken from, and naturally principally from, the life of Harlem.

The first big tune I ever used was *East St. Louis Toddle-O,* a number that I still use as my radio theme song. But since that time, I have advanced far from my song titles, looking to the everyday life and customs of the Negro to supply my inspiration. Of all people, the Negro is most given to leg-pulling, this word has been added to my vocabulary since I have been here—a very pleasant way of passing the time. In local dialect this is known as "jive," and from this I derived *Jive Stomp. Send Me* comes from an expression used only to show the heights of ecstasy.

You have in England a very old proverb which runs "Every man for himself," and we have a saying just as old, "Every tub must stand on its own bottom"—which means the same thing. I have a great success with *Every Tub,* taken from this source.

A "swanky" person is known in America as "ritzy," in Harlem as "dicty," and this was the basis of my *Dicty Glide.* Of course, a large part of the meaning is conveyed not only by the music and singing, but by the dance itself, for which certain steps fitting to the rhythm should be used. A lofty carriage is needed for this particular dance. The word "moocher" became familiar to you some time ago through a popular dance tune,[1] but I doubt whether many people knew the real meaning of it, which is "swindler." From the same basis I named a song, *The Mooch,* but here the meaning is slightly different, representing a certain lazy gait peculiar to some of the folk of Harlem.[2]

Those old Negroes who work in the fields for year upon year, and are tired at the end of their day's labour, may be seen walking home at night with a broken, limping step locally known as the "toddle-O," with the accent on the last syllable. I was able to get a new rhythm from this, and what better title could I find than the original?[3]

Another of my tunes, *The Birmingham Break-down,* may seem easy enough to understand, but here the word "break-down" typifies a fast, unrestrained dance in which all the dancers are out to do their hottest work. It is nothing less than a race. But there are other negro moods which are quieter.

---

[1] Cab Calloway's *Minnie the Moocher,* recorded in 1931.

[2] The dancer James Barton remembered seeing the comedian Bert Williams perform a dance called the Mooche in 1898, describing it as "a sort of shuffle, combining rubberlegs with rotating hips." See Marshall and Jean Stearns, *Jazz Dance: The Story of American Vernacular Dance* (New York: Macmillan, 1968), 197–99.

[3] See §6, footnote 3.

We have affectionate terms. I took the title *Ducky Wucky,* equivalent in affectionate value to the English "my darling," from the "Amos 'n' Andy" hour on the American radio.

I have been told that in England the words "black and tan" recall memories of the voluntary force that went to Ireland during the rebellion immediately after the war, and that it can also mean a familiar term for the Manchester terrier. But in *Black and Tan Fantasy* the words have a very different meaning. There are in Harlem certain places after the style of night clubs patronised by both white and coloured amusement seekers, and these are colloquially known as "black and tans."

Another custom is the *Breakfast Dance* which commences about four in the morning and continues until about nine o'clock, with intervals for breakfast. And what a time they have! From these impromptu dances taking place solely in Harlem I have derived much inspiration. There are *Rent Party Blues, Parlour Social Stomp,* and *Saturday Nite Function,* all of which mean more or less the same thing. The Negro who owes his rent does not run the risk of being thrown out by his landlord. He merely organises one of these gatherings. The neighbours all come, pay a standard rate for their tickets of admission and have a swell time. You can imagine how pleased the unfortunate host is to be able to pay his rent. He stands with a happy grin on his face watching the proceedings. The party spirit is not allowed to flag. Owing the rent is here more a case for rejoicing than for despair, and is as much an excuse for a party as it is a means of raising money. It really is a source of income as pleasant as it is novel. You have the basis of the idea when you give "bottle parties."

The first tune I ever wrote specially for microphone transmission was *Mood Indigo,* a title which explains itself. But my latest composition *Sophisticated Lady* may not be so obvious in its meaning, for my idea of sophistication may differ from yours. My conception of the word is the blasé type.

You are all familiar with the word "swing," but in *It Don't Mean a Thing If It Ain't Got That Swing,* there is a slight difference. Here the swing does not influence the rhythm, for the rhythm is still there without it, nor does it wholly describe the step. It is a subtle combination of the two, best described as a buoyant rhythm.

Since I have been in England I have composed a new number entitled *Best Wishes,*[4] which was played and broadcast on June 14 for the first time. The lyric is by Ted Koehler, one of the writers of *Stormy Weather.* I have dedicated this song to Britain — the title, not the lyrics — and I hope that the visit of my orchestra has given you a better insight into the Negro mind. For it is through the medium of my music that I want to give you a better understanding of my race.

[4] *Best Wishes* had been recorded the previous year, on 17 May 1932.

IV. Into the Swing Era (1933–1942)

Bolstered by their successes abroad, Ellington and his musicians resumed the strenuous schedule of a big band in the thirties: traveling to one-nighters across the United States, appearing in hotels, theaters, dance halls, and nightclubs, making radio broadcasts, and recording in studios from New York to Chicago to Los Angeles. Following appearances in two Hollywood films, *Murder at the Vanities* and *Belle of the Nineties* (both 1934), the Ellington orchestra made a Paramount short on its own, *Symphony in Black* (1934, released in 1935), featuring the young Billie Holiday. It also returned to the Cotton Club in 1937 and 1938, now located downtown on 48th Street after closing in Harlem.

Throughout this period Ellington kept composing steadily, producing instrumentals and songs tailored to the three-minute length of a 78-rpm record, also extending these boundaries with the four-part *Reminiscing in Tempo* (1935) and the two-part *Diminuendo and Crescendo in Blue* (1937). Although he kept telling interviewers about other large-scale projects, it was not until the early forties—with the musical *Jump for Joy* (1941) and the "tone parallel" *Black, Brown and Beige* (1943)—that works of greater dimensions emerged. Yet Ellington hardly needed a broader canvas to prove himself as a composer. In the late thirties and early forties he wrote dozens of short works that brilliantly exploited the resources of his orchestra, among them *Echoes of Harlem* (1936), *Azure* (1937), *Braggin' in Brass* (1938), *Battle of Swing, Blue Light,* and *The Sergeant Was Shy* (1939), *Jack the Bear, Harlem Air Shaft, Concerto for Cootie, Ko-Ko,* and *Cotton Tail* (1940), and *Main Stem* (1942). He also recorded in pared-down musical settings: small groups, duets for piano and bass, occasionally as solo pianist.

Many writers have described the years around 1940 as a creative peak for Ellington and his orchestra. This judgment stems partly from the consistent excellence of Ellington's compositions at this time, partly from the superior performances of his orchestra.[1] For Ellington, of course, composing and performing were interrelated parts of the same process. Clearly the general stability of personnel in the thirties helped him as a writer, just as the arrival of such new members as cornetist Rex Stewart (in 1934), bassist Jimmy Blanton (1939), and tenor saxophonist Ben Webster (1940) fired his imagination.

Another crucial player took the stage at this time: Billy Strayhorn, the young composer, arranger, and pianist who joined the organization in 1939 and would remain until his death in 1967. Strayhorn not only relieved Ellington of routine arranging chores—providing fresh orchestrations of popular songs and dance tunes—but made substantial original contributions with such works as *Chelsea Bridge, Raincheck,* and a new theme for the orchestra, *Take the "A" Train* (all from 1941).

Personally this was a difficult time. Ellington's parents both died in close succession,

---

[1] For an assessment by Lawrence Gushee of Ellington in 1940, see §86.

Daisy in 1935 and J.E. in 1937. The loss of his mother was especially traumatic, resulting in a period of mourning during which few new works appeared. Since the late twenties Ellington had been separated from his wife Edna and living with Mildred Dixon, a dancer he had met at the Cotton Club. In 1938 he left her for another dancer, Beatrice "Evie" Ellis, who would become his lifetime companion. A different kind of parting occurred in 1939 when, following a second trip to Europe, Ellington broke with manager Irving Mills, who had played a major role in promoting his career since 1926. Ellington signed with the William Morris Agency and moved to the publisher Jack Robbins.

While America's entry into World War II in 1941 affected all aspects of society, the Ellington orchestra by and large continued to function as before. A recording like *A Slip of the Lip (May Sink a Ship)* (1942) reflected wartime conditions, of course, and the draft would eventually claim clarinetist Chauncey Haughton and trumpeter Harold "Shorty" Baker (in 1943 and 1944, respectively).[2] But two lesser conflicts may have made a greater impact on Ellington: the dispute between radio broadcasters and the American Society of Composers and Publishers in 1941, which stimulated the composition of new pieces since much of Ellington's previous ASCAP-licensed repertory was banned from the airwaves; and the musicians' union strike of 1942–1944, which led to a recording hiatus of nearly a year and a half.[3]

[2] In his memoirs, Rex Stewart wrote that Wallace Jones was also drafted (*Boy Meets Horn* (Ann Arbor: University of Michigan Press, 1991), 214).

[3] The orchestra appeared on a few film soundtracks and late in 1943 recorded a number of transcriptions for World Broadcasting System, but otherwise did not record in the studio between 28 July 1942 and 1 December 1944. Many air checks from public performances, however, survive. See *ERMDE*, 47–62.

20. Wilder Hobson:
"Introducing Duke Ellington" (1933)

W hile Ellington was feted in Europe during the summer of 1933, he was not exactly a "prophet without honor in his own country," as Spike Hughes had claimed.[1] Two articles, in particular, indicated how seriously Ellington was being taken at home: R. D. Darrell's "Black Beauty," published in 1932 before the journey abroad, and an expansive profile by Wilder Hobson that appeared the following year in *Fortune*.[2]

Several features made Hobson's piece notable: the figures on Ellington's income, sure to interest readers of *Fortune;* the attempt, mingling fact and fantasy, to explain how Ellington's orchestra played difficult arrangements from memory; and the information, presumably taken from press material or interviews, about two works-in-progress, one a "Negro musical show" to be produced for John Hammond (nothing came of this), the other a five-part suite on themes from black history which anticipated *Black, Brown and Beige* by ten years.

Wilder Hobson (1906–1964) became interested in jazz while a student at Yale. Author of *American Jazz Music* (1939), he also contributed two chapters to *Jazzmen* (1939; see §36) and served on the writing staffs of *Fortune, Time,* and *Newsweek.*

Hobson devoted one section of the article to a brief history of jazz. Since it bears little on Ellington and offers no fresh information it has been omitted here.

. . . Before the money changers failed us, it was customary to call this the Jazz Age. The etymology of the word jazz is obscure. It was once jass, and some say this was the corrupted nickname of a Negro musician called Charles. Others think the word has lecherous origins. However that may be, jazz means different things to different people. To some it means the whole cocktail-swilling deportment of the post-War era. To others it suggests loud and rowdy dance music. Many people go so far as to divide all music into "jazz" or "classical." By "classical" they mean any music which sounds reasonably serious, be it *Hearts and Flowers* or Bach's *B Minor Mass,* while their use of "jazz" includes both Duke Ellington's Afric brass and Rudy Vallée crooning *I'm a Dreamer, Aren't We All?*

Source: [Wilder Hobson], "Introducing Duke Ellington," *Fortune* (August 1933), 47–48, 90, 94, 95.

[1] See §§13 and 14.

[2] An abridged version of the article was reprinted in Ralph de Toledano's *Frontiers of Jazz* (New York: Oliver Durrell, 1947; 2nd rev. ed., New York: Frederick Ungar, 1962), 137–47. In introducing it, Toledano wrote: "When in August of 1933, *Fortune* published a long and sympathetic article on Duke Ellington and hot jazz, it was an event. For years after, the article was discussed and avid collectors combed secondhand magazine shops to get their hands on a copy" (137).

It may not have been entirely coincidental that Hobson's piece appeared on the heels of Ellington's successful tour abroad.

But Duke Ellington bears just about as much relation to Vallée as the *B Minor Mass* to *Hearts and Flowers*. The curly-headed Vallée has made a fortune dispensing popular ballads to the vast public which always adores them. In this respect he resembles Guy Lombardo, Russ Columbo, Bing Crosby, and various other radio and tea-dancing idols. On the other hand, Mr. Ellington and his orchestra offer rich, original music, music of pulse and gusto, stemming out of the lyricism of the Negro and played with great virtuosity. Ellington's music is jazz; it is the best jazz.

Ellington has just undertaken his first tour of Europe, where he was resoundingly greeted in Great Britain and France. Said the London *Times:* "Mr. Duke Ellington . . . is exceptionally and remarkably efficient in his own line . . . And the excitement and exacerbation of the nerves which are caused by the performances of his orchestra are the more disquieting by reason of his complete control and precision. It is not an orgy, but a scientific application of measured and dangerous stimuli." It is no paradox that Ellington should arouse a special personal interest abroad. He is an idol of the jazz cult, which has developed a critical canon as precise and exacting as that applied to porcelains or plain song. The jazz cult is apathetic to nine-tenths of modern dance music—just as apathetic as the old lady who never cared much for a bass drum. But the cultist will often go to preposterous lengths to hear or collect records of the remaining tenth, the genuine *hot* music. Furthermore, the jazz cult is international. It has no boundaries. In Europe, which is more critical and discriminating about all kinds of music than the U.S., there are many jazz connoisseurs. England and France have magazines strictly devoted to *hot* music. A Belgian lawyer, Robert Goffin, has written the only knowing volume on the subject *(Aux Frontières du Jazz)*, which makes such American jazz apologists as Gilbert Seldes and Carl Van Vechten seem positively unlettered. Apropos of Ellington, M. Goffin remarks: "Sans extravagance, avec des moyens tout en douceur et en demi-teintes, Duke a atteint le pinacle de la gloire."

As for the U.S., Duke Ellington and his orchestra have appeared in every large Paramount, Loew's, and Keith theatre in the country; they have played dance engagements from Bowdoin College, Maine, to Frank Sebastian's Cotton Club in Los Angeles; they shared a double bill with Maurice Chevalier in New York and have broadcast innumerable hours over various radio chains; they were featured in Amos 'n' Andy's motion picture *Check and Double Check* and in the late Florenz Ziegfeld's *Show Girl*. All of which means that Ellington is a commercial success. Cleverly managed by Irving Mills, he has grossed as much as $250,000 a year, and the band's price for a week's theatre engagement runs as high as $5,500.[3] These figures are, of course, scarcely to be compared with Rudy Vallée's receipts (with a much smaller band he is estimated to have grossed $312,000 in 1931). But what is remarkable is the fact that Ellington has never compromised with the public taste for watery popular songs, for "show bands" combining music with scenic effects, low

[3] One of the article's captions accompanying a photo of Ellington sidemen stated: "The top salary in this group is $125 per week—approximately equal to the best symphonic wages."

comedy, and flag drills. He has played *hot* music, his own music, all the way along: *Lazy Rhapsody* in San Francisco, *Hot and Bothered* in Chicago, and *It Don't Mean a Thing if It Ain't Got That Swing* in New York. Moreover, Ellington himself, a robust, well-poised Negro of Paul Robeson's stripe, is not a showman; he has no such fopperies as Paul Whiteman's three-foot baton and still plays the piano in his orchestra.

His success with a type of music not noted for its box-office appeal may be partly attributed to the fact that he is assisted in his theatrical tours by feature singers such as Ivie Anderson and dancers like the gelatinous "Snake Hips" Tucker. These performers plus the band constitute the highest grade Negro entertainment, which always has a market of its own. But there can be little doubt that Ellington's success is mainly due to his music itself. It is the final development of a moving, spirited, wholly American musical form. . . .

Various names [in the history of jazz] are worth mention—Don Redman, Louis Armstrong, Fletcher Henderson, Earl Hines—but it is Duke Ellington, a veritable prince of pulsation, who probably deserves to be called the first figure in jazz today. When Ellington and his orchestra played before Percy Grainger's music classes at New York University, Mr. Grainger drew some casual comparisons with the music of Bach and Delius. "I'll have to find out about this Delius," said Mr. Ellington. The chances are he has never made the investigation. So busy is he with his band and his own musical ideas that he seldom troubles to hear his own phonograph records.

Edward Kennedy ("Duke") Ellington lives in a large Harlem apartment at 381 Edgecombe Avenue—and therefore New York may lay claim to being the jazz capital of the world. Separated from his wife, he makes his home with his parents, a nineteen-year-old sister Ruth, and a fourteen-year-old son Mercer, who prefers drawing to music (even his father's). For many years Duke Ellington's father was a blueprint maker at the Washington, D.C., Navy Yard. Edward Kennedy Ellington was born in the capital in April, 1900 [*recte* 1899]. He began studying the piano at the age of eight under a Mr. Grant and a Mrs. Chinkscales [Clinkscales]. At Armstrong High School he veered away toward painting, etching, and all kinds of athletics, but his mother kept him on the piano stool. At sixteen he began to play raggy music for Washington society with Louis Thomas' orchestra. These were the years when jazz entered the North; the Original Dixieland [Jazz Band] was enjoying its New York heyday, and in 1918 the late Lieutenant Jim Europe, famous Negro bandmaster of the A.E.F. [American Expeditionary Force], returned from overseas with a group of black boys who had discovered the New Orleans brand of nerve tonic before the War. One fine day in France, when several bands of the allied nations were assembled in concert, Jim Europe had stopped the show with *St. Louis Blues*. He played it again in Boston a year or so later, and after the performance his drummer stabbed him in the back.

Jim Europe and the Original Dixieland convinced Ellington that jazz was his medium. In 1923 he toured with one of the earlier and more raucous jazz bands, directed by Wilbur C. Sweatman, a mammoth Negro whose specialty was a number in which he found room for three clarinets in his mouth at once. This feat was not so interesting to Ellington as the pliable idiom of jazz, which barred no experiment and allowed each player to formulate his own rules. The fact that a man could squeeze a living from such irregular music was almost too good to be true. Back in Washington a little later, he formed his own band, the Washingtonians, with trumpeter Arthur Whetsel, clarinetist Barney Bigard, saxophonist Otto Hardwick, and drummer Sonny Greer. All of these men are with him today.[4]

The local success of the Washingtonians encouraged Duke to move on to New York. He opened at the Kentucky Club in 1926 [*recte* 1923, when it was still called the Hollywood], and was soon verging on bankruptcy. Almost any New York success requires press-agentry, and Ellington's jazz had no ballyhoo. Fortunately before it was too late a press agent appeared. Irving Mills is not a musician himself, but he knows what is distinctive and is an experienced showman. No one needed to convince him that Ellington was highly potential: he had heard the band.

The problem was one of sales, and Mills believed that with a larger orchestra and a distinctive location, Ellington could be made a drawing card. For a while he flirted with the idea of forming a musical bureau to be known as the Royal Orchestras—led off by Benny "King" Carter. Once and for all, therefore, Ellington became "Duke," a *sobriquet* first earned in his Washington school days. The Royal Orchestras never materialized, but Mills augmented Ellington's band to twelve pieces, placed him at the Cotton Club in Harlem (where rents were low), and installed a Negro floor show, fast, agile, and undressed. A dozen men were what Ellington needed to give body to his ideas; the radio spread his name and music throughout the East, and between the floor show and the band—undeniably the most toe-tickling in the city—the Cotton Club attracted a large downtown clientele.

Ellington had arrived, and subsequently only one other Negro bandmaster has had a comparable success. This is Cab Calloway, also managed by Irving Mills. In many places, including New York, Calloway's gate exceeds Ellington's. Draped in such fascinating haberdashery as a snow-white dress suit with extra long tails, Calloway weaves gracefully before his orchestra and in a high, spasmodic voice emits *hot* arias like *Minnie the Moocher* and *Kicking the Gong Around*. He usually plays no instrument and, as a composer, has boasted only of the lyrics to the chorus of *Minnie*. They begin as follows: *Hi-de-hi-de-hi—ho-de-ho-de-ho*. Calloway's vocalizing is sensational; his band is not to be compared with Ellington's.

Ellington composes perhaps half the music his orchestra plays, and stamps his personality unmistakably on the rest. In addition to those already mentioned, among his best numbers are *Mood Indigo, The Mystery Song, The Dicty Glide, It's Glory* (Victor records), and *Blue Tune, Lightnin'*, and *Ducky-Wucky* (Brunswick records). His best recorded versions of other music include

[4] Bigard was not a member of the original Washingtonians. He joined Ellington at the Cotton Club some time between 29 December 1927 and 9 January 1928.

Limehouse Blues and *Three Little Words* (Victor), and *Rose Room, The Sheik,* and *Blackbirds Medley* (Brunswick). Ellington uses fourteen men—three trumpets, three trombones, four saxophones (doubling on all manner of reeds), piano, guitar, string bass, and drums. Very frequently the sections are employed in unison, the six-part brass team playing in counterpoint against the four reeds with the remaining players acting as percussion. But Ellington has no set rules of orchestration. His conceptions are miniatures; and in the titivating mysteries of rhythm, tone color, and interweaving voices, Ellington is an adept. R. D. Darrell, writing in the magazine *Disques* declares: "To me . . . the most daring experiments of the modernists rarely approach the imaginative originality, mated to pure musicianship, of a dozen arresting moments in Ellington's works" [see §12].

While Ellington's music is personal and finished to the *n*th degree, there are always *hot* solos by the players—the jazz fundamental is preserved. Ellington's instrument is not so much subservient to him as sympathetic. The understanding between the men is uncanny: Ellington and his drummer, Sonny Greer, for instance, engage in a constant signaling with eyebrows, hands, or grimaces. It is no exaggeration to say that his band of fourteen can *fake* (improvise) as adroitly as the early five-piece combinations. Usually the music is a striking blend of arrangement and invention, typical of which is a trumpet player stabbing bright patterns through lustrous curtains of tone.

Ellington hates the spade work of writing music. At rehearsals, which are frequently called for three o'clock in the morning, after the night's work is done, no scores are visible. The leader seats himself at the piano and runs over the theme he wishes to develop, shows the men what he thinks the saxophones might play here and the brasses there. Perhaps Barney Bigard, the solo clarinetist, suggests a rolling phrase on the reeds at a certain point; it is tried and judged by general opinion. Freddy Jenkins, the electric little trumpeter, may favor muting the brass in various passages. Each man has his say. After four to five hours of this informal process, a new number has been perfected—suavely and intricately arranged, played with the utmost technical command. Ellington believes his men memorize more easily this way than they would by using prepared scores. Most of his famous arrangements have never been written down; sometimes, after five or six months, Manager Mills succeeds in persuading Ellington to put one on paper. The *hot* solo passages are, of course, left blank, with some such notation as "*get off.*"

But there is really very little reason why Ellington should bother to score his arrangements. They are so difficult that few other dance bands can play them at all, and very few with anything approaching the ease and spirit of Ellington's musicians. Reading his scores, other orchestras quickly discover that he continually expects things from his men which even the best players elsewhere are seldom called upon to deliver. He conceives his music, for instance, in terms of piano chords and indicates certain notes for the fourth saxophone, regardless of whether the intervals and sequences are convenient for a saxophonist to play. Ellington knows his men can play them; other leaders are not so fortunate. Manager Mills wastes considerable money buying Ellington special arrangements of standard tunes. By the time the orchestra plays them they are Ellingtonian—lustered with his own harmonies, pungent with his rhythm.

Ellington spends his spare moments writing a score for a Negro musical show to be produced next season by John Henry Hammond Jr., son of the New York lawyer John Henry Hammond, and one of the leading jazz connoisseurs of the country. Ellington is also conceiving a suite in five parts, tentatively entitled *Africa, The Slave Ship, The Plantation, Harlem*—the last being a climactic restatement of themes. Whether this will be arranged for his band as now constituted or for an augmented group has not been decided. The composer expects to leave the piano, taking a baton in the form of a drumstick which, while conducting, he will beat on an elaborate choir of tom-toms. And he is trying desperately to find a reed instrument lower even than a contrabassoon with which to produce voodoo accents in the opening section. His friends say he will ultimately invent one.

With this suite in his repertoire, Ellington may some day make his Carnegie Hall début. It will be an occasion—but, depend on it, there will be no concert-hall piety about the affair. Harlem offers a foretaste of it this very day. In Harlem hot music survives. In Harlem argument survives—the jazz boys debate the merits of two Negro pianists, the partially blind Art Tatum and Willie Smith, somewhat terrifyingly known as The Lion. And in Harlem Duke Ellington and his men have a traditional place in the purple glow lamps of the Cotton Club. Presiding high above his fellows is the dapper Sonny Greer, surrounded like an alchemist with his tom-tom crucibles and tympanic retorts. In the delicacy and pertinence with which he approaches these instruments he is the very symbol of elegant, seething syncopation. There, while Ellington's brass sprays out the steaming measures of *Ring Dem Bells* and Greer titillates the chimes, listeners may remember their Aldous Huxley and cry out: "What songs! What gongs! . . . What blasts of Bantu melody!"

21. The "Secret" of the Ellington Orchestra (1933)

Several months after Ellington had returned to the United States from his European tour, the journalist H. A. Overstreet addressed a subject that had baffled English observers: the Ellington orchestra's uncanny ability to play a great many pieces without using scores. Apparently some listeners had believed the group improvised everything—an "orchestra of Louis Armstrongs," as Overstreet put it.

In explaining the "secret" behind this phenomenon, Overstreet gave one of the earliest detailed explanations of Ellington's working methods, emphasizing two important aspects: Ellington's practice of evolving pieces collectively in rehearsal and his reliance on writing

Source: H. A. Overstreet, "Touching Tomorrow's Frontiers Is Duke Ellington's Music," *Metronome* (October 1933), 31, 52.

down arrangements. The source for Overstreet's information is not known. Perhaps he spoke with members of the orchestra or with Ellington himself, or drew upon first-hand observations.

Overstreet's article appeared in the *Metronome,* an American magazine founded in 1885 and aimed at professionals in the fields of popular music and entertainment. In the pre-swing era it focused mainly on white dance bands; later in the forties and fifties, under editors Barry Ulanov and Leonard Feather, it provided more integrated jazz coverage.

The following excerpt omits a section reviewing highlights from Ellington's trip abroad.

. . . Because of the fact that regular Sunday performances are not permitted in British music halls, concerts were arranged for the open Sundays of the band, and the most spectacular of these was the one under the auspices of a British musical weekly [*Melody Maker*], which was planned particularly for musicians. Seats were on sale for six weeks before the band landed in England and eight weeks before the concert, and although London's Trocadero Theatre, at which it was held, is the largest theatre in all of Europe, with 4,000 seats and accommodations for nearly 1,000 standees, it was completely sold out.

At this concert [25 June 1933] the orchestra played twenty-eight numbers, all of them Ellington arrangements, and twenty-one of them Ellington compositions. Musicians who had caught performances of the band at the Palladium and marvelled at the fact that the orchestra used no music or music stands for a performance lasting nearly an hour, marvelled even more at the concert when the orchestra referred to written arrangements for only four or five of their older and more lengthy selections which are not used frequently by the band and are therefore not included in the musicians' memorized repertoire.

The virtuosity of the individual musicians, the brilliant brass section, the amazingly proficient reed group and the rhythm section's torrid tempo, described abroad as "a revolution in rhythm," came in for their share of attention and acclaim, but the fact that the stands were not encumbered with orchestrations gave rise to more discussion than any one thing. For the previous acquaintance of these British musicians with the Ellington orchestra had been solely with their records, and these many of them had played so often that they knew them virtually by heart. In these records, they had ascribed the incredible flights of the Ellington soloists as pure improvisation, conceived and simultaneously executed in the recording studio.

Their pre-conception of the band, gained from records, had been a generally accepted idea that it was an entire orchestra of Louis Armstrongs, performing on trombone, saxophone and clarinet as well as trumpet, and somehow welded together by Duke Ellington.

Yet here on the concert stage was the orchestra, playing the recorded arrangements they knew so well, and playing them note for note, figure for figure, both as an ensemble and as soloists—a blow to their theory of pure improvisation. But the orchestrations from which the performance stemmed still were not in evidence.

The explanation—which some British musicians are still seeking, although the journals of the musical world there have gone into it extensively—is contained in one word: *rehearsal*. But when the word rehearsal is applied to the pre-performance activity of Duke Ellington and his band, the word itself takes on a wider meaning, and requires explanation.

Duke Ellington and his orchestra are a product of the night clubs of New York. For years they went to work at midnight, finished at four or five in the morning. After Irving Mills placed the orchestra in the Cotton Club and it began to attract nation-wide attention on the air, they went into theatres as well, but still doubled into the Harlem rendezvous. As a result of their years of nocturnal activity, they have simply turned their lives upside down, so that now, no matter what they are engaged in at the moment, they sleep through the day until it's time to go to work. When their work is officially over, their day is still young—so they keep on working. To the outsider, they're rehearsing, but it's more than that.

Even when the orchestra is touring theatres, as at present, it sticks to this schedule. Material is constantly needed for phonograph recordings, an immensely important phase of the band's activity, in view of the enormous sale of their records abroad, where radio hasn't wrought the havoc with records that it has here.

After the last show is over, the band assembles in the rehearsal room, if the theatre has one, and if not, on the stage. If Duke Ellington has an idea for a tune, the men sit in with him until he finishes it, accepting criticisms and suggestions from each. With a popular tune, the procedure from then on is the same.

The men take up their instruments, and the arrangement is started. Ellington takes the men by sections, first the reeds, then the trumpets, then the trombones, and gives each man his notes for four bars. The men play them singly, then as a section, with remarkable rapidity. Any necessary changes are made section by section; the men make suggestions and from time to time Ellington turns to the piano to trace out an idea. The arrangement of from sixteen bars to a full chorus will be completed in this manner, by sections, before the orchestra plays it as a whole. Then they play it a sufficient number of times to fix it firmly in their memories.

While the other sections are at work, Juan Tizol, the Puerto Rican valve trombonist, will have been busy with a score, taking down the arrangement as it is made for the other sections, sometimes writing down the trombone parts, sometimes indicating them sketchily, for elaboration later. This rough score serves many purposes; for the moment it is used for reference in settling arguments, for there are plenty of these until the entire arrangement is completed.

These arguments would be politely termed exchanges of ideas, but they sound like arguments. Remarkable as the musical memories of the individual musicians are, Ellington's is even more remarkable, and he is able to detect any deviation from the parts as he outlines them. If the deviation is an improvement, it stays in; if not, it's out.

There's protest, too, as, for instance, when one of the saxophone players gets a note below the range of his instrument. If the Duke follows any general rule in arranging, it's that if he can play it on the piano, it can be played somehow by the man he's writing for, on his particular instrument. When one of these situations arises, that particular section holds a conclave to see if Duke's idea can possibly be carried out on their instrument. The many special mutes which Ellington has devised come to the aid of the brass section, but the saxophones have their troubles. That's why, in some Ellington arrangements, you see a saxophonist suddenly thrust his fist into the bell of his completely closed instrument, sounding perfectly a note which any musician will promptly tell you is impossible on that instrument.

At any rate, when an Ellington arrangement has been completed, it has also been completely memorized, but also written. Then Duke takes the score home with him, to see if any further refinements are possible. About noon the day after he went to work on the tune he has polished it to his satisfaction, sometimes entirely rewriting parts of it, and goes to bed.

At the next rehearsal the following night, the arrangement is again rehearsed time after time, from the orchestration if the parts have already been extracted, and if not, from memory, with the score on the piano for reference. Changes and improvements are constantly made, until the finished arrangement is not only written but perfectly memorized. Then, and not until then, is the number ready for stage, radio and recording.

Of course this procedure is varied, often greatly. If the band is playing for dancing, and someone requests a tune that only one man knows, the orchestra will play it, often brilliantly, as happened in the case of Duke Ellington's version of Old Man River. It was requested at the Cotton Club by someone who had heard it at a party, before *Show Boat* opened, even before the score was in print. He sang it for Duke. Ellington played it on the piano. Then the orchestra played it, and so successfully that in that form, with a few very slight changes, it has remained in the band's repertoire ever since.[1]

Again, if the tune being arranged is a popular one, sure to be discarded later for a newer tune, the arrangement is rarely written, unless the number is to be recorded. And on occasion, getting home about dawn, Duke Ellington will compose a number and arrange it completely, before going to bed, handing the completed score to one of his men for extraction the following day.

With such dependence, successful as it may be, upon intensive rehearsal and memorizing, one wonders why a score is written at all. But the written arrangement is useful in many ways: if it is an Ellington composition, it forms the basis for the commercial orchestration printed by the publisher. And although each of the orchestras managed by the firm which handles Ellington

[1] *Show Boat*, by Jerome Kern and Oscar Hammerstein II, opened 27 December 1927, during the Ellington orchestra's first month at the Cotton Club. Although *Ol' Man River* was recorded by a Cootie Williams small group in 1938, the full Ellington orchestra did not record it until 1951. Overstreet, however, may be alluding to an arrangement of the song that went unrecorded in the thirties. (There are a few parts from a "Showboat Medley" in the Smithsonian's Duke Ellington Collection, probably from the thirties and copied in Juan Tizol's hand, apparently never recorded.)

cultivates its own particular style, the arrangements are often useful to the other bands, eventually finding a permanent place, of course, in the Ellington library. The human equation is not overlooked, and should the men become rusty in a number which is not ideal for theatres, it can be worked up on short notice for special radio or concert presentation.

If there is any secret to the Ellington method, it is this: for every hour of actual performance there are at least two hours of intensive rehearsal.

22. Warren W. Scholl: Profile of Ellington in the *Music Lovers' Guide* (1934)

Writing for an audience of classical-music devotees, as R. D. Darrell had done earlier in "Black Beauty" (1932), Warren W. Scholl described Ellington's recent successes and evaluated selected recordings. In stating that Ellington failed when he "expands to larger forms"—referring to *Creole Rhapsody* (1931) and the twelve-inch versions of *Creole Love Call* and *St. Louis Blues* (both 1932)—Scholl voiced a criticism that would run throughout the composer's career.

The *Music Lovers' Guide* was begun in 1932 by R. D. Darrell and Axel Johnson (former editors of *Phonograph Monthly Review*). In 1935 it changed its name to the *American Music Lover,* and to this journal Warren Scholl (b. 1913) contributed important early discographies of Bix Beiderbecke and Benny Goodman. Scholl also served as New York correspondent for England's *Melody Maker* during the thirties and wrote feature articles for *Down Beat*.

A biographical section summarizing Ellington's career has been omitted.

Duke Ellington occupies a unique position in the realm of hot jazz. His band is distinctive and unusual, and everything about Ellington and his band savors of originality and interest.

In ten years Duke Ellington has worked himself up from a small time band leader to the position of a first-rate conductor in the hot jazz field. . . .

Ellington's band is inimitable. There are many colored orchestras in America, but none can compare favorably with this one. Louis Armstrong, Cab Calloway, and Don Redmond [*recte* Redman] are showmen. Ellington at his best is a refined interpreter of hot jazz, representing the finest orchestra of its kind in the world. This may sound like an exaggerated statement, but it is true. When the Duke visited England and Europe last summer, he received greater response from audiences than Paul Whiteman or Ted Lewis did when they visited these countries. Here in America, where the best in hot jazz emanates, no other band (colored or white) can boast the originality and versatility of Ellington. As jazz king, he has superseded Paul Whiteman.

Records by the Ellington outfit outsell all others abroad. So great has the

Source: Warren W. Scholl, "Duke Ellington—A Unique Personality," *Music Lovers' Guide* II/6 (February 1934), 169–70, 176.

demand become for records by this band, that the Columbia Phonograph Company (American) has signed Ellington to make a special series of records, to be released only abroad. When Victor and Parlophone can issue complete albums of records by Ellington, one can hardly deny that this aggregation occupies a peculiar and enviable position in the hot jazz field. No other organization, foreign or domestic, has ever been able to vaunt this distinction.

For a single broadcast over the B.B.C. Ellington received a higher salary than any other orchestra previously had been paid. At the conclusion of the program the band was playing *Mood Indigo*. Time was running short, but the officials of the station allowed him to play the complete arrangement, which ran five minutes overtime into a scheduled commercial broadcast. Such is the singularity of Ellington.

Duke Ellington and his band has had the privilege of playing for Percy Grainger at New York University. Grainger approved of Ellington and even compared some of his characteristics with Bach and Haydn. What other contemporary leader has played such a concert?

The repertoire of this organization is more distinctive and varied than that of any other band in this field. Every number played is a special arrangement by Ellington in collaboration with other members of the band. About one-half the selections featured are original compositions written by Ellington. The versatility of this man is amazing. Considering the prodigious number of original works he has written, he still manages to be fresh in his newer compositions.

As composer, the Duke is most widely known for his *Mood Indigo, Black and Tan Fantasy, It Don't Mean a Thing,* and *Sophisticated Lady.* Original and excellent as they are, they are by no means his best efforts. His records of these selections outsold many of his others, but this is a misleading indication. His record of *Slippery Horn* or *Black Beauty* is far superior from a strictly musical standpoint. Consider the opening introduction and the three trombone passage following in *Slippery Horn.* The intricate theme played and the phrasing used here is far more ingenious than the saccharine strains of *Sophisticated Lady,* for instance.

Black Beauty represents Ellington in a happy, carefree mood. The lilting muted trumpet solo with saxophones in the background, and the variation which the clarinet weaves around the theme are surely better than the hot measures of *It Don't Mean a Thing.* Among his many compositions his best are *Swanee Rhapsody, Blue Ramble, Blue Tune, Creole Love Call, Drop Me Off at Harlem, Lightnin', The Mooche,* and *Rude Interlude* (his latest opus).

Ellington had the honor of being represented last summer in a concert by the New York Philharmonic Symphonic society augmented by Paul Whiteman's orchestra. His *Mood Indigo* was a part of the program which included music by Gershwin, Grofé, and William Grant Still. It is no overstatement to say that Ellington has a significant place in the field of modern American music.

The Ellington combination is the only one of its kind which has never stooped to that lowly bugbear known as the general public. He has always played what he wanted as he wished, and the public has liked it. No commercial arrangements are featured by his band. The few popular selections that he does present are played in the typical Ellington tradition. I recall his breath-taking version of that trite, insipid ballad *Just an Echo in the Valley*. Hearing him play it as he did, convinced me that he can make anything sound listenable if he can make tripe like *Echo in the Valley* sound as it did.

A trait peculiar to Ellington's compositions is that his is the only band that can properly perform them. They were written with this express combination in mind. Since there is no corresponding orchestra to compare with Ellington's, his is really the only band qualified to properly interpret his numbers.

Every man in the band is a thorough musician. Each memorizes his part of an arrangement before playing it publicly. At recent concerts given in England, entire programs of over an hour's length were played from memory. English musicians were astounded when they learned this.

Ellington has a very extensive and representative phonograph record repertoire. His first discs for the major companies were made for Okeh, under his own name. Then there followed a contract with Victor. However, he continued recording for Okeh under the pseudonym of The Harlem Footwarmers. Likewise he recorded for Columbia using the name of Sonny Greer for some discs, and that of Joe Turner and his Memphis Men for others. At the same time the band was making records for Brunswick under the alias of The Jungle Band.

When his Victor contract expired a year and a half ago, he signed up exclusively with Brunswick. This fall that contract expired and he signed up with Victor again. He has made two twelve-inch records, neither of which is successful. When he expands to larger forms, he is out of his field. His *Creole Rhapsody* (Victor) is very flimsy as concert material. On Brunswick his *Creole Love Call* and *St. Louis Blues* offer evidence of his shortcomings in the longer phases of arranging. Among his best records of selections not his own are: *The Sheik, Bugle Call Rag, Limehouse Blues, 12th St. Rag, Sam and Delilah,* and *Three Little Words*.

In the past four years there has been a decided improvement in the finish and polish of the orchestra. Records of the 1928–1929 period show that Ellington was still inclined towards roughness and crudeness. His newest releases compared with his older ones offer conclusive evidence of this. Contrast Ellington's 1929 [*recte* 1930] Brunswick record of *Mood Indigo* with his long-playing Victor recording of the same selection and you will be convinced for yourself.

At present the band has grace, charm, and a sophisticated subtlety. When it "goes to town" it does so in a gentlemanly fashion. Never for one moment does any ad-libbing soloist "get lost" in the fervor of his hot passages. Each man knows precisely where he is going and why.

One somewhat annoying feature of Ellington's that has been remedied is the growling, wah-wah effects his trumpets formerly indulged in. These noises have been cleaned up considerably, but not entirely. Many people consider these effects as much a part of Ellington as cadenzas were a part of Liszt.

Vocalizing is merely an incidental phase with the Ellington aggregation. Ivy Anderson takes care of what vocalizing there is. Only a small percentage of

Ellington's records have any singing in them. Many bands employ three or four vocal combinations with their outfits and usually push the orchestra into the background. But Ellington reverses the situation. It minimizes singing and emphasizes the orchestral selections.

Duke Ellington is currently working on the score of a new Harlem musical comedy which is being directed and sponsored by Mr. John Henry Hammond, Jr., an ardent admirer of Ellington's. Judging from past performances, there ought to be some interesting material in this new opus.

As conductor, composer, and arranger, Duke Ellington unquestionably occupies an enviable niche in the field of hot American jazz, and leads an orchestra which is the finest of its type in the world.

All of which admits of no comparisons.

23. Roger Pryor Dodge on *Black and Tan Fantasy*, from "Harpsichords and Jazz Trumpets" (1934)

 What role does improvisation play in jazz composition? How might jazz performance practice resemble that of earlier European musical traditions? How does one seriously discuss jazz as music?

These were some of the questions addressed by Roger Pryor Dodge in "Harpsichords and Jazz Trumpets," first published in the American little magazine *Hound & Horn* (July–September 1934) and later reprinted in Ralph de Toledano's *Frontiers of Jazz* (1947). The centerpiece of this celebrated essay was an analysis of *Black and Tan Fantasy*, the 1927 composition by Ellington and trumpeter Bubber Miley (although here Dodge attributed it to Miley alone).

Dodge built his discussion around solos he had notated from recordings. Although the musical examples are rough in form and contain errors—the theme, for example, should be in B-flat minor, not major—they represent an early use of transcription for the purpose of jazz analysis.

Dodge (1898–1974) was a dancer in ballet and vaudeville, later a critic who wrote on jazz from the mid-twenties through the fifties. His acquaintance with Bubber Miley dated from 1931 when the two performed together in Billy Rose's show *Sweet and Low*. Dodge produced an early historiography of jazz, "Consider the Critics," that appeared as the final chapter in Frederic Ramsey, Jr., and Charles Edward Smith's *Jazzmen* (1939). Later he wrote for *H.R.S. Rag, Jazz, The Record Changer*, and other small jazz publications.[1]

The recorded sources for Dodge's four transcribed solos of *Black and Tan Fantasy* are as follows:

1. 3 November 1927, OKeh 8521 (C take).
2. 3 November 1927, OKeh 40955 (B take).

Source: Roger Pryor Dodge, from "Harpsichords and Jazz Trumpets," *Hound & Horn* (July–September 1934), 602–6.

[1] See §90 for another article by Dodge.

Black and Tan Fantasy

Fig. 1

Bubber Miley

Fig. 1 (cont.)

3. 26 October 1927, Victor 21137.
4. A private recording Miley apparently made for Dodge.

The excerpt below comes after Dodge has compared jazz with baroque and classical music and briefly discussed composing for jazz orchestra.

. . . The four solos that follow are notated from records made by Bubber Miley. He said they were variations on a Spiritual his mother used to sing, called Hosanna, but the Spiritual turns out to be a part of Stephen Adams' "Holy City" commencing at the seventeenth bar. There the tune is in four-four time and eight bars long, but Miley's version has about two bars taken out next to the last bar and the remaining six bars drawn out to twelve by dividing each bar into two. In the composition "Black and Tan Fantasy" (fig. 1) this theme is announced in the minor, but his hot solos (variations) are on the original major. As he improvises these solos the orchestra simply plays a "vamp" rhythmic accompaniment. I have written them out under each other as in an orchestral score, with the theme on top, in order to facilitate inter-comparison; but it must be understood that these are pure improvisations out of a folk school, with no idea of adequate notation. All of these solos are by Bubber Miley except the first twelve bars of No. 2 which is [sic] by Joseph Nanton, a trombonist in Duke Ellington's orchestra.[2] As I have said, negro improvisations are either on the melody or on the harmony, and it would appear that Miley paid no attention to the melody, so far removed are his variations; but by playing certain parts of the theme, then the corresponding part in any one of the hot solos, you will find that many times he did have the theme in mind.

In No. 1, all through the first twelve bars, there is a vague resemblance to the theme. The thirteenth and fifteenth bars are exactly the same as the theme but his treatment of these bars takes the startling form of blasts. In No. 3, if we play the fifth and sixth bars of the theme, and then his corresponding variations, we again see a melodic resemblance, but it is curious how this is his first melodic attack after the four-bar hold; that is, instead of continuing with the melody, he is starting one.

In the thirteenth bar of No. 3 he wonderfully distorts the B-flat in the theme, to an E natural. Here is a take-off of the most extreme kind, and accordingly he followed the harmony until he could catch up with the melody. This he did at the twenty-first bar, finishing with a jazzed up version of the theme.

A typical Jazz distortion of the given melody is to lengthen the time value of one note by stealing from another, thereby sometimes reducing the melody to an organ point. Though this was practiced prior to Miley, it is interesting

---

[2] Dodge later acknowledged that he had erred in assigning the first of these solos to Miley, when in fact it was played by trumpeter Jabbo Smith, substituting for Miley on this date. It is also Smith who plays measures 13–24 of No. 2, following trombonist Nanton's first chorus. See Dodge, "Bubber Miley," *Jazz Monthly* (May 1958), 5.

Fig. 2

J.S. Bach

to see how the whole note in the first bar of the theme is held longer and longer until in No. 4 he is holding it seven bars. Notice how the improvisations do not have any break between the twelfth and thirteenth bars, that is, where the theme begins its repeat.

It seems to me the little phrases in bars eight, nine and ten of No. 1, where he plays with his melody at either end of the octave, can only be found elsewhere in such music as Bach's "Goldberg Variations" (fig. 2).[3]

Joseph Nanton's twelve-bar variation in No. 2 seems to be on the harmony. It is followed by Miley's [*recte* Jabbo Smith's] beautiful entrance, a slow trill on the original B-flat. In No. 4, which he made for me, the little coda to the long note is the purest music I have ever heard in Jazz. I speak of purity in its resemblance to the opening of the Credo for soprano voices in Palestrina's "Missa Papae Marcelli" (fig. 3). You will observe that the thirteenth bars of both No. 3 and No. 4 are the same. The freedom leading up to the C in the fifteenth bar is amazing and the A-flat in the nineteenth bar, after all the agitation, is no less surprising.

There were two elements essential for this freedom of thought; harmony and rhythm. Miley told me he needed the strictest beat and at least a three-part harmony. Though the piano could give him this, he was always better, however, with the orchestra and its background of drums, etc. Whereas the academy now might be able to compose parts like this, write them down and with a little shaping make something very inventive, no folk artist could do so, as his improvising in such a manner that rhythm and melody are torn apart, really demands these two elements. We can now understand how a person like Duke Ellington was indispensable to Miley—"When I get off the Duke is always there." The Duke's co-operation, in fact, inspired Miley to the best work he ever did and neither of them sustained very well their unfortunate parting of the ways. The Duke has never since touched the heights that he and Bubber Miley reached in such records as "East St. Louis Toodle-O,"

Fig. 3

Palestrina

---

[3] The excerpt is from the second half of the Aria that opens Bach's *Goldberg Variations*, measures 1–8.

"Flaming Youth," "Got Everything But You," "Yellow Dog Blues," etc., etc.—and of course the many "Black and Tan Fantasys." The sudden and tragic death of Bubber Miley [1903–1932] put a stop to his career before he was thirty—though without the guidance of the Duke, who is a real Diaghileff in a small way, perhaps he would have slipped backwards too. . . .[4]

24. Constant Lambert on Ellington (1934)

I n the early thirties composers in the classical field began recognizing Ellington's talent. One was the Australian-born Percy Grainger (1882–1961), who in 1932 ranked Ellington as one of the three greatest composers in the history of music, sharing honors with J. S. Bach and Frederick Delius.[1]

Another was the British composer and critic Constant Lambert (1905–1951), who met Ellington in 1933 and reviewed his orchestra favorably in several articles. The following year, in *Music Ho! A Study of Music in Decline*, Lambert paid tribute to Ellington in the course of a quirky, patronizing, bigoted, occasionally insightful discussion of jazz. Like the Swiss conductor Ernest Ansermet and his 1919 appreciation of Sidney Bechet,[2] Lambert offered a striking example of a conservatory-trained European seeking to validate the work of a black American jazz musician.

. . . An artist like Louis Armstrong, who is one of the most remarkable virtuosi of the present day, enthralls us at a first hearing, but after a few records one realizes that all his improvisations are based on the same restricted circle of ideas, and in the end there is no music which more quickly provokes a state of exasperation and ennui. The best records of Duke Ellington, on the other hand, can be listened to again and again because they are not just decorations of a familiar shape but a new arrangement of shapes. Ellington, in fact, is a real composer, the first jazz composer of distinction, and the first Negro composer of distinction. His works—apart from a few minor details—are not left to the caprice or ear of the instrumentalist; they are scored and written out, and though, in the course of time, variants may creep in—Ellington's works

---

[4] Earlier in the article Dodge had compared the great Russian choreographer and impresario Sergei Diaghilev to the leader of a jazz orchestra: "[Diaghilev] managed the financing, he controlled and selected the great artists, smoothing out their differences, and he proved himself a rare man; probably more rare than any single one of the artists. But important as he was to the life of the organization, students will always pick out the important separate creators and give them their due credit, for these were the people who were the backbone of the organization and upon whom all lasting significance depends."

Source: Constant Lambert, "The Spirit of Jazz," from *Music Ho! A Study of Music in Decline* (London: Faber, 1934; rpt., London: Hogarth Press, 1985), 186–88.

[1] John Bird, *Percy Grainger: The Man and the Music* (London: Paul Elek, 1976), 204.
[2] "Bechet and Jazz Visit Europe, 1919," in Ralph de Toledano, ed., *Frontiers of Jazz* (New York: Oliver Durrell, 1947; 2nd rev. ed., New York: Frederick Ungar, 1962), 115–22.

in this respect are as difficult to codify as those of Liszt—the first American records of his music may be taken definitively, like a full score, and are the only jazz records worth studying for their form as well as their texture. Ellington himself being an executant of the second rank has probably not been tempted to interrupt the continuity of his texture with bravura passages for the piano, and although his instrumentalists are of the finest quality their solos are rarely demonstrations of virtuosity for its own sake.

The real interest of Ellington's records lies not so much in their colour, brilliant though it may be, as in the amazingly skilful proportions in which the colour is used. I do not only mean skilful as compared with other jazz composers, but as compared with so-called highbrow composers. I know of nothing in Ravel so dexterous in treatment as the varied solos in the middle of the ebullient *Hot and Bothered* and nothing in Stravinsky more dynamic than the final section. The combination of themes at this moment is one of the most ingenious pieces of writing in modern music. It is not a question, either, of setting two rhythmic patterns working against each other in the mathematical Aaron Copland manner—it is genuine melodic and rhythmic counterpoint which, to use an old-fashioned phrase, "fits" perfectly.

The exquisitely tired and four-in-the-morning *Mood Indigo* is an equally remarkable piece of writing of a lyrical and harmonic order, yet it is palpably from the same hand. How well we know those composers whose slow movements seem to be written by someone else—who change in the course of the same section from slow Vaughan Williams to quick Stravinsky and from quick Hindemith to slow César Franck. The ability to maintain the same style in totally different moods is one of the hallmarks of the genuine composer, whether major or minor.

Ellington's best works are written in what may be called ten-inch record form, and he is perhaps the only composer to raise this insignificant disc to the dignity of a definite genre. Into this three and a half minutes he compresses the utmost, but beyond its limits he is inclined to fumble. The double-sided ten-inch *Creole Rhapsody* [on Brunswick] is an exception, but the twelve-inch expansion of the same piece [Victor] is nothing more than a potpourri without any of the nervous tension of the original version. Ellington has shown no sign of expanding his formal conceptions, and perhaps it is as well, for his works might then lose their peculiar concentrated savour. He is definitely a petit maître, but that, after all, is considerably more than many people thought either jazz or the coloured race would ever produce. He has crystallized the popular music of our time and set up a standard by which we may judge not only other jazz composers but also those highbrow composers, whether American or European, who indulge in what is roughly known as "symphonic jazz." . . .

25. Ellington's Response to Lambert (1935)

Certain writers—John Hammond, for one (see §27)—claimed that Ellington began to take himself seriously as a composer only after receiving praise from such composer-critics as Constant Lambert, Percy Grainger, and Spike Hughes. But Ellington's wry responses to a reporter who read him excerpts from Lambert's *Music Ho!* indicate that, by 1935 at least, he was still keeping such accolades in perspective. Here, as in the *Christian Science Monitor* interview with Janet Mabie five years earlier (§8), he stated his credo with simple directness: "A black man feels [a] black man's music most, and that's what I want to write."

Duke Ellington, gifted Negro musician, paid a flying visit to Philadelphia last week, accompanied by that "hot and sweet" aggregation of inspired toe-ticklers who play in his "Cotton Club" band.

When Duke was making life gayer for the patrons of exclusive London night clubs last year [*recte* two years ago], he had a strange experience. He was taken up by the musical intelligentsia of the British capital. He was "discovered" by the highbrows, and great was the hue and cry thereof. It was the greatest British triumph since Dr. Livingstone's adventures in Darkest Africa.

Constant Lambert, English composer and critic, who is a very brilliant but very young man, wrote a book about modern music ("Music Ho!"). He had a lot of nice things to say about Duke's music, practically smothering the jazz boy's "Blues" in an admiring avalanche of fancy critical verbiage.

The fashionable and ultra-sophisticated Sitwells blew perfumed critical kisses in Duke's direction.

Percy Grainger went overboard with a splash, comparing Duke's melodic line to that of Bach. Others followed with tributes to the jazz composer that ranked him with Stravinsky and Ravel.

Apparently all this adulation left honest Duke slightly bewildered. Your correspondent found the idol of Mayfair one night last week in a local temple far removed from Kensington Gardens, Hyde Park or the studios of London's Bohemia. In fact, your correspondent found the dusky maestro in a rather select but noisy night club in Manayunk,[1] doing his stuff in a smoke-laden, purple-lighted cabaret to the syncopated delight of a crowded dance floor.

During an intermission your reporter cornered Duke in his dressing room, confronted him with Critic Lambert's book, and proceeded to read excerpts. Duke listened to the rhapsodies about himself as best he could amid the distraction of passing cigarette girls and shouting waiters.

"I know nothing in Ravel," read your reporter (from Lambert's pages), "so dextrous in treatment as the varied solos in Ellington's ebullient 'Hot and

Source: Gama Gilbert, " 'Hot Damn!' Says Ellington When Ranked with Bach," *Philadelphia Record*, 17 May 1935.

[1] A town close to central Philadelphia along the Schuylkill River.

Bothered,' and nothing in Stravinsky more dynamic than the final section . . . It is genuine melodic and rhythmic counterpoint."[2]

A look of simple wonder appeared on Duke's countenance. "Is that so," he gasped. "Say, that fellow Lambert is quite a writer, isn't he?"

Your reporter read some more. "In Ellington's compositions jazz has produced the most distinguished popular music since Johann Strauss."

Duke's face lit up in a broad grin. "Hot damn!" he said, "I guess that makes me pretty good, doesn't it?"

"Ellington (this was still reading Lambert) is a real composer, the first jazz composer of distinction and the first Negro composer of distinction."

"Well," said the Duke, "all I can tell you about that is that when I was in London, Lambert and a lot of other English fellows got interested in my music. They used to come around and see me. I didn't know who they were, but they were nice fellows and they asked me a lot of questions, and I answered them all the best I could.

"At first, they didn't know what I was driving at. They wanted to know how I made this sound and why I used that chord and all, and there was an awful lot of drinking and talking. But finally I made 'em see my way and listen my way. I only found out afterward I'd been talking to a lot of musical editorial writers."

"What about this, Mr. Ellington, Lambert says here: 'Ellington's first American records may be taken definitively as a full score and are the only jazz records worth studying for their form as well as their texture.'"

"I guess he's right," said Duke, "he's a musical editorial writer and he ought to know. But I'll tell you a hot one about the records we made of 'Mood Indigo.' There was a funny sound in the first record we made, and we busted eight more recordings before we found the trouble. There was a loose plunger in the 'mike,' and we couldn't get rid of it nohow, so what did we do but transpose the piece to another key so the goofy mike sound fitted and it made a swell effect."

"Yes," we said, "that was what one English critic called 'Ellington's weird and dulcet harmonizations such as never were [heard] on land or sea, recalling the opalescent subtleties of Debussy.'"

"How come?" said Duke.

"That's what an English critic said about that record."

"Is zat so?" said Duke. "Opalescent subtleties. Don't those London fellows push a mean pen?"

Asked about his own ideas of music, Ellington said:

"A black man feels [a] black man's music most, and that's what I want to write. My aim is not only to make jazz. It is to make new, unadulterated music expressing the character and moods of the Negro. It's hard for me to get other kinds of music. Take Stravinsky, he has a terrific conception and he sure knows how to handle his material, but I really can't feel his music with

---

[2] In this quote and the following ones Gilbert slightly alters Lambert's language in *Music Ho!*. For the original wording, see §24.

my heart. I'm wild about some of it though. What's that bird . . . 'Firebird'— that's it. Great stuff!"

The intermission was over. The reporter left. But the Duke still lingered. Stretched out in his chair with a dreamy expression in his eyes, he was scratching his head, "The greatest popular dance music since Johann Strauss—hot damn!" he said.

26. Ellington on Gershwin's *Porgy and Bess*—and a Response from the Office of Irving Mills (1935/1936)

O ver the years Ellington maintained a fairly consistent persona in interviews. With beguiling charm he would answer a journalist's questions politely or deflect them with humor, often concealing his true feelings behind an effusive verbal smoke-screen. His interest in creating positive impressions extended to his memoirs, *Music Is My Mistress*, which in its 500-plus pages hardly contains a discouraging word about any person or event in Ellington's life. (Ellington realized the fairy-tale quality of his story, once telling his son Mercer, "We've written the Good Book . . . and now let's write the Bad Book!"[1])

One notable lapse from his customary discretion, however, occurred in remarks he allegedly made about George Gershwin's opera *Porgy and Bess* that appeared in 1935 in the left-wing magazine *New Theatre*. Responding to interviewer Edward Morrow's leading line of questioning—"Would you say that an honest Negro musical play would have to contain social criticism?"—Ellington came down hard on the Gershwin work premiered earlier that year.

This outspokenness was so unusual for Ellington as to raise questions about the interview's authenticity. According to Richard Mack, director of advertising for Mills Artists, Ellington was upset about being quoted inaccurately by Morrow—and off the record, at that. Mack's claim appeared in an *Orchestra World* publicity profile that he characterized as "a sincere study of *Duke Ellington, the man*."

Are the quotes attributed to Ellington in Morrow's article genuine? While the frank tone is surprising, the manner of delivery would seem to be Ellington's own.

Duke Ellington on Gershwin's "Porgy"

When the Theatre Guild launched the George Gershwin musical version of DuBose and Dorothy Heyward's play *Porgy* recently, and rechristened it *Porgy and Bess,* the cult of critical Negrophiles went into journalistic rhapsodies, hailed it as a "native American opera," avowed it "typical" of a "child-like,

---

Sources: Edward Morrow, "Duke Ellington on Gershwin's 'Porgy,'" *New Theatre* (December 1935), 5–6; Richard Mack, "Duke Ellington—In Person," *Orchestra World* (May 1936), [n.p.].

[1] *DEP*, 172.

quaint" Negro people and declared it "caught the spirit" of a "primitive" group. The huzzas filled the columns, were quoted by second-hand *intelligentsia,* and echoed in the banalities of the subscribers. No one, however, thought to ask Negro musicians, composers and singers their opinions of the Gershwin masterpiece.

Accordingly, I sought out Edward Kennedy ("Duke") Ellington, Negro orchestra leader and composer. He has neither axes to grind nor pretensions to support, but busies himself reproducing and creating the most genuine Negro jazz music in the world. Objective critics have likened his work to Sibelius; his band is distinctive. Unfettered by hot-cha exploitation, his energies might be released to the serious efforts his genius warrants.

"Well, Duke," I began, "now that you have seen *Porgy and Bess,* what do you think of it?"

"Grand music and a swell play, I guess, but the two don't go together—I mean that the music did not hitch with the mood and spirit of the story." Then he added: "Maybe I'm wrong, or perhaps there is something wrong with me, but I have noted this in other things lately too. So I am not singling out *Porgy and Bess.*"

"But sticking to *Porgy and Bess,* Duke, just what ails it?"

"The first thing that gives it away is that it does not use the Negro musical idiom," replied Ellington. "It was not the music of Catfish Row or any other kind of Negroes."

"Then I don't suppose it could be very true to the spirit, scene or setting of impoverished Charleston Negroes if the musical expression failed to consider the underlying emotions and social forces of the Gullah Negroes," I suggested.

"That might be it at that," agreed Ellington, "but I can say it better in my own way. For instance, how could you possibly express in decent English the same thing I express when I tell my band, 'Now you cats swing the verse, then go to town on the gutbucket chorus'!"

"You would intend for the boys to play the verse in rhythm, and finish the final chorus with improvisations, accented beats and a *crescendo,*" I laughed.

"Sure, but for all your fifteen-dollar words you didn't give the same impression, did you?" he argued. "If you hadn't been around the band and if you did not know the backgrounds of the musicians you couldn't interpret them or use their idioms, could you?"

"I think I get your viewpoint," I answered, "but why did you say the music was 'grand'?"

"Why shouldn't it be?" he smiled amiably, "It was taken from some of the best and a few of the worst. Gershwin surely didn't discriminate: he borrowed from everyone from Liszt to Dickie Wells' kazoo band."[2]

Ellington turned to the piano, and playing said: "Hear this? These are passages from *Rhapsody in Blue.* Well, here is where they came from—the

---

[2] A reference to "Dickey Wells' Shim Shammers," a group that recorded a few sides for Columbia in 1933 (no relation to the trombonist Dicky—or Dickie—Wells who played with Fletcher Henderson and Count Basie).

Negro song *Where Has My Easy Rider Gone?* Now listen to this—this is what I call a 'gut-bucket waltz.' See, it's a waltz, but it still has the Negro idiom. I have taken the method but I have not stolen or borrowed." He played on, evidently pleased with his innovation.

"Will you ever write an opera or a symphony?" I asked.

"No," Ellington declared positively. "I have to make a living and so I have to have an audience. I do not believe people honestly like, much less understand, things like *Porgy and Bess*. The critics and some of the people who are supposed to know have told them they should like the stuff. So they say it's wonderful. I prefer to go right on putting down my ideas, moods and themes and letting the critics call them what they will. Furthermore, an opera would not express the kind of things I have in mind."[3]

"Where would you consider *Porgy and Bess* offered opportunities that you should have used that Gershwin missed?" I asked.

"Several places," Ellington said, "he missed beautiful chances to really do something. There was one place, though, where he made the most of his music: the hurricane passages, when no one was on the stage. But when he tried to build up the characterizations he failed. What happened when the girl selling strawberries came on the stage? Did he get the rhythm, the speech, and the 'swing' of the street-vendor? No, sir, he did not; he went dramatic! Gershwin had the girl stop cold, take her stance, and sing an *aria* in the Italian, would-be Negro manner."

Ellington warmed up to his subject. "Bubbles [John Sublett], who is a great dancer, built up the character of Sportin' Life with his dance. The music did not do that. And other actors had to make their own characterizations too. There was a crap game such as no one has ever seen or heard. It might have been opera, but it wasn't a crap game. The music went one way and the action another. If a singer had lost his place, he never would have found it in that score. Still, the audience gasped: 'Don't the people get right into their parts?' and 'Aren't they emotional!'"

"Would you say that an honest Negro musical play would have to contain social criticism?" I asked.

"Absolutely," declared Ellington. "That is, if it is expected to hold up. In one of my forthcoming movie 'shorts' I have an episode which concerns the death of a baby.[4] That is the high spot and should have come last, but that would not have been 'commercial,' as the managers say. However, I put into the dirge all the misery, sorrow and undertones of the conditions that went

---

[3] Soon after this article appeared, Ellington seems to have changed his opinion. A journalist interviewing him in 1936 reported that "Duke is living for the day when he can write an opera" (Carl Cons, "A Black Genius in a White Man's World," *Down Beat* (July 1936), 6), and two years later an article stated that Ellington had just completed an opera that "deals with the history of the American Negro" ("Ellington Completes Negro Opera at Bedside," *Down Beat* (October 1938), 2). The latter may have been a premature announcement regarding the never-produced, probably never-finished opera *Boola*.

[4] The "Hymn of Sorrow" segment from the film *Symphony in Black*, released in September 1935, after this interview took place.

with the baby's death. It was true to and of the life of the people it depicted. The same thing can not be said for *Porgy and Bess*."

It was very evident that here was one colored composer who realized the cramping forces of exploitation which handicap not only him and his colleagues, but the Negro masses as well. That is why their expression is filled with protest. He is also fully conscious that there are imitators and chiselers, always ready to capitalize on specious products purporting to "represent" the Negro. They are totally lacking in social vision, and their art is phony.

No Negro could possibly be fooled by *Porgy and Bess*. [Rouben] Mamoulian's direction has added nothing to his old superficial tricks of animating inanimate objects, such as rocking chairs, with rhythmical motion to fit a song. (This business was used in *Porgy* which he directed in 1927.) His Negroes still wave their arms in shadowed frenzy during the wake. The production is cooked up, flavored and seasoned to be palmed off as "authentic" of the Charleston Gullah Negroes—who are, one supposes, "odd beasts."

But the times are here to debunk such tripe as Gershwin's lamp-black Negroisms, and the melodramatic trash of the script of *Porgy*. The Negro artists are becoming socially-conscious and class-conscious, and more courageous. Broadway will find it harder to keep them on the chain-gang of the hot-cha merchants. The Ellingtons and the [Langston] Hughes' will take their themes from their blood. There will be fewer generalized gin-guzzling, homicidal maniacs, and more understanding of rotten socio-economic conditions which give rise to neurotic escapists, compensating for overwrought nerves. There will be fewer wicked, hip-swinging "yellow-gal hustler" stereotypes, but more economically isolated girls, forced into prostitution. These themes are universal. They will be particularized and vivified in ringing language, and charged with the truth of realities. The music will express terror and defiance in colorful Negro musical idioms which have remained melodious despite a life of injustices. They will compose and write these things because they feel the consequences of an existence which is a weird combination of brutality and beauty.

Duke Ellington—In Person

... Though we are not trying to give you the notion that Duke Ellington is an angel ex-officio, we must insist that his nature is almost entirely free from bitterness. He sincerely believes that his verbal attackers have as much right to express their opinions as have his constant boosters. In addition he feels that there is still much for him to learn and adverse criticism often has the power of suggesting constructive and creative ideas.

In any close-up of Duke, his pet aversions must be noted. He hates being misquoted in interviews. Very often a reviewer will ask Duke to express his opinion on some subject and in the reviewer's elaboration of Duke's statements the writer will add ideas of his own. The Ellington "Porgy and Bess" interview is an example of this. Ellington was asked his reaction to the music of that production (and, at that, not for publication). Duke said, in praising

Gershwin's score for the show, that he felt that Gershwin's music, though grand, was not distinctly or definitely negroid in character. The reviewer then proceeded to add pet notions of his own and credited them to Duke, finally appearing with a so-called statement by Ellington accusing Gershwin of being everything from a bad musician to an obvious plagiarist. Duke was very unhappy over these uncalled-for misquotations and feverishly rushed to straighten matters out. Though months have passed since this event, Duke feels the injustice of it to this date and constantly expresses the hope that "Gershwin didn't take any stock in those things I was supposed to have said." . . .

27. John Hammond: "The Tragedy of Duke Ellington" (1935)

Ellington's interest in writing pieces longer than roughly three minutes—the length permitted by one side of a ten-inch, 78-rpm recording—proved a divisive issue for critics. While some rallied to the defense of Ellington's "extended works," as they came to be called, others pronounced them shapeless, overblown, or contrary to the spirit of jazz.

The first "extended" piece to generate considerable controversy was not *Creole Rhapsody* (1931)—though it had caused grumbling in some quarters—but *Reminiscing in Tempo* (1935), which took up four record sides and lasted nearly thirteen minutes.[1] Ellington composed it following the death of his mother Daisy in May, writing it as his orchestra traveled by train on a series of one-nighters through the South.[2] Although gentle and reflective in character, *Reminiscing in Tempo* provoked violent reactions from writers who earlier had admired Ellington's shorter works. No one was more incensed than Spike Hughes, Ellington's former booster in England, who branded the piece "a long, rambling monstrosity" and threatened not to review any more Ellington records "until Duke realizes it is not 'smart' to write this sort of music."[3]

In the United States one young writer deeply disappointed by *Reminiscing in Tempo* was John Hammond (1910–1987), a jazz enthusiast, record producer, and social crusader who also served as American correspondent for the *Melody Maker*. Although not as outraged as Spike Hughes, Hammond called *Reminiscing in Tempo* "formless and shallow," citing it as an example of how Ellington avoided, both in his music and life, "the troubles of his people or mankind in general." Hammond also criticized Ellington for allowing himself

Source: John Hammond, "The Tragedy of Duke Ellington, the 'Black Prince of Jazz,'" *Down Beat* (November 1935), 1, 6. Originally published in the *Brooklyn Eagle*, 3 November 1935.

[1] Other "extended" recorded performances were the two-part *Tiger Rag* in 1929 and the two medleys made for Victor with experimental 33⅓-rpm technology in 1932. For more on the latter, see Brad Kay's liner notes to *Reflections in Ellington* (Everybodys EV 3005).
[2] *MM*, 85–86.
[3] "Mike" [Spike Hughes], "Ellington on the Spot," *Melody Maker* (14 December 1935), 5.

and his orchestra members to be exploited by powers in the music business, especially (though he goes unnamed here) manager Irving Mills.[4]

With this article a rift developed between Hammond and Ellington that would widen steadily over the years. The process can be seen in 1939 when Ellington lambasted Hammond in Down Beat (see §34) and again in 1943 when Hammond attacked Black, Brown and Beige in his article, "Is the Duke Deserting Jazz?" (see §43).

Of all our native popular composers Duke Ellington is probably the most gifted and original. For more than ten years, he has been producing, with the aid of the most accomplished orchestra in America, songs and arrangements quite unlike those of any other musician, black or white. His work has been received with international acclamation, in some cases, less than it deserved and in a few, considerable more.

Unlike so many of his contemporaries, Ellington is a hard-working, ambitious individual. Confronted with the undiscriminating praise of critics like Constant Lambert, he felt it necessary to go out and prove that he could write really important music, far removed from the simplicity and charm of his earlier tunes. "Daybreak Express," and "Rude Interlude," were the first signs of this, but even they could not prepare us for the pretension of his new 12-minute work, "Reminiscing [in Tempo]," which Brunswick has just seen fit to release on two ten-inch records. The saddest part of the tale is that the composer considers it his most important contribution to the field of music.

The reasons for the complete sterility of this new opus are so numerous that it is difficult to know exactly where to begin. The most logical place would be with the Duke himself, since his life during the last eight years is almost the ideal example of what the modern composer, Negro or white should avoid at all costs.

As a person, Ellington is one of the most completely charming I have ever come across. His disposition is without rival among artists, for he has never been known to lose his temper or do conscious ill to anyone. He suffers abuse and exploitation with an Olympian calm and fortitude, never deigning to fight back or stand up for even his most elemental rights. Unpleasantness of any sort he flees from; he would greatly prefer not seeing the seamier side of existence and has spent most of his recent years in escaping from the harsh reality that faces even the most secure among Negroes.

The Duke has been exploited in a way that is absolutely appalling to anyone not thoroughly conversant with the ethics of Broadway. Although he and his orchestra have earned between five and ten thousand dollars a week consistently for the last eight years, he has received disgracefully little himself. His living habits are exceedingly modest for one in his position, and yet he has accumulated nothing.

[4] For two rebuttals of Hammond, see E. Burley Edwards, "Ellington Defended," Melody Maker (18 January 1936), 6–7, and H. M. [Helen] Oakley, "Critics Tear Hair Over 'Dukes' [sic] New Tunes—Simplicity Upsets Them," Down Beat (March 1936), 1–2.

Ellington is fully conscious of the fact that Broadway has not treated him fairly, knowing many of the sordid details. And yet he did not lift a finger to protect himself because he has the completely defeatist outlook which chokes so many of the artists of his race.

It is easier to accept abuse without fighting back than to go through the unpleasantness of rows with associates. As a result, Duke has no time for rest and contemplation; he must be steadily on the run, hopping from one spot to the other in grinding one night stands, picking up work when it can be had in theaters, and never getting down to any sustained labor. Since his music is losing the distinctive flavor it once had, both because of the fact that he has added slick, un-negroid musicians to his band and because he himself is aping Tin Pan Alley composers for commercial reasons, he and his music are definitely losing favor with a once idolatrous public. And unless there are definite changes very soon he will be in a very precarious position.

But the real trouble with Duke's music is the fact that he has purposely kept himself from any contact with the troubles of his people or mankind in general. It would probably take a Granville Hicks[5] or Langston Hughes to describe the way he shuts his eyes to the abuses being heaped upon his race and his original class. He consciously keeps himself from thinking about such problems as those of the southern share croppers, the Scottsboro boys, intolerable working and relief conditions in the North and South, although he is too intelligent not to know that these all do exist. He has very real fears as to his own future, and yet he has never shown any desire of aligning himself with forces that are seeking to remove the causes of these disgraceful conditions.

Consequently Ellington's music has become vapid and without the slightest semblance of guts. His newer stuff bears superficial resemblance to Debussy and Delius without any of the peculiar vitality that used to pervade his work. The Duke is afraid even to think about himself, his struggles and his disappointments, and that is why his "Reminiscing" is so formless and shallow a piece of music.

There is one extremely significant factor regardless of whatever worth there still exists in Ellington's orchestra. The majority of the musicians do not accept unfair dealings with the equanimity of their leader. Within the past year they have struck together twice in my knowledge and won their demands from an unwilling manager. Even the most highly paid among Harlem musicians do not forget the fact that they come from a race that has been traditionally exploited and that a determined fight has to be waged to preserve even their present status.

[5] Writer and critic Granville Hicks (1901–1982) was literary editor of *New Masses* in the thirties.

28. Enzo Archetti: "In Defense of Ellington and His 'Reminiscing in Tempo'" (1936)

O ne American writer who admired *Reminiscing in Tempo* was Enzo Archetti, a music enthusiast who worked for a New York life insurance company. Archetti wrote regularly for R. D. Darrell and Axel Johnson's *American Music Lover;* in a July 1935 column for this magazine he had credited Ellington with producing "the most significant *American* music being created today."[1]

Apparently *Reminiscing in Tempo* caused no change in Archetti's high opinion, which he justified by quoting extensively from a favorable review by the British critic Leonard Hibbs that had appeared in *Swing Music* (December 1935).

For a more recent defense of *Reminiscing in Tempo* that looks closely at issues of structural unity, harmonic invention, and orchestration, see Gunther Schuller, *The Swing Era: The Development of Jazz, 1930–1945* (New York: Oxford University Press, 1989), 74–83.

The release of Duke Ellington's latest work *Reminiscing in Tempo* on Brunswick 7546 and 7547 has been the occasion for a storm of protests and jeremiads in various periodicals, which are characteristic of the general stupidity, intolerance, and narrow-mindedness of those swing-music fans who, because of prejudice, will not admit to or permit any change or progress in the style of a creator of swing music. To such persons Louis Armstrong is a washout because he no longer plays as he did years ago. To them Duke Ellington is a failure and betrayer of *The Cause* because he no longer writes any *Black and Tans* or *Mood Indigos*. It is remarkable, that with very few exceptions in all the "reviews," or opinions printed so far Ellington's *Reminiscing* has been scathingly dismissed as a failure without any attempt being made to analyze or understand the work. To them it was something in which the rhythm could not be tapped out with a foot nor the melody whistled. Fortunately, Ellington is too great an artist and too important a creator to be influenced by such reactions.

The exceptions to the general run of "reviews" are few, and these are noteworthy for their sincerity only and not because they betray any great understanding of the work. In this group we can include John Hammond's review in *Down Beat* and Edgar Jackson's in *The Gramophone*.[2] Edgar Jackson frankly admits he does not understand this new piece. Hammond condemns it with well chosen words, but with no attempt to analyze it. On the other hand, a few reviewers have hailed it as a great work in empty words, like Van (Horace Van Norman) in his review in this magazine in [the] Decem-

---

Source: Enzo Archetti, "In Defense of Ellington and His 'Reminiscing in Tempo,'" *American Music Lover* 1 (April 1936), 359–60, 364.

[1] Cited in Ronald G. Welburn, "American Jazz Criticism, 1914–1940" (Ph.D. diss., New York University, 1983), 65.

[2] Edgar Jackson (1895–1967) became the first editor of *Melody Maker* in 1926. In the thirties he wrote a column, "Dance and Popular Rhythmic Records," for *The Gramophone*.

ber 1935 issue, but this type of review also fails for the very same reason—
i.e., it did not analyze or explain.

On one point only do all the reviewers—pro and con—agree: that only the
last of the four sides of *Reminiscing* is satisfying and somewhat understandable, but again the reason is very carefully neglected.

Up to this time, only one review has appeared in print which is at all worthy
of consideration from every angle. This is Leonard Hibbs' review in the
December issue of the magazine *Swing Music* which appears under the heading
of *Conversation About Jazz*. It is a fair, intelligent analysis and the only one
so far which indicates that an honest attempt was made to understand the
work; the only article which has conceded that Ellington has a great mind
and that he has the right to change it from time to time when he creates new
music. Except for an article from the Duke himself explaining his work, this
is surely the most satisfactory. Admittedly, it is a personal opinion, but one
so well expressed and so sincere that it deserves to be quoted:

"Readers of record reviews are roughly divided into two groups. Those
who when they disagree with the critic think that he is nuts, and those who
are so unwilling to think for themselves that they blindly follow his judgments
without stopping to think whether the critic is right or wrong or why. The
latter class is the most dangerous because they hang on to an idea long after
the critic in question is quite willing to admit he was wrong, or the artist or
band whom he once praised has deteriorated. For example, there are
thousands who believe in the Divine right of Duke, because his best work has
been lauded to the skies in highbrow language, which the majority of them
do not understand. . . . In spite of their childlike faith, the Duke *can* go wrong.
What neither group appears to realize is that any review is only the opinion
of one critic . . .

"Apart from the many, more or less, stereotyped issues (just good, medium,
and indifferent jazz) there are several examples of superlatively good swing
music. That is to say jazz at its very best—but still—Jazz. Then there is the
new Ellington work on four sides of two records. With the exception of the
last side this is certainly not swing music, so as it is not jazz proper it must
be reviewed as music and there are quite a lot of moderns writing music proper
who know much more about it than Duke . . .

"Which brings me back to the absurdity of blindly accepting one critic's
views, and what is more absurd the acceptance of *my* views. Because if anyone
ever approached jazz from a strictly personal view—then I do.

"I know of no jazz work on records which has the capacity to thrill me the
way that the new Koussevitzky recording of Sibelius Symphony in *D Major*
does. The way in which Sibelius writes for brass is for me quite the most
tremendous thing I know in music. I do not even faintly agree with those who
say that jazz is the only real music of our time. I do not think that Ellington
can be seriously regarded as one of the great composers of the twentieth
century . . .

"But I do think that in its own way jazz is the most active and *alive* musical
movement of our time. I do not think that Ellington in his better movements
is a composer who is worthy of the serious attention of every school of musical

thought. I do think that jazz has injected fresh life into a branch of music which had become stagnant. The art of improvisation! . . .

"This will be the first review of *Reminiscing in Tempo* to appear in print.* In my anxiety to hear it I made elaborate and expensive arrangements to steal the first copies to be pressed in this country. For days before I attempted to write a word about it, I played it and played it, but frankly I couldn't make head or tail out of it. I regret to say that I wrote to at least three friends to say how disappointed I was. I said it was dull and meaningless, and I still think it is dull but to an infinitely less extent. It wasn't jazz and it wasn't music. It wasn't jazz because there was little about it other than the instrumentation that was remotely connected with jazz. It wasn't music because it got nowhere. It got pretty desperate when the time to write this review got nearer and nearer. I was torn between the resolve to postpone the review until next month, as I could have done, and the desire to scoop my fellow scribes by being the first to review the records. At the same time, I had too high an opinion of Duke to think that he would willingly perpetrate anything like the pointless joke that this appeared to be . . .

"So, working on the hypothesis that Duke knew what he was doing if he had not expressed himself well enough for my lesser mind to grasp what he was about, I stuck to my guns until I saw a ray of light—quite suddenly—just like that—and from that ray of light a theory was formed. A theory which is at least substantiated by the music itself . . .

"The first obvious thing that strikes me is that there are several closely related tunes. The second thing to strike me was that the greater part of the work was rather unnecessary.

"Then as you were playing each side quite a lot, it might occur to you that only one of the four sides was complete in itself. And that side was the last side. You would be quite right. Side four is a complete 10-inch Ellington work in itself. It begins, it is developed, and it comes to a proper end. Incidentally, if it had been issued on its own it would have been one of the best things that Duke has ever turned out—and it still is. But why the first three sides?

"The title should give a clue to that surely. But as far as I can see it is a very indirect one.

"I have said that side four is complete in itself. It is. It has everything that we have grown to expect from Ellington. It has the gentle swing which characterises his music in certain moods. It has a melody of the wistful kind which he conceives better than anyone else I know. The development and construction are typical Ellingtonian. And yet side one is swingless, formless and almost without tempo.

"My suggestion is that, if we accept side four as being a complete opus in itself, then in the whole of this four-sided work, Duke is reminiscing over the various stages of its building up in his mind and instead of just presenting us with a new work taking up one side of a record, he is giving us the lowdown on how he builds up those little 10-inch masterpieces of his.

---

* *Swing Music* is a British magazine. Mr. Hibbs means, of course, that this is the first review to appear in Great Britain.

"Now let us play the records over together and just see how this theory of mine fits in with the actual music.

"Side one opens with a rhythmic figure played by Duke on the piano. Call it a secondary tune if you like. Personally, I like to think of Duke going to his piano in the throes of inspiration with a new tune floating around in his head but tantalising by being just out of reach. He can't nail it down. It's there but it won't take shape. Suddenly, he thinks he has it and he thinks of it as the trumpet would play it and we hear his mind at work. Then as the trumpet evolves this melody, the saxes take up the rhythmic figure that he has suggested on the piano. Yes, that's not bad, he says to himself, now give the melody to the clarinets and see how that bass figure sounds on a trombone. H'm, not bad! Now the basses take over the original piano theme while Duke suggests ensemble treatments for the melody.

"No! That's no good, says Duke, and the music stops.

"And starts again with the trombone playing a fresh melody which is closely related to the first one. Actually, of course, it is the same melody with a few changes. And once again the missing parts are dovetailed in to see how it would sound this way. But this does not satisfy him, and so we come to the end of the first side.

"After another short introduction by the piano, a muted trumpet plays yet another form of the melody (let's call it Tune No. 3). I think that Duke might well have been content with this one, it's a lovely, plaintive thing. Just about ten times as good as 'Solitude.'

"This also is followed by ideas of proper clothing in the form of ensemble variations. Then Duke decides to stick to the piano. In his solo, which carries us over to side three, he elaborates his original bass figure and works hard on the melody. Adding something here and taking away there. This solo on its own is quite a textbook of piano ideas.

"The ensemble passages which follow are, to me, quite meaningless unless some such explanation as I have offered is applied. If you accept my theory, then they are the logical outcome of a musical mind striving to perfect an idea. If you have Tune No. 3 at the back of your mind as you listen to them, then it is not so difficult to see what he is getting at.

"The melody which we hear played by the clarinet as this side comes to an end is a reminder of Tune No. 3.

"Side four is, I believe, the brain child itself. A solo trumpet gives out the melody which Duke evolved in his long solo, and which now goes through the customary development after which the work comes to an end.

"What interests me is that all the way through this last side you can trace the *thoughts* that have gone to make up the first three sides.

"Very briefly, I believe that Duke has allowed us to 'tune-in' on his mind at work."

Add to this, that during his reminiscing, Duke was influenced by thoughts of Delius (Ellington is known to be a great admirer of Delius' works), Stravinsky, and Debussy (all of whom can be traced in Ellington's orchestration), and we have a complete mental picture of Duke's *Reminiscing in Tempo.*[3]

29. Helen Oakley (Dance):
The Ellington Orchestra at the Apollo (1936)

During the thirties Ellington and his orchestra made many appearances in theaters. Sharing a bill with dancers, singers, and comedians, they offered audiences a polished stage show often featuring Ellington's popular songs and instrumental hits. Helen Oakley described both the musical and theatrical aspects of one such show presented in 1936 at Harlem's celebrated Apollo Theatre, on 125th Street.

Oakley (b. 1917) left her native Toronto in 1933 for Chicago, where she began writing about jazz for *Down Beat* and the *Chicago Herald and Examiner*. By doing so she entered a field that has included few women. In 1936 she moved to New York and began working for Irving Mills, producing a number of important Ellington small-group record dates for his Variety label. Oakley and her husband Stanley Dance (whom she married in 1947) have long been involved in chronicling Ellington's life and music; they collaborated on *The World of Duke Ellington,* a collection of interviews and articles published in 1970. She has also written a biography of bluesman T-Bone Walker, *Stormy Monday: The T-Bone Walker Story* (1987).

Duke Ellington opened the Apollo Theatre, Friday, September 11, to a crowded and enthusiastic house.

The first big hand from the house went to Duke himself as the composer and arranger of the hits grouped together in the opening number. Opening with *Harlem Speaks* or *East St. Louis Toodle-Oo,* the theme, the band modulated into *Sophisticated Lady,* bringing the house down with Lawrence Brown's brilliant trombone solo. A change of tempo, and *Rockin' in Rhythm* introduced the Four Step Brothers, four weaving and interchanging figures, shadowy behind a darkened scrim. A few haunting strains, and the house enthusiastically showed its appreciation of Duke's number one hit tune, *Solitude.* Scarcely had the murmur subsided before the band swung into that early and prophetic Ellington brainchild, *It Don't Mean a Thing If It Ain't Got That Swing.* The ever popular Ivy Anderson went into her dance, and,

---

[3] Although there is no compelling evidence showing that Ellington was influenced by Delius, since the thirties many critics have linked the two composers. One early source for the comparison is R. D. Darrell's "Black Beauty" (see §12). See also Barry Ulanov's discussion of English critic John Cheatle (*DE*, 143–44) and Burnett James, "Ellington's Place as a Composer," in Peter Gammond, ed., *Duke Ellington: His Life and Music* (London: Phoenix House, 1958; rpt., New York: Da Capo, 1977), 149–50. According to John Bird, Percy Grainger sparked Ellington's interest in Delius in 1932 (see John Bird, *Percy Grainger,* 204).

As for Stravinsky, Ellington mentioned the composer's *The Firebird* in a 1935 interview (see §25) and *Le Sacre du Printemps* in 1937 (§31).

Source: Helen Oakley, "Duke Ellington at the Apollo," *Metronome* (October 1936), 45.

giving a taste of those famous lyrics, Duke's message of yesteryear has now become the slogan of the day, *Swing Is the Thing.*

The opening number proves a potpourri of all that is to follow. The scrim disappears, the lights go up, the band moves forward, and the show is on. Duke now presents one of his greatest numbers, written several years ago, a recorded masterpiece, recently revised during his Chicago stay at the Congress Hotel, where it proved to be a "killer." Duke announces it himself, "Ladies and Gentlemen, *Merry-Go-Round.*" Very few of Duke's compositions show to any greater advantage the magnificent team work of which his reed and brass sections are capable. The intonation and power in the brass section are consistently amazing to even those most familiar with the band, and the blend and flexibility of the reeds could not be bettered by any unit playing today.

This number is an outstanding example of swing music, but since Duke has been playing in this manner for a great many years and has never in the past had to resort to this current classification to identify his medium, it should not be necessary now to so standardize it. In scoring of this type, Duke avails himself of extremely powerful rhythms, carried out to great advantage by two magnificent bass players, and the rhythmic beats are further accentuated by the sectional scoring. This results in a massive swing contributed by the entire band, almost a march tempo, and of such power as to be almost unbelievable.

The dancers are up next, and they are a talented quartet. As such the house appreciates them; they take several calls. Duke now presents one of his several numbers which feature extensively the soloists in the band.

It may be the *St. Louis Blues,* it may be the *Mooche,* but it more than likely is the *Black and Tan Fantasy.* Duke may call on Johnny Hodges, alto saxophonist without par (and one who can perform miracles on the soprano sax); he may call upon Barney Bigard, a master technician on the clarinet, or perhaps it may be the turn of Harry Carney, the very young and inspired musician, who has managed to do so much with the baritone. In the brass section there are two trumpeters, Charles (Cootie) Williams, and Rex Stewart. Cootie has a conception of savagery and force on the instrument that cannot be equalled. His work with the wa-wa mute is more expressive than speech (*Echo[e]s of Harlem,* Brunswick). Rex, probably the only trumpet player who ever truly approached the spirit of "Bix" Beiderbecke on the horn, has a beautiful tone, unlimited imagination and unbelievable technical ability. In addition to these men, Duke boasts two exceptional bass players. The first, Bill Taylor, who is extremely solid and is possessed of a beautiful tone, and Hayes Alvis, a brilliant player with plenty of technique.

The next number on the program is Duke's hit tune of the year, *In a Sentimental Mood.* The new medium and the delicate scoring in this composition are merely new proof of the Ellington versatility.

Now it is Ivy who is up; she is singing *Sad Night in Harlem* or perhaps *My Old Flame.* Ivy always gets a big hand. She is a great singer and a great showman, completely natural both on and off the stage. Her second number is a specialty, with Sonny Greer backing.

Showmanship being inherent in Duke, he finishes the program with what is commonly called a "screamer." Probably *Some of These Days.* Rex comes down front and plays a couple of high-note choruses and ends up on high whatever you wish, and the show is over.

In short: tremendous musical values and fine showmanship. A great stage presentation.

30. R. D. Darrell: Ellington in an Encyclopedia (1936)

R. D. Darrell's *The Gramophone Shop Encyclopedia of Recorded Music* of 1936 was the first comprehensive discography published in the United States. For each composer Darrell provided a brief annotation and a list of representative recordings. Aware that some of his readers might wonder why Ellington appeared in such a volume, Darrell offered a typically feisty rationale.

Darrell later claimed that his encyclopedia was "perhaps the first reference work of almost any kind to include—among the so-called classical or serious composers—Duke Ellington."[1]

For a biographical note on Darrell, see §6.

While recorded jazz, dance and popular music does not fall within the scope of this Encyclopedia, the compiler would be stupid indeed arbitrarily to rule out a considerable number of works of this type which soar far above the levels set by the ordinary machine-products of Tin Pan Alley, and which reveal incomparable powers of rhapsodic melodic invention and an instinct for tonal nuances and orchestral ingenuities equal to the most brilliant flights of Rimsky-Korsakov's or Richard Strauss' imagination. This would be ineptly named "Encyclopedia of the World's Best Recorded Music" if it included many a work of very minor genius, merely because it happened to be signed by the name of some celebrated "serious" composer, and dogmatically ruled out works of superb fantasy and exuberant vitality because they happened to be cast in the smaller and highly limited forms of modern dance music.

A few composers, such as Gershwin, have done much to lift the popular songs into the class of the art-song, but the most notable efforts to invest American jazz with the imagination and craftsmanship vital to aesthetic worth, have been made by the young Negro pianist, dance orchestra leader, and composer: Duke Ellington. Ellington has written scores of dance pieces, some of which are commercial products of little artistic value, but many others of which are of unique significance for their poly-timbres, their complex texture, the spontaneous and rhapsodic flow of their melodies, the homogeneity of

Source: R. D. Darrell, "Duke Ellington," *The Gramophone Shop Encyclopedia of Recorded Music* (New York: The Gramophone Shop, 1936), 152.

[1] Letter to Ronald G. Welburn, 12 May 1980, reproduced in Welburn, "American Jazz Criticism, 1914–1940" (Ph.D. diss., New York University, 1983), 183.

their style, and above all for their sensitive and poignant revelation of pure feeling in tone. A group of the most important is listed below in condensed form.

Awful Sad
Birmingham Breakdown
Black and Tan Fantasy
Black Beauty
Blues I Love to Sing
Creole Love Call
Creole Rhapsody
Daybreak Express
Drop Me Off at Harlem
East St. Louis Toodle-O
Hot and Bothered
In a Sentimental Mood

It Don't Mean a Thing
(The) Mooche
Mood Indigo
(The) Mystery Song
Old Man Blues
Reminiscing in Tempo
Rockin' in Rhythm
Rude Interlude
Saddest Tale
Solitude
Sophisticated Lady
Swanee Rhapsody
Take It Easy

31. "Ellington Refutes Cry That Swing Started Sex Crimes!" (1937)

The belief that jazz could be a dangerous influence upon America's youth emerged in the early twenties then gradually waned over the next decade. It did not disappear altogether, though, as shown by the above sensational headline from *Down Beat* in 1937. After a New York music teacher claimed that "hot" music caused criminal behavior, Ellington's widely recognized dignity, impeccable manners, and high artistic standards made him a well-qualified respondent.

While Ellington never attended college, as the article states, the polished eloquence of his quoted remarks shows how he might have given people this impression.

In refutation to the hue and cry against swing music by Arthur Cremin, of the New York Schools for Music, in which the instructor attributed the recent wave of sex crimes to the current "hot" jazz vogue, Duke Ellington, prominent composer-pianist-bandsman, denounced Cremin's psychological experiments as being totally unfair and completely lacking in authoritative material.

Cremin, in his recent attack, said he would prove through tests he conducted, that swing music developed debased emotions in human beings. He is reported to have placed a young man and woman in a room, alone, first playing a series of symphonic recordings followed by a set of swing records. According to the teacher, the young couple remained formal throughout the

Source: "Ellington Refutes Cry That Swing Started Sex Crimes!" *Down Beat* (December 1937), 2.

first renditions, but as the music turned to jazz, they became familiar and more personal toward one another.

"If this experiment is earnestly offered as proof for the ill effects derived from swing music," said Duke Ellington, in discussing the matter before the Musician's Circle in New York, "then the facts must be totally discounted as not being a true psychology test, for there was no 'proper constant'—a prerequisite of an accurate experiment of this nature."

Ellington, who studied psychology during his collegiate courses at Howard University, further explained that in true tests, persons under observation are usually selected because of identical characteristics, but in this case, two persons were picked at random. Also, he pointed out, that it was an established fact that a body of people will respond to a given act in various manners and consequently a group of persons would not be affected in the same way.

Music is known to be a stimulant, but in recent case histories of convicted and known sex criminals, not one showed preference for music of any sort. "Music invigorates emotions to certain degrees," continued Ellington, "but on the other hand, so do baseball and football games. If music can be proved a neurotic influence then I'm certain you will find Stravinsky's 'Le Sacre du Printemps' a great deal more exciting, emotionally, than a slow 'ride' arrangement of 'Body and Soul' or even a fast rendition of 'Tiger Rag.'"

To complete his denouncement of Cremin's derogatory statements, Ellington illustrated that, in observing hundreds of audiences in theatres and ballrooms during the past two years, he noticed a transition that has come over mass attendances. Before swing music made such enormous strides in the jazz world, dancers and audiences, in general, were of a noisier type than is found today.

"This recent change to relative quietude may be attributed to the fact," concluded Ellington, "that 'hot' jazz affords a great deal more interest in music, due to the individual solos and more interesting harmonic patterns in the music. Audiences, today, invariably crowd around the bandstand, eager to grasp every solo note and orchestral trick and certain to 'shush' down any rowdiness that may hamper the enjoyment of the music." The new jazz movement has served to enlarge the public's knowledge of music, mainly in the world of modern American jazz, which is being accepted, at present, as a recognized form of music.

During his recent theatre engagements in New York, Duke Ellington's orchestra spent a day in the recording studios, where they recorded, among other selections, two new compositions, "Crescendo in Blue" and "Diminuendo in Blue." His present tour will keep him in the hinterlands until late Winter, when it is expected he will return to New York for the next Cotton Club show.

32. Aaron Copland on Ellington (1938)

I n the pages of *Modern Music* (1924–1946), the little magazine sponsored by the League of Composers and edited by Minna Lederman, writers focused on developments in contemporary concert music. But throughout its existence *Modern Music* also included commentary on popular music for film, theater, radio, and dancing. Among those who wrote on such topics were the composers Virgil Thomson, Paul Bowles, Colin McPhee, and Aaron Copland.[1]

In works from the twenties, such as *Music for the Theatre* and the Concerto for Piano and Orchestra, Copland (1900–1990) borrowed and transformed jazz materials. Although in subsequent decades his own music moved away from jazz, Copland apparently kept up with popular-music trends, as shown by his 1938 assessment of Ellington's position among "swing" bandleaders. Copland emphasized Ellington's contribution as a composer.

Two paragraphs on recent recordings by other bandleaders have been omitted.

Since the record makers persist in forgetting *la musique moderne* during the holidays (according to them, Bach makes an appropriate gift, but Bartok does not) this is a good moment to see what the swing bands have been up to recently.

When swing was new, it was little more than "hot jazz" masquerading under a new name. Since then things have happened. The jazz boys have learned how to incorporate what was once a reckless kind of improvised playing into their regular commercial product. The result has been a freshening of the older pre-swing variety of jazz, particularly along harmonic and instrumental lines. . . .

. . . [T]he master of them all is still Duke Ellington. The others, by comparison, are hardly more than composer-arrangers. Ellington is a composer, by which I mean, he comes nearer to knowing how to make a piece hang together than the others. His recent *Diminuendo in Blue—Crescendo in Blue* (Brunswick) cannot be placed in the completely successful category with his *Mood Indigo* or the amazing *Clarinet Lament*—but they are far from being dull pieces nevertheless. (The end of the *Diminuendo* is particularly inventive.) These records all indicate that Swing is here to stay—at any rate until something more startling comes along.

Source: Aaron Copland, "Scores and Records," *Modern Music* (January–February 1938), 109–10.

[1] For writings in this volume by Bowles and McPhee, see §§42 and 48.

33. Ellington: "From Where I Lie" (1938)

R. D. Darrell, Percy Grainger, and other white commentators tended to perceive Ellington within a European context—comparing his music, for example, to that of Delius, Ravel, Debussy, and Stravinsky. Ellington, by contrast, located himself solidly within the African-American artistic heritage. A reflective statement written from a hospital bed in 1938 made his stance clear.

The "Editor's note" below appears in the original.

(Editor's Note: Duke Ellington was scheduled to leave Wickersham hospital, where he underwent a hernia operation last month, Friday, July 15. During the first real vacation he has had in ten years, he had a chance to muse. Below are some of his musings. After reading through it we were sorely tempted to label it "Music Maestro Pleases," for he is as facile with the typewriter as he is at the keyboard.)

The sky-line from my windows in the Wickersham hospital is an inspiring sight. I have spent three weeks in bed here, not too ill to be thrilled daily by a view of these skyscrapers, and with plenty of time for ample meditation.

It is natural, perhaps, that I should think of many subjects, some serious, some fanciful. I spent some time comparing the marvelous sky-line to our race, likening the Chrysler tower, the Empire State building and other lofty structures to the lives of Bert Williams, Florence Mills and other immortals of the entertainment field.

I mused over the qualities which these stars possessed that enabled them to tower as far above their fellow artists as do these buildings above the sky-line.

And it seemed to me, from where I was lying, that in addition to their great talent, the qualities which have made really great stars are those of simplicity, sincerity, and a rigid adherence to the traditions of our own people.

We are children of the sun and our race has a definite tradition of beauty and glory and vitality that is as rich and powerful as the sun itself. These traditions are ours to express, and will enrich our careers in proportion to the sincerity and faithfulness with which we interpret them.

Source: Duke Ellington, "From Where I Lie," *The Negro Actor* 1/1 (15 July 1938), 4.

34. Ellington in *Down Beat:* On Swing and Its Critics (1939)

Ellington presented his views on "swing" and music criticism in three articles written for *Down Beat* in 1939.

In the first, "Duke Says Swing Is Stagnant" (February), Ellington charts the growth of jazz and its "striving toward legitimate acceptance, in proportion to its own merits." He begins by stating that "swing," as an offshoot of jazz, has been productive in raising the level of musicianship in bands and improving the public's taste. Then abruptly he proceeds to criticize the commercialization that swing has introduced, claiming that the responsibility for change lies with critics. Toward the end he discusses his own orchestra, taking care to separate out its repertory from familiar musical categories: "We are not interested primarily in the playing of jazz or swing music, but in producing musically a genuine contribution from our race."

In the second article, "Situation Between the Critics and Musicians Is Laughable," published in April (during the orchestra's European tour) and May 1939, Ellington adopts a more aggressive stance.[1] In it he attacks critics who judge musicians by a uniform standard rather than taking into account individual goals. He points out the shortcomings of half a dozen writers, reserving his harshest words for John Hammond, whose article "The Tragedy of Duke Ellington" had appeared in *Down Beat* a few years earlier (see §27). To air such negative opinions publicly was rare for Ellington.

After seeking in the second article to set up general critical guidelines, Ellington attempts to follow them himself in the third, "Duke Becomes a Critic!" (July). The effort fails, however, since Ellington dons the familiar smiling mask of diplomacy, praising virtually every band he mentions. The only hint of judgment comes from reading between the lines, as in the case of Guy Lombardo—"He eliminated all superfluous figures and we all know the results"—and in the ambiguous concluding sentence on Paul Whiteman: "He is still Mr. Whiteman." Otherwise, the article reads like a toastmaster's speech at an awards banquet: "[A]ll the above-mentioned bands deserve endearing tribute for their sincere efforts to preserve a definite spirit of musical independence, and toward furthering the progress of the dance-medium as a musical element."

February 1939

The most significant thing that can be said about swing music today is that it has become stagnant.

Sources: Duke Ellington, "Duke Says Swing Is Stagnant," *Down Beat* (February 1939), 2, 16–17; Ellington, " 'Situation Between the Critics and Musicians Is Laughable'—Ellington," *Down Beat* (April 1939), 4, 9; Ellington, "Duke Concludes Criticism of the Critics," *Down Beat* (May 1939), 14; Ellington, "Duke Becomes a Critic," *Down Beat* (July 1939), 8, 35.

[1] An editor's note in the May issue explained that the article appeared in two installments due to a mechanical error. The second part is called "Duke Concludes Criticism of the Critics." The editor also stated that Ellington wrote it shortly before sailing for Europe (i.e., on 23 March 1939).

Nothing of importance, nothing new, nothing either original or creative has occurred in the swing field during the last two years.

It becomes necessary to adopt a far-seeing and mature point of view when considering the current popularity of swing, revising in the mind's eye its inception, the conditions and circumstances surrounding its birth and growth and the completion of the cycle as it appears today. Much has been written about swing, it has been defined 1,999 times and it has been the subject of much controversy.

An ironic twist to the situation has bitten deeply into the minds of many of the actual purveyors of swing music. Those musicians who were "swinging" on their instruments 10 and 15 years ago (before the appellation "swing" had any significance other than that of inferring in what style the music was to be played) today look on, some with amusement, others with intolerance, at the farce which is being played out to the full on that merry-go-round known as the amusement world.

What is important is the fact that Jazz has something to say. It speaks in many manners, taking always original and authentic form. Still in the throes of development and formation, it has fought its way upwards through the effortful struggles of sincere and irate musicians, has fought to escape mal-judgment at the hands of its own "causified critics," those fanatical fans who have woven about it interminable toils. It has striven in a world of other values, to get across its own message, and in so doing, is striving, toward legitimate acceptance, in proportion to its own merits.

Granted then that Child Jazz shows promise, let's swing the spotlight over toward the adolescent youth, Swing. It's not so very difficult to understand the evolution of Jazz into Swing. Ten years ago, when this type of music was flourishing, albeit amidst adverse conditions and surrounded by hearty indifference, there were yet those few enthusiasts in whom the music struck a responsive chord.

These enthusiasts were scattered sparsely over this nation and through Europe. Fired with enthusiasm and belief, these supporters drew more closely together, combining their efforts to popularize jazz music, so that musicians might feel free to follow their inclinations in this field without the pressure of economic considerations to deter them.

Little by little, these people gathered about them more interested and zealous fans. They commenced to publish small trade magazines, dealing with their own particular "high-priests of jazz." The European fans, familiar with this form of American music solely through the medium of phonograph recordings, nevertheless adopted a typical European attitude of seriousness in evaluating our "renegade child."

Over a period of several years, these groups of enthusiasts swelled to amazing proportions. Hot musicians became conscious of a fair percentage of laymen who knew of their background and of what they were trying to do. This encouraging enthusiasm and sympathetic viewpoint, coming from outside the profession as it did, seemed to afford musicians the moral courage and incentive necessary to the open adoption of swing as a style of playing.

As is so often the case, the sweeping wave of popularity lost sight of the genuine values of its popular hero, and much that is false came into prominence. On fire with the new craze, writers, faddists, bandmanagers, night club proprietors, entertainers and newspapermen entered the field with a vengeance. Genuine values became distorted and false ones set up in their places.

Before proceeding to explain why I feel that the music is stagnant at the present time, it is only fair to recognize certain beneficial effects which the swing craze has brought about. Without any question, qualifications for playing swing music demand superior musicianship than that heretofore required. Greater flexibility, superior tone and range, intelligence in the use of phrasing and dynamics, are all qualities that are far more consistently demanded from the swing musician than they were in the past from the average player.

Accordingly, the myriad of bands throughout the country today, who are modeling themselves along the lines of a Benny Goodman or a Red Norvo, rather than along the lines of any out-and-out popular dance band, are cultivating a higher standard of musicianship among the younger professionals who are striving, musically speaking, to get their feet on the ground. Young bands trying to make their way these days are more apt to play cleanly and in tune than has been the habit in the past.

It stands to reason that since, during the last couple of years, the public has listened to so much music played according to these standards that they themselves are becoming more discerning, discriminating and appreciative. The ear of the lay public is becoming accustomed to the rhythms and forms adopted in swing. They are quicker to pick out riffs, and rhythmic variations, and therefore, slowly but definitely, the standards of musicianship for bands demanded by the public should elevate, and should eventually attain a far higher standard.

I believe that there has been little or no progress in swing music of late. It is the repetition and monotony of the present day swing arrangements which bode ill for the future. The mechanics of most of the current "killer-dillers" are similar and of elementary quality.

Once again, it is proven that when the artistic point of view gains commercial standing, artistry itself bows out, leaving inspiration to die a slow death. The present dearth of creative and original music is not, I'm convinced, due to a lack of talent.

The adage "necessity is the mother of invention" can very aptly be applied to our situation. The responsibility of improving audience level lies with the critics who might well give their particular job more serious consideration. When audience level improves, it will likely inspire our artists to a high level. Swing is merely one element in good dance music. Pure swing is monotonous. I feel strongly that the swing "craze" has been harmful since it has done two or three damaging things to popular music.

It has thwarted the improvement of many good bands, which for commercial reasons remain in the same uninspired groove and refuse to risk rising above the current public taste.

It is, however, encouraging to note that there has been a closer affinity between the exponent of swing music and the exponent of legitimate music. It is pleasant to hope that the series of lectures and concerts promoted by

Walter N. Neumberg [*recte* Walter W. Naumberg] of the Town Hall music committee, and other prominent musical personalities, now being conducted in New York's Town Hall, devoted to a study of Jazz as a native American art, will perhaps encourage the general public to give more serious thought to the music of today, and to show further discrimination and to seek high levels in the music which they have made popular.[2]

Benny Goodman's performance with the Budapest string quartet, rendering Mozart's *Quintet for Clarinet and Strings,* was still another step in the right direction, demanding serious approbation for the swing musician. There is being shown at the present time a definite trend in this direction which offers some promise for the future of swing. Without any doubt, progress must await audience development.

We are not concerned personally with these conditions, because our aim has always been the development of an authentic Negro music, of which swing is only one element. We are not interested primarily in the playing of jazz or swing music, but in producing musically a genuine contribution from our race. Our music is always intended to be definitely and purely racial. We try to complete a cycle.

As a group of musicians we understand each other well. We have identical feelings and beliefs in music. Our inspiration is derived from our lives, and the lives of those about us, and those that went before us. The boys in our band play in a certain style, the music I write is inspired by those things they play. We write the music for the men in our band, it is inspired by those men, and they play it with the realization and understanding that they are playing their own music.

Those things which we have to say, we try to express musically with the greatest possible degree of freedom of inspiration and individuality. We thus attempt to achieve a form of individual expression presented by the entire band, both as individuals and as a whole. I believe a significant future for the swing music of today is largely dependent upon the strength of character, depth of artistic integrity, and purity of creative inspiration existent today in that body of musicians most concerned with swing.

These same musicians have spent years studying music, perfecting themselves on their instruments, many of them also delving deeply into the subject of harmony and composition. It stands to reason that these men are well equipped to know what they are doing and what they want to do in their own field. It is up to these musicians to carry out their beliefs in music to the fullest possible extent, remembering to ignore those critics, who, lacking a musical education and foundation, might want to confound them and attempt to influence them in perhaps the wrong direction.

[2] Walter W. Naumberg, chair of the Town Hall music committee, had launched a lecture-recital series entitled "From Early Folk-Songs to Modern Jazz" in the fall of 1938. Although the concerts were devoted primarily to classical music, Benny Goodman's orchestra had performed for the final event, "The Rise of Jazz and Swing," on 14 December 1938.

April 1939

The situation which exists between the "swing critics" and the professional musician has reached proportions which have become laughable.

It is an exaggerated situation, with the feeling on both sides attaining an ill-proportioned intensity of thought. A situation now exists which is resented by both the musicians and critics, and which has slowly grown up out of innumerable minor situations.

These situations have been of secondary importance. The most dominating attitude has been that of the musicians who question the right of musical amateurs to pass judgment upon their efforts. The professional claims that a "man who doesn't know how to play an instrument has no business telling the man who does, how to play." The pro also claims that the critic seldom maintains an objective viewpoint and that, accordingly, his opinion is often damaging where no foundation exists for adverse judgment.

The musician feels that criticism should be based most particularly upon the status of what a man is trying to do. If the musician in question is trying to earn his living by attempting to intrigue and win the approbation of the public, he feels that criticism of his work should not be based upon the degree of sincerity involved in the music which he is presenting, since he is obviously not directing his efforts with this particular goal in view.

He feels that if he is to be the object of fair criticism, it must be stated in front what he is trying to do, that the criticism to follow must be based upon the degree of success which he is achieving in that particular field he is attempting to conquer.

The critics, on the other hand, feel it is their duty to constantly "expose" all musicians attempting to earn their living in any other manner than a strictly musical one. It may be, and probably is justifiable, to accord the highest praise to the greatest standard of musicianship, but, on the other hand, it is unfair to condemn completely the lesser product whose aims are admittedly less exalted. The critics ignore all individual goals and judge musicians entirely by their own personal standards.

The professional musician rightly objects to such thoughtless, unconsidered and casually personal criticism of his most serious and considered efforts. The musician, however, forgets to view the situation from a sane and mature standpoint. When angered it is only human to show prejudice and to over-stress. The musician indignantly inquires "what right has the so-called 'critic' to print his opinion of a man's work, when his knowledge is seldom based on anything other than personal predilections or prejudice?"

He demands to know why the musician should be subjected to criticism of any kind, and he demands musical qualifications in any person entitled to offer criticism. Here we find the faulty judgment to be lying [in] the direction of the musician. For it is an established fact that any art worthy of the name requires its own critics, whose responsibility it is to "maintain and elevate standards," the same principle applying to any respected profession.

The musician is basing his thoughts upon false premises when he insists that there is no need for the critics, and demands that he no longer be subjected to their hysterical and prejudiced outpourings. These thoughts are the direct result of a prejudiced opinion of a situation which, growing up, as it did, out of nothing, has never been properly clarified, and has finally grown to achieve worrisome proportions. What the musician probably means, and what he is entirely entitled to demand, is: "Give Us Better Critics."

Give us honest persons, with a certain fundamental knowledge of music, its foundations, its requirements, and the requirements of the music business itself. Give us conscientious persons who properly realize they have a job to fulfill. Give us those who may understand that they are responsible to us for maintaining certain high standards in the profession. Give us critics who by *constructive criticism* will help to elevate former standards, whose sympathetic and encouraging advice will inspire the artist to strike out for higher levels, with the assurance that his efforts will not go unappreciated, and with confidence that the critics will do their utmost to show the great paying public in what direction it should accord its appreciation and approbation.

A musician seldom makes a good critic, since he naturally has his own ideas of how music should be played. Accordingly, the musician should accept the fact that a critic is not necessarily required to play an instrument in order to properly fulfill the job of "critic." In fact, the critic is more likely to deliver impartially if he is not personally musically talented.

The swing critic who perhaps has stirred up the greatest resentment, while at the same time was earning the deepest gratitude of others, has been John Henry Hammond, Jr., son of a prominent New York family and possessed of wealth in his own right. To properly judge the "modus operandi" of Hammond, it is necessary to devote some thought to the man himself. He appears to be an ardent propagandist and champion of the "lost cause." He apparently has consistently identified himself with the interests of the minorities, the Negro peoples, to a lesser degree, the Jew, and to the underdog, in the form of the Communist party.[3]

Perhaps due to the "fever of battle," Hammond's judgment may have become slightly warped, and his enthusiasm and prejudices a little bit unwieldy to control.

May 1939

Whether or not that may be the case, it has become apparent that John has identified himself so strongly in certain directions that he no longer enjoys an impartial status which would entitle him to the role of critic. He has continued to publicise his opinions of musical units other than those to which he has been attached, freely condemning and condoning, ignoring the fact that he has forfeited the right to do this. Such tactics would not be tolerated from the

[3] In his autobiography co-written with Irving Townsend, *John Hammond on Record* (New York: Summit Books, 1977), Hammond recalled his involvement with various social and political causes during the thirties, among them organizing miners in Kentucky (77–80) and working on behalf of the Scottsboro boys (82–87, 95–105).

business man and they are doubly unappreciated when employed by one whose name and position allow him to remain immune from counter-attack.

Lack of impartiality is not, however, the only failing exhibited by the swing critics. Many of these fans mean well and are not lacking in sincerity but due perhaps to lack of experience, youth or impulsiveness they often render their criticisms ineffectual. Devoting a passing thought to the writings of some of the names familiar to us, I feel there are certain comments to be made. In the case of Marshall Stearns, his verdicts are often influenced by misinformation or inaccuracy. Helen Oakley may be found guilty of hasty judgment and of impressionability. George Frazier indulges in fragrant [sic] overstatement as witness his remarks anent the subject of Martha Tilton. Al Brackman may be accused of lack of discrimination. Hughes Pannassie [recte Hugues Panassié] preserves a closed mind on many musical subjects, judging all things according to certain preconceived conceptions.

I'd like to appeal to the present day and future critics to study seriously their function and the responsibility which is upon them. To throw out former "prejudices" and to think for themselves; to try to base their opinions on definite knowledge, and to judge a man's work according to what he is attempting to do. Speaking as a musician, I don't believe I can be far wrong in saying that one of today's urgencies in our own particular field consists of a crying need for "Bigger and Better Critics."

July 1939

The only outstanding conviction that we know concerning the contemporary dance field is that it is essentially as yet unexplored. There is so much that remains to be done, and even to be attempted. We have previously stated that we consider the influence of commercialism the most flourishing and potent evil to be combatted in our field of endeavor. Standardized commercial requirements are apt to dull the ambitions of our outstanding musicians and influence them to satisfy themselves with a musical formula calculated to please, not themselves, but the general public.

It is to be hoped that those musicians who are today standing at the top of the ladder of success will continue to permit their musical spirit of independence to function sufficiently to allow for constant experimentation and innovation, which qualities are the principal ingredients of musical progress. In commenting upon the better aspects of the outstanding contemporary bands of today we herald with a musical fanfare every significant instance of the spirit of musical independence.

Tommy Dorsey: Tommy has won, and justly so, the appreciation of all sincere musicians by his policy of attempting to play well many and varied types of music. His renditions of beautiful melodies in a style which is pleasing to the lay ear [have] won many a convert over into resulting appreciation of the more complicated swing-music ... which, incidentally, he does so adroitly.

Benny Goodman: Benny has outstandingly proven himself to be a great leader by the fact that he has consciously separated himself, one-by-one, from the stars in his band and yet still shows himself to be tops. His practice of offering his own renditions of all the worthwhile music he encounters during his career of musical activities also deserves sincere tribute.

Paul Whiteman: Mr. Whiteman deserves credit for discovering and recognizing ability or genius in composers whose works would not normally be acceptable to dance bands. Whiteman makes it possible to commercialize these works. We confess he has maintained a "higher level" for many years, and we think there is no doubt but that he has carried jazz to the highest position it ever has enjoyed. He put it in the ears of the serious audience and they liked it. He is still Mr. Whiteman.

Guy Lombardo: Lombardo deserves credit for having a keen eye in recognizing the value of a simple trick. At a time when musical ornamentation was all the rage, he showed foresight in employing musical-simplification to the "nth degree." He eliminated all superfluous musical figures and we all know the results.

Bob Crosby: A band with an amazing amount of color. We feel that here the tan has attained a very luxurious lustre, perhaps through absorption. However that may be, a truly gutbucket band, capable of really getting down there. Band shows a strong blues influence, and also possesses notable musical background. Just different somehow.

Hal Kemp: Kemp has achieved a very nice medium. He has reached a pleasing musical middle. Not overserious, but tasteful, with no hard lines. Band sounds always musicianly and acceptable, never awkward or ugly.

Jimmie Lunceford: A greatly underrated band. Capable of mighty fine interpretations obviously the result of sincere thought and of rehearsal to the perfection-point; rehearsal until the arrangements are matured. Much of the music of this band has been overlooked. He has developed a definitely individual style, mood, and color, and has never been successfully imitated.

Fred Waring: Waring has shown broad scope and wide range, notably having put the popular-music glee club on the musical map. He is uncontrovertibly [*sic*] the finished product of the stage.

Count Basie: Basie's outstanding musical quality has been unpretentiousness and he and his boys have stuck to their guns all the way through to success. Undoubtedly the greatest rhythm section in the business, they are the greatest exponents of that emotional element of bouncing buoyancy, otherwise known as swing.

Fletcher Henderson: Fletcher is another man who has a good band and who also is the victim of sensationalism, in another form, which deprives him of the tribute of leadership. It is difficult for him to combat his present reputation as an arranger. Fletcher has had bands which have been the inspiration for many bands; our own, for one.

Artie Shaw: Artie has used his band to great advantage in rhapsodizing his solos to the point of making them finished products in the concerto classification.

Don Redman: Redman has performed phenomenal feats in orchestration and has created several magnificent things, many of which have been copied although Redman has rated no credit lines. We shall never forget the *Chant of the Weed* and its effectiveness.

Cab Calloway: Calloway is definitely the most dynamic personality ever to front a band. He established characters who existed in the realm of dreams, characters who attained their altitude on a curl of smoke, but to us it seems unfortunate because his almost immortal characterizations have overshadowed his better singing. His band continues to improve all along but only to be overshadowed by Calloway's tremendous personality. I always resent the statement that *Minnie the Moocher* is not pure jazz.

Louis Armstrong: Louis also is a great personality, we say also great, not because he is lesser, but because we cannot think of further terms. Unless possibly to say he is heroic-size standard in trumpet. He is also a brilliant comedian. We heard his band recently and were favorably impressed.

There are many other fine bands today which deserve considerable rating here, such as those of Bunny Berigan, Charlie Barnet, Bobby Hackett, Jack Teagarden, Harry James, Red Norvo and others, but space does not permit. However in conclusion, we would like to say that all the above-mentioned bands deserve endearing tribute for their sincere efforts to preserve a definite spirit of musical independence, and toward furthering the progress of the dance-medium as a musical element.

35. The Parting of Ellington and Irving Mills (1939)

I rving Mills (1894–1985) had been a key figure in Ellington's career since 1926, when he began managing the band at the Kentucky Club. He waged an intensive advertising and promotional campaign, secured recording and performing opportunities, and published Ellington's music. A shrewd, tough, tenacious businessman, Mills alienated some members of the Ellington organization while apparently maintaining cordial relations with its leader.

But as the Ellington orchestra was returning from Europe in May of 1939, the announcement came that Ellington and Mills had ended their partnership. England's *Melody Maker* carried a brief, incomplete account of the event. According to biographer Barry Ulanov, Ellington cited Mills's "lack of attention" as a reason for leaving, possibly his unfair business practices as well.[1]

For Mills's version of the split, see §56.

Yesterday, Thursday, Duke Ellington and his Band passed through London on their way home to New York. Off the S.S. "*Britannia*," they arrived early in the morning at Tilbury and left Waterloo at 4.30 in the afternoon to board the "Ile de France" at Southampton, thereby concluding a European barn-

---

Source: "Irving Mills and Duke Ellington Sever Association," *Melody Maker* (6 May 1939), 1.

[1] *DE*, 206–7.

storming tour which has taken in towns never before visited by a first-class band.

Excluding expenses, the band has received £1,500 a week from the Scandinavian bookers who brought them over.

It has now just become known that Ellington and Irving Mills have severed their long business association, which has resulted in the famous Negro band-leader and composer becoming a world-wide attraction.

From the time Ellington reaches New York he will be one of the attractions of the noted William Morris office, said to be out to compete, through a new band department, with the terrific Music Corporation of America organisation which controls some 70 per cent of the best white band attractions of the U.S.A.

The circumstances under which Ellington and Mills are parting are too much a matter of hearsay at the moment to warrant recounting. Until duly checked up, the "M.M." [*Melody Maker*] is in no position to print the exact truth of it.

Hitherto, the connection between Mills and Ellington has been secured through a company known as Ellington, Inc., in which they each owned 45 per cent of the stock, an American lawyer holding the balance. Under this arrangement Ellington also has had a piece in Cab Calloway, Inc., the company which exploits the Prince of Hi-de-ho's music.

The man in the William Morris organisation who will handle Ellington in future is Willard Alexander, a remarkable figure who has great discernment where swing bands are concerned and who has been associated with the rapid rise of such as Benny Goodman and Count Basie.

The publication of Ellington's compositions and his band records will, it is said, remain under the control of Irving Mills.[2]

36. Wilder Hobson on Ellington, from *Jazzmen* (1939)

 ne of the landmarks of literature about jazz was *Jazzmen* (1939), a collection of essays, edited by Frederic Ramsey, Jr., and Charles Edward Smith, which gave an overview of jazz history, profiled several notable figures, and assessed the contemporary scene. Its contributors included prominent jazz historians, critics, and discographers, among them Roger Pryor Dodge, Otis Ferguson, and William Russell.

One contributor, Wilder Hobson, documented the rise of hot jazz in New York, discussing Ellington's orchestra as one of three important big bands to emerge there in the twenties (together with those of Fletcher Henderson and Luis Russell).

[2] Ellington moved to the publisher Robbins, then started his own company, Tempo Music, in 1942.

Source: Wilder Hobson, excerpt from Chapter 9, "New York Turns on the Heat," in *Jazzmen*, ed. Frederic Ramsey, Jr., and Charles Edward Smith (New York: Harcourt, Brace, 1939), 217–19.

Compared with Hobson's 1933 profile of Ellington in *Fortune* (see §20), the tone here was slightly more muted. Like some other critics, Hobson may not have cared for Ellington's recent music, perhaps believing that in becoming "suave, elaborate, and virtuoso" the orchestra had forsaken its appealing "folk-musical sources" of the late twenties.

For a biographical note on Hobson, see §20.

. . . Edward Kennedy Duke Ellington, the son of a Negro worker in the Washington, D.C., Navy Yard, opened with his band at the Cotton Club in Harlem in 1927, when [Fletcher] Henderson's band had long since become a byword with other jazz players. Apart from musicians, however, Henderson's music was known mostly to a limited dance hall audience. It had had no effective promotion. Ellington, on the other hand, had Irving Mills' plugging management, a bandstand in the purple glow lamps of the Cotton Club which was a center of the Harlem entertainment vogue, and widespread radio facilities. Also, in addition to being the leader of a remarkable combination, Ellington was a composer of decided interest. In a short time his radio hookups brought him a large, national audience—his was the first large hot band to attract any such attention.

He has since had all kinds of salutes. Recently it has often been said that Ellington's music has lost the genuineness which characterized it in the late twenties, that it has become overly suave, elaborate, and virtuoso. In a recent appearance at the downtown Cotton Club on Broadway, Ellington's boys wore white jackets, boiled shirts and dress ties, crimson trousers and shoes. Duke himself opened the evening in a light gray coat and black trousers, moved on to full dress, and finished in a henna jacket and the blacks. The trumpets appeared to be made of platinum, heavily embossed, perhaps suitably inscribed and possibly taken out of Tiffany's each day and put back after the night's work. Even the instrument cases were handsomely lettered in metal. The only feature which marred the general splendor was a battered platter which Rex Stewart produced from some hiding place and waved over the bell of his trumpet during the last chorus *tutti* of *The Sheik of Araby*.

These trappings may have little to do with music, but I think they are fitting and proper in this case. If any musician ever earned the right to a dress uniform, Ellington's boys have earned their crimson pants and fancy instrument cases. They have been and are an epitome of a sort. The jazz language, coming out of folk-musical sources, by its own nature bred a lot of remarkable improvising talent. As the players grew more and more interested in the combination of instruments in sections, jazz inevitably acquired considerable orchestral sophistication. Jazz musicians are bound to be more and more experimental *orchestrally*. And it is probably natural that some one organization should most vividly represent *all* the elements of this process in which a folk-music is gradually moving into general musical currents. It seems to me that the band which does this is Ellington's. In it you hear improvising in many spirits, the "low-down" rhythmic playing of trumpeter "Cootie" Williams and trombonist Joe Nanton, the spirited, melodic inventions of the saxophonists Johnny Hodges and Harry Carney, and the floridity of trumpeter

Rex Stewart, trombonist Lawrence Brown, and clarinetist Barney Bigard. Also, this is certainly the most striking *ensemble* in jazz, with a brilliance, finish and ease resulting from long collaboration. Finally, I don't know of any jazz orchestrator as musically fertile as Ellington. His ideas may seldom get sustained development, may often be loosely strung together and over-rich for the thematic material which is carrying them. But in an Ellington performance it is a rare three minutes in which something of *orchestral* fascination doesn't occur. Of how many other bands can the same be said? . . .

37. A Celebrity Interview (1941)

Beginning in the thirties, Ellington's fame and popularity made him the frequent subject of "personality profiles" in the press. Writers of these articles would routinely comment on his extravagant wardrobe, elegant conversation, nocturnal working hours, tremendous appetite, superstitious beliefs, and relationships with women.

Some of these topics turned up in a 1941 article by Almena Davis published in the black newspaper the *California Eagle*. But in addition to noting the "fantastic design" of Ellington's bathrobe and his "wicked" good looks, Davis passed along items of musical interest: Ellington's comments on a recent *Down Beat* article claiming that black bands were losing ground to white ensembles; on his new arranging partner, Billy Strayhorn; and on his practice of writing music for individuals rather than instruments.

At the time of this interview (6 January 1941) the Ellington orchestra was based temporarily in Los Angeles, where it performed at the Casa Mañana in Culver City and recorded a few times in Hollywood.

Davis's style relies heavily on ellipses; accordingly, in the version below, editorial deletions are marked by bracketed ellipses [. . .].

Duke Ellington is a very fascinating person. This may not be news to thousands of females who've swooned over his sophisticated pan in the newspapers and swung limp and hysterical, before bandstands from coast to coast and overseas. It's not news to me. It merely confirms a suspicion I had about the composer of that wistfully-world weary "Sophisticated Lady," that bizarre piece of satire, "Black and Tan Fantasy," of "Solitude," "In a Sentimental Mood," "It Don't Mean a Thing," "Mood Indigo" . . . music which calls out our joy or sorrow and blows it away on the high notes of a trumpet or drowns it in the piano's bass . . .

He received me in the sitting room of his suite in the Dunbar Hotel. Impressive sentence, that! I sat down without being asked. I wonder, could that have accounted for the startled look on his face? . . . Or perhaps it was my bright and glowing youth . . . or maybe I resembled his Aunt Maggie. At any rate,

Source: Almena Davis, "Duke Ellington Fascinates Interviewer as He Takes 'Downbeat' Writer to Task," *California Eagle*, 9 January 1941.

we started the interview off amicably enough, with him traipsing off to the bedroom to answer the phone while I fidgeted without.

That telephone rendered yeoman service as a punctuation mark or a mechanical paragrapher for this interview. Every time I figured I had about heard enough from our hero on any one subject, the phone would ring. By the time he had returned from being hearty to acquaintances who'd met him "at Whoozis' house when he was here in '37 and just heard he was in town and just thought they'd call to see what he was doing tomorrow night" . . . I'd framed another question.

I understand Mr. Ellington is quite a fashion plate. Well, gather around, boys, while I describe minutely the Ellington attire on the afternoon of January 6. He wore a bathrobe of the fantastic design affected by bathrobes with extremely extroverted personalities. From the neck of it peeked the collar of his beige pajama top and from the skirt of said bathrobe, there protruded two thin and unattractive legs. It does beat all how unattractive men's legs are. It's downright disillusioning![. . .]

The Ellington face is not quite so elemental. Rather, it's awfully wicked looking, like that of a bronze Bacchus. Long and complex, it has two outstanding achievements: a pair of eyes perched upon two ponderous pouches that are gleefully wicked and surgically intelligent, by turns, and a mouth that epitomizes what a lady novelist would have described with exclamation points in the days when there were lady novelists as sensuous.

Having found himself some cigarettes and an ash tray and draped his ranging person over a sofa, we fell to talking.[. . .]

Question No. 1 concerned the article by R. L. Larkin in *Down Beat* magazine which contended that Ellington, Basie, Lunceford, and the rest of the fair-haired Senegambians of the popular music field are slipping . . . no longer the box office attractions of former years . . . poor showmen . . . no longer distinctive . . . and are being booted out in the cold by the white folks who are "stealing their stuff."[1]

From the Ellington lips there was emitted a loud pooh-pooh. In the first place, the Duke doubts that Brother Larkin knows whereof he speaks. He thinks it hardly likely that any booker would give out the kind of information that would enable Larkin to speak authoritatively. And as far as his own band is concerned he knows the brother is all wet.

Like anything else in this inconstant world, the popularity of bands waxes and wanes. From 1930 to '34 Ellington enjoyed a heyday, riding the crest both financially and artistically. From '34 to '37 there were no tremendous profits. '37 to '38 were good, '39 slow—. Then 1940 saw that whimsical wench, Mistress Public, take the Duke to her bosom again. For confirmation of this, see story in this paper concerning the 1940 *Down Beat* poll, in which the Ellington outfit was voted the second greatest in the world; and the *Chicago Defender,* which last week reported the Duke No. 1 for 1940; and then there's *Swing* magazine's award of 17 "whole notes" (100 per cent—excellence) out of 24 in 1940 to Ellington.

[1] R. L. Larkin, "Are Colored Bands Doomed as Big Money Makers?," *Down Beat* (1 December 1940), 2, 23.

In the second place, Ellington continued, Mr. Larkin is wrong because white bands are NOT stealing Negro stuff. They can't. "The only way to play Negro music is to be a Negro."

The Duke did not rationalize that very controversial statement. He just spit it out like a blast from Cootie Williams' trumpet, and in a breath revived the old argument about whether jazz and swing, the commercial terms for the popular music of the day, are Negro music . . . and whether Negro music is all swing and jazz.

He thinks not. His band, he claims, "doesn't make any attempt at playing jazz or swing." What it plays is "unadulterated American Negro music." It just happens that this music is danceable and therefore popular.

It is danceable, he explained, because it is "rhythmic" and "in strict tempo." Spirituals, if they are sung as the singer feels them and "not as he has been taught" have this same danceable quality . . . and the "shouts" of the old fashioned church, the same.

"Swing is only an emotional element, not a type of music. The emotional element is a strong part of Negro music, but it isn't Negro music."

White bands are not stealing the Ellington style for another reason . . . because they can't get to it even if they wanted to. He and a youngster whom he is developing and whom he considers one of the finest arrangers in the country, one Billy Strayhorn, do all the arranging for the Ellington group and they DON'T SELL ARRANGEMENTS.[2]

I was interested in his method of arranging. He says he writes a piece not for the instruments, but for the MAN who is to be featured. Take the case of Cootie Williams, the great trumpeter, for instance. During the years Cootie was with Duke, the pieces in which he starred were written for him. Recently gone over to Benny Goodman's sextet (not the orchestra), Cootie, according to critics, is experiencing great difficulty conforming to Goodman's style.

In Cootie's place, Ellington has a Chicago youth named Ray Nance, who plays the violin as well as the trumpet.[3] There has heretofore been no fiddle in the Ellington music but the Duke is writing something now that will star Nance on that instrument.

Asked which of his countless compositions he is most fond, the composer said whichever one he is currently working on. He usually works after playing hours, two or three a.m. He has practically finished a full-length opera based on the history of the American Negro, and is readying a synopsis of it to submit to a prospective producer.

There's another musician coming up rapidly in the Ellington family, son Mercer, a 20-year-old Juilliard and Columbia student, who joined his dad here Tuesday. Mercer has been composing a lot lately and his father plans to play and perhaps record some of the young man's efforts. Duke's sister Ruth,

[2] Strayhorn (1915–1967) began contributing arrangements and compositions to the Ellington orchestra in 1939. Among the first to be recorded were *Like a Ship in the Night* and *Savoy Strut* (by Johnny Hodges-led small groups, on 27 February and 21 March 1939, respectively), and *Something to Live For* (by the full orchestra with Strayhorn on piano, 21 March 1939).

[3] Nance (1913–1976) joined the Ellington orchestra in November 1940. His first recorded appearance—perhaps his first performance with Ellington—was 7 November 1940 at the Crystal Ballroom in Fargo, North Dakota.

well known here, is opening a music publishing business in New York for the express purpose of publishing Mercer's work. . . .[4]

38. Ellington: "We, Too, Sing 'America'" (1941)

In a talk given before black church-goers in Los Angeles for their Annual Lincoln Day Services (falling near Lincoln's birthday on 12 February 1941), Ellington expounded on contributions made by blacks to American culture, especially their patriotism, industry, and creative achievements. These themes would find musical expression in various works over the years, most notably in *Black, Brown and Beige* (1943) and *My People* (1963). While the basic thrust of Ellington's message was positive, ominous references to events abroad foreshadowed America's involvement in the war.

For the text of his speech, Ellington glossed the line "I, Too, Sing America," from the epilogue to Langston Hughes's *The Weary Blues* (1926). Ellington had met Hughes (1902–1967) as early as 1936, when the two planned collaborating on *Cock o' the World,* a musical that never materialized. Later in 1941 Ellington wrote music for a text by Hughes and Charles Leonard, "Mad Scene from Woolworth's," which was briefly featured in the revue *Jump for Joy* (see §39).[1]

The abrupt ending suggests the *Eagle* may not have reprinted Ellington's entire text; ellipses are reprinted here as they appeared in the *Eagle.*

First of all, I should like to extend my sincere appreciation to the Rev. Karl Downs for the opportunity to appear on this very fine program and express myself in a manner not often at my disposal. Music is my business, my profession, my life . . . but, even though it means so much to me, I often feel that I'd like to say something, have my say, on some of the burning issues confronting us, in another language . . . in words of mouth.

There is a good deal of talk in the world today. Some view that as a bad sign. One of the Persian poets, lamenting the great activity of men's tongues, cautioned them to be silent with the reminder that, "In much of your talking, thinking is half murdered." This is true no doubt. Yet, in this day when so many men are silent because they are afraid to speak, indeed, have been forbidden to speak, I view the volubility of the unrestricted with great satisfaction. Here in America, the silence of Europe, silent that is except for the harsh echoes of the dictators' voices, has made us conscious of our privileges

---

[4] The company, Tempo Music, ended up publishing not only Mercer's music but that of Duke, Billy Strayhorn, Johnny Hodges, and many others within the Ellington orbit.

Source: Duke Ellington, "We, Too, Sing 'America,'" delivered on Annual Lincoln Day Services, Scott Methodist Church, Los Angeles, 9 February; published as the "Speech of the Week" in the *California Eagle,* 13 February 1941.

[1] For more on Ellington's links with Hughes, see Arnold Rampersad's two-volume biography, *The Life of Langston Hughes: I, Too, Sing America* (New York: Oxford University Press, 1986) and *I Dream a World* (New York: Oxford University Press, 1988).

of free speech, and like the dumb suddenly given tongue, or the tongue-tied eased of restraint, we babble and bay to beat the band. Singly, as individuals, we don't say much of consequence perhaps, but put together, heard in chorus, the blustering half-truths, the lame and halting logic, the painfully-sincere convictions of Joe and Mary Doaks . . . compose a powerful symphony which, like the small boy's brave whistle in the dark, serves notice on the hobgoblins that we are not asleep, not prey to unchallenged attack. And, so it is, with the idea in mind of adding my bit to the meaningful chorus, that I address you briefly this evening.

I have been asked to take as the subject of my remarks the title of a very significant poem, "We, Too, Sing America," written by the distinguished poet and author, Langston Hughes.

In the poem, Mr. Hughes argues the case for democratic recognition of the Negro on the basis of the Negro's contribution to America, a contribution of labor, valor, and culture. One hears that argument repeated frequently in the Race press, from the pulpit and rostrum. America is reminded of the feats of Crispus Attucks, Peter Salem, black armies in the Revolution, the War of 1812, the Civil War, the Spanish-American War, the World War. Further, forgetful America is reminded that we sing without false notes, as borne out by the fact that there are no records of black traitors in the archives of American history. This is all well and good, but I believe it to be only half the story.

We play more than a minority role, in singing "America." Although numerically but 10 per cent of the mammoth chorus that today, with an eye overseas, sings "America" with fervor and thanksgiving, I say our 10 per cent is the very heart of the chorus: the sopranos, so to speak, carrying the melody, the rhythm section of the band, the violins, pointing the way.

I contend that the Negro is the creative voice of America, is creative America, and it was a happy day in America when the first unhappy slave was landed on its shores.

There, in our tortured induction into this "land of liberty," we built its most graceful civilization. Its wealth, its flowering fields and handsome homes; its pretty traditions; its guarded leisure and its music, were all our creations.

We stirred in our shackles and our unrest awakened Justice in the hearts of a courageous few, and we recreated in America the desire for true democracy, freedom for all, the brotherhood of man, principles on which the country had been founded.

We were freed and as before, we fought America's wars, provided her labor, gave her music, kept alive her flickering conscience, prodded her on toward the yet unachieved goal, democracy—until we became more than a part of America! We—this kicking, yelling, touchy, sensitive, scrupulously-demanding minority—are the personification of the ideal begun by the Pilgrims almost 350 years ago.

It is our voice that sang "America" when America grew too lazy, satisfied and confident to sing . . . before the dark threats and fire-lined clouds of destruction frightened it into a thin, panicky quaver.

We are more than a few isolated instances of courage, valor, achievement. We're the injection, the shot in the arm, that has kept America and its forgotten principles alive in the fat and corrupt years intervening between our divine conception and our near tragic present.

39. Interview in Los Angeles: On *Jump for Joy*, Opera, and Dissonance as a "Way of Life" (1941)

Ellington took special pride in *Jump for Joy*, describing it in his memoirs as the "first social significance show."[1] The revue opened 10 July 1941 at the Mayan Theater in Los Angeles and closed nearly twelve weeks later on 27 September. As Ellington explained, the show was intended to "take Uncle Tom out of the theatre, eliminate the stereotyped image that had been exploited by Hollywood and Broadway, and say things that would make the audience think."[2]

During the run of *Jump for Joy* Ellington stayed at the Dunbar Hotel. Interviewed there by reporter John Pittman, Ellington discussed the challenge of writing a musical and touched upon other current projects.

The article's final section describing Ellington's method of composing for specific players—a topic explored elsewhere in this volume[3]—has been omitted. Two intriguing sentences, however, bear quoting: "Youngest member [of the Ellington band] is young Billy Strayhorn, a pianist who is writing a thesis for a degree in music from the Pittsburgh Conservatory [*recte* Pittsburgh Musical Institute]. His thesis will be called 'Ellingtonian Orchestration.'" It is not known whether Strayhorn actually undertook or ever finished this project.

When Edward Kennedy Ellington came to San Francisco this week to head the stage show at the Golden Gate Theater, that was big news in the entertainment world. It's always big news in the entertainment world of every city— here and abroad—when the Duke arrives. Ellington's name is a synonym for the best in modern popular music. To attempt to "gild the lily" would be presumptuous.

Yet, there are certain aspects of Ellington's work, several sides of the man himself, which are not generally known, but which entitle him to the respect of his fellows and the high place he holds in the theater far more than the popular success of his band.

What one senses first about the Duke, once the ice of formality has been broken, is a person of considerable stature as a man.

One has to look for this, because Ellington has acquired the knack of

Source: John Pittman, "The Duke Will Stay on Top!" Unidentified clipping, probably San Francisco, August or September 1941.

[1] *MM*, 460.
[2] *MM*, 175.
[3] See, for example, §§20, 22, 37, 53, and 63.

interviewing the interviewer, and unless you're on guard, you'll do most of the talking yourself.

What strikes you most forcibly after penetrating the Duke's carefully guarded exterior is the man's genuine humility, his capacity for work—and for growth.

Ellington, mind you, has played for European royalty and American economic royalty. He was a "success" several years ago. But you won't learn that from Ellington. He is always asking for your opinion on his work, no matter whether you are Winthrop Rockefeller or a member of the Los Angeles dog-catching department.

"Some bands make a name and settle back," he says. "They get in a rut and soon they're finished."

No danger of the Duke's band ever doing that. Every new idea enters the sieve of his brain, to come out in some form or other in his latest composition. And the value of a new idea is tested by hours and days of experimentation, study, practice, rehearsal.

The Duke works like a longshoreman loading tanks for the Red Army. His apartment in the Dunbar Hotel in Los Angeles looked like a work shop. Sheets of music, finished and half-finished compositions, trays of cigarette butts, a piano and a record-playing machine, records and more records, pencil stubs!

"Sorry the place looks like this," he said at noon on Sunday. "I just got to bed."

He was as suave in a silk dressing gown as in the white sports suit he wore on the stage of the Mayan Theater.

"I'm pretty much at it these days. Three jobs, you see. 'Jump for Joy,' a film with Orson Welles, and a job of my own. Then there's the band and rehearsals."

He elaborated.

"'Jump for Joy' provided quite a few problems. There was the first and greatest problem of trying to give an American audience entertainment without compromising the dignity of the Negro people. Needless to say, this is the problem every Negro artist faces. He runs afoul of offensive stereotypes, instilled in the American mind by whole centuries of ridicule and derogation. The American audience has been taught to expect a Negro on the stage to clown and 'Uncle Tom,' that is, to enact the role of a servile, yet lovable, inferior."

This problem worried the Duke no end. How to present the Negro as he is, without sacrificing entertainment features, was his principal objective in producing "Jump for Joy." . . .

The same motive characterized his interest in the Welles film. He was writing the third part of the film with Welles, tracing the history of Jazz to the Negro, and featuring the life of Louis Armstrong, King of Trumpeteers [sic].[4]

---

[4] The film project with Welles, to be called *It's All True*, was never finished. Ellington took up the same story, however, in 1956 with *A Drum Is a Woman*. See Patricia Willard's essay accompanying the *Jump for Joy* recording issued by the Smithsonian (LPR 037), 23–24.

But it was mainly in his "own special job" that something else about the character of Ellington was revealed. This something else is the fact that Ellington is a "race man."

That term speaks volumes to America's 15,000,000 Negroes. It means national loyalty, patriotism, devotion to the ideals of the nation. Ellington is all of those things. Another way of putting it is to say that the Duke is no Uncle Tom. He abhors "Uncle Tomism." He deeply resents any slur against the Negro people. He respects his nation. He works to make this respect universal.

His "special job" is an opera. It is the story of the Negro people. It traces the history of this great nation from its beginnings here through chattel slavery, reconstruction, to the present.

Ellington is still working on this opera. He is looking for ideas. He admits having trouble in representing the Negro American as he is today, what he wants, what he's got, what he's tried to get and didn't, how he is going to get it.

This is something only a very few people have been able to do in prose. Imagine its difficulty in song and music!

That the Duke will finish his opera, and that it will fulfill its purpose, seems to be in the cards. Because Ellington's humility and capacity for work are implemented by certain other characteristics which virtually guarantee continuing achievements in his field.

Between the bowl of peaches and pears—they are his favorite breakfast— and the coffee and cigarette, Ellington revealed these other characteristics of his work and his life.

To an observation that his music was distinguished by its preoccupation with dissonance, he gave an illustrated "lecture" on his theory of music.

As the recording machine played one of his most recent compositions, a combination of Cuban music and the unmistakable Ellington rhythm, he talked about dissonance.[5]

"That's the Negro's life," he said. "Hear that chord!"—he set the needle back to replay the chord—"That's us."

"Dissonance is our way of life in America. We are something apart, yet an integral part."

Perhaps he didn't know it, but he was expressing the political theory which most realistically defines the concept of "nation within a nation," that is, the political status of Negro Americans.

"Then you believe the Negro's contribution to music can be traced back to the culture of African people?"

"Yes and no. Occasionally a strain breaks through that sounds primitive.

[5] The piece might have been *Bakiff* (1941), composed by Ellington's valve trombonist Juan Tizol, Ellington's *The Flaming Sword* (1940), or possibly *Conga Brava* (1940) or *Moon Over Cuba* (1941), both Ellington–Tizol collaborations.

But Negro music is American. It developed out of the life of the people here in this country."

This seemed a profound observation, not the sort of idea that would come from a man whose work had consisted chiefly of writing pleasing popular compositions. It distinguishes the Duke from the majority of other popular band leaders. . . .

V. *Black, Brown and Beige* (1943)

Since the early thirties Ellington had spoken of plans to write a large piece depicting the story of blacks in America.[1] The work was described variously as a suite or an opera—*Down Beat,* in fact, announced in 1938 that he had completed an opera after working on it for the past six years, one that dealt with "the history of the American Negro, starting with the Negro back in the jungles of Africa, and following through to the modern Harlemite."[2]

The announcement was premature. With the premiere of *Black, Brown and Beige,* however, on 23 January 1943, Ellington finally realized his long-stated goal. The work marked an auspicious occasion, Ellington's debut at Carnegie Hall, which in turn culminated New York's celebration of "Ellington Week," from 17–23 January. Proceeds from the concert went to Russian War Relief. The event was highly publicized, with celebrities and jazz fans filling the hall and many of New York's music critics reviewing the concert afterward, devoting special attention to Ellington's ambitious new piece.

Other jazz and popular musicians, of course, had already performed in Carnegie Hall: the black bandleader James Reese Europe and his Clef Club Orchestra in 1912–1914, Benny Goodman's orchestra in 1938, and various jazz, blues, and gospel artists in the two "Spirituals to Swing" concerts produced by John Hammond in 1938 and 1939. But Ellington's debut marked the first time a major black composer would present an evening of original music in New York's most prestigious concert hall. Moreover, this was a black composer who worked in the jazz idiom and whose works usually were heard in nightclubs, ballrooms, and theaters rather than in temples of high art.

The story of *Black, Brown and Beige*—its musical content, critical reception, and subsequent revisions over the years—forms one of the most fascinating chapters in the Ellington saga. Some of the issues it raised and controversies it sparked emerge in the following articles, which span three decades, ranging from previews and reviews in 1943 to later evaluations by Robert Crowley in 1959 and by Brian Priestley and Alan Cohen in the mid-seventies.

The orchestra that performed *Black, Brown and Beige* had undergone several recent personnel changes. Veteran clarinetist Barney Bigard left in July 1942, his chair taken by Chauncey Haughton (who would be replaced by Jimmy Hamilton in May 1943). Harold "Shorty" Baker joined in October 1942, expanding Ellington's trumpet section to four. New vocalists included Betty Roché (featured in the "Blues" section of *Black, Brown and Beige*) and Jimmy Britton. An important new figure working behind the scenes was Tom Whaley, who in 1941 took over the demanding copying chores from trombonist Juan Tizol.

---

[1] See, for example, his 1930 interview in the *New York Evening Graphic* (§8) and Wilder Hobson's "Introducing Duke Ellington" (§20).
[2] "Ellington Completes Negro Opera at Bedside," *Down Beat* (October 1938), 2.

40. Previews of the First Carnegie Hall Concert (1943)

Two articles previewing Ellington's first Carnegie Hall concert emphasized different aspects of the event.

In *Down Beat,* Helen Oakley focused on the major new work to be unveiled, here titled simply "A Tone Parallel" with its three movements identified as "Black, Brown and Beige." Plans for the concert were still taking shape, as two items toward the end indicate. First, Ellington apparently intended to write a portrait of the black entertainer Florence Mills featuring saxophonist Johnny Hodges. Instead, probably under time pressure, he used *Black Beauty* of 1928 for the purpose, placing it after his 1940 portraits of comedian Bert Williams and dancer Bill "Bojangles" Robinson. Second, Oakley stated that three pieces by Billy Strayhorn would be featured: "dirge, folk dance and light jump." The Carnegie Hall program listed the second of these as "Nocturne," but as it turned out, only *Dirge* and the "light jump"—otherwise known as *Johnny Come Lately* (1942)—were played.

Writing for the *New York Times Magazine,* Howard Taubman provided a basic introduction to Ellington and his working methods. Even after Ellington's triumphant European tours in 1933 and 1939, some *Times* readers, it seems, may have been unfamiliar with Ellington and his music. Taubman visited Ellington at home in Harlem and captured a sense of the controlled chaos preceding the Carnegie debut.[1]

In the version of Taubman's article presented below, two sections of biographical summary have been omitted.

Helen Oakley (Dance) in *Down Beat*

On the 23rd of January, 1943, Duke Ellington is contracted to appear on the stage of New York's Carnegie Hall to perform an initial American concert presentation of his own works. The occasion will mark the first public performance of the long attended, widely discussed *Tone Parallel,* the latest and to date most significant work yet delivered from the pen of the famed negro composer.

Because of the sharp musical interest and discerning attention which always have been noticeable features of the English and European receptions accorded the American Duke, the latter admits to a preference to a continental audience. "They exhibit," he says, "a surprisingly keen interest in what we are attempt-

Sources: Helen M. Oakley, "Ellington to Offer 'Tone Parallel,'" *Down Beat* (15 January 1943), 13; Howard Taubman, "The 'Duke' Invades Carnegie Hall," *New York Times Magazine* (17 January 1943), 10, 30.

[1] See also Leonard Feather's description of the concert and its preparations in his liner notes to *The Duke Ellington Carnegie Hall Concerts, January 1943* (Prestige CD 34004-2 or LP P-34004).

ing to do." He adds, with an engaging smile, "and more surprising still, they are generally aware of our short-comings and successes. Audiences of such caliber are an inspiration. We're stimulated to superior performance by their sound musical intelligence."

Unlike the [Benny] Goodman offering and those of others in the dance field who have advanced on Carnegie, the Ellington performance will be a serious program hailing the attention of Carnegie's customary patrons.[2] Regardless of the box-office returns, if a sincere interest and an intellectual discernment are not notably factors of the New York audience reaction, it will be, Duke Ellington is quoted as saying, a great disappointment to him and he considers a deterrent to the ambition of all progressing American musicians. In his most recent contribution to American music, *A Tone Parallel* written expressly for the concert and concerning which wide-spread interest has been evinced by critic and public alike, the renowned musician-composer, celebrated for his *American Lullaby, Blue Bell[e]s of Harlem, Reminiscing in Tempo, Solitude* and *Sophisticated Lady,* introduces a pioneer form.[3]

Acknowledging an aversion to identifying [his] music . . . with any accepted classic form, Duke designates his latest work a *Tone Parallel.* It is to be presented in three movements, but he emphasizes, this construction has been used simply because it satisfactorily lent itself to the presentation of his ideas. "The things we use," Ellington says, "are purely Negroid—we want to stay in character. We are, in the final analysis, the only serious exponents of Negro music."

Disclaiming the symphonic idea on the grounds such a designation implies complex orchestration involving 110 pieces, he states his *Tone Parallel* may be conceived a symphony only inasmuch as a symphony involving no more than 16 pieces can be conceived. "We are not attempting," he clarifies, "to produce a magnificent affair. We desire to remain true to self. The music was inspired by the character of the playing of the men in the band and is characteristic of ourselves, and we hope, of the saga which motivates our effort. Quite simply, we are weaving a musical thread which runs parallel to the history of the American Negro."

Designating the three movements of the *Tone Parallel,* Black, Brown and Beige, in the first, the composer advances two themes, the Work Song and the Spiritual. The second movement is punctuated by four short fanfares which represent war, the four wars which occur during the time-span represented— the Revolutionary, the Civil, the Spanish-American and World War No. I. Following the fanfare introducing the Revolutionary War, a first theme is ushered in displaying the strong West Indian influence predominant throughout this period.

The fanfare heralding the Civil War assumes the proportions of a gigantic rocket which, ultimately spluttering into a thousand pinpoints of color, represents the countless, conglomerate aspects of mood, of station, of life itself

[2] Benny Goodman's celebrated 16 January 1938 concert had featured his orchestra's regular repertory, together with standard jazz instrumentals and arrangements of popular songs.
[3] See below in Oakley's text for descriptions of *American Lullaby* and *Blue Belles of Harlem.*

which incorporated, made up the turbulent aftermath which sequelled the awesome Civil struggle. The predominant musical note struck here is that of humor, light laughter-ringing pathos sounded only in the strain of bewilderment and fear involved by the frightened old folk, told to go free and uncomprehending where or how to proceed.

The third theme is a blues strain that depicts the heartaches and sorrow that ensued from the "love-triangles" which characterized the post-war conditions of a battle-scarred nation. The second movement is climaxed finally in the upheaval that signals World War No. I and the calm of exhaustion that succeeded it, when the American Negro found time to stop and think.

In the third movement a subtle and sophisticated mood is introduced. A purposeful false theme signals what Ellington phraseology terms "the recognition of the Harlem Hotcha," the profound inculcation impressed at that time upon public opinion, the musical note sounded as blatant, noisy, fictitious. Musical portraiture of a boisterous and chaotic care-freedom symbolizes the erroneous conception of the American Negro then universally entertained.

Progressively the looming hilarity is dispersed in the findings of research and understanding which reveal the race, in general, bent on education and culture, spiritual and material. It is revealed there are more churches in Harlem than the vaunted cabarets. The people respond not at all to the tom-tom, the schools claim their allegiance. "Without," Duke Ellington says, "enough food, with no clothes at all, with hardly a roof over his head, even the poorest sharecropper struggles to put his kids through school."

The penultimate musical strain comes down to earth. A deep sincerity advances the motif, a note instinct with strength, stability and purpose. Progressively, the melodies from the first movement are brought forward, complimenting [sic] the sum of the present with the strains of the traits and heritages that went before, and here, in the complex interchange of melody and counter-melodies, the confusion of the struggle of solidarity is revealed. While wish advances on fulfillment, yet again America, the native land, finds herself thrown into war and, as always in the past, the true spirit of the American Negro rises once more to protect the flag. The magnificent Black, Brown and Beige again prove themselves to be Red, White and Blue and the *Tone Parallel* moves on to its close.[4]

In addition to premiering the widely-discussed *Parallel* which is presently scheduled to precede the half-way programatic [sic] break, Duke Ellington will perform his *American Lullaby,* occasioned originally in the demand for American forms by ten American composers and commissioned into being together with offerings from the pens of Ferde Grofé, [Peter] DeRose and many others. Conducting the L.A. Philharmonic in the Hollywood Bowl, Meredith Willson [recte Wilson] recently performed this entire sequence of works with signal success, subsequently recording them. Duke will also present the band in his own *Blue Bell[e]s of Harlem* which was written at the request of Paul Whiteman on the occasion of the latter's 1938 Carnegie performance.

---

[4] A section in which singer Jimmy Britton proclaimed "Black, Brown and Beige" for the "Red, White and Blue" was cut before the premiere (*DE*, 250–51).

Three portraitures will also be included in the Ellington program. Those of Bert Williams and Bill Robinson [*A Portrait of Bert Williams* and *Bojangles,* both 1940] are known already to the public, and the third, a portrait inspired by the memory of Florence Mills and designed to feature Johnny Hodges, has been written expressly for this occasion. Also commissioned for initial performance will be three compositions, dirge, folk dance and light jump, from the pen of the youthful Ellington protégé, Billy Strayhorn. In addition, as wind-up, there will be characteristic display of Ellington band virtuosity.

The program notes are to be authored by Irving Kolodin, music critic with the *New York Sun.* Scheduled also to perform in Boston at Symphony Hall on January 28, Ellington will likely present, excepting a few minor changes, his full Carnegie program. A third concert appearance for the band has been set for the stage of the Municipal Auditorium in Cleveland, Ohio, on the evening of February 20.

Howard Taubman in the *New York Times Magazine*

When Edward Kennedy Ellington, known everywhere as Duke Ellington, and his band invade Carnegie Hall next Saturday evening in a concert for Russian War Relief, Bach, Beethoven and Brahms will have to step aside for jazz. But not for the first time. Paul Whiteman, Benny Goodman, Fats Waller, John Kirby, Eddie Condon and many others, including scat singers and disciples of boogie-woogie, have proved that now and then the old masters have to make room for an indigenous American art in their traditional precincts. . . .

The name of Ellington has become a trade-mark for the best in jazz. Duke does not know how many pieces he has written. Asked to hazard a guess, he thought, "Maybe a thousand." A member of the band exclaimed, "Naw, nearer five thousand!" Ellington and his band have made something like 10,000 [*recte ca.* 650] master recordings, many especially for European markets. Ardent fans have been gathering in Ellington disks from the start, and the early ones are collectors' items, like the first recordings of Caruso.

Ellington's music and band must be discussed as a unit, for they have been made for each other during the past twenty years. Though it may shock the idolaters of the masters, it is fair to say that Ellington is a composer in the tradition of Bach and Haydn. The eighteenth-century masters wrote most of their music for specific occasions, for performances by themselves and ensembles under their leadership and often under pressure of a deadline. That's the way Ellington works. His public wants new pieces. Ellington turns them out at the last minute. He writes them only with his own band in mind.

Even the copying out of the parts of a new Ellington composition is reminiscent of the way Bach is supposed to have worked. Bach's sons copied out parts even as their father composed. Members of Duke's band sat up with him through an all-night session, as he wrote a fairly long new piece, and extracted the parts for the individual players as fast as Duke set down the music on the master score. Several times, when Duke's muse seemed to be slowing up, his copyists jogged him, "C'mon, Duke," they said, "you're holding us up." And Ellington worked a little faster.

Ellington's music can be hot and it can be languid. It can blaze and it can be insinuating. It is always distinctive, made with subtlety and with a tremendous flair for rhythm and color. The hepcats say that over the years he has had the highest average for being "groovey." They call him "a terrific character." A learned critic of The Times of London [reviewing a June 1933 performance at the Palladium] phrased it more seriously ten years ago: "Mr. Duke Ellington is exceptionally and remarkably efficient in his own line. . . . And the excitement and exacerbation of the nerves which are caused by the performances of his orchestra are the more disquieting by reason of his complete control and precision. It is not an orgy but a scientific application of measured and dangerous stimuli."

Ellington's acceptance as an ace practitioner of his art by low brow and high gives him the right to an opinion on the directions of jazz. It took some time to get his opinion, because on the day of my visit to his apartment in Harlem he was still asleep at 1 p.m. He had worked all the previous night, knocking off at 9 a.m. Since the band had had a night off, Duke had spent it writing music for the Carnegie Hall concert. The piano was still in the corridor where it had been pushed so as not to disturb members of his family. Sheets of freshly written music were on the piano, under the telephone, in the living room. As we chatted, members of Ellington's band drifted in, and from the kitchen they could be heard humming parts of the new score and arguing over how to do it.

The Duke is a husky fellow, with a chuckle in his eyes and a hearty, friendly manner. Obviously he can be playful, but he spoke seriously of the directions of "jazz" and "swing," though he helped to give the latter term currency when he wrote a piece in 1931 entitled, "It Don't Mean a Thing If It Ain't Got That Swing." He prefers to call his own work "Negro music."

"Our band came along," he said, "just when Paul Whiteman and his orchestra had popularized the symphonic style. And don't let them kid you about Whiteman. He has been a big man in our music. He's done a lot for it, especially with his concerts where he gave composers a chance to write new, extended works.

"But as I was saying, we came in with a new style. Our playing was stark and wild and tense. That's the way our boys had to play, and we planned our music that way. We tried new effects. One of our trombones turned up one night with an ordinary kitchen pot for his sliphorn. It sounded good. We let him keep it, until we could get him a handsome gadget that gave him the same effects.

"We put the Negro feeling and spirit in our music. We were not the first to do that, but maybe we added some more. We did it in a different way. Other bands came along later and did similar things, though not quite the same. Now some of them play pretty much as we do. Once in a while I tune in on a band, and for a few measures I think it's us."

Ellington believes that dance music has its cycles and keeps changing in small ways from one year to the next.

"It has calmed down lately," he said. "The hotcha period is out for a while. Maybe because of the war, maybe because that was coming anyhow. Our music is still plenty hot, but more subtly so."

He has the utmost faith in the future of this music. He believes that it has already played a big part in all music. He says he has heard "hot jazz in Stravinsky and other long-haired composers." He contends that there may be some combination of the classic and the jazz forms in the post-war world which will be a landmark in American music.

"One thing's sure," he said, "it will be original.". . .

Ellington does not write for choirs—saxes, trumpets, trombones—as others do. Each member of the orchestra has a different part, written for his particular style and talents. I saw the parts of a new composition. They were not marked for the instrument but with the name of the player; Barney [Bigard], Juan [Tizol], Chauncey [Haughton], Johnny [Hodges], Rex [Stewart], etc. Sometimes Duke jots down a few chords, and brings them in to a session and lets the boys go to work on them. Some of the bandsmen write music, and Duke's son, Mercer, now in the Army, composes.

Ellington's most elaborate composition is an opera, still unproduced, called "Boola." It deals with the history of the Negro in America, a subject on which Duke has read extensively. He has taken some of the music from this opera and turned it into a half-hour tone poem for his band, and he will unveil it at Carnegie Hall. It is called, "Black, Brown and Beige." The first movement tells of the sorrows and joys of the Negro on first being brought, in slavery, to the colonies. Here Duke uses work songs and spirituals. In the second movement Duke deals with the recurring hopes and disappointments between American wars—the whippings, the escapes, the emancipation, the hardships, Jim Crowism; in other words, alternations of jubilation and blues. The last movement sings of Harlem, and Duke does not like the conventional attitude toward this part of our town.

"I always say," he says, "that there are more churches in Harlem than cabarets. The Negro is not merely a singing and dancing wizard but a loyal American in spite of his social position. I want to tell America how the Negro feels about it."

41. Program for the First
Carnegie Hall Concert (23 January 1943)

llington's Carnegie Hall debut was subtitled, "Twentieth Anniversary Concert," a reference to 1923 when the Washingtonians first came to New York and opened at the Kentucky Club (at the time still called the Hollywood).

The actual performance departed from the printed program in a number of ways: the national anthem preceded *Black and Tan Fantasy*; *Moon Mist* replaced *Blue Serge*; *Ko-Ko* replaced *The Flaming Sword*; Strayhorn's *Nocturne* was deleted; *Boy Meets Horn*, a feature

Source: Program for the Ellington orchestra's 23 January 1943 Carnegie Hall concert, Duke Ellington Collection, Smithsonian.

DUKE ELLINGTON AND HIS ORCHESTRA

Twentieth Anniversary Concert

CARNEGIE HALL

New York

Saturday Evening, January 23, 1943

at 8:45 o'clock

Proceeds for Russian War Relief

PROGRAM

I.

Black and Tan Fantasy	Ellington-Miley
Rockin' in Rhythm	Ellington-Carney
Blue Serge	Mercer Ellington
Jumpin' Punkins	Mercer Ellington

II.

Portrait of Bert Williams	Ellington
Portrait of Bojangles	
Portrait of Florence Mills	

III.

Black, Brown and Beige	Ellington
(A Tone Parallel to the History of the Negro in America.)	

—— Intermission ——

IV.

The Flaming Sword	Ellington
Dirge	Billy Strayhorn
Nocturne	
Stomp	

V.

Are You Stickin'?	Ellington
(Chauncey Haughton, clarinet)	
Bakiff	Tizol
(Juan Tizol, valve trombone; Ray Nance, violin)	
Jack the Bear	Ellington
(Alvin Raglin, string bass)	
Blue Belles of Harlem	Ellington
(Duke Ellington, piano)	
Cotton Tail	Ellington
(Ben Webster, tenor saxophone)	
Day Dream	Ellington-Strayhorn
(Johnny Hodges, alto saxophone)	
Rose of the Rio Grande	Warren-Gorman-Leslie
(Lawrence Brown, trombone)	
Trumpet in Spades	Ellington
(Rex Stewart, cornet)	

VI.

Don't Get Around Much Any More	Ellington
Goin' Up	
Mood Indigo	

(Duke Ellington and his orchestra are under the exclusive management of the William Morris Agency, Inc.)

A NOTE ON ELLINGTON

By Irving Kolodin

The twenty years of Edward Kennedy Ellington which are embodied in this concert comprise one of the most remarkable careers in American music. Whether it concerns the plaintive "Mood Indigo" or the elegant "Sophisticated Lady" which have become a part of the mass culture of this country, or the more intricate works which have stirred what Ellington calls the "jive sages" to futile search for gaudy enough adjectives, it can scarcely be contested that his voice is an individual one, his touch utterly distinctive, his fertility and invention without parallel in the field in which he works.

Perhaps the very identity of Ellington with the day-to-day life of America over a period which embraces a boom, a depression and a second World War has led to an acceptance of him much too casual for his real importance. Whether Ellington is a greater composer than Delius, say, whom he greatly respects, this writer can't say definitively; but he will acknowledge that the very thought of Delius engenders a more imposing picture than that of a man who is a band-leader, who appears in vaudeville theatres and makes black label records.

As in the case of Poe, who received his first considered approbation in foreign lands, Ellington's worth has been proclaimed most insistently by such non-Americans as Percy Grainger; the English critic, conductor and composer Constant Lambert; the French *savant* of jazz Hugues Panassié. It would be grossly inaccurate to say that Ellington is without honor in his native land, but it is our foreign brethren who have been mostly completely convinced that he is a prophet.

Virtually all the music to be heard tonight is the product of Ellington, his disciple-arranger Billy Strayhorn, or a member of the band. But the creative process involved has been the subject of so much misunderstanding and confusion that some clarification is in order.

The notion that most of the fine Ellington works are inspirations of the moment, in a recording studio while the wax is spinning, can be dismissed as a romantic idealization of a practical necessity. That necessity involves the character of the music itself, and the fact that the individual soloists in the band are encouraged to express their particular strain of talent within the structure of an idea which Ellington has conceived. Thus it may be said that an idea which occurs to Ellington is developed according to his knowledge of what a certain soloist can do with it—without saying that the idea, per se, belongs to them.

On the other side, a certain group of pieces, such as "Rockin' in Rhythm" on this program, have emerged from ideas conceived by one or another members of the band. These men themselves, however, are frank to admit that the molding and shaping that goes on under Ellington's direction produces something which would be quite beyond the capacity of any single musician, working independently. The subjective result of all this is that the performances are intensely personal, in a way that formal music knows nothing about.

This concert tonight then, as well as exemplifying the amount of real feeling and artistry that can be conveyed within the range of Negro music, also portrays the kind of creative effort that would be in force were conditions adjusted for it. As much individual effort as is contained in a given piece, it is still the sum of the creative energy of nearly twenty men, working together for a common purpose.

161

NOTES ON THE PROGRAM

By IRVING KOLODIN

BLACK AND TAN FANTASY **Ellington-Miley**

In its first form, "Black and Tan" dates to a period more than fifteen years removed in Ellington's output. I say in its "first" form, for it has since given rise to at least two descendants: "Prologue to Black and Tan Fantasy" and "New Black and Tan Fantasy." Moody and mournful, it has deep overtones of sadness which give it cause to be called "Basic" Ellington. After the opening piano and clarinet duet, the band contributes to a steady surge of feeling which culminates in an ironic quotation of a theme certainly appropriate to these surroundings. (N.B. It's by Chopin). The first form of the work was strongly influenced by the great trumpet player "Bubber" Miley who was then a member of the Ellington band, and given a part-credit for composition on the first recordings.

ROCKIN' IN RHYTHM **Ellington-Carney**

One of the most celebrated of Ellington recordings was of a tune by himself called "It Don't Mean a Thing If It Ain't Got that Swing." His use of the term antedated the current popularization of it by at least three or four years—and such a piece as this shows why. The "Rock" is unmistakable and so is the "Rhythm." The currently celebrated band-leader Harry James acknowledged to me that the idea for the tune "Peckin'" with which he achieved his first fame about 1936, came from this piece, though the association may be obscure in the arrangement played tonight. Harry Carney, the fine baritone sax player, had the original idea from which this piece evolved.

BLUE SERGE **Mercer Ellington**

In a direct baronial line, the twenty-three year old son of "Duke" Ellington should perhaps have become known as "Earl" Ellington; but Mercer is his baptismal name. However, he can offer, in a line of succession, the talent manifested in this pair of pieces attributed to him. The first, with its rather deceptively non-committal title, pursues a languid course, in which a tenor saxophone solo is the prominent feature.

JUMPIN' PUNKINS **Mercer Ellington**

Though Ellington, Sr., is known essentially as a composer and band-leader, he is a pianist of distinctive style and individual inclinations. That much is indicated in the opening strain of this piece, which is in what our British friends call "tempo"—meaning a gentle bounce gait that engages the attention without exciting it. Bass and piano are conspicuous throughout, if the amount of discretion embodied in this playing can be called "conspicuous."

PORTRAITS

BERT WILLIAMS **Ellington**

This group of pieces represents a new departure for the talent of Ellington—new, that is, as of the period when the first two were recorded, about two years ago. It seems fair to say that the great Negro actor and comedian never enjoyed such a background piece for his pantomime as Ellington has created in this whimsical, concise estimate of his unforgettable talent. One can almost visualize him shuffling onto the stage of the Palace to its opening strains, and easing into the marvellous pantomime of a poker game which was one of his most brilliant creations.

BOJANGLES **Ellington**

"Bojangles" is, of course, the unaging Mayor of Harlem and points west, the nimble Bill Robinson of the mischievous feet. All that is needed to complete this picture is the tip-titled derby of the buoyant Bill, his balance-wheel of a cane, the dry tap of his feet on a hardwood floor. But lacking those, one can fairly see him in this agile, sharpwitted piece with its one line of thought and positive good humor.

FLORENCE MILLS **Ellington**

To complete this tryptich of "Portraits," Ellington has revived a piece originally titled "Black Beauty" as suitable to the character of the fine singer Florence Mills who died within the last few years. In its altered form the main feature is a trumpet solo which leads the band.

BLACK, BROWN AND BEIGE **Ellington**

This newest work of Ellington, and the most ambitious of his career, has its inception in an unproduced opera which has been stirring in his mind since 1932. The title "Boola" is exemplary of the work as a whole, for "Boola" is the term Negroes use to symbolize the perpetual spirit of the race through time. Thus when a discussion of some important phase of American history is under way—Valley Forge, for example—one of the group is sure to say: "Yes, 'Boola' was there all right"—referring to some heroic Negro little known to the white man who made a valiant contribution to the Revolutionary cause.

In this "tone parallel to the history of the American Negro," three main periods of Negro evolution are projected against a background of the nation's history. "Black" depicts the period from 1620 to the Revolutionary War, when the Negro was brought from his homelands, and sold into slavery. Here he developed the "work" songs, to assuage his spirit while he toiled; and then the "spirituals" to foster his belief that there was a reward after death, if not in life. "Brown" covers the period from the Revolution to the first World War, and shows the emergence of the Negro heroes who rose to the needs of these critical phases of our national history. "Beige" brings us to the contemporary scene, and comments on the common misconception of the Negro which has left a confused impression of his true character and abilities. The climax reminds us that even though the Negro is "Black, Brown and Beige," he is also "Red, White and Blue"—asserting the same loyalty that characterized him in the days when he fought for those who enslaved him.

A musical synopsis of "Black, Brown and Beige" must account for the following factors, as guides to the programatic ideas the work embodies:

Black:

Work songs first—different songs according to different kinds of work—driving spikes, piling cotton, simple housework. A baritone saxophone solo by Harry Carney is prominent in this section, and finally the "tired out" work song, on the trombone of "Tricky Sam" Nanton.

The spirituals arise out of what the composer describes as the "Church Window" mood—the Negroes looked in from outside, but the windows were pretty, anyway. Toby Hardwicke's saxophone sets this mood. The full spiritual theme comes from muted brass, restated by the valve trombone and developed by the alto sax of Johnny Hodges against an inspired background of guitar and bass. All the themes, work and spiritual, are combined in the final section.

Brown:

The purpose of marking the wars of the past here is to bring out the Negro heroes who have participated in each. The Revolutionary war is suggested, then followed by the introduction of the West Indian influence, an important one to the whole Negro character. Two trumpets and a trombone are utilized here. "Swanee River" and "Yankee Doodle" are cited to establish the period of the Civil War. Emancipation was not an unmixed blessing, for it left the older Negroes with freedom but no security. A duet of baritone and tenor saxes tells the story of the old people's attitude toward Emancipation. Trombone and trumpet (Nanton and Stewart) take up the younger folk's happier side. Out of the Spanish-American war period and the emergence of the Negro into urban life comes the Blues, expressed through the voice of Betty Roche. The Ellington text is sufficiently noteworthy to be reproduced here:

"The Blues . . . .
The Blues ain't . . . .
The Blues ain't nothing . . . .
The Blues ain't nothing but a cold grey day
And all night long it stays that way."

"The Blues . . . .
The Blues don't . . . .
The Blues don't know . . . .
The Blues don't know nobody as a friend
Ain't been nowhere where they're welcome back again."
(Saxes cry out, trombone wails, trumpets bark on the theme of "Low, ugly mean blues.")

"The Blues ain't sump'n that you sing in rhyme
The Blues ain't nothin' but a dark cloud markin' time

The Blues is a one-way ticket from your love to nowhere
The Blues ain't nothing' but a black crepe veil ready to wear"
The Blues ain't nothin' . . . .
The Blues . . . ."

Beige:

This section brings the Negro from the World War down to the present. The Harlem of the '20s, hotcha, excitement, razz-ma-tazz, is mirrored in tom-toms and screaming brass, according to the common misconception that every Negro can sing wonderfully or dance phenomenally. We come closer to this Negro metropolis, to the tinkle of a piano in a gin mill. But, as Ellington says, there are more churches in Harlem than gin-mills. As for the Negro of the bands and the stage, Ellington has the epigram: "All they hear really is a few people trying to make a living." A waltz shows the striving to sophistication, but underneath is the clamor of feeling which is yet undisciplined according to European standards. It is a panorama of life—a longer "Harlem Air Shaft," showing the struggles for expression, the yearning for education which can rarely be used, the true straight line of the Negro's character which is too often turned aside and deflected by his surroundings. Finally, the voice of Jimmy Britton proclaims the theme of "Black, Brown and Beige," but still "Red, White and Blue."

THE FLAMING SWORD — Ellington

A stay at the Sherman House in Chicago provided the title for this work two or three years ago. It is a band piece, in a slightly Cuban rhythm, which exhibits the virtuosity of the orchestra as a whole.

DIRGE — NOCTURNE — STOMP — Strayhorn

Billy Strayhorn is the one talent of the day who has reacted to the genius of Ellington with comparable fervor and versatility. He is now 27 years old. Ellington found him in Pittsburgh in 1938, and gradually has worked him into the Ellington organization as arranger, some-time composer and handy-man. His assimilation of Ellington's mannerisms and his expression of them in ideas of his own has progressed to the point where members of the band can't be sure themselves whether a certain new creation is the work of Ellington or Strayhorn.

Fame knows him as the creator of such successes as "Take the 'A' Train," which has now become the orchestra's theme in theatre appearances, and "Chelsea Bridge." The titles of these new pieces are sufficiently explanatory to be intelligible without further annotation.

CONCERTOS

As many of the most famous sections of certain Ellington compositions were dictated by the talents of a certain performer in the band, so whole works have been built up around the personality of one virtuoso or another. These have come to be known among Ellingtonians as "concertos," in the sense that a single instrumentalist dominates the whole tonal scheme.

ARE YOU STICKIN'? Ellington

Originally conceived for the fluid clarinet of Barney Bigard, this piece is now played by Chauncey Haughton, a reed player of considerable distinction, who joined the Ellington ensemble last summer. It is in jump tempo, brightly maintained throughout.

BAKIFF Tizol

As well as being Ellington's choice as "my only extractor" (meaning that he can take a rough Ellington score and divine just what was meant to be written into each voice) Juan Tizol is a brilliant exponent of that odd instrument, the valve trombone. Here he is heard utilizing the flexibility permitted by the addition of valves to the slide trombone with great originality.

JACK THE BEAR Ellington

This is built around the solo bass, played by Junior Raglin. The original recording by the late, greatly admired Jimmy Blanton, is extended by a solo for the violinist Ray Nance.

BLUE BELLES OF HARLEM Ellington

As Ellington says, this piece features the "pianist in the band"—namely, Ellington himself. It was written in 1938 at the invitation of Paul Whiteman for a concert which that band-leader gave in this hall, and was part of a "Bells" suite distributed among various celebrated composers. It embodies a reflective mood, developed in an improvisatory spirit.

COTTON TAIL Ellington

Ben Webster's insistent saxophone is the motivating influence in this piece, which was written around it. It moves forcefully throughout, with the saxes battling brass and piano individually, and as a section.

DAY DREAM Ellington-Strayhorn

The lovely sensitive quality which Johnny Hodges draws from his alto saxophone—a truly unique sound in modern dance music—is here exploited fully. The mood of reverie in which Hodges excels is set off by the background provided by the band.

ROSE OF THE RIO GRANDE Warren-Gorman-Leslie

One is almost inclined to put a star beside this title, for it is the one work on the program which is not the creation of Ellington or one of his direct co-workers. However, it has come to be associated with the trombone playing of Lawrence Brown, one of the Ellington inseparables. In this version he takes two choruses, supplanting the vocal once sung by Ivy Anderson.

TRUMPET IN SPADES Ellington

In his career as a brilliant brass-man with Ellington, Rex Stewart has developed a unique technic on his instrument which is exemplified in this piece. By depressing the valve of his trumpet halfway, Stewart produces a strangulated, expressive sound which is usually associated with mechanical mutes or a plunger. Many trumpeters have imitated, without real success, the effects that Stewart produces in such a piece as this.

FINAL GROUP

DON'T GET AROUND MUCH ANY MORE Ellington

This work began its career as a Johnny Hodges specialty called "Never No Lament," under which title it still must be sought for in its recorded form. However its pure melodic quality and really distinctive construction led to a vocal version which resulted in the title noted above.

GOIN' UP Ellington

The forthcoming film "Cabin in the Sky," in which the Ellington band appeared, is the source of this piece, which embodies the virtuosity of the whole ensemble. It utilizes three tempos, beginning in a medium bounce, slowing down somewhat, and then picking up sharply at the conclusion. Piano, four trumpets, five saxes, the trombone of "Tricky Sam," Hodges, the ensemble, Lawrence Brown, Nance, Webster and Stewart all have a part in the succession of episodes.

MOOD INDIGO Ellington

This fitting conclusion to the record of Ellingtonia included on this program includes what the composer calls the "one new effect in modern dance music." By this he means the utilization of the special sound contributed by the early microphones (in use when the work was first recorded) to the whole sound that was heard. This "tone," which could not otherwise be isolated, was figured into the voicing of the instruments, and played a part in the final effect. Barney Bigard contributed the phrase which may be described as the "verse" of the piece—the contrasting arpeggiated idea.

for cornetist Rex Stewart, came in between *Day Dream* and *Rose of the Rio Grande; Trumpet in Spades* was dropped.[1]

The program annotator was Irving Kolodin (1908–1988), who a few years earlier had assisted Benny Goodman with his autobiography, *The Kingdom of Swing* (1939). At the time on the staff of the *New York Sun,* Kolodin later served as music critic for the *Saturday Review* from 1947 to 1982. While generally sympathetic toward Ellington, Kolodin expressed reservations about a composer "who is a band-leader, who appears in vaudeville theatres and makes black label records." The Ellington-Delius comparison was by now commonplace (see §28, note 3), but Kolodin stretched it further by claiming that Ellington "greatly respects" the English composer.

Except for the description of *Black, Brown and Beige,* presumably based on press materials, Kolodin's observations on individual pieces probably came from close listening to Ellington's recordings.

42. Two Reviews (1943)

 llington's Carnegie Hall debut drew extremely mixed reactions. While most critics acknowledged the orchestra's virtuosity and originality, a number expressed disappointment over Ellington's handling of large-scale composition.

One of the latter was the composer and writer Paul Bowles (b. 1910), who reviewed the event in the *New York Herald-Tribune.* Challenging the very notion of fusing "jazz as a form with art music," Bowles attacked Ellington's new work while praising the more familiar jazz and dance numbers.

In *Down Beat,* Mike Levin testified for the defense. Those who found fault with *Black, Brown and Beige,* wrote Levin, judged too quickly and lacked basic knowledge about both Ellington and jazz. Repeated listenings to recordings made during the Carnegie concert had convinced Levin that Ellington's new piece was a success, even while aspects of the performance could be criticized. Levin's argument relied more on emotional assertions than on informed musical commentary. But it plainly demonstrated how a concert intending to unite classical and jazz contingents instead had driven a wedge between them.

Levin also appended a detailed report on each selection played by the orchestra at the concert; it has been omitted here.

Paul Bowles in the *New York Herald-Tribune*

Duke Ellington is the only jazz musician whose programs have enough musical interest to be judged by the same standards one applies to art music. He is the composer of many of the finest popular melodies of the last fifteen years,

[1] A nearly complete recording of the concert is offered on *The Duke Ellington Carnegie Hall Concerts, January 1943.*

Sources: Paul Bowles, "Duke Ellington in Recital for Russian War Relief," *New York Herald-Tribune,* 25 January 1943; Mike Levin, "Duke Fuses Classical and Jazz!," *Down Beat* (15 February 1943), 12–13.

and he is the pianist, arranger and conductor of what has consistently been and still is the greatest jazz orchestra in the country. His conscious search for harmonies, rhythms and sonorities hitherto unused in jazz has been eminently successful, because he has a musically creative intelligence which has protected him from the pitfalls of commercialization. His greatest achievement is to have been able to invent tirelessly and incorporate his discoveries into the medium without his music losing the flavor, directness and dignity of early jazz.

Precisely because of all these things one expected more from the important number on Saturday evening's program, "Black, Brown and Beige (a tone parallel to the history of the Negro in America)." It lasted the better part of an hour and contained enough bright ideas for several short pieces. But presented as one number it was formless and meaningless. In spite of Mr. Ellington's ideological comments before each "movement," nothing emerged but a gaudy potpourri of tutti dance passages and solo virtuoso work. (The dance parts used some pretty corny riffs, too.) There were countless unprovoked modulations, a passage in 5/4, paraphrases on well-known tunes that were as trite as the tunes themselves, and recurrent climaxes that impeded the piece's progress. Between dance numbers there were "symphonic" bridges played out of tempo. This dangerous tendency to tamper with the tempo within a piece showed itself far too many times during the evening. If there is no regular beat, there can be no syncopation, and thus no tension, no jazz. The whole attempt to fuse jazz as a form with art music should be discouraged. The two exist at such different distance from the listener's faculties of comprehension that he cannot get them both clearly into focus at the same time. One might say they operate on different wave lengths; it is impossible to tune them in simultaneously.

Fortunately there were other things on the program. The arrangements, barring tempo changes, were, of course, excellent. Such numbers as "Rockin' in Rhythm," "Ko-Ko" and "Black Beauty" showed the band in all its glory. The instrumental give and take was never hysterical and the rhythms never jumpy or breathless. The saxes often played in unison, which eliminated the thick-sounding choir these instruments form in many bands.

There was Jimmy [sic] Hodges, whose perfect, smooth alto sax playing reached a high at the end of "Don't Get Around Much Any More." Rex Stewart did some superb musical clowning in a piece whose figures were based on the familiar noises made by a beginner on the cornet. Perhaps the most impressive solo playing was by Joe Nanton, who made his trombone sound like a protesting wild beast. He has always supplied more atmosphere for the band than any other one man.

The audience was so vociferous in its approval both during and after numbers that one could never hear the cadences.

Mike Levin in Down Beat

New York—Duke Ellington has taught me a lesson I'll never forget—namely, never blow your top before the third time over lightly. Three weeks ago he and his band gave a concert in Carnegie Hall. It lasted for three hours, including a 48 minute work entitled *Black, Brown and Beige*. At three minutes to 12, an exhausted audience filed out of the hall, each excitedly asking the other what his opinion was.

It was obvious that most were a little confused, but in general delighted with the last half of the program. Of *BBB*, the more honest ones said, "I don't get it." Others, vociferously liked certain portions, many, including ace musicians and writers, said it was a complete failure.

The critics said:

Robert Bagar *(World-Telegram)*: "It is too long a piece. . . . Mr. Ellington can make some two dozen brief, airtight compositions out of *BBB*. He should. . . . It is far from being an in toto symphonic creation."

John Briggs *(N.Y. Post)*: "Mr. Ellington was saying musically the same thing he had said earlier in the evening, only this time he took forty-five minutes to do it."

Paul Bowles *(N.Y. Herald-Tribune)*: "Formless and meaningless . . . Nothing but a potpourri of tutti dance passages and solo virtuoso work. The dance part used some pretty corny riffs too. . . . [1]

Henry Simon *(PM)*: "First movement all but falls to pieces . . . can't compare with the second movement . . . but there's no doubt of his importance to American music."

Abel Green (editor of *Variety,* a theatrical fan magazine, who after devoting his lead paragraph to disapproving of the band's uniforms in strict hep jive, went on to say): "A bit self-conscious, as these tone poems usually are . . . a bit fulsome . . ."

Irving Kolodin *(N.Y. Sun)*: "*Brown* and *Beige* were the best sections . . . *Black* needs a little trimming . . . One can only conclude that the work would be much better if scored for full orchestra with solo parts as indicated by Ellington."

And so on, much too far into the night.

With the exception of Kolodin, who wrote the program notes, none of these gentry know much about jazz and even less about Ellington other than that his brass men make unusual noises now and then. Bagar and Simon are acquainted with the stuff, and did their honest best. Others, not quoted here, wrote greater literary epics.

Abel Green came up with this gem: "For a different reaction to the performance of the band and its soloists, it was interesting to watch the faces of noted musicians. As the outstanding instrumentalists took solos, the auditors' feelings were plainly evident."

Abel was given New York City's fence-sitting trophy last month.

Maybe it isn't ethical to make cracks about other scribes. But I honestly feel that they made fools out of themselves, and were unfair as hell to Duke in the process.

I know—I made the same mistake.

Coming out of the concert, my first reaction was letdown. Too much music,

---

[1] Levin goes on to paraphrase a number of Bowles's sentences. See above for the original.

too much intermission chattering, [sent] me for some fresh air. Outside it started. Everybody was looking for an opinion, so they could be sure of what to think themselves. The well-known tunes were "wonderful" — *BBB* had wonderful ideas mind you, but was "formless, don't you think, Jack?"

That night I had heard things I liked — also things I didn't like. I didn't dig at least half of *Black,* and parts of the rest of the suite. And I wasn't sure that I understood what Duke was trying to do with the rest of the program.

I talked to musicians, arrangers, critics, record fans, and just people. They disagreed violently on the second half of the concert, a series of Duke's best-known records. But they all seemed to agree *BBB* had pretty ideas and nothing else.

So I oiled up the old portable and prepared to give Duke hell for betraying his public. Then I began to remember that the boss had never tried to pan a band without hearing it at least four times first. And that here was something much more complex musically than any dance band ever served up — which I was judging on one hearing at a jammed concert hall.

Brother, believe me, the gremlins had me but good. To pan the Duke, the most fertile figure in American music, or to duck the review completely. The boss wouldn't let me do the latter, and I hated like heck to do the former. The only answer was either that I had to write a pan, and a bad one at that, or prove my own opinion was wrong.

It was!

Danny James, Duke's manager, had a set of records made at the concert. Being a good guy, and also having a terrific laugh at the way I was squirming, he lent me the records. Since then, I have listened to that concert exactly six times over.

Anybody who says that *BBB* doesn't have form and continuity simply doesn't know what he's talking about. That's no question of opinion or anything controversial. That's a question of musical fact, and is easily settled by listening enough times to the records. There are a lot of things about the form that I don't like. Duke has a habit of shifting tempos with solo instruments, and of throwing recaps right smack on top of a developing theme.

But the principal trouble was one of dynamics, rather than writing. The Ellington band is famous for its shadings and colorings. There were very few of these present in *BBB.* That is not the music's fault. That was a question of rehearsal, and familiarity with the score. Duke didn't really get it set until three weeks before the concert, and new parts and sections were added several days before the concert itself.

The abrupt shifts from loud to soft and back again with no shading, and the trick of either playing completely out of tempo, or "jumping" the particular groove hit, made it all but impossible to detect the various ideas moving in the score.

Therefore when Duke read the unfavorable reviews the next morning and said, "Well, I guess they didn't dig it," and nothing more, he was perfectly correct. But it wasn't all the critics' fault. The band didn't give *BBB* the performance it should have had. It isn't perfect. But it is a tremendous step forward for music and for Ellington.

Some of the critics said that it was too much for a dance band, limited by size, to attempt, that it couldn't achieve enough color. This time that was true. Duke's outfit didn't have all the color it should have, not even enough to make *BBB* clear, even with its defects. This was a tragedy, knowing of what they are capable.

Some said that Duke was abandoning jazz for a bastard classical form. I was ready to agree with this myself for a couple of days. But listening to the concert again, I don't think it's true. *BBB* is not the final step by any means. Duke is working towards music where he can use all the rich scoring and harmonic advantages of the classical tradition, plus the guts, poignance, and emotional drive of great hot jazz, specifically the solo.

The *Blues* section of *Brown*, sung wonderfully by Betty Roche, was an admirable example of this. Purists screamed because it wasn't strict blues in the old shouting fashion. No, but what you had was a woman singing about what was worrying her heart, backed by some powerful cadences similar to those used by Stravinsky in his pre-war stuff.

Look to music like this for the first undeniable American expression I've heard in a concert hall. I played the discs for [vibraphonist and band leader] Red Norvo. Came the blues. Said Norvo, an impeccable musician: "Those are the blues the way they hit me. That's it."

There was plenty wrong with this concert. It was too long. The programming was not too good. Instead of playing ten "personal concerto" numbers, Duke should have included more of the works which make his band really outstanding. *Reminiscing in Tempo* is an example of something sorely missed. Certainly the program couldn't be too heavy, but ten "concertos" are a lot to wade through too!

There were various things done by individual members of the band, including Duke himself, that struck me as not too good. *BBB* was written and rehearsed too hastily. Even Duke can't take 48 minutes of composition in a few weeks, and make it as completely polished as he does a three minute disk. Tonal colors usually present were missing. The rhythm section often wavered. There was plenty of scuffling in the brass, noticeably on the last bars of *Beige, Blue Bell[e]s of Harlem*, and *Goin' Up*. Also it's one thing to be relaxed, another to stand in the center of the stage talking while Duke plays an interlude, as Harold Baker, Rex Stewart, and Joe Nanton did during *Mood Indigo*. Sonny Greer still plays much too loudly on occasion (especially on the first five numbers), and is too concerned with the way his drumming looks, instead of the way it sounds. Many of the smaller tunes were played at tempos apparently picked for their novelty. *Ko-Ko* suffered especially from this, played at such break-neck speed that even Duke's brass could barely stand the gaff.

Johnny Hodges stole the show for the crowd on *Day Dream* and *Don't Get Around Much Anymore*. His playing there struck me as being over-phrased, much better in *BBB,* and cut to shreds all evening long by Harry Carney's superlative baritoning. Carney plays some baritone and clarinet passages in *BBB* that for purity of phrasing and delicacy of taste are unsurpassed even in Ellingtonia.

One trouble in judging whether *BBB* has any "form" is the story that Duke has attached to the work. Taken from the plan of his opera *Boola, Black* represents the early Negro period, with work songs coming first in the period of slavery, and then the spirituals to make up for the dreary life. *Brown* is concerned with the Civil War, the West Indian influences, and the spread of Negro life to the city, with its urban blues. *Beige* is built around the "hotcha" idea of colored life, and Duke's pointing out that Harlem has more churches than joints. The waltz is to show the desire for "good living," while the ending unites *Black, Brown,* and *Beige* with Red, White, and Blue.

I don't think the music needs any such "programmatic" prop. It stands by itself as good music with development in the piece itself and not depending on color effects to tell people what is going on. This is a horrible pit into which men as excellent as Tschaikovsky fell. Fortunately Duke has avoided it for the most part.

Concert-goers noticed little snatches of his own tunes all over *BBB*. And why not? Duke has been shaping to write this and other works for years. Why not use all that he has built in the interim? If Sibelius can do it without censure, so can Duke.

Mistakes such as Paul Bowles' statement that, if there is no syncopation there can be no jazz, can be skipped. (How about slow blues?) It's a common fallacy of people who want to hold jazz back to only what it has done in the past.

But what strikes me as the wrong the critics did Duke (with the exception of Kolodin) was that they judged him on one not-too-good hearing—most of them not even too familiar with his band or previous works. I don't claim to be any better critic than the rest of them. I do claim that anybody who says he can listen to *BBB* once and evaluate it fairly is a very, very unhappy square.

I further think that Duke should get the concert tour that the William Morris office finally has summoned the guts to attempt. I further think that as much as possible, he and the band should give up straight dance work, and work on the sort of thing they tried in *BBB*. Only by actual writing can Duke work it out and can the band learn to play it. Like it or not, this looks like not only a fusion of the American classical and jazz traditions, but also the first road without a dead-end close by. It would be a tragedy to drown it in one-nighters and theater dates.

43. The Debate in *Jazz* (1943)

S ome of the most spirited responses to Ellington's Carnegie Hall debut appeared in the American magazine *Jazz*, edited by Bob Thiele. Between May and December 1943 a series of articles demonstrated that the concert not only had roused classical-music devotees but also had sent shock waves through the jazz community.

For some jazz writers, the issue was not simply whether Ellington could write a suc-

Sources: John Hammond, "Is the Duke Deserting Jazz?," *Jazz* 1/8 (May 1943), 15; Leonard Feather [a rebuttal of Hammond]," *Jazz* 1/8 (May 1943), 14, 20; Bob Thiele, "The Case of Jazz Music," *Jazz* 1/9 ([July] 1943), 19–20.

cessful large-scale piece but whether he should be appearing in concert halls at all. John Hammond framed the question in the title of an article, "Is the Duke Deserting Jazz?," published in the May 1943 issue of *Jazz*. Hammond had previously criticized Ellington's *Reminiscing in Tempo* for not showing a commitment to social causes (see §27). Now, faced with *Black, Brown and Beige,* a work that did just that, Hammond attacked from another direction. He charged Ellington with abandoning jazz: ever since Ellington had been lauded by European composers, Hammond maintained, his music had become more complex and less connected to its original function for dancing.

Leonard Feather (b. 1914) responded to Hammond with a fierce rebuttal which touched on some of the possible personal reasons behind the latter's assessment of Ellington. At the time Feather was working both as a critic and as a press agent for Ellington.[1]

After the somewhat extreme positions taken by Hammond and Feather, *Jazz*'s editor Bob Thiele offered a more moderate view in "The Case of Jazz Music," attempting to sort out those defining traits of jazz Ellington had called into question through his Carnegie Hall appearance. Like Hammond, though, Thiele affirmed his belief that jazz was rooted in "folk music" and cautioned against "falling in love with the hybrid in jazz music."

Three other articles not reprinted here contributed to the *Jazz* debate. In "Ellington Hits the Top, and the Bottom" (May 1943), Jake Trussell, Jr., linked Ellington's recent decline to various personnel losses (Cootie Williams, Jimmy Blanton, Barney Bigard) and additions (Ben Webster, Herb Jeffries), claiming that the final blow came when Ellington appeared in Carnegie Hall, "the sacrosanct, hypocritical hideout of everything and everybody that hates jazz music." Needless to say, Trussell's opinion of *Black, Brown and Beige* was not charitable. Trussell's subsequent article, "In Defense of Hammond" ([July] 1943), mounted an offensive against Leonard Feather.

Finally, in "Jazz and Ellingtonia" (December 1943) Jim Weaver took issue with some of Thiele's criteria for jazz, countering that Ellington's main innovations in the field had come from expanding its formal possibilities beyond the limited structures previously found in dance music.

John Hammond: "Is the Duke Deserting Jazz?"

Jazz had the most ambitious evening in its history when Duke Ellington gave his concert at Carnegie Hall. The whole town turned out for the event, and the auditorium itself could have been sold many times over. At long last the music world has paid proper homage to Duke Ellington, its most distinguished bandleader and composer.

Rather than review the concert in detail, we would like to dwell upon the development in Ellington which led to this event. In the first half of his career as a bandleader, Duke was content to be leader of the finest dance unit ever

[1] Feather later wrote of his attack on Hammond: "I was as guilty of bias and poor taste in defending Duke and denouncing Hammond as I had found him to be in jumping to hasty conclusions after a single hearing" (from his notes to *The Duke Ellington Carnegie Hall Concerts, January 1943*). Indeed, the tone of this piece is unusually shrill for this well-known and prolific writer on jazz.

produced. He was able to mould soloists like Bubber Miley, Johnny Hodges, Barney Bigard, Joe Nanton, to name only a few, into a cohesive group, whose prime function was to express his ideas. Both as arranger and composer Duke had a tremendous melodic gift, unequalled by any other popular composer of the day, and his band had a distinctive style that set it apart from any other in the land.

He started out in 1923 as pianist in Elmer Snowden's Washingtonians at the small Club Kentucky and Barron's Exclusive Club. In a very short time his talent for organization led him to take over the band and change it from seven soloists to a large, disciplined group relying on his arrangements and ideas. When he opened the Cotton Club in the late twenties his success was assured, for he became not only a great dance orchestra, but the greatest show band of all times.

Success was a great stimulus both to Ellington the composer and Ellington the bandleader. His great popular song successes were written during this period, and through his records, he became a musical hero at home and in Europe. In 1933 he finally took his band to England and started a new phase of his career.

Until that time Duke had been content with dance music as his medium of expression. Blues and other folk music had been his primary sources of inspiration, and he was quite happy at being known as a popular composer.

Serious composers and musicians turned hand-springs over him. Spike Hughes, Cecil Gray, Constant Lambert, and even the dean of English critics, Ernest Newman, wrote profound articles about him, complaining that his talent was being restricted by dance tempo and the thirty-two-bar form.

Unfortunately for jazz, Duke took this advice to heart. During the last ten years he has been adding men to his once compact group, has introduced complex harmonies solely for effect and has experimented with material farther and farther away from dance music, and although he has earned the fervent praise of trade paper critics he has alienated a good part of his dancing public.

It took courage to do this, and one could only wish that he were being rewarded by the quality of his product increasing with his ambition. But the more complicated his music becomes the less feeling his soloists are able to impart to their work. Wonderful musical thrills can still be had from the band, but they are by no means as consistent as they once were.

"Black, Brown and Beige," Duke's panorama of Negro life in America, sprawls along for more than three quarters of an hour. In it are many exciting ideas, some penetrating wit, and several marvelous tunes, but all are lost in the shuffle because they are not woven together into a cohesive whole. It was unfortunate that Duke saw fit to tamper with the blues form in order to produce music of greater "significance."

The concert did begin with a bang. *Black and Tan Fantasy,* although it has become far more fancy, still packs a tremendous wallop, particularly when Joe Nanton makes his own special contribution. *Rockin' in Rhythm,* the second number, had more gusto than any other number and came closest to the real Ellington. But in *Jumpin' Punkins* the rhythm section went completely to pieces, and Sonny Greer's obstreperous drumming nearly wrecked a couple of the soloists. The three musical portraits of Bert Williams, Bojangles and Florence Mills were delightful examples of sensitive, direct writing and playing.

It was the second half of the concert which disturbed me most. *Ko-Ko* is not distinguished jazz, while Billy Strayhorn's three tunes had little to contribute except unconventional harmonies. Very few of all the various concertos written for soloists in his band came off. Chauncey Haughton's clarinet playing is stiff and technical, with none of the easy confidence Barney Bigard possesses. Tizol's *Bakiff* is little more than dressed-up movie music, but the composer played magnificently. Ray Nance's fiddle playing is all right in small doses, but there was far too much of it during the evening. Junior Raglin is a good bass player despite his snapping of strings and twirling his instrument.

Duke was not at his best as a pianist in *Blue Belles of Harlem,* but Ben Webster was fine in the uninteresting *Cotton Tail* which would have been exciting if the band had been swinging behind him. Johnny Hodges, who is my favorite of all alto men, decided to turn on the schmaltz in *Day Dreams* [*sic*], with the result that every note was smeared and glissed. It's only fair to say that the audience loved it and would gladly have had an encore. Rex Stewart clowned around in *Boy Meets Horn,* and seemed content to play for effects rather than from the heart. But Lawrence Brown was superb in *Rose of the Rio Grande,* which closed the group. Unfortunately, Harry Carney, one of the greatest musicians in jazz, had little chance to play, and even Ben Webster had fewer solos than one might have expected.

The conclusion that one can draw from this concert is that Duke is dissatisfied with dance music as a medium for expression and is trying to achieve something of greater significance. No one can justly criticize him for this approach if he keeps up the quality of his music for dancing. My feeling is that by becoming more complex he has robbed jazz of most of its basic virtue and lost contact with his audience.

Despite all that I have said, Duke is still the greatest creative force in jazz, and his band is a wonderful instrument tonally, if not rhythmically. I hope that some day he will be able to find himself once again and continue his contributions to the folk—or people's—music of our time.

Leonard Feather Rebuts Hammond

By now many of you will have heard about, or read, John Hammond's article suggesting that Duke Ellington is deserting jazz. The article appeared in the "People's Voice," the Harlem newspaper in which Hammond has a financial interest, and also in Art Hodes' interesting new publication, "The Jazz Record" (Feb. 15 issue).

I wrote an answer to Hammond which the "Voice" published. Hammond called up the theatrical editor, furious because he had not been shown my article before publication. It didn't occur to him that he had omitted to show his own article to Ellington before publication. In the following week's "Voice" Hammond tried to refute my arguments by pointing out that I am Ellington's press agent.

This excuse is palpably idiotic, for two reasons: (1) I was calling Duke's band the greatest in the world, and writing at great length about it, for ten years, before I had the remotest business with Duke. One such article appeared in the London "Melody Maker" in 1934. Another appeared a year or so ago in the "Victor Record Review" and was reproduced in the all-Ellington issue of "Jazz." I did not start working with Duke until October 1942, and I didn't need to be his paid press agent to know that he has the greatest band in the world. (2) As a press agent, I have never sent out critical opinions; only factual and informative press releases. My critical articles were all specially written, and still are being written, for people who still respect my integrity as a critic although they are perfectly well aware that I have been doing publicity work too.

Now I am going to say a few things which couldn't be said in the "Voice," because the "Voice" is not a musician's paper and these matters are of specialized interest to people who know plenty about jazz and the men who are mixed up in the jazz game.

To come to the point, I think it is a dirty rotten, lowdown no-good shame that somebody like John Hammond, who has done so much to eliminate race prejudice in music, should be so completely befuddled by personal prejudices himself.

Hammond's prejudices against certain musicians and bands are mostly motivated by his inability to run their bands or their careers for them. The proofs of this have been all too numerous.

Take the Ellington case first. Duke is a man of fine intellect, alert, ambitious and aware of his own abilities and potentialities. Hammond, who at one time was a great admirer of Duke and his band, tried to get him to make certain changes in it. Duke thought he knew better than Hammond how to run the Ellington band.

The climax came one day in the Columbia recording studios when Duke was making "Serenade to Sweden" [recorded on 6 June 1939]. John Hammond, who was working for Columbia at the time, was supervising the recording, and at one point he told Duke that one of the soloists was departing too far from the melody, and that Duke should have him keep it straight.

Duke fixed Hammond with a cool grin and said: "John, you're getting more and more like Irving Mills every day."

According to those who were in the studio at the time, John never quite got over that. . . .

John's attitude toward anything the Ellington band may do is one of extreme readiness to find fault at the drop of a mute because he doesn't get along with Duke the way he does with Count [Basie]. But, in addition to being prejudiced, his judgment was ridiculously hasty. At the time he wrote his review of the concert he had heard it exactly once. To criticize such a monumental work as the fifty-minute Black, Brown and Beige on one hearing is, as Mike Levin pointed out in "Down Beat," entirely unfair.

Personally, I have sat with musicians such as Cootie Williams, Billy Stray-horn and others both in and out of Duke's band, listening to *Black, Brown and Beige* a dozen times, and every one of us gets an increasing thrill out of it that can't be compared with anything else in jazz. Rex Stewart, whom Hammond accuses of lack of feeling, told me that the first time he heard Johnny Hodges play the glorious *Come Sunday* theme in the first movement, tears came to his eyes.

There is music like that all the way through *Black, Brown and Beige*, music that is deep and stirring, music that has so many complexities of form and fascinating developments in melodic continuity that it is nothing short of wicked to dismiss it by saying that it "sprawls along" for three quarters of an hour. And John avoided any mention of Betty Roché, whose singing has been praised by everyone I have spoken to. All he could find to complain about was Duke's alleged "tampering" with the blues form—which isn't even true since one of the loveliest parts of the second movement, shortly before the end, is based strictly on the traditional twelve-bar pattern.

Anybody who knows something about jazz is perfectly entitled to criticize *Black, Brown and Beige* or any other part of the concert. John was right in some of his criticisms, but in his characteristic manner he drew careful attention to the faults and soft-pedalled the virtues; and in talking about *Black, Brown and Beige* he was on dangerous ground—almost as dangerous as if he had never heard it at all.

Finally, there is his absurd complaint about the "quality of Duke's music for dancing." Who the hell wants to dance in Carnegie Hall? And what does Hammond know about music for dancing, since he doesn't even dance? Duke's music has gone a little beyond the stage where it has to tickle the toes of a mob of jitterbugs. It is the only jazz that has combined the fundamental qualities of this musical idiom with the progress and advancement that are necessary to save it from stagnation. Ellington the man, and Ellington's music, will be remembered longer than the puny attempts of the Hammonds to attempt to dictate to him, or belittle him when the attempts a[t] dictatorship fail.

Right?

Or do you have to be Ellington's paid press agent to feel that way?

Bob Thiele: "The Case of Jazz Music"

I intended to title this article "The Case of Duke Ellington" and add my bit to the current Ellington controversy being carried on in "Jazz." In this article, besides stating my viewpoints on the situation, I intend also to add to some of the points in the articles written by John Hammond, Leonard Feather and Jake Trussell in the last issue. I will do all of this and more, because I feel that the Ellington discussion leads up to factors important to the good of Jazz music. . . .

Critics have been preaching about Duke's music for years and now that he has finally been recognized as a great musician, composer and arranger he has come down from Jazz Heaven to walk with us mortals. This is just so much "hokum."

As far as I am concerned Duke Ellington was and always will be the most powerful force in jazz music. He is an ingenious arranger, a brilliant composer and a pianist of talent. He has proven over and over again that his orchestra has never lost freedom and spontaneity, the essence of jazz. He writes with a feeling for jazz and his musicians interpret the music with the same feeling. Duke also leaves plenty of room for improvisation. However, in the past few years it has become quite evident that Duke is filling his ambition to work in more extended orchestral forms. Many of his arrangements are definitely influenced by modern composers.

In years past Duke's band has always strived to present individual and ensemble performances that were innovating and yet played in a true jazz style. But lately, many of Duke's arrangements present a love of exaggerated coloring, tending toward a sort of varied, over-rich layer cake of ideas and tones. I am afraid I have no sympathetic appreciation of this type arrangement, for it is in direct opposition to the fundamentals of jazz. I am inclined to agree with John Hammond, when he states that Duke is drifting further and further away from dance music. After all, jazz is dance music. Leonard Feather complains that Hammond doesn't know how to dance and no one cares to dance in Carnegie Hall. This may be true, but Leonard also stated in his article, "Duke's music has gone a little beyond the stage where it has to tickle the toes of a mob of jitterbugs." That is just the point. True jazz must contain that beat, and once it reaches the concert form, it is no longer dance music. Jazz must be free and exciting; spontaneous and spirited. As a musician, Duke merits the warmest commendation for trying to better himself in the field of music, but let's not say *Black, Brown and Beige* is a thrill that cannot be compared with anything else in jazz.

The conclusion that I have come to concerning the present Ellington situation is that, by becoming more and more involved with music by the modern composers, Duke Ellington is slowly losing contact with the basic fundamentals of hot jazz.

In answering the articles by John Hammond and Leonard Feather I make the following sincere suggestions. It might be wise for Leonard Feather to listen to more healthy bursts of New Orleans music and for John Hammond to go and listen to Duke under proper conditions. I recently heard Duke's band play two one-nighters and can honestly say it was the most exciting music I have heard in many years. Duke's band can definitely "swing" and I feel that if John should happen to hear it when it is "swinging" he might change a few of his opinions.

I realize that Leonard Feather doesn't like the idea of John Hammond suggesting what men to use to an orchestra leader, but I am about to do the same thing, for I feel that all jazz enthusiasts have a right to make suggestions.

I agree with Jake Trussell [in the May 1943 issue] because I feel that many of the men who are leaving Duke cannot be replaced and can rightly be called a part of "Ellingtonia." Jake's article was humorously exaggerated, but he is correct about the effect the absence of these musicians will have on Duke's music. Cootie Williams, Rex Stewart, Barney Bigard, Jimmy Blanton and Otto Hardwicke are no longer with the band. Recently I spoke with Duke for an hour or more and he told me that when Otto Hardwicke left the band it would be necessary to re-write the entire lead sheet [i.e., lead alto parts], because, as Duke explained, he wrote the sheet for no one but Otto Hardwicke. It is not beyond the realm of possibility that Duke may be able to build new soloists out of the group he has at the present time. Time will tell.

It wouldn't be necessary to wait if Duke had picked exceptional musicians to replace his great soloists of years gone by. It would be impossible to replace Cootie and Rex, but a clarinet player with a fluid, effortless style could have been found to replace Bigard. At the present time Duke is using Jimmy Hamilton. Jimmy told me two years ago, while he was playing at the Village Vanguard and studying at the Juilliard School, that he was striving for a semi-classical tone and a technique comparable to Benny Goodman. Two years later I find that he has almost achieved his goal and he should fit into typical Ellington mood-numbers very well. Junior Ragland [Raglin] is not up to the past standards of Ellington bassists. Duke has added two sax players that shouldn't be anywhere near the great Ellington band.[2] However, in the singing of Betty Roche, Duke has an ideal replacement for Ivie Anderson. Betty has a very definite feeling for the blues and her voice is strong enough to take her out of the Harlem jump singer category.

All this leads up to an important question: what constitutes the music we are talking and writing about?

Jazz music springs from folk music and still contains many of its qualities. It is spontaneous, full of improvisation. It is music that springs from the *soul* of musicians. It represents America: Negro spirituals, marches, Tin Pan Alley. It is living American music. It is hard music, beat out for hard dancing. It is free music. It is comparatively new and different. It is rough and exciting.

I feel that jazz must always contain many, if not all, of these fundamentals or it is not real jazz. Unfortunately, present day musicians are forgetting this, and so are many of the critics. They feel that when Duke Ellington plays a "different" chord it is truly great; *Black, Brown and Beige* is a thrill that cannot be compared with anything else in jazz. *Black, Brown and Beige* is not true jazz. Louis Armstrong improvising the blues is jazz. Billie Holiday's singing is jazz. Why is it hard for musicians and critics to grasp the ideas that constitute real jazz?

"Technique! The very word is like the shriek of outraged art." At times how true this statement rings in my ears. Most musicians who think they are playing wonderful music are merely stressing technique and what they consider to be a good tone. It seems that the wilder, louder and the more notes he can inject into a chorus make him a great artist. These musicians are too weak to try to create something of beauty; they are content to forget about music that was played in the past. If some present day musicians would take the time to listen to the mighty jazzmen, who hadn't much theory of technique,

---

[2] Thiele probably refers to Sax Mallard and Nat Jones, the former with Ellington from April to June 1943, the latter from June to September 1943.

they might find themselves in a new world of music. However, many of the new crop of so-called jazz musicians are just innately dull.

I do not want my readers to feel that I am intimating that such musicians as Art Tatum should be placed in the above category. Definitely not. But why must musicians rave about Tatum's technique, which *is* extraordinary, when he plays so much *music*? Why must young trumpet players base their styles after Roy Eldridge when Louis Armstrong is still playing? I wonder if some of these youngsters ever knew that Joe Smith had more finish and subtlety than Eldridge will ever have. Smith had a marvelous tone, round and full. Joe would stand up in the last row of the old Fletcher Henderson band and improvise two choruses and you could just about hear a pin drop. Not, "Take another, Joe."

The fact that a musician can send his fingers down the keyboard in a few seconds without missing a note doesn't mean he is a great jazz musician. Because a musician plays the same descending figures on every chorus, combined with a brass-pipe tone, does not make him a great jazz musician either. Remember, it is all very interesting music, but ask yourself if it's jazz. Let's not follow in the footsteps of Panassie by falling in love with the hybrid in jazz music.

It might be wise to adhere to a few simple words of wisdom uttered by [trombonist] Benny Morton.

"Jazz is Negro music. It has a tempo that's been handed down for a generation. It's easy and it rocks. There's no need to blow hard. Relax. Close your eyes and improvise melodies of beauty. Jack Teagarden still plays jazz."

44. *Black, Brown and Beige* in a List of "Classical Records" (1946)

A few years after Ellington's Carnegie Hall debut, the debate over *Black, Brown and Beige* had cooled somewhat. In part this resulted from Ellington's paring down of the work after its premiere. Indeed, he would never again perform the original, forty-five-minute version.

In 1946 a review of *Black, Brown and Beige* appeared in Kurt List's "Classical Records" column for the magazine *Listen: The Guide to Good Music*. The version discussed by List was the first commercial disc of *Black, Brown and Beige* to reach the public, made for Victor in December 1944, after the recording ban had been lifted. (The 1943 performances from Carnegie Hall and Boston's Symphony Hall were not issued commercially until 1977, although a bootleg source had circulated earlier.)

The 1944 Victor *Black, Brown and Beige* consisted of four sections drawn from the longer work, each filling one side of a twelve-inch, 78-rpm disc: "Work Song," "Come Sun-

---

Source: K. L. [Kurt List], review of *Black, Brown and Beige*, "Classical Records," *Listen* VII/6 (April 1946), 13.

day," "The Blues," and "Three Dances" (combining "West Indian Dance," "Emancipation Celebration," and "Sugar Hill Penthouse"). Interestingly, List chose to review it under the "Classical Records" category, together with music by Borodin, Chopin, Liszt, and Offenbach.

Born in Austria, List had studied composition with Alban Berg and musicology at the University of Vienna. He began his association with *Listen* in 1944.

If memory serves right this is a thoroughly shortened version of Ellington's composition which he presented in Carnegie Hall several years ago. Neither jazz nor symphonic, it is still a remarkable work which should have attracted the attention of many more musicians than it actually did. If jazz has anything to offer to serious music, then it certainly lies more along the road on which Ellington proceeds, than that of Leonard Bernstein or George Gershwin. The work is remarkable, not because it transcends the actual jazz clichés, which it does not, but because it endows them with a great deal of imagination and with a wealth of invention clearly borrowed from the vocabulary of modern serious music. Yet it has an originality of its own which finds its most genuine expression in the sonorities of the solo instruments of which the saxophone sounds most overwhelming. Paul Bowles, the critic, once took Ellington to task for this work. Bowles wrote: "If there is no regular beat there can be no syncopation . . . no jazz." But this is precisely where Ellington has made a great advance over the jazz clichés. By overstepping the rigid demands of the meter he has given the work a rhythmic fluctuation of an improvisatory character which is the work's chief strength.

It is unfortunate that the Duke has not recorded the work in its original entirety. But even in its present form it should prove to be of importance to every collector and an implicit prophecy to every honest and serious musician.

45. Robert D. Crowley: *"Black, Brown and Beige* After 16 Years" (1959)

I n 1959 Robert Crowley, a composer and teacher in Portland, Oregon, compared a new version of *Black, Brown and Beige* on Columbia (CL 1162) to the 1944 Victor recordings. Like earlier commentators, Crowley sidestepped a discussion of the work's musical features and pronounced its form problematic. But he praised Ellington for undertaking such an ambitious composition and credited him with inspiring younger musicians—among them John Lewis, Charles Mingus, and Jimmy Giuffre—to "create an art music in the jazz idiom."

Crowley (b. 1921) was educated at Reed College and the University of California,

Source: Robert D. Crowley, *"Black, Brown and Beige* After 16 Years," *Jazz* 2 (1959), 98–104.

Berkeley. His article appeared in critic Ralph J. Gleason's short-lived publication *Jazz: A Quarterly of American Music* (1958–1960).

Black, Brown and Beige was first performed at Duke Ellington's first Carnegie Hall concert on January 23, 1943. It was understood to be the extensive work relating to Negro history Ellington had been discussing with his associates since the mid-thirties. Material originally planned for an opera to be called *Boola* was said to be incorporated in it.* The piece was advertised in *Metronome*** as "Duke Ellington's first symphony," and its premiere was anticipated with great excitement. The 23rd was the last day of Ellington Week in New York, a commemoration of his first 20 years in popular music.

The regular critics of all the New York papers panned the piece, especially for its excessive length—48 minutes—and for its discontinuity and formlessness.† The most capable musician who wrote about it, Paul Bowles, was harshest. The popular music reviewers wrote of it with approval, but it is clear that Mike Levin of *Down Beat* and Barry Ulanov, in his Ellington biography, lacked the technical equipment to defend it effectively.

Alec Wilder, a musician predisposed to admiration of everything Ellingtonian, wrote on the subject some years later and corroborated the unfavorable first impressions of the concert reviewers. While not condoning the fact that *B, B and B* had been presented as it had, he showed insight into some of the reasons for its deficiencies: "Like the other great talents of American popular music—Gershwin especially—his technique is mostly self-acquired, shaped to functional ends. So long as he spends half his life and more as a public performer, with trains, buses, and theater dressing rooms in between, it's not likely to change much."‡

That Ellington's compositional aspirations were not satisfied by the production of fine popular songs and three-minute instrumentals had been apparent since 1931, the year of *Creole Rhapsody*. This "two-side" piece was followed four years later by one which needed four sides, *Reminiscing in Tempo* and again by *Diminuendo and Crescendo in Blue*, recorded on two 78 rpm sides in 1937. These works, like *B, B and B,* have been generally dismissed by heavy critics and music historians—including Gilbert Chase, the latest and best writer of American music history—as "pretentious."[1]

---

* *DE,* 253.
** January 1943.
† As cited by Ulanov in *DE,* 257–58, and Mike Levin in *Down Beat* (15 February 1943), 12–13 [see §42].
‡ Alec Wilder, "A Look at the Duke," *Saturday Review* (28 August 1948), 43–44 [see §55].
[1] Crowley's source is Gilbert Chase, *America's Music: From the Pilgrims to the Present* (New York: McGraw-Hill, 1955), 485: "Pretentious in its aping of modern European composers and the conventional tone poem, [*Black, Brown and Beige*] is more contrived than creative. The same may be said of other compositions by Ellington in the larger forms, such as *Reminiscing in Tempo* and *Diminuendo and Crescendo in Blue.*"
   By the time of the second revised edition of *America's Music* (1966), however, Chase had modified this opinion, and in the third (Urbana: University of Illinois Press, 1987) he took a stance radically different from that of 1955: "Eventually [Ellington] would become a great jazz

At the time of *B, B and B*'s premiere, union musicians were on strike against the recording industry. It was not recorded until nearly two years later and then in very abbreviated form.* I had heard the 1943 Carnegie concert, with slight alterations, in Chicago later in the winter, and remembered enough to be bitterly disappointed by this Victor recording on four twelve-inch, 78 rpm sides.

The present recording seems to be an uncut, perhaps somewhat revised, version of the first part of the work, "Black," dealing with slave days and early Negro Christianity, according to Ellington's programmatic outline. The "Brown" section, an elaborate blues; and "Beige," which was supposed to deal with modern-day urban, prosperous Negroes, are not touched upon, hence the label misrepresents the contents of the record.

On the second side of the record under discussion the "Come Sunday" portion of "Black" is presented twice more, once with words sung by Mahalia Jackson and once as a violin improvisation by Ray Nance. Miss Jackson's singing seems as inappropriate to me in this setting as Pete Seeger's would, and the words, what one can understand of them, are troubling in that they exemplify the preposterous gulf that always seems to divide jazz music from its "lyrics." Nance's violin behind Miss Jackson simpers. On its own it's nice, but an unrewarding subject for discussion.

My opinion is that the second side was a "gimmick" planned by somebody at Columbia to help sell the record and that Ellington complied in order to have another chance at the music on the first side, and/or out of sheer senti-ment with regard to Miss Jackson. Her improvisation of a tune for the Twenty-third Psalm, the last thing on the second side, is a real catastrophe; it resembles, more than anything else, Al Hibbler's old specialty, "My Heart Sings."

Several factors make it desirable to know and enjoy both recordings. The Victor is more or less a "sampler," while the Columbia now at hand offers a self-contained fragment. Two performers of the utmost importance to the Ellington style play on the Victor but not on the Columbia, namely Joseph Nanton and Sonny Greer. Another, who played the 1943 concerts but missed the 1944 recording because of Army service, is gloriously present on the new recording: Harold Baker. Not only are Baker's tone and articulation of exem-plary purity and precision, virtues in themselves; he adds a voice to the band that is evidently an integral part of Ellington's conception; the voice brought, before my time, by Arthur Whetsol.** Trombonists Quentin Jackson and John Sanders distinguish themselves in the new recording, despite Jackson's persis-tent trouble with his lip.

One may applaud Jackson's energetic humor on the plunger-mute solos without qualifying one's admiration for Tricky Sam Nanton's playing on the older recording. Nanton learned the wa-wa business at its source and applied it with matchlessly droll profundity. Harry Carney plays as well this time as

composer in the classical meaning of the term, while maintaining the group participation and collabora-tive effort that constitute the core of jazz" (512).

* In New York, 11–12 December 1944. See *DE,* 309.

** See *DE,* 203.

he did thirteen years ago: that is, perfectly. His interpretation of his part is now somewhat less powerful but more expressive than it was then.

All my musical life I have heard discussions on the question: who is the indispensable man in the Ellington band? Cootie Williams, Barney Bigard, Otto Hardwicke, Ben Webster, Lawrence Brown? In general the same musicians who least impress the younger generation today were the candidates. To a degree each of them was indispensable. But the man missed most calamitously on this new recording of *B, B and B* is the one most maligned of all by the bop and cool luminaries. Without Sonny Greer, it's a different Ellington. A comparison of the opening passages on the two recordings is enough to demonstrate the fact. Sam Woodyard, who is using tom-toms where Greer used timpani, sounds emaciated and ineffectual. But it is much more than a matter of timbre and resonance. As the piece progresses Greer gets a marvelous two-four effect that seems to be unique with him. With less stress on this beat, and with the collaboration of Jimmy Blanton, Greer produces, on records like "Blue Goose," and "Flamingo," a truly magical, floating, quality never heard elsewhere.

Unfortunately the beat, magical or otherwise, is not allowed to persist long enough to make any kind of point on either recording, and this is probably the crux of the matter when *B, B and B*'s overall structure is called in question. The individual in-tempo sections are so brief and so thoroughly negated by the bridge passages that the rhythm section becomes an annoyance when it does play. This is less noticeable on the old recording. Sonny Greer's instruments seem better integrated with the ensemble. He seems to be able to make his contribution without being separately discernible.

The principal subject raised by the new recording, however, is certainly not one of performance or of the relative merits of various *virtuosi,* but that of jazz composition itself. Ellington wanted to present a "big" work, and in it to interpret the Negro people to themselves and to the rest of the country. His motivations were surely, in large part, musical ones; but the musical ones were mixed with others of a distinctly social nature. For a jazz band, indeed for a *Negro* jazz band, to play a work of symphonic proportions, written by its leader, in Carnegie Hall! If one can imagine the audacity of this idea as it seemed before it became an accomplished fact, one can well understand the excitement aroused by its announcement. There can be no question but that, as a social and political event, the concert was a positive milestone for the Negro people.

The specifically musical quality of *B, B and B* was, from this standpoint, of secondary importance. The significance of the occasion would have been only slightly enhanced if this work had been whole-heartedly acclaimed by the musical press. As a matter of fact it was not acclaimed except in the popular music trade papers, and the more astute the critic, the more adverse was the criticism of the only really relevant aspect of the piece, its form or structure. (Paul Bowles's comments on the scoring are just peevish; the piece is a comprehensive anthology of Ellington's original and very personal methods of instrumentation.)

Ellington had, whether he realized it or not, chosen a superman-sized dilemma to wrestle with, and he lacked the knowledge and experience necessary for victory. Unity in a large scale work, organic transition, appropriate proportions, variety and strategic placement of climaxes—the skill to secure these is not congenital, as are a good ear and melodic inventiveness. This compositional skill has to be learned, by most of us through patient and wisely-directed study. Even the genius has to learn it, if only subconsciously via thorough absorption of the works which embody its principles. These works are the great compositions of, roughly, 19th century Europe, works which are, because of superficial features and the social conditions of their perpetuation, anathema to almost all jazz musicians. They were certainly of little interest to Ellington in his formative years.

What Ellington produced in *B, B and B* is distinguished from the work of many other jazz musicians and green-horn longhairs only by its magnitude and by the delightful originality of its details. It is a long series of loosely related or unrelated smaller pieces, interrupted rather than integrated by arbitrary "classical" transitions. Since reiteration is almost the only means of extension used, the music, especially on the Columbia disc, seems excessively repetitious. The program on the Victor record jacket is absolutely essential to one's accepting it as a single work.[2] It swings too briefly to allow the development of the special cumulative impact we enjoy in good jazz, hence it fails in both categories.

Nevertheless, it seems shameful to me to dismiss the whole thing as "pretentious." Anything audacious and ambitious has a tincture of pretentiousness in it. Any less than arrogant composer must sometimes feel, "Who the hell am I to set forth this mess of little-learning, guess-work and hope, and expect hundreds of people to listen to it in awe?" It is essential to human progress that aspiration should overcome this attitude. But it is also essential that the motivation towards audacity should be an inner, authentic one rather than an outer, specious one. A musical impulse which demands that certain material be treated in complicated, lengthy fashion is of the former order. A feeling of persecution, no matter how intense or how well founded, is of the latter order.

As mentioned above, I believe Ellington's motivations were mixed. Perhaps "persecution" is too strong a word, but jazz musicians are conscious of their inferior status as compared with so-called "classical" musicians. Their usually superior economic situation does not entirely compensate. They also tend to be almost desperately serious about their work and hence are constantly outraged by their night-club audiences and their employers. They yearn for acceptance and recognition as artists. They discover that they have more to say than can be said in the routine format. They want to be considered intellectuals, and are encouraged in the desire by the *Playboy* type of mentality, or, as Charlie Miller once categorized this element, the advertising agency intellectuals.

Ellington, discounting the faking of Paul Whiteman, was the first and is

---

[2] The "program" consisted of brief picturesque descriptions of the four sections. It was introduced in the liner notes as "the Duke's own interpretation, as reported by Inez Cavanaugh." For more on Cavanaugh, see §93.

still the most energetic jazz musician to demonstrate these tendencies in public by presenting ambitious musical works. He laid out the ground, one might say, in a way that has undoubtedly guided jazz musicians with aspirations towards composition ever since. Nothing else on the scale of *B, B and B* has been attempted, even though jazz musicians have, in recent years, grown unprecedentedly "serious." (Ellington has always had too much wit and *élan* to be so comically "serious.")

The musical nephews of Ellington—men attempting to create an art music in the jazz idiom—are today more numerous than ever before. My belief is that the average young jazz musician is still relatively ignorant. More often now than in Ellington's youth he has had fine teaching on his instrument and "knows his chords," but he has no real skill in harmony or counterpoint and knows nothing of music history. The reasons for this are in part economic and in part personal: his parents were either too poor to provide training or too prudent to prepare him for a moribund profession; or else he himself rejected "all that boring long-hair crap." Finding himself, at about 22, with the urge to do something "bigger" than arranging or "getting away" on popular tunes, he finds himself in more or less the position Ellington was in when he conceived the general idea of *B, B and B*. This is roughly the position of the individual who, when asked whether he could play the violin, gamely replied, "I don't know; I never tried." He hasn't paid the dues.

At this point, if he has the intelligence and the humility, he may settle down to the arduous work of acquiring all the traditional compositional skills. ("Traditional" sounds pretty stodgy, but remember that without a tradition each generation starts roughly where the previous one did, rather than where it left off.) When this happens, recent history shows, he is probably lost to jazz, his experience in which will prove to be only a handicap. His mature music will be concert music in the contemporary international idiom. Examples are Mel Powell and Bill (William Overton) Smith.

On the other hand, especially if he has achieved some notoriety as a jazz figure or faces the handicaps still confronting the Negro musician, he may attempt to defeat the odds through main strength, experimenting, borrowing willy-nilly from post-Debussy concert music he happens to encounter and feel some identification with. Perhaps the most familiar figures in this group are John Lewis, Charlie Mingus, and Jimmy Giuffre. They are talented, industrious, and even, in an unstandardized way, somewhat learned. They enjoy fame, the employability that is the envy of their non-jazz colleagues, but their work is strictly limited because of the poverty of the idiom. Jazz is too rigid, too narrow in all phases of expressive nuance to allow for formal growth. I believe this poverty to be technically inherent; it is economically essential, in any case, since greater flexibility and variety would immediately make the product less popular, and there is little philanthropic support available for jazz.

The most vivid illustration of this I know of took place at a performance of the Modern Jazz Quartet a couple of years ago. John Lewis gave a long and high-flown introduction of "Fontessa," including a lot of information about the Commedia dell'Arte, of all things, and about how various figures were to be presented by various historical jazz styles, etc. When they started to play, it was just the MJQ again, as instantly identifiable as [George] Shearing. John Lewis was John Lewis, blowing cool piano, and Milt Jackson was just Bags, getting away on vibes, with no hint of Columbine or the swing era, or whatever he was supposed to represent. There was not the most rudimentary hint of the kind of contrast that can be exploited compositionally.

This is the other horn of the dilemma, mentioned above: even for the most sophisticated the idiom is not amenable. Ellington's bold pioneer work helped to indicate this fact, I think, and hence it has a musical relevance, as well as a social relevance, that goes beyond itself and its intrinsic merits.

Ellington's permanent reputation will be based on his songs, which have stood out of the banal morass of commercial music for 30 years because of their vigor and poignance. I feel that he has also played a vital role as a great public figure. Somewhat in the manner of Franklin D. Roosevelt he has, in his expansive zest for life, his resilience, his perennially unexpected response to events, and his creative execution of everyday tasks, set an example of human potentialities for thousands of people. Certainly he is the main reason I, for one, am a musician.

46. Brian Priestley and Alan Cohen: "Black, Brown & Beige" (1974–1975)

The first serious analytical article on *Black, Brown and Beige* appeared in 1974, three decades after the work's premiere (and the year of Ellington's death). The British writer and pianist Brian Priestley (b. 1946) and composer-arranger Alan Cohen (b. 1934) had become familiar with the piece through listening to and transcribing various recordings, also through studying a score issued by Tempo Music, Ellington's publishing company. Cohen's orchestra also recorded the work in 1972 with Priestley on piano.

The authors' hands-on experience with *Black, Brown and Beige* put them at an advantage over earlier commentators with more limited access to the work. The result is a densely detailed, section-by-section discussion giving special attention to Ellington's thematic treatment and unifying techniques.

This article was originally commissioned for the British journal *Jazz & Blues*, edited by Max Harrison, but when the periodical ceased publication it appeared instead in *Composer*—the bulletin of the Composers' Guild of Great Britain—in three installments. For the reprinting of their article in this volume, Priestley and Cohen made minor editorial adjustments and added a number of footnotes, indicated by asterisks.

Priestley and Cohen's principal recorded sources for *Black, Brown and Beige* included the following: the 23 January 1943 premiere, issued on FDC 1004 (later on Prestige LP P-34004, which for the first movement incorporated part of a 28 January 1943 performance from Boston's Symphony Hall); the four twelve-inch sides made for Victor in December 1944; the 1958 Columbia recording (with Mahalia Jackson); portions of the First Sacred

Source: Brian Priestley and Alan Cohen, "Black, Brown & Beige," *Composer* 51 (Spring 1974), 33–37; 52 (Summer 1974), 29–32; 53 (Winter 1974–1975), 29–32.

Concert in 1965, issued by RCA Victor; a 1972 re-creation by the Alan Cohen band (Argo ZDA 159). For more information, see Priestley and Cohen's "References" section in "Black, Brown & Beige," *Composer* 51 (Spring 1974), 33–34. For a chronological discography of *Black, Brown and Beige*, see Wolfram Knauer, "Simulated Improvisation in Duke Ellington's *Black, Brown and Beige*," *The Black Perspective in Music* 18/1–2 (1990), 34–37.

Black, Brown and Beige has been described as a significant work, a work unique in the history of jazz composition and unique in the output of Duke Ellington. But, despite the lip service paid to it, it is not a well-known work.

The reason for this unfamiliarity is clearly stated in Barry Ulanov's description of its premiere.[1] "One listening, most people felt, was not enough. Unfortunately, only a privileged few were ever to hear the complete work again . . . When most of the New York critics were so severe in their reviews of *Black, Brown and Beige*, [Ellington] quickly accepted their criticism. He broke the work into a series of excerpts of less than half the length of the original . . ."

As well as distorting our impression of the music, this has had the effect of silencing discussion on all sorts of questions in which even listeners not especially partisan about the work would be extremely interested. For example, how closely does the inspiration of the composition—the history of the American Negro—relate to the actual detail of the music? And how aware was Ellington of antecedents for the various compositional techniques he used, bearing in mind that one can have spoken "prose" for years without realizing it's called prose?

Another of the endless possibilities for speculation concerns the relationship of *Black, Brown and Beige* to the rest of Ellington's work during the period of its composition, and indeed the possible length of this period. Ulanov quotes a newspaper interview that Duke gave in Dallas in the autumn of 1933 which touched on his plans for a "negro suite . . . five parts . . . [which] will trace negro music from its source in the African jungle . . . I shall look into the future for the fifth and last movement, probably a hundred years from now, and give an apotheosis aiming to put the negro in a more comfortable place among the people of the world and a return to something he lost when he became a slave." When Ellington had a spell in hospital in the summer of 1938 he was still talking in terms of five movements, beginning with Africa, while claiming "as he always had for three or four years" that the actual writing was almost completed.

Obviously the projected first and fifth movements of this conception are not a part of the finished version of *Black, Brown and Beige*, which Ulanov points out "had much in it of the opera he had been preparing for an even longer period," identifying the famous "Ko-Ko," too, as "an excerpt from the incomplete score of Ellington's opera *Boola*." What is intriguing is that the tom-tom figure and unison trumpet motif which open "Work Song," and form a virtual motto-theme for the entire composition, are found in embryonic form in the first movement of Ellington's music for the 1935 film short called *Sym-*

[1] All Ulanov citations come from *DE*.

phony in Black, the one in which Billie Holiday appears with the Ellington band and to which she refers in her autobiography, *Lady Sings the Blues.*[2] Unfortunately, Ulanov does not discuss this music, but *Symphony in Black* is also intended to portray Negro life, and in fact the first movement depicts visually the kind of physical labouring which gave rise to the work-song.* . . .

Black

"That kind of talk stinks up the place"; of course, we are familiar with Ellington's dictum about musical analysis and it will become obvious from the few thousand words which follow that we are unrepentant. But it is a dictum too many people have sheltered behind too long, for any Ellington initiate knows that there is much in this composer's music that could usefully be approached in this manner, whether one wishes to read the results or not. And it is unrealistic to expect the artist himself to have much interest in retracing publicly a mental process that is, for him, over and done with; pianist Charles Rosen put it a slightly different way: — "To what extent a composer can describe his working habits is more dependent on chance, the right interviewer, or an irrelevant talent with words than upon any distinction between reason and instinct."[3]

It may seem to some listeners, however, that the existence of a programmatic content or story-line in relation to *Black, Brown and Beige* is sufficient for focussing their listening, that one only needs to hear, say, "Work Song" in terms of its (very real) progression from aggressive to mournful to resigned, in order to understand that it describes the first 100 years or so of the Negro in America. This is well and good, except that any approach to musical appreciation can prove inadequate taken in isolation; one may start wondering at which point exactly in "Come Sunday" do "the workers have a church of their own," and whether the aggressive bit before the alto solo is another work-song to suggest the building of the church. (The comment is not facetious but cautionary: after all, Brian Rust's *Jazz Records* 1897–1942 demonstrates that Duke's genuinely poetic description of "Harlem Air Shaft" was concocted, probably in reply to an interviewer, to stimulate interest in a piece which was originally intended to be called, according to the Victor files, "Rumpus in Richmond.")

It is worth remarking, though, that the programmatic content here, especially in "Black," is untypical for Ellington, consisting not of specific vignettes

---

[2] Billie Holiday with William Dufty, *Lady Sings the Blues* (Garden City, N.Y.: Doubleday, 1956), 62.

* More than that: the section in question is developed from the same figure shown below as *x,* and the outline of the *B.B.&B.* motto-theme (ex. 1b) is heard behind Hodges's solo. In fact *Symphony in Black* (the soundtrack of which was not available to us when writing the article) must be regarded as a preliminary sketch for *B.B.&B.* since, in addition to the work-song, it contains a slow vocal blues and an instrumental spiritual theme. The latter, furthermore, is based on figure *zz* (see ex. 8) which occurs throughout the second movement and recurs in the third movement of "Black."

[3] Charles Rosen, *The Classical Style* (New York: Viking Press, 1971), 405.

Ex. 1a

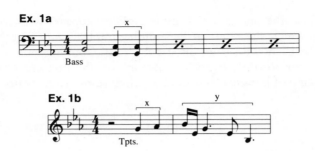

Ex. 1b

but of generalized history, and requiring techniques that were new to the composer. *B. B. & B.* is not only a work of symphonic scale but, of all Ellington's extended compositions, the one most profitably influenced by symphonic devices. Although there is no obvious labouring of such parallels by Duke himself, "Brown" contains the simple dance pieces and slow movement which occupy the centre of a traditional symphony, and "Beige" is a lively but episodic Finale, while "Black" has the closely argued thematic development typical of an opening movement (and, like some nineteenth-century examples, it lasts long enough to be a miniature symphony in itself, which is why it made sense for Ellington to play it as a separate piece on the 1965 European tour).

It may well be indeed that this format arose, not from any direct aping of earlier models, but from the demands of the programmatic motivation itself. In other words, that the fragmentation and development of short thematic motifs in "Black" is intended to represent musically the fragmentation of African tradition on American soil; similarly, the conflict during "Work Song" between motifs referring to the blues scale (exx. 3b, 4a and 6a) and those affirming the major mode (exx. 1b, 3a, 6b and 7—while exx. 2a, 2b and 4b express the conflict within the space of a single phrase) may just be a metaphor for the clash between two cultures. Beyond this general point, we have made little attempt to underline the emotional significance of various passages (except for the occasional adjective where some conjecture of this kind seems helpful), believing that the sensitive listener can best do this for himself.

1st MOVEMENT. The short introduction to "Work Song" contains much of the thematic material not only of "Black" but of the entire work. One particular feature of "Work Song" itself is the incessant use of a two-beat rhythmic

Ex. 2a

Ex. 2b

Ex. 3a

Ex. 3b

figure x (see exx. 1a–7), which may occur either in the first or the second half of a bar (creating considerable metric variety, not to say ambiguity) but which always carries a powerful, built-in accent on the up-beat (giving the illusion of a self-perpetuating form like that of a genuine work-song). After the opening bass and tom-tom figure (ex. 1a) and the motto-theme which is heard three times (ex. 1b), the tempo picks up slightly with a transition for the saxes (ex. 2a) interrupted by an important unison trombone phrase (ex. 2b). Saxes and trumpets then exchange comments on ex. 1b and y of ex. 2a, while a harmonic detour down a semitone to D major (paralleled many times later on in the work) builds back to a call-and-answer version of the motto-theme (ex. 1b), with the trombones taking over the backing figure (ex. 1a).

At this point (the point at which the Victor recording commences) comes the first substantial melody, a long and asymmetrical sax-section line which nevertheless contains short rhythmic cells (exx. 3a, 3b, $y + x$ of ex. 2a). A trombone chord interrupts the beat, and leads to a brief and initially violent transition (omitted in the Victor version) in which the brass imply D minor before the saxes resolve into E-flat again, capped by a quieter trombone chord. The tom-toms, having underpinned almost all the foregoing, now reintroduce the *B. B. & B.* motto-theme as first played by the trumpets.

[Harry] Carney's solo*—the first of several solo passages which are thematic and therefore (inflections apart) written out—begins during a four-bar break and immediately introduces a new four-note figure (z of ex. 4a), which

Ex. 4a

Ex. 4b

---

* References are to the soloists in the 1943 Carnegie Hall premiere unless otherwise stated.

Ex. 5

develops into a fully fledged second theme in the relative minor with references to earlier motifs. Indeed, it is itself incorporated into a version of the motto-theme (y of ex. 4b) shortly before the cadential trumpet re-entry and the saxes' bridge back to E-flat. A final restatement of the motto-theme then leads to a short out-of-tempo interlude featuring Harold Baker (although a most ingenious cut in the Victor score jumps straight from the motto-theme to the third bar of [Joe] Nanton's solo below).

Although new material is still being introduced, one could say in symphonic terms that this interlude marks the start of the development. Baker quickly takes the band back into tempo with $y + x$ of ex. 2a and, after dialoguing with the saxes for a few bars, makes way for a sax-section passage based on ex. 2b in the relative minor. This leads directly to Nanton's plunger-muted trombone entry (ex. 5) with a blues-inflected version of ex. 1b and, at half-tempo, $y + x$ of ex. 2a and y of ex. 1b, backed by an important chromatic countermelody loosely related to ex. 4a. A sudden lurch into D major (again) is marked simultaneously by the trombones with ex. 2b and the saxes with y of ex. 1b, both at the original tempo and, as the trumpets carry through the modulation to C major, they are left to play an unaccompanied eight-bar passage based on the earlier solo trumpet interlude.

As the rhythm re-enters with quiet saxes swinging the backing figure (ex. 1a), Nanton begins a new episode with a bluesy motif which is extremely difficult to notate as it sounds (ex. 6a). This forms the basis of a fifteen-bar section (omitted on Victor) and then comes Nanton's second figure (ex. 6b), which is not only the most work-song-like of the whole movement thanks to the interjections of the ensemble but is remarkably similar to the Miley theme of "East St. Louis Toodle-Oo" (at the slower tempo of the 1937 recording). This figure is also seen to be related in shape to the first bar of ex. 2b and particularly to the motto-theme (ex. 1b), which becomes evident when it is taken up by unison trumpets and the orchestration, together with an abrupt key-change *up* a semitone, gives the feeling of a recapitulation after development.

Ex. 6a   **Ex. 6b**

Ex. 7

A further brief cut in the Victor version finds Nanton meandering through new keys and introducing a figure obviously related to what has gone before but new in this form (ex. 7), and the ensemble challenging his final allegiance to the major mode (ex. 6b) with an anguished blues version of *y* of ex. 1b. A coda marked in the score *religioso* ends the movement (as it did the first side of the Victor 78s); unaccompanied saxes play a virtual inversion of the "Come Sunday" theme, closing with an ambiguously incomplete modulation to E-flat.

2nd MOVEMENT. The original version of "Come Sunday" begins with the theme played quietly by tightly muted brass accompanied only by Sonny Greer's tubular bells marking the chord-changes (ex. 8).[4] And, while the shortened Victor recording cuts the whole movement up to the violin solo, the 1958 and 1965 records omit just the opening eleven bars. This has all the air of a deliberate revision: Ellington may have felt that the chimes, unavailable since Greer's departure, were an essential part of the orchestration or, more likely, that the feeling of a bridge passage here duplicated the function of the "Work Song" coda; he may equally have felt it a weakness to begin "Come Sunday" in the same key as "Work Song" and indeed the aforementioned sax-section coda leads more seamlessly into the obliquely harmonized theme-statement by valve-trombone and saxes in F, the home key of the first half of "Come Sunday." The cut, however, does also remove the first explicit references to a descending scale (*zz* of ex. 8) which becomes more important later.

Juan Tizol's slow theme-statement ends with the first of several brief allusions throughout the work to folk material, in this case to "Swing Low, Sweet Chariot" (not without its similarities to certain "Work Song" motifs, especially ex. 7). This is terminated by a saxophone interlude with clarinet lead (its first appearance) which, though at a faster, swinging tempo, has the same yearning quality as the rest of the movement thanks to its descending scale figures (ex. 9). When the rhythm-section drops out, the saxes take the tempo

Ex. 8

---

[4] The Prestige recording differs in several ways from the transcription in Ex. 8 (based on the Tempo score and the FDC issue of *BBB*): in m. 2 the lower note is A-natural instead of A-flat; in m. 3 the valve trombone enters on the B-flat on beat three; in m. 4 the tempo doubles, with eighth note now equaling quarter.

Ex. 9

down again as their harmonies drop through two octaves to allude to "East St. Louis Toodle-Oo" behind Ray Nance's violin solo, which is the central section of the movement.

These 24 bars begin with pizzicato except, doubtless because of the acoustics, in the Carnegie Hall performance which is entirely bowed (another exception is the 1965 *Sacred Concert* where Jimmy Hamilton has the impossible task of re-creating the violin part on clarinet). After the opening reference to ex. 2b in the relative minor, the violin develops a long spiralling line (again consisting mostly of descending phrases) which becomes a countermelody when the valve-trombone re-enters in the major with the "Come Sunday" theme: this is now rewritten and reharmonized, its rising aspirations underscored by the expansive descending bass-line, while a third solo instrumentalist (Rex Stewart) holds a quiet muted line starting from a single long note (ex. 10). It might be mentioned that the acoustic equilibrium between the four elements in this lovely passage is difficult to realize outside the recording studio and, of the recordings, only the Victor approaches the ideal.

The reverie is rudely interrupted by crashing chords from the piano answered by menacing brass, but the piano quickly calms the multitude with an improvised half-close on A7. Instead of the implied move to D major, this prepares a drop of a semitone to A-flat7, the first chord of Johnny Hodges's full 32-bar chorus of the "Come Sunday" theme with a middle-8 related to the saxophone interlude earlier (ex. 11). His accompaniment in the original performance is restricted to bowed bass and strummed guitar, with muted trombones marking the phrase-ends and a chromatic countermelody in the middle-8 from Carney leading to brief support from the other saxes; however, with Hodges out of action for the 1958 recording and his solo taken by Carney, the countermelody was redistributed then and thereafter to Paul Gonsalves. On the other hand, the use of the three trombones (four in 1965) throughout to replace the guitar on the later recordings is already indicated in the score, along with muted trumpet chords in the second and third 8s which sound less offensive than one might have imagined (cf. Cohen 1972

Ex. 10

Ex. 11

LP). It must be assumed that the striking bass-and-guitar-only idea was the result of a last-minute amendment to the score.

A five-note "Amen" by the saxes closes the movement (and was included on the Victor 78s, only to be left off the LP reissue, perhaps because of a damaged master) and its last chord is overlapped by the start of Harold Baker's unaccompanied cadenza, not written out in the score although it assumes a form closely copied in the 1958 recording and the 1963 version of "Light," which it introduces.

3rd MOVEMENT. This final movement of "Black" does indeed give the impression of being "Light" compared with what has preceded, and at least initially it is simpler and more swinging, much of it being in eight-bar phrases. Nevertheless, the thematic cross references come thick and fast—to such an extent that a detailed run-down would be unreadable—and the listener who becomes completely familiar with this movement will recognize versions of almost all the motifs quoted so far. It falls loosely into five sections and the first section brings up once again the question of the musical genesis of the work or, to put it another way, the question of self-borrowing.

The trumpet cadenza pauses on a high note and leads into a swing tempo by way of eight bars of exchanges with the ensemble in B-flat, based on material from "Work Song," and a further eight bars' ensemble completes the introduction. An AABA[1] chorus (with B as a middle-16) sees another trumpet, or rather Stewart's muted cornet, using both y of ex. 1b and ex. 2a as the basis of a countermelody to a tightly voiced ensemble. The ensemble introduces material new to *B. B. & B.* (ex. 12) but what they play is in fact closely related to the final chorus of "Ridin' on a Blue Note," recorded just five years earlier—indeed, the last eight bars are all but identical; add to this the fact that the sax figure in the middle-16 (ex. 13) is the same as their backing in the second chorus of the earlier piece and, even more remarkably, that the introduction to "Ridin'" has a trumpet-and-ensemble exchange with the trumpet playing ex. 2a from "Work Song"! Perhaps this makes more credible Ellington's statements that he was actually writing the extended composition already in the 30s or perhaps "Ridin'," like "Ko-Ko," was created for the unfinished opera and then incorporated into *B. B. & B.*

The fully notated bass solo which follows illustrates the density of the

Ex. 12

Brass & Saxes

Ex. 13

thematic references in this movement. It begins in the one-bar break with a quotation of ex. 2a and continues with four phrases, each in a different key, based in turn on exx. 7, 2b, 1b, 3a and again 2b.

The ensemble returns in the home key in a more transitional mood, but with a chorus that can still be seen as an AA¹ BA² form, though it may not have been conceived in those terms. A finds unison saxes essaying a blues version of ex. 7 with trombones adapting ex. 12 as a backing; A¹ is in similar vein for the first four bars, but after the trombones quote *zz* of ex. 8, there is a bar of silence followed by four bars of unaccompanied trumpets reminiscent of their appearance in the first movement but based this time on *y* of ex. 1b; the rhythm-section returns for B (again sixteen bars) which begins with ex. 11 rhythmically dislocated (i.e., swung) by saxes and clarinet, and this first reference in the present movement to "Come Sunday" is followed by the relative minor version of ex. 2b, now also swung; finally Lawrence Brown's trombone, having entered with a countermelody, then takes the lead with the "Come Sunday" theme, the harmonization being as in ex. 10 but swung so as to sound like a variant of ex. 12 (which justifies thinking of this as the last 8 of a chorus, i.e. A² rather than C). However, as well as having a two-bar tag, the phrase is extended by the majestic entry of the brass with *zz* of ex. 8 in a ritard which includes bars of waltz-time, before pausing altogether.

At a new slow tempo, Brown continues with a broader version of "Come Sunday" now harmonized as in the Hodges solo, and a sax-section tag rephrasing *zz* of ex. 8. Then the full might of the ensemble combines the "Come Sunday" theme on unison trombones with the trumpets in harmony varying the *B. B. & B.* motto (ex. 14—incidentally, in the score the trumpet counterpoint was also pitted against Brown's solo above, but a wise decision saved it for this one appearance); the climactic moment is prolonged when the rhythm hangs suspended while the saxes play ex. 7 in half tempo against the trumpets' repeated references to *y* of ex. 1b. Before the tension evaporates, a slight increase in tempo initiates a most unexpected two-bar key change down

Ex. 14

a semitone to A minor and the start of a briefly discordant version of the "Come Sunday" middle-8 dominated by clarinet-led saxes, ending with a calmly drawn-out cadence in C major.

The final 56-bar section begins abruptly in A-flat at a swinging tempo which was originally hardly quicker than the start of this movement, but has been taken much faster since it became the Finale of the only section of the work that Ellington plays any longer. The new combination of previously heard material starts with a call-and-response pattern between the trombones (y of ex. 1b) and tenors (ex. 2a) while the altos quietly hum "Come Sunday" at half tempo, and it even manages to incorporate both ex. 3b (saxes in bar 18) and ex. 4a (saxes in bar 30). The delightful writing here needs to be heard rather than described, for this is a section that Ellington could equally well have recorded as a separate number, and it illustrates the fact that what distinguishes this whole movement, and what keeps it moving, is the variety of rhythmic transformation the material undergoes.

Brown

The shortest part of the triptych presents the two dances and the slow "Blues," which have long been familiar from the Victor recording where they are presented virtually complete, except for introductory and linking material. They form a welcome change of pace after the long and involved first part for, although "Light" may represent the light at the end of the tunnel as far as the historical programme of the work is concerned, it was still pretty heavy musically.

This is undoubtedly why Ellington chose the two dances as the only extracts to be repeated at the second Carnegie Hall concert [11 December 1943], playing them as separate numbers with improvised piano intros rather than the appropriate ensemble passages of the original score. In his announcements at this second concert, Ellington is not only less suave than in later years, but sounds almost apologetic at the mere mention of *Black, Brown and Beige* and its social message: — "We thought it would be better to wait until the story was a little more familiar until we did the whole thing again." And, of course, he never has to this day, despite using some of the material for related projects such as *My People* and the *Sacred Concert*.

Duke introduces the first dance as follows: — "This particular sketch is one that we dedicate to the 700 Negroes who came from Haiti to save Savannah, Georgia during the Revolutionary War, so we call it 'The West Indian Influence.'" Ellington's announcements at the premiere were clearly very similar, judging by Ulanov's description (although his relation of them to the actual music is rather garbled at this point), and we are particularly fortunate that his description of "Emancipation Celebration" was preserved on record. "And now another short portion of 'Brown' which represents the period after the Civil War, where we find many young free Negroes who are happy with so much opportunity in front of them, and just behind them a couple of very old people who are free but have nothing and no place to go, and of course it's

Ex. 15

very dark for them. And we find a duet representing the old people and the solos representing the younger people. This is 'The Lighter Attitude.'"

One may suspect, of course, that this is another case of Ellington "selling" the piece to a musically unsophisticated audience, especially with the changed title making it all sound ominously humorous. But it seems likely, given the nature of the work as a whole, that this is a genuine example of a programmatic inspiration which then undergoes a purely musical development. The "Blues," on the other hand, may derive from a musical inspiration initially, although in context it denotes not only the era which created the blues but the state of mind caused by an illusory Emancipation.

4th MOVEMENT. The "West Indian Dance" begins, in the complete version, with 4 bars of march time from Greer, followed by Chauncey Haughton's clarinet quoting a song dating from the Revolutionary War (or, as we call it over here, the War of Independence), "The Girl I Left Behind Me." But the valve-trombone interrupts, leading the Haitian regiment with an introductory reference to the Latin-American rhythm of the tenor-and-baritone theme. The movement, in fact, gains much of its impetus from the alternation of a predominant 8-to-the-bar rhythm with the occasional "straight 4" and indeed, on the Victor recording, the first 24 bars of the theme (intro. omitted) have Latin-American percussion either overdubbed or played by additional musicians.

The material and structure here is relatively simple, and, for this reason, the figure introduced by [Ben] Webster and Carney sounds like a new invention (ex. 15). Comparison with ex. 14, however, shows that it is merely a syncopated, blues version of the "Come Sunday" theme which, in the earlier manifestation, sacrificed its first note for rhythmic (i.e. dramatic) reasons; it is harmonized this time with an F maj. 7 so that it can lead via the circle of fifths to the key of A-flat, now the most prominent note of the theme. This develops into a 32-bar chorus (ABA¹C where B is ex. 3b played as a brass riff) and the last two bars introduce a two-trombone pedal figure which underpins an 8-bar bridge passage by the reeds.

The second chorus does not maintain the 32-bar format but continues the pedal-figure for a further eight bars and introduces a variant of ex. 15 in the saxes and a new theme played by the "pep" section (Nanton, Stewart and Nance, all with plungers—ex. 16). Incidentally, at the premiere performance, the brass lost their place during the pedal-figure and the entry of the pep section is four bars late (not made up till the coda), which affords a revealing glimpse of the complexity of even Ellington's simpler pieces! After the end of this theme, the pep section has a 4-bar bridge before the other trombones play ex. 15 in its original two-part harmony (answered by Latin-American-sounding muted trumpet fills) and extend this also for an extra four bars. A further

Ex. 16

12-bar phrase has the reeds harmonizing a new figure, with the pep section filling in, which sounds as if it might be a ride-out chorus from "Stompy Jones," but what would be the last four bars are replaced by a recapitulation of the three-way counterpoint which began this half (ex. 16). The irrepressible energy of this conclusion is then dismissed, rather than dissipated, by an 8-bar coda of tag-endings (two bars only on Victor).

5th MOVEMENT. The staccato last chord of "West Indian Dance" leaves Carney holding a high note which turns out to be the start of a quote from "Swanee River" (in minor), challenged by the brass with "Yankee Doodle" (in the much more jaunty whole-tone scale), and then the reeds slowly stumble, as if from slumber, into the opening theme of "Emancipation Celebration" before describing a vertiginous chromatic ascent which leads into the dance.

This movement, which makes impressive use of breaks and constantly changing call-and-response patterns, is entirely constructed in 8-bar phrases (with two partial exceptions) and might be justifiably likened to a scherzo and trio. Almost everything grows logically from the first few bars, with Rex Stewart introducing what is to all intents and purposes new material (*p* of ex. 17), though it's worth pointing out that its key notes (the 5th of the scale, the tonic and the 6th) perform exactly the same function in the much-used ex. 7. Moreover, the saxophone backing-figure *q* has a similar shape to *y* of ex. 1b, a fact which becomes clearer when the saxes reply to the cornet theme with another version of their own figure, this time rhythmically much closer to *y* of ex. 1b. If one calls these the first two elements of an ABA^{1}C chorus, then C becomes the cornet-and-trombone duet based on a simple inversion of *r* of ex. 17, the saxes adapting *p* for the fills.

However, there is no real chorus format and the development just continues from there: the saxes now reverse the roles by adopting C with breaks for cornet and trombone (trombone only after the premiere, logically enough since his is the next solo). Then, while the saxes return to B, the brass play a new figure which hardly sounds new in context and could be considered a variant

Ex. 17

of C influenced rhythmically by B. It is this figure which the saxes then take up to back Nanton's brief solo. The "trio" section (featuring just three instruments, as it happens) has solo breaks for Junior Raglin on bass, and Stewart and Nanton playing what might be termed a variant of B in the rhythm of A. This is then taken up by the full brass section to provide the climax of the movement, and introduces a recapitulation of C, heard three times (the two repeats omitted on Victor to save space, as is the repeat in the bass solo). Interestingly, the joyous return of A shown in the score at the very end of the movement was cut by Ellington, doubtless for sound programmatic reasons, although at the premiere he sketched it in gently on piano *during* the last repeat of C; apart from anything else, this is a bold illustration of the musical unity of the movement, for it seems that any one figure could be combined with any other at the drop of a hat.

6th MOVEMENT. The "Blues," also known at the time as "Mauve" (just to confuse the colour scheme), is obviously the movement which lends itself best to being played as a separate excerpt and requires little in the way of analytical comment. It gives the impression of being a freely developed, open-ended piece like the folk-blues, but its relationship to the 12-bar form is quite subtle: the first four bars of A ("The blues . . . The blues ain't . . . The blues ain't nothin") are a hesitant lead-in to 12 bars which, despite the almost out-of-tempo recitative of the vocal, actually follow the standard blues chord-sequence.

The only direct connection with the rest of the work, however, lies in the fact that the brass-dominated introduction (regrettably omitted on Victor) seems to establish the key of D-flat, but it immediately drops down a semitone, the same relationship noted in the first three movements; this time, however, the lower key (C minor) is given greater prominence commensurate with the subject-matter and only works its way back to D-flat halfway through the movement. The introduction ends with an inverted pyramid sustaining the 7th degree of the scale and the 4th, and Betty Roche's vocal begins with eight bars (A) centred on the 7th and eight bars (B) emphasizing the 4th. A^1 follows immediately and has slight changes in the accompaniment to lead into a bridge passage consisting of one extra vocal phrase ("Low ugly mean blues," backed by valve-trombone originally but baritone on Victor), an ensemble quotation from the 1939 "Way Low" and an out-of-tempo lead-in to the 17-bar Webster interlude; this, incidentally modulates to D-flat but ends in B-flat.*

The blues chorus by the trombones (later called "Carnegie Blues") is the focal point of the movement, firmly in D-flat but starting on the 7th of the scale which is, of course, the key-note of the previous minor section. A further two bars of tenor in the original performance (12 bars in the 1963 recording, but either way not written into the score) brings back the vocal with the long-delayed B^1 section; this too ends in B-flat, but in minor to prepare us for the mysterious modulation back to C minor and the briefest of recapitulations in

---

* Andrew Homzy has shown, in a paper delivered at the 1991 International Duke Ellington Conference in Los Angeles, that this solo already existed in *Concerto for Klinkers* from *Jump for Joy* (1941). This further evidence of the gradual coalescence of *B.B.&B.* should be viewed in conjunction with the fact that the opening phrase of the tenor solo, heard in each of its first three bars, repeats the same pitches as the setting of the words "Blues ain't nothin'."

reverse ("The blues ain't nothin'. . . . The blues ain't. . . . The blues"). The striking close is a reminder that, while this movement is far from being complex, harmonically and orchestrally it is fascinating.

Beige

"Beige" is the least well-known part of the work, having been almost totally excluded from the Victor recordings and indeed, apart from the "Sugar Hill Penthouse" section, never played at all after the initial performances.* One has to bear in mind again the mixed reception accorded the work and the fact that such comments as "a gaudy potpourri" (Paul Bowles, quoted by Ulanov), if there is any justice in them at all, would seem to apply most forcefully to this final segment of the piece. It may also be, especially if it were the last part to be written, that it did not live up entirely to Ellington's own standards and was therefore partially suppressed (the official score contains little more than one-third of the original version).

Nevertheless, the experience of both the present authors was remarkably similar, namely that what at first hearing seemed to be a rather unsatisfactory medley of sketchy ideas is, when one comes to know it, not only musically attractive but worthy of serious consideration as the true finale of an important composition. Like each of the other two broad divisions of the piece, it has its own unique flavour and, while "Brown" featured less formal, more typically jazz-style construction than "Black," "Beige" goes even further towards a loose, episodic kind of development with almost no obvious combination or repetition of material. It takes the form of one continuous movement lasting some 13–14 minutes and containing many different tempos and different moods, which towards its close refers back to motifs from the first part of the work in order to unify the conception of the whole.

Once again Ulanov's description based on Duke's own introductions is a valuable aid to understanding the motivation of the composer. "Beige," he tells us, "depicts the contemporary Negro, the United States between two world wars and during the second. . . . The twenties meant gin-mills, the pseudo-African movement, the Charleston, the party life . . . the lonely plaint of the single drinkers, the sad tinkle of a people sad beneath the temblors of their night-life. Here is a new dignity, the serious side of Negro life . . . the Negro's striving for sophistication . . . yearning for education, the shouts of the underfed and poorly clothed and miserably housed, the kept woman in a Sugar Hill penthouse . . . Finally, a brief patriotic motto, 'The Black, Brown and Beige are Red, White and Blue,' signifies Duke's awareness of the war and the Negro's participation in his country's destiny . . ."

Although these programmatic details cannot, of course, excuse any weak-

---

* At the time of writing, it was not known that Ellington had re-recorded several extracts from "Beige" in May 1965, now titled *Cy Runs Rock Waltz* (corresponding to ex. 19), *Beige* (being the "new waltz theme" section we have described), and *Sugar Hill Penthouse* (beginning from ex. 20 to the end of the Victor extract at ex. 21). The opening of the movement (see ex. 18) was also recorded, but regrettably not included on *The Private Collection*, Vol. 10 (Saja 7 91234-2).

Ex. 18

Tbns. & Bari.

ness in the music (if such there be), they do explain the episodic structure of the movement. Just as the fragmentation of motifs in "Work Song" and the opposition of major scale with blues scale may derive from the ideological background of the composition, so here the description of twentieth-century life means a picture of sharp contrasts, violent contradiction and rapid change. And, though Ulanov's almost contemporary comments make the finale of the piece sound time-locked in the circumstances of 1943, this is not in fact true of the music itself any more than it was of "Black" or "Brown."

7th MOVEMENT. As befits a closing movement, "Beige" begins in the same tonality as "Black" (although in minor) and ends in the same key as "Black" ends, thus balancing the many and varied tonal relationships of the work as a whole. The opening of the movement is an ensemble with a double-tempo "jungle" feel in E-flat minor (cf. "Ko-Ko"), featuring an important four-note phrase from trombones and baritone (*xx* of ex. 18). After a climax based on this phrase a held chord introduces a piano cadenza and a few bars of discordant ragtime;* but this dissolves into a repetition of the four-note phrase on the piano, which is taken up by mournful saxes led by Webster's tenor, ending again on a held chord.

A medium waltz-tempo abruptly establishes the key of B-flat and supports Harold Baker's trumpet playing another four-note phrase (*yy* of ex. 19) which develops into a 32-bar ABCA¹ chorus with lilting saxophone accompaniment harking back to earlier countermelodies. A bridge-passage, including a descending arpeggio on unison saxes, introduces Lawrence Brown's trombone lead for a second chorus, now 48-bars long with a trumpet countermelody at A and with a different B section taken by the piano. Again a held chord, and

Ex. 19

* Mark Tucker has shown (in *Ellington: The Early Years*) that the "discordant ragtime" is an earlier composition titled *Bitches' Ball*. A much lengthier (1'50") version of this theme was recorded in March 1957, which may or (given its eventual issued title, *Piano Improvisations Part IV*) may not represent the original form of the piece. Compare also with Ellington's eight-bar solo on the 1948 Carnegie Hall version of *Cotton Tail*.

In view of Tucker's suggestion that this "could have been a piece Ellington heard other pianists play," it is instructive to note Fats Waller's 1923 piano roll of the Spencer Williams tune *Your Time Now;* it ends with a 22-second up-tempo coda, quite out of context, which begins virtually identically to the Ellington solos cited, although the chord sequence develops somewhat differently.

Ex. 20

Baker links into a brief variation of the waltz theme but in a slow-medium 4/4, only to be interrupted by a short Ben Webster cadenza which negotiates simultaneously a return to 3/4 and a key change (down a semitone). A new waltz theme presented by clarinet-led saxes, slightly faster and more "striving" than the trumpet theme, works its way back to E-flat and is climaxed by a brilliant brass-dominated ensemble. Then all feeling of key and tempo is lost during a longer cadenza from Webster, which comes to rest in F major.

An Ellington solo intro leads into a clarinet theme played by Carney rather than Haughton, which turns out to be a 38-bar chorus based on a combination of *xx* of ex. 18, now lightly swung and harmonized in the relative major, with the downward arpeggio heard earlier in the saxophone bridge-passage (ex. 20). A transitional 20 bars beginning with three muted trumpets in harmony, and including brief development of the clarinet theme, prepares a new theme in the same mood on open trumpets in unison. And then this longest continuously in-tempo section of the movement concludes with "Sugar Hill Penthouse" in the version familiar from the Victor recording: this is none other than the entire chorus of the trumpet theme, sensuously harmonized and rephrased in 4/4 by Carney's clarinet and the saxophones (ex. 21).

A banal "everyone-on-stage-for-the-finale" fanfare leaves the solo piano to introduce a short but exact reprise of "Come Sunday" played by Hodges and answered by meditative muted trumpet. Then the most bombastic piano cadenza of all announces what is, whichever way one looks at it, the masterstroke (ex. 22): with martial-sounding accompaniment, trombones and baritone pound out an immensely long line in A-flat beginning with yet another four-note phrase (actually identical to *zz* of ex. 8 but in the form used in "Light" immediately prior to the combination of "Come Sunday" with the "Work Song" motto theme). The trombones and baritone also incorporate in passing ex. 2a, *y* of ex. 1b and ex. 2b and, when they have almost outstayed their welcome, they are suddenly deflated by a few bars of "floor-show" music and, with final reminders of both "Work Song" and "Come Sunday," the movement swings to a carefree conclusion similar in mood to that of "Light."

As well as the parts of "Beige" which seem to have been forgotten imme-

Ex. 21

Ex. 22

diately after the event, Ulanov notes that singer Jimmy Britton (who replaced Herb Jeffries in the Ellington band) "was cut out of the finale of *Black, Brown and Beige* at the dress rehearsal performance at Rye High School the night before the Carnegie Hall concert . . . he had been assigned some gaudy flag-waving lyrics in the patriotic splurge with which *B. B. & B.* concluded. They had to go." And, although the mind boggles at the thought of the contents, this clearly indicates that the last movement was undergoing revision at the time of the premiere.

"Beige" does appear less balanced, though not less coherent, than the other two parts of the work, but this should not preclude a re-evaluation thirty years later; nearly all the material is memorable, and it would indeed have been intriguing to see Ellington reworking it in later life. As usual with program-matic music, it is difficult for the forewarned listener to hear without being constantly influenced by the story-line. But the psychological development of the final movement seems clear to listeners who have not been so influenced, and certainly the underlying vein of "black" humour in its kaleidoscopic jux-tapositions finally becomes inescapable with the riposte to the patriotic anthem.

When one comes to ask what are the distinguishing qualities of the work as a whole, one of them is very definitely the use of contrast and surprise, balanced as it is by an unshakeable sense of forward movement. With the exception of the anthem and of the "Come Sunday" melody, there is no such thing as a static "tune," intended to go down in history as the "Theme from *Black, Brown and Beige*." Even the manner in which the 32-bar version of "Come Sunday" is led up to by intimations earlier in the movement (including a suggestion of the middle-eight) seems to justify its final flowering. "The Blues," on the other hand, is slow but not static and the fact that the early part of the vocal gives the impression of being out-of-tempo tends to obscure its simple construction—until, when the listener is just getting used to the shape and confidently anticipating the B^1 section, it is dropped in favour of a bridge-passage and a tenor solo that lasts 17 bars instead of the usual 16 (and, by the way, it is extremely difficult to be dogmatic about which is the "extra" bar).

This sort of thing is entirely typical. The clarinet theme of "Beige" (ex. 20) starts in regular four-bar phrases and bids fair to develop into a regular 32-bar chorus: certainly, bars 17 to 24 are an obvious middle-eight but what follows, instead of a repetition of the first eight, is a bridge-passage of four bars and then an amended version of the second eight—plus a two-bar tag! Not only is it impossible to say whether this sounds more like $ABCA^1B^1$ or $ABCDB^1$ or even $A(16)B(8)A^1(14)$, but this technique of avoiding the obvious is just a hair's breadth away from a conventional one-chorus tune of the kind that leads inevitably to another chorus of the same. In this context, note also the opening of "Emancipation Celebration," where the last note of the cornet theme coincides with the start of a saxophone phrase which sounds initially like a one-bar break to fill the eighth bar. In fact, it turns out to be the next eight bars starting a bar early, so that the habitual sensation of "odd" and "even" bars is upset and then, when one has accepted the new phrase by virtue of its repetition, comes the real break at the 14th bar (i.e. at the seventh not the eighth bar of this section, but the fact that it is a two-bar break gives the required feeling of restored balance although we are still a bar "short" somewhere).

A lot more needs to be said about the rhythmic aspect of the writing, but one is hampered by the fact that critical vocabulary in this area is so sparse as to be non-existent. Most of our analysis concerns melodic and harmonic matters—and even here the problem has been what to leave out. However, the internal rhythm is very much part of the overall structure, both the harmonic rhythm which determines the rate of chord-changes and key changes, and the various melodic rhythms which typically differentiate one movement from another. "Work Song" is the most obvious example, with the tremendous lift (and the equally buoyant undercurrent at other times) provided by the two-beat figure x; the rhythmic relationship between its rising intensity and the falling motif y explains not only the bursting energy of the motto-theme but, for instance, the naturalness of the polyrhythms at ex. 5 and elsewhere.

This really requires an essay of its own, as does the orchestration. Listen, for one example, to the different uses of the saxophone section in the "Work Song" melody (ex. 3a etc.), where Hodges leads and Webster and Carney add tremendous body to voicings contained within the octave, and to the spread chords in the "religioso" coda of "Work Song" with Otto Hardwicke playing lead. Also related is the marvellous integration of solo passages and ensemble, frequently by means of comments on each other and inter-change of motifs, which is not a technique of orchestration alone so much as composition in all its aspects.

The question that arises with the last few comments is to determine the extent to which they are unique in *Black, Brown and Beige*, and how far they are typical of Ellington's work in general at this period. Relying on the ear alone, one might be led to two diametrically opposed conclusions and yet, without a large body of analytical writing to draw upon, there is no other method of immediate comparison. Obviously there is much in this piece that is recognizable as Ellington within the space of a few bars, and it may be that what is finally most impressive about *Black, Brown and Beige* is the breadth of the conception and, only secondarily, the immense and hard-won skill with which it was carried through.

As to the developmental techniques which were new to Ellington at the time, their use remains rare in his work (*The Tattooed Bride*, though on a smaller scale, is possibly even more thorough-going). What must be borne in mind is the cheerfully unacademic nature of his whole approach to the large-scale work: just as his harmonies are perennially unorthodox, and his counterpoint no more classical than his touch at the piano, so the form of each movement seems to have been created spontaneously. Unlike certain other jazz "composers," Ellington was pre-eminently a composer who was also a "jazzman."

VI. The Hot Bach (1943–1949)

After making his debut at Carnegie Hall on 23 January 1943, Ellington performed there at regular, near-annual intervals over the next five years. These appearances inspired him to write a series of large works for the concert hall, among them *New World A-Coming* (premiered 11 December 1943), *Perfume Suite* (19 December 1944), *Deep South Suite* (23 November 1946), *Liberian Suite* (27 December 1947), and *The Tattooed Bride* (13 November 1948). In the aftermath of *Black, Brown and Beige,* the Carnegie events kept alive the debate about such issues as the merits of jazz versus "serious" music, the place of jazz in the concert hall, and Ellington's ability (or lack thereof) to compose extended works. Increasingly, Ellington found himself in the position of discussing his music in the context of the "classical" European tradition (see his "Defense of Jazz" (§47) and "Certainly It's Music!" (§50)). His growing reputation as a serious composer who happened to write for jazz orchestra led the writer Richard O. Boyer, in an extensive 1944 profile in *The New Yorker,* to dub Ellington "The Hot Bach."

Throughout this period the Ellington orchestra continued to perform in a variety of venues across the country, including the Casa Mañana in Culver City, California, Denver's El Patio Ballroom, Chicago's Civic Opera House, and the Percy Jones Hospital Center in Battle Creek, Michigan. Longer engagements were at New York's Hurricane Club (in 1943 and 1944) and the Club Zanzibar (1945), both featuring regular radio broadcasts. Radio became especially important in 1948 when a second recording ban when into effect (no commercial recordings were made between December 1947 and September 1949).

In contrast to the relative stability of personnel during the thirties, Ellington's orchestra experienced a great deal of flux in the mid- to late forties. Among the major defections were Ben Webster (in 1943), Juan Tizol (1944), Rex Stewart (1945), and Otto Hardwick (1946); Joe "Tricky Sam" Nanton died on 20 July 1946 while on tour in California. Key additions to the band included vocalist Kay Davis (1944), high-note trumpeter William "Cat" Anderson (1945), saxophonist and clarinetist Russell Procope (1945), and trombonists Tyree Glenn (1947) and Quentin "Butter" Jackson (1948).

Another notable change took place in 1946 when Ellington left the Victor record company after his contract expired. After a brief association with the Musicraft label he signed with Columbia the following year.

47. Ellington's "Defense of Jazz" (1943/1944)

I n October 1943 a provocatively titled article, "Is Jazz Music?," appeared in the *American Mercury*, the journal founded by H. L. Mencken. Its author, Winthrop Sargeant (1903–1986), had already published a pioneering study, *Jazz: Hot & Hybrid* (1938), and would later serve as *The New Yorker*'s chief music critic from 1947 to 1972.

In the *American Mercury* article Sargeant criticized those who drew close connections between jazz and classical music. Following the example of certain writers in the twenties and thirties, he classified jazz as a "variety of folk music," outlining those aspects—"one-cell" melodies, repetitive structures, narrow emotional range—that made it vastly different from the European art tradition.[1]

The excerpt below captures the general tone of Sargeant's article and underscores one of his main points: that with more educational opportunities, black musicians would outgrow jazz and turn to more "civilized concert music."[2]

In a letter to the editor a few months later, Ellington responded to Sargeant's elitism with a gentle rebuttal, graciously ceding some points to the critic while effectively countering his thesis.

Winthrop Sargeant: Is Jazz Music?

. . . Perhaps the most striking peculiarity of jazz as opposed to "classical" music, however, is the extremely limited nature of its emotional vocabulary. As a musical language, jazz is graphic and colorful, but, in poetic resources, it is about as rich as pidgin English. A great deal of it makes its appeal exclusively to the motor impulses without affecting the emotions at all. When it does affect the emotions it is limited to the expression of a few elementary moods—sexual excitement, exhilaration, sorrow (in the blues), and a sort of hypnotic intoxication. Its vocabulary does not encompass religious awe, trag-

---

Source: Winthrop Sargeant, "Is Jazz Music?," *American Mercury* LVII/238 (October 1943), 403–9; Duke Ellington, "Defense of Jazz," *American Mercury* LVII/241 (January 1944), 124.

[1] Sargeant, consciously or not, echoed the sentiments of Paul Rosenfeld writing in the late twenties: "American music is not jazz. Jazz is not music. Jazz remains a striking indigenous product, a small, sounding folk-chaos, counterpart of other national developments. What we call *music*, however, is a force, adjusted to the stream of the world in which materials float and elements play, and active like them upon the human situation . . ." (*An Hour with American Music* (Philadelphia: J. B. Lippincott, 1929), 11–12).

[2] Sargeant's conservative position was apparently too tolerant for the reactionary composer and educator Daniel Gregory Mason (1873–1953), who in a letter to the periodical's "Open Forum" chided Sargeant for taking popular music seriously and called jazz "the academic routine of the illiterate" (*American Mercury* LVII/240 (December 1943), 761).

edy, romantic nostalgia, metaphysical contemplation, grandeur, wonder, patriotic or humanitarian fervor, profound grief, horror, exaltation, delicate shades of humor—all of them more or less stock-in-trade expressions of high-brow symphonic or operatic music.

The mistake of the fashionable jazz aesthetes has been to take jazz out of the simple sidewalk and dance hall milieu where it belongs and pretend that it is a complex, civilized art. In its own surroundings, jazz need make no apologies. It is the most vital folk music of our time; it is distinctly and indigenously American, and it speaks a new, infectious dialect that is fresher than anything of the sort Europe has evolved in centuries. It is, I think, something of a pity that, in a watered-down commercial form, jazz has virtually drowned out every other form of American popular music. The flood of musical bilge that emanates from Hollywood and the commercial dance band business has practically swamped the creation of more light-hearted and elegant types of entertainment music. Curiously enough, the mass-produced, commercialized product is also tending to swamp what is left of real, improvised jazz. It is already obvious that the fresh, ingenuous type of jazz the Negroes of New Orleans and Chicago played a generation ago is unlikely ever to be heard again except in phonograph records. Thus, the original spring of jazz has run dry—and for very logical reasons. The musical dialect of jazz, like verbal dialects, owes its development to its remoteness from standardized education. One of its most important ingredients has been the rather colorful awkwardness—the lack of technical polish—with which it is played. And that awkwardness, when genuine, is the fruit of ignorance.

Jazz appeared in the first place because the poor Southern Negro couldn't get a regular musical education, and decided to make his own homemade kind of music without it. His ingenuity has proved him to be one of the world's most gifted instinctive musicians. But as his lot improves, and with it his facilities for musical education, he is bound to be attracted by the bigger scope and intricacy of civilized concert music. Give him the chance to study, and the Negro will soon turn from boogie woogie to Beethoven.

Ellington: Defense of Jazz

SIR: Mr. Sargeant in his article, "Is Jazz Music?" (September issue), has definitely hit upon some truth. It was evident from the start, however, that the article could not be entirely true, since the object was to prove that jazz is *not* music. But how could this be, when the dictionary (I quote from *Webster's New International*) states that music is "Lyric poetry set and sung to music; a tone or tones having any or all of the features of rhythm, melody, or consonance. . . ."? Obviously, jazz fulfills these basic requirements.

There were certain special points Mr. Sargeant made, with which I differ very much. He states that jazz "grows like a weed or a wild flower, exhibits no intellectual complexities," and that jazz is not subject to intellectual criticism because it doesn't contain "the creative ingenuity and technique of an unusual, trained musical mind." Mr. Sargeant has evidently not been exposed to some of the more intelligent jazz, nor is he aware of the amazing musical background of some of our foremost composers and arrangers, in the popular field.

Again, he says that "harmony in jazz is restricted to four or five monotonous patterns," and names the blues, to substantiate this strange statement. I would be interested in knowing how he has managed to arrive at his classifications. Everyone knows that the blues is built upon a set pattern, as is, for example, the sonnet form in poetry. Yet this hasn't seemed to limit poetry to four or five monotonous patterns, nor, do I think is jazz so limited.

But it was when Mr. Sargeant remarked that jazz doesn't encompass such emotions as tragedy, romantic nostalgia, wonder, delicate shades of humor, etc., that I felt badly. Either Mr. Sargeant stuck his neck out, in making such a statement, or we composers in the popular field have in trying to write music that expressed these particular emotions.

Mr. Sargeant is definitely correct in his remarks concerning much of Hollywood's musical products, and I was amused at his use of the term "colorful awkwardness." Part of the tone-poem *Black, Brown and Beige* contains a theme called "Graceful Awkwardness."

Most of all, I was struck by Mr. Sargeant's concluding statement, that given a chance to study, the Negro will soon turn from boogie woogie to Beethoven. Maybe so, but what a shame! There is so much that is good in a musical expression in the popular field.

New York City   DUKE ELLINGTON

48. Carnegie Revisited (1943/1944)

 n 11 December 1943 Ellington returned to Carnegie Hall with a new extended composition, *New World A-Coming*, together with two excerpts from *Black, Brown and Beige* ("West Indian Influence" and "The Lighter Attitude," both from "Brown") and a number of shorter works.

A generally favorable account of the event was given by Barry Ulanov (b. 1918), the editor of *Metronome* who soon would be Ellington's first biographer. Ulanov praised *New World A-Coming* and singled out individual soloists for their work. But he was disappointed in Ellington's decision to offer a "dance program" instead of more ambitious fare—a sign, according to Ulanov, that John Hammond's criticism earlier that year (see §43) had found its mark.

The Canadian-American composer Colin McPhee (1900–1964), writing under the pseudonym "Mercure," took a different stance in his regular column about popular idioms for *Modern Music*. Like his colleague Paul Bowles he looked skeptically at jazz presented as

Sources: Barry Ulanov, "Ellington's Carnegie Hall Concert a Glorified Stage Show," *Metronome* (January 1944), 8, 48; "Mercure" [Colin McPhee], "The Torrid Zone," *Modern Music* XXI/2 (January–February 1944), 121; M.A.S. [Mark Schubart], "Ellington Concert at Carnegie Hall," *New York Times,* 20 December 1944.

concert music, criticizing not only *New World A-Coming* but the setting in which it was premiered.

After Ellington's subsequent Carnegie concert on 19 December 1944, the critic Marc Schubart expressed similar reservations in the *New York Times,* although keeping the overall tone of his review positive.

Ellington's Carnegie Hall Concert (11 December 1943) a Glorified Stage Show

Two hours of Ellington are, by definition, 120 minutes of wonderful music, and Duke's Carnegie Hall concert on December 11 was just that. It was not, however, by any stretch of the imagination, a bona fide concert; it was, rather, an expanded stage show. With the exception of the fifteen minute *New World A-Coming,* the program consisted entirely of brief pieces, most of them conceived for records and of routine record length, three minutes or thereabouts.

The Carnegie Hall stage show opened with Duke's opening theme, *Take the "A" Train,* and closed with his signoff, *Things Ain't What They Used to Be.* Sandwiched in between were the familiar specialties of Duke's current repertoire, the pop songs, the vehicles for the various Ellington soloists, the excerpts from *Black, Brown and Beige,* a couple of the old-time hits, some of the new, and *New World.* It was a program that would have pleased John Hammond mightily; it was a dance program; it was a tacit admission on Duke's part that he agreed with and accepted John's criticism of the last concert, viz.:

> The conclusion that one can draw from this concert is that Duke is dissatisfied with dance music as a medium for expression and is trying to achieve something of greater significance. No one can justly criticize him for this approach if he keeps up the quality of his music for dancing. My feeling is that by becoming more complex he has robbed jazz of most of its basic virtues and lost contact with his audience.[1]

Only once on this program did Duke attempt what the second-string critic of the *New York Herald-Tribune* so bitterly decried in his review of the January concert. "The whole attempt to fuse jazz as a form with art music," said Paul Bowles pompously, "should be discouraged." Fortunately, Duke was not discouraged. For Carnegie this time, he composed one of his most artful pieces, a facile set of variations on a charming theme. In spite of a folksy title that belies both the maturity of Duke Ellington's thinking and the quality of his verbalization, *New World A-Coming* is a successful work. "It is inspired by a great writer [Roi Ottley] and a great book [*New World A-Coming*]," Duke announced. "We accepted the title as a possibility," he continued. "We, very optimistically, anticipated a better future," Duke explained the program of his music. *New World* is optimistic; it suggests halcyon days to come for the colored people, a world of peace and good will, of languorous contentment.

[1] From "Is the Duke Deserting Jazz?," *Jazz* 1/8 (May 1943), 15. See §43.

Those are pleasant things, but they reflect a political ingenuousness which it is better to forget in contemplating this music.

Regarded purely as music, and surely that is the way to accept this or any other Ellington composition, *New World* consists of a series of florid piano passages, in and out of tempo, amplified with great tonal beauty by the orchestra, rich in its chord structure, in its soft, sensuous mood. The whole is not unlike Duke's lovely *Blue Belles of Harlem,* with overtones suggestive of Ravel. It might be called *Fox-Trots Nobles et Sentimentales.* My only cavil with the piece is its fragmentary quality; some of the changes of tempo I found awkward, abrupt. But as a whole I think it is first-rate Ellington, and excellent music, a perfectly successful fusion of "jazz as a form with art music."

There were twenty other numbers, in this order and with these credits:

Take the "A" Train: familiar theme, marred by Ray Nance's skipping of the top notes in his trumpet solo; it was a cold night and Ray's lips were undoubtedly stiff.

Moon Mist: a miserable public address system made Nance's fine fiddle just about inaudible to half the house; Johnny Hodges and Lawrence Brown could be heard, happily.

Variations on Tea for Two: brilliant muted trumpet by Taft Jordan, backed by a fine Strayhorn arrangement of the [Vincent] Youmans standard, voicing clarinet, alto and bass clarinet with the brass delightfully.

Variations on Honeysuckle Rose: Jimmy Hamilton's tight, saxless scoring of [Fats Waller's] tune was far more effective than his underfed clarinet solo.

Variations on Stardust: two choruses of beautiful trumpeting by Harold Baker in a pretty setting designed by Mrs. Baker (Mary Lou Williams).

C Jam Blues: in spite of Duke's apology ("one of our more or less trite things") the successor to [Basie's] *One O'Clock Jump* in popularity as a band instrumental was altogether fine; good solos by Nance and Hamilton and Tricky [Sam Nanton], a fair tenor exercise by Skippy Williams and another marvelous muted trumpet bit by Taft.

Black, Brown and Beige: from the middle section, *Brown, The West Indian Influence* and *The Lighter Attitude;* the first with superb plunger scoring for two trumpets and trombone; the second with more plunger passages, this time ineffably poignant, contrasted with Rex [Stewart]'s bouncy half-valve cornet. Betty Roche's illness necessitated the cancellation of the scheduled blues excerpt from *BBB, Mauve.*

Floor Show: best known as *Goin' Up,* this is the instrumental that was featured in aborted form in the film, *Cabin in the Sky.* Stunning once more were Lawrence Brown's unaccompanied trombone in the middle of the number, and the sixteen measures of Nance violin that follow it.

Don't Get Around Much Any More: the first half of the program was brought to a conclusion with Duke's Hit Parade leader; as usual, Johnny's alto elicited capsizing sighs from the audience.

Ring Dem Bells: highlight of the up-to-date version of this Ellington standard was Nance's scatting and his plunger trumpet.

Award Winning Compositions: the same dreary, cheap potpourri of top Ellington hits (*In a Sentimental Mood, Mood Indigo, Sophisticated Lady,*

Caravan, Solitude, I Let a Song Go Out of My Heart) which Duke features in all his stage shows and cafe appearances.

Jack the Bear: in which Jr. Raglin revealed himself as no Jimmy Blanton on bass, but proved he was somewhere, unlike the legendary Jack the Bear.[2]

Do Nothing Till You Hear from Me: a beautiful chorus by Lawrence Brown, a tolerable vocal by Albert Hibbler, who does seem to be improving.

Summertime: as if to deny the impression of *Do Nothing,* another and entirely horrendous, larynx-straining vocal by Hibbler.

Cotton Tail: too fast for tenor Skippy Williams, who never really got going; Harry Carney did, however, on baritone, contributing the number's most effective moments in this performance.

Black and Tan Fantasy: Toby Hardwicke's exquisite alto introduced the Ellington classic, Tricky Sam's bumptious trombone brought it to its mournful conclusion.

Rockin' in Rhythm: the great power of the present-day Ellington band was unleashed in this favorite of an earlier day; five trumpets especially effective; usual complement of good solos, Carney on clarinet, Tricky, Nance on trumpet.

Sentimental Lady: Johnny Hodges and Rex Stewart took the solo bows, and deserved them; as on the record, affecting music amply justifying its bright title.

Trumpet in Spades: the old virtuoso piece starring Rex, gliding from top to low register with consummate ease and great humor; Duke explained its program as "the picture of 47th and South Parkway at noon in Chicago," the music reflecting "the changes in crowd and car traffic" by changes in tempo and tone.

Things Ain't What They Used to Be: "everybody hums it but nobody knows its title," Duke said with wistful melancholy of his closing theme. Taft Jordan's brash, moving open trumpet highlighted the last number of a concert in which he had distinguished himself greatly, and had demonstrated his proper inclusion among the Ellington stars.

The greatest disappointment of the program was that Duke did not play *BBB.* His explanation, "I don't think too many people are familiar with its story; I want to wait until the story is more familiar to play it again," doesn't satisfy me at all. One needn't follow the history of the American Negro, to which *BBB* is "a tone parallel," to enjoy and appreciate and, indeed, to understand the music. It is actually, I think, far more successful listened to simply as music, without Duke's relentless programming between sections.

For his second Carnegie Hall concert, Duke Ellington should have been more, not less ambitious. Though he presented much wonderful music, the sum of same was a glorified one-nighter. Whether he meant to or not, in this dance program Duke acknowledged the captious carping of his least well-wishing critics. By so doing, I think, he demeaned himself.

---

[2] Various musical personalities went by the name of "Jack the Bear," among them an early stride pianist based in New York and a bass-playing tailor who had a shop in Harlem.

The Torrid Zone (review of 11 December 1943 concert)

Carnegie Hall was jammed for the recent Ellington concert; even the stage was filled, with seats at two-fifty. Outside of the much-heralded *New World A-Coming*, there was little that was new on the two-hour program, but the fan-audience was perfectly happy to listen to the long string of record-length three-minute pieces they already knew by heart. The band got off to a fair start with *Take the "A" Train*, grew sweet and intimate for *Moon Mist* and *Sentimental Lady*, jumped in *C Jam Blues* and *Rockin' in Rhythm*. High spots were the solos of Johnny Hodges, Lawrence Brown, Jimmy Hamilton and Ray Nance; the low-spot—the Duke's new composition, florid, lush and formless. Somehow, the concert was dim and tepid; both audience and band were on their best behavior; hands that elsewhere would have been clapping to the beat were clutching programs and program-notes. It's not easy to dispel the pall of Carnegie Hall.

Ellington Concert at Carnegie Hall (19 December 1944)

Duke Ellington and his orchestra gave a concert at Carnegie Hall last night and the occasion was one which showed clearly why Mr. Ellington is one of the most imposing figures in the world of jazz today. Like most jazz concerts, this one was too long; for it is highly questionable whether listening to swing music in the constraining atmosphere of a concert hall for well over two hours is a pleasurable experience. Nevertheless, Mr. Ellington compiled an admirably varied program for the occasion, and presented it with commendable precision.

Unlike other jazz artists, Mr. Ellington's music makes no pretence at spontaneity and includes virtually no improvisation. His orchestrations are skillfully contrived for effect, and little is left to chance, except that he makes use of the individual styles of performance of the various men in his band. However, his music (and, with the exception of a few pieces by Billy Strayhorn, his colleague and arranger, there was nothing else on the program) is remarkably free of the sterile blight of the so-called "commercial" arrangement. There were vigorous swing numbers, plaintive blues and innumerable solos designed to fit the capacities of his soloists.

There are those who seek in Mr. Ellington's music a growing affinity between jazz and serious music. Actually, the unmistakable style and distinction of his work is based on and derived from the jazz idiom only and employs an instrumental technique utterly different from that of symphonic music. In last night's concert, for example, there were some magnificent solos by Ray Nance, trumpeter; Joseph Nanton, trombone; and Johnny Hodges, saxophonist. There were wailing glissandi and strange effects achieved with mutes and blocks. But whereas in jazz this off-pitch attack and careless sounding intonation is necessary, it can find no place in the present-day symphonic technique, unless the composer is deliberately trying to capture the flavor and atmosphere of jazz.

Among major offerings on Mr. Ellington's program were his "Perfume Suite" and selections from his well-known "Black, Brown and Beige." In the former, there is an ingratiating little piece called "Dancers in Love" which gives Mr. Ellington a chance to display his pianistic talents, as well as a startling trumpet solo in the final section, "Coloratura," played by William ["Cat"] Anderson. Space does not permit mention of all the vocal and instrumental soloists. Suffice it to say, they acquitted themselves with honor, to the obvious enjoyment of the capacity audience.

49. Richard O. Boyer: "The Hot Bach" (1944)

Few writers have depicted Ellington and his world as vividly as Richard O. Boyer in "The Hot Bach," a three-part profile published in *The New Yorker* during the summer of 1944. Boyer not only interviewed Ellington extensively but traveled with the orchestra, observed rehearsals and performances, spoke with musicians, and jotted down overheard conversations. (In the text Boyer refers to himself as the "Boswellian friend of Duke's" and "friend with a historical turn of mind.") The result is a richly textured, candid portrait of Ellington offstage, out of the public eye.

Boyer deftly captures the group spirit of Ellington's musicians on the road, showing their extraordinary resilience in the face of monotony, physical discomfort, and racial discrimination. He highlights the important supporting roles played by Ellington's road manager Jack Boyd, his valet Richard Bowden Jones ("Jonesy"), and especially his writing partner Billy Strayhorn. Boyer's expert touch with description and dialogue brings to life scenes rarely observed by outsiders, such as activities before and after a typical dance job, and the collective working-out of a new piece in the middle of the night.

In this "jumpy atmosphere," as Boyer calls it, Ellington forms the calm center—patiently enduring a myriad of distractions, steadily making art out of chaos.

An abridged version of the article was included in Peter Gammond's *Duke Ellington: His Life and Music* (1958). Following is the complete text.

I

Duke Ellington, whose contours have something of the swell and sweep of a large, erect bear and whose color is that of coffee with a strong dash of cream, has been described by European music critics as one of the world's immortals. More explicitly, he is a composer of jazz music and the leader of a jazz band. For over twenty-three years, Duke, christened Edward Kennedy Ellington, has spent his days and nights on trains rattling across the continent with his band

Source: Richard O. Boyer, "The Hot Bach—1," *The New Yorker* (24 June 1944), 30–34, 37–38, 40, 42, 44; "The Hot Bach—2," *The New Yorker* (1 July 1944), 26–32, 34; "The Hot Bach—3," *The New Yorker* (8 July 1944), 26–31.

on an endless sequence of one-night stands at dances, and playing in movie theatres, where he does up to five shows a day; in the night clubs of Broadway and Harlem and in hotels around the country; in radio stations and Hollywood movie studios; in rehearsal halls and in recording studios, where his band has made some eleven hundred records, which have sold twenty million copies; and even, in recent years, in concert halls such as Carnegie and the Boston Symphony. His music has the virtue of pleasing both the jitterbugs, whose cadenced bouncing often makes an entire building shudder, and the intellectuals, who read into it profound comments on transcendental matters. In 1939, two consecutive engagements Ellington played were a dance in a tobacco warehouse in North Carolina, where his product was greeted with shouts of "Yeah man!," and a concert in Paris, where it was greeted as revealing "the very secret of the cosmos" and as being related to "the rhythm of the atom." On the second occasion, Jacques-Henri Lévesque, a Paris critic, professed to hear all this in the golden bray of trombones and trumpets and in the steady beat of drums, bass, and piano, and Blaise Cendrars, a surrealist poet, said, "Such music is not only a new art form but a new reason for living." A French reporter asked Tricky Sam Nanton, one of Ellington's trombonists, if his boss was a genius. "He's a genius, all right," Sam said, and then he happened to remember that Ellington once ate thirty-two sandwiches during an intermission at a dance in Old Orchard Beach, Maine. "He's a genius, all right," he said, "but Jesus, how he eats!"

Ellington is a calm man of forty-five who laughs easily and hates to hurry. His movements are so deliberate that his steps are usually dogged by his road manager, Jack Boyd, a hard, brisk, red-faced little white man from Texas, whose right index finger was shortened by a planing machine twenty years ago. Boyd, who has been an Ellington employee for some years, yaps and yips at his heels in an effort, for example, to hurry him to a train which in fifteen minutes is leaving a station five miles away. Boyd also lives in fear that Ellington may fall asleep at the wrong time, and since it usually takes an hour of the most ingenious torture to put the slumbering band leader on his feet, the manager's apprehension is not unreasonable. In general, Boyd's life is not a happy one. It is his job to herd about the country a score of highly spirited, highly individual artists, whose colors range from light beige to a deep, blue black, whose tastes range from quiet study to explosive conviviality, and whose one common denominator is a complete disregard of train schedules. Often Duke finishes his breakfast in a taxi. Frequently, driven from the table in his hotel room by the jittery, henlike cluckings of Boyd, he wraps a half-finished chop in a florid handkerchief and tucks it in the pocket of his jacket, from which it protrudes, its nattiness not at all impaired by the fact that it conceals a greasy piece of meat. Not long ago this habit astonished an Icelandic music student who happened to be on a train that Duke had barely caught. The Icelander, after asking for Ellington's autograph, had said, "Mr. Ellington, aren't there marked similarities between you and Bach?" Duke moved his right hand to the handkerchief frothing out of his jacket. "Well, Bach and myself," he said, unwrapping the handkerchief and revealing the chop, "Bach and myself both"—he took a bite from the chop—"write with individual performers in mind."

It is in this jumpy atmosphere that Ellington composes, and some of his best pieces have been written against the glass partitions of offices in recording studios, on darkened overnight buses, with illumination supplied by a companion holding an interminable chain of matches, and in sweltering, clattering day coaches. Sometimes writing a song in no more than fifteen minutes and sometimes finishing concert pieces only a few hours before their performance, he has composed around twelve hundred pieces, many of them of such worth that Stokowski, Grainger, Stravinsky, and Milhaud have called him one of the greatest modern composers. There are many musicians who have even gone as far as to argue that he is the only great living American composer. His career almost spans the life of jazz and has figured prominently in the surge which has brought jazz from the bawdy houses of New Orleans to the Metropolitan Opera House and even to Buckingham Palace. King George, who has one of the world's largest collections of Ellington records, is often found bending over a revolving disc so that he can hear more clearly the characteristically dry, dull thud of the band's bass fiddle pulsing under an Ellington theme or the intricate sinuosity of a tenor saxophone as it curls in and out of the ensemble. To Ellington devotees in Europe, which he toured in 1933 and in 1939, identifying him as a mere writer and player of jazz (his instrument is the piano) is like identifying Einstein as a nice old man. Some notion of their fervor is apparent in the words of a London critic reporting an Ellington concert at the Palladium. "His music has a truly Shakespearean universality," he wrote, "and as he sounded the gamut, girls wept and young chaps sank to their knees." The American counterparts of these European devotees prefer to emphasize the air of gaudy sin that surrounded the birth of jazz instead of likening it to the music of the spheres. They like to dwell on Madam White's Mahogany Hall in New Orleans, a resort which offered its patrons jazz music, and on Buddy Bolden's extravagant love life (Bolden was an early jazz cornettist), and they find pleasure in the belief that most jazz musicians smoke marijuana and die spectacularly in a madhouse. They try to ignore the ugly fact that several of Ellington's musicians learned how to play in Boy Scout bands. In endowing the late Bubber Miley, originator of the growl style on the trumpet and one of the early members of Ellington's band, with an almost legendary aura, although he has been dead less than ten years, they are grateful for the fact that he at least was a very heavy drinker. Anyone who is now forty-five has lived through the entire history of jazz, but this does not prevent the followers of the art from speaking, for example, of the trumpet player King Oliver, who died in 1938, as if he were a Pilgrim Father. In the jazz world, 1910 is the Stone Age and 1923 is medieval. The men in Ellington's band, which was playing when Benny Goodman was in short trousers and when the word "swing" was unknown, have aroused such admiration individually that there are many collectors who spend their time searching for old Ellington records not because they want to listen to the band as a whole but to savor the thirty seconds in which their particular hero takes a solo. As he plays, they mew and whimper in a painful ecstasy or, as they themselves put it, they are sent.

Ellington has, like most entertainers, a stage self and a real self. On the stage, at least when he supplies the "flesh"—the trade term for personal appearances in movie houses—he presents himself as a smiling, carefree African, tingling to his fingertips with a gay, syncopated throb that he can scarcely control. As the spotlight picks him out of the gloom, the audience sees a wide, irrepressible grin, but when the light moves away, Ellington's face instantly sags into immobility. He has given a lot of thought to achieving serenity and equipoise in a life that gives him neither repose nor privacy. He craves peace. He will not argue with anyone in his band, and his road manager, on whom most of the burdens fall, repeatedly sums up his problem in the phrase "Trouble with this band is it has no boss." The arguments which Duke refuses to have, and which, to Boyd's acute distress, he concedes beforehand, usually involve overtime pay or a request for an advance on next week's salary. When Boyd tries to persuade Duke to take a militant attitude, Ellington usually says, in a tone of wheezy complaint, "I won't let these goddam musicians upset me! Why should I knock myself out in an argument about fifteen dollars when in the same time I can probably write a fifteen-hundred-dollar song?" Besides, Ellington contends that an argument may mean the difference between a musician's giving a remarkable performance and just a performance. Furthermore, doctors will tell you that there is a definite relation between anger and ulcers. "Anyway," he will add, in a final desperate defense of his pacific nature, "why should I pit my puny strength against the great Power that runs the universe?" Ellington wears a gold cross beneath his flamboyant plaids and bold checks, reads the Bible every day, along with Winchell and the comics, and has been known to say, "I'd be afraid to sit in a house with people who don't believe. Afraid the house would fall down." He broods about man's final dissolution, and in an effort to stave his own off he has a complete physical examination every three months.

Part of Duke's character goes well enough with the onstage Ellington who periodically throws back his head and emits a long-drawn-out "Ah-h-h!" as if the spirit of hot had forced wordless exultation from his lips. He likes to eat to excess and to drink in moderation. He is also fond of what he calls "the chicks," and when they follow him to the station, as they often do, he stands on the back platform of his train and, as it pulls out, throws them big, gusty, smacking kisses. (He is married, but he has been separated from his wife for fifteen years.) He has a passion for color and clothes. He has forty-five suits and more than a thousand ties, the latter collected in forty-seven states of the Union and seven European countries, and his shoes, hats, shirts, and even his toilet water are all custom-made. His usual manner is one of ambassadorial urbanity, but it is occasionally punctuated by deep despair. In explaining his moods, he says, "A Negro can be too low to speak one minute and laughing fit to kill the next, and mean both." Few people know that he is a student of Negro history. He is a member of one of the first families of

Virginia, for his ancestors arrived at Jamestown in 1619, a year before the pilgrims landed on Plymouth Rock. He has written music commemorating Negro heroes such as Crispus Attucks, the first American killed in the American Revolution; Barzillai Lew, one of the men depicted in the painting called "The Spirit of '76"; and Harriet Tubman, Nat Turner, Denmark Vesey, Frederick Douglass, and other Negro fighters for freedom.[1] He has also written an unproduced opera, "Boola," which tells the story of the American Negro, and a long symphonic work entitled "Black, Brown and Beige," which he says is "a tone parallel to the history of the Negro." His concern for his race is not entirely impersonal, since he and his band are constantly faced, even in the North, by the institution of Jim Crow. "You have to try not to think about it," Duke says, "or you'll knock yourself out."

Because Duke likes peace and repose, he tries to avoid the endless controversies that go on in the world of jazz. The followers of jazz cannot even agree on the fundamental point of what it is. To keep out of this dispute in particular, Duke frequently says, when people try to pin him down, "I don't write jazz. I write Negro folk music." There are those who insist that the only "righteous jazz," as they call it, is performed by bands of no more than six or seven men whose music is as spontaneous, unpremeditated, and unrehearsed as that of Shelley's skylark. Yet the very aficionados who insist that all real jazz is improvised and that all the solos must be impromptu often claim that Duke's artistry is the genuine, blown-in-the-bottle stuff, brushing aside his own statement that almost all the music his seventeen-piece band plays has been scored. Partly because of this bickering, Ellington always feels that he has found sanctuary when he boards a train. He says that then peace descends upon him and that the train's metallic rhythm soothes him. He likes to hear the whistle up ahead, particularly at night, when it screeches through the blackness as the train gathers speed. "Specially in the South," he says. "There the firemen play blues on the engine whistle—big, smeary things like a goddam woman singing in the night." He likes, too, to sit next to the window, his chin in his hand, and, in a trancelike state, to stare for hours at the telephone poles flashing by and at the pattern of the curving wires as they alternately drop and ascend. Even at night, particularly if his train is passing through certain sections of Ohio or Indiana, he will remain at the window (shifting to the smoker if the berths are made up), for he likes the flames of the steel furnaces. "I think of music sometimes in terms of color," he says, "and I like to see the flames licking yellow in the dark and then pulsing down to a kind of red glow." Duke has a theory that such sights stimulate composition. "The memory of things gone is important to a jazz musician," he says. "Things like the old folks singing in the moonlight in the back yard on a hot night, or something someone said long ago. I remember I once wrote a sixty-four-bar piece about a memory of when I was a little boy in bed and heard a man whistling on the street outside, his footsteps echoing away. Things like these may be more important to a musician than technique."

[1] Beyond *Barzallai Lou* (as Ellington spelled the name) and the historically panoramic *Black, Brown and Beige* (both 1943), it is not clear which other pieces Boyer had in mind that commemorated various "Negro fighters for freedom."

Perhaps Duke will still be awake at three in the morning, when his train stops for fifteen minutes at a junction. If there is an all-night lunchroom, he will get off the train, straddle a stool, his Burberry topcoat sagging like a surplice, a pearl-gray fedora on the back of his head, and direct the waitress in the creation of an Ellington dessert. The composition of an Ellington dessert depends upon the materials available. If, as is often the case, there is a stale mess of sliced oranges and grapefruit floating in juice at the bottom of a pan, he will accept it as a base. To this he will have the girl add some applesauce, a whole package of Fig Newtons, a dab of ice cream, and a cup of custard. When Duke is back on the train, Boyd, who has stayed up for the purpose, will beg him to go to bed, if they are on a sleeper, or to take a nap, if the band is travelling by day coach, as is often necessary in wartime. Ellington not infrequently takes out a pad of music-manuscript paper, fishes in his pockets for the stub of a lead pencil, and begins composing, and Boyd departs, complaining to the world that "Ellington is a hard man to get to bed and a harder man to get out of it." Frowning, his hat on the back of his head, swaying from side to side with the motion of the car, occasionally sucking his pencil and trying to write firmly despite the bouncing of the train, humming experimentally, America's latter-day Bach will work the night through.

It was on a day coach, rolling through the Ohio and Pennsylvania night, that Ellington wrote most of "New World A-Coming," a symphonic work which had its premiere at Carnegie Hall last December. A Boswellian friend of Duke's who was travelling with him at the time took notes on the scene. Across the aisle from Duke as he worked, four men in the band were playing tonk, a form of gin rummy, at a dollar a hand. In front of him a harassed mother was trying to soothe a crying baby and behind him two little boys, in the great day-coach tradition, were eating oranges. Nearby, Lawrence Brown, an Ellington trombonist, a husky, dignified man who looks like a doctor and says he would like to be one, was reading the *Atlantic Monthly,* while Junior Raglin, a chunky youth who plays the bass fiddle, was scowling over a comic magazine. Sonny Greer, Ellington's jaunty, jouncy drummer, looked up from the card game and said to Duke, "What you doing, Dumpy?" Duke grunted, then said, "Oh, just fooling around on a new piece." The other card players looked over and in succession asked, "How's it going, Pops?," "Getting any-where, Sandhead?," and "You sending 'em, Fatso?" The band members, who sometimes speak of Duke as The Duke, also address him as Phony, which is short for the Phony Duke, and Ze Grand, a contraction of Ze Grand Duke. Duke didn't reply to any of the questions; he just kept on working, swearing whenever the rocking of the train made him blur his notations. Not far away, a group of soldiers were swarming around Estrelita, whom publicity men know as the Sepia Gypsy Rose Lee or the South American Bombshell and whom the band calls Skookums. She is a part of a vaudeville act that occa-sionally tours with Ellington. Down the aisle a way, Albert Hibbler, a blind singer in the band, was balancing himself on the arm of a seat occupied by Betty Roche, Ellington's blues singer, whose customary white dress highlights the deep black of her skin, and at one end of the car Wallace Jones, Harold

Baker, and Rex Stewart, trumpets, and Juan Tizol, trombone (a musician, of course, takes the name of his instrument), were discussing the occupational hazards of their trade.

"When we don't sleep," said Tizol, who is a Puerto Rican and the only white man in the band, "seems like our lips get even stronger. Get a lot of sleep and damn if they don't crumple."

"I got a salve I like," Jones said. "Prevents muscles of the lip going dead. But the muscles of my lip just wouldn't vibrate last night, just wouldn't vibrate. That damn hall was too cold."

Baker began talking about the difficulty he had had in learning the trumpet. "I breathed all wrong," he said, "and it strained the whole side of my face. It used to hurt so. I blew from too low and I couldn't learn to keep my stomach tight. I used to blow with my jaw as hard as a wall and my teacher would walk up and bang the trumpet right out of my mouth. I pressed so hard against my teeth that they were sore all the time. To cure myself, I hang my trumpet on a string from the ceiling. Just walk up to it and blow it without touching it with my hands.

"Music is bad for the nerves," he went on. "My nerves are bad now. You gotta do so many things at once. You gotta think about how to fill your horn, about harmony. You gotta look pretty and keep the guy next to you satisfied. You sneak each other that ole go-to-hell look, then flash the public that ole full-of-joy look. I dunno. It's just rush and then rush some more. Never no sleep. Feel like I want to quit sometime." No one spoke for a moment and there was no sound except the rattling of the train. Then Baker said musingly, "Always wanted to play like Joe Smith, but seemed like my notes would crack on me. Joe's notes were so clear and clean." Rex Stewart, a ball of a man with a mustache and a slow, pleasant smile, said comfortingly, "Well, Harold, I'm always missing something, too. Never get exactly the right thing out. Never sounds exactly like I imagine before I play."

The train rounded a long curve and Duke stopped writing. He began again and then evidently decided he wanted to try the music out on someone. "Swee-pea? Sweepea!" he called. Sweepea is William Strayhorn, the staff arranger and a talented composer in his own right. Strayhorn, who, incidentally, does not play in the band, is a small, scholarly, tweedy young man with gold-rimmed spectacles. He got his nickname from a character in a comic strip. Strayhorn, who had been trying to sleep, staggered uncertainly down the aisle in answer to his boss's summons.

"I got a wonderful part here," Duke said to him. "Listen to this." In a functional, squeaky voice that tried for exposition and not for beauty, Duke chanted, "Dah dee dah dah dah, deedle dee deedle dee boom, bah bah bah, boom, boom!" He laughed, frankly pleased by what he had produced, and said, "Boy, that son of a bitch has got a million twists."

Strayhorn, still swaying sleepily in the aisle, pulled himself together in an attempt to offer an intelligent observation. Finally he said drowsily, "It's so simple, that's why."

Duke laughed again and said, "I really sent myself on that. Would you like to see the first eight bars?"

"Ah yes! Ah yes!" Strayhorn said resignedly, and took the manuscript. He looked at it blankly. Duke misinterpreted Sweepea's expression as one of severity.

"Don't look at it that way, Sweepea," he said. "It's not like that."

"Why don't you reverse this figure?" asked Strayhorn sleepily. "Like this." He sang shakily, "Dah dee dah dah dah, dah dee dah dah dah, boomty boomty boomty, boom!"

"Why not dah dee dah dah dah, deedle dee deedle dee dee, boom bah bah bah, boom?" Duke said.

"Dah dee dah dah dah!" sang Strayhorn stubbornly.

"Deedle dee deedle dee dee!" Duke answered.

"Dah dee dah dah dah!" Strayhorn insisted.

Duke did not reply; he just leaned eagerly forward and, pointing to a spot on the manuscript with his pencil, said, "Here's where the long piano part comes in. Here's where I pick up the first theme and restate it and then begin the major theme. Dah dee dah, deedle dee deedle dee, boom!"

The train lurched suddenly. Sweepea collapsed into a seat and closed his eyes. "Ah yes!" he said weakly. "Ah yes!"

Duke retrieved his manuscript from him and went back to work. The blackness outside was changing to gray, and presently the music slipped from his hand and his head dropped forward as if his neck was broken. Some time later Boyd bustled through the coach, shouting to the band that the train would be in New York in half an hour. He was brought to a halt by the sight of Ellington's sleeping form. He began to shake Duke. "Damn if I don't let him stay here!" Boyd said to Duke's friend after a moment. "Damn if I don't do what I did in Tacoma! Let him stay there that time until the train was switched to a siding five miles away. He had to walk back. Damn if you wouldn't think that'd cure him!" He loosened his clutch on Duke's collar and the big man sagged forward. Boyd glared at him. "Once in San Francisco," he said, "Ellington slept that way and when he got off the train he was so sleepy he got in a line of men that were being herded into a van. They were prisoners for San Quentin. When Ellington tried to get out, the guard wouldn't let him. Damn if I should of rescued him! Should of let him go to prison. It would of taught him."

Boyd tries to arrange things so that the band will arrive at its destination at about six or seven in the evening, making it possible for Duke to sleep an hour or two before the night's engagement. If the town is in the North, Ellington can occasionally get into a hotel, since his name is well and favorably known, but the other members of the band have to scurry around the Negro section of the town, if there is one, and make their own arrangements for lodgings. Usually they can get rooms in the households of amiable colored citizens, and if they can't do that they often pass the time in some public place like a railway station or a city hall. Most dances begin at nine and run until two in the morning. On dance nights, Boyd has an assignment that almost tears him in two. He is supposed to "stand on the door" and check the number of admissions to the dance, but he is also supposed to have Duke awake and at the dance hall. At about eight-thirty, after a half hour's futile effort to rouse his boss, he is in a frenzy. Then, with the strength of desperation—Boyd is a small man and Duke is six feet tall and weighs two hundred and ten pounds— he props the unconscious band leader in a sitting position on the edge of his bed and, grabbing his arms, pulls him out of bed and onto his feet and walks him across the floor. This usually restores a degree of consciousness, which slowly spreads through the rest of Ellington's system. At this point, Boyd tears off to the dance hall, leaving some hanger-on behind to see that Ellington does not go to sleep again.

Duke thereupon pads sleepily about the room, groping for his red bathrobe and red slippers. His bare shanks show from beneath what appears to be a short, old-fashioned nightshirt, but if anyone calls it a nightshirt Duke is insulted. He says sulkily, "It's an Oriental sleeping coat. Not a nightshirt. Have 'em specially made for me." When he gathers himself together, he reaches for a phone and orders what for him is breakfast—fruit, cornflakes, and black tea with cream. While he is on the phone, he may pick up a pencil and scribble a few bars of music on the pad before him. After humming a bit of what he has just written down, he may say, "Always like to use the voice instead of the piano when writing. Piano holds you too much to what falls naturally under the fingers." With an almost imperceptible increase in tempo, he will eat his breakfast, and then, at a faster pace, he will shave and take a shower. He usually trots out of the bathroom, flings himself on his bed, and douses himself with talcum powder. He also sprays himself with toilet water. Then he may say, "Tell you about me and toilet water. It must have two properties. It must have a nice, clean fragrance, and it must be pleasant to the taste. Have mine blended for me. Call it Warm Valley. After one of my pieces." When he has dressed, he grabs a hat, flings it away, takes another one, and says, "Tell you what goes with me and hats. I pay twenty-five or thirty dollars for a specially tailored hat and then throw it away and buy one of these dollar-ninety-five corduroy porkies. I love these little porkies."

Duke usually arrives at a dance a trifle late, a common practice among band leaders and one they justify by arguing that they can make a more dramatic entrance after the band has been playing awhile. Most of the dances Ellington plays for are held in auditoriums, dance halls, or armories that accommodate anything from two to ten thousand people. When Duke arrives, someone tells the men in the band, and after a minute or two they call a halt and explode into the band's dressing room. They are very intense. As Sonny Greer explains, "To give anything, you gotta give everything." Their intensity is expressed by a weird cacophony in which some of the musicians shriek like steam whistles, some of them imitate the pantings of locomotives, some sing like saxophones or trombones, and some make sounds so complicated and unearthly that it seems impossible that they come from a human throat. There is a good deal of horsing around and pushing, and occasionally a bottle is passed. While all this is going on, Albert Hibbler may still be dressing and complaining, "I can't see my uniform." Somebody may say with rough affection, "Shut up, you squarehead. You don't need no uniform," and hunt it up for him. If someone tells Duke that there is a big crowd on the floor, he starts to yell, "Hurry up!

Hurry up! I want to make my entrance!" No one pays much attention to him. Lawrence Brown, who is one of the best trombones in the profession, usually stands apart from the rumpus, as if he disapproved. "I don't care anything about the band business," he says. "I sometimes think I may still study medicine." Brown, who is thirty-six, a college graduate, and the son of a minister, used to play trombone for Aimee Semple McPherson in the Angelus Temple in Los Angeles, a fact which disturbs some of his admirers, who, with the reverse morality of jazz fanciers, would prefer that he had begun his career in a sporting house. While his mates riot in the dressing room, Brown may say with quiet pride, "I do not curse, drink, or smoke." Not long ago he said that if he couldn't become a doctor, he would be a dentist or an undertaker.

In general, or so its members like to think, the more exhausted the Ellington band is, the better it plays. Ordinarily, the tempo at the beginning of a dance is rather slow; both players and dancers have to warm up to their interdependent climax. By midnight both are in their stride. Then the trumpets screech upward in waves, sometimes providing a background for a solo, soft and sensuous, by tough little Johnny Hodges, alto saxophonist, who advances toward the front of the stage threateningly and who holds his instrument as if it were a machine gun with which he was about to spray the crowd. Johnny is fond of addressing his fans as "Bub" or "Bubber" when they come up to talk to him at a dance. Junior Raglin's bass fiddle beats dully, like a giant pulse. Junior's eyes are closed and his face is screwed up as if he were in pain. Duke's face is dominated by an absorbed, sensual scowl as he plays his piano. Sonny Greer, a cigarette waggling before an impassive face, jounces up and down on his stool so hard that he seems to be on a galloping horse, and Rex Stewart, as the night advances, becomes progressively more cocky and springy as he takes his solos. Sometimes the excitement among the dancers reaches a pitch that threatens literally to bring down the house. Two years ago, a dance in a hall in Arkansas was stopped when the floor began to collapse under the feet of the jitterbugs, and five years ago, in Bluefield, West Virginia, so many people crowded about Duke on the stage that it caved in, fortunately without casualties. Almost always a group of serious thinkers who attend these affairs just for the music and not for the dancing gather before the bandstand in front of Duke and make profound comments. "The guy is really deep here," one will say, over the howling of the jitterbugs. Another will murmur, "Terrific mood, terrific content, terrific musicianship." Prim little colored girls sitting along the wall with their mammas—many of Duke's dances in the North are attended by both Negroes and white people—will get up and really throw it around when they are asked to dance, and then will return demurely to their mammas. The serious thinkers disapprove of the jitterbug and his activities, but Duke says, "If they'd been told it was a Balkan folk dance, they'd think it was wonderful." Every now and then there is a wail from Tricky Sam Nanton's trombone, a sad wa-wa melody which sometimes sounds like an infant crying, sometimes like the bubbly, inane laugh of an idiot, and sometimes like someone calling for help. Sam says, "It's a sad tale with a little mirth. When I play it, I think of a man in a dungeon calling out a cell window." Usually a dance ends peacefully, but more than once, in the Southwest, cowboys have brought the festivities to an abrupt ending by firing their guns at the ceiling. On such occasions, the band gets off the stage in a hurry, which is probably a good idea. Once in a while, in the South, a gentleman draws a gun and insists that the band play only his favorite tunes. Unpleasantness, however, is not confined to regions below the Mason-Dixon line. During prohibition, a group of gangsters tried to shake Duke down when he was in Chicago. They presented their demand to Sam Fleischnick, who was then Duke's road manager. Fleischnick refused. "All our boys carry guns," he told the gangsters. "If you want to shoot it out, we'll shoot it out." Ellington considered getting out of town when he heard of Fleischnick's declaration of war against the gang, but he finally solved the problem in more sensible fashion. He telephoned the influential owner of a New York night club where Duke and his band once had played and the owner arranged for Ellington to have the freedom of Chicago without cost.

When a dance is over, Boyd and his Negro assistant, Richard Jones, or Jonesy, who doubles as Duke's valet, begin packing the instruments, uniforms, scores, stands, and the like so that they can be transported to the next town the band is playing. "If the band gets four hours' sleep," Boyd often says, "me and Jonesy don't get any. When the band walks out, they're through, but me and Jonesy have to get the baggage on the train and often we don't get to bed at all." After work, Ellington and Strayhorn are likely to go to some Negro all-night spot, if they are in Buffalo, Cleveland, Chicago, New Orleans, Pittsburgh, San Francisco, or some other big town which affords such a luxury. Duke, who is always worrying about keeping his weight down, may announce that he intends to have nothing but Shredded Wheat and black tea. When his order arrives, he looks at it glumly, then bows his head and says grace. After he has finished his snack, his expression of virtuous determination slowly dissolves into wistfulness as he watches Strayhorn eat a steak. Duke's resolution about not overeating frequently collapses at this point. When it does, he orders a steak, and after finishing it he engages in another moral struggle for about five minutes. Then he really begins to eat. He has another steak, smothered in onions, a double portion of fried potatoes, a salad, a bowl of sliced tomatoes, a giant lobster and melted butter, coffee, and an Ellington dessert—perhaps a combination of pie, cake, ice cream, custard, pastry, jello, fruit, and cheese. His appetite really whetted, he may order ham and eggs, a half-dozen pancakes, waffles and syrup, and some hot biscuits. Then, determined to get back on his diet, he will finish, as he began, with Shredded Wheat and black tea. Long before this, he is usually surrounded by an admiring crowd, which watches him with friendly awe. He chats with the chicks in the group and may turn from his steak or lobster to say pleasantly to one of them, "You make that dress look so beautiful." He is not a bit embarrassed by the fact that he said the same thing the night before to another chick in another town. Sometimes he will pause before eating a dessert awash in rich yellow cream and say to a girl, "I never knew an angel could be so luscious." At the end of his supper, he may lean back, satisfied at last, and sing out to Strayhorn, "Dah dah dee dee dee, tah tahdle tah boom, deedle dee, deedle dee, boom!"

"Why not deedle dee deedle dee dee, deedle dee deedle dee dee, dumtah dumtah dumtah, boom?" Billy asked recently on such an occasion.

"I don't think that's right for a trio," Duke said. "This is a trio."

"I don't think your strain is melodic enough," Billy said.

"I think it's a nice strain. Then it goes backward." Duke said, and sang, "Boom, dee deedle, dee deedle, boom tah tahdle tah, dee dee dee dah dah!"

"I still think it has too many notes for a trio," Billy said. "I'm looking for something small that goes up a half tone."

Sometimes Duke and Strayhorn have adjoining rooms at a hotel. It will be bright daylight when they climb into their beds, Duke first having said his prayers. Ellington may stare up at the ceiling a moment before he falls asleep and then call to Billy, in the next room, "Sweepea! How about dah dee dah dah, dah dee dah dah dah as an opening fanfare?"

"Why not deedle dee deedle dee deedle dee, deedle dee dee?" sings Sweepea sleepily. Then there is silence.

II

There are times when Duke Ellington exudes such calm contentment that a colleague, under the influence of the benign radiation, once murmured drowsily, "Duke make me sleepy, like rain on the roof." His nerves and laughter are so loose and easy that members of his jazz band believe that they got that way because of his physical makeup rather than because of the quality of his spirit. "His pulse is so low he can't get excited," they explain. "His heart beat slower than an ordinary man's." Only something in the flow of the blood, they are sure, could explain a calm that has survived twenty-three years in the band business—years in which Duke and his seventeen-piece band have again and again clattered on tour from one end of the country to the other. Duke believes that his calm is an acquired characteristic, attained through practice, but whether acquired or inborn, it is his monumental placidity, which is only occasionally shattered, that enables Duke to compose much of his music in an atmosphere of strident confusion. Most composers, alone with their souls and their grand pianos, regard composition as a private activity. Often, when Duke is working out the details of a composition or an arrangement, the sixteen other members of his band not only are present but may even participate, and the occasion sometimes sounds like a political convention, sometimes like a zoo at feeding time. Ordinarily, Duke completes the melody and the basic arrangement of a composition before he tries it out on the band at a rehearsal; then, as he polishes, or "sets," the arrangement, he is likely to let the men in the band make suggestions in a creative free-for-all that has no counterpart anywhere in the world of jazz or classical music. Perhaps a musician will get up and say, "No, Duke! It just can't be that way!," and demonstrate on his instrument his conception of the phrase or bar under consideration. Often, too, this idea may outrage a colleague, who replies on *his* instrument with *his* conception, and the two players argue back and forth not with words but with blasts from trumpet or trombone. Duke, whom European music critics have called the American Bach, will resolve the debate by sitting down at his piano, perhaps taking something from each suggestion, perhaps modifying and reconciling the ideas of the two men, but always putting the Ellington stamp on the music before passing on to the next part of the work in progress. Duke sometimes quotes Bach. "As Bach says," he may remark, speaking about piano playing, "if you ain't got a left hand, you ain't worth a hoot in hell."

The band rarely works out an entire arrangement collectively, but when it does, the phenomenon is something that makes other musicians marvel. This collective arranging may take place anywhere—in a dance hall in Gary, Indiana, in an empty theatre in Mobile, or in a Broadway night club. It will usually be after a performance, at about three in the morning. Duke, sitting at his piano and facing his band, will play a new melody, perhaps, or possibly just an idea consisting of only eight bars. After playing the eight bars, he may say, "Now this is sad. It's about one guy sitting alone in his room in Harlem. He's waiting for his chick, but she doesn't show. He's got everything fixed for her." Duke sounds intent and absorbed. His tired band begins to sympathize with the waiting man in Harlem. "Two glasses of whiskey are on his little dresser before his bed," Duke says, and again plays the eight bars, which will be full of weird and mournful chords. Then he goes on to eight new bars. "He has one of those blue lights turned on in the gloom of his room," Duke says softly, "and he has a little pot of incense so it will smell nice for the chick." Again he plays the mournful chords, developing his melody. "But she doesn't show," he says, "she doesn't show. The guy just sits there, maybe an hour, hunched over on his bed, all alone." The melody is finished and it is time to work out an arrangement for it. Lawrence Brown rises with his trombone and gives out a compact, warm phrase. Duke shakes his head. "Lawrence, I want something like the treatment you gave in 'Awful Sad,'" he says.[2] Brown amends his suggestion and in turn is amended by Tricky Sam Nanton, also a trombone who puts a smear and a wa-wa lament on the phrase suggested by Brown. Juan Tizol, a third trombone, says, "I'd like to see a little ritard on it." Duke may incorporate some variation of one of the suggestions. Then he'll say, "Come on, you guys. Get sincere. Come on down here, Floor Show"—he is addressing Ray Nance—"and talk to me with your trumpet." In a moment or so the air is hideous as trombone and clarinet, saxophone and trumpet clash, their players simultaneously trying variations on the theme. Johnny Hodges suggests a bar on his alto saxophone, serpentine, firm, and ingratiating, and tied closely to Duke's theme. Harry Carney, baritone sax, may say it is too virtuoso for the whole sax section and clean it up a little, making it simpler. "Come on, you guys. Let's play so far," Duke says. As the band plays in unison, the players stimulate one another and new qualities appear; an experienced ear can hear Rex Stewart, trumpet, take an idea from Brown and embellish it a bit and give it his own twist. Duke raises his hand and the band

---

[2] *Awful Sad,* first recorded in 1928 featuring trumpeter Arthur Whetsol, had also been recorded for Victor in 1933—when Brown was in the orchestra—but not issued.

stops playing. "On that last part—" he says, "trumpets, put a little more top on it, will ya?" He turns to Junior Raglin, the scowling bass player, and says, "Tie it way down, Junior, tie it way down." Again the play, and now the bray of the trumpets becomes bolder and more sure, the trombones more liquid and clearer, the saxophones mellower, and at the bottom there is the steady beat, beat, beat, beat, four to a bar, of the drums, bass and guitar, and the precise, silvery notes of Ellington on the piano, all of it growing, developing, fitting closer together, until Duke suddenly halts them by shouting, "Too much trombone!" Juan Tizol, a glum white man and the only player in the band who likes to play sweet, complains, "I think it's too gutbucket for this kind of piece. I'd like it more legit." He plays a smooth, clear curlicue on his valve trombone. "Well, maybe you're right," Duke says, "but I still think that when Sam gets into that plunger part, he should give it some smear." Again the band begins at the beginning, and as the boys play, Duke calls out directions. "Like old Dusty," he may say (Dusty is a long-dead jazz musician), and even as he says it the emphasis and shaping will change. Or he may lean forward and say to one man, "Like you did in 'The Mooche,'" or he may shout over to Carney, who doubles on the clarinet, "The clarinet is under Tricky too much!" As the music begins to move along, he shouts, "Get sincere! Give your heart! Let go your soul!" His hands flicker over the keyboard, sometimes coming in close together while he hunches his broad, quivering shoulders, one shoulder twisted higher than the other, an absorbed half-smile upon his face. At a signal from Duke, various players, with the theme now solidly in mind, will get up and take solos. He points at the soloist he wants and raises his right index finger, and as long as the player doesn't get too far away from the theme, Duke lets him have his way. Perhaps two hours have gone by. The sky is getting gray, but the boys have the feel of the piece and can't let it alone. They play on and on, their coats off, their hats on the backs of their heads, some with their shoes off, their stocking feet slapping up and down on the floor, their eyes closed, their feet wide apart and braced when they stand for a solo, rearing back as if they could blast farther and better that way. Now Juan Tizol grabs a piece of paper and a pencil and begins to write down the orchestration, while the band is still playing it. Whenever the band stops for a breather, Duke experiments with rich new chords, perhaps adopts them, perhaps rejects, perhaps works out a piano solo that fits, clear and rippling, into little slots of silence, while the brass and reeds talk back and forth. By the time Tizol has finished getting the orchestration down on paper, it is already out of date. The men begin to play again, and then someone may shout "How about that train?" and there is a rush for a train that will carry the band to another engagement.

Duke enjoys the rhythm of a train as it rolls across the country and on one occasion he even scored it, putting notes on paper as he bounced and swayed along, listening to all the metallic variations of sound. He called the piece that resulted "Daybreak Express." The continental nature of Duke's profession is indicated by his itinerary for 1942. He began on January 1st in Kansas City, Missouri, and then, playing one-night stands and engagements that lasted as long as six weeks, rattled along to Junction City, Kansas; Omaha, Nebraska; Madison, Wisconsin; Waukegan, Illinois; Elkhart, Indiana; Chicago; Detroit; Canton, Ohio; Pittsburgh; Uniontown, Pennsylvania; Boston; Lawrence, Massachusetts; Portland, Maine; Worcester, Massachusetts; Boston, Toronto, Buffalo, Washington, Baltimore, Philadelphia, Pittsburgh; Moline, Illinois; South Gate, San Diego, San Francisco, Stockton, and Sacramento, all in California; Portland, Oregon; Vancouver; Seattle and Tacoma; Salem in Oregon; and then back to King City, Vallejo, San Jose, Los Angeles, and Ocean Park, in California; Salt Lake City, Denver, Chicago, Milwaukee, Chicago, Cleveland, Dayton, Fort Wayne, Chicago, St. Louis; Moberly and Kansas City, in Missouri; Topeka, Kansas; back once more to California to play at Long Beach, Los Angeles, Hollywood, Sacramento, Oakland, and San Jose; then to Salt Lake City, St. Louis, Omaha; Storm Lake and Fort Dodge, in Iowa; St. Paul, Madison, Chicago, Toledo, Cincinnati, Youngstown; Toronto and Kitchener, in Canada; down to Buffalo, Fort Dix, Philadelphia, Baltimore, Washington, Hartford, Bridgeport, Harrisburg, Columbus, and, on the last day of 1942, to Detroit.

Duke likes trains because, as he says, "Folks can't rush you until you get off." He likes them, too, because dining-car waiters know about his love for food and he is apt to get very special attention. His journeys are punctuated by people who shove bits of paper at him for his autograph. Not long ago, travelling between Cleveland and Pittsburgh on a day coach, a German refugee with sad, weak blue eyes who had once played chamber music in Stuttgart sat down next to Duke and asked him for his autograph, and the two men got into conversation. A friend of Duke's with a historical turn of mind happened to be along on the trip and took notes on what the two men said. The refugee knew little about jazz, but he did know that Stokowski, Stravinsky, and Milhaud had described Ellington as one of the greatest modern composers.

"You can't write music right," Duke said, explaining his methods of composition, "unless you know how the man that'll play it plays poker."

"*Absolut phantastisch!*" the German murmured. Duke seemed startled, then laughed.

"Vot a varm, simple laugh you haf," the refugee said enviously.

Duke laughed again. "No, what I mean is," he said, "you've got to write with certain men in mind. You write just for their abilities and natural tendencies and give them places where they do their best—certain entrances and exits and background stuff. You got to know each man to know what he'll react well to. One guy likes very simple ornamentation; another guy likes ornamentation better than the theme because it gives him a feeling of being a second mind. Every musician has his favorite licks and you gotta write to them."

"His own licks? *Licks?*" asked the refugee.

"His own favorite figures," Duke said. He looked out the window. "I sure hated to leave that chick," he said affably. "I'd just met her. She was all wrapped up for me. All wrapped up in cellophane."

"Please?" asked the German.

"I know what sounds well on a trombone and I know what sounds well on a trumpet and they are not the same," Duke said. "I know what Tricky Sam can play on a trombone and I know what Lawrence Brown can play on a trombone and they are not the same, either."

"Don't you ever write just for inspiration?"

"I write for my band," Duke said. "For instance, I might think of a wonderful thing for an oboe, but I ain't got no oboe and it doesn't interest me. My band is my instrument. My band is my instrument even more than the piano. Tell you about me and music—I'm something like a farmer."

"A farmer that grows things?"

"A farmer that grows things. He plants his seed and I plant mine. He has to wait until spring to see his come up, but I can see mine right after I plant it. That night. I don't have to wait. That's the payoff for me."

"Mr. Ellington, how do you get those lovely melodic passages?"

"If you want to do a mellow cluster with a mixture of trombones and saxes, it will work very well," Duke said. "A real derby, not an aluminum one, will give you a big, round, hollow effect."

"A real derby?"

"A real derby."

"Not an aluminum derby?"

"Not an aluminum derby."

"*Phantastisch!*" the exile said.

Duke laughed. He called to Sonny Greer, his drummer, sitting up ahead, "I sure hated to miss that chick," he said. "She was all wrapped up in cellophane."

The refugee's pale blue eyes stared steadily at Duke. "When inspiration comes, Mr. Ellington," he said finally, "you write, *natürlich?*"

"It's mostly all written down, because it saves time," Duke said. He seemed eager to get away, but the coach was crowded and there wasn't another place to sit. "It's written down if it's only a basis for a change. There's no set system. Most times I write it and arrange it. Sometimes I write it and the band and I collaborate on the arrangement. Sometimes Billy Strayhorn, my staff arranger, does the arrangement. When we're all working together, a guy may have an idea and he plays it on his horn. Another guy may add to it and make something out of it. Someone may play a riff and ask, 'How do you like this?' The trumpets may try something together and say, 'Listen to this.' There may be a difference of opinion on what kind of mute to use. Someone may advocate extending a note or cutting it off. The sax section may want to put an additional smear on it."

"Schmear?"

"Smear," Duke said.

Duke tried a few times to end the discussion, but the exile's questioning kept bringing him back to his exposition, and he was still explaining when the train pulled into Pittsburgh, where he and his band were to give a concert at Carnegie Hall. The hall is a resplendent place. It has tall, gray marble columns with gilt Corinthian capitals, and on its walls are inscribed the names of Schubert, Brahms, Bach, Beethoven, Mozart, and Chopin. As the band trooped through the building to the dressing rooms, Duke glanced at the list of his predecessors and remarked, "Boys, we're in fast company."

When the band is doing five shows a day in a movie house, Duke can take a hot, stuffy dressing room, often windowless and small, and give it the pleasant atmosphere of a neighborhood saloon. As soon as a show is over, Jonesy, his valet, who always wears a hat on the back of his head and a leather windbreaker, helps him undress and holds his red bathrobe up while he slips into it. Then Duke will lie down on a cot, a towel over his eyes to shield them from the light. Jonesy goes out to get him beer and sandwiches, and by the time he returns Duke is usually up playing a game of cassino with someone in his band. Other members of the band will keep walking in and out. "My honor is here. My honor is here," Duke mumbles, as he examines his cards, in a voice that has the lulling drone of an electric fan. Sometimes he varies this refrain with the more firmly voiced observation, "I will now do something to straighten this out." He keeps the door of his dressing room closed, but even so there is always the presence of the mechanical voice in the movie, faint yet powerful, and, now and then, the brash canned music of the newsreel. Sometimes, too, down the corridor, the deep voice of Estrelita, the South American Bombshell, who is part of an act that occasionally travels with Duke, may be heard as she sings, "Doan be so hasty. Yo' kisses so tasty!" Jimmy Hamilton's clarinet is often heard as he walks up and down outside the room like a bagpiper, practicing Grieg or some other classical composer. Someone in Duke's dressing room will open the door and say, "Jimmy, can't you get those squeaky mice outa that reed? They musta built a nest in it." Jimmy, a solemn youth, will not reply. Duke, his big face relaxed, will say sleepily, "I think I'll rest my spine awhile," and lie down again on his cot. Billy Strayhorn will be working quietly over the score of some new tune in a corner. After a time a masseur will come in, and perhaps a newspaper reporter. Duke, his voice shaking as the masseur kneads him, will be interviewed as he lies naked on his cot. Recently a young reporter asked him what he had in mind when he wrote "Mood Indigo." "It's just a little story about a little girl and a little boy," Duke said. "They're about eight and the little girl loves the little boy. They never speak of it, of course, but she just likes the way he wears his hat. Every day he comes by her house at a certain time and she sits in her window and waits." Duke's voice dropped solemnly. The masseur, sensing the climax, eased up, and Duke said evenly, "Then one day he doesn't come." There was silence until Duke added, " 'Mood Indigo' just tells how she feels."

When the reporter left, Duke said, "Jesus, did you see the tears come into his eyes when I spoke about 'Mood Indigo'? That's what I like. Great big ole tears. That's why I liked Whetsol." Whetsol is a trumpet player now dead. "When he played the funeral march in 'Black and Tan Fantasy,' I used to see great, big ole tears running down people's faces." Duke chuckled. In such moods as this, Duke and the older members of his band are almost sure to talk about the musicians who played with them when the band began. Their conversation has something of the nostalgic, elegiac atmosphere that surrounds a group of old Yale grads talking about football players of other years. "Bubber Miley!" Duke exclaimed on one of these occasions. (Bubber, too, is dead.) "Bubber used to say, 'If it ain't got swing, it ain't worth playin'; if it ain't got gutbucket, it ain't worth doin.'" Freddie Guy, guitarist, was present and, as Duke went on to speak of great trombone players and great trumpet players, with never a word for the rhythm section, Freddie at last mumbled regretfully, "Duke sure love his brass! Duke sure love his brass!"

The world of jazz is sentimental. When Cootie Williams, another great trumpet player, left the Ellington band three and a half years ago to go with another band [Benny Goodman sextet], a composer who had nothing to do with either band [Raymond Scott] wrote a sad piece called "When Cootie Left the Duke." Duke still finds it hard to talk of Cootie's departure. Both Bubber and Cootie were known for their "growl" effect. Duke occasionally says, "Cootie gave the growl more beauty than anyone, more melodic magnificence. He had a sort of majestic folk quality. His open horn was wonderful—wonderful loud and wonderful soft. He had a hell of a style." Such adoring reminiscence sometimes bothers the newer members of the band. Juan Tizol once asked gloomily, at one of the dressing-room sessions, "What do you see in my playing anyway, Duke? I don't call myself a hot man anyway." There was a hurt tone in his voice. "Not for me. I take all my solos straight. Sweet style."

"Well, Juan," Duke said gently, "there are times when a writer wants to hear something exactly as it's written. You want to hear it clean, not with smears and slides on it. Besides, your style is good contrast to the more physical style of Johnny Hodges."

"I play with a legit tone," Juan said, as though accusing himself of something rather unforgivable. "Duke, what is there about my trombone tone?"

"You get an entirely different quality," Duke said. "It's real accurate. So many look on the valve trombone as an auxiliary instrument, and it's your main instrument. That's a hell of an obligation. You got to live up to those valves and you do, Juan, you do. You know how many slide trombonists use the slide so they can fake, and when you object they say, 'Watta ya think this has got on it—valves?'"

"If there was any room in legit, I'd still go back to legit," Tizol said. He seemed inconsolable. "I like legit because I could feature myself better in legit than in a jazz band. I don't feel the pop tunes, but I feel 'La Gioconda' and 'La Bohème.' I like pure romantic flavor. I can feel that better."

Duke said to the room at large, "Juan's got inhibitions. He won't ad-lib. Once, on the 'Twelfth Street Rag,' he did some ad-libbing. Only time he ever did."

Jack Boyd, Ellington's road manager, a small, brisk white man from Texas, knocked on the door and said, "Five is in, folks"—five minutes before the band was due onstage for another performance. Jonesy came in to dress Duke, and Tizol rose to go. "You're a hell of a good man, Tizol," Duke said, making a final effort to comfort his trombone. "We need a man who plays according to Hoyle. A guy who does only one thing but does it for sure, that's it."

"I'm only legit," Tizol said.

There are times when Duke's cheery calm is shaken and when his dressing room is more like a prison cell than a friendly saloon. A few months ago the band arrived in St. Louis to play at the Fox Theatre. As the train pulled into the Union Station, Ellington's two white employees — Tizol and Boyd — immediately got a taxi and went to one of the town's good hotels. Duke and the band members got taxis only after an hour and considerable begging, since most of the drivers didn't want Negroes as passengers, and then they were taken to a rickety hotel in the Negro section. The next day, when the colored members of the band went out for lunch after the first performance, they couldn't find a restaurant in the neighborhood that would serve them. They didn't have time to get over to the segregated district before they were due onstage again. They returned to the theatre and arranged for a white man to go out to buy sandwiches at a drugstore. When the proprietor of the store, making inquiry, found that the sandwiches were for a Negro band, he refused to fill the order. A few minutes later the men went back to work, hungry, the curtain rose, and from the white audience out front there came a burst of applause. The crowd cheered, whistled, and stamped its feet. As the curtain was going up, the dejection on the faces of the players vanished, and, as swiftly as an electric light is switched on, it was replaced by a look of joy. The music blared, Duke smiled, threw back his head, and shouted "Ah-h-h!," Rex Stewart took off on a solo that was greeted with fervor, and as he bowed, the musician next to him muttered out of the side of his mouth, "Bend, you hungry fathead! Bend!" Everything was flash and brightness until the curtain came down. Then the joy was switched off and there was just a group of angry, hungry Negroes arguing their right to food.

"Can't we eat in our own country?" Rex Stewart said.

"And my son is in the Army!" another man said.

"Are we prisoners or something?" Harry Carney asked.

The band milled around in the gloom backstage. "Gee," said Stewart, "I'd like to go to a valley hemmed in by mountains, just me myself. That would be Utopia." The manager of the theatre was called, and admitted that if the band was to work it should be allowed to eat. He arranged for food to be sent in. A few minutes later, Boyd was in a saloon overlooking the stage door when a man in the band came out and got into a taxi.

"Did you see that?" asked a woman on a stool at the bar.

"See what?" Boyd said.

"See that nigra get in that cab?"

"Well, he's a pretty nice fellow. He's a member of the Ellington band. Some people think he's a very great artist."

"A very great artist? Well, I don't know what you think, but I always say that the worst white man is better than the best nigra."

Duke tries to forget things like that, and if he doesn't quite succeed, he pretends he does. An hour after the show, Duke was introduced to a policeman who said enthusiastically, "If you'd been a white man, Duke, you'd been a great musician." Duke's smile was wide and steady as he answered quietly, "I guess things would have been different if I'd been a white man."

Once Duke is aboard a train, soothed by the ministrations of admiring porters and dining-car waiters, he likes to relax and talk about his music. He is somewhat given to making set speeches and often, when he is asked if he can recall an incident, he remembers what he is in the habit of saying about it rather than the event itself. He enjoys telling how he happened to write any of his compositions. "In my writing," he said not long ago on a train, in the presence of his historian friend, "there's always a mental picture. That's the way I was raised up in music. In the old days, when a guy made a lick, he'd say what it reminded him of. He'd make the lick and say, 'It sounds like my old man falling downstairs' or 'It sounds like a crazy guy doing this or that.' I remember ole Bubber Miley taking a lick and saying, 'That reminds me of Miss Jones singin' in church.' That's the way I was raised up in music. I always have a mental picture."

He looked out the window at a drab village through which the train was speeding. A woman stood on a porch, holding a tablecloth which she seemed about to flourish. Before she completed her motion, she was out of sight. "I'd like to write something about that," Duke said. "You know, people moving in a train, other people standing still, and you see them for just an instant and then you rush on forever. Sometimes you look right into their goddam eyes. Seems for a minute like you know them. Then they're gone." He kept staring out the window. After a while he pointed at a tree and said, "Looks like a band leader." Again he was moodily silent. Then he suddenly said, "Take 'Eerie Moan' [recorded 1933]. I wrote that in 1930, when I was at the Cotton Club. It's the voice of New York City. You're lying in bed all by yourself. The window is open. It's summer. If there was someone in bed with you, you'd be contented. But you're alone and it's very late and you listen and listen and you hear something out there that comes from millions of people sleeping, from manhole covers that give a double click as a taxi shoots over them, from tugboats far away when they whistle hoarse. You really don't hear anything single, just a kind of general breathing. You feel very alone. You moan and it seems like that's the sound you're hearing from all the city outside in the night. Only place you can hear it is New York City."

Boyd lurched down the aisle. Duke caught him by the arm. "What time have we got to catch the train tomorrow?" Duke asked. "Seven in the morning," Boyd said cheerfully. "God damn!" said Duke. "You can't sleep after the birds wake up, so you don't want anyone else to! You're not normal. You can't sleep after sunrise." Duke's voice was bitter. "You change that train or we won't get any sleep!" Boyd continued down the aisle, muttering to himself, and Duke mumbled, "He can't sleep after sunrise and he doesn't want anyone else to."

Two young soldiers came up to ask for his autograph. After Duke had given it to them, they hung around to talk. "My favorite piece," one of the soldiers said, "is 'In a Sentimental Mood.'"

"It was one of those spontaneous things," Duke said. "It was after a dance at Durham, North Carolina, and they gave me a private party. Something was wrong with it. Two girls weren't speaking to each other. One girl had cut in on the other girl's guy and the other girl kept saying, 'Of all the people in the world! That *she* should take my man!' I was sitting at the piano, one girl on each side, and I'm trying to patch 'em up, see? And I said, 'Let's do a song' and that was the outcome, and when I finished they kissed and made up."

Other passengers had become aware that Duke was talking about his music and a little group crowded around, its members occasionally clutching at each other and at the seats to steady themselves.

"How about 'Clarinet Lament'?" someone asked.

"It was just something for Barney to play," Duke said. Barney is Barney Bigard, a famous clarinettist who used to be with the band. "We sort of worked it out together. You sit down and try this and that and finally you run upon something and write it out."

"How about 'Awful Sad'?"

"It's a beautiful thing," Duke said. "Very little to be said beyond the title. After I wrote it I said, 'What'll I call it?,' and someone said, 'It's awful sad.' I fingered it out on the piano. It was late at night. It had a beautiful part for Whetsol, a beautiful, tender part. It gives me a chill when I hear it."

Someone asked him about "Solitude" and he said, "I wrote it in Chicago in twenty minutes while waiting for a recording date. The other band, the one ahead of us, was late coming out and I wrote it holding a sheet of music paper against a glass wall. When we went in, it was the first thing we made. The sound engineer was half crying. It filled everybody up. To make people cry, that's music at its highest. My songs had a tendency in those days to be laments. There was always that melancholy in them. You look at the same melancholy again and again from a different perspective."

Duke seemed to feel that the conversation had taken too sombre a turn and he began speaking of his appetite, documenting his claim that it is national, even international, in scope. "I have special places marked for special dishes," he said. "In Taunton, Massachusetts, you can get the best chicken stew in the United States. For chow mein with pigeon's blood, I go to Johnny Cann's Cathay House in San Francisco. I get my crab cakes at Bolton's—that's in San Francisco, too. I know a place in Chicago where you get the best barbecued ribs west of Cleveland and the best shrimp Creole outside New Orleans. There's a wonderful place in Memphis, too, for barbecued ribs. I get my Chinook salmon in Portland, Oregon. In Toronto I get duck orange, and the best fried chicken in the world is in Louisville, Kentucky. I get myself a half-dozen chickens and a gallon jar of potato salad, so I can feed the sea gulls. You know, the guys who reach over your shoulder. There's a place in Chicago, the Southway Hotel, that's got the best cinnamon rolls and the best filet mignon in the world. Then there's Ivy Anderson's chicken shack in Los Angeles, where they have hot biscuits with honey and very fine chicken-liver omelets. In New Orleans there's gumbo filé. I like it so well that I always take a pail of it out with me when I leave. In New York I send over to the Turf Restaurant at Forty-ninth and Broadway a couple of times a week to get their broiled lamb chops. I guess I'm a little freakish with lamb chops. I prefer to eat them in the dressing room, where I have plenty of room and can really let myself go. In Washington, at Harrison's, they have devilled crab and Virginia ham. They're terrific things. On the Ile-de-France, when we went to Europe, they had the best crêpes Suzette in the world and it took a dozen at a time to satisfy me. The Café Royal, in the Hague, has the best hors d'œuvres in the world—eighty-five different kinds, and it takes a long time to eat some of each. There's a place on West Forty-ninth Street in New York that has wonderful curried food and wonderful chutney. There's a place in Paris that has the best octopus soup. And oh, my, the smörgåsbord in Sweden! At Old Orchard Beach, Maine, I got the reputation of eating more hot dogs than any man in America. A Mrs. Wagner there makes a toasted bun that's the best of its kind in America. She has a toasted bun, then a slice of onion, then a hamburger, then a tomato, then melted cheese, then another hamburger, then a slice of onion, more cheese, more tomato, and then the other side of the bun. Her hot dogs have two dogs to a bun. I ate thirty-two one night. She has very fine baked beans. When I eat with Mrs. Wagner, I begin with ham and eggs for an appetizer, then the baked beans, then fried chicken, then a steak—her steaks are two inches thick—and then a dessert of applesauce, ice cream, chocolate cake, and custard, mixed with rich, yellow country cream. I like veal with an egg on it. Monseigneur's, in London, has very fine mutton. Durgin-Park's, in Boston, has very fine roast beef. I get the best baked ham, cabbage, and corn bread at a little place near Biloxi. St. Petersburg, Florida, has the best fried fish. It's just a little shack, but they can sure fry fish. I really hurt myself when I go there."

Duke's audience seemed awed at his recital, and he looked rather impressed himself. "Gee," he said admiringly, "I really sent myself on that, didn't I?"

Some of the passengers wanted to ask more questions, but Duke had worked himself up to the point of having to go to the diner. There, between bites, he resumed the discussion of his music with one of his new acquaintances, who had gone along with him. "Take 'Harlem Air Shaft,'" Duke said. "So much goes on in a Harlem air shaft. You get the full essence of Harlem in an air shaft. You hear fights, you smell dinner, you hear people making love. You hear intimate gossip floating down. You hear the radio. An air shaft is one great big loudspeaker. You see your neighbors' laundry. You hear the janitor's dogs. The man upstairs' aerial falls down and breaks your window. You smell coffee. A wonderful thing, that smell. An air shaft has got every contrast. One guy is cooking dried fish and rice and another guy's got a great big turkey. Guy-with-fish's wife is a terrific cooker but the guy's wife with the turkey is doing a sad job." Duke laughed. "You hear people praying, fighting, snoring. Jitterbugs are jumping up and down always over you, never below you. That's a funny thing about jitterbugs. They're always above you. I tried to put all that in 'Harlem Air Shaft.'"

It was dark outside now, and Duke looked out at the night. When he saw that the moon was up, he said, "Bomber's moon. I'm going to write a song about that." Duke's companion asked him about "Saturday Night Function." "That's from the old rent-party days," he said. "When I was young, I travelled around with a character named Lippy and with James P. Johnson, one of the world's great piano players. He really can play plenty of piano. I can still hear Lippy coming into a tenement at four in the morning and shouting, 'It's Lippy, and James P. is with me!' We'd be in bed and hear that ole click, clack, click of those triple locks and when they'd open up, Lippy would shout, 'Wake up everybody and dust off that piano so James P. can play!' Everybody would crowd around and James P. would milk 'em around, kind of teasing 'em when they asked for a piece, saying 'Is this what you mean?' and 'Or is this the number?' and then finally bang into it. That's real dramatic timing."

Duke lit a cigarette. "That's the way the whole world should be," he said.

"James P. was an artist and the people wanted to hear him at any hour. Now everybody wants to know your pedigree. I think I'll build a city like that. A guy has a new painting or a poem that he wants people to enjoy at four in the morning, and it's all right. I'll have nothing but bungalows, so we can always knock on windows and walk in and sit down and start playing on a man's piano without offending anybody." He was silent for a moment and then said, "I like that city idea." He thought awhile. "I really like that city idea. I think I'll call it Peaceful Haven."

III

Duke Ellington and the sixteen other men in his jazz band are rather surprised at the research that has been expended on bringing to light the drunks, hang-overs, and frolics of their youth. The research has been done by earnest his-torians who are eager to determine the precise connection between dissipation and the creation of art. It is a source of mild regret to Duke and his colleagues that their escapades simply did not have that purple extravagance which is supposedly in the best tradition of jazz. Try as they would, Hugues Panassié, the French critic, and Robert Goffin, the Belgian critic, could not discover about Ellington and his band anything to match the attractive degeneracy of Buddy Bolden, a famous early cornettist and the Paul Bunyan of the jazz world, who kept himself so busy with the ladies that he had little time left for music, or of Leon Rappolo, an early clarinettist, who became insane from smoking marijuana, or even anything to equal the career of Bix Beiderbecke, another famous cornettist, who died in 1931 of drink. Ellington is apologetic. He feels that if he had only known years ago the artistic importance of his infrequent sprees he would have paid more attention to them and remembered more for posterity. He regrets that he did not know at the time that his befuddlement was the stuff of history. He can dredge up little for the archives. "I should have kept a diary," he says.

Ellington is also surprised at critics who claim in columns of rococo prose that jazz is the American equivalent of the glory that was Greece and the grandeur that was Rome. A few weeks ago such a critique was read to Duke, a tall, broad, coffee-colored man of forty-five, as he lolled on a cot in his dressing room at the Hurricane, a Broadway night club in which he and his band were playing an engagement. The author maintained that when New York is but a memory, or at best a forest of rusty steel ascending to a quiet sky, the perceptive archæologist will be able to recreate American civilization if he is fortunate enough to find one Ellington record amid the deserted ruins. In the record's pulsing rhythms, the article said, he will hear the throb of long-stilled traffic, see the flash of neon signs, get some suggestion of the subway, and will understand, when a solo soars above the theme and then sinks back again, how the individual of the vanished past yearned for the stars but was limited to a banal earth. Duke listened impatiently. When the final sentence had been read, he said, "I don't know. May be something to it. But it seems to me such talk stinks up the place."

In the field of jazz there is an exceptionally wide discrepancy between the art as practiced and the art as the writers write about it. The performers sweat, and may even rehearse, for every effect they get. The writers say that their music is as effortless as a bird's. The performers devote their lives to developing their technique. The writers present them as simple children of nature who blow their primitive souls out through their horns. The performers, most of whom spent the era of prohibition working in night clubs, know the world not only in terms of music but in terms of Mickey Finns and bouncers. The writers, who consider themselves intellectuals, range all the way from surrealist poets in Paris to Yale graduates on *Fortune*. Negro jazz musicians, who have found it best to take no part in the peculiar caprices of a white world, usually have nothing to say when they are told that there is a difference of opinion about whether they were the first surrealists, as is maintained in France. They view such assertions as just one more example of an inexplicable order which simultaneously gives them adoration and Jim Crow. They find it hard to reconcile life deep in the heart of Texas, where they must say "Yassuh, Boss," and life in Paris, where they have been told they are comparable to Bach, Beethoven, and Brahms. During a European tour of the Ellington band, the conductor of a Paris symphony orchestra once bowed to Johnny Hodges on the street and respectfully asked him for an explanation of his artistry on the alto saxophone. "I just lucked up on it, Bubber, I just lucked up on it," Johnny told him. The conductor, writing about the incident later, said, "It is a unique experience to stand before this black boy, and upon asking him to explain his amazing virtuosity, to be told, 'I just lucked up on it, Bubber.'" Duke himself got into the spirit of things when he was asked, in London, in 1933, "What is hot?" He replied, "Hot is a part of music, just as the root is part of a tree and the twigs and the leaves and the trunk. Hot is to music as a root, a trunk, a twig, a leaf is to a tree."

Despite Duke's own doubts, it is possible that that archæologist of the future may be able to reconstruct something of the present from Ellington's music, if as is arguable, a composer's music does to some extent reflect his environment. For Duke's environment has been as American as a Model T Ford and, in a sense, as standardized. He spent his boyhood on the swarming tenement pavements in Washington, D.C., and his first job was jerking soda. He liked the pavements, and to this day he has an aversion to green because it reminds him of grass. "When I was eight," he says, "I decided that grass was unnatural. It always makes me feel sort of creepy. It reminds me of graves." From his early youth his days and nights have been spent, for the most part, far from grass, in cafés, cabarets, speakeasies, night clubs, drugstores, all-night lunch stands, hotel lobbies, railway depots, day coaches, subways, dance halls, movie theatres, dressing rooms, pool rooms, taxis, and buses. Duke sometimes says, "I've had three educations—the street corner, going to school, and the Bible. The Bible is most important. It taught me to look at a man's insides instead of the cut of his suit."

Duke sometimes thinks that it is good business to conceal his interest in the Bible, just as he conceals his interest in American Negro history. He doubts if it adds to his popularity in Arkansas, say, to have it known that in books he has read about Negro slave revolts he has heavily underlined paragraphs about the exploits of Nat Turner and Denmark Vesey. In public he usually sets his beige-colored face in a grin as wide as possible. He claims that the flashiness of his clothes is not self-gratification but rather a selfless effort to play up to the rôle the public expects him to assume, a claim his friends don't take too seriously. He has two general modes of dress—one for the public, which a member of his band has described as "very sharp and fly," one for rehearsing or composing. At work, he likes to wear a cheap hat, the brim turned up all around, a sports shirt without a tie, the points of the collar long enough to reach almost to his chest, brown suède shoes, a blue or maroon pullover sweater, and a sports suit so tailored that it makes him look slender. When he is leading his band at rehearsal, his expression varies between a grin, a pouty sleepiness in which every muscle droops and sags, and a fey daintiness. In this last mood he arches his eyebrows and has a coy look that is meant to be a silent appeal to his band for a delicate musical effect. As he plays the piano, his expression is often one of quizzical pleasure, as if he is surprised and delighted by the sounds he creates. "I really get wrapped up in it," Duke says. There are times when Duke laughs naturally and exuberantly; for example, when the boys in the band, sitting around a dressing room, are competing to see who can whistle the lowest note. "I knock myself out," he says. Then he truly seems the simple Afro-American without a care in the world. New acquaintances are always surprised when they learn that Duke has written poetry in which he advances the thesis that the rhythm of jazz has been beaten into the Negro race by three centuries of oppression. The four beats to a bar in jazz are also found, he maintains in verse, in the Negro pulse. Duke doesn't like to show people his poetry. "You can say anything you want on the trombone, but you gotta be careful with words," he explains.

Duke was born in Washington, in 1899, when Buddy Bolden was sounding on his cornet those uncouth notes which historians say were the beginning of jazz. While the new music moved slowly north from New Orleans, first to St. Louis and Memphis, then spreading out to Chicago, New York, and Europe, Duke was attending public school and, at his mother's instigation, taking lessons on the piano from a woman he insists was named Miss Klinkscale [Marietta Clinkscales]. He was christened Edward Kennedy Ellington, but he has been called Duke since he was twelve, when his elegance and aplomb began to attract the attention of his playmates. His earliest musical memory, he says, goes back to when, at the age of four, he heard his mother playing "The Rosary" on the piano. "It was so pretty I bust out crying," he says. Duke occasionally speaks of his father as Uncle Ed. This is because Duke, who has only one sister and no brothers, had twenty-eight cousins who were so frequently around the Ellington house that Duke and his sister picked up the name. Duke's father worked for the Navy Department as a blueprint developer. "Uncle Ed sure provided for his family," Duke says. "We didn't want for anything."

When Duke was fifteen, he attended a rent party, which in Washington was called a "hop" or a "shout." The guests paid ten or fifteen cents to their host. On this occasion a man named Lester Dishman was at the piano. "He was terrific—really good," Duke says. "The piano jumped. The air shook. With his left hand he really yum-yummed, while with his right he played intricately woven melodic things. But fast!" After hearing Dishman, Duke went to all the rent parties he could and heard Clarence Bowser, Doc Perry, Louis Brown, Louis Thomas, and other gifted pianists. "Bowser's music was majestic," Ellington recalls. "I used to think, if only I could just get on to that 'Sticky Mack' style of his. They got three, four, five dollars a night. When they played at these shouts, they never had a thought in the world, drinking gin and playing and things getting wild, so that someday serious writers in Europe would investigate them, writing monographs and things.

"Doc Perry," Ellington continues, "taught me to read notes, not just spell 'em out." Duke composed his first piece shortly after hearing Dishman, while he was fifteen. It was during a summer vacation from high school. Duke remembers that he began by moving the family upright into his own room. It had a player attachment, and Duke commenced his studies by slowing down a roll of James P. Johnson playing his own "Carolina Shout." For a week Duke studied the anatomy of "Carolina Shout." "Then I locked myself in my room for two weeks and when I came out I had a shout of my own," Duke says. (A "shout" in this sense is a composition to be played at a rent party.) He had not yet named it a few weeks later when he got a job as a soda jerker in the Poodle Dog Café, an establishment near the Senators' ball park, and in honor of this event he called it "Soda Fountain Rag." His early admirers thought he had written several shouts, for he played the piece first in blues time, then in waltz time, then straight, and finally what is now known as hot. "They never knew it was the same piece," Duke says. When the summer was over, Duke returned to high school, from which he graduated in 1917, when he was eighteen. While he was still in school, he got the notion that he might become a designer of advertising posters. He showed a certain amount of painting talent in class and won a scholarship to the Pratt Institute in Brooklyn for the study of commercial art. When the United States entered the first World War and Washington became a boom town, people there were so dance-crazy that jazz bands were in great demand, and Duke decided he could make more money by heading a band than he could as a commercial artist. He never used his scholarship to Pratt.

The first Ellington band consisted of Sonny Greer, a dapper, sporty young fellow who was and still is the drummer; Otto Hardwicke, a mild, dentisty gentleman who played the alto saxophone for Ellington, and still does; Charlie Irvis, trombone, now dead; Elmer Snowden, banjo, who now plays the guitar in another band; Arthur Whetsol, trumpet, now dead; and Duke, piano. Duke enjoys telling how he recruited Sonny, who was greatly admired by Ellington and the other young men in the band because he came from New York. "Sonny was a very fly drummer," Duke says, "but we wanted to be sure that he had really played in Harlem. He was playing in the pit band at the Howard Theatre in Washington and we waited on the street outside to grill him. I take the lead in conversation because I'm sure I'm a killer in my new shepherd's-plaid suit, bought on time. Sonny comes back at us with a line of jive on

Harlem that lays us low. So we decide he's O.K. and he comes with the band."
Duke was soon clearing as much as two hundred dollars a week. "As a result
of prosperity," he says, "everybody in our band at that time became a juice
hound, juice meaning any kind of firewater." Otto Hardwicke bought a car
which the band called Dupadilly, and when Dupadilly broke down he bought
one that was called Dear Me. During the next few years the band played in
one small Washington cabaret after another, and in 1923 it moved to New
York, where a young man named Bubber Miley replaced Arthur Whetsol.
"Bubber was temperamental," Duke recalls. "He liked his liquor. He used to
get under the piano and go to sleep any time he felt like it. In fact, all our
horn blowers were lushies."

Duke, Sonny, and Otto (who holds that his name should be pronounced
as if it were spelled O-toe) like to sit around and recall the golden days of
their youth. All three have described in detail every hangover they can remember to those writers who want to believe that the pressure of jazz is so intense
that young Negroes take to alcohol and dope in an effort to attain the proper
mood to produce their fevered art, but their efforts to satisfy these writers are
lame and they know it. Sonny sometimes sums up the distressing normality
of their early days in New York by saying, "We scuffled around trying to
make a buck, but we had a happy time. That's how it was." Occasionally he
says, "Many's the time we split a hot dog six ways—but reluctantly." In a
more mellow mood, he insists that they always ate as much as they could
hold. "Duke drew people to him like flies to sugar," Sonny says. "Duke would
turn on the old charm and then we would all eat." As a matter of fact, the
band, which didn't get off to a particularly successful start in New York, lived
for three months without visible means of support. They were supported,
actually, by a legendary gentleman whom Duke refers to as "Mr. Gunion."
"A Mr. Gunion," Duke says, "is any guy who throws his money around. Mr.
Gunion supported us while we were spending most of our time hanging
around, playing now and then, just for fun, at Harlem places like Mexico's,
the Capitol Club, Barron's, and Smalls' Paradise." However, Mr. Gunion's
support was precarious and at the end of the three months, Duke, Otto, and
Sonny returned to Washington "to fatten up." As Duke, who values his food,
recreates this happy occasion, he sounds like a Kentucky colonel remembering
mint juleps on the pillared veranda. "We got to Washington on a Sunday
morning," he says. "Otto went to his home, because he lived in Washington,
and Sonny came home with me. I still remember the smell of hot biscuits when
we walked in. There was butter and honey. My mother broiled six mackerel.
There was lots of coffee. Uncle Ed got out the old decanter and we lay there
drinking corn in the sunshine. It was nice."

The band reassembled in New York when they got news of a job at a place
called the Hollywood Club, at Forty-ninth Street and Broadway. It was at this
cabaret, later the Kentucky Club, that the Ellington band began to take on its
permanent form. There it first went on the air, over national radio hookups,
on early-morning sustaining programs, and there Bubber Miley, who was then
the spark plug of the group, stamped his character on the band, by means of
the growl of his trumpet and his gutbucket technique. The band's manner of

playing came to be known as "the jungle style." It played at the Kentucky Club for four years and the only unpleasant events were four small fires, each of which managed to burn up Sonny Greer's drums.

It was during this period that Freddie Guy, a slim, light-brown guitarist, joined the band. He is still with it, and today he says, "I grew up with this little band, and if they're going to hell, I'm going, too. Been everywhere else with 'em. When my wife says, as we start on a trip, 'Please don't go,' I say, 'All right. Hand me my suitcase.'" Guy remembers that the Kentucky Club had a line of twelve girls and that everyone worked till he dropped. "Once you put your horn in your mouth, you didn't take it out until," he says. He waits for his listener to ask, "Until when?" Then he says, "Until you quit. Until period. You started at nine and played until."

While Duke was at the Kentucky Club, he began writing at the pace that has enabled him to turn out a total of more than twelve hundred pieces. In 1927, his last year there, he wrote, among other pieces, "Black and Tan Fantasy," "Creole Love Call," "East St. Louis Toodle-Oo," "Hop Head," "Down in Our Alley Blues," "Jubilee Stomp," "Black Beauty," "Blues I Love to Sing," "Birmingham Breakdown," and "The Creeper."[3] Duke is proud of the fact that he never had any conservatory training. He likes to say, "I got most of my instruction riding around Central Park in a taxi." His instructor on these occasions was Will M[arion] Cook, who once broke his violin into pieces after reading an article in the *Times* calling him the greatest Negro violinist in the world. "What I've been trying to be," he explained, "is the greatest violinist, not the greatest Negro violinist." "Will never wore a hat," Duke says, "and when people asked him why, he'd say because he didn't have the money to buy one. They'd give him five dollars and then he and I would get in a taxi and ride around Central Park and he'd give me lectures in music. I'd sing a melody in its simplest form and he'd stop me and say, 'Reverse your figures.' He was a brief but a strong influence. His language had to be pretty straight for me to know what he was talking about. Some of the things he used to tell me I never got a chance to use until years later, when I wrote the tone poem 'Black, Brown, and Beige.'"

In 1927, the band went on the road under the management of Irving Mills, an agent who specialized in Negro entertainment. It was playing at a theatre in Philadelphia when the proprietors of the Cotton Club in Harlem, which was just about to open, decided that they wanted to engage it. They had been persuaded by Jimmy McHugh, who had written the score of the show that was to open the new club. Duke couldn't go because he had a contract with the owner of the Philadelphia theatre which ran for a week beyond the date of the Cotton Club's opening, and the owner declared with considerable heat that nothing on earth could persuade him to release Ellington. The Cotton Club people acted with the forthrightness that was characteristic of the prohibition era. They called Boo Boo Hoff, a friend and an underworld power

[3] Only five of these titles were first recorded in 1927. The others date from 1926 (*East St. Louis Toodle-O, Birmingham Breakdown, The Creeper*) and 1928 (*Jubilee Stomp, Black Beauty*).

in Philadelphia, and Boo Boo sent an emissary known as Yankee Schwarz to the theatre man. "Be big," Yankee Schwarz pleaded. "Be big or," he mumbled embarrassedly, "you'll be dead." The choice presented no dilemma to the theatre man. Duke's band arrived at the Cotton Club a few minutes before the opening. Because of their excitement and exhaustion, the musicians didn't play well that opening night. One of the proprietors, a man with an Irish soul, didn't respond to their music, which seemed to him jangling and dissonant. His customers didn't seem to enjoy it, either. Before the night was over, he grimly expressed a wish for something more melodic and McHugh rushed up to Ellington. "For God's sake!" he cried. "Play 'Mother Machree' or I'm a goner!" Ellington did the best he could with it.

Both Ellington and McHugh survived the opening, and after a shaky beginning, the band soon reached heights that some of its admirers say it has never surpassed. Duke played five years at the Cotton Club, and there many of the band's most famous men joined it. Tricky Sam Nanton, trombone, and Harry Carney, baritone saxophone, had already signed up at the Kentucky Club, and now Wellman Braud, bass; Johnny Hodges, alto and soprano sax; Barney Bigard, clarinet; Juan Tizol, valve trombone; and Cootie Williams, trumpet, made their appearance. The boys from Harvard and Princeton discovered the orchestra and made weekend trips to Harlem to hear it play. Soon it was said that Duke's music, chromatically rich and often containing two or three themes in a delicate balance, had so modified jazz that he had created a new art form. Amid the prohibition frenzy that exploded each morning in the Cotton Club, there was always a serious little group of intellectuals who listened to "Mood Indigo," "The Mooche," "Awful Sad," "Sophisticated Lady," "Shout 'Em, Aunt Tillie," "Ring Dem Bells," "Cotton Club Stomp," "Flaming Youth," "Doin' the Voom Voom," and a hundred other Ellington pieces with a veneration theretofore reserved for Beethoven's Fifth.

"At first," Duke says, "I was happy. There were lots of pretty women and champagne and nice people and plenty of money." But some time in 1932, a year in which Duke made sixty thousand dollars, the life began to pall. The endless succession of drunks who demanded the right to drape their weaving bodies over him, whispering hoarsely in his ear, began to wear him down. He became moody. His friends started to worry about him. He frequently proclaimed that life was nothing but a racket, and he felt that he had things to say in music but that the commercialism of his trade was so overwhelming that he was not permitted to say them. "I'd bring something I thought was good to the music publishers," he recalls, "and they'd ask, 'Can an eight-year-old child sing it?' I'd bring something new to them and they'd say, 'This ain't what we're looking for. We want something like Gazookus wrote last week.' I'd see guys writing little pop numbers that were going over big. I didn't see why I should try to do something good. I thought I'd stop writing. Music publishers would come around with little tunes and say, 'If you'll put your name on it, we'll make it our Number One plug.' If something bad was plugged, it would go over better than something good that wasn't. I felt it was all a racket. I was on the point of giving up." Duke's mood in those days was so low that he was even irritated by his most ardent admirers, those who practically dedicated their lives to collecting and savoring the records that he and his band had been making ever since 1926. "One of these guys," Duke says, "would come up after you had played a number and say, 'Why did Barney hit an E-flat natural in the thirteenth bar? He didn't do it on the record.' If you did something new, it made 'em mad."

Duke's friends decided that a tour of Europe for him and his band might be the solution of the problem. The thought of such a thing alarmed Duke, who had an almost psychopathic fear of the ocean. His explanation was that when he was sixteen he had read a book about the suffering of those who went down on the Titanic. "What about icebergs?" he asked his friends. He was unconvinced when told that a collision was not inevitable. Nevertheless, Mills booked him and his band for a European tour, and they finally boarded the Olympic, bound for England, in the summer of 1933. Duke was full of foreboding. His anxiety grew when a passenger told him that at night the ship was steered not by human hands but by an automatic pilot. "I couldn't understand," Duke says, "how an automatic pilot could see an iceberg. I decided that I wasn't gonna take any chances by sleeping at night. I slept in the day and stayed up all night, but it was very lonesome." Duke tried to keep the band awake and alert through the dark hours by buying the boys quantities of a drink composed of Bass ale, brandy, and champagne, but the plan was self-defeating. One by one, Duke's companions would succumb to sleep, and by four or five in the morning he would find himself deserted. He would pace the deck miserably, waiting for daylight, when the robot helmsman would be relieved by a human being, who could see icebergs.

The reception Ellington got in England was vastly encouraging to him. A large crowd met him at the dock in Southampton and he was followed through the streets of London. He found that his desire to write sincerely, which he had felt was not appreciated, was understood and valued three thousand miles from the Cotton Club. He received an ovation when he walked out on the stage before his band to conduct a concert in London's Palladium. There were demonstrations at his concerts in Liverpool and Glasgow. He liked leading his band in "God Save the King" and told a British reporter, "I am very sincere when I play the King." He and his band went on to France, where he found that he was considered the originator of one of the only two art forms that had stemmed from America. (The other was the animated cartoon, as developed by Walt Disney.) He heard for the first time that he and his band were surrealists, because their music rose from the unconscious rather than the conscious.

The event in Europe Duke enjoyed most was a party given by Lord Beaverbrook for the Prince of Wales, at which the Ellington band provided the music. "It was very ducky," Duke told reporters on his return to the United States. "We were way up, feeling mellow, the result of plenty of nectar." Duke says that King George, then Duke of York, asked him to do a solo of "Swampy River," an Ellington composition. Duke did not recognize him and refused. "I gave him the light fluff," Duke recalls, "and said, 'You know, I never do solos.'" All in all, the present King had a bad time at the party. He had set his heart on going along with the band to a recording studio after the party to watch it make a record, but the Scotland Yard detectives wouldn't let him. They said there would be too big a crowd. "The Prince of Wales," Duke remembers, "wanted to show Sonny Greer how to beat those drums. We expected some Little Lord Fauntleroy stuff, but he really gave out some low-down Charleston."

When Duke returned to the United States in the fall, he felt better. He now was certain that there was a breed of folk the world over who listened to his records and knew what he was driving at. For two years, which he spent on tour, he was in fine fettle. Then, in 1935, his mother, to whom he had been very close, died and he fell into a state of depression again. He had always felt that he and his activities were the special concern of a benevolent God. In the face of this tragedy, he began to doubt it. He wondered whether his luck had permanently changed. It was then that he began wearing the little gold cross that always hangs around his neck. He read his Bible through three times in 1935 in an effort to regain his equilibrium. "I wrote 'Reminiscing in Tempo' that year," Duke says. "It was one of my first ambitious things. It was written in a soliloquizing mood. My mother's death was the greatest shock. I didn't do anything but brood. The music is representative of that. It begins with pleasant thoughts. Then something awful gets you down. Then you snap out of it, and it ends affirmatively."

It took Duke some time to snap out of it. "When my mother died," he says, "the bottom dropped out. I had no ambition. Before that I'd compete with anybody. I'd say, 'You wanna fight? O.K., because I'm fighting for my mother and the money I get will go to her.'" When his father died, in 1937, Ellington suffered an emotional relapse and lost whatever ground he had gained. For a time he did almost no composing. In 1939, again at the urging of his friends, he decided to repeat the European cure. The band toured France, Belgium, Holland, Denmark, Sweden, and Norway, and once more Duke was restored. "You have to be a Negro to understand why," Rex Stewart, one of Ellington's trumpet men, once said. "Europe is a different world. You can go anywhere, do anything, talk to anybody. You can't believe it. You are like a guy who has eaten hot dogs all his life and is suddenly offered caviar. You can't believe it."

"Things have happened to me in such a way," Duke said on his return, "as to prove religion to me. I have stood alone and had things come out all right. I'm certain religion gives you strength. It makes you feel that if you are God's son you are strong and don't have to worry."

Duke has made nearly a million dollars in the last twenty years, but he has spent it as he made it. He has received about a half million in royalties from phonograph records; almost twenty million of his records have been sold. He has received a quarter of a million in sheet-music royalties. For one-night stands—dances and concerts—which have taken up most of the band's time in recent years, Duke collects between $1,250 and $2,000, depending on the attendance. He may gross as much as $10,000 a week from one-nighters, but the band's payroll and expenses are so heavy that he is fortunate if he breaks even on the road. Duke's men receive between $125 and $185 a week and expenses when travelling, while he draws $600, $250 from the current receipts, the remainder in the form of an allowance from the auditor—a white man named William Mittler—who handles all his financial affairs. He spends money lavishly, supports a good many hangers-on, lends money freely, gets it back infrequently, and is usually broke when the weekly pay day rolls around. In 1939, a year in which the band came out even, he took in $160,000; in 1940 he grossed $185,000, but his payroll had ascended from $80,000 to $98,000, and travel expenses had increased from $25,000 to $30,000. The following year he took in only $135,000 and ended up with a loss of $1,500, and in 1942 he grossed $210,000 and netted only $4,000. He is now under the management of the William Morris agency. In order to sell his records and sheet music, Duke must remain before the public even when it costs him money. He lost $18,000, for example, on a six-month engagement at the Hurricane in 1943, but he figured that it was a good investment because of the Broadway address and the free radio time and publicity.

Ellington lives in a large, airy apartment at 935 St. Nicholas Avenue. The furnishings, which include gold-and-blue rugs and tapestries from Sweden, are modern. He was married in 1918, but for the past fifteen years he has been separated from his wife, who lives in Washington. They have one son, Mercer, also a composer and now a sergeant in the Army. Occasionally, around four or five in the morning, when the band is in New York, the men go up to Duke's apartment and talk, drink, and eat until almost noon. Many of their remarks are apt to begin, "Do you remember when . . ." and the stories they introduce may concern anything from the time that Tricky Sam, after a good deal of schnapps in Copenhagen, joined a confusing Danish folk dance, to the time Harold Baker blasted out a trumpet solo to quell a riot on a boat on the Mississippi. Junior Raglin, as bulky as a football player and as black as Jack Johnson, may tell how he misplaced his bull fiddle in Boise, Idaho, and Rex Stewart is almost sure to speak of his experiences while trouping with Gene Bedini's "Peek-a-Boo" girl show through Pennsylvania when he was fifteen years old.

As the morning progresses, the gigantic Junior may confide his ambition to play the Italian harp in a symphony orchestra, and Jimmy Hamilton, Duke's intense young clarinettist, will probably become involved in an argument over his favorite instrument. "The clarinet," he will say, "is a very intelligent instrument." Nicknames are a good deal in evidence and it develops that Johnny Hodges is known as Rabbit, that Sonny is called Nasty, that Rex is known as Fatstuff, and that Otto Hardwicke is Professor Boozay. When Sonny and Otto join forces to roam Harlem in search of diversion, their nicknames change to Spruce and Juice. There is a lot of laughter and a lot of noise at these gatherings, but almost inevitably there are solemn interludes in which the men complain that the band can't get a radio sponsor because its members are Negroes. Duke thinks that winning the war will change this and much more. When he was working several months ago on a composition called "New World A-Coming," he liked to repeat the title and then say, "And I mean it."

50. Ellington: "Certainly It's Music!" (1944)

E llington's two Carnegie Hall appearances in 1943 may have prompted the following article, commissioned by *Listen: The Guide to Good Music*, a magazine aimed at classical music-lovers and record-buyers. The title seems a response to the question posed in 1943 by Winthrop Sargeant in the *American Mercury*, "Is Jazz Music?" (see §47).

The main subject addressed by Ellington is his relationship to European composers. With characteristic elusiveness he both invites the comparison ("that I owe a debt to the classical composers is not to be denied") and rejects it ("the musical devices that have been handed down by serious composers have little bearing on modern swing"). Yet Ellington is adamant that a homegrown musical tradition not be judged by imported critical standards: "To attempt to elevate the status of the jazz musician by forcing the level of his best work into comparisons with classical music is to deny him his rightful share of originality."

Some of the syntax and individual phrases—"Schoenbergian 'images,'" the "Duke of Hot"—seem out of character for Ellington. Perhaps he collaborated with another writer or his prose was heavily edited.

Whoever started the rumor the music of Duke Ellington bears some resemblances to the compositions of such masters as Bach, Ravel and Stravinsky always puzzles me. Even though I appreciate the compliment, no amount of self-examination seems to bear out the contention. Having been asked to base this article on the relationship between my own work and that of the classical composers, I find it necessary to make a few perhaps dangerous comparisons. Since I am not running for public office, however, I shall content myself with praising my "loyal opposition" and leaving such matters as musical evaluations to my readers.

When Johann Sebastian Bach constructed his compositions along strict and formal lines; when he introduced dominant sevenths, tonic and some altered sevenths for harmonic interest, I am sure that he, of course, never visualized their translation into the medium of jazz. Whether or not he would have been happy to hear similar rhythms licked out by a hot band is a good subject for a high school debate, and let us leave it to academic circles to thrash out that particular problem. Nevertheless, when I sit down to compose or arrange a piece of my own, the striking of a few chords does not conjure up in my mind visions of Duke Ellington as a maestro of the old school.

Frankly, I prefer to regard my compositions as strictly, "yours truly," as does any creative musician. I am not writing classical music, and the musical devices that have been handed down by serious composers have little bearing on modern swing. Nevertheless, no composer can help but repeat to some extent some things from the subconscious accumulation of years of listening to the music of others. If anyone finds Schoenbergian "images" in "Solitude," "Mood Indigo" or any other of my compositions, they should charge it to

Source: Duke Ellington, "Certainly It's Music!," *Listen* IV/12 (October 1944), 5–6.

subconscious activity. I did not intend them and in all probability they do not exist anywhere but in the minds of self-important, over-sophisticated musicologists who like to make an occasional comparison.

That I owe a debt to the classical composers is not to be denied but it is the same debt that many composers, for generations, have owed to Brahms, Beethoven, Debussy and others of their calibre. They have furnished us with wholesome musical patterns in our minds and have given us a definite basis upon which to judge all music, regardless of its origin.

If there is any characteristic of my own music that I would like to associate with that of the old masters, it is a conscious attempt on my part always to imbue my work with disciplined structure and orchestration. That in itself does not make my compositions unique—it simply means that I assume a responsibility that all composers of any school owe to their own good craftsmanship. To me, a musical instrument is in a sense a color instrument, and orchestral music should be scored to give full value to every possible shading and blending. That is true of symphonic music; it is true of chamber music—and it should be true of modern composition.

I warned you that comparisons, especially in the case of a "hot" composer, are dangerous; let us take up the case of Ellington vs. Wagner (the professional jazz critics haven't gotten around to that one yet, although they have put me on the witness stand in the case of Bach, Ravel, Stravinsky, Sibelius, and quite a few others). Wagner gave full scope to the range of his instrument; his harmony and counterpoint are involved and intricate. The "Duke of Hot," on the other hand, practices an economy of instrumentation and virtuosity—and his music never sounds cluttered up because there is never too much going on at the same time.

So what? It makes it seem that the "long-hair" Wagner went in for a lot of hot licks and jive stuff and the "short-hair" Ellington is just an old schoolmarm playing a harmonica out at a Sunday School picnic.

It is very flattering to read such things about one's self as this choice quotation I have picked out at random: "If any so-called 'long-hair' musician really wants to be able to distinguish Ellington's band from any other he needs only to listen for the one that sounds most like Rimsky-Korsakov."

If I seem a little shy about being displayed on a critical platform with the classical big shots, let me also dispel the notion that I hesitate to place the jazz medium in a top musical category. I have displayed my wares on the stage of Carnegie Hall, as have Benny Goodman and others of our contemporaries. My orchestra and I air our stuff regularly over the same wave lengths as the New York Philharmonic, the Metropolitan Opera and other illustrious musical organizations. So does every name band in the country. Jazz, swing, jive and every other musical phenomenon of American musical life are as much an art medium as are the most profound works of the famous classical composers. To attempt to elevate the status of the jazz musician by forcing the level of his best work into comparisons with classical music is to deny him his rightful share of originality. Let us remember that many "long-hair" composers (still current) freely admit that they have been influenced by the jazz idiom. That, it seems to me, puts the shoe on the other foot.

Music, like any other art form, reflects the mood, temperament and environment of its creators. I could no more compose like Brahms than he could beat out the jive in a 52nd Street night spot. So let's forget about comparisons and leave each man to his trade, huh?

51. Ellington: "Swing Is My Beat!" (1944)

The October 1944 issue of *New Advance*, a Canadian publication sponsored by the International Youth Council, featured a short article by Ellington together with such offerings as "Does High School Education Prepare You for Marriage?" and "Playing Better Football."

Curiously, Ellington's well-known aversion to categories and stylistic labels is little present here. He refers to two major types of American music—jazz and "the concert hall variety"—aligns himself with "swing" rather than "jazz in the popular sense of the word," then claims to be "carrying on the tradition of American folk music, particularly the music of my people." The recent controversy over *Black, Brown and Beige* and the debate over jazz's place in the concert hall inform Ellington's efforts at self-explanation.

One notable feature is the brief discussion of composing methods—a subject Ellington usually avoided.

Americans have always listened to music, when they aren't busy making it. This is part of our culture. For some, hearing "live" music is a luxury. For others it's part of the daily diet. Everything depends on how the budget stacks up against the price of admission to Carnegie Hall or the cover charge at nightclubs giving out with the "hot" brand of music.

Well, when the war came along, a few years back, people wondered whether music was going to be one of the casualties. Would it have to take a back seat for a while? Would we have to sacrifice it at a time when bombs and bullets had an A-1 priority over Boogie-Woogie and Bach? I think these last few years have proved that music doesn't kick up its heels and call it quits under crisis. Music is staying by popular request of the fighting men and the folks they left behind. And that goes for all music.

Ours is a country of two major types of music—the concert hall variety and what goes under the general heading of "jazz." It wouldn't be right to draw too thick a line between them because nowadays we are beginning to see "jazz" moving into the Concert Hall—into the scores played by symphony orchestras, and the other way around. My own Carnegie Hall concert, recently, is an example of what I mean.

Swing is my beat. Not jazz in the popular sense of the word, which usually means a chatty combination of instruments knocking out a tune. Swing, as I like to make it and play it, is an expression of sentiment and ideas—modern

Source: Duke Ellington, "Swing Is My Beat!," *New Advance* (October 1944), 1, 14.

ideas. It's the kind of music that catches the rhythm of the way people feel and live today. It's American music because it grew out of our folk music, picking up a little from every section of the country as it traveled from New Orleans to Chicago to Kansas City to New York.

Swing came along as a new brand of jazz. It wasn't the "hot" type, the "sweet" style and the so-called popular music that the boy friend was singing to his girl on a park bench. At the start, people said it was a fad and scheduled for a short life—if a happy one. But it fooled them, as any real style will. It didn't date but instead has become a brand of music in which people are creating as hardily as pioneers in any new field.

What swings? Rhythm. A few notes, a chord combination, a simple musical phrase is developed into a series of rhythm patterns which creates a form that is listened to as seriously as a concert hall piece. Part of the reason is that this rhythm hits home to the people who hear it. It speaks their language and tells their story. It's the musician and his audience talking things over.

When I get an idea, I write the melody and often work out the arrangement, too. But sometimes the band and I collaborate on the arrangement. I write the melody down and play it at rehearsal. Then the boys will start making suggestions in a "free-for-all." One of them might get up and demonstrate his idea of what a measure should be like. Then another one of the boys will pick it up and maybe fix it a little. Sometimes we'll all argue back and forth with our instruments, each one playing a couple of bars his own way.

Still other times I might just sit down at the piano and start composing a little melody, telling a story about it at the same time to give the mood of the piece. I'll play eight bars, talk a bit, then play another eight and soon the melody is finished. Then the boys go to work on it, improvising, adding a phrase here and there. We don't write like this very often and when we do it's usually three o'clock in the morning after we've finished a date.

But this is a little off the point. What I am trying to get across is that music for me is a language. It expresses more than just sound. I often think of tones as colors or memories, and all that helps in composing.

I said that swing is my beat. But because of all the confusion about what swing is and isn't, I prefer to say that I am carrying on the tradition of American folk music, particularly the folk music of my people. In my tone poem "Black, Brown and Beige" I tried to parallel the history of the Negro in music. My opera, "Boola," which is still unproduced, tells the story of the Negro in America.

What's the future of swing?

It has been said that it has no future because it's too narrow in its form. I don't think that's right. Swing at its best is "free" within the form itself. Take, for example, the lyrical "Stardust" and then take the more recent "Your Socks Don't Match." The two are completely opposite in sentiment, mood, and character, but they are both a product of swing.

A number of composers have been experimenting with these new musical ideas on a large scale. I spoke of my own tone poem and opera. Then there's the work of Gershwin which is not the same but moves in the same general direction. There are others, too, and I am convinced that still others will come along and their music will stick. For swing is a product of its time. Whether it's a jam session brand which is its purest state, or music written down on paper for a market, it's alive, creative and that's what gives it its future.

52. An Ellington Solo Piano Transcription in *Down Beat* (1944)

Transcribed solos became a regular feature in *Down Beat* beginning in September 1936, with a notated version of Louis Armstrong's *West End Blues*. One of the contributing transcribers in the late thirties and early forties was Sharon A. Pease, a Chicago-based teacher whose column "Swing Piano Styles" presented brief solos and discussed their characteristics.[1]

Late in 1944 Pease featured Ellington's solo on *Frankie and Johnny,* taken from a "concerto type arrangement" Ellington had been performing at least since 1941, when he appeared on Bing Crosby's Kraft Music Hall radio program. Together with some of the musical examples in Billy Strayhorn and Leonard Feather's *Duke Ellington Piano Method for Blues* (1942), this was among the earliest published Ellington piano transcriptions.

For a comparison of Pease's transcription with recorded sources, hear Ellington's performance from 17 September 1941 (Standard Program Library P-169) or from the 19 December 1944 Carnegie Hall concert (Prestige P-24073 or 2PCD 24073).

A standard biographical summary in the first part of the article has been omitted here.

. . . During his current theater tour, Duke is featuring a concerto type arrangement on the standard *Frankie and Johnny* (fig. 1). The accompanying style example, one of his solo choruses, contains the melodic-harmonic treatment that is characteristic of Ellington's composition and arrangements. It reflects Duke's ability to think of his orchestra as a single instrument with multiple colorings and extensive harmonic possibilities. For example: the basic harmony, played by the left hand, is simple and, with the exception of abundant chromatics, quite conventional; the treble harmony, generally speaking, gives unusual coloring by the addition of sevenths, ninths, and elevenths. The introduction establishes the key and the mood without the commonly used principal theme and authentic cadence. The first six measures of the chorus retain much of the original melody but with a new harmonization. The next two measures employ the original harmony with coloring added by means of treble

Source: Sharon A. Pease, "Technical Skill and Invention Boost Ellington," *Down Beat* (1 November 1944), 12.

[1] A collection of these solos appeared in *88 Keys to Fame* (New York: Leeds Music Corporation, 1943).

Fig. 1

variation. The following two measures are completely divorced from the original composition and form a progression into the improvised ending. The ending is formulated from the material used in the introduction. Here is a little masterpiece of good form and modern harmony.

53. "Why Duke Ellington Avoided Music Schools" (1945)

This mid-forties portrait of the famous musician at home in Harlem has the standard ingredients of a personality piece: descriptions of Ellington's clothes, his taste in furnishings, even his breakfast preferences. Yet it also contains revealing statements by Ellington about the training of young musicians, the process of composing, and the relationship of jazz to "serious" music.

The piece, by an unidentified writer, appeared in the New York newspaper *PM*, published from 1940 to 1948.

It was around 4 p.m. when we reached Duke Ellington's apartment on St. Nicholas Ave. the other day. The building he lives in has an old, ornate, rather dilapidated facade. The halls are narrow and dark, with tile floors.

Mr. Ellington was just getting up, the maid said. Would we wait? We said we would, and walked through an entrance hall painted a stark, gleaming white.

A small spinet piano stood against one wall of the hall. Fluffy yellow scatter rugs were on the floor. One set of French doors led into a bedroom with modern furniture in it. Another opened into the living room, also modern. One wall was lined with shelves of books.

When the Duke appeared he was wearing a red and orange flowered dressing gown with a yellow bath towel over his head. He ducked into the living room to ask if we wanted breakfast and we noticed the gold cross, which he always wears, on a chain around his neck.

"Four o'clock is a good time for breakfast," he said, "I always eat this time, I'm up all night writing."

He went away to take a shower, then returned a few minutes later immaculate in gray trousers, full and pleated around his fairly ample girth, and pegged in at the ankles. A white sport shirt was monogrammed in blue. The initials were E.K.E., for Edward Kennedy Ellington. The Duke won his nickname through the dandified dress he wore when he was a schoolboy in Washington.

We asked him about the following statement Mark Schubart had made in

Source: "Why Duke Ellington Avoided Music Schools," *PM*, 9 December 1945.

the *New York Times* after the Duke's last concert at Carnegie Hall [see §48]:

"There are those who seek in Mr. Ellington's music a growing affinity between jazz and serious music. Actually, the unmistakable style and distinction of his work is based on and derived from the jazz idiom only, and employs an instrumental technique utterly different from that of symphonic music."

The Duke listened to the quotation with a smile.

"I guess *serious* is a confusing word," he said. "We take our American music seriously. If *serious* means European music, I'm not interested in that. Some people mix up the words *serious* and *classical*. They're a lot different. Classical music is supposed to be 200 years old. There is no such thing as modern classical music. There is great, serious music. That is all.

"Critics are a funny bunch of people. They use words to their own advantage. They live in one world and we live in another. We don't understand what they are talking about. I don't think the public does, either. All music critics think jazz musicians are trying to get into the symphonic field. Ninety-nine per cent of the jazz people aren't interested in symphony techniques at all.

"Jazz is like the automobile and airplane. It is modern and it is American. I don't like the word *jazz* but it is the one that is usually used. Jazz is freedom. Jazz is the freedom to play anything, whether it has been done before or not. It gives you freedom. I remember in the old days when I was struggling to write something entirely new. I would try something that hadn't been done before. I felt like an intruder in a new land. No—more like an illiterate.

"I'm not the offspring of a conservatory. I've avoided music schools and conservatories. I didn't want to be influenced away from what I felt inside. Back in 1915, 1920 when I was getting started in Washington, there were two schools of jazz. There were the disciplined jazz musicians who played exactly what was written. They had all the good work. I got kicked out of a couple of those bands.

"Then there was another group of musicians that didn't know music. Some of them could only play in one key. But they played precious things. I was in between. My greatest influence came from the ragtime piano players. I was trying to play ragtime. That's what I was trying to do, but it came out a little different.

"I wouldn't have been a good musician if I'd gone to a conservatory and studied in the usual way. I haven't the discipline."

In that case, we said, why had he recently established three scholarships for graduates of New York high schools at the Juilliard School of Music?

"Things are different now," he said. "A musician coming along today has to learn a lot. Even if he has loads of natural ability, he has to develop great skill to be eligible for a good job. If he goes about it the way I did, it will take him much too long. Juilliard is a fine school. The people there are aware of American music. They won't hold anyone back. I developed the helter-skelter way. I don't think everyone should be allowed to do that. Most people learn faster and more at school."

The men in his band have been his strongest inspiration, the Duke said. Three of them have been with him since he started to attract public attention in 1927.[1] Almost all have been with him for more than 10 years. The unity of the Ellington band is apparent in all of the Duke's conversation. He uses the pronoun *we* much more than *I*. "We are more interested in folk music." "We play a lot of descriptive music." "We get a kick out of the jitterbugs and try to describe the different styles of dancing in our music."

"We've tried to absorb the styles of all the individuals in the band," the Duke went on. "I don't write for anyone else but the band. When I'm writing a trumpet part, for instance, I don't write within the radius of the horn, but for the man behind the horn.

"Our music grew out of the personalities in the band. We see an old man walking along the street. We play a song that goes with the man.

"Playing is demonstration," said the Duke. "But writing is the real thing. Writing is a matter of adjusting yourself, settling down to do it. You have to have a contented feeling. You get your mind set on writing, then you do it. There is no formula for it. I go for long stretches without writing. I'm a great procrastinator. I have great ideas, but nothing ever happens. Then I get an idea or I promise to do a piece and I do it. I try to write fast. Usually I work walking up and down, humming to myself and drinking Coca-Cola.

"I don't believe in working at the piano. A piano is more or less of a hindrance in composing. It limits you to what your fingers fall on. Unless you're an awfully good pianist, your suggestion is stunted. You're too apt to follow familiar harmony. I can imagine a lot of sounds I wouldn't play offhand on the piano."

Religion has helped him in his work, the Duke told us. He doesn't go to church, though; he "just believes."

"Religion helps my spirit of independence," he explained. "Helps me do things people call *daring*. For instance, say musicians just don't put a ninth in a particular place, and we do it. Religion helps me. I guess it gives me the proper inflation when I need it."

Negro life, rhythm and melodies have been an important source of his music, the Duke says, but he prefers to think of it as American music.

"Twenty years ago when jazz was finding an audience, it may have had more of a Negro character," he said. "The Negro element is still important. But jazz has become a part of America. There are as many white musicians playing it as Negro. Charley [Charlie] Barnet does so well on my stuff it sometimes scares me.[2] We are all working along more or less the same lines. We learn from each other. Jazz is American now. *American* is the big word."

Willie Manning, a wiry, middle-aged man in a big, double-breasted gray suit, who had been running in and out, giving the Duke telephone messages and arranging appointments, came in to insist that the Duke eat breakfast.

---

[1] Harry Carney, Sonny Greer, and Fred Guy. Otto Hardwick was another longtime Ellingtonian still playing with the orchestra in 1945, but he had left the band between 1928 and 1932.
[2] Bandleader Barnet (1913–1991) featured a number of Ellington (and Ellington-influenced) pieces in his repertory, among them *The Sergeant Was Shy, Harlem Speaks,* and *Drop Me Off in Harlem.*

We went into the kitchen where the Duke ate an enormous plate of Shred-ded Wheat, sliced bananas and cream.

"I love a good breakfast in the morning," he observed. He also answered all telephone calls with "good morning." Just then, Willie reminded him that it was almost 6 p.m. and he had to broadcast.[3]

The Duke put on a roomy gray tweed sports jacket, a light beige camel hair overcoat and a porkpie hat. It wasn't until he had his coat on and was standing up beside us that we realized how big he is. He is tall (6 feet) and portly (200 pounds) and has the lazy ease of a large man who is not very active. His only exercise is walking down the four flights of stairs from his apartment to the street. "But I don't walk up," he added. "That would be too much exercise."

54. "Interpretations in Jazz: A Conference with Duke Ellington" (1947)

With a 1947 interview for the *Etude*, a magazine issued by publisher Theodore Presser and read by music teachers and students across America, Ellington once again crossed the barrier dividing serious and popular music. Addressing an audience that might have misunderstood the role of spontaneity in jazz, Ellington stressed traits his readers probably valued, emphasizing the importance of study and disci-pline in the life of a jazz musician. While on other occasions Ellington rejected the "jazz" label as delimiting, here he embraced it and argued for a broad interpretation of the term. Jazz stood for "freedom of musical speech," Ellington claimed, and thus encompassed many different forms and styles.

An editor's note introducing Ellington to readers of the *Etude* has been omitted below. Worthy of mention, however, is the news that Ellington had recently "established an instru-mental scholarship at the Juilliard School of Music, the first living artist to do so."

Jazz today is no longer the jazz of twenty years ago. When I began my work jazz was a stunt, something different. Not everybody cared for jazz and those who did felt that it wasn't the real thing unless they were given a shock sensation of loudness or unpredictability along with the music. For that rea-son, I feel that I was extremely lucky to enter the picture when I did! I had to teach myself to read music. I relied on instinct rather than knowledge to guide me, and had to develop many techniques in spotlight positions. When I was playing at the Cotton Club, for instance, I had the luck to be engaged for three days at a theater in mid-town. All went well, and on the third day,

---

[3] The broadcast was probably from the Club Zanzibar, 49th Street and Broadway, where Elling-ton's orchestra had been appearing often that fall.

Source: Gunnar Askland, "Interpretations in Jazz: A Conference with Duke Ellington," *Etude* (March 1947), 134, 172.

they told me I was scheduled to open at the Palace Theater *tomorrow!* Now in those days the Palace was the country's ranking vaudeville theater: the goal of every seasoned player. I was completely bewildered by the idea of opening there with no special preparation—but I had to be ready.

Nor was that all! I was also told that it would be my duty to announce my own numbers. Up to that time, I had never spoken a word from a stage. Still, I had to do it. In trepidation, I groped my way toward the footlights, trusting to Providence to put the right word into my mouth at the right moment. After, I was praised for a new kind of style of announcing! I have no idea what kind of "style" it was! Again, the first time I ever lifted a baton was when I conducted the personal appearance opening of Maurice Chevalier [at the Fulton Theater in 1930]. Again, I had no idea what to do—but I did it! I was lucky, indeed, to begin when I did. But perhaps I should define my notion of luck; to me, it means being at the right place at the right time, and doing the right thing before the right people. If all four "rights" are in good order, you may count yourself lucky. And this, precisely, brings me to the question of luck, or rightness, as it concerns the youngster of today who dreams of a career in jazz.

He still needs to be lucky to get to the top—but the value of these "rights" has changed so that the chances for a start like mine no longer exist.

Jazz today is by no means the formless, chancy, irresponsible medium it was around 1920. It is impossible to stress this sufficiently. A certain psychological element enters into jazz which can work great harm to the chances of the enthusiastic young player; there is a vague feeling that "classical" music means hard work while jazz represents the livelier aspects of pure fun. Well, that may be so—to the listener! It certainly is *not* the case as far as the performer is concerned. The jazz musician today needs the most thorough musical background he can possibly get. He needs to be more than moderately expert on his instrument, whatever that may be; he needs to have the kind of theoretic mastery that can solve all sorts of harmonic and arrangement problems without a moment's hesitation; most of all, he needs to be acutely aware of musical history and the position of jazz in that history.

What, exactly, is jazz? A matter of trick rhythms, blues-notes, and unorthodox harmonies? I think not. Those matters may enter into it, but only in the nature of a result and not of a cause. To my mind, jazz is simply the expression of an age, in music. Think of the terms classical music, romantic music. An entire picture comes to mind—a picture of the way people thought and felt; an expression of human reactions to the conditions under which they lived. You wouldn't dream of associating a certain rhythm, or a fixed tone quality with either of them. Jazz is exactly the same—not in its forms, of course, but in the large, overall pattern of its expression. Just as the classic form represents strict adherence to a structural standard, just as romantic music represents a rebellion against fixed forms in favor of more personal utterance, so jazz continues the pattern of barrier-breaking and emerges as the freest musical expression we have yet seen. To me, then, jazz means simply freedom of musical speech! And it is precisely because of this freedom that so many varied forms of jazz exist. The important thing to remember, however, is that not one of these forms represents jazz by itself. Jazz means simply the freedom to have many forms.

Let us go a step further. In its opening the way for many kinds of free musical expression jazz is peculiarly American. Thus, the American character of jazz derives simply from its freedom rather than from any specifically American line of musical descent. In the case of other lands, we say their music is typically French, Italian, or English, if it follows a traditional pattern (whether of melodic line, harmonization, arrangement, rhythm, or anything at all). We say that music is typically jazz, or typically American, if it follows no pattern at all! Even the Negroid element in jazz turns out to be less African than American. Actually, there is no more of an essentially African strain in the typical American Negro than there is an essentially French or Italian strain in the American of those ancestries. The pure African beat of rhythm and line of melody have become absorbed in its American environment. It is this that I have tried to emphasize in my own writings. In *Black, Brown and Beige,* I have tried to show the development of the Negro in America; I have shown him as he is supposed to be—and as he is. The opening themes of the third movement reflect the supposed-to-be-Negro—the unbridled, noisy confusion of the Harlem cabaret which must have plenty of "atmosphere" if it is to live up to the tourist's expectation. But—there are, by numerical count, more churches than cabarets in Harlem, there are more well-educated and ambitious Negroes than wastrels. And my fantasy gradually changes its character to introduce the Negro as he is—part of America, with the hopes and dreams and love of freedom that have made America for all of us. But what has this to do with the development of jazz?

Simply this: that it requires a great deal more than off-beat rhythms and loud hoots to make jazz. It requires, basically, two separate kinds of awareness. First, the thorough musical awareness that twenty-five years of steady development have brought in jazz. And, in second place, an awareness of the contemporary scene with all its shadings of feeling. When the young jazz musician comes out of the Conservatory, he still needs to learn much that cannot be taught by books and masters. He needs to learn what people are thinking and feeling; he needs to adjust to the *contemporariness* of the times and the people whom he wishes to express, and for whom he wishes to interpret life. And human needs of feeling can change overnight! Hence, no doubt, the many kinds of jazz freedoms we find. It's like moving a person from a room with a red light, into another room lit by amber light. It's the same person, but he looks different. And the many jazz forms we find, each with its distinguishing harmonic or stylistic device, represent varying moods, or colors, of the same human scene.

In this sense, then, it becomes increasingly difficult to say just where "good music" leaves off and jazz begins. Jazz *is* good music—when it sets itself, as earnestly as any other form, to explore and to express the feelings and the conditions of its time. There is good and worthless jazz just as there is good and bad music in the purely classical and romantic styles. But for good jazz, the hit-or-miss days of making a noise and being "different" are gone. Expressive jazz requires as much scholarship, as much musicianship, as any other kind of music. In addition, it requires a peculiar awareness of form and of the human thoughts and feelings these forms express. The young musician will do well to reflect on the needs of jazz before he gets himself a drum and starts out on a career. If his "rights" are in order, he'll have luck!

55. Alec Wilder on Ellington (1948)

I n the course of a record review, the composer and songwriter Alec Wilder (1907–1980) offered a probing assessment of Ellington. Although an admirer of Ellington's music since the late twenties, Wilder criticized Ellington for accepting limitations imposed by popular taste—writing pieces, for example, based on "the thirty-two-measure convention of Broadway and the radio, with slight extensions and variations." At the same time, Wilder found Ellington's longer compositions lacking in development and integration. These shortcomings led him to question Ellington's credentials as a composer, even while, somewhat paradoxically, granting his ability to produce "fine melodies, interesting rhythms, new orchestral sounds."

For another example of Wilder's critical writing about Ellington, similarly equivocal in tone, see American Popular Song: The Great Innovators, 1900–1950 (New York: Oxford University Press, 1972), 412–16.

The following biographical note accompanied Wilder's article: "Alec Wilder, composer, arranger, and songwriter, is a product of the Eastman School of Music. He is known for such songs as 'Trouble Is a Man,' 'Soft as Spring' and 'It's So Peaceful in the Country' and for a collection of pieces conducted by Frank Sinatra."

Twenty years is a long time in the career of any man, especially a career involving so fluctuating a field as popular music. It is all of twenty years since I first heard the music of Duke Ellington, and it has been, for most of that time, so much a source of delight to me that I've never consciously criticized it. I only listened and was pleased. From the Cotton Club days down through all the recordings, I've listened and been happy or sad, according to the Duke and his moods.

Then, on a famous occasion, I visited Carnegie Hall and heard the disciples and the sycophants moon and mewl over his "larger musical forms," and I came away unconvinced. For this time, instead of merely listening, I listened critically. And while I don't hold with the scared people who label all short form composers as "miniaturists," at the same time I feel, and feel profoundly, that Ellington was unhappy and unconvincing when he attempted the larger, longer forms. It was, I thought, unsuitable and even pretentious of him to develop his thematic material in terms of so-called "serious" music. What resulted were fragments, many of them interesting, colorful, even exciting; but each fragment or section remained isolated, unintegrated with the others. From this I would except the slow movement, which had a text to keep it

Source: Alec Wilder, "A Look at the Duke," Saturday Review (28 August 1948), 43–44.

together ["The Blues," from the middle movement of *Black, Brown and Beige*].

Perhaps a little background would be in order. Ellington has now been a name of consequence in popular music for more than twenty years. When he emerged from Washington, the Whiteman vogue was close to its peak (about 1927). He has since survived both swing and bebop. Unique among American bands and band leaders, he is celebrated both for his music and for the way it is played. It is almost a certainty, when the band is playing at its best, that it will be playing something devised by Ellington, or evolved from an idea contributed by one of his men. More recently, his disciple and associate Billy Strayhorn has contributed material of worth, but numerically its quantity is still small.

"Devise" and "evolve" are almost inevitable words to use in speaking of Ellington's creations, for his method of work is as unusual as some of the results it has produced. That method consists, as is well known, of arriving at a record date (where most of the well-known things have been created) with only fragmentary ideas—sometimes with none at all—and going to work really from scratch.[1] Sometimes Ellington will sit at a piano, idly, for half an hour, till a promising thought occurs; then he will start working it out for his men, assigning a trumpet here, a saxophone there, while indicating the kind of color background he wants, in blending and timbres—clarinets, saxes, trombones.

If this method was successful for the many miraculous short pieces from "Jig Walk" (his very first record)[2] through "East St. Louis Toodle-Oo," "Birmingham Breakdown," "Daybreak Express," the more recent "Sepia Panorama" and "Jack the Bear," it was hardly sufficient for the extended "Black, Brown and Beige." Now we have another collection of new short pieces, and the opportunity to evaluate what Ellington is of now—or at least of the late months of last year when this album was recorded ("Mood Ellington," Columbia B 164).

They are, on the whole, representative Ellington, showing that the man has the knack, as always, for creating lovely melodic lines, strong unusual rhythms, and unique orchestral effects. "Lady of the Lavender Mist" is a charming nostalgic melody of the elegant kind he writes so well; "Three-Cent Stomp" has great drive, is cleanly played, and in the realm of rhythmic pieces, satisfying; "Golden Cress" is, again, typical Ellington, if a little dated; in "[On a] Turquoise Cloud" a very ingenious use is made of soprano voice with clarinet and trombone, later with bass clarinet added; "Progressive Gavotte" has a clever idea, but bothered me (perhaps it shouldn't, as titles like this are not meant to be taken too seriously) for being neither very progressive nor

---

[1] This "working from scratch" method was by no means the only way Ellington composed, or even the most common procedure (see Richard O. Boyer's *New Yorker* profile (§49) and Ellington's article for *New Advance* (§51)). Its novelty, though, made it a favorite with writers.

[2] As of this writing, no early commercial recording of *Jig Walk* by Ellington has turned up; at least three later air checks survive (see *ERMDE*). The song was written by Ellington and Jo Trent in 1925 for *Chocolate Kiddies*, a show that traveled to Europe with a cast of black singers and dancers accompanied by Sam Wooding's orchestra. Curiously, the cornetist Rex Stewart also mentioned an early recording of the song by Ellington (see §95).

much of a gavotte. "Hy'a Sue" and "New York City Blues" are strictly band pieces, largely discussable in terms of the solos that make up each side.

But can you call them compositions? And can you call the man who put them together a composer? To me, the works of Ellington in terms of composition extend only as far as the song form extends, that is, the thirty-two-measure convention of Broadway and the radio, with slight extensions and variations. Beyond this, I find little integration or growth of ideas, and nothing that can be called structure. Over all, his music remains improvisatory . . . there is no elision, or development of thematic material, or interweaving of it, rarely any comment on or reappraisal of a starting thought.

Since Ellington has pleased millions of people, myself included, and has never departed from playing music his way, the way he felt a dance band should sound, the distinction may be gratuitous. But we are dealing, for the moment, with a straw man created by the young men without horns, the self-appointed critics who have made a persistent point of intellectualizing Ellington's music. To be sure, what he has done by instinct, and native taste, and experience, has been rhythmically and instrumentally a potent influence on popular music in this country, but I do not believe he is a composer in the essential sense of the word. Fine melodies, interesting rhythms, new orchestral sounds? Yes. But composition, no.

Perhaps what I am basically unhappy about is the sameness of objective in these new pieces as in the old, the willingness to be confined within the eight-measure phrase, the three-minute or the four-minute record. I am not reverting to the "larger form" delusion of "Black, Brown and Beige" as the desirable alternative, but I firmly believe that within the scope of his own talent there is a possibility of growth which he has never realized.

Some of this may be inherent in the nature of jazz music itself, which is a subject for a scholarly thesis not in my line. Can one say, for instance, that Louis Armstrong is a greater musician than he was in 1930, or Jack Teagarden, or _____ (fill in your own name)? The nature of jazz seems to be that the great men find their expression at a comparatively early age, ascend swiftly to a certain, distinctive level of expression, and continue on that plateau as long as they can. It is almost the highest praise to say of a venerated jazz man that he is "as good as ever," implying no retrogression. But "better than ever"? *That's* a rarity.

However, I do not think that it is enough for a man of Duke's talent to be "as good as ever." As a creator of wonderful sounds, he has no equal in the whole nervous history of our popular music. His sound is definite, it is unique, and it is, moreover, a form of communication. It is completely honest, strong and self-aware. He hasn't been caught up in the directionless revolt of bebop, and he hasn't fallen into the pseudo-scientific delusion of Schillinger-derived formulae.[3] He remains himself—humble, clear, and creative. But not, to my mind, evolving and experimenting.

[3] In the thirties and forties a number of American musicians had come under the influence of a mathematically based compositional system devised by Joseph Schillinger (1895–1943), among them George Gershwin, Glenn Miller, and Tommy Dorsey.

There will be the counter-objection that music for the dance band suffers the limitation that it is music for dancing, and the terms of the contract are fairly rigid. But is it, really? How much dancing is still actually done to the music of our so-called dance bands? Isn't it the fact that most of it is played in theatres and heard over the radio, that it has become, essentially, music for listening, as is most every other kind of music?

In this case, then, it would appear easily possible for Ellington to rid himself of some conventional restraints, to work in terms of more freedom and daring. It might even be that his fortunate alliance with Columbia, with its Long Playing record, on which he can go on for six, eight, or eleven minutes (if that is his choice) could be a determinative factor when he starts recording again.

But more than mechanics is the matter of mores. Is it possible for the band man, with his life of alternate ease and tension, of exhilarating "kicks" and grueling routine, to look upon his work as more than a means to an end? The end, of course, being the best living possible. Working through and with the men whom he has been associated with for years, Ellington has come to know their weaknesses as well as their strengths. He may have some remote concern with art, but it is, after all, only their living.

Catch him in an off-moment and he's likely to tell you that he decided a long time ago he wasn't going to "beat his brains out" working against the conditions that prevail in this most peculiar business. If he took the making of popular music with the complete seriousness and conscientiousness which his order of talent merits, that irresponsibility which dwells in even the best jazz musicians would "bring him down" — and the trade expression is the only accurate one — in no time. The ensembles might sound fine on a record which is the product of perhaps four hours' work and even more "takes," but they don't always sound find in the "Aquarium" or the "Fish Bowl" or the "Glass Slipper" or whatever else they chose to call some of the places in which such a band pursues its calling. Blow his top? Why? It'll probably sound better next time. Boys will be boys.

At the same time, he'll ask you, somewhat wistfully, what about strings and oboes and the other devices that live on the other side of the musical tracks? You catch his thought that maybe he could do something with them, but he'd have to learn how first. But it's just a vagrant thought, and gone again. Like the other great talents of American popular music — Gershwin especially — his technique is mostly self-acquired, shaped to functional ends. So long as he spends half his life and more as a public performer, with trains, buses, and theatre dressing rooms in between, it's not likely to change much.

Who is to urge him to change? Not me, certainly. There's always the beautiful sound, and the lovely tunes, and the interesting rhythms, and the vague speculation about what might have come of them.

VII. The Fifties

By the fifties the heyday of the big bands was over. Economic pressures had caused many established groups to break up in the late forties. Younger audiences now preferred to dance to rhythm and blues and rock 'n' roll, and individual singers like Frank Sinatra and Doris Day became more popular than the ensembles that had launched their careers. While Ellington, Count Basie, Woody Herman, and a few other bandleaders still found steady work, they faced new problems during this period.

The less favorable economic climate for big-band musicians may have contributed to personnel changes Ellington experienced early in the decade. In 1951 three key figures departed—Johnny Hodges, Lawrence Brown, and Sonny Greer—as did the trombonist Tyree Glenn, who had taken over Joe Nanton's plunger role in 1947. The arrival of such newcomers as tenor saxophonist Paul Gonsalves (1950), trombonist Britt Woodman (1951), trumpeter Clark Terry (1951), and drummers Louie Bellson (1951) and Sam Woodyard (1955) offset these losses somewhat. Also, Juan Tizol came back to the fold in 1951, as did both Hodges (1955) and Brown (1960). But the steadily shifting membership changed the orchestra's sound and style and left its mark on Ellington's composing, which was tailored to specific instrumental voices in the ensemble. (The reed section proved an area of stability, however, as the trio of Harry Carney, Russell Procope, and Jimmy Hamilton stayed intact well into the sixties.)

As in the forties, Ellington continued to turn out longer works, though now for occasions other than his orchestra's appearances at Carnegie Hall. These included *Harlem* (1951), *Such Sweet Thunder* (1957), *Toot Suite* (1959), and *Idiom '59* (1959). Ellington also explored other outlets for his compositions, writing *Night Creature* (1955) for combined symphony and jazz orchestras, *A Drum Is a Woman* (1956) for a television production, and *Anatomy of a Murder* (1959) for a Hollywood film directed by Otto Preminger.

While critics gave mixed marks to the new band members and works—some citing a decline in previous standards, others defending the changes—they generally agreed that Ellington's triumphant appearance at the 1956 Newport Jazz Festival provided a much-needed boost of morale. Soon after, Ellington appeared as the subject of a *Time* magazine cover story which pronounced the concert a "turning point in a career," demonstrating that "Ellington himself had emerged from a long period of quiescence and was once again bursting with ideas and inspiration."[1]

Ellington's recording alliances shifted during the fifties. He began the decade with Columbia, moved to Capitol in 1953 (the first session produced *Satin Doll*), then went back to Columbia in 1956. He also recorded two albums for Bethlehem and a handful of small-group sessions for the Mercer label, run by his son and Leonard Feather.

As in previous years, the orchestra traveled constantly, criss-crossing North America and making trips to Europe in 1950 (for the first time since 1939) and in 1958 and 1959.

[1] [Carter Harman], "Mood Indigo & Beyond," *Time* (20 August 1956), 54.

56. Ellington's Silver Jubilee in *Down Beat* (1952)

I n 1952 *Down Beat* celebrated Ellington's twenty-five years in the music business—dating from the Cotton Club opening on 4 December 1927—by devoting
an entire issue to him. Included were articles by Ellington and Strayhorn, tributes
by well-known musicians and critics, and a discography of recent recordings compiled by
regular *Down Beat* columnist George Hoefer. Highlights from the issue follow.

Many lists appeared in the Ellington "Silver Jubilee" issue—not surprising for a magazine famous for its annual popularity polls. Critics and celebrities ranked their favorite
recordings and Ellington played the game as well, beginning with an account of ten memorable events from the last twenty-five years. In this career retrospective, Ellington described
significant performances at home and abroad, mentioning at the end some of the noteworthy people he had met along the way.

Ellington on Career Highlights

I have been asked to list the ten events that seem most memorable to me out
of everything that has happened since we originally opened at the Cotton
Club.

This is a task of considerable magnitude, since we have been fortunate
enough to be on the receiving end of a large variety of honors. If I recall
certain events and pay tribute to certain beautiful people I may be unconsciously offending certain other beautiful people. However, I shall search my
mind for the ten occasions that stand out as personal memories.

Of course, our values today are greatly changed, but in those days there
were certain things you had heard about that you always wanted to experience, and one of these was playing the Palace Theatre on Broadway. It meant
reaching the peak for any artist who worked vaudeville, since the Palace was
the ultimate in that field. So perhaps our first very big moment after the Cotton
Club opening was the day we first played the Palace, in 1929.

We opened the show with *Dear Old Southland*. I remember the men hadn't
memorized their parts on this, and the show opened on a darkened stage.
When I gave the downbeat, nothing happened—the men couldn't see a note!
Then somebody called for the lights and the show went on.

The next highlight, I believe, was our trip to the west coast to make our
film movie. It was the Amos and Andy feature, *Check and Double Check*,
and we did *Ring Dem Bells* and *Three Little Words*. Later, of course, we were

Source: *Down Beat* (5 November 1952), 1, 7, 18.

in Hollywood for *Murder at the Vanities,* Mae West's *Belle of the Nineties* and several other pictures; but there was a special kick out of making our screen debut.

We took time out from the Cotton Club to make *Check and Double Check.* Aside from that, we were at the club right along from our opening in December 1927 until early in 1931. We doubled into Ziegfeld's *Show Girl* and various theatre dates. All that time, we were on the air from the Cotton Club.

Broadcasting was a lot simpler in those days; you didn't have to clear all your numbers a day or two in advance. I can remember times when Ted Husing[1] would turn around to me in the middle of a broadcast and say "Duke, how about playing so-and-so?" and we'd go right into it.

The next big moment was our opening night at the London Palladium. This was a night that scared the devil out of the whole band, the applause was so terrifying—it was applause *beyond* applause. On our first show there was 10 minutes of continuous applause. It was a tremendous thrill. In fact, that entire first European tour in 1933 was a tremendous uplift for all our spirits.

Europe was responsible for the next big kick I can recall, too. It was my [fortieth] birthday celebration in Stockholm, April 29, 1939. I was awakened by a 16-piece band from the local radio station which marched into my hotel room serenading me with *Happy Birthday.* All day long, at the hotel and at the Concert House where we were playing, huge bouquets of flowers kept arriving, and hundreds of people flocked to the dressing room. The whole audience rose to sing *Happy Birthday* and there was a ceremony onstage, followed by a big banquet for the entire orchestra and numerous guests at the Crown Prince Cafe. It all brought a very glowing ending to our second European tour.

Two years later, in 1941, we got a very special kick out of the opening of *Jump for Joy.* This was the revue in which the whole band took part. A number of critics felt this was the hippest Negro musical and has remained so to this day. We had some great lyrics for our songs, thanks largely to Paul Francis Webster; some fine writing by Sid Kuller, and such artists as Marie Bryant and Paul White, Joe Turner, Herb Jeffries, Dorothy Dandridge and Wonderful Smith.

The sixth important occasion was the first Carnegie Hall concert—first of what turned out to be an annual series. This enabled me to present my Tone Parallel to the history of the American Negro, *Black, Brown and Beige,* which as originally presented at Carnegie ran about 50 minutes. We only recorded excerpts from it for the RCA Victor album, but the entire concert was recorded privately and we hope some day to have this recording released generally so that everybody can hear *B, B & B* in its original form.

That first night at Carnegie was the only time in my life that I didn't have stage fright. I just didn't have time—I couldn't afford the luxury of being scared. Dr. Arthur Logan, an old friend and our personal physician, was standing around backstage handing out pills to everybody in the band. He even took one himself. He offered one to me and I refused it. I wasn't ner-

---

[1] One of the announcers for Ellington's radio broadcasts from the Cotton Club.

vous—not at all. But I did walk onstage without my music. Somebody signalled to me from the wings that they had it—but I didn't need it anyway; I remembered it all.

This first concert, in January 1943, turned out to be a milestone that paved the way for other regular concert series, so that by now an annual jazz concert at Carnegie has become a permanent thing for several other organizations. One thing that hasn't been duplicated, however, is the audience we had on that opening night and at our subsequent concerts. The quality of the appreciation, the attentiveness of the entire crowd of 3,000 people to every note we played, was a model of audience reaction that has proved hard to duplicate.

At the time of that concert, too, the music business celebrated a national Ellington week, and during the performance at Carnegie we were privileged to receive a plaque inscribed by some of our well-wishers from every branch of music—among them John Charles Thomas, William Grant S[t]ill, Deems Taylor, Marian Anderson, Albert Coates, Kurt Weill, Dean Dixon, Aaron Copland, Paul Whiteman, Benny Goodman, Count Basie, Earl Hines, Artie Shaw, Morton Gould and Marjorie Lawrence.

There was a similarly jubilant occasion in January 1945, when we took part in the annual *Esquire* jazz awards concert, at the Philharmonic Auditorium in Los Angeles. Most of the presentations of "Eskies" to individual winners were made by Hollywood personalities. Billy Strayhorn received his from Lena Horne, mine was presented by Lionel Barrymore.

There was another great evening, in 1949, when we played at Robin Hood Dell in Philadelphia with this beautiful 96-piece symphony orchestra, conducted by Russ Case, wrapped around ours.

I spent a lot of time listening, that evening, when I should have been playing. I wrote a bop thing for them, using the same jump-blues theme we recorded on one of the small band dates as *Who Struck John*. They played it perfectly.

Ninth on our list of significant moments would be the concert at the Metropolitan Opera House early last year. Our audience numbered over 3,500 including Mayor Impellitteri, who paid a special tribute to us onstage, and we introduced a new concert work, *Harlem,* which I later performed with the NBC Symphony orchestra.

Tenth and last, I recall with special delight another Philadelphia story— this one was the annual Musical Festival held by the *Philadelphia Inquirer* at the Municipal Stadium, with a tremendous show for an audience of 125,000 people, all admitted free. There were, if I remember right, three symphony orchestras as well as Benny Goodman, Perry Como, Mindy Carson and a big Indian war dance routine. I was especially impressed by the fact that when I did *Monologue* I had the whole audience giggling—and believe me, it's quite impressive to hear 125,000 people giggling.

It is a somewhat arbitrary decision to select ten events over a 25-year span, but these are the ones that came to mind. Of course, I could go into many details about some of the great people we've met through the years.

There was my meeting with the Pope, on my last visit to Europe, when the Pope had a great deal to say to me, but I must have been overawed because later I didn't remember a single thing he had said. There was my private audience with President Truman, whom I found very affable and very musically informed. There was the party in London when I fluffed off the guy who kept asking me to play *Swampy River,* and then found out he was Prince George. Later that evening the Duke of Windsor (then Prince of Wales) sat in with us on drums and surprised everybody, including Sonny Greer.

There was the time we were playing the downtown Cotton Club in 1937 when Leopold Stokowski came in alone and listened to our band. Later he discussed our music and invited me to attend his concert the next evening, when I heard him conducting the Philadelphia orchestra at Carnegie Hall.

But I don't want to go on name-dropping, because what has impressed me most through all these years has been not the renown of these people, but the sincerity of their interest in our music, and the interest of all the audiences who have helped to make our achievements possible. I can best sum it up by saying that the days since that long-ago Cotton Club opening have provided 25 years of eminently happy memories.

In addition to the preceding article, Ellington provided *Down Beat* with two lists. The first showed preferences among his own recordings. Curiously, all were drawn from the pre-1942 repertory, including such lesser-knowns as *Showboat Shuffle, Country Gal,* and *The Brownskin Gal.* The editors explained the selection process and supplied dates and labels for each.

Lists of Favorites

For many years Duke Ellington's answer to fans, disc jockeys and interviewers who asked him to name his own favorite Ellington records has been: "The one coming up."

When *Down Beat* approached him to select his five preferences, his first comment was "The five coming up." But eventually he broke his long-standing rule of evasion and drew up a list of records for which he has the most personal affection. It happens to run to a total of 11 records.[2] It follows: *Birmingham Breakdown* (1927, Brunswick); *Old Man Blues* (1930, Victor); *Creole Rhapsody* (1931, Victor); *Reminiscing in Tempo* (1935, Brunswick); *Showboat Shuffle* (1935, Brunswick); *Harmony in Harlem* (1937, Brunswick); *I Let a Song Go Out of My Heart* (1938, Brunswick); *Something to Live For* (1939, Brunswick); *Country Gal* (1939, Columbia); *Flamingo* (1940, Victor); *The Brownskin Gal* (1941, Victor).

In another list, Ellington cited "his special preferences in classical music," showing a distinct taste for early twentieth-century programmatic works: Ravel, *Daphnis and Chloe* (1909–12);

Source: *Down Beat* (5 November 1952), 2–4.

[2] Of these eleven, Billy Strayhorn composed *Something to Live For* and arranged *Flamingo.*

Delius, *In a Summer Garden* (1908); Debussy, *La Mer* (1903–5); Debussy, *Prelude to the Afternoon of a Faun* (1892–94); Holst, *The Planets* (1914–16).

• • •

After polling roughly fifty celebrities for their five favorite Ellington recordings, the *Down Beat* editors made a cumulative tally of those placing in the top ten. All but one—*The Hawk Talks,* drummer Louie Bellson's composition recorded in 1951—dated from 1941 or earlier.

It is a significant tribute both to the quality and quantity of Duke Ellington's works that 108 different titles were named by the 50 and more celebrities who submitted their lists of five favorite Ellington records.

The following [are] the results of *Down Beat's* polling to find the favorites of the Ellington favorites:

1. *Mood Indigo, Sophisticated Lady* (tied with 15 mentions each.)
2. *Solitude* (13)
3. *All Too Soon* (12)
4. *Take the "A" Train* (11)
5. *Warm Valley, Cotton Tail* (tied with 10 each.)
6. *Jack the Bear* (9)
7. *Ring Dem Bells* (8)
8. *I Got It Bad, Black & Tan Fantasy* (tied with 7 each.)
9. *Caravan, The Hawk Talks* (tied with 6 each.)
10. *Chelsea Bridge, East St. Louis Toodle-Oo, Flamingo,* and *The Mooche* (tied with 5 each.)

Among the various Ellington tributes, three were written by close associates: the composer-arranger Billy Strayhorn, the publicity agent Ned Williams, and the manager, publisher, and recording executive Irving Mills.[3]

Strayhorn's statement—one of the few published writings by him—contained a line that would be repeated often by commentators: "Ellington plays the piano, but his real instrument is his band."

Billy Strayhorn: "The Ellington Effect"

In 1934, in Pittsburgh, I heard and saw the Ellington band perform for my first time. Nothing before or since has affected my life so much. In 1939, I became his protégé, enabling me to be closer and see more.

His first, last and only formal instruction for me was embodied in one word: observe. I did just that, and came to know one of the most fascinating and original minds in American music.

Source: *Down Beat* (5 November 1952), 2.

[3] Strayhorn's and Williams's articles were later reprinted in *Hear Me Talkin' to Ya* (1955), edited by Nat Shapiro and Nat Hentoff. Williams's article was slightly abridged there; here it appears in its entirety. Shapiro and Hentoff also excerpted three paragraphs from Irving Mills's piece.

Ellington plays the piano, but his real instrument is his band. Each member of his band is to him a distinctive tone color and set of emotions, which he mixes with others equally distinctive to produce a third thing, which I like to call the Ellington Effect.

Sometimes this mixing happens on paper and frequently right on the bandstand. I have often seen him exchange parts in the middle of a piece because the man and the part weren't the same character.

Ellington's concern is with the individual musician, and what happens when they put their musical characters together. Watching him on the bandstand, the listener might think that his movements are stock ones used by everyone in front of a band. However, the extremely observant may well detect the flick of the finger that may draw the sound he wants from a musician.

By letting his men play naturally and relaxed Ellington is able to probe the intimate recesses of their minds and find things that not even the musicians thought were there.

Lately, personnel changes have prompted the comment that what I call the Ellington Effect has been replaced by something different. This, I believe, comes about from listening with the eyes instead of the ears. The same thing has happened every time there has been a change during my stay, and, even before my time, the advent into the band of the very people who have left brought forth the same remarks.

The same comment accompanied my arrival, but has long since simmered down to a whodunit game indulged in by the band (which always puzzles me, because I think my playing and writing style is totally different from Ellington's).

The Ellington Effect has touched many people, both listeners and performers, princes and paupers, the loved and the unloved, and will, as long as there is, and after there is . . . . . . Ellington.

Under the auspices of Irving Mills, the publicist Ned Williams began working on Ellington's behalf in the early thirties. His memories of hearing Ellington, however, dated back to 1927 at the Cotton Club. The *Down Beat* editors introduced Williams's article as follows:

> "Ned Williams was an important figure in Duke's life in the 30's," says Barry Ulanov in his biography of Duke Ellington. "He was Irving Mills' publicity chief . . . he sold Duke to magazine and newspaper editors . . . there was something about his own personality that generally got across, and thus got Mr. Ellington across."[4] Ned was managing editor of *Down Beat* for 10 years, from 1942 until last spring.

Williams's anecdotal account focused on some of Ellington's distinctive character traits.

Source: *Down Beat* (5 November 1952), 14.

[4] *DE,* 169.

Ned Williams on "Early Ellingtonia"

For a chap who never professed to play jazz, Edward Kennedy Ellington has created more than his share of the stuff in the quarter-century career which this issue of *Down Beat* acknowledges. Duke's story always has been that he and his boys are attempting to project the music of their race, nothing more, nothing less. The fact that it has turned out to be the bulk of the great jazz created in this particular period is purely co-incidental.

This will not be an attempt to document the history, musical or otherwise, of Duke Ellington. Duke dislikes biography or even the mention of it, which is why he withdrew his collaboration on Barry Ulanov's book before the first few chapters had been completed.

"My story isn't finished," he will say. "Why should any attempt be made to write it down?"

So this will be just a rambling reminiscence of the more than 20 years in which I have been privileged to call Duke Ellington my friend, more than half of them in close association.

I first heard the Ellington band in 1927, which was the year it made its debut at the famous Cotton Club in Harlem. That year I was the press agent for the celebrated song team of Van & Schenck, and for the Silver Slipper, where Gus and Joe were appearing in the heart of Times Square.

Dan Healy was the producer of the floor show at the Slipper, and it was as his guest that I visited Harlem. We were driven there by an affable member of the Slipper mob, Johnny Irish, who had his girl friend with him, the dancing star of the Slipper show, Ruby Keeler, who a few months later became the bride of Al Jolson.

I can't say that I was too much impressed with the Ellington crew on that visit. It definitely didn't have the form and the polish that it acquired later, of course. I was bewildered by the elaborate floor revue at the Cotton Club, even then comparable with the top Broadway musicals, and fascinated by the dispatch and lack of commotion with which a belligerent drunken guest was subdued and evicted by the club attaches.

The next time I heard Ellington was three years later on the stage of the Oriental theater in Chicago. That occasion was memorable for the rendition of *Mood Indigo* by the original trombone, clarinet, trumpet combination, Tricky Sam Nanton, Barney Bigard and Artie Whetsol. It never has sounded the same since.

Duke's opening date for that engagement was Friday the thirteenth, which fixed that date as a lucky one in his normally superstitious mind, for he played that same theater five more times in that one year, with an increased gross business each return. To this day a Friday the thirteenth is his favorite date to make decisions, sign contracts or open engagements.

Ellington's superstitions have not always operated as advantageously as this one. He never has appraised his friends and associates solely on their traits or their merits. An individual usually is regarded as lucky or unlucky to him, depending upon the state of Ellington's fortunes at the time.

Thus he often has not enjoyed full advantage of some friendships because those concerned were loyal enough but unfortunate enough to have stayed close to Duke during rugged periods. Others, comparatively less worthy, sometimes have received undue regard because they have been on hand in prosperous times, even though not directly responsible for the good fortune.

Generally speaking, however, Duke, a deeply religious soul, has been singularly loyal to friends and far above average in his devotion to members of his family and to relatives.

Subsequently I was to hear the fabulous Ellington band on countless occasions, in rehearsals, recording sessions, theaters, one-nighters, and in the Cotton Club during its hey-day. There was the early era in which the Duke had just received general fame, when Paul Whiteman and his arranger, Ferde Grofé, visited the Cotton Club nightly for more than a week, finally admitted that they couldn't steal even two bars of the amazing music.

There was the unforgettable night when Ethel Waters stood in the spotlight, with the Ellington band pulsating behind her, and sang, for the first time in public, a song by Harold Arlen and Ted Koehler called *Stormy Weather*. I heard Ed Sullivan introduce Arlen on television the other night, merely as the writer of *Over the Rainbow!* Oh, well.

Then there was that later night at the Cotton Club, when the entire brass section of the Ellington band arose and delivered such an intricate and unbelievably integrated chorus that the late Eddie Duchin, usually a poised and dignified musician, actually and literally rolled on the floor under his table in ecstasy.

Duke always has had a penchant for pinning nicknames on those most closely associated with him, usually nicknames that stick. Thus Freddy Jenkins, the little trumpet player who held the uninhibited spot in the band later graced by Ray Nance, became Posey. Johnny Hodges, alto star now out on his own, still is called Rabbit by those closest to him.

The late Richard Jones, Duke's valet for years, jumped only to the call of Bowden, and Jack Boyd, erstwhile manager of the band, whose given name is Charles, for no explainable reason was always just Elmer to the Duke. It was Elmer in turn who dubbed Ellington as Dumpy, and I can't remember when I've called him anything else in direct communication.

It may be a signal honor, but Duke went into a big corporation routine for me, never addresses me nor refers to me except by my first two initials, N.E. Another leader, while playing trumpet for Ellington, won the name which he still uses professionally, Cootie Williams, and there are many other instances. For favored feminine acquaintances, Duke lapses into the old southern custom of adding May to everything, Daisy May, Evie May, Willie May, no matter if the resemblance to your own given name is very slight. Even the antiquated revolver, toted around in the trunks of the troupe for years against possible hold-ups (no one knows who would use it) always has been designated Sweetie May.

Another odd instance of the 13 (Friday or not) superstition in the Ellington make-up comes to mind. It was the year [1938] that he was writing, with the collaboration of Henry Nemo and others, the entire score for a Cotton Club show. He had completed twelve songs, but he decided that unless he turned out 13, it wouldn't be lucky.

So he composed a thirteenth song, which strangely enough never was presented as a production number in that show, since the producer and the dance directors already were spinning on their heels with the wealth of Ellington material. But it was played regularly on the nightly broadcasts from the Cotton Club.

It was called *I Let a Song Go Out of My Heart.*

Speaking of song titles reminds me of the amusing go around we experienced with radio censorship about 15 years ago, when we were celebrating Duke's 10th anniversary in music business (and his birthday) with a matinee party at the Cotton Club and a special broadcast to England through the facilities of B.B.C.

We had cleared the numbers for the broadcast in customary fashion when this worried girl assistant phoned from the station. They were in serious doubt, it seemed, about the propriety of two of the titles scheduled, *Hip Chick* and *Dinah's in a Jam.*

My efforts to assure her (and the censor board) that the *Hip* in the first title had nothing to do with hips, and that the jam version of *Dinah* was not even remotely connected with pregnancy were unavailing. Since both were instrumental numbers, we switched the titles to more innocuous ones and played them anyway.

I've often wondered since about the condition of the wigs of the busy radio censors if they ever learned the truth about the significance of such recorded titles as *The Skrontch, T.T. on Toast, Warm Valley,* and others.

My former staff at *Down Beat* expressed an opinion about me earlier this year, and I quote: "We suspect that he has only one strong musical conviction—that Duke Ellington is the greatest thing that ever happened to American jazz."

They were so right—and still are!

Irving Mills (1884–1985) was a central figure in Ellington's career, serving as manager, publicist, and publisher from 1926 to 1939. For the "Silver Jubilee" issue he gave an overview of his professional association with Ellington, including the ostensible reasons for ending it in 1939.

Mills's statements about his role as creative and artistic advisor to Ellington seem self-serving, to put it mildly. The same person who in 1952 claimed never to want Ellington to "sacrifice his integrity . . . to find a short-cut to commercial success" had earlier influenced Ellington to record popular and novelty numbers from the Mills catalog, even appearing as vocalist on such discs as *When You're Smiling* and *Three Little Words* (both 1930).

In his memoirs, Ellington took a characteristically generous view of Mills. He credited the latter with a string of accomplishments—among them, Mills's insistence that Ellington perform and record only his own music—and wrote about the end of their partnership as follows: "Irving Mills and I had come to the parting of the ways some years before. He gave me his 50 percent of Duke Ellington, Inc., in exchange for my 50 percent of Mills-Calloway

Source: *Down Beat* (5 November 1952), 6.

Enterprises, Inc. We dissolved our business relationship agreeably and, in spite of how much he had made on me, I respected the way he had operated. He had always preserved the dignity of my name. Duke Ellington had an unblemished image, and that is the most anybody can do for anybody."[5]

Irving Mills: "I Split with Duke When Music Began Sidetracking"

The story of my long association with Duke Ellington, an association which covered the period [during] which he rose from obscurity to a position of eminence in the music world that was completely unique, is of special interest at this time. There are many factors in the story that could be of help to those who are trying at present to re-vitalize the music business, which we all know has been in a slump, both financially and artistically.

Naturally, many readers will want to know why our long and happy business relationship came to an end a few years ago. In connection with that, I want to state first that our close friendship and personal relationship never has come to an end. Every time he comes to Hollywood, Duke always spends a long, friendly visit with me at my home.

The Duke Ellington story, and the part I played in it, has been told many times before, but to give a clear explanation of why I withdrew from my managerial activities with Duke, I must retell some of it.

The first time I heard Duke Ellington was at the Kentucky Club in New York, where he had come in with the five-piece band he had been appearing with in Washington D.C. I had gone to the Kentucky Club that night with the late Sime Silverman of *Variety* who, like most newspaper men, liked to go out for an evening of relaxation after putting his paper "to bed" for another deadline. I think the number that caught my attention that night was *Black and Tan Fantasy*. When I learned that it was Duke's composition, I immediately recognized that I had encountered a great creative artist—and the first American composer to catch in his music the true jazz spirit.

What was equally important about that meeting was that Duke felt that in me he had found not only someone capable of handling his professional career but someone who also understood and thoroughly appreciated the significance of his creative efforts as a musician.

Shortly after that, when I was producing a new show for the Cotton Club, I built as much of it as possible around Duke's band and his music. The budget, incidentally, did not provide for a band as large as Duke felt he needed—10 pieces. I paid the salaries of the additional musicians out of my share of the project. I did it gladly, because I had complete faith in Duke Ellington and firmly believed that together we were launching something more than just a dance orchestra.

I was convinced that we were launching a great musical organization espe-

[5] *MM*, 89.

cially designed to interpret something new and great in American music—the music of Duke Ellington.

And I was never more sure of it than I am now—on the 25th anniversary of that event.

For those who are active in any branch of the management or booking business nowadays, I want to stress the fact that I never thought of the organization as just a dance band, even though it was completely successful as such in those days. Nor did I ever think of Duke as just a band leader, a songwriter, or personality, though he was indeed all of them.

For me, the development of Duke Ellington's career was an over-all operation consisting of much more than merely securing engagements for him or selling his songs. Anyone could have done that. My exploitation campaign was aimed at presenting the public a great musician who was making a lasting contribution to American music. I was able to guide Duke Ellington to the top in his field, a field in which he was the first to be accepted as an authentic artist, because I made his importance as an artist the primary consideration.

I never tried to persuade Duke to sacrifice his integrity as Duke Ellington, the musician, for the sake of trying to find a short-cut to commercial success. There might be something there for some of today's personal managers, booking agents and press agents to think about.

Too many of them think solely in terms of developing and exploiting musicians as commercial attractions.

I think Duke will agree that I did give him sound advice when he himself was in doubt as to what represented his best work. Many great musicians have turned out material that was not up to their best standards.

I felt that one of my important functions with Duke was to be in the recording studio when we were putting out those records, which were to make him a unique and important figure in music, and see to it that nothing went into a record that did not add to his stature as a musician. I wanted every Ellington record to have that quality that in later years would rightfully earn the tribute we express when we say: "This is the real Duke Ellington!"

When I withdrew from my managerial relationship with Duke, it was because I sensed that Duke had fallen into a different attitude toward his music, and was taking off in what I thought was a wrong direction. For an example—not necessarily his best—let's take his *Reminiscing in Tempo*. It had many good things in it, and one of these days Duke will go back and extract the good things from it and use them to better advantage. But that recording never should have been released. It was one of the points [at] which Duke lost touch with the huge, loyal following that loved genuine Ellington music.

I did not try to stop Duke, because I understood exactly what he was trying to do. He was trying to break out of what he thought were bonds placed on his creative ability by the patterns in which he had been working. Those of us who know and love the real Duke Ellington feel that his mistake was turning from the idiom . . . to the concert works to which he has practically confined his writing in recent years.

But those of us who know and understand Duke, also know why it was important—even necessary—for him to try that path.

Now Duke has had his fling. I think he now knows more clearly where his best efforts should be directed. One of these days we'll be back together again. It almost happened the last time he came out to the Coast. When he's ready, I'll be glad to start all over again with Duke Ellington, and to assist him to gain his proper place as one of the most important figures in contemporary music.

57. André Hodeir: "A Masterpiece: *Concerto for Cootie*" (1954)

 ndré Hodeir's essay on *Concerto for Cootie* marked a milestone in the literature about Ellington. While earlier writers had conducted serious examinations of Ellington's music, Hodeir was the first to scrutinize so closely a single composition.

Trained as a composer at the Paris Conservatoire, Hodeir (b. 1921) applied to jazz aesthetic precepts and artistic standards derived from his study of the European classical tradition. His critical method for approaching jazz, grounded in the experience of close listening to recordings, made a strong impact on such American writers as Martin Williams and Gunther Schuller.

Hodeir's essay first appeared in *Hommes et Problèmes du Jazz* (1954); the book came out two years later in the United States as *Jazz: Its Evolution and Essence,* translated by David Noakes.

Ups and Downs of the Concerto

Some pieces of music grow old; others stay young. At times we can hardly believe it possible that once we actually enjoyed listening to a page of music or a chorus that now seems overwhelmingly long on faults and short on merits. To make up for this, some works seem more and more attractive to us as time goes by. For one thing, we are more difficult to please at thirty than we were at twenty. Instead of liking a hundred records, we no longer like more than five or six; but perhaps we like them better. Judging by my own experience, there can be no doubt that the test of time has favored Ellington's *Concerto for Cootie*—more, perhaps, than any other work, and this is a sure sign of merit. It has become clear to me that this piece is one of the high points in Ellington's output, which has been vast and rich in flashes of genius, but unequal and occasionally disappointing. I would even say that it offers a striking epitome of certain essential aspects of his work.

Source: André Hodeir, "A Masterpiece: *Concerto for Cootie*," in *Jazz: Its Evolution and Essence,* translated by David Noakes (New York: Grove Press, 1956; rev. ed., 1979), 77–98.

The concerto formula—that is, a composition centered around a single soloist accompanied by large orchestra—is widely used these days. There is almost no repertory that does not include a certain number of arrangements conceived with an eye toward the possibilities, the style, and the ambitions of such and such a popular soloist. In 1940, even though it wasn't exceptional, the concerto was rarer. It was only four years before then that Ellington had recorded his first concertos, one of which, *Echoes of Harlem,* had already been designed for Cootie Williams. Admittedly, the appearance of these compositions did not constitute an innovation in the form. Before Ellington, Armstrong had recorded solos that had all the concerto's appearances. But the Ellington style of concerto, from the very beginning, not only introduced a markedly different musical climate but also laid the foundation for an infinitely richer conception. In it, far from merely serving to set off the soloist as in Armstrong's records, the orchestra worked in close collaboration with him. Naturally, it would be impossible to state positively that Duke Ellington and his group grasped from the beginning all the possibilities that this kind of composition offered, but it seems probable all the same. In any case, the fact is that, after several years of varyingly successful experiments (the detestable *Trumpet in Spades,* in which Rex [Stewart] trumpeted to such poor advantage, comes to mind), the orchestra recorded, on March 15, 1940, this *Concerto for Cootie,* which still strikes us, a decade and a half later, as the masterpiece of jazz concertos and as being, along with *Ko-Ko,* the most important composition that Duke Ellington has turned out.

The concerto formula is not faultless; to be more precise, it invites esthetic lapses that the arranger and the soloist do not always manage to avoid, even when they are fully aware of the lurking danger. Fear of monotony engenders an abusive use of effects; the difficulty a soloist has in improvising freely against too melodically and harmonically rich an orchestral background leads to the greatest possible reduction of the orchestra's part. In this way, a kind of by-product of the concerto is produced, with a virtual elimination of all dialogue between the soloist and the orchestra, which is actually the basic reason for the form's existence. On the other hand, the fact that the arranger conceives the concerto in terms of a single soloist—of such and such a special soloist—makes it possible to attain most easily in this form that cardinal virtue of any work of art, unity. Perhaps it will be objected that this is a classical composer's idea, but I think I have had enough experience with jazz to affirm that the notion of unity is just as important in this music as in European music. Is it possible to believe that a record joining the talents of Armstrong and Parker, even at the top of their form, would constitute a composition, in the real sense of the word? Certainly not. We could go further and say that, in actuality, such a confrontation would immediately be recognized as unfruitful. Neither Armstrong nor Parker would really be in top form; it is much more likely that neither would be able to play at all. True, I have purposely taken an extreme example; but records have given us many specimens of similar though less extreme confrontations, and I don't remember a single successful one in the lot.

In the light of this, it is easy for me to say in what way *Concerto for Cootie* rates my qualification as a masterpiece. *Concerto for Cootie* is a masterpiece because everything in it is pure; because it doesn't have that slight touch of softness which is enough to make so many other deserving records insipid. *Concerto for Cootie* is a masterpiece because the arranger and the soloist have refused in it any temptation to achieve an easy effect, and because the musical substance of it is so rich that not for one instant does the listener have an impression of monotony. *Concerto for Cootie* is a masterpiece because it shows the game being played for all it is worth, without anything's being held back, and because the game is won. We have here a real concerto in which the orchestra is not a simple background, in which the soloist doesn't waste his time in technical acrobatics or in gratuitous effects. Both have something to say, they say it well, and what they say is beautiful. Finally, *Concerto for Cootie* is a masterpiece because what the orchestra says is the indispensable complement to what the soloist says; because nothing is out of place or superfluous in it; and because the composition thus attains unity.

Structure of *Concerto for Cootie*

Concerto for Cootie should not be considered as an ordinary arrangement. Its unusual structure, the polish of its composition, the liberties with certain well-established rules that are taken in it, the refusal to improvise—these characteristics are enough to place it rather on the level of original composition as this term is understood by artists of classical training. *Concerto for Cootie* is not derived from any earlier melody. True, *Do Nothin' Till You Hear from Me* uses the same melodic figure; but this song, composed by Ellington, is several years later than the orchestral work. There can be no doubt that it was adapted from it.* *Do Nothin'* is in a way the commercial version of the guiding idea behind *Concerto for Cootie*. Indeed, it retains only the initial phrase. We wouldn't even have mentioned the song here but for the fact that this phrase had to be revised to conform to the traditional framework of the thirty-two-bar song. We shall be able to appreciate the original better by comparing it with this popularized version.

This initial phrase, which constitutes the principal theme of the *Concerto*, undergoes numerous transformations in the course of the composition. We shall call it theme A at its first exposition, A', A", and A''' in what follows. Figure B, which comes between the second and third exposition of A, serves merely as an episode; actually, it comes where the bridge would have if *Do Nothin'* had preceded the *Concerto*. On the contrary, theme C is extremely important. Played in a new key—and one that is not even neighboring—it completely changes the lighting and atmosphere of the composition. The lyricism of its lines, its range spread over a whole octave, and its being diatonic form a perfect contrast with the restraint of the first theme, which is static, chromatic, and confined within the limits of a fourth except for its last phrase. Finally, the re-exposition of A is immediately followed by a final coda that

---

* *Do Nothin'* was recorded by the Ellington band, with a vocal by Al Hibbler, in 1947. [Air checks and transcriptions of the song, however, date back to 1943. —Ed.]

borrows its components from Ellington's *Moon Glow,* put out in 1934 by Brunswick. Here, in outline form, is how these various elements are joined together:

Plan of CONCERTO FOR COOTIE

Introduction	8 bars
I. *Exposition* (F major)	
Theme *A*	10 bars
followed by *A'*	10 bars
followed by *B*	8 bars
followed by *A"*	10 bars
followed by a modulatory transition	2 bars
II. *Middle section* (D♭ major)	
Theme *C*	16 bars
followed by a modulatory transition	2 bars
III. *Re-exposition and coda* (F major)	
A'''	6 bars
Coda	10 bars

For a number of reasons, this construction is the furthest thing from being customary in jazz. The notion of variation scarcely subsists in it at all. As for the concept of chorus, it has disappeared without a trace. For that matter, since improvisation doesn't play any active role here, there would have been no reason for Ellington to preserve the traditional division in choruses. It was logical to adopt a more flexible structure, one more closely related to the "composed" nature of the piece. The mold chosen calls to mind the da capo form of the eighteenth-century Italians, although the recurrence of *A* after the middle section *C* is hardly more than suggested.

Another surprising thing is the use of ten-bar phrases, an unprecedented practice in the history of jazz arrangements. This innovation is even bolder than it seems at first encounter. The initial phrase, as it appears in the printed edition of *Do Nothin',* does indeed comprise eight bars. The two extra bars of *A* and *A'* could therefore be considered as little orchestral codas added as an afterthought, constituting a kind of rebound of the phrase played by the soloist, even though they fit in—it would not be enough to say merely that they follow—so perfectly that the ear is aware of no break. But a closer analysis of the phrase's articulation reveals that its final turn in the *Do Nothin'* version is completely different from the original ending. The new turn is, for that matter, pretty weak, and there can be no doubt that it was added in order to re-establish a rhythmic equilibrium of the conventional kind that the *Concerto,* a free composition, deliberately ignored. Notice (fig. 1) that in *Concerto for Cootie* the final note comes one bar sooner than is customary. Ending a phrase like this on a weak measure was, in 1939 [*recte* 1940], absolutely revolutionary, and yet no one seems to have noticed it, because the band takes up the phrase right away and goes ahead with it as naturally as can be. The listener who hasn't been forewarned is not aware that the real phrase ends in the sixth measure, and the forewarned listener doesn't react much differently. It would almost seem as though seven-bar melodies had been heard since the beginning of jazz.

Fig. 1

Fig. 1

Top line: the melody of *Do Nothin' Till You Hear from Me* as published by Francis Day. Middle line: the initial phrase (*A*) of *Concerto for Cootie*. Bottom line: the same phrase as played in its second exposition (*A'*). N.B.—The vertical arrows indicate measures that reproduce the ones above exactly.

The second exposition of *A*—that is, *A'*—fits in with the traditional rules; the twofold repetition, in the sixth measure, of a group of four eighth notes is enough to create anew the usual symmetry. The little orchestral coda remains, though, making the section cover ten bars. *A"*, on paper, differs from *A* only in these last two measures, which prepare the transition to *C*. However, the performance gives the phrase quite a different aspect. In addition to the question of sonority, which we shall consider later, it must be noticed that Cootie here gives back to the notes their rhythmic values, which he had deliberately distorted during the first exposition of the theme. Finally, *A'''* is a merely suggested restatement of *A*. After four bars, which include a melodic variant, there is a sudden branching out to the coda—a conclusion for which the way has been prepared by the changing harmonies that underline this restatement.

Simplicity and Subtlety of the Harmony

The harmonic language of *Concerto for Cootie* is, on the whole, extremely simple. Apart from the introduction, the general climate of the piece is as resolutely consonant as *Ko-Ko*, Ellington's other masterpiece of that period, was the opposite. In the *Concerto*, dissonance plays a secondary role; it does not constitute the foundation of the harmony. It does not serve to create a feeling of tension, but operates as a means of adding color. Nonetheless, the many dissonances to be found in the work are not there for nothing: there can be no doubt that their suppression would weaken it considerably. It is they, certainly, that by contrast make the consonances sound so bright and fresh. This over-all harmonic simplicity doesn't rule out subtlety of detail. Certain passages have presented problems to the best-trained ears. The little phrase in contrary motion in the seventh and eighth measures of the coda, which is harmonically a real gem, would provide a test in musical dictation for the greatest specialists in this ticklish sport; but I want to call attention merely to its musical beauty, which I like to think any listener will appreciate.

Another exceptional passage is the measure just before the exposition of theme C. I doubt that there are many examples of modulations more striking than this one, not only in jazz but in all music. On paper, it seems extremely simple, and no doubt it actually is. Listening to it, one has to admire the abruptness and rigor of this turning; and its effect is all the more astonishing because Ellington has put before it a two-beat rest that constitutes — taking into consideration the completely inconclusive phrase just preceding it — the most effective break you could ask for between one part of a piece and another that you would have expected to follow without any break at all. To call this a stroke of genius is, for once, not to misuse the phrase.

It would be possible to mention a number of other harmonic finds. In spite of its ambiguous character and a certain acidity that does not lack charm, the introduction is not the most successful part of the composition. I prefer certain details in the purely accompanying part: the saxes' dissonances behind phrase A' or a complementary phrase like the one in the eighth measure of C, which has a melodic, harmonic, and instrumental savor that is truly penetrating. Attention should also be called to the occasional use of blue notes in some of the trombones' punctuation of phrases A and A''. Although, basically, *Concerto for Cootie* has no more connection with the blues than [Coleman] Hawkins' *Body and Soul*, these blue notes are by no means out of place; the faint touch of the blues that they introduce fits into the atmosphere of the piece perfectly.

There remains the added-sixth chord, which is put to considerable use here. This harmonic combination, which generally raises my hackles, fills me with joy in the *Concerto*. It is true that Ellington sometimes uses it in a regrettably Gershwin-like way, but that certainly is not the case here. Why? I couldn't say for sure; that sort of thing is more easily felt than explained. Perhaps the consonant climate of the piece accounts for a large part of it; perhaps the general feeling and the orchestration itself play a decisive role. What must be remembered is that no chord, however flaccid, is inherently ugly; the only thing that counts is the use made of it.

The Orchestra at the Soloist's Service

There is no point in dwelling on the orchestra's role in *Concerto for Cootie*. What we have already said is enough to define it. In this piece, as in most jazz concertos, the orchestra never dominates the soloist; it introduces him, supports him, continues where he leaves off, provides a connection between two of his phrases—in a word, it is at his service. Notice that the orchestra states no theme; when it happens to sketch one of the main motifs, it does so as a reply, not as a statement. The soloist always takes the initiative. Like a good servant, the orchestra is satisfied with approving. Even the admirable modulation that precedes the entry of C is not, from a structural point of view, anything but the opening of a door; once the guest of honor is shown in, the servant fades away into the background.

Still, this servant, though he may not obtrude, says exactly what must be said, and his clothes may not be sumptuous but they are exceptionally elegant. The orchestra's bearing is equaled in sobriety only by the orchestration. In both respects, *Concerto for Cootie* is a model of discretion and authenticity. It displays an economy of means that is the sign of real classicism. To me, the little syncopated figure that is given alternately to the saxes and the brasses to punctuate each exposition of A is infinitely more valuable than the overloaded backgrounds that the big modern band does not always know how to do without; it achieves a maximum of effectiveness without using more than two chords, although it is true that these are renewed each time. Judged by the same standards, the orchestral background of B is possibly even more successful. And what is there to say about the countermelody of C, where the saxes, in their chromatic movement, support Cootie's lyric flight so majestically?

Another cause for admiring astonishment is the incomparable co-ordination between the harmony and the orchestration. In order to express the nuances of a clear harmony in which there are nonetheless plenty of half-tints, the composer has everywhere hit upon just the instrumentation called for. Orchestral color and harmonic color blend in a way that delights the amateur in me as I observe what this combination brings to the piece and that impresses the professional in me as I remember how rare such a combination is. Actually, this blending is the principal virtue of an orchestration that doesn't offer any sensational innovations but that can still boast some captivating details. I shall mention only the orchestra's big descent at the end of A' (cf. fig. 1), in which the principal motif, taken by the clarinet, does not emerge clearly from the cloud of enveloping chromatic lines but is delicately suggested; the imitation of the theme is guessed at rather than actually heard.

If I have stressed the lesson in simplicity that the *Concerto* presents in both its harmony and its orchestration, it is because that is precisely what the piece has to teach. However, it is all too easy to confuse what is simple with what is merely simplified. *Concerto for Cootie* demonstrates the possibility of achieving a real orchestral language while observing the strictest economy of means. It constitutes, indeed, a summit that few musicians have reached. In this respect, Duke Ellington here makes one think of Mozart. I don't know whether the jazz fan will appreciate the significance of such a comparison, but I feel safe in making it because this composition deserves to be considered not merely as a specimen of jazz, which is only one kind of music, but as a specimen of music, period.

Strong and Weak Points of the Performance

We have just considered the orchestral part of the *Concerto* in its conception. But we must not forget that the conception of a work of jazz cannot be separated from its execution. When Ellington wrote the trumpet part, he wasn't thinking of anyone but Cootie, and similarly he didn't design the work as a whole for any orchestra but his own. Whether the *Concerto* was composed by one man or by a whole group is a good question. It has been and will continue to be asked, although the answer can be provided only by those who were present when the piece was created, either as participants or witnesses. The only thing we can be sure of is that the whole band, then in its great period, took part in the performance. Wallace Jones and Rex Stewart were on trumpet, Joe Nanton, Juan Tizol, and Lawrence Brown on trombone, Barney Bigard on clarinet, Otto Hardwicke, Johnny Hodges, Ben Webster, and Harry Carney on sax, Duke Ellington at the piano, Fred Guy on guitar, Jimmy Blanton on bass, and Sonny Greer on drums; and we mustn't forget, of course, Cootie Williams on solo trumpet. Listing these names and remembering that we are now going to talk about performance brings us right to the heart of jazz. Let us accordingly abandon the very general approach we adopted when talking about the problems offered by the harmonic and orchestral aspects of the piece.

I don't know exactly when the *Concerto* was composed or when it began to be performed, so it would be hard for me to prove that it was not completely broken in when it was recorded, but this seems likely.[1] If so, perhaps the record would have been the better for being put off until after enough performances to correct the occasional lack of preciseness of which the band is guilty. But it is not certain that the result would have been very different. Even at that time, the Ellington orchestra was frequently somewhat easygoing in its performance as a group; it rarely had [Jimmie] Lunceford's kind of precision. On the other hand, there is no way of knowing whether Cootie would have played his part with the same spirit after another twenty run-throughs; his fire might have died down along the way, and it must be admitted that this would have been completely regrettable.[2] For that matter, the flaws I have referred to are notably few; they are venial and easily overlooked. If they cause regrets in spite of this, it is because they are the only thing to be criticized in a record that otherwise calls only for praise. But you would have to be particularly narrow-minded to let the beauties of this piece be obscured by paying too much attention to the fact that the saxes, for example, scurry after one another in the scale leading to the coda. Alongside these slight defects, the playing in *Concerto for Cootie* actually has many solid virtues. The balance among the players and their fine sound in both loud and muted passages are highlighted by an excellent recording technique. Nuances are performed with

---

[1] As of this writing no air checks of *Concerto for Cootie* have surfaced before the first recording for Victor, 15 March 1940.

[2] Air checks of *Concerto for Cootie* from the summer and fall of 1940 show Williams still playing the piece with spirit, also revising and embellishing his part in new ways. For dates, see *ERMDE*, 418.

sensitivity and taste. The band seems to be one man following or, even better, anticipating the leader's wishes.

The tempo of *Concerto for Cootie* is "slow moderato," a difficult one to keep to, but just right for the piece. There are few records in which the rhythm section of the band plays in quite such a relaxed way, and by the same token there are few in which the band phrases with as much swing. Naturally, this is not a torrid record like [Lionel] Hampton's *Air Mail Special*. That kind of exaltation, which has its own appeal, is only rarely Duke Ellington's line. But *Concerto for Cootie* is a perfect example of a performance that is full of swing in a gentle climate.

The rhythmic success of the performance is based largely on Jimmy Blanton's playing, of which this is certainly one of the best recorded examples. It is fascinating to follow the bass's admirable part, curiously aired out as it is with whole bars of silence. At each exposition of theme *A*, Blanton stops playing, only to put in a discreet but effective reappearance at the fifth bar. Such details might constitute the whole attraction of an ordinary record. Here, they almost pass unobserved. I remember that, when I once put Pierre Gérardot on the spot by asking whether the tempo of *Concerto for Cootie* was slow or medium, he had to stop and think a moment before being able to answer. If I had asked him such a question about some run-of-the-mill record that had just appeared, he would doubtless have replied right off; but the *Concerto*, for him as for me, was in a world apart from the jazz of every day.

An Authentic Composition and the Interpreter's Part in It

The time has come to turn to the soloist's part and ask questions about it just as we did about the orchestra's role. We have just seen that one of the essential characteristics of *Concerto for Cootie* is the elimination of improvisation. There is nothing arbitrary about this; it was imposed upon Ellington by circumstances. As we have already said, partly because it is a kind of concert music but even more because of its very form, the jazz concerto (at least when the orchestra plays more than a merely passive role) seems to require of the soloist greater circumspection than he usually shows in a simple chorus-after-chorus performance. It is appropriate to mention that most of the concertos that came before this one were already notable for the extent to which they had been worked out. No one would believe, for instance, that Barney Bigard's part in *Clarinet Lament* was spontaneously improvised from one end to the other in the studio. Nevertheless, a large part was surely left to the moment's inspiration. *Concerto for Cootie* has every appearance of being the first jazz record with an important solo part in which improvisation does not figure at all.

Does that mean that we have here a European-style concerto, a composition worked out in private, then written down, and finally rehearsed and performed? Yes and no. Undoubtedly Ellington realized that such a piece had to be thought out from the first to the last, right up to and including the solo part. Whether this part was put down in black and white or memorized makes little difference. The only thing that counts is its character, which, as far as the melody is concerned, is that of something fixed and final. There seems nothing unwarranted in saying that one performance must have differed from another only in minor expressive details that are left to the interpreter in other kinds of music as well. It remains to be determined whether the trumpet part, of which at least the actual notes were decided on before the recording, is the work of Cootie, of Duke, or of several hands. The question is not easy for anyone who wasn't there when the composition was created. It is hard to believe that a piece of music so perfectly unified as to be almost without parallel in the whole jazz repertory should not be the work of a single man; and that man would have to be Duke Ellington. True, anyone who is familiar with the way that famous band works would have to think twice before positively rejecting the possibility of a collective effort; but, all things considered, this kind of gestation seems unlikely. Pending definite information to the contrary, we shall regard *Concerto for Cootie* as a real *composition* as European musicians understand this word.

However, if the notes of this trumpet part were decided on before the recording, it was still only the notes that were. This feature is what takes us far away from European conceptions. Ernest Ansermet had the right idea when he observed, more than thirty years ago, that even though the work of jazz may be written down, it is not fixed. Unlike the European concerto, in which the composer's intention dominates the interpreter's, the jazz concerto makes the soloist a kind of second creator, often more important than the first, even when the part he has to play doesn't leave him any melodic initiative. Perhaps Cootie had nothing to do with the melody of the *Concerto;* he probably doesn't stray from it an inch; and still it would be impossible to imagine *Concerto for Cootie* without him.

We here touch upon one of those mysteries of jazz that classical musicians have so much trouble in recognizing but that are basically simplicity itself. For the European musician, sound is a means of expression that is distinct from the creation of a work; for the jazz musician, it is an essential part of this creation. That difference is enough to create a gulf between two conceptions that in other respects seem to work together in the piece we are talking about. No interpreter of European music, whatever his genius, will tell us as much about himself as Cootie does in these three minutes. It is the expressionist conception of jazz that allows the interpreter to substitute himself for the composer, to express his personality completely, to make himself a creator. Some people condemn expressionism of any kind, regarding it as a debasement. To do so is to condemn almost all jazz. Although many soloists may have abused the possibilities offered them, the greatest have managed to stay within certain limits; but these limits themselves are broader than some ears, convinced of the absolute superiority of European art, can tolerate in a musical manifestation that is judged, a priori, to be inferior.

Don't misunderstand me: I don't in the least claim, like most specialized critics, that jazz is *the* music of our time. On the contrary, I want very much to stress, even though I were to be accused of "racial prejudice," that, to me, the riches of jazz, however precious, cannot for a moment match the riches of contemporary European music. But it is perhaps worth while to recall that several centuries of European music had passed before the mind of a genius, Arnold Schoenberg, gave birth to the idea of a "melody of timbres" (*Klang-farbenmelodie*)—that is, a musical sequence in which each sound is expressed by a different timbre. Isn't that, in a different way, what jazz musicians accomplished spontaneously by giving to the sonority of one instrument the most varied possible aspects?

A Bouquet of Sonorities

Few records do more than the *Concerto* to make possible an appreciation of how great a role sonority can play in the creation of jazz. The trumpet part is a true bouquet of sonorities. The phrases given to it by Ellington, which have a melodic beauty of their own that should not be overlooked, are completely taken over by Cootie. He makes them shine forth in dazzling colors, then plunges them in the shade, plays around with them, makes them glitter or delicately tones them down; and each time what he shows us is something new. Even if he had had to put up with a less charming melody, his art would have been enough to make us forget its banality. But it mustn't be thought that this gamut of sonority is merely decorative, artificial, gratuitous. The sonorities he imposes on the melody were conceived in terms of the melody itself. A different melody would have been treated differently; but this particular one, under his fingers, could not have been treated in any other way.

It is interesting to note that there is a different sonority corresponding to each of the three themes. The reason is easy to understand. It is appropriate that theme A, which we have already described as static, should be handled in subdued colors; that theme B, which is savagely harsh, should invite free use of the muted wa-wa's stridencies, which here have an extra brutality; and the lyricism of theme C can be fully expressed only in the upper register of the trumpet, played open. But there are other, more subtle details. Why is there such a diversity of expression in the different expositions of A? (Only A' and A''' are played in the same spirit.) Why does the trumpet have such a violent vibrato in A, whereas A' is played with an even sonority that almost prefigures the way modern trumpets sound? Why, in A'', is there that sound held like a thread, which is so disconcerting that it is rather hard to believe it is a muted trumpet rather than a violin? To ask such questions, which come naturally to the classically trained listener, would show ignorance of the fact that *Concerto for Cootie,* like many works of jazz, owes it vitality to the contrast of sonorities—a contrast that does not in the least affect its basic unity.

Furthermore, with what taste, with what a sense of proportion Cootie uses his amazing technique for producing different timbres! How admirably he knows how to bring to bear on expressive detail the resources of an art that, used with less discipline, would risk being nothing more than an advanced exercise—far from ordinary, to be sure, but without special significance! Unreserved admiration is the only possible reaction to his discreet and sensitive use of the glissando, which is scarcely noticeable in the various versions of A, is more developed in B, and becomes in C an essential part of his lyricism. This judicious use of sonorities is perfectly paralleled by the intelligence of his phrasing. We have already noted that Cootie deliberately twisted the rhythmic values of theme *A*. It is not easy to bring off that sort of treatment. Even when the melody lends itself to it—and this one does—there is the constant danger of being corny in the worst possible way. Cootie's performance does not for a moment seem in the least bit mannered. From the very first, the listener cannot doubt that the kind of vibrato he uses is profoundly felt.

How the Piece Stands

Let's try to place the *Concerto* now, first of all among the great trumpeter's performances. The job is not so simple as it might seem at first. The *Concerto* seems to represent a synthesis. Nowhere else has Cootie appeared under more varying aspects; nowhere else has he succeeded in bringing into such radical opposition serenity and passion, lyricism and simple tenderness. Nonetheless, what traces are to be found here of the magical, incantatory Cootie of *Echoes of Harlem,* of the mocking Cootie of *Moon Glow,* of the hell-bent-for-leather Cootie of *It's a Glory,* and of all the other Cooties that there isn't room to mention? At the most there is, from time to time, an intonation or the fragment of a phrase to serve as a furtive reminder that it is, after all, the same artist. And yet, who could make any mistake? What soloist leaves a more indelible imprint on his work than this disconcerting Cootie? In a way, he is one of those who constantly show the public a different face. Someone like Louis Armstrong is always more or less himself. It is his incomparable inventive gift that saves him from being repetitious; it doesn't take any time to recognize his triumphal accent, his straightforward phrasing. Cootie covers a wider range; he seems always to be discovering something. For all that, he doesn't lose his identity. This man of a thousand sonorities is still one whose particular sonority you would recognize in a thousand.

In any case, the *Concerto* is certainly one of the most successful records Cootie has made. It can be said that he completely lives up to the music that Duke Ellington wrote for him and surrounded him with. He attains real greatness here, both in feeling and in taste; there is nothing in this music that is not authentic. I don't know of many soloists who rate such praise.

Before concluding, it might be appropriate to try to refute two objections that will surely occur to those who, taking advantage of the similarities we have more than once indicated, would like to place this work in relation to the classical concerto. These objections are not unimportant; it is simply that they don't apply to the scale of values by which jazz is to be judged.

The first objection would be that *Concerto for Cootie* is a sample of "easy" music; in other words, a work without depth, one of those that reveal all their secrets at a single hearing, and to any kind of listener, without requiring any effort. That may be. By comparison with the great pages of contemporary music, the *Concerto* is not a complex work, and it is even less a revolutionary work. Neither its harmonic system nor its perfectly tonal melody can offer the slightest problem to a trained person. The classical critic, accustomed to judging modern music by certain criteria, will naturally be disappointed at failing to find here, apart from effects of sonority, anything that can't be grasped immediately.

But, in an age when creators have got so far ahead of the public that the bridges threaten to be cut off for some time, is it not fortunate that a composer can resume contact with a more accessible kind of music and give us a well-balanced work that is simple in idiom, sound and not bare of nobility in thought, admittedly easy to understand but individual, even original, and savorful in a way that withstands repeated listening? Isn't there room, along-side Schoenberg's *Suite for Seven Instruments* and Webern's *Chamber Symphony,* for an art designed to please without making any concessions to vulgarity or bombast? Doesn't the *Concerto* satisfy this definition just as do certain pieces by Haydn and Mozart that are not scholarly music but have nonetheless withstood the test of almost two centuries of listening?

The other objection is less important. It has to do with the piece's proportions. *Concerto for Cootie* takes only one side of a ten-inch seventy-eight—three minutes. Judged by the standards of European music, by which a symphonic idea of no great significance may well be stretched over more than a quarter of an hour, that is not very much. But what is such a criterion worth? It is to be feared that attaching so much importance to size is one of the prejudices of the European mind, which is under the influence of several grandiose achievements. The *St. Matthew Passion* [of J. S. Bach] is not a masterpiece because it lasts almost four hours; it is a masterpiece because it is the *St. Matthew Passion.* For that matter, this prejudice has been gravely breached even in Europe. Didn't Schoenberg, in reaction to the bombast of post-Romanticism, say he would like to see a novel expressed "in a single sigh"? Didn't Webern make some of his compositions incredibly brief? Speaking little makes no difference if a great deal is said. Though it is no miracle of condensation, *Concerto for Cootie* says more in three minutes than such a long and uneven fresco as the *Liberian Suite.*

All that remains is to place *Concerto for Cootie* as jazz. Almost twenty years of experience were required before orchestral jazz produced, within a few days of each other, its two most important works. The first is *Ko-Ko.* It has less freshness and serenity, but perhaps more breadth and grandeur. The second is the *Concerto.* In the perfection of its form and the quality of its ideas, the *Concerto,* which combines classicism and innovation, stands head and shoulders above other pieces played by big bands. It has almost all the good features found in the best jazz, and others besides that are not generally found in Negro music. It makes up for the elements it doesn't use by the admirable way in which it exploits those that constitute its real substance. Isn't that exactly what a masterpiece is supposed to do?

58. An African View of Ellington (1955)

The Ellington orchestra turned up in a scene from the novel *Mirages de Paris* (1955) by Ousmane Socé, former Senegalese ambassador to the United States. Socé's fictional account of a performance in Paris may have been based on the band's appearance there in 1950 (although the banjo reference implies an earlier date). Around this time Ellington was featuring an arrangement of Rodgers and Hart's *Blue Moon*, mentioned in the text.

This selection was brought to my attention and translated from the French by the late Mercer Cook, scholar, former U.S. ambassador to Niger and Senegal, and the son of composer Will Marion Cook, Ellington's one-time mentor. As a teenager in Washington, D.C. (Dunbar High School, Class of 1920), Mercer Cook had heard the young Ellington playing at the True Reformers' Hall and the Howard Theater. Cook also saw Ellington and his orchestra in Dakar, Senegal, when they appeared there in 1966 for the World Festival of Negro Arts.

. . . To cure [Fara's] depression, a group of friends decided to offer him some distraction. So it was that they took him one evening to the Salle Pleyel where Duke Ellington was presenting a gala program of American Negro music.

They reached the concert hall at about nine p.m. To get good seats they had paid dearly, despite their meager scholarship stipends. Fara looked around with the eyes of one from another world. Jacqueline's death, changing the normal course of his life, was also changing his perceptions. Huge white silk curtains hid the stage. In the hall he could see Frenchmen, foreigners, and among the latter, many Anglo-Saxons.

The silence of expectancy was swept away by the crash of a brass cymbal. Slowly the white curtains opened, the black musicians appeared in white tuxedos. Stepping out to the front of the stage, Duke Ellington looked very much like a prince.

He gave the orchestra the down-beat: trumpets, saxophone, clarinet, banjo broke into a stampede of wild horses, a mad gallop, dashing over paths of wet sand. Full speed ahead, at one turn, the gallop struck against an impenetrable forest; and while the applause exploded, the musicians bowed, thanking the audience with a line of pearly white smiles.

After a moment's rest, the jazz began to imitate sounds as grotesque and expressive as the masks of black sculptors. Without warning, the soloists (trumpet, saxophone, and clarinet) each in turn, moved down stage and whispered tender romances. The lights had lowered, the harsh daylight had been transformed into a starlit night:

> *Blue moon*
> *You saw me standing alone*
> *Without a dream in my heart*
> *Without a love of my own*

Source: Ousmane Socé, *Mirages de Paris* (Paris: Nouvelles Editions Latines, 1955), 224–26. Translated by Mercer Cook.

Sweet jazz, as diversified as life itself, a jazz that jokes, exults, complains and dreams!

Twenty minutes intermission. The concert then continues with miracles of musical onomatopoeia: hyena howls, elephant trumpeting, heart-rending appeals of men calling out in anguish, cries of tormented souls: poets, musicians, and all those in the clutch of despair.

The next number moved with leonine strides under hurricane-laden skies, a sparkling shift as the brass section imitated flashes of lightning, with raindrops falling in the tempo of a deluge, and the drums pedaled at break-neck speed as if to escape the flood. . . .

The talent of the black musicians, thought Fara, lay in their mastery of life's rhythms. Rhythms are to time what lighting is to space. There are rhythms which make time fast or slow, bright or somber—rhythms which make it sweet as a sip of tender words, others which make it bitter.

59. George Avakian: Ellington at Newport (1956)

Ellington's appearance at the Newport Jazz Festival on 7 July 1956 turned out to be a high point of his performing career—comparable in some ways to the opening at London's Palladium in 1933 and the Carnegie Hall debut in 1943. The piece that especially roused the audience was *Diminuendo and Crescendo in Blue* of 1937, which Ellington extended on this occasion by having tenor saxophonist Paul Gonsalves take a lengthy solo between the work's two halves.

Present at the event was critic and record producer George Avakian (b. 1919), who provided an eyewitness account when Columbia issued a recording of the concert, *Ellington at Newport*. Avakian's emphasis on the important role played by Count Basie's drummer Jo Jones was echoed by Ellington in *Music Is My Mistress*: "Jo Jones was the driving force behind our big success at Newport in 1956, the man with a blueprint for a bouncing, boiling bash, the man in the pit with the git-wit-it git" (241).

Overshadowing everything else, including the introduction of a new work written expressly for this recording at Newport, Duke Ellington's performance of *Diminuendo and Crescendo in Blue* in the last set of the 1956 Festival turned into one of the most extraordinary moments in the history of this annual event.

Within an hour, reporters and critics were buzzing about it. By next morning, it was generally conceded to have been one of the most exciting performances any of them had ever heard. All were agreed that it was a triumph of the good old rocking (R & B, if you will) blues beat which has been too often

---

Source: George Avakian, from the liner notes to *Ellington at Newport* (Columbia CL 934).

missing in jazz in the last fifteen years. All were also agreed that it couldn't have happened to a nicer guy.

Typically, Duke was enjoying a perfectly successful appearance when he announced this 1937 medium-tempo blues (Duke said 1938, but it was written a year earlier) but no one was planning to break out the champagne or wave flags. Duke opened with four introductory choruses on piano; by the second, the rhythm section had already laid down a rocking beat and Duke had served notice of what was to come. Three minutes later, following the long series of ensemble choruses, Duke took over for two more rocking choruses that kicked off Paul Gonsalves playing one of the longest and most unusual tenor sax solos ever captured on record.

Gonsalves played for 27 straight choruses. Of that, more later, for there are three levels at least from which this extraordinary feat must be viewed. (It should, of course, also be heard.) At about his seventh chorus, the tension, which had been building both onstage and in the audience since Duke kicked off the piece, suddenly broke. A platinum-blonde girl in a black dress began dancing in one of the boxes (the last place you'd expect that in Newport!) and a moment later somebody else started in another part of the audience. Large sections of the crowd had already been on their feet; now their cheering was doubled and redoubled as the inter-reacting stimulus of a rocking performance and crowd response heightened the excitement.

Throughout the rest of the performance, there were frequent bursts of wild dancing, and literally acres of people stood on their chairs, cheering and clapping. Yet this was no rock 'n' roll reaction; despite the unbridled enthusiasm, there was a controlled, clean quality to the crowd; they were listening to Duke as well as enjoying the swirling surge of activity around them. Crouched just off the edge of the stage, where I could signal back to the engineers if anything unexpected happened onstage during our recording, I had a rare view of the audience (at least 7,000 were still there, about midnight of the last night). Halfway through Paul's solo, it had become an enormous single living organism, reacting in waves like huge ripples to the music played before it.

But the management and the police, unable to sense the true atmosphere of that crowd as it felt from the stage, grew more apprehensive with every chorus. Fearful of a serious injury in the milling crowd, which by now had pressed forward down the aisles (the open area between the boxes and the elevated stage was already jammed with leaping fans), producer George Wein and one of the officers tried to signal Duke to stop. Duke, sensing that to stop now might really cause a riot, chose instead to soothe the crowd down with a couple of quiet numbers.

Out of sight of the crowd was an unsung hero who is quite possibly the person most responsible for this explosive performance. No one will ever know for sure, but perhaps the Ellington band might never have generated that terrific beat if it weren't for Jo Jones, who had played drums that night with Teddy Wilson. Jo happened to be in a little runway below the left front of the stage, at the base of the steps leading up from the musicians' tent behind the bandstand. From this vantage point, hidden from the crowd by a high canvas, but visible from the shoulders up to the musicians, Jo egged on the band with nothing more than appreciation and a rolled-up copy of the *Christian Science Monitor*. As Duke (whose voice you can hear from time to time) drove the band in the early stages of *Diminuendo and Crescendo,* first the reed section and then the trombones and finally the rest of the band picked up on Jo, who was shouting encouragement and swatting the edge of the stage with the newspaper, about eighteen inches from my squatting haunch. (As this target has grown more inviting with the years, I was careful to stay an arm and a half's length clear of Jo at all times.) The saxes began hollering back at Jo, then the rest of the band joined in, and by the time Gonsalves had sprung the dancers loose it seemed that bassist Jimmy Woode and drummer Sam Woodyard were playing to Jo as much as to anyone else. Even the super-placid Johnny Hodges, who will probably not raise a half-masted eyelid come millennium-time, smiled and beat time back at Jo.

Gonsalves dug in harder and harder, and when he finally gave way to Duke, the release was electric. But only for an instant, for Duke himself was swinging, and when the band pitched in with the low-register clarinets plumbing *misterioso* depths, the tension built anew. (Don't miss the rhythm section's excruciatingly-delayed return after the first chorus with the clarinets. What would normally be a 4-bar break turns into 7!) With Duke and Jo still whipping up the band from opposite sides of the stage, the last choruses climbed to a climax topped by Cat Anderson, Duke's high-note specialist, who booted everybody home after the 59th chorus. Flat here and there? Nobody complained then, and don't bother us now, boy!

As we were saying about eight hundred words ago, Paul Gonsalves rates some examination on his own. His staunchest fans would never rate Paul among the giants of the saxophone, but after his feat at Newport one wonders who else could have sustained 27 choruses without honking or squealing or trying to take the play away from what really counted—the beat. I can think of two or three others who might have done it—but I just as easily can imagine them running into complications of their own making. But that matters little, because the point is that Paul did it.

The key, obviously, lies in knowing how to tread the narrow path between Spartan simplicity and embroidery to a degree just short of destroying the hypnotic effect that Gonsalves achieves by adhering to the rhythm section's conception. This is not the place for the soloist to take over: he cannot grab the spotlight; he must remain one with the driving beat and yet not fall into dullness. A "display" saxophonist would probably have burned himself out within ten choruses, thus reducing the permanent value of this performance as it happened to develop (although the crowd might have enjoyed it just as much at the time).

Thus the Paul Gonsalves solo is not really a solo at all, but a leading voice supported by many parts, and never letting down the conception of those parts: the beat laid down by the drums, bass, and occasionally Duke's piano, and equally important the reacting support of the crowd, the girl who danced, the enthusiasm of the rest of the band (which did not play at all behind Paul, but which kept the beat with him and drove him on with shouts of encouragement which Paul must have sensed were something more than just routine showmanship), and Jo Jones's wadded *Monitor*.

60. Ellington: "The Race for Space" (ca. late 1957)

Sometime between October 1957, when the Soviet Union launched its satellite *Sputnik I,* and January 1958, when the U.S. put its first satellite, *Explorer,* into orbit, Ellington joined the then-vigorous debate on "the race for space." His article may have been commissioned by a magazine or newspaper; a published source for it, however, has not been located. Yet a date for the article can be suggested because Ellington alludes to the launching of both satellites, also to his "newest jazz opus," the "Ballet of the Flying Saucers" from *A Drum Is a Woman,* which had been recorded in 1956 and telecast in May 1957.

Although ostensibly addressing U.S. efforts to match the Soviet Union's scientific achievements, Ellington seems more concerned here with race relations, showing more anger and frustration on the subject than anywhere else in his writings. He keeps returning to inequities in the American social system and shortcomings of the federal government. Toward the end he finally turns to music, citing the racial and musical mix within a jazz orchestra as a model for society.

Someone, possibly Ellington, edited the typescript, crossing out and striking over some of the most militant phrases, softening the overall tone of the piece. In the following version, these deletions have been reinstated, with crossed-out lines and struck-over passages marked off by { }. Also, roughly half a dozen spelling errors have been corrected.

As a musician, jazz, that is, there would rightly be some question as to what Duke Ellington is doing in a serious discussion on the race for space. As the most adequate answer I can think of, I'm talking about the race for space for the logical reason that what happens in the race for the moon and other planets and the control of space affects me as well as every other American and like you and others reading this, I most certainly don't want Russian "moons" and other space projectiles circling around over my head.

And being what might be called a musical opportunist, I'm way ahead of a lot of my contemporary composers because my newest jazz opus, "{Dance} Ballet of the Flying Saucers" is now in its polishing up stage. And I'm reasonably sure I premiered it long before the United States [got] around to putting its first satellite into a space orbit.[1] That, more or less, is a summation of why I'm concerned in this controversy over the control of space.

Sounds presumptuous. Well, sort of. But that is how it is, for in my medium, jazz, the viewpoint is also competitive and primarily creative as well as unbe-

---

Source: Duke Ellington, "The Race for Space" (ca. 1957), typescript in the Duke Ellington Collection, Smithsonian Institution.

[1] The original sentence in the typescript reads: "And I'm reasonably sure I'll be able to premiere it long before," etc. Someone has changed the tense to "I premiered it," also crossing out the word "long" and drawing a line to the following handwritten phrase: "think I stole a match on all of this [?] in Jan[uary?] Drum is a Woman." While these alterations suggest that the editing of Ellington's article occurred some time after it was first written, they still leave the time frame somewhat vague.

lievably liberal. Which, I suppose, the scientists working on space vehicles and the like may very well envy, seeing that on my side of the fence we musicians are seldom hampered by congressional committees checking on what we're having for dinner {or whether we played for a mixed dance in Mississippi or not the other night}.

Which adds up that the field of jazz has not yet become an arena of the sort of racial conflicts based on color, national origin and the like that I sincerely believe along with many other Negroes is pinning the United States to the earth. Meanwhile, the Russians show their contempt for ou[r] inability to straighten out our race problems and keep ap[a]ce of them, by even sending a dog into space!

For as I see it, and mind you my view is strictly that of a musician, a citizen of the United States and a descendant of a family of this country's earliest and most loyal settlers—we Negroes—the dreary bickerings over the morals, ancestry, beliefs, thinkings and affiliations of the men whom we have to depend upon for our very existence makes me all the more thankful that I'm in jazz and not in science.

In jazz, as in the sciences, I am in a medium for creators. Those who write the great symphonies and those who write the jazz classics are of the same creative mold of the men who put Sputnik into space and those who will follow this mighty {Russian} achievement with other space satellites and miracles. All of them—musicians, physicists, mathematicians, geneticists, biologists, geologists, astronomers, atomic researchers—are motivated by the same burning urge to create. Whether in science or in jazz.

I consider Sputnik a work of art in the same sense that I view a great painting, read a great poem or listen to a great work of music. For it is in the nature of man to worship the accomplishment while considering the means, the method, the condition in which the accomplishment was achieved as something secondary. Similarly, we marvel at the Pyramids as an unbelievable feat of ancient engineering skills.

While we acknowledge that thousands and thousands of slaves pushed, pulled, lifted and rolled those tremendous blocks of granite into position in the building of these all-time monuments to the glory of the Pharoahs, we don't make a production of the inhumanity of it. Instead, we hail the Pyramids as one of the Seven Wonders of the World.

In the same sense, people today marvel at Sputnik without giving a thought to the human sacrifice in living standards, regimentation of thought and the brutal subjugation of the individual to the state, the Reds put their people through in order to accomplish Sputnik.

But this same regimentation has brought about its fantastic results perhaps because it doesn't permit race prejudice as we know it {inside Russia} to interfere with scientific progress. For, as in music, harmony—harmony of thought, must have prevailed in order for the scientists to make a moon that would work. To attain harmony, the notes are blended in such a fashion that there is no room for discord.

{In America we simply don't have this all essential harmony. We don't have it in politics, we don't have it in our social life nor in the (free) daily business of living. In religion where it should be a shining example, we have Catholics against Protestants against Jews and all of them against the Negro. In politics Democrats hate Republicans, and Dixiecrats hate both.}

Because so many Americans persist in the notion of the master race, millions of Negroes are deprived of proper schooling, denied the right to vote on who will spend their tax money and are the last hired and first fired in those industries necessary for the progress of the country.

When you stop and think of the way southern congressmen and senators tie up Congress with filibusters and delaying tactics against the passage of civil rights measures to protect minorities from persecution, when you think of the lost time and effort President Eisenhower spent trying to settle the Little Rock situation;[2] in fact the time being lost all over the South as well as places in the North over the school desegregation issue ordered by the Supreme Court in 1954, you'll get an idea of how and why the Russians may be having breakfast on the moon by the time you read this.

It seems to me that the problem of America's inability so far to go ahead of or at least keep abreast of Russia in the race for space can be traced directly to this racial problem which has been given top priority not only throughout the country but by Washington, itself. They're spending so much time trying to figure whether the potential Negro vote is worth making the South mad by opening white schools to Negro kids, by dropping the color bar in restaurants, railroad and bus stations, in white collar jobs and in political appointments that those in charge of the missile and nuclear programs don't know which way to go.

Especially when they are at the same time being insulted, policed and spied upon by congressional committees, the FBI, the American Legion, the White Citizens Councils and everybody else who know as much about advanced science as I know about parsing a Russian noun!

Put it this way. Jazz is a good barometer of freedom. When pure jazz is not accepted and pseudo jazz with political and dogmatic coatings take[s] over, you can look for freedom of expression to step out of the picture. In its beginnings the USA spawned certain ideals of freedom and independence through which, eventually, jazz was evolved and the music is so free that many people say it is the only unhampered, unhindered expression of complete freedom yet produced in this country. But if I were told to play my music in only the keys of F-sharp the monotony and frustration of it would force me right out of jazz. Yet there are some people who in effect are permitted to express themselves freely in only one key.

This denial of expression of freedom, of movement and the creative process {not only dulls the intellect but upsets any balance between them} not only dulls the intellect but makes for deep resentment that sometimes pays off in driving people mad from frustration or keeping the psychiatrist couches as busy as a 50 cent flophouse bed. By that I mean we're not going to get much done so long as discrimination keeps 16 million Americans looking at the

---

[2] In 1957 President Dwight D. Eisenhower sent troops to Little Rock, Arkansas, after Governor Orval Faubus defied a Supreme Court order to desegregate public schools.

game from knotholes. Everybody has to get in the game if we are playing to win.

Which brings me to the theme of the Man with the Different Sound. I pick a trumpet player to fill a spot because I think he's got a different sound and because he may be the right man for the right spot in my band. I wouldn't, nor would any other bandleaders, pick a man for a chair in the band just because he went to a music school and has a diploma showing he can play his instrument. We need first to know how he sounds for some of the best musicians in history never went to school at all.

And this sound you hear so much about in music circles today is not merely the simple tooting of a horn, plunking of a piano or bass fiddle or beating drums. It's an inclusive term taking in the temperament, the personality of the man we are planning to hire. We want to know how he thinks and what he thinks about. For we plan to keep him as a member of our band or team and we need to know all we can about a fellow who is going to eat, sleep and travel with us on long trips across the country or abroad. Just like the men who make the first trip through space to the moon. They will have to be selected according to their individual outlook and temperament and then blended in the same way we write harmony in music if they are to sound right.

But beyond that, we don't care what he looks like, what color he is, what race he belongs to or even what language he speaks best. Music is bigger than all those things and the successful band has but one requirement for its personnel: can it play the music? We concede we will have prima donnas, fellows with the big head or shy guys meek as mice. We'll have some who go around with chips on their shoulders and others who won't say anything at all unless forced to. Bands are made up of all kinds of personalities. And this is also true of basketball, football, baseball and hockey teams. It is true, too, of business, religious [groups?] and explorers, whether in Africa or in the Arctic. And it has been proven that teamwork required for success in scientific endeavors takes in all kinds of combinations of people. I have heard of engineering firms, or research teams in various phases of atomic, genetic and other studies that are made up of Chinese, German, British, Italian and American scientists. And there are jazz bands which achieve that so essentially different sound made up of a polyglot of racial elements that includes Indians, Germans, Jews, Negroes, Swedes, Frenchmen, Belgians and southern whites. All harmony, too, for they have freed themselves from the suspicions of racial differences and dedicated themselves to the business of discovering, arranging and playing of that different sound. The sound of harmony.

So, this is my view on the race for space. We'll never get it until we Americans, collectively and individually[,] get us a new sound. A new sound of harmony, brotherly love, common respect and consideration for the dignity and freedom of men.

61. André Hodeir: "Why Did Ellington 'Remake' His Masterpiece?" (1958)

I n his introduction to *Toward Jazz* (1962), André Hodeir described the book as a departure from his previous work, *Jazz: Its Evolution and Essence* (1954/1956): "I am no longer concerned, as I used to be, with objectivity; I am trying to define a truly personal attitude toward the phenomenon of jazz." That "personal attitude" pervaded his chapter in *Toward Jazz* on Ellington—originally published in the Paris weekly *Arts* in 1958—in which earlier praise gave way to scathing criticism and bitter disappointment.

The specific target of Hodeir's attack was Ellington's 1956 re-recording of *Ko-Ko* (1940) on the album *Historically Speaking*, issued by Bethlehem (BCP 60). (Also included on the set were new versions of *Creole Love Call, East St. Louis Toodle-Oo, Jack the Bear,* and other pieces the Ellington orchestra had recorded earlier.) According to Hodeir, this performance was inferior and symptomatic of Ellington's general decline over the past decade, resulting from the composer's "diminution of musical sensibility." Elsewhere in the book, Hodeir identified someone "capable of filling the vacancy left by Duke Ellington": Gil Evans.

The pieces in *Toward Jazz* contain two kinds of footnotes: those dating from the first publication of the individual essays, and Hodeir's "Self-Critical Notes and Other Particulars" written later for the published collection in 1962. In the version below, the original notes are represented by asterisks, the "Self-Critical" ones by numerals in parentheses.

For a refutation of Hodeir's position on the Bethlehem recordings, see Gary Giddins's liner notes to *The Bethlehem Years, Vol. 1* (Bethlehem BCP-6013, 1976).

Duke Ellington holds a privileged position in the history of jazz. He was its first *composer* in the strict sense of the term, and for a long time he was its only composer. Fats Waller was not a composer, he merely *wrote tunes.* Ernie Wilkins is an *arranger* who works with other people's ideas.[1] A composer is a musician who makes full use of a capacity which neither the tune writer nor, with very few exceptions, the arranger possesses, a capacity which might be defined as that of *endowing jazz with an additional dimension.* This dimension, which gives a work new depth and greater possibilities for development, is form. Jazz history may be summed up as follows: Armstrong created jazz, Ellington created form in jazz; Parker and Davis re-created jazz, while Monk is trying to re-create form in jazz.

In order to create his music, the Duke forged himself a double-edged tool. On the one hand, he had a flair for orchestration and handled tone color imaginatively; by working on these natural gifts he was able to transform them into an orchestral language. On the other, he benefited by that respect which a bandleader can earn by combining a smiling authority with an indisputable musical superiority; he used it to build an orchestra which, for fifteen

Source: André Hodeir, "Why Did Ellington 'Remake' His Masterpiece?" [1958], in *Toward Jazz* (New York: Grove Press, 1962; rpt., New York: Da Capo, (1976)), 25–32.

[1] In the fifties Wilkins (b. 1922) composed and arranged for the orchestras of Count Basie, Dizzy Gillespie, Tommy Dorsey, Harry James, and others.

years, was absolutely unique in jazz. His musical language was as integral a part of his orchestra as his orchestra was of the works he produced. There may have been other jazzmen with the equipment necessary to equal the Duke as a composer, but if so they lacked the organizational flair necessary to create a means of expressing themselves. Anyone can bring a score to a bandleader; the only way to be really creative in jazz is to have an orchestra at one's disposal. And if one has built that orchestra all by oneself, one may be in a position to make a substantial contribution to the language of jazz. Having an orchestra at one's disposal is not sufficient, however. Don Redman, Fletcher Henderson, Sy Oliver, and several others have attempted to break new ground in the field of form, which had been by-passed by the early jazzmen. Their praiseworthy efforts, however, lacked any deeply felt inspiration. It was thanks to Duke Ellington that we have been able to avoid doing the same spade work over again today. Single-handed he changed the face of a desert and brought forth the first fruit of that multidimensional music which may one day supplant every other form of jazz; and though at times the fruits were bitter, at others they were sweet indeed.

Duke Ellington was a brilliant precursor, though he hit his full stride in only a few, rare instances, as against hundreds of errors (errors which were nevertheless full of original touches and partial achievements); the Duke was once a great musician, but now fatigue seems to have gotten the best of him.

I understand the reasons for this fatigue, but I must also observe its effects. What I cannot bear is to watch Ellington the middle-aged bandleader debase the work of Ellington the artist. The fact that for the past ten years he has written nothing worth-while—has so declined, in fact, that there have been doubts that he actually wrote certain pieces of trash signed Ellington—would not in itself be very exceptional. Composers as great as Stravinsky, Bartók, and Schönberg each reached the point in their careers where they mysteriously seemed to lose their best creative powers forever. With Ellington, however, one would have thought that even after the creator in him had succumbed to the exhausting life he has led, the musician would survive. The Duke had been the only composer; we would still have liked to regard him as the greatest orchestra leader.

And yet two years ago . . . but this is a sorrowful tale. The directors of a large recording firm [Bethlehem] persuaded Ellington to record a set of pieces taken from his past. The idea was a rather poor one to begin with, but did have a positive side which might have deserved serious thought. After all, works as rich in sound texture as In a Mellotone or Ko-Ko might well reveal new dimensions when enhanced with the glamour of high fidelity.

I wish to call the reader's attention to the last-named piece. As he must know, the original version of Ko-Ko was recorded in 1940; it constitutes the most perfect example of Duke Ellington's language (then at the height of its development) and remains one of the undisputed masterpieces of orchestral jazz. Every jazz fan knows the 1940 Ko-Ko by heart.

This is where our story takes a preposterous turn, for as it happens there was at least one man who had forgotten that unique moment of beauty in the history of jazz, and that man was Duke Ellington himself! So far as I know, neither Rembrandt nor Cézanne ever did a watered-down copy of an early painting containing a vision that was already perfect in itself. Great works of architecture have, it is true, been altered, but the architects were already dead when this was done. The Duke has done *Ko-Ko* over again, and the result is a hideous copy which makes a mockery of his own masterpiece. Moreover, he has allowed this new version to be issued on a record, the mere title of which — *Historically Speaking* — is an insult to his great name.*

The whole thing is so unthinkable that I am assailed by a doubt: perhaps he did it purposely, in a conscious effort at self-debunking. In that case this article would be ludicrous, and there would be nothing left for me but to crawl into a hole for having written it. But then, who has ever attained such a summit of greatness? Not even Nietzsche. No, I'm afraid that the obvious explanation of this desecration is not a credit to Ellington. There is only one possible alternative: either the Duke has simply lost the remarkable musical sensibility which lay at the heart of his genius, or else he was never really conscious of the beauty of his music.

My love and respect for Duke Ellington and his music make me inclined to doubt this last hypothesis. The contemporary artist has one anguishing advantage over his predecessors, and this is a sense of historical perspective which enables him to situate himself with regard to the past. Duke Ellington is not a pure creature of instinct like Armstrong or Parker; whether we like it or not, every composer is an intellectual, a person capable of meditation. I should hate to think that Ellington never knew *who he was*. And if he did know, how can he have forgotten? Can he have lost, not only his creative powers, but his musical awareness as well, becoming oblivious to his own mistakes — I should say, his *crimes?*

But the hardest part of my task remains undone. I hope no one will think I am performing it with the bitter gusto that one can take in pulling down minor idols; Jimmy Noone and Mezz Mezzrow are mere straw men; we are dealing here with something that was once very important.(1) I was a very young musician when I first heard Ellington's *Ko-Ko* sixteen years ago, and I immediately succumbed to the magic spell of that long-awaited vision. Suddenly I saw jazz in a new light; Ellington's music had reached fulfillment at last, and there was reason to hope that this achievement foreshadowed the revelation of an even more exciting musical universe.

The years have passed and the Duke's music has failed to keep its promise, but it would be unfair to hold this against him; the important thing, after all, is the tremendous contribution he did make. (I cannot help smiling when I think of the indignant article I published after the Duke's stay in Paris in 1950; my anger at his decline was justified, but in giving vent to it, I lacked proper perspective. This is not the case today, however, for the matter at hand is far more serious.)

The 1940 version of *Ko-Ko* was splendidly strange and violent.** The intro-

* Bethlehem BCP 60.
(1) The allusion to Noone and Mezzrow refers to a series of polemical articles which appeared in *Jazz Hot* between 1948 and 1952.
** RCA Victor LPM 1715 [originally Victor 26577].

duction seemed to come from another world, while Tricky Sam's (Joe Nanton) solo had a wail that was more than merely exotic, and even the Duke's piano had an unearthly sound to it. Above all, this was the first time that anyone had really *written for a jazz orchestra;* the beauty of Blanton's famous break was due entirely to the rigorous conception that had guided the Duke's hand throughout the previous choruses.

Listening to the 1956 version of *Ko-Ko* is one of the most painful ordeals imaginable to anyone for whom jazz and music are *living* experiences. Nothing is left of the qualities I have just mentioned (very briefly, I'm afraid, but then every jazz fan, I hope, will know what I'm talking about), nothing save an atrocious caricature. What was once magnificent becomes grotesque, the epic spirit gives way to stupid gesticulation, and the sense of mystery to mere vulgarity. Yet scarcely a note of the score itself has been changed. Never have two *versions* of a single piece constituted two such different *works;* only in jazz, I feel, is such a distortion of creative concept possible. What is unbelievable is that both versions should be the work of one and the same musician. One may object that Ellington no longer had the same musicians at his disposal. Tricky Sam and Blanton are dead. But in that case he shouldn't have re-recorded *Ko-Ko!* Whichever way you look at it, the Duke alone is responsible. In 1956 he had good material at his disposal. Quentin Jackson is a very respectable trombonist. The burden of his disgraceful, buffoonish interpretation of a solo which constituted one of the high points of Tricky Sam's career, must be borne by the Duke as well, for it was he who put Jackson in an impossible situation from the very moment when he snapped his fingers for the down-beat.

This is the crucial point. The reader does not realize, perhaps, that this moment of a performance, which does not appear on a recording, determines in one out of two cases the quality of the work about to be played. If the leader does not hit the right *tempo,* if his finger-snapping is a bit too slow or a bit too fast, his musicians will be thrown off balance with little hope of recovery. A bandleader worthy of the name almost always sets the right tempo at the very outset. In 1940 the Duke had a marvelous intuitive grasp of his composition; the tempo chosen was just right and his orchestra, which didn't always "swing it" (*In a Mellotone* was one of many pieces spoiled by a drummer who sounded like a frustrated drum major), immediately hit the right pace. The 1940 version of *Ko-Ko* remains one of the most swinging records of the swing era. As for the *Ko-Ko* of 1956 . . .

What can possibly have happened? I don't think this disaster can be explained by practical considerations. Had recording techniques shrunk as they developed, making it necessary to play the arrangement in a shorter space of time, the Duke's decision to speed up his tempo would have been understandable, though not acceptable. If the Duke had not had the old recording at his disposal, one might think he had simply made an equally inexcusable error of judgment. Why this insane choice? Perhaps the Duke wanted to prove that his present orchestra had greater technical virtuosity than the earlier group; I find this unbelievable, but if it is true, what a dismal failure for the sake of such a trivial demonstration!

None of these explanations is satisfactory. No, there is only one possible reason for this choice, and that is a *diminution of musical sensibility;* it would not be the first time I have encountered such a thing.* How can a great musician have become so insensitive? I cannot carry this explanation any further, for the truth is that the whole thing is as puzzling to me as it is painful. I can only observe the results of the Duke's choice and these are disastrous.

Not only is Quentin Jackson's solo made *impossible* (as against Tricky Sam's, which we cannot avoid hearing "in our head"), but the whole arrangement is *inevitably* performed in a jarring, jerky style devoid of any swing. Ellington's broad phrasing can no longer draw its deep, even breath, but gasps and pants laboriously; once lovely figures are now twisted and contorted, a veil of ugliness has fallen over the work as a whole.

What did the Duke have to say about all this? Did he stand helplessly by, watching this farcical desecration of what ought to be his favorite score? Did he rush into the studio to put a stop to it, begin again from scratch, or even ... call the whole thing off? Not a bit of it. He had already accepted—or even suggested—two "improvements" on the original, two changes which could not fail to disfigure it: a ridiculous introduction on the drums, and an affected clarinet solo which now dominates that stupendous fourth orchestral chorus (which, in the earlier version, was punctuated by percussive piano work of a splendidly aggressive character). After that, what was to stop him from ruining his own music completely with a bad choice of tempo? And why should he object to the record being issued?

For me, the title *Historically Speaking* means "The Duke Judged by His Past."(2) I'll never forget the musician who did the original *Ko-Ko*, but now

---

* Does anyone remember what happened to Trummy Young's famous trombone solo on *Margie* (which he once recorded with Jimmy Lunceford), when he played it last year [1957] at the Olympia with Louis Armstrong? Here again the notes were exactly the same, but the tempo was such that what had once been a supple play of ambiguities now became a mere skeleton, devoid of any musical meaning. True, it was only Trummy Young.

(2) I do not know whether or not Duke Ellington was referring to this piece when he wrote, in "A Royal View of Jazz" (*Jazz: A Quarterly of American Music,* No. 2, Spring 1959): "I don't want to be modern ... futuristic ... and neither do I want to be hung by the plaintiveness of something we might have done years ago, even with success. I don't want to feel obliged to play something with the same styling that we became identified with at some specific period. I have no ambition to reach some intellectual plateau and look down on people. And, by the same token, I don't want anyone to challenge my right to sound completely mad, to screech like a wild man, to create the mauve melody of a simpering idiot, or to write a song that praises God, if I so desire. I only want to enjoy what any other American artist wants—and that is freedom of expression and of communication with our audience."

If he was referring to my article, then he was probably the victim of a hasty translation which distorted its meaning. This is not the first time that this sort of thing has happened to me. I therefore hope he will take the opportunity to read this chapter in its present translation.

Still and all, the Duke's definition of freedom hardly seems acceptable in the light of modern philosophy. It was certainly not Nietzsche's approach to the problem, when he put these words in the mouth of Zarathustra: "Tell me not from what thou hast freed thyself, but why hast thou done so." (I am quoting from memory.) Zarathustra was inviting man to enjoy the highest freedom of all, but that freedom is conceivable only in terms of rigor. The existentialist philosophers have defined, far better than I could ever do, the limitations which a free man imposes upon himself. Only the irresponsible artist's freedom is absolute; only rigor can preserve art from anarchy.

Moreover, if Duke Ellington has every right to debase his masterpieces, why do not I have the right to protest against this debasement? After all, anyone should be allowed to criticize a work of art once it has been made public.

I can never forget the one who agreed to sign this new version. I hope I've made myself clear. This is not just another bad record, it is the sign of a dereliction which confirms once and for all the decadence of a great musician.

We have the right to demand a great deal only of those who have done great things. There should be no doubt about it; the present article constitutes an unprecedented tribute to the Duke in his golden age. But it is also meant to put the reader on his guard against the enticements of a once glorious name which now represents only an endless succession of mistakes. This was the most ghastly mistake of all, for nothing can ever redeem it.

62. Selections from *The Jazz Review* (1959)

During its relatively brief life, *The Jazz Review* (November 1958–January 1961), edited by Martin Williams and Nat Hentoff, published a number of articles on Ellington's music. Most extensive of these was "Early Duke,"[1] Gunther Schuller's three-part survey of Ellington's music to 1931, which became the final chapter in *Early Jazz: Its Roots and Musical Development* (1968).

Three other notable contributions to the Ellington literature from the pages of this periodical follow.

• • •

Together with Schuller's "Early Duke," Mimi Clar's "The Style of Duke Ellington" (April 1959) represented one of the first efforts to identify precisely those orchestrational and harmonic devices that gave Ellington's music its distinctive qualities. While André Hodeir had touched on these topics in his 1954 essay on *Concerto for Cootie* (§57), Clar strove to be more specific, both through her prose description and her use of transcribed musical examples.

Clar's transcriptions—like those of Roger Pryor Dodge in "Harpsichords and Jazz Trumpets" (see §23)—tend to give rough, over-simplified, sometimes incorrect versions of Ellington's orchestrations.[2] Despite such technical shortcomings, however, many of her musical observations remain sound. The recordings listed by Clar as sources for her transcriptions were: Victor 12" LPM 1364; Columbia 12" ML 4369; Victor 10" LPT 3017; Victor EPBT 1004 (45 rpm); Capitol EAP 1-638 (45 rpm).

A pianist and critic, Clar (b. *ca.* 1935) graduated from the University of California at Los Angeles and contributed several analytical articles to *The Jazz Review*.

Source: Mimi Clar, "The Style of Duke Ellington," *The Jazz Review* 2/3 (April 1959), 6–10.

[1] [Part 1], *The Jazz Review* (December 1959), 6–14; Part 2 (January 1960), 18–22; Part 3 (February 1960), 18–25. The article also appeared as "The Ellington Style: Its Origins and Early Development," in *Jazz,* edited by Nat Hentoff and Albert McCarthy (1959).

[2] For example, Clar transcribes the introduction to *Ko-Ko* (Ex. 1a) for three trumpets and trombone instead of for three trombones. Then, curiously, she puts the first chorus (Ex. 1b) in e minor rather than e-flat minor.

Mimi Clar: "The Style of Duke Ellington"

The problem of talking about Duke Ellington's style is neatly summed up by
Andre Previn:[3]

> "You know," he said, "Stan Kenton can stand in front of a thousand fiddles and
> a thousand brass and make a dramatic gesture and every studio arranger can nod
> his head and say, 'Oh, yes, that's done like this.' But Duke merely lifts his finger,
> three horns make a sound, and I don't know what it is!"

Much has already been written about how the Ellington orchestra reflects
the styles of the men within the band; how at an Ellington rehearsal the
composition and orchestration occur simultaneously; how an arrangement
usually doesn't get written into the Ellington book until a certain amount of
experimentation has taken place before live audiences; how Duke builds his
arrangements around the strengths and weaknesses of his orchestra members;
and how the force of his own personality seems to bring out the best in each
single man yet moulds him to advantage into the orchestral whole. These
factors contribute to the intangibles that defy the printed word or note.

Also eluding the analyst's pen, and forming the key to the Ellington sound,
are the tone colors of the band. Duke's men produce a collective and individual
intonation which cannot be easily duplicated by outsiders. Individually, the
sound of each artist is free from the restriction of ensemble conformity: an
infinite number of false notes, out-of-range notes, muted brass growls, reed
slurs, smears, slides, laughing, crying, preaching, and talking emanates from
every instrumentalist. Thus the stylistic attributes of the men infuse themselves
into the overall aural picture: Rex Stewart with his peculiar in-between notes;
Johnny Hodges' singing alto; Harry Carney's swooping baritone; Lawrence
Brown's alternatingly sweet and barrelhouse trombone; Tricky Sam Nanton's,
Cootie Williams', and Ray Nance's gutbucket jungle inflections; Jimmy Blanton's bedrock bass; Cat Anderson's shrieks; Ben Webster's and Paul Gonsalves' warm tenors; not to mention Duke's own romping piano. These men,
to mention only a few, at one time or another have become an integral part
of the Ellington sound.

Collectively, the Ellington sound reflects not only the written notes being
exercised, but the timbres of each instrument, the various overtones of each
instrument and each note, plus the intonation of the group (which differs from
individual intonation in that if off-pitch, the notes must be blued simultaneously to the same degree by each person—no routine task). The complexity
of the sound arises from the overtones and intonation more than from the
notes themselves. For example, the brass section can change its overtones and
inflections by the use of mutes, much as an organist pushes in or pulls out the
stops of his instrument. The mutes impart to the orchestra a quality of balance
in volume and color between the brass and the reeds.

[3] Nat Hentoff and Nat Shapiro, *The Jazz Makers* (New York: Holt, Rinehart & Winston, 1957;
rpt., New York: Da Capo Press, 1979), 200. The original source for this quote is an article by
Ralph J. Gleason, "Duke Excites, Mystifies Without Any Pretension," in the special Ellington
"Silver Jubilee" issue of *Down Beat* (5 November 1952), 18.

Ex. 1 Reed and brass combinations, voicings:
Ko-Ko (a, b); *Bojangles* (c)

Among the many contrasted instrumental combinations within the band may be found alto solo with clarinet obbligato above; alto solo and muted trombone behind; alto solo backed by two clarinets on top, trombones in the middle, baritone on the bottom; duets between high muted trumpet and low baritone sax, between clarinet and string bass; piano combined with baritone sax; clarinet, muted trumpet, and muted trombone (*Mood Indigo*); sections employed in unison; brass played in counterpart against reeds. The typical Ellington reed sound of the forties and fifties springs from the blend of two altos in the top voices[,] two tenors in the middle, and the baritone on the bottom. The well-known "jungle style" arising in the late twenties developed with the beat of the rhythm and plaintive wail of the reeds, as well as with the muted growls, dirty tones, and wah-wah lines in the brass (ex. 1).

As for the notes that the sections or combinations play, Duke conceives

Ex. 2 Melody note in 9th, 11th, 13th of chord:
Chelsea Bridge

much of his music in terms of piano chords; he indicates certain notes to be blown regardless of whether the intervals or sequences are convenient or conventional for the instruments to execute. His men proceed to play them, unmindful that all the rules say such things are impossible. (Duke remembers trombonists complaining, "Man, this thing ain't got no keys on it, you know.")

Duke frequently constructs the chords so that the melody lands in the bottom or middle voices. As the melody is so subdued, the sound of the harmony is automatically pronounced. When the melody note falls in the upper voice, it enriches the harmony by forming the ninth, eleventh, or thirteenth of the chord. *Chelsea Bridge* and *Passion Flower* [both by Billy Strayhorn] present the latter concept to advantage (ex. 2).

It takes many listenings to absorb all that takes place in an Ellington performance. After initially stating the main theme or tune Ellington elaborates upon it or develops it by introducing counter-melodies, by interchanging the theme between soloist and ensemble, by combining parts of the theme so that several versions of it are showcased simultaneously, melodically and/or rhythmically. The themes are developed through *both* solo and ensemble; when a section or single instrument undertakes the solo chores, the remaining sections or instruments rather than merely outlining harmonic changes or dropping out altogether, contribute vitally to the goings-on, either in subordinate melodic activity, in antiphonal interplay, in tonal or harmonic foundations, or in rhythmic impetus.

Duke's recording of *I Don't Know What Kind of Blues I've Got* is unusually rewarding in its multi-thematic aspects. The vari-textured layers of musical strata so effectively carry out the message and mood of the title and lyrics as sung by Herb Jeffries:

> There's two kind of woman, there's two kind of man,
> There's two kind of romance since time began:
> There's the real true love, and that good old jive;
> One tries to kill you, one helps to keep you alive.
> I don't know—what kind of blues I've got.
> (Instrumental Interlude)
> There's no rest for the weary; I'm going to see Snake Mary;
> 'Cause I don't know what kind of blues I've got.

Ex. 3 Counter melody, antiphony:
I Don't Know What Kind of Blues I've Got

After the moody piano introduction, the low clarinet simply and lucidly establishes the lovely theme which is perpetuated by various instruments as a sort of repeated passacaglia-like ground throughout the record: a melody, neither major nor minor, which further reflects the perplexity expressed in the title. Different blues spring forth almost immediately as the trombone cries a counter-melody to the clarinet (ex. 3). A slight variation of the ground is delegated to the muted brass section as the tenor takes up the counter-melody in the second chorus. Next, the clarinet, this time in a high register, again repeats the ground to a trombone counterpoint. Following a brass and reed introduction, Jeffries enters for a vocal chorus which rides over the omnipresent ground (still in the saxophone, which is later joined by more reeds, then brass). An instrumental interlude wherein the unison reeds catch up the "real-true-love" ground with the brass riffing the "good-old-jive" counter-rhythms (ex. 4) intensifies the dualism in the sung text and spans a final vocal passage by Jeffries, whose voice travels in contrary motion to the terminating bars of the slightly varied tenor ground.

Harlem Air Shaft affords another illustration of how Duke volleys thematic assignments from one end of the band to the other. The brass repeat riff-like figures over a light singing unison reed melody during the choruses, which are interspersed with a bridge where the reed section statements are exchanged with muted brass replies. Reed section and trumpet share solo assignments

Ex. 4 Counter rhythms:
I Don't Know What Kind of Blues I've Got

throughout, with drum breaks strategically placed here and there. The record closes polyphonically, with the clarinet improvising above repetitive brass theme motifs and buoyant unison reed lines.

Ellington compositions and orchestrations reflect both conservatory-approved techniques and typical jazz unorthodoxies. In the conservatory traditions, some Ellington melodies are very diatonic in nature, the lines conforming to the strict rules of counterpoint (i.e., careful closure of leaps, making certain that ascending phrases descend and vice versa, etc.); harmonies in which the voices move in contrary motion; canonic entrances among several voices (vocal in *It Don't Mean a Thing*); consecutive bass lines, both ascending and descending; and melodies very much on-the-beat, in the manner of Bach chorales. Turning from the conservatory to jazz, we discover the rhythms of which Ellington is fond: ragtime, tango, rhumba, stop-time, not to mention the poly-, off-, and cross-rhythms in his works (exx. 5–8).

Duke has a penchant for chromatic and syncopated melodies (*The Mooche* and *Prelude to a Kiss* = former; *Cotton Tail* = latter). Ellington's melodies have continuity and unity, simplicity and complexity, tonality and atonality. (*C Jam Blues,* about as tonal and simple as one can get, sharply contrasts with the chromatic *Passion Flower,* which is of a very indecisive tonality when

Ex. 5 Accents on off-beats:
Perdido intro

Ex. 6 Piano accompaniment rhythms:

Ex. 7 Muted brass accompaniment rhythms:
Sophisticated Lady

Ex. 8 Rhythm section beat:
Bojangles

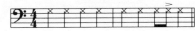

Ex. 9 Syncopated melody:

Cotton Tail

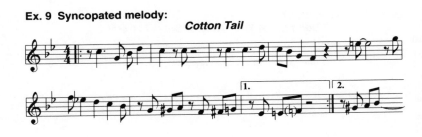

Ex. 10 Tonal melody:

C Jam Blues

played without the harmonies.) *In a Mellotone,* with its diatonic melody, offers a clear example of how Duke unifies a composition by transferring a brief melodic idea from one chordal structure to the next. The same holds true for *Sophisticated Lady* (exx. 9–12).

Besides diatonic, chromatic, tonal, atonal, and sequential melodies (alone or in combination), Duke's lines often spell out harmonic changes or specific chords within themselves. (Examples: *Things Ain't What They Used To Be, It Don't Mean a Thing, Black and Tan Fantasy.*) Some Ellington melodies

Ex. 11 Atonal, chromatic melody:

Passion Flower

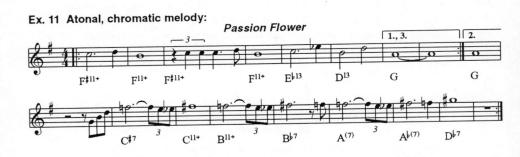

Ex. 12 Diatonic melody:

In a Mellotone

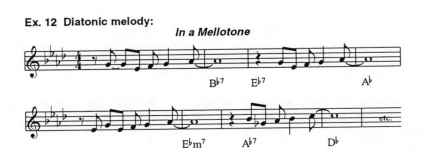

require a slow languid tempo while others demand faster execution; the latter maintain a heavy rhythm as solos and ensembles are planned to fit within this rhythmic niche.

Instrumental color heightens the tonal variety in an Ellington orchestration. The string bass occupies a paramount position in driving the orchestra, for it is in the bass that much of the band's rhythmic energy is harnessed. I believe at one period Duke used two basses, but upon Jimmy Blanton's arrival, the band boasted an equivalent of four or five bass players in one. Blanton, as we all know, not only swung powerfully but transformed his instrument into a blowing melodic voice. Jimmy can be heard to best advantage with the orchestra on *Jack the Bear* and *Chloe,* where his bass lines (sometimes re-enforced by corresponding piano notes) ring out even behind the ensemble passages, as well as illuminating their assigned solo spots. After Blanton's unfortunate demise, succeeding bass men have retained an active role by playing riffs and subordinate melodies, as well as straight rhythm.

Ellington's device of maneuvering the brass section into a rhythmic function shows up on [Billy Strayhorn's] *Boo-Dah,* where muted brass enters on off-beats during the last eight bars of the first chorus. Brass riffs frequently double as melodic embellishments and rhythmic punctuations.

Ray Nance's solo violin definitely lies off the beaten track in the jazz scene. His bluer-than-blue bowings plus a few mischievously plucked strings in *Caravan* lend a touch of subtle humor, in addition to new color dimensions. (Ray's violin is also present in *It Don't Mean a Thing,* to mention but one more example.)

Duke's piano forms the undercoat for the orchestral painting. Besides an economical accompaniment which prods, supports, and lifts the bandsmen at exactly the proper spots, Ellington supplies piano interjections over, under, and in-between the entire band, which enhance the overall hue and texture of the orchestra. Some such Ellington pianisms are: chords built on fourths *(Caravan);* tremoloed minor ninths *(Stormy Weather* intro); single notes inserted for rhythm as well as polytonal effects *(Caravan);* pungent harmonic voicings *(The Mooche);* polytonal chords (ending of *The Mooche*); major seconds *(Jack the Bear);* and runs seemingly polytonal in sound relationship to the rest of the band (endings on *Ko-Ko, Chloe*). In solo, Duke's piano is a myriad of fluttering arpeggios, cantering chords, pretty runs—a florid rambunctious style availing itself of the entire range of the instrument (exx. 13–18).

I have treated Duke Ellington within this text as a composer and as a performer. The two facets of his career can hardly be divorced, since Duke writes with the band in mind or composes on the spot with the cooperation and inspiration of the band members. The band is his instrument and means of expression. Indeed, with Ellington, it is always "we" (not he as an individual) who achieves his musical accomplishments. While dealing with the Ellington compositions themselves, we must bear in mind that whether a piece be of Ellington origin or not, it will become thoroughly inundated with the stylistic harmonies, tone colors, inflections, and emotional interpretations of the Ellington orchestra.

Ex. 13 Chords built on 4ths:
Caravan

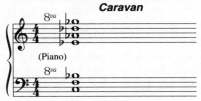

Ex. 14 Inversions: chords used in backing solos

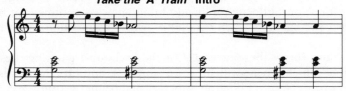

Ex. 15 Inversions & whole-tone scale:
Take the 'A' Train intro

Ex. 16 A. Broken piano chords:
Flamingo

B. Series of augmented chords:
Flamingo

Ex. 17 Minor 9ths tremoloed:
Flamingo

Ex. 18 Minor 9ths broken:
Things Ain't What They Used to Be

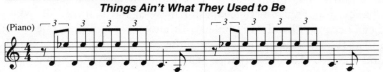

The noted arranger Quincy Jones (b. 1933) was twenty-six when he wrote the following record review. To this assignment he brought his experience working in and writing for big bands, also his instrumental training under Clark Terry, a member of Ellington's trumpet section from 1951 to 1959. Although clearly an Ellington admirer, Jones delivered some blunt judgments of the 1958 orchestra, and like Hodeir (see §61) had some discouraging words about the recent remake of *Ko-Ko*.

(Incidentally, in the same issue Jones reviewed Ornette Coleman's first LP, *Something Else!!!!*.)

Quincy Jones on *Newport 1958*

I think "Cat" Anderson ought to have his own band. I don't think, incidentally, that he's a jazz musician. He's a good trumpet player and certainly an impressive exhibitionist, but for me, he's never played jazz. I realize Duke knows how to make everybody an integral part of the orchestra, but "Cat" doesn't stay in the realm Duke conceives for him. If he did, he'd be very functional; but he seems to spend most of his time trying to break out of what Duke has set for him. "Cat" is like a Father Flanagan trying to run Vassar while his hands were still full with Boys' Town. Duke's given him enough to do.

"Cat's" *El Gato* stopped the show in Paris. All the trumpet players in the audience were gassed by it. They ran backstage and wanted to know what mouthpiece "Cat" used. He wouldn't show it to them, and that made them mad. But none of that has anything to do with jazz. Duke *does* have a beautiful trumpet player in the section—Clark Terry—but he doesn't use him enough. Clark has never sounded like anyone else; he's always been himself. I love his humor and his tone. He was the man who taught me to play in Seattle. He

Source: Quincy Jones, review of Duke Ellington, *Newport 1958*, in *The Jazz Review* 2/4 (May 1959), 30.

was with Basie's sextet then, and was in and out of the town. To me, he's got such deep roots, confidence and authority. Back to *El Gato*. Musically, what is it?

Paul Gonsalves on *Happy Reunion*. I love Paul. His conception of sound. Just a few of the young guys have it. Most have thrown sound away for other things. Basically, I guess, I'm a romanticist. I like beauty—pretty music, pretty women.

Billy Strayhorn wrote *Multicolored Blue*. Billy to me is the boss of the arrangers. I'd like to really know just what's what in that little lab of theirs. I'd like to know how much Billy is responsible for in Duke's work these days. Ozzie Bailey, the singer in this, doesn't fit with the band at all. Maybe I'm prejudiced because I liked Al Hibbler with Duke. He had the same sound with the band as [Harry] Carney's baritone—the coarseness, the deep-rooted earthiness and warmth. About Strayhorn again, I bet he orchestrates a lot of Duke's things. It sometimes feels to me that Duke plays a lot of things to Strayhorn on the piano, and then Billy takes over. I hear a lot of piano-style things in those arrangements.

Listen to the trombone section. It's very, very good. And the rhythm section. [Sam] Woodyard and [Jimmy] Woode definitely understand what Duke is trying to do. Not many young drummers could fit into Duke's band. In a drummer, Duke needs a man with fullness and drive who is also tasty. Many younger drummers would be too busy, too self-conscious. On bass, Duke needs a man who won't just walk all the time.

Jazz Festival Jazz sounds like something Tom Whaley (the copyist) whipped up when he was asleep on the bus on the way to Newport. I don't think this kind of program as a whole, by the way, indicates that Duke is putting on Newport. He'd do it anywhere. If he had the time, he'd do it well. If he doesn't have the time, it'll always look and sound like Ellington even when it isn't fully.

I dig *Mr. Gentle and Mr. Cool*. I'm a sucker for transparency. It's fantastic how effective simplicity is. I'm glad to see Harold Baker back in the band. It seems as if with some of Duke's sheep, it's not possible for them to stray effectively. Speaking of using space, I love Duke as a pianist. His playing reflects his writing so much. He has so much taste. He always knows when *not* to play. That's just as important.

I like the feeling with which Ray Nance plays the violin, but I don't like his technique. For a trumpet player, he plays good violin. But as a trumpet player, he's fine. He's distinctive, identifiable. He has such a definite thing, like his solo on "*A*" *Train* which is a classic. Ray is another example of a jazz fact—if a guy is himself and sincere, he doesn't have to play too much on his horn. But if he doesn't have real identification, he has to be a real virtuoso and you have to judge him by how well he knows his horn. It's the penalty he has to pay for not being individual.

Juniflip is Clark Terry's, and as I said before, I love him. He's a natural musician. The Carney-Mulligan baritone duet on *Prima Bara Dubla* I don't like. It's a gimmick. I might appreciate it better except for the fact that when you have these two plus the Ellington orchestra plus Duke as a composer and player, what happens here is not enough. It's trite thematically; it sounds contrived; and when you're playing in a tempo like this in a minor key, if there isn't real emotion, it just dies. This died. And they wind up in thirds at the end. Now that's very "original." It implies real "organization." As for *Hi Fi Fo Fum,* I've never heard a drum solo arrangement I've liked.

As for the performance as a whole, this was the place where it was desirable for the band to make an impression, and I'm sure Duke did. But musically, this is the outside of the band. They didn't let the people all the way in. And yet it is a fantastic band. Even when you're hearing just the outside, it's so nostalgic and the nostalgia is so powerful it almost covers up any flaws that might be in the band. By the way, I dig [Johnny] Hodges more and more. I didn't get the message at first, but his feeling and his conception are very impressive.

What I resent in the current Duke is when he takes masterpieces of his own and soups them up in hi-fi and destroys the original feeling. The *Ko-Ko* on Bethlehem, for example. It's unbelievable. I don't know why he does it.

But even in a performance like this one, even when they're just opening the doors a little and not playing what the band is really capable of, you always know there's *something* there.

Beginning in September 1959 the English critic Max Harrison contributed regular record reviews to *The Jazz Review,* among them two devoted to Ellington. Harrison's closely argued, rather exacting evaluation of Ellington's score for the Otto Preminger film *Anatomy of a Murder* is characteristic. For his other Ellington piece in *The Jazz Review,* see the issue of March–April 1960 where a review appeared of *Back to Back* by Ellington and Johnny Hodges.

Although chiefly active as a classical-music critic, Harrison has published extensively on jazz in such periodicals as *Jazz Monthly, The Jazz Review,* and *The Wire.* His writings include the first published monograph on Charlie Parker (1960), the main entry on "Jazz" for *The New Grove Dictionary of Music and Musicians* (1980; revised and enlarged for *The New Grove Gospel, Blues and Jazz,* 1987), and, with Charles Fox and Eric Thacker, *Essential Jazz Records, Vol. 1: Ragtime to Swing* (1984).

The following revised version of the 1959 review was made by Harrison in 1991.

Max Harrison on *Anatomy of a Murder*

This selection of pieces from the soundtrack of Otto Preminger's *Anatomy of a Murder* is disappointing when considered in the perspective of Ellington's past accomplishments as the leading jazz composer. Though superior to what almost any immediate rival might have done, this music scarcely ever displays the originality or sense of adventure found in, say, the best moments of *Such*

Source: Max Harrison, "Ellington's Music for *Anatomy of a Murder,*" *The Jazz Review* 2/10 (November 1959), 35–36. Revised by the author in 1991.

Sweet Thunder or in any of his finest work. The invention is nearly as plentiful as ever, yet the actual ideas fall short, in terms of melody, harmony and orchestration, of the sheer personal distinction of the idiom that he evolved over a long period of years.

There is, indeed, a thread of commonplace running through most of these items which may in the last analysis be due to Ellington having to compromise with the, for him, unaccustomed requirements of music for films. In the *American Weekly Entertainment Guide* for August 1st, 1959, he was quoted as saying, "Music in pictures should say something without being obviously music, you know, and this was all new to me." In other words, film music has to make its contribution, on the levels of emotion, atmosphere, or whatever, to the cinematic moment without drawing attention to itself. Excellent music has been written for films that went on to lead a life of its own away from the screen, instances being Sergei Prokofiev's for Sergei Eisenstein's *Alexander Nevsky,* Arthur Bliss's for Alexander Korda's *Things to Come,* Virgil Thomson's for Robert Flaherty's *Louisiana Story*—and John Lewis's for Roger Vadim's *Sait-on Jamais.* But such achievements are rare, and that Ellington was conscious of the curiously negative impression left by some of his music when heard away from Preminger's film is suggested by his further statement, "The next one will be better. I'll try another one and then I'll show them."

None of which explains, however, why the actual performance of his score sounds like one of the most uncommitted this band has recorded, and certainly the worst since *A Drum Is a Woman* (1956). Individual and ensemble execution is generally good, yet on most tracks lack of enthusiasm is apparent in a heaviness of effect that cannot be entirely accounted for by the oddly thick scoring Ellington often adopts.

The music for the main title opens somewhat rhetorically with strongly marked ensemble chords, wa-wa fanfares and the drummer pounding the offbeats relentlessly. These give way to an ostinato reed figure with brass interjections, and Ray Nance has a good wa-wa solo in the form of a dialogue with these latter. The movement undergoes an abrupt shift of emphasis as both ostinato and drum-hammering are silenced and Ellington takes one of those wry, quizzical solos that were typical of his later years, saying much with very few notes. *Flirtibird* is more unified, and is a sufficiently well composed vehicle for Johnny Hodges to make one regret that he did not take fuller advantage of it. The pervading lack of enthusiasm, let alone communicative fire, is again evident in his perfunctory phrases and uncharacteristically hard tone. The score has four main themes and *Flirtibird* introduces one of them, a six-note motive that is used here antiphonally in three dialogues. The first is between Ellington, who states it several times with variations, and the ensemble, which offers a different response to each of these. Hodges then takes his leader's place and provides further variants but still keeping the idea recognisable. Finally band and soloist reverse places.

That same six-note motive is employed in Harold Baker's feature, *Almost Cried,* yet not in such an interesting way either here or in the introduction to *Way Early Subtone.* This latter has a beautiful section by Russell Procope on the clarinet but otherwise is mostly disconnected padding. In contrast, *Hero to Zero,* one of the best movements, is a good piece of atmospheric writing. It has no central melodic idea until the theme appears towards the end, and mostly Harry Carney's and Paul Gonsalves's lines are simply the most prominent threads in the texture rather than the focal points. Thematically related to this are *Low Key Lightly* and *Haupé,* the former having a lengthy piano introduction leading to some rather graceful schmaltz from Nance on his violin. *Haupé* is another Hodges feature, less resourcefully composed than *Flirtibird* yet drawing much better playing from him, the melodic line more sensitively inflected, the tone softer, warmer.

A simple vehicle for improvisation, *Happy Anatomy* has solos from Gonsalves and Clark Terry with good backgrounds, the trumpets behind Gonsalves, for example, being particularly effective. Terry's solo is the finest on this record, but the drummer is too heavy again. *Midnight Indigo* opens with the lovely combination of xylophone, bass clarinet and string bass leading to a dialogue between piano and xylophone. There are also some rich, quietly sustained ensemble chords, and the delicacy of texture here is almost worthy of earlier landmarks such as the 1940 band's *Dusk.* In unhappy contrast, *Sunswept Sunday* is stodgy non-jazz, aptly featuring Jimmy Hamilton. Within the context of music for a film it is not an adverse comment to say this is not jazz, yet it remains poor material for Ellington's band. Worse follows, however, in the shape of *Grace Valse,* a heavily conventional piece of salon music, and *Upper and Outest.* This last is patched together from various of the above elements, the ostinato figure, the six-note motive, the heavy drumming and so forth, all in a discouragingly offhand rehash.

As will have been noticed, several of these movements are in the long familiar pattern of Ellington's vehicles for his leading soloists. Given the quality of improvisation of which these men had so many times shown themselves capable, this was, to an extent, understandable. But it also seems like a stock response, or even, remembering the unfamiliar circumstances into which Ellington's music was being projected, an evasion. Instead merely of providing another set of miniature concertos for his famous sidemen, he should have been more concerned with enhancing the dramatic and visual specifics of Preminger's film. This was in fact done in *Hero to Zero* and *Midnight Indigo,* which, significantly enough, work excellently both in the film and as independent pieces. Yet twice is not enough. Needed here was less of the Ellingtonians as soloists and more of Ellington as composer.

VIII. The Late Years (1960–1974)

When he reached his sixties, an age at which many contemplate retirement, Ellington kept up the relentless schedule of composing, performing, recording, and traveling he had followed for over thirty years. During this time he was showered with awards, prizes, and honorary degrees,[1] and celebrated both at home and abroad for his musical achievements. He also embarked on more international tours than at any earlier period in his career, traveling often to Europe, also to the Middle East and India in 1963, Japan in 1964, Latin America and Mexico in 1968, and the Soviet Union in 1971. These journeys sometimes inspired new compositions, as with the *Far East Suite* (1964), the *Latin American Suite* (1968), *The Afro-Eurasian Eclipse* (1970), and the *Goutelas Suite* (1971).

The most dramatic musical change of these last years was Ellington's turn toward liturgical music, notably a series of three Sacred Concerts between 1965 and 1973. Performances took place in various churches and cathedrals and featured his orchestra, vocal soloists, choirs, and dancers. Anticipating this development was the show *My People,* written in 1963 for the Century of Negro Progress Exposition in Chicago. It included such religious numbers as *Ain't But the One, Will You Be There?,* and *David Danced Before the Lord.* Up until this time Ellington's faith had been a private matter. With these late sacred works he found a public forum for expressing long-held personal beliefs.

In addition to the suites and sacred music, Ellington produced new songs and instrumentals, arranged popular material from the Beatles and Walt Disney's *Mary Poppins* to Tchaikovsky's *Nutcracker* Suite, and collaborated with choreographer Alvin Ailey on the ballet *The River* (1970). He also recorded with various other musicians, among them Louis Armstrong, Ella Fitzgerald, Coleman Hawkins, and such younger luminaries as John Coltrane, Charles Mingus, and Max Roach. As of this writing, however, few of Ellington's later recording projects, compositions, and arrangements have received extensive critical attention beyond the initial reviews.

Ellington's orchestra in this period included a mixture of veterans and newcomers. Trumpeter Cootie Williams, absent since 1940, returned in 1962, and the great reed section of the fifties—Johnny Hodges, Russell Procope, Jimmy Hamilton, Paul Gonsalves, and Harry Carney—lasted until 1968 (when Hamilton left). Among the notable new voices were the Swedish singer Alice Babs, featured in the second and third Sacred Concerts, and tenor saxophonist Harold Ashby.

During Ellington's last decade three of his closest associates died: his personal physician Dr. Arthur Logan in 1973, Johnny Hodges in 1970, and, perhaps the hardest loss of all, Billy Strayhorn in 1967. Ellington paid tribute to these individuals, and to many he had known and worked with throughout his career, in his memoirs, *Music Is My Mistress.* These were published in 1973, a year before his own death from cancer on 24 May 1974.

[1] He received most of these after 1959. See *MM,* 476–89.

63. Irving Townsend: "When Duke Records" (1960)

ver the years many stories circulated about Ellington's unusual methods of composing, recording, and editing in the studio. The following account by Irving Townsend, who produced a number of Ellington's records for Columbia in the late fifties and early sixties, helps clarify aspects of a process that often became distorted through retelling. As Townsend points out, Ellington never came to a session unprepared, contrary to those who claimed he created something from scratch each time he recorded. Townsend supports the assertion with detailed descriptions of sessions he supervised.

In addition to producing records for Columbia, Townsend (1920–1981) served as vice president of the company's West Coast division. He assisted John Hammond with his autobiography, *John Hammond on Record* (1977), and wrote a memoir of country life, *The Less Expensive Spread* (1971). For another piece by Townsend on Ellington, see "Duke's Sweet Thunder," *Horizon* (November 1979), 50–57.

I, like most people who listen to records, was brought up on stories of how Duke Ellington makes a record, and the more incredible the latest episode was, the more I came to believe that Duke and his band usually arrive at a recording studio totally unprepared. The miraculous process of writing an arrangement in front of the band, playing it four bars at a time, and recording it in the last few minutes of the session is the sort of tale any jazz lover likes to believe, and I, and probably you, did.

I have now officiated at countless record sessions of Duke Ellington's orchestra, and, in the belief that truth may be more fascinating than half-truth, I will describe the processes by which we finally arrive with enough music to release a new Ellington album. To say the least, there has never been a record date like these of Duke's, any more than there has ever been a man or a band like this one.

An Ellington record session often begins in an empty studio, or almost empty. The bandstand, with brass to the right, saxes to the left and drums and bass between, forms a semi-circle around the piano. Behind the piano stool are two small tables, one for the copyist, or "extractor," as Duke describes him, to work and one for an Ellington dining-table, where, usually while the band warms up, Ellington will eat his steak, grapefruit, cheese, and coffee stuffed with wedges of lemon. At the far end of the studio a dozen chairs are set in a row for the audience. More about them later.

Duke Ellington arrives at a record date with the same sense of timing he

Source: Irving Townsend: "When Duke Records," *Just Jazz 4*, eds. Sinclair Traill and the Hon. Gerald Lascelles (London: Souvenir Press, 1960), 16–21.

follows for every appearance, whether it be from the wings of a theatre, or out of a taxi, or out of a shower. Ellington likes to remember that he got his first job at New York's Cotton Club by being late. The owner, also late, missed the other band's audition, arrived as Duke arrived, and hired him. He has nurtured the reputation he has made for always being late because it allows him the freedom to time his entrance to suit his sense of drama. Actually, Duke is often late and often on time, but I believe he has reversed the old vaudevillian adage which warns "Always leave them wanting more." Duke likes to arrive at that point. In our years of recording together, I've know Duke to arrive an hour early, two hours late, and at every point between these two extremes. I have never known him to arrive anywhere at the wrong moment.

Duke Ellington, for all his eccentric behaviour in a recording studio, takes records more seriously than anyone I have ever recorded. He knows that what he leaves behind after each session will be heard around the world for as long as music is played. He knows he cannot erase an inferior performance if it is released on record, and he is at the height of his creative powers in a recording studio. He listens intently to playbacks, his head resting on his hands over the piano keyboard, his eyes shut. Most of the time he raises his head slowly as the music stops, holds up a single index finger, and we try again.

Records made in one take are rare, particularly for any large musical group, and rarer for Ellington. But there have been some examples. One I remember particularly is the *Come Sunday* section of *Black, Brown and Beige* [recorded 1958], sung by Mahalia Jackson. Duke treated this first performance like a kind of divine revelation and would not let Mahalia repeat it until the next day. Then, he asked her to sing it not for records but for him. She sang the never-used Take 2 of *Come Sunday* the following afternoon without a light in the studio and without a sound from the band. It was one of those unpredictable moments which seem to bloom when Ellington is around.

Duke believes that singers should record a performance only once. Never afterward, in his opinion, does the singer give quite the same meaning to a song as in that first, heartfelt Take 1, and many of the vocal sequences in *A Drum Is a Woman* [1956] were recorded only once. Which reminds me of *Drum,* the most complex, probably least understood of all Ellington's major recordings. *Drum* first appeared written out in longhand on hotel stationery, lyrics included with narration. The writing and recording progressed almost simultaneously for many weeks, and there are still many minutes of wonderful orchestral music never used, as well as many choice examples of Duke's colourful prose. (He was determined to use the phrase "largo eloquence" somewhere in the work, but we never found a suitable place for it.) Ellington took three months to write, record and edit *A Drum Is a Woman,* including one session where he and the band worked all night, leaving the studio at seven in the morning. I think he is still more proud of this work than any other, and I think I know why, for it not only combines every talent he possesses on one record, but it contains much of his sense of humour and many of his personal opinions, properly attired in a confounding array of fiction and musicianship. Like a painted jungle, *Drum* should be viewed often and from a distance. Then the brush strokes disappear and things begin to happen.

The long-debated question about how much of Ellington's work is written by Billy Strayhorn will not be answered here, except to clarify their relationship, as it pertains to Duke's records. The two men work together on virtually all major recording projects, and often it is impossible for an acute listener to tell which parts were written by which man. That is the way they want it, and as it should be. Little of what either writes is left unchanged by the other, and Billy and Duke are present at all sessions. Duke is careful to give Billy composing credit officially, and neither man has any interest in taking credit from the other for anything they've done. But this is a composing team, unique in musical history, and only by keeping their output intact and their contributions undivided can the team function. Billy has written parts of every album we've done, sometimes in the form of entire pieces, sometimes, as in the case of *Drum* and *Anatomy* [*of a Murder*, 1959] short passages interwoven with the whole. Billy has also played piano on most albums, usually with the whole band playing, while Duke escapes from the keyboard to conduct a difficult passage. Both write music or lyrics, both arrange and orchestrate, and Ellington uses the pronoun "we" advisedly.

The recording of Ellington's Shakespearean Suite called *Such Sweet Thunder* [1957] climaxed several weeks during which Duke and Billy read Shakespeare. I never quite discovered how they read it, for Duke's summaries of the plays and characters were unlike any I had heard before. Ellington gathered together a series of short pieces descriptive of various impressions he had received from his quick course in the Bard, and we recorded them under such temporary titles as "Cleo," "Puck," and "Hamlet." We all searched later for the final titles, and I found "Such Sweet Thunder" in Bartlett's Quotations. To appreciate the Suite in its final form, one must listen to the music as a statement of what Duke got out of Shakespeare, a uniquely personal, yet deeply perceptive encounter. To overlay someone else's concept of the characters described in *Thunder* is deceptive and unfair. Duke likes Lady Macbeth, whether you're supposed to like her or not, and he treats her right.

In one aspect of record making, Ellington is never on time. This is the selection of titles for the new pieces we record. Usually such a piece, and there have been a hundred of them, is identified on the manuscript by a single word or by a letter or a number. *Blues in Orbit* [1959], the title of a piece in his newest album, was called *Tender* when we made it. At the end of the session I corner Duke and try to get titles settled, but it is usually to no avail, and we discuss titles back and forth by telephone for days or weeks afterward before one is finally chosen. There were no titles on any of the pieces in the *Anatomy* album when it was made, no final titles for *Drum* or *Thunder*, no title for *Copout, Toot Suite*, and so on. But Duke's usual reply at sessions about titles is, "Oh, we'll think of something," and one of us usually does.

Ellington never arrives at a record session unprepared. He may not have anything copied out for the band, and at best he never has a complete arrangement immune to changes, but if anything he prepares too much. His music for the soundtrack of *Anatomy of a Murder*, for example, would fill the time of a picture twice its length. But the final polishing of any Ellington arrangement is done as the band plays it, and Duke, to the bewilderment of people who have watched him record, writes and rehearses music in small segments, usually of eight measures and almost always without a written conclusion. His first studio rundowns of new music trail off as his musicians reach the end of a phrase at different moments and come to a limping stop. Then, knowing the length of each segment and how it sounds, Ellington proceeds to move his parts around. A typical example, although fictitious, of Duke's final instructions for a performance might go as follows: "Start at letter C. Then go to A and play it twice, only the second time leave off the last two bars. These bars are the beginning of a sheet you have marked X. After X I'll play until I bring you in at C again and you go out with letter D. Any questions?"

Part of the accepted reason for Duke Ellington's famous on-the-spot composition is the widely held belief that he cannot compose or arrange without his band. Duke considers himself to be fortunate in having fourteen men always available to play whatever he writes moments after he writes it, and he also believes that each man in the band makes a sound suited to some particular aspect of his music. He hires individual sounds, and in an album such as *Bal Masque* [1958] he demonstrates what he means by making Jimmy Hamilton's clarinet the butterfly in *Poor Butterfly,* Shorty Baker's trumpet the sadness in *Willow Weep for Me,* and Johnny Hodges' alto the *Gypsy Sweetheart.* Duke's men are the personification of an emotional gamut, and it is little wonder that he uses them in his writing. He can and often does write away from the band, but whereas most conductor-arrangers stop writing when they enter a recording studio, Ellington sees no reason to. His band includes several copyists and several arrangers, to say nothing of at least two composers, and everybody is busy before and during the recording. Recently, he recorded the score of a pilot television film at MGM Studios in Hollywood. He arrived with a box of music at noon. At midnight he left the studio having recorded half of what he brought with him and half of what he put together in the studio. I don't think one segment was finally used just as it was written before the session, but all could have been. Duke simply thought of a better way of doing the same thing after he wrote the music, so he changed it.

One of the Ellington characteristics which has contributed to his legendary tactics in a recording studio is to make use of all available material on hand. This is heroically exemplified in his *Jazz Party* [1959] album, which began as a regular Ellington session and ended as an informal jazz festival. Dizzy Gillespie and Jimmy Rushing happened to be there listening, so he used them, but not by incorporating them into the music he intended to record. Instead, he put together arrangements of tunes suited to them on the spot and thereby made the most of his unexpected guests. Jimmy Jones dropped in while Duke was playing the introduction to a blues, so while the record was being made he motioned to him and had him sit in on piano without Jones knowing we were recording the only Take. If there is an extra drummer in the studio, Duke uses him. If there is no bass player on hand, Ellington finds a piece to record which doesn't need a bass. If an instrument key breaks, as Russell Procope's clarinet key did in the record of *Toot Suite* in the *Festival Session* album [1959], Duke decides to use the clicking of the broken key as a part of the score. So adept is Ellington at adjusting to the demands of the moment that he turns handicaps and sudden crises into gems of inspiration. He has been doing it ever since the night in Washington, D.C., long ago when he arrived to play a job where there was no piano and he wound up playing the banjo all evening. Knowing Duke, I imagine his audience was convinced he had never played anything but banjo before and that the piano was no longer desirable in a jazz band.

And speaking of audiences, Duke has a special one for record sessions. I have recorded Ellington at every hour of the day and in some very unlikely places, but I have never recorded without a loyal dozen or so sitting in those chairs at the end of the studio. His doctor, Arthur Logan, is a regular member of the audience, as is his press agent, Joe Morgen, and his band boy, Bobby Boyd. But the rest of the group may include a couple of ex-Ellington sidemen, a couple of wives of members of the band, a policeman or two, and a variety of anonymous fans who sit motionless through the sessions. At some point in every session Duke walks over to this gallery and kisses each girl, greets each man and signs autographs, contracts, and cheques. Word of an Ellington record date seems to pass as soon as the date is set, and it is never too late or too early for an Ellington fan to get to a session.

Ellington devotes the first half-hour of every record session to the piano, where he plays by himself and oblivious of the din around him. This pianistic ritual sometimes relates to the music we are to record, but more often it has nothing to do with it. After he has played alone for a while, he usually calls over one of the musicians to play with him, and they soar away to their own special musical oasis and remain there for minutes on end. Then, as if a signal had sounded, Duke asks no one in particular if everybody has arrived. He pounds out the band call on the piano, claps his hands, whistles, and walks swiftly around the studio as if he had just arrived at that moment. At the end of the date he usually goes back to the piano alone and plays again what he played at the beginning, never quite finishing it, but as in everything, decisively inconclusive.

Ellington usually leaves the editing, sequence of selections, and all sound problems to me. And he seldom shows any disappointment over a recorded performance after he leaves the studio. This, like lying down while he talks on the telephone, is part of his formula for avoiding useless and enervating irritation. Duke is seldom completely satisfied with a record, although he is also not seriously dissatisfied either. But part of his philosophy is to ignore what is past correction and to use mistakes as lessons. An acetate of all records made at each date is prepared and sent to him. Sometimes he doesn't get around to hearing it until the record is released because of his schedule, but when he listens, he does so usually without comment.

Nowadays when I am asked if Duke Ellington really creates his music in a recording studio I have to reaffirm what has been said many times. He does compose, orchestrate, and create his sounds on the spot. But obviously he does not arrive to record unprepared. Music is always handed out, parts are ready for the band. But Ellington saves the final editing of his music until he hears it, and he reserves the right and has the ability to rewrite anything he believes could be better.

If you ask him before a recording date whether or not he is ready, he will invariably answer, "I hope so."

He means just that. He has written more than enough music for the date, and all that remains is to listen to it, put the segments together, and perhaps write an ending or an introduction. And of course find a title.

64. Ellington: "Where Is Jazz Going?" (1962)

T he early sixties is usually thought of as a period of violent upheaval in jazz, characterized by the radical experimentation of John Coltrane and Ornette Coleman, the volatile statements of Charles Mingus, and the energized outpourings of Cecil Taylor and Eric Dolphy, among others.

Such developments, however, were far from Ellington's mind in "Where Is Jazz Going?," an article that appeared in *Music Journal* in 1962 (perhaps commissioned by its then-editor, the writer and popular-music historian Sigmund Spaeth). Instead, Ellington mused about various uncontroversial topics in a kind of unleashed stream-of-consciousness: jazz's relationship to rock 'n' roll and the roots of both in folk music; the improved technical training of young musicians; aspects of performing jazz that made it "thoughtful creation, not mere unaided instinct." By the end of his meandering monologue Ellington returned to a favorite subject—the futility of categories—by way of addressing the main question of the article.

Where is jazz going? Questions of this kind are never easy to answer, and in this case it might be easier to answer another question, namely: where is jazz coming from? Because one of the most important distinctions between the musical scenes of yesterday and today is that the average young musician nowadays comes equipped with conservatory experience, with a background of educational equipment that is way out ahead of the training most of the musicians had not too many years ago.

As far as the future of jazz is concerned, it is by no means certain that this will be the only factor in determining which way things will go. Whether jazz will be more folklike in nature, or less, whether it will be less or more mechanical, is not important.

What is important is that it must live, and the only way it can live is with the existence of an ever larger and more keenly interested audience, to give it the support that must always be its life blood.

Jazz, like any other form of art, has to be subsidized. If there are more intelligent listeners, of course, it will move in a more intelligent direction. This does not necessarily mean, however, that it will leave the realm of folk music and tend to become a more mechanical thing.

Recently I was asked whether I felt that jazz had moved a great distance away from its folk origins. With the present state of Rock 'n' Roll music I don't know how anyone can even consider asking such a question! Rock 'n'

Source: Duke Ellington, "Where Is Jazz Going?," *Music Journal* (March 1962), 31, 96.

Roll is the most raucous form of jazz, beyond a doubt; it maintains a link with the folk origins, and I believe that no other form of jazz has ever been accepted so enthusiastically by so many.

This is probably an easy medium of musical semantics for the people to assimilate. I'm not trying to imply by this that Rock 'n' Roll shows any single trend, or indicates the only direction in which things are moving. It is simply one aspect of many.

I have written a number of Rock 'n' Roll things myself, but am saving them for possible use in a show. As far as my own music in general is concerned, I would categorize it as Negro music. It represents what I absorbed as a child and have grown up with among the people around me who were musicians; and beyond that, my own self and my surroundings have been injected into it.

There have been many rebellions concerning our music through the years. As far back as 1933, when I said I was playing Negro music, some critics complained, "*Sophisticated Lady* is not Negro music." But the fact remains that *Sophisticated Lady* is Negro music—it's the Negro I know, and my interpretation.

No matter how many controversies may rage about the direction in which our music, or jazz in general, is going, the music will continue to develop along natural lines. Some of it may become more complex, and some of it will remain simple. There will always be some kind of folk music around, be it Rock 'n' Roll or western or hillbilly music.

Actually the word "simple" is sometimes misleading and is subject to many interpretations. Take, for instance, a recent composition entitled *Night Creature* [1955]. We gave this number its premiere at Carnegie Hall, performed by our orchestra combined with the Symphony of the Air—a total of 111 men.

Despite this, I feel that *Night Creature* basically was done in quite a simple manner. It could have been developed into something far more complex and elaborate; but essentially it tried to tell a rather simple story in fairly simple language. The main purpose of it was to try to make the symphony swing, which I believe we did very successfully.

What we did with *Night Creature* was, in effect, a new argument, on a much larger scale than ever before against the theory that jazz cannot be written. There are still a few diehards around who believe in this; in fact, not long ago I made up a little story to interpret their attitude.

There was a little raggedy boy out in the middle of a field. He was wandering through the grass and stumbled over what appeared to be a black stick. He picked it up and sat down under a weeping willow tree. We, of course, know that it was a clarinet he was holding; but he didn't know what it was. But somehow or other, intuition told him to just blow on it—and when he blew, out came jazz! And that's the way jazz is supposed to be, according to these diehards—it's not supposed to be prepared or planned in any way.

Another theory they hold is that there is such a thing as unadulterated improvisation without any preparation or anticipation. It is my firm belief that there has never been anybody who has blown even two bars worth listening to who didn't have some idea about what he was going to play, before he started.

If you just ramble through the scales or play around the chords, that's nothing more than musical exercises. Improvisation really consists of picking out a device here and connecting it with a device there, changing the rhythm here and pausing there; there has to be some thought preceding each phrase that is played, otherwise it is meaningless.

So, as I say, jazz today, as always in the past, is a matter of thoughtful creation, not mere unaided instinct; and although it is impossible for me or anyone else to paint any accurate picture of things to come, I am sure that it will develop into something very big and beautiful.

As you may know, I have always been against any attempt to categorize or pigeonhole music, so I won't attempt to say whether the music of the future will be jazz or not jazz, whether it will merge or not merge with classical music.

There are simply two kinds of music, good music and the other kind. Classical writers may venture into classical territory, but the only yardstick by which the result should be judged is simply that of how it sounds. If it sounds good it's successful; if it doesn't it has failed. As long as the writing and playing is honest, whether it's done according to Hoyle or not, if a musician has an idea, let him write it down.

And let's not worry about whether the result is jazz or this or that type of performance. Let's just say that what we're all trying to create, in one way or another, is music.

65. Pete Welding: "On the Road with the Duke Ellington Orchestra" (1962)

The Ellington orchestra's frequent road trips often included spouses, friends, business associates, relatives, assistants, and occasionally journalists. Those who traveled along tended to emphasize the tremendous physical strain involved, as when Stanley Dance reported on a 1968 tour of Latin America[1] or Ernest Borneman gave a near-incredulous description of following the Ellington entourage around Paris in 1948.[2]

In April 1962, *Down Beat* assistant editor Pete Welding spent several days with the Ellington band as it performed a series of one-nighters near Chicago. His account captures various strategies used by Ellington's musicians to cope with the numbing grind of their schedule. Throughout Welding's narrative, Ellington—who traveled separately from his musicians, in a car driven by baritone saxophonist Harry Carney—remains a distant figure, appearing only once at the start of a performance to galvanize his tired troops into action.

Source: Pete Welding, "Long Day's Journey: On the Road with the Duke Ellington Orchestra," *Down Beat* (7 June 1962), 24–25, 43.

[1] *WDE*, 261–82.
[2] Ernest Borneman, "Diary—68 Hours without Sleep," *Down Beat* (25 August 1948), 6–7.

Welding (b. 1935) served as assistant editor for Down Beat from 1962 to 1965. He has written extensively on the blues in liner notes and specialist publications.

The personnel of the orchestra during Welding's trip consisted of Ray Nance, Eddie Mullens, Bill Berry, Roy Burrowes, trumpets; Lawrence Brown, Leon Cox, Chuck Connors, trombones; Johnny Hodges, Jimmy Hamilton, Russell Procope, Paul Gonsalves, Harry Carney, reeds; Ellington, piano; Aaron Bell, bass; Sam Woodyard, drums; Milt Grayson, vocals.

It was approaching 11 a.m. when I arrived at the small, nondescript hotel where the Ellington band was staying. The April day was sharp and still, and the sky above the small Indiana town of Rensselaer was a sullen, pallid gray. Surely we'd have rain before night.

The night before, I had traveled from Chicago to join the band for a stay of several days, to observe at first hand and from the vantage point of a seat on the band bus that unique phenomenon, the Duke Ellington Orchestra. The men had traveled more than 18 hours the previous day, coming by bus from New York City for a series of one-nighters in the Chicago area. Their first engagement had been a two-hour concert at Rensselaer's St. Joseph's College.

Entering the Hoosier Inn, the town's only hotel, I found myself in a fusty sitting-room-lobby occupied by three persons. Eddie Mullens, a trumpet veteran of many years' services in various big bands and now a member of the Ellington brass section, was leafing through a picture magazine under the baleful scrutiny of two withered village elders. As I conversed with Mullens their merciless gaze never left us. It was a bit unnerving; I felt like an exotic bird under the observation of a pair of sharp-eyed ornithologists.

Dolorous flute strains floated thinly from somewhere above us. After a few tentative starts, it launched into the theme from *Exodus*. I nodded quizzically. "That's Jimmy Hamilton," Eddie explained. "He's always working on his flute—anytime, anywhere."

"You'll find out," he said and winked.

I remarked that though the scheduled departure time was drawing near, no one in the band except him appeared to be up and about.

"That's another thing you'll find out soon enough," he said. "This band is *always* late. Like today. The band call is for 11 . . . so that means we'll leave about 12:30."

(He was within 10 minutes of being right. It was 12:40 p.m. before the bus, bearing on its side the legend "Duke Ellington and his Famous Orchestra," departed Rensselaer.) One by one, band members had straggled down from their rooms, to mill about in the tiny lobby or on the sidewalk after stowing their luggage and instruments on the bus.

Finally, after everyone had been herded into the bus by the band's road manager, Al Celley, and his assistant, the rotund Bobby Boyd, and after a frantic last-minute nose count, we pushed off.

Another concert was scheduled for the evening, this one at a small college in Dubuque, Iowa. The ride, northwest across Illinois, was sure to take six hours at least. Knowing this, the men settled themselves as comfortably as possible in preparation for the monotonous afternoon.

I had heard that there was a rigid seating arrangement in force on the bus, the prized seats being awarded on a seniority basis. This is true—to a degree. The coveted seats are the first four on the right-hand side of the bus and are occupied by Johnny Hodges, Russell Procope, Lawrence Brown, and Jimmy Hamilton, in that order. (Harry Carney, oldest member in point of service, rarely travels in the bus; he and Ellington travel in Carney's Chrysler. They had driven into Chicago the previous evening and would join the band in Dubuque.) After these first four, the seniority system falls off, and the other men choose seats almost indiscriminately, though permanently.

Brown, aloof, dignified, a seeming refutation of the aphorism "no man is an island," quickly became absorbed in a copy of *Popular Mechanics*. Hamilton fished out his flute and resumed *Exodus,* then moved into *Moon River.*

Conversation was intermittent, lagged, died. Most of the men either read, slept, or gazed dully at the flat ochre monotony of the landscape. The sky darkened to a somber plum color, though it was still early afternoon. The torpor was a palpable thing. It had begun to drizzle lightly.

Sam Woodyard alone refused to allow his high spirits to be dampened. He was holding forth on his favorite topic—Life.

"Look," he said to no one in particular, "that's what we've lost in this modern age—the art of living. Nobody knows how to enjoy life any more. People don't want you to. They think there's something wrong with you if you're happy . . . and that's because they're so unhappy themselves. They want you to be unhappy too. They see you smiling, happy, glad to be alive, and they come up to you and say, 'What are you so happy about?'"

He spat out the offending words venomously.

"That's what they ask—'What are you so happy about?'" he continued. "Did you ever hear such a stupid question?"

He paused dramatically. No response. He plunged ahead. "As if just being alive, able to work, and do your best weren't enough," he thundered, warming to his subject. "Why, just the fact of being able to get up out of bed in the morning to face life, to earn your bread, to do battle—why, that's plenty to rejoice in! Now, most people miss the significance of getting out of bed. It's a *very* positive thing. It means you're ready to continue, to take what life has to offer. . . ."

As the dissertation continued, some stirred. Leon Cox interrupted with his best imitation of a pompous radio announcer: "Thank you, Mr. Sam Woodyard. Ladies and gentlemen, you've just heard more words of undying wisdom from the wailing Watusi. Tune in tomorr . . ."

He got no further, for by now Woodyard had swung into a vocalized drum solo. "Chung-a-chung-a-chung." His whole body rocked to the rhythm. Cox joined in good-naturedly, then began to sing a risque parody of *Tenderly.*

"It's time again," he announced, "for another installment of Leon's Lewd Lyrics," and proceeded to render several short, though highly improper, versions of standards. Several requests were answered, and then, as suddenly as the outburst had started, it subsided.

Hamilton had put away his flute, donned a hooded sweatshirt and, looking like a giant pixie, was explaining the principles of electricity to trumpeter Roy Burrowes, who had joined the band just a week before, taking Cat Anderson's place as lead trumpet while Anderson underwent minor surgery. Burrowes listened raptly as Hamilton explained direct and alternating currents, transformers and rectifiers, describing wave patterns in the air with his hands, and illustrating his remarks with drawings on a pad of paper.

Across the aisle from me, Ray Nance was sleeping, his checked hat pulled down over his eyes. Paul Gonsalves, behind him, and Bill Berry were reading paperback novels. Woodyard and Cox were now talking quietly.

The afternoon wore on. The drizzle became a heavy, slanting rain. Evening deepened, and driving became difficult. At times the bus seemed barely to crawl along the narrow ribbon of road between the rolling fields of corn.

Five p.m. passed and then six, seven, and still we drove on. The bus driver, a sharp-featured, bluff Irishman named Dick, had miscalculated the road time, had missed several turnoffs in the rain, which meant delays while the route was retraced, and it soon became apparent that there would be no time for supper before the concert. Tempers frayed, snapped, and, after a babble of indignant voices, sullen silence descended.

This was the mood of the band when the bus at last nosed into the parking lot behind the auditorium where the concert was to be held. The men changed into tuxedos in the darkened bus. There was a frantic scramble to get drums, music stands, and music in place on the bandstand.

"We thought you'd never get here," said a young collegian to Bobby Boyd, whom he was assisting in unloading the gear from the bus bay. "*You* thought we'd never get here," rumbled Boyd in mock surprise. "How about us? Still, we're only 15 minutes late." Everything was accomplished with a dispatch that indicated that this was not a rare occurrence.

Ellington also had been delayed by the storm and arrived a few minutes later, while all was being readied. Appraising the situation, he joked quietly with the men backstage, made light of the situation with a few well-chosen words, and ushered them on-stage with an encouraging "Let's go get 'em, gang."

And they did, roaring through the concert program with bite and passion beyond the routine.

"We should play on empty stomachs all the time," one of the men said during intermission, while all were gleefully wolfing down the sandwiches and coffee the school provided. Excitement was high, for the band was playing particularly well that evening, and no one knew it better than its members.

For the most part the Ellington orchestra plays either concert or dance engagements, mostly one-night appearances, and only rarely settles in one place for any length of time.

The concerts are formulized two-hour affairs: Several old Ellington staples, new material like the *Asphalt Jungle* and *Paris Blues* themes that Ellington is currently featuring, and numbers showcasing individual soloists.

I asked Russell Procope if playing the same set of tunes night after night proved monotonous.

"No," he replied, "it's not so much that it's boring or monotonous. That's an attitude of mind. See, it's the sort of thing you expect in big-band work.

You *have* to work from arrangements, and so your satisfaction arises from your professionalism. You know, just how well you play the charts . . . that sort of thing. These are good tunes and good arrangements, and there's a challenge to them.

"Besides, everyone gets a chance to solo, to say his piece. And, remember, the arrangements are always changing too. As new guys come into the band, Duke will either write new pieces to showcase their talents or will completely re-arrange older numbers for them. That's one reason why there are so many different arrangements of the same tunes in the book. They were individually tailored for particular soloists."

I expressed curiosity as to why Ray Nance doesn't use either music or stand. "Ray's got a retentive memory," Russell replied. "He plays an arrangement a few times and he remembers it. He doesn't need it after that."

Another member advanced a different theory, "No, it's just that all Ray's parts have gotten lost. By accident or design, I don't know."

The second half of the concert proceeded without hitch, the men feeling somewhat better for the little food.

Afterwards, there was a rush to get the gear stowed on board.

While Boyd was dismantling stands, collecting music, packing, and loading the bus, the band members hastily changed to street clothes, cleaned instruments, packed, joked, and talked with relish about the gargantuan meals they were about to consume. Finally, all was ready, and we pulled out.

Celley had gotten directions to an all-night restaurant, and he in turn directed the driver to it. The night was clear and bright, and a sharp chill was in the air as we hurried into the garishly-lit diner. The rain had stopped.

After the tension of the preceding hours, the warmth and brightness of the restaurant and the imminence of a hot meal brought on a kind of collective giddiness, or at least an expansive good humor. Dick, the bus driver, took a good deal of kidding about his map-reading abilities, and it was roundly suggested that in the future Celley—who is very near-sighted, and not the least bit sensitive about it—should drive.

Conversation then moved to previous drivers the band had had. Jimmy Hamilton recalled, "We had this one guy who used to drive sideways. Used to sit up there at the wheel with his feet out in the aisle." Jimmy demonstrated on the stool, swinging around at a 90-degree angle to the counter, his arms twisted behind him gripping an imaginary wheel some inches above his plate. "I guess he was afraid he was going to miss something going on in the bus, so he sat that way. We used to call him 'Old Sidesaddle,' but he sure scared me some—driving that way."

Mullens, who had been eating and laughing quietly all the while, suddenly broke in with several stories of his travels through Europe with the Lionel Hampton Band.

". . . So we were driving through all these little French villages," he was saying, "and all the people were standing waving and shouting at us. We couldn't understand what they were saying. We figured they were just yelling hello or cheering the band—'cause there was a big banner on the side of the bus—so we just waved back and kept on going. But it was strange, I thought, that everybody should stop and make signs to us. And sure enough, when we finally did slow down, this guy came running up to tell us that the bus was on fire. Flames were shooting out about 10 feet behind us. That's what everybody had been pointing at. And all the time, Lionel and Gladys [Hampton's wife] were up there smiling and waving back at all the nice people. It was too much!"

There followed a rash of stories about Europe. Finally Celley began to urge the men onto the bus for the long trip back to Chicago. It was nearly 1:30 a.m., and the drive would take more than five hours. Everyone was reluctant to leave the pleasant warmth of the diner, but at last all were on board and we left Dubuque.

After the rush of conversation, something that accompanied every departure, weariness descended, and all was quiet, except for the muffled sound of the motor and the angry, insistent whine of the tires on the highway. The few reading lamps that had been lit were extinguished, and most of the men settled down for whatever sleep they could catch as the bus careened through the dark night. Few cars were on the road.

Paul Gonsalves, sitting directly behind me, leaned over to offer me a drink. "Can't sleep either?" he asked quietly. I could barely make out his features in the gloom. Across the aisle Sam Woodyard slept soundly, his figure huddled in his seat. I nodded, pulling at the bottle. "It's always like this after playing," he explained. "I get too wound up. The excitement has to wear off, and then I can sleep."

We conversed in near whispers. "You know," Gonsalves said, "this may sound strange coming from me, but I've always wanted to write. Serious writing, I mean. You have a lot of time on your hands when you're on the road, and you see an awful lot, too. A lot of life.

"Now me, I have always tried to reflect, analyze, and think about what I see going on around me. You know, there are many different ways of interpreting a given situation. There's your way of looking at something . . . and as many other points of view as there are persons involved. Everyone brings their own personality, their own experience, their own way of looking at things—they bring all this, you see, to a situation. And you have to consider their points of view as well as your own—at least if you are an intelligent man."

He paused, lit a cigaret, and continued, "Now, for a long time I've wanted to write a book about my experiences, and I *have* seen a lot and thought about what I've seen. The way I would do this book would be to have two characters tell the same story—on opposite pages—each telling it his own way. One guy would have the left-hand page and the other the right, all the way through the book. It would be the same story, you see, but it would be totally different because of the personalities of the two narrators. Each would have to see the same series of events entirely different from the other. Probably call it *Pro and Con*, or something like that."

Dawn broke slowly. We rode the last hour in a dull opalescent light. It was strangely quiet, but as six a.m. and Chicago neared, there appeared an increasing number of cars and trucks. The city was coming to life as we woodenly trooped off to bed.

The next several days flew by in a rush of what was to me unreality.

Breakfast in the early afternoon, a long ride to the night's engagement, meals bolted, a wearying ride back to the drab Chicago hotel where the band was staying. A rough way of life. As the strangeness of the situation wore off, I was able to observe the men in the band with a new awareness. I saw that every one of them is a strong personality, an individualist fiercely determined to preserve his own identity.

A more disparate collection of egos and temperaments could hardly be imagined, yet once they come together on the bandstand, there is not a more cohesive and balanced union conceivable. All the men seem to function best in their roles as members of the orchestra.

The band is the submerged total of all their strong, proud, overweening personalities. Ellington's great genius, as was borne home to me, resides in his ability to weld together, yet subtly to emphasize and bring to the fore in his music, this collection of individuals.

Every man in the orchestra knows two things: first, that he is an Ellington-ian; and second, that his own personality is being respected and taken into account. This attitude is reflected in his playing, his regard for Ellington, and his intense pride in the band.

For, after all, these men *are* the Duke Ellington Orchestra.

66. Ellington with Stanley Dance: "The Art Is in the Cooking" (1962)

O ne of Ellington's most trusted associates was the English author and critic Stan-ley Dance (b. 1910), who first visited the United States in 1937 and moved there in 1959. Dance often accompanied the Ellington orchestra on tours, befriended individual members, and later assisted both Duke and his son Mercer in compiling their memoirs (*Music Is My Mistress* and *Duke Ellington in Person: An Intimate Memoir,* respec-tively). Because of Dance's intimate knowledge of the jazz scene, his interviews with musi-cians—collected in such volumes as *The World of Swing* (1974), *The World of Earl Hines* (1977), and *The World of Count Basie* (1980)—often yielded information and insights unavailable elsewhere.

Dance conducted the following interview with Ellington in New York City during an appearance by the orchestra at Basin Street East in 1962. In it, Ellington wove one of his most whimsical verbal tapestries on the subject of musical categories, taking two side-trips to comment on his plunger-mute brass players and to reminisce about the twenties.

Duke Ellington's frequently expressed impatience with categorization in jazz is jus-tified, or made understandable, by both his band and music. Neither belongs under any of the flags of convenience flown on the angry seas of criticism. Dixieland, traditional, Chicago style, hot, swing, Kansas City, bop, progressive, modern, cool,

Source: Duke Ellington, in collaboration with Stanley Dance, "The Art Is in the Cooking," *Down Beat* (7 June 1962), 13–15. Also reprinted in *WDE*, 3–11.

West Coast, East Coast, mainstream, hard bop, funky, soul, and Third Stream are some of the terms critics have employed through the years, in communicating with the public, as labor-saving reference tags. Sometimes, too, these tags have served as rallying cries, or as slogans in calculated and systematic promotions. But to Duke and many other musicians, they represent divisions, ill-defined and indefensible, which tend to restrict the artist's prerogative of freedom.—S.D.

People are told that they must never drink anything but a white wine with fish or a red wine with beef. The people who don't know, who've never been told that, who've never been educated along these lines—they drink *anything*. I suspect they get as much joy out of their eating and drinking as the other people.

It's just like people who listen to music. They don't necessarily *know* what they're listening to. They don't have to know that a guy is blowing a flatted fifth or a minor third, but they enjoy it, and this I consider healthy and normal listening. A listener who has first to decide whether this is proper form when a musician plays or writes something—that's not good. It's a matter of "how does it sound?," and, of course, the sound is modified by the taste of the listener.

The listener may like things that are pretty, what we consider pretty or schmaltzy. Another may like a graceful melodic line, with agreeable harmony under it and probably a little romantic element. A third may like subtle dissonance, while a fourth may go for out-and-out dissonance. A fifth may have a broad appreciation and enjoy all kinds. But what is really involved here, I think, is personal taste rather than categories.

Music itself is a category of sound, but everything that goes into the ear is not music. Music is music, and that's it. If it sounds good, it's good music, and it depends on who's listening *how* good it sounds.

Now let me put this right. Music can sound good to somebody who likes nothing but cacophony, but it doesn't necessarily have to sound good to the man sitting next to him. There are quite a few people who really dig distortion. Everybody in the world doesn't like pretty. Everybody in the world doesn't like sweet. There are some people who don't like either one ever, but they are all entitled to their likes and dislikes.

Some people, you know, don't even like to get along with others. They're not happy unless they're fighting all the time. Some people are a little sadistic, shall we say, and some are a little masochistic. I've often suspected that when people have said something about others, they've said it deliberately, expecting them to come back with something ugly, so that they could get their kicks.

Now, let's consider your imaginary customer who goes into the restaurant. He looks at the menu and finds the dishes classified under such headings as fish, fowl, and meat. That's a convenience for him. Right? He orders steak, but, after a few minutes, here comes the waiter with a plate of fish. When he complains, the chef—and the chef is the important cat!—comes out of the kitchen with a big carving knife in his hand. The chef tells him to eat up, because it's good food, because if he were starving, he wouldn't care if it were fish *or* steak.

If a man has some very hungry ears for what he considers jazz, or for a

334 / THE LATE YEARS (1960–1974)

pleasant noise that makes him feel he wants to swing (and we have there possibly a reasonable definition of jazz), then almost anything would suffice. At least, if he were starving he would tolerate it for one take. But if he were not starving, and if he were now like a gourmet in a gourmet restaurant, and he ordered fish, and *they* brought him fish, and the minute he tasted it he said, "No, this is not cooked by Pierre! Who is the chef today? This is not the way I like it. I like it the way Pierre cooks it." What then?

This is not a matter of categories. This is personal. He wants his fish cooked a particular way, just as some people want their trumpet played by Louis Armstrong, some by Dizzy Gillespie, some by Harry James, some by Miles Davis, and some by Maynard Ferguson. And I know a lot of people who like to hear Ray Nance play trumpet.

Some people have been raised on nothing but fish. There's been nothing else available where they live. Some people have been raised on nothing but beef, because sheep aren't allowed in their territory. Some people have been raised on fowl, because it's the only thing they can get, and they have to shoot it down.

Each of these people may develop a taste for the food they've been accustomed to, and when they experience one of the others they may find it strange and distasteful. They may possibly decide that beef hasn't the delicacy of fish, but maybe they don't put it down. Maybe they say, "This is something new. This is something I never tasted before, and I like it." And they acquire a taste for it.

I don't really regard these three—fish, fowl, and meat—as three different categories of food. Maybe I'm too basic, too primitive. They're all prey. Maybe I still think in terms of killing the animal and eating it half an hour later.

You could divide up the meat section of that menu under beef, lamb, pork, and so on, under hot and cold, or according to the way they were cooked—grilled, roasted, baked, boiled, etc.—and maybe that's a service to the customer, but to multiply divisions that way in music, in my opinion, merely multiplies confusion. Fish, fowl, and meat may provide us with a parallel, but never forget that *the art is in the cooking*. And what is convenient for the listener, or the critic, is not necessarily helpful to the musician.

I'm sure critics have their purpose, and they're supposed to do what they do, but sometimes they get a little carried away with what they think someone *should* have done, rather than concerning themselves with what he did.

Those trumpet players we mentioned don't come out of the same egg. It isn't that at all. If you like what Louis Armstrong plays, you like that on trumpet. If you like what Dizzy Gillespie plays, you like that on trumpet. So this is more a matter of personal identification, which means that you like not a category but Louis Armstrong trumpet and that anyone else who plays like Louis Armstrong should be labeled "imitation of Louis Armstrong." And anyone who plays like Dizzy Gillespie should be labeled "imitation of Dizzy Gillespie."

This is a matter of imitation, not category. When a guy has invented a style, or become identified with a style, somebody else cannot come along and be a great member of this democratic world of sound that he has created; it's *his* world. Anyone else who uses his creation is an imitator and should be labeled as such. We'll come back to the modifications, but this, I feel, completely destroys the category business. It's a matter of *personal* sound.

It's the same even where you have bands and clusters of sounds. A certain sound comes out of a big band. It may be the character given it by a large brass section or by a particularly skillful group of saxophones. The minute you change the men in the section, it doesn't sound the same, although you may have the same arranger. What happens to the category? The arranger can continue to write in the same style, and someone else who has studied his scores can copy the style, but that brings us back to imitation.

Imitation, influence, and inspiration? Where do you draw the lines now? That's one thing I'd like to know. Yes, just about every musician has been inspired by another musician, has adopted characteristics of his style and clothed them in his own personality. Some people have done it very skillfully and deliberately. Others have done it, you might say, grabbing at a straw. It may surprise you, but I think those who have done it grabbing at a straw are the ones who have come up with the nearest thing to something new.

Take the people you hear playing plungers in the band. They derive their styles in part from Bubber Miley and Tricky Sam Nanton, but Charlie Irvis was first.

Nobody ever really picked up on Charlie Irvis. He used an object that was very effective, and he played in a different register of the horn. There was a kind of mute they built at that time to go into the trombone and make it sound like a saxophone, but he dropped his one night, and the darn thing broke into a million parts. So he picked up the biggest part that was left and started using it. This was his device and it was greater than the original thing. He got a great, big, fat sound at the bottom of the trombone—melodic, masculine, full of tremendous authority. I wish I could find someone to do it now. When he was with me, we weren't making many records, and I don't know if he was on those with Bubber Miley and Mae Barnes.[1]

But Bubber and Tricky were the first to get really wide recognition for the plunger thing. They had such beautiful teamwork together. Everything they played represented a mood, a person, a picture. As a matter of fact, everything we used to do in the old days had a picture. We'd be riding along and see a name on a sign. We used to spend a lot of time up in New England, around Boston, and we'd see this sign, "Lewando Cleaners," and every time we saw it we'd start singing: "Oh, Lee-wan-*do!*"

Out of that came *East St. Louis Toddle-Oo*. Probably it would have been better if he had called it *Lewando* and got some advertising money from it.

Everything was like that then. The guys would be walking up Broadway after work and see this old man coming down the street, and there was the beginning of *Old Man Blues*.[2] Everything had a picture or was descriptive of something. Always.

---

[1] Ellington may have been thinking of records Miley made with Josie Miley, Monette Moore, Sara Martin, or some other singer during the period 1924–26. Miley is not known to have recorded with Barnes.

[2] Ellington used a similar description for the inspiration behind *East St. Louis Toodle-O* (see §67).

A lot of guys heard and listened to Bubber and Tricky's thing. When Cootie Williams first came into the band, taking Bubber's place, he picked up the plunger and became so expert. He did things with a greater range than Bubber. Tricky was there all through this, and he was followed by Tyree Glenn.

Tyree, to me, is a very beautiful trombone player. He plays real good, legit trombone, and when he applied the plunger to it, his tone remained very precise and clean, so that you were tempted to like it better than Tricky's, because it was so clean. But then Tricky's was so very plaintive. Tyree is a very agile-minded musician, and he always wants to do a lot of things. I'm sure he had enjoyed Tricky before. He must have, because he couldn't have done the plunger work so well if he hadn't enjoyed doing it. He still uses the plunger, and he is one of the most effective plunger trombones I have ever heard.

After Tyree came, Butter [Quentin Jackson] and he returned us to a little of Tricky's plaintiveness. Then there was Booty Wood, and he had more of a gutty thing in his playing.

Some people hesitate to take the plunger role. Maybe they've heard it for years and they have a thing in their minds, and it all seems mysterious to them. But those who have come in and picked up on it have really done it from a *gracious* point of view, of carrying on where someone else has left off. It has to do with conforming to a character and a styling, which they obviously enjoy doing. It is sometimes considered a traditional device with us, both as regards the growl solo and the section with plungers, which we call the "pep" section. A lot of guys come in, and they know the part before they get here. They don't need an arrangement, and, if they did, in most instances there wouldn't be one anyway.

We've been very fortunate that way, to find guys in there who wanted to be there. Take Paul Gonsalves. When he came into the band, the first night, he played Ben Webster's solos, every solo, identical with Ben's. He knew them all. He knew everything in the book. But he's no imitator. You hear him today. That was a matter of musicianship and ear.

Of course, if I said everyone who has adopted some of Louis Armstrong's things was an imitator, I would be damning a whole lot of wonderful people.

Certain modifications can be made to that. I don't even think the imitators of Louis form a specific category, because they divide up by personalities. If someone took one of these big, fat IBM machines and worked it down (with time, I'm sure it could be done), you could say that so-and-so had a style based on Louis Armstrong's to a certain point, to 75.439 percent blah-blah-blah, beyond which he developed a new perspective that now boils down to 19 figures with a decimal point. This is so-and-so, but it all comes back to individual people. There is no category. There is one of every style. If two people are playing identically the same, one is an imitator.

Some people really don't give much credit to the creative element. I've known them to say the imitation was better than the original. Are you going to say the son has better blood than the father?

It is possible, because it's not all the father's blood. The mother can raise the quality. And certain parts of the blood's potency may not have come forward until possibly the third generation, so the father never enjoyed it, yet he had it all the time. Things like that are in the Bible.

Anyway, I think we've solved our problem. I think it's something I've been trying to say for a long time. You cannot say that two performers who play in an identical way are out of the same mold. What you can say is that of these two, one is an imitator.

Yes, there were some very good Lester Young imitators. Lester was one of the very potent influences. Charlie Parker had plenty of imitators. Johnny Hodges too. And there was a time when there was hardly a tenor player in the world who didn't try to sound like Coleman Hawkins.

But we mustn't leave out the greatest—Sidney Bechet! The greatest of all the originators, Bechet, the symbol of jazz.

I heard him before I left Washington. He always played the same way— the same way then as just before he died. I remember hearing him play *I'm Coming, Virginia* in 1921—the greatest thing I ever heard in my life. I'd never heard anything like it. It knocked me out.

He played clarinet back in New Orleans, and later on he still played it occasionally, but when he got on soprano he wouldn't get off it. He was just as great a clarinet player. He had a wonderful tone—all wood, a sound you don't hear anymore. The New Orleans guys absorbed something down there along with the Albert system.

I consider Bechet the foundation. His things were all soul, all from the inside. It was very, very difficult to find anyone who could really keep up with him. He'd get something organized in his mind while someone else was playing, and then he'd play one or two choruses—or more—that would be just too much.

He played with us in 1926, when I had a band up in New England. Johnny Hodges learned a lot from him, particularly on soprano. We had Toby Hardwicke, Bubber Miley, Tricky Sam, Sonny Greer, and the tuba player Mack Shaw. The police, gangsters, or somebody had caught Mack out in Chicago, beaten his face in and broken up all the bones. This cat would be blowing his tuba and blow out a loose bone. He had a whole lot of loose bones in his face, and he'd just put them together again and continue blowing! We had a terrific band then.

It had to be terrific in those days, because that was when Mal Hallett had a band up in New England, and you had to play alongside him. The big dance territories were in Massachusetts and Pennsylvania. Charlie Shribman put on dances, and they'd have battles of music. All these big bands used to come up from New York, and Mal Hallett would blow them right out over the Charles River. He just played big, fat arrangements of dance music, and most of his guys were legit, but they'd open up with a flag-waver, and that was *it!* Paul Whiteman came up there with 28 pieces one night, but Mal was too much for him with his novelties and everything.

We had a six-piece band, and we used to play him contrast-wise. He'd know we were coming on, and he'd blow up a storm and lift the roof off. Then we'd crawl up there with our six pieces and begin softly, and develop it, so that when we did play loud it would seem as though we were playing louder than we actually were.

That was a long time ago. Then as now, it's hard if you don't keep with it. If you just stay home for a while and listen to what the other kids are doing out there on the battlefield, you may see where this one made a lot of mistakes or where that one missed a great opportunity. But on the other hand you get more fears. You may read where so-and-so lost this particular battle and so many men were washed away, and it's all a little terrifying. If you come out from home cold—bang!—and all the other cats have been roaming around the jungle, fighting the different animals who're growling with their plungers, honking with their tenors, screeching with their flutes and clarinets, then these animals can sound pretty wild after the comforts of home.

You see the time? I've got to go and marshal the front-line forces over at Basin Street right now![3]

67. Ellington on the Air in Vancouver (1962)

I n 1962 the Canadian broadcaster Jack Cullen conducted a lengthy radio interview with Ellington during the latter's visit to Vancouver with his orchestra. The interview took place in the middle of the night at the studio of station CKNW, with Cullen proceeding chronogically through Ellington's career and prompting the composer to say a few words about well-known pieces.

The following edited transcript presents some of Ellington's comments on the circumstances behind selected compositions and record dates.

On *East St. Louis Toodle-O* (1926)

"What actually happened, we started out calling it the 'Todalo,' and of course, the printer obviously made a mistake and put another 'o' in it or something. I never spelled it for him, actually. 'Todalo,' you know, is a broken walk.

"In those days—well, now we do the same thing—practically everything we wrote was supposed to be a picture of something, or it represented a character of something. . . . We were walking up Broadway one night after playing the Kentucky Club, and we were talking about this old man, after a hard day's work in the field, where he and his broken walk [are] coming up the road. But he's strong, in spite of being so tired, because he's headed [home] to get his feet under the table and to get that hot dinner that's waiting for him. And that's the *East St. Louis Todalo*, actually,

---

[3] The last two sentences here were omitted in the version of the article that appeared in *Down Beat,* but included in the *WDE* reprinting.

Source: Interview by Jack Cullen for station CKNW, Vancouver, Canada, 30 October 1962. Issued on Varèse International recordings (VS 81007).

but since it was misspelled we've been compromising it, and we call it *Todalo, Toodle-Oo. . . .*"

On *Creole Love Call* (1927)

"We had to do something to employ Adelaide Hall, and of course, she wasn't a regular member of the group. . . . She went to Europe with a show I wrote called *Chocolate Kiddies* [1925], and she came back, and then she was a star. . . .

"I always say that we are primitive artists, we only employ the materials at hand. And when someone comes in—just like when Kay Davis came in, she was a soprano, so we employed her in her natural character. . . . The band is an accumulation of personalities, tonal devices. As a result of a certain musician applied to a certain instrument, you get a definite tonal character."

On the Cotton Club band in 1930

"We were very, very fortunate, because we were on the Columbia Broadcasting System, and at that particular period all the other bands in the country were trying to imitate Paul Whiteman, and naturally they were souped up with a lot of grandiose fanfares and all that sort of thing. But we had a very, very plaintive sort of style, and out of contrast alone we stuck out, and caught on."

On *Three Little Words,* from the film *Check and Double Check* (1930)

"[Bert Kalmar and Harry Ruby] wrote *Three Little Words* for Sonny [Greer] to sing, because he was a singing drummer in those days. We got to Hollywood, and he got mike fright, light fright, Hollywood fright, and all sorts of funny [things], and he said, 'Man, I can't sing, I'm not a singer, I'm a drummer,' and he was just scared to death. So we said, 'Well, tell you what we'll do, let's go over and get Bing [Crosby].' So we went over to the Cocoanut Grove and got Bing, and he came over and made the track.

"The next day the director heard the record—the track—and he says, 'This guy can't sing a note by himself.' He says, 'Go get the three of them.' So then we went back and got the three guys and brought them back over there, and they made the track—the Rhythm Boys [Bing Crosby, Harry Barris, Al Rinker] made the track, and they photographed it as our three trumpet players singing."

Mood Indigo (1930)

"When we made *Black and Tan Fantasy* . . . [we used] the plunger [mute] in the trumpet and in the trombone in that duet [and] always got a 'mike' sound. . . . They hadn't conquered this yet, and so they messed up a lot of masters because every time they'd get the mike sound they'd throw it out and have to make it again, staying there all night long making the thing. . . .

"We had a little six-piece date in 1930 at OKeh. So we went down, and that night when I was waiting for my mother to cook dinner, why, I said, 'Yeah, I need another number, I better scratch out something while I wait.' So I did the orchestration in fifteen minutes. And the aim, of course, was to employ these instruments in such a way, at such a distance, that the mike tone would set itself in definite pitch — so that it wouldn't spoil the record. Lucky again, it happened."

On Mitchell Parish's Lyrics for *Mood Indigo*

"It's very funny about the *Mood Indigo* record. . . . I saw Mike [Mitchell Parish] in Paris a couple of years ago, and he had just signed his renewals with Mills. He got a nice fat chunk of money, you know. He's sitting there, smoking his cigarette, drinking his champagne. And you know, I'm a rat at heart. So the guy's very happy about the deal he made, he got this money, so I said, 'What did you do about *Mood Indigo*?' Man, he hit the ceiling! He said, 'Damn, I forgot that!' Because he doesn't get anything from *Mood Indigo*.

"At the time [he wrote the lyrics] he was signed with the company — Mills Music — and so they just bought him outright, and he was on a regular stipend, on a salary. These things happen. I wrote a couple of things and sold them outright, too."

Sophisticated Lady (1933)

"We were playing in Chicago. In between the shows, in the theater, I used to go up in a room that they had — I think it was the pit-orchestra leader's room and he had a piano — and I was up there and writing something.

"I said, I have to write a thing to capture a real sophisticated lady, you know, one who is traveled and learned. And I took as an example some friends of mine whom I knew at that time, who were school teachers in Washington. These kids were very, very sophisticated. They used to fly off to their weekends around the country and summer in Europe. I thought that was a real example of [a] 'sophisticated lady.'"

Solitude (1934)

"I wrote that in twenty minutes standing up. . . . It was another one of those things.

"We were in Chicago, in the Victor studio. Someone else was late getting out of the recording studio, and I needed a fourth number. So I was leaning up against one of those glass office enclosures, and I wrote it out — what orchestration there was of it."

In a Sentimental Mood (1935)

"That was written very spontaneously. One playing—zhwoop!—just like that. The occasion was in Durham, [North] Carolina. After this dance we went up to the North Carolina Mutual building, an insurance building—some friends of mine were executives up there—and we had a party, a lot of ladies and gentlemen, and we were having a bit of sipping.

"It was a rather gay party, with the exception of two girls and one fellow. And it seemed—they were all friends of mine—that one girl had been engaged to this young man for a long time, and suddenly her best friend was now going to take him away from her. And so I had the two chicks, one on each side of me, and I said, 'Just listen to this. You girls are too good friends to let anything like this come between you.' And this is what I played for them. I played it and I remembered it, and then I put it down."

I Let a Song Go Out of My Heart (1938)

"The tune was written in Memphis, Tennessee, in a little hotel owned by an old friend of mine . . . and I had a certain amount of inspiration. (I'm seldom alone. I'm extremely partial to extremely pretty people.)

"We did the song, and played it, and we came back to New York and . . . decided to put it into the show, the Cotton Club show. . . . The Cotton Club had moved down on Broadway then, they were no longer up in Harlem. . . .

"[Henry Nemo] liked this melody and wrote this lyric to it for the show. Out of all the numbers we wrote—you know, you write about twenty numbers—this was the only one that was thrown out of the show, and in its place they put a thing called, what was it—*Swingtime in Honolulu*. But this is the tune that got to be the big hit, *I Let a Song Go Out of My Heart*."

On the Musicraft Recordings (1946)

"I was completely satisfied with everything we did at Musicraft. . . . This was a wonderful thing for me, they were wonderful people to deal with, everybody was wonderful and had tremendous artistic respect. I got Bob Stephens, who was a master recorder, to sit in the monitor room with the engineer to make sure everything was just as we wanted it on every date. I was very pleased with everything that went into Musicraft, and I had the world's greatest contract (I'll never have a contract like that again). I had a contract, something like—they had to guarantee me a hundred thousand dollars a year in royalties, and if I failed to earn a hundred thousand dollars in royalties, they had to pay a penalty of fifty thousand dollars."

68. Eddie Lambert: "Duke Ellington—1963" (1963)

F ive years after previously visiting England, the Ellington orchestra returned to perform in various cities—London, Manchester, Liverpool, Bristol—before moving on to France, Germany, and Scandinavia. The trip was reviewed favorably, though not uncritically, by Eddie Lambert, who gave a detailed report on the orchestra's repertory, sound, and personnel, singling out two musicians for special mention: the majestic trumpeter Cootie Williams (who had rejoined Ellington after a twenty-two-year absence) and the indispensable baritone saxophonist Harry Carney.

Lambert (1930–1987) wrote frequently about Ellington for the British periodicals *Jazz Monthly* and *Jazz Journal*. In 1959 he published a monograph on Ellington for the "Kings of Jazz" series, and later completed a massive work—*Duke Ellington's Music on Record, 1924–1974*—to be issued by Scarecrow Press. A passionate devotee of Ellington's music, Lambert took an active role in international "Ellington Study Group" conferences and hosted one in Oldham, England, in 1985.

The presence of Duke Ellington and his musicians was enough to warm up even a January so cold as that just experienced, and as one drove, walked, stumbled and cursed through snow, ice, fog and slush to attend the various concerts, one could, for once, feel assured that it would all be very worthwhile. The sound of this Ellington band is now a memory, to be stored along with those of the 1958 orchestra. On that tour, as we all know, many writers were highly critical of Duke's policy and the band was adjudged disappointing in the context of the programmes presented. This year the critics did an about face and in considering the Ellington band sans ballad medley decided that now the Duke was really presenting his music in undiluted form. Four years ago I was frankly bowled over, for the sound of the band was so much more glorious than even the finest records suggested and despite the medley and the drum solo found their concerts to be the finest I had ever experienced in the jazz field. One does not always agree with Ellington's programming, but before going on to criticise what Duke did place before our ears in 1963 we should remember that this music comes from a road band leading the unsettled existence of all touring orchestras. Whatever criticisms one may make of Ellington the fact remains that his concerts still have more "meat," more musical substance than those of any other figure in jazz.

The most disappointing features of this year's tour, apart from the drum solos and mediocre vocals, were the repeated programmes at most concerts and the lack of solo space given to Russell Procope and Ray Nance. Later on in the tour I am told Duke featured the great themes of *Sweet Thursday,* an emotional *Echoes of Harlem* with Cootie [Williams], *Just A-Settin' and A-Rockin'* and several fresh scores of old favourites for his TV show, but although I attended five concerts the only variants were the length of the *Kinda*

Source: Eddie Lambert, "Duke Ellington—1963," *Jazz Journal* 16/3 (March 1963), 1–3.

Dukish prelude to *Rockin' in Rhythm* and the omission of *Pretty and the Wolf* from some of the concerts. Appearances for a prolonged stay at a music festival would seem to be the only way of giving Ellington the opportunity he deserves to show off his greater works, but in the meantime he has a considerable repertoire of shorter works, both old and new, which might have been paraded for the benefit of those who attended several concerts.

Although [Sam] Woodyard's drum solo (an inevitable evil at jazz concerts these days) was perhaps superior to Milt Grayson's vocals, the latter had the inestimable benefit of Duke's perfect piano accompaniments, to which the ear attuned with delight during the singing. Cat Anderson too must take responsibility for some of the duller moments—not for his high note work, which I hope no one finds dull, but for the mediocrity of his feature number *The Eighth Veil*. On the previous tour we had to contend with the almost unendurable *La Virgen de la Macarena*; at least *The Eighth Veil* was an improvement on that, if only for the superior orchestral backing, but why greater use is not made of Cat's abilities as a jazz musician one cannot imagine. Here is a player with a fiery variant of the Armstrong style and an attractive ballad manner who is also a growl specialist of considerable accomplishment. When on the 1958 tour *Madness in Great Ones* replaced *La Virgen* the value of the concert was enhanced by the creative use of Cat's talents. Certainly some such number as this or *A Gathering in a Clearing* would be the ideal setting in which to feature Anderson.

The most notable difference from the 1958 performances so far as the soloists were concerned was the drastic reduction in the amount of space accorded to Ray Nance. A long violin solo in *Guitar Amour,* the *Perdido* chase chorus and two or three odd choruses elsewhere were all we heard from Ray—the hilarious vocals had gone, while the features for his growl horn from the "before my time" selection of the previous tour were also absent. Some of one's warmest memories of the 1958 tour were of Nance's sweet, singing trumpet in such numbers as *Such Sweet Thunder* and while one appreciates the difficulty of featuring all the soloists in the band adequately, several of the items in the programme were a good deal less entertaining than Ray's singing, while there seems no reason why his horn should not be heard "down front" at least once during a concert.

The overall sound of the Ellington orchestra was different from that of 1958, the texture less mellow, the tone colours bolder but less subtle. The trombone section of [Britt] Woodman, [Quentin "Butter"] Jackson and [John] Sanders, which will surely go down as one of the great teams in jazz history, has wholly disappeared and in their place we had a less well blended section led by Lawrence Brown. Brown's is of course an Ellington voice, the long association between him and Duke enabling him to realise his part in the band to perfection. Chuck Connors played bass trombone, which gave a greater depth to the section, but he was not heard in solo. The third member of the team was Buster Cooper, who on the evidence of two short solos would appear to be a player of vigour if little individuality, yet it would be highly uncharitable to dismiss this young musician on so brief an acquaintance for he has as yet had little opportunity to really settle into the band. The lack of a growl specialist in the section (a temporary infirmity one trusts) has led to Lawrence Brown taking over the muted solo in *Rockin' in Rhythm*, a task he performs remarkably well for one who, to use his own words, "does not *feel* that style." The brief trombone statement of *Pyramid* and the full chorus solo during Milt Grayson's *Do Nothing 'til You Hear from Me* were more characteristic of Brown's rich, burnished tone and beautifully melodic sense. His solo in *Pyramid* was a mere eight-bar theme statement played muted, but it was so wholly characteristic of Lawrence that no other trombonist in jazz could possibly have realised the passage in this perfect manner.

The trumpet section too had changed, only Ray Nance and Cat Anderson remaining from the 1958 band. The loss of the mercurial Clark Terry and the lyrical Shorty Baker was bound to change the character of the section. Roy Burrows fills Clark Terry's chair, but lacks the latter's strength of musical character. While playing as part of the sax section in *The Asphalt Jungle Theme* one was aware only of the addition of a mild brass flavouring; when Terry used to play such parts a completely new sonority was heard, his voice in the section being as distinctive as those of Hodges or Carney. Burrows played a pleasant solo in *Jam with Sam* in the loose chromatic manner favoured by the younger players, but the chase chorus with Ray Nance in *Perdido* revealed him as a player lacking in tone, ideas and swing. To be "carved" by a man of Nance's vast experience and talents is hardly a disgrace, but Burrows sounded too tentative and too derivative a player for this band. This is unfortunate, for Clark Terry has created a need for a modern trumpet in the Ellington band which is now as much a part of the tradition as the growl brass specialists.

The second change in the trumpet section is probably the most talked about personnel change in jazz since Cootie Williams left Duke in 1940. The return of this commanding figure to the forefront of the jazz scene is long overdue. If anyone thought that the general delight caused by the reunion of Ellington and Williams was simply nostalgia their illusion must have been shattered by Cootie's solos, which were among the high spots of these concerts. Most of his playing was muted in the growl manner, revealing a vast wealth of sonorities which were in themselves beautiful to hear, while the very *power* of Cootie's trumpet is remarkable, filling the largest of halls with full, radiant tone. His phrasing and dynamics are perfectly balanced, his playing as individual as any in jazz. For two brief choruses he played open trumpet and it was evident at once that the great majesty of his open style has lost nothing in his many years of obscurity. Only Louis Armstrong and Roy Eldridge at their best share the serene, majestic carriage of Cootie Williams' authoritative solos and one hopes that his playing taught something of jazz essentials to those whose prime delight is the boosting of thin toned, half hearted trumpet players. Here indeed was a display of commanding mastery.

The fabulous reed section was unchanged and a few notes proved that the description of them as the finest in jazz history is no exaggeration. The infinite range of sonorities, the nonchalant perfection of their phrasing, the uncanny way in which the voices blend with whoever is leading the section and the glorious warmth and swing of their playing are quite inimitable. Of the soloists, Johnny Hodges was, as ever, outstanding. His work has a mature professionalism which many take, incorrectly, to be a lack of concern with the essentials of his art. Utterly without showmanship Hodges simply plays music without any "arty" or vaudeville trimmings, this straightforward approach being mistaken too often for boredom. There were three Hodges feature numbers—*Star-Crossed Lovers* with its rich colours and brooding orchestral background, a bouncing *Things Ain't What They Used To Be* with ebullient brass accompaniment and *All of Me,* which featured fine playing from the trombones. Minor variations in the solo parts could be heard at each concert, while in his two-chorus solo in *Main Stem* Hodges wrought considerable changes, the basic framework remaining the same but the amount of elaboration depending apparently on mood.

During section passages Johnny Hodges can be heard distinctly, his dynamic phrasing and rich tone enhancing the work of the team. But the vital spark of this section, indeed of the whole band, is Harry Carney. It would be foolhardy to suggest that Duke is dependant on any one of his musicians but Carney would surely be the most difficult man to replace in the entire Ellington organisation. Not only does his baritone serve as the basis on which the entire ensemble is balanced and provide a powerful weapon in the armoury of Ellingtonian sonorities, but his obvious zest for playing and his unfailing swing inspire the orchestra constantly. In these concerts Carney's principal solo was during *Pyramid* and he performed with characteristic skill, taste and authority. A man with more than enough talent to become one of the leading jazz primadonnas, Carney has chosen instead to follow the less spectacular path of a great bandsman; of all the outstanding figures who have passed through the ranks of this finest of jazz orchestras none has contributed more than this modest, dedicated musician.

Of the remaining reed players Paul Gonsalves was given the greatest prominence, notably in the up-tempo solos in *Cop-Out, Perdido* and *One More Time:* the former was of course a tenor marathon in which Paul's relentless swing and peculiar harmonic approach were evident. But Gonsalves is a far more satisfying musician in a calmer context and the extent of his talents could be more clearly grasped from brief passages in *Pyramid* and *Guitar Amour,* and during the middle section of *Star-Crossed Lovers* when the tenor is the leading voice in the ensemble. Here his beautiful tone and exact rhythmic placing are heard to the greatest advantage, for while there are many tenor players who could equal or excel Gonsalves in his frantic vein, the less lauded aspects of his playing reveal a far more attractive musical personality.

The value of Jimmy Hamilton's precise musicianship and clarinet virtuosity are at a premium in the more complex Ellington scores and as these were not produced during the tour a feature number, *Calinè* [a.k.a. *Silk Lace*], played with refreshing clarity and lucidity, and a couple of up-tempo choruses were all we heard from him. In parenthesis one might utter a slight regret at not hearing a short solo from Hamilton's tenor, if only for the revealing contrast it provides both with his precise clarinet style and with the more elaborate methods of Paul Gonsalves. Russell Procope produced the current version of his *Jam with Sam* alto chorus but was otherwise confined to section playing.

Frequently the lead voice in the section, his alto is an important and essential part of the band, but it was regrettable that Russell was not heard in his prime solo function as clarinettist in the [Barney] Bigard manner. Of course, one cannot expect everything in one Ellington programme, but Procope's distinctive clarinet is surely too excellent a solo voice to be entirely neglected.

In the rhythm section the enigmatic Sam Woodyard held forth and on occasion his drive at up-tempo was a tremendous force, hurling the band forward with immense verve and attack. On other occasions he seemed almost a decorative accessory leaving the swing to the horns; at such moments Harry Carney's presence was felt in no uncertain manner. Sometimes Woodyard plays so well that one is convinced that he is the finest drummer yet to play with Ellington, but at others his heavy off-beat accentuation seems inappropriate and poorly balanced. Sam Woodyard's virtues outweigh his defects by a considerable margin, however, and overall he is a considerable asset, his inconsistencies being due in part to Ellington's rather unusual concept of the drums as an arm of the orchestra rather than its rhythmic heart. Ernie Shepard on bass is the most recent recruit to the band and appeared somewhat over-awed at filling his vital spot in the Ellington orchestra. With characteristic tact Duke left less prominent places for the bass than is usual with him, but on several occasions he could be seen encouraging Shepard when his playing brought forth Ducal approval.

"Our piano player," as Duke introduced himself, remains an all embracing and inimitable stylist, his accompaniments to Grayson's vocals, his *Kinda Dukish* feature and his work in the band revealed that mastery which we have learned to appreciate on records. The effect on the orchestra when he sits in on piano is electric and he remains the greatest band pianist yet heard in jazz.

This then was Ellingtonia '63—provoking minor criticisms but above all reaffirming the eminence of the man and the orchestra in the field of jazz. There has never been anything in music quite like this ensemble and to be able to hear what they really sound like "in the flesh" was a delight and a privilege. Here were concerts by a band which embodies everything that jazz has been yet refreshes itself unendingly in new endeavours. Duke Ellington and his orchestra do not so much represent one aspect of jazz as embody the very spirit of the music.

69. A. J. Bishop: "Duke's *Creole Rhapsody*" (1963)

The English writer A. J. Bishop published several analytical articles about Ellington's music during the sixties.[1] In the following essay written for *Jazz Monthly,* he compared two versions of *Creole Rhapsody* (1931), Ellington's first "extended" work. Bishop gave close consideration to formal aspects, pointing out innovations in Ellington's approach to phrasing and his means of achieving sectional contrast.

For another appraisal of *Creole Rhapsody,* more critical in tone, see Gunther Schuller's discussion in *Early Jazz* (New York: Oxford University Press, 1968), 353–54.

The score for *Creole Rhapsody,* which was Duke's first extended composition, was probably completed late in 1930. In January 1931 the band recorded the piece for Brunswick, and in this version it covered two 10-inch 78 rpm sides. The structure of the composition in broad outline is ABABCBA, an outline which is close to the "Sonata Rondo" form of classical music. More specifically it was an extension of the form already used by Duke in *Misty Morning* [1928] (ABABA), with the addition of an extra episode, C.

The first and main theme is not, strictly speaking, a theme at all. It consists simply of an eight-bar harmonic skeleton, in which three different chords, each repeated three times, are decorated by a soloist, and which is rounded off by a cadential figure. This eight-bar sentence is presented in much the same way each time it is played, the differences being in the arabesques performed by the soloists — [Barney] Bigard, [Johnny] Hodges, Freddy Jenkins and [Harry] Carney. The first section is subtly shaded dynamically. At the opening the band is playing quite loudly, and this is followed by a gradual diminuendo, leading into a piano solo which is a free variation on the harmonies of the theme.

B, the second theme, is a very beautiful and characteristic Ellington blues, which follows A after a brief modulation, and is presented by two soloists; first Bigard, then Cootie Williams. Ellington's technique of using short linking phrases to knit together diverse episodes, a technique he developed in the late twenties, is consistently used in *Creole Rhapsody.* Such a linking phrase connects the blues section with the second exposition of A, which re-appears in conventional thirty-two-bar song-form, with a bridge passage (or "middle-eight") in which the scoring is more complex. Here again, the dynamic treatment is very subtle. The music rises to a crescendo in the more melodic interlude, which has a wider span than the main sentence, and falls back in the last eight bars to close the first side of the record.

The second side opens with an introduction on the solo piano, based on theme A, which then goes into a variation on the blues theme. A modulation

Source: A. J. Bishop, "Duke's *Creole Rhapsody*," *Jazz Monthly* (November 1963), 12–13.

[1] See §71, also "The Protean Imagination of Duke Ellington: The Early Years," *Jazz Journal* 10 (October 1971), 2–4, and *Jazz Journal* 12 (December 1971), 12–14.

and a four-bar interlude lead into theme C, which is extremely interesting in two ways. Firstly, it is scored as a trombone duet, one of the first in recorded jazz. Secondly, from a structural viewpoint: C is sixteen bars long but divided in a very unusual way. Instead of being divided into four four-bar phrases, it is made up of two five-bar phrases, a four-bar phrase, and a two-bar rounding-off phrase. The effect of hearing a prolongation of the normal four-bar phrase is a very curious one. Our ears are so conditioned to hearing jazz in a succession of four-bar units, both rhythmically and harmonically, that any departure from this norm leaves us with a feeling of disorientation. It is worth looking at this section more closely. At first it seems as though the initial phrase is going to fit into the normal pattern. The last note of the phrase starts on the third beat of bar four. Instead of ending within the bar, it continues over the bar-line, stretching across five beats and ending on the third beat of bar five. The fact that this note is not strongly attacked, and that it fades perceptibly, gives an inconclusive feeling which leads one to expect that the phrase will be further extended. But it is repeated from bar six, and played in the same way again, this time ending on the third beat of bar ten. The conventions of jazz phrasing have been completely shattered, and in the most brutal and surprising way. We don't quite know what is going to happen next. In bar eleven, which is normally harmonically weak, the trombones take up a new phrase, which is balanced in the conventional way, in four bars. This feeling of balance is reinforced by the final two-bar rounding-off phrase, and we are back in the world of everyday jazz again after a brief but thought-provoking interlude. We will return to this point again later.

The trumpet section enters now, tightly muted, playing a variation on the blues theme. At the end of this a modulation leads back to the A theme, which is presented for the last time, in thirty-two-bar form. The bridge is different from the previous one, and again the whole section is well shaded dynamically. The first eight bars are mezzo-forte, played by saxes and solo trumpet, and in the second eight bars fortissimo brass chords alternate with solo baritone sax. There is a diminuendo in the bridge, where open trumpet, clarinet and piano follow each other. Fortissimo chords return in the last eight bars, now alternating with and almost absorbing the solo clarinet part.

The record ends with a short coda, in which lightly played cadential chords are punctuated by brush figures in a final diminuendo.

Six months later *Creole Rhapsody* was recorded again, this time for Victor. The Victor version is so different from the previous one that it is virtually a new composition. The score was completely revised, and extended to cover two 12-inch 78-rpm sides. Apparently Duke was not satisfied with the composition in its original form, and the changes he made throw an entirely different light on the piece.

The A theme, which was the backbone of the original *Rhapsody*, loses a great deal of its importance in the second recording, because it is not repeated in the final section. Theme B (the blues) is retained, but only in a twenty-four-bar section in the first part. The muted trumpet variation of B, which was used on the second side of the first recording, is not heard. Theme C disappears completely. Instead there is a new third theme with an entirely different character; a broad, flowing thirty-two-bar melody, which is one of the finest that Duke has ever written. Duke also self-effacingly cut out his solo piano parts, and is only heard in a supporting part, playing interludes which modulate and change the tempo, and he plays a duet with Barney Bigard.

The use of contrasting tempi for the different themes was one of the great innovations of the Victor recording. The antiphonal A theme is played fast, the blues at a moderate tempo, and the new third theme very slowly, as befits its lyrical character. Bearing these changes in mind, the first part is generally the same as the first side of the Brunswick recording. The entry of the slow melody introduces a mood that was previously absent, as Arthur Whetsol sensitively unfolds the theme in his inimitable way, cushioned against a quiet reed background. After a brass fanfare this melody is presented a second time, by reeds and muted valve trombone. This wonderful slow movement has the quiet beauty and restful quality of a peaceful rustic scene, a scene painted with the most delicate nuances and combinations of timbre; a delicacy which is enhanced by subtle dissonances evoking pangs of nostalgia.

Another innovation is an interlude played by Johnny Hodges at a very fast tempo, and this is followed by a third treatment of C played as a free two-part, out of tempo variation by Duke and Barney. The last minute of the record is a kind of recapitulation, in which the bridge passage used as a "middle-eight" to A in the earlier version, and parts of C are alternated with fanfares based on A, which modulate upwards at each appearance. This final section borrows elements from the link between the middle and final parts of Gershwin's *Rhapsody in Blue,* and has a feeling of heavy-handed pretentiousness which was absent from the first recording, and this, together with its jerky stop and go character, does a lot to spoil the Victor record. Perhaps this explains why many critics prefer the earlier recording.

Both versions of the *Rhapsody* are important, because together they give us an insight into Duke's musical ideas and aspirations. The first version certainly hangs together more satisfactorily, but the performance has many crudities and many indifferently performed passages; in particular, the solo trumpet parts on side two; and the ensemble playing in the final twenty-four bars, which lacks clarity and spaciousness, vitally necessary qualities in this kind of broad climax. It is obvious, too, that Duke was not satisfied with his C theme for the original *Rhapsody,* which has an undeniably experimental character, and is quite undistinguished, with its stilted melody and jerky rhythms. From a structural viewpoint it was a praiseworthy attempt to escape from the four-bar strait jacket; but it cannot be considered to be a successful attempt. The two opening phrases are really extended four-bar phrases rather than truly melodic five-bar phrases. Duke returned to this problem again, four years later, and used similar ideas in a much more integrated and satisfying way in *Reminiscing in Tempo.*

Despite the tempo changes, which were quite as unusual in the jazz of 1931 as they are in the jazz of 1963, and the more complex harmonies and tone-colours, the performance on the Victor recording is far more relaxed and polished, and it is one of the most interesting jazz compositions ever recorded.

70. Dan Morgenstern on *The Ellington Era* (1963)

Columbia's release in 1963 of *The Ellington Era, Volume 1,* a set of recordings made between 1927 and 1940, prompted a thoughtful review-essay by Dan Morgenstern in the short-lived classical-music magazine *Listen: A Music Monthly.*[1]
Before discussing specific pieces, Morgenstern established a critical and historical context for readers unfamiliar with Ellington's work and with jazz in general. The result goes far beyond a standard introduction, however, as Morgenstern provides both a succinct overview of Ellington's career and a critique of what he calls the "progressivist" theory of jazz, which values the quality of "innovation" above all else.

Born in Germany in 1929, Morgenstern came to the U.S. in 1947 and began writing about jazz while still in his twenties. A contributor to various periodicals in the late fifties and early sixties, among them *Jazz Journal,* the *Jazz Review,* and *Jazz,* he served as editor of *Down Beat* from 1964 to 1973 and since 1976 has been director of the Institute of Jazz Studies at Rutgers University-Newark in New Jersey.

For many years jazz had to fight an uphill battle for official recognition as a bona-fide "art form." In light of the current state of affairs in the jazz world, this recognition might well appear to some observers as a mixed blessing indeed. It has largely removed jazz from its original context—the functionality of entertainment and dance music—and has placed this music and its creators adrift in the aesthetic, philosophic, semantic and economic miasms which constitute the contemporary environment of art and "art appreciation."

Though it is a very young art, jazz has already been tightly strapped into the rigid bed of formalistic "history" and evolutionary theory. This framework—often sloppily and haphazardly erected—has supplied the intellectual justification for the demand for constant "innovation" which goes hand in hand with the promotion of all forms of art in this country. This need for novelty—commercial in nature but beefed up by the prattling of befuddled "spokesmen" for the arts—results in the swift condemnation to obsolescence of all but the latest style and mode.

In this atmosphere, jazz history becomes nothing but a tracing of influences pointing to the latest genius and the searching jazz musician is confronted with a process of evaluation which equates music with technology and robs him of the benefits of a viable tradition.

The more's the pity, since jazz is the possessor of an exceptionally strong and durable tradition which counts among its pillars a number of artists still active and still in full command of their creative resources.

Outstanding among these "old masters" is the 64-year-old orchestra leader-composer-pianist-arranger Duke Ellington, who, alongside the indestructible Louis Armstrong, could well be called the greatest living exponent of jazz.

Source: Dan Morgenstern, "The Ellington Era," *Listen: A Music Monthly* 1 (December 1963), 15–16.

[1] Morgenstern reviewed the same collection in *Down Beat* (February 1964), 13–14.

Ellington's career as a bandleader dates back 40 years and is exceptionally well-documented on phonograph records.

Columbia Records—the only American record company aware of its responsibilities to the present as curator of past treasures—has now made available, in a handsomely boxed and annotated set of three long-playing records, 48 pieces of Ellingtonia dating from the period 1927–1940, under the title *The Ellington Era, Volume 1*. Some of the music—very little—sounds dated. But the impact of the freshness, vitality and beauty of these "old" works constitutes a most effective refutation of the progressivist theory of jazz.

Newcomers to the world of Ellington's music might well assume that this collection is a carefully chosen sampling of "the best" from the period in question. Not so. Not counting his small-group efforts, Ellington recorded over 400 selections in those years, and Columbia is readying another collection to follow this set.[2] It is a representative sampling—nothing more or less. In fact, every Ellington collector will miss more than one of his favorites—and there are many such collectors.

These remarks are made only by way of indicating the richness of Ellington's contribution to jazz, which began around 1925 and by no means ended in 1940. In fact, it seems a bit arbitrary of Columbia not to have broadened their perspective and included some of the works from 1947 to 1952, when the band was once again under their banner, or, for that matter, from 1956 to 1962. But these, one hopes, will come later—the "Ellington Era" is still in full swing.

Ellington is one of the few jazz veterans who has escaped from the prevalent theory of obsolescence—though there was a time, in the late 1940's and early 1950's, when it was considered "in" to label him as "passé." Yet, the continuing appreciation of Ellington has, as often as not, been mainly based on his current work. Even in the booklet accompanying this collection one finds a reflection of this attitude. Leonard Feather—never a man not to keep up with the demands of the times—talks of "seemingly primitive exercises" and "the tremendously advanced sensitivity of present-day ears." In view of the staggering amount of pretentious trash which these "sensitive" ears have so readily accepted, this seems a peculiar apologia—when none is needed. Happily, Stanley Dance does not water down his appreciation of the music in the informative program notes.

What strikes the listener first about Ellington's music is his mastery of form. These recordings were all made at a time when the limits of 78-rpm techniques still applied. The average length of the pieces is three minutes (only the two-part *Diminuendo in Blue/Crescendo in Blue* is an exception). But though seemingly to be a limitation, this time-stricture actually provided a disciplinary framework for Ellington's imagination. It coincided with a truth about the nature of jazz which has often been forgotten: jazz is an immensely concentrated music. Western—late western—assumptions about the superior value of large, complex and time-consuming structures in music gave jazz an inferiority complex. But no jazz composer—including Ellington himself—has yet

[2] *The Ellington Era, Volume 2* (Columbia C3L-39), released in 1966.

created a "large" work of merit and stature comparable to the three-minute masterpieces of classic jazz. (It needn't be *three* minutes—six or seven will do, too. I have in mind the jazz suites and such.) In his most successful longer works, Ellington still remains the master of the cameo form—in *Such Sweet Thunder* and *Suite Thursday* it is the individual segments one returns to.

The three-minute form also coincided with the function of jazz, if one may be allowed to introduce such a concept. The conditions which made possible Ellington's development as an artist are interwoven with the "function" of his orchestra. For almost five years, from late 1927 until 1932, Duke Ellington and his orchestra performed at the Cotton Club in Harlem, playing for floor shows and dancing. The "jazz concert" was not a workaday reality then. Even today, the band still plays for dancing. But dancers don't stay on the floor for more than a few minutes at a time, nor do night-club acts occupy the stage for the length of a symphony. And many an Ellington classic had its origin as "special material" for a dancer, or background to a juggling act. To imply that such origins reduce the "artistic" stature of these works is to demonstrate gross ignorance of the history of art, which has always—until it became a commodity in itself—had "functional" roots.

Ellington thus made a virtue of a necessity. He didn't invent the jazz orchestra, either. The basic instrumentation was given, and the development of Ellington's band (from two trumpets, one trombone and three reeds plus four rhythm to a proportional increase in all but the rhythm section) followed that of jazz bands in general. His originality expressed itself in what he did with this format and instrumentation, which was to imbue it with an unprecedented (and still unmatched) richness of timbre, texture and expressiveness.

One of his chief means for so doing was to cultivate a steady personnel. Throughout the years, there have been remarkably few shifts and changes in the Ellington band, and during the 1930's there were only three defections (two due to illness) from the ranks. The remaining changes were additions. No orchestra in jazz history can point to a similar record. But the Ellington men were not just steady employables. Each member of the ensemble was an individual voice, each had a special gift, each contributed to the totality of what could well be called an organism as well as an organization.

The orchestra thus soon became a continuous workshop in which ideas could be introduced, amended, polished and reworked; an interpretative instrument unique both within jazz itself and in music as a whole. Indeed, the conception of the band as an "organism" became so rooted in the consciousness of its admirers during the 1930's that it was considered a major and unamendable catastrophe when such key men as trumpeter Cootie Williams (who left in 1940 and rejoined last year) and clarinetist Barney Bigard departed from the fold. But these critics underestimated Ellington the catalyst. The band never lost its personality.

In addition to his seemingly inexhaustible gifts as a melodist and composer, his talents as a pianist (which only recently have been duly appreciated by jazz critics), his organizational capacities, and his personal charm and urbanity, Ellington is one of the great orchestrators of all times. The unique sound of his orchestra—it has never been duplicated, though often imitated—springs in large degree from his profound understanding of harmony and, as Sidney Finkelstein (one of the few musically perceptive writers on jazz) has pointed out, harmony related to instrumental timbre.[3] He is a veritable poet of sounds, and the range of his sensibility is astonishing. He can be tender (what band ever sounded sweeter than Ellington's in *Blue Tune*), brash, biting, sly, humorous, nostalgic . . . whatever the mood, there is an Ellington piece to fit it.

In his understanding of the overwhelming importance of sound can be found the secret of Ellington's success as a recording artist. (The history of jazz runs parallel to that of the phonograph; more than likely, one would have been impossible without the other.) From the beginning of its career, the Ellington band recorded better than any other (its chief early competitor, Fletcher Henderson's orchestra, never came through on records), and one might well say that Ellington was the first a&r [artist and repertory] man in jazz, for there can be no doubt that he was the one who saw to it that the balance was judiciously adjusted, the soloists properly placed, and the atmosphere relaxed and congenial.

Thus, Ellington's records, in contrast to most jazz discs, do give a good reproduction of the music itself. And what music it is! Among the best of these 48 pieces one might cite, in chronological order, the joyous *Old Man Blues* (with its striking use of polytonality); *It Don't Mean a Thing* (after 31 years still the definitive version, including Duke's own later attempts); *Harlem Speaks* (with a brilliant contribution from trombonist "Tricky Sam" Nanton); the amazing *Clarinet Lament* (with its unearthly opening fanfare); the playful *In a Jam*; the aforementioned *Diminuendo/Crescendo in Blue* (a startling study in dynamics, displaying the virtuosity of the orchestra to the fullest); the poignant *Subtle Lament; Portrait of the Lion* (first in the Ellington portrait gallery, dedicated to the great Harlem pianist and early influence on the composer, Willie "The Lion" Smith), and *The Sergeant Was Shy* (a demonstration of humor and swing).

There are, of course, the famous "hit" numbers: *Mood Indigo, Solitude, I Let a Song Go Out of My Heart, Caravan* and *Sophisticated Lady*, proving that as a "songwriter" Ellington can hold his own among the best. (Though it must be noted, in all fairness, that some of the band's sidemen had a hand in several: Barney Bigard in *Indigo* [originally recorded as *Dreamy Blues*], Juan Tizol in *Caravan*, and Otto Hardwick and Lawrence Brown in *Sophisticated Lady*.)

A few words about the great sidemen. Of the featured soloists, Johnny Hodges, on alto saxophone (and occasionally, soprano sax as well), and trumpeter Cootie Williams (as fine on open horn as in his well-known role of "growl" specialist) are outstanding. Both are with Ellington today. The late trombonist Joseph "Tricky Sam" Nanton was a unique musician; like Williams, he specialized in the use of the plunger mute, with which he produced a sound closely approximating the human voice, yet wholly instrumental—it could be either humorous or deeply moving. Harry Carney, unquestionably

---

[3] See Sidney Finkelstein, *Jazz: A People's Music* (New York: Citadel Press, 1948; rpt., New York: Da Capo, 1975), 195.

the greatest baritone saxophonist in jazz, has been with Ellington uninterruptedly since 1926 [*recte* 1927]. A tower of strength in the ensemble, he is a warm and affecting soloist. Trombonist Lawrence Brown, who joined in 1932 and is back in the fold once again today, has a big, ripe sound and brilliant instrumental technique. Barney Bigard, one of the great New Orleans clarinetists, never regained the heights he reached during his Ellington tenure. His sound is unequaled.

These were the stars. Trumpeter Bubber Miley, who left the band in 1929 and died in 1932, was the most important early member. He was a gifted writer as well as a very personal soloist, and his *Black and Tan Fantasy* and *East St. Louis Toodle-Oo* remain in the Ellington repertoire as his legacy. Arthur Whetsol, also a trumpeter, was a sensitive and lyrical player, who, like Miley, died young. Sonny Greer, the band's drummer from the start to 1951 (he met Ellington in 1919 and worked with him from then on), was an integral part of the Ellington sound, and no drummer since Greer has quite filled his shoes. Bassist Wellman Braud, from New Orleans and the oldest musician in the band, has often been maligned by critics of modernistic persuasions. But Ellington featured him as no other band leader had ever featured a bassist, and his big tone and propulsive swing were the rhythmic foundations of the band in its early years. The great Jimmy Blanton only appears on two selections, and not in a featured role. The late Ivie Anderson, the vocalist, was as different from the average band singer as the orchestra she sang with was different from the average swing band. She appears on three selections, and one would like to hear more of her.

Alongside such RCA Victor albums as "The Indispensable Duke Ellington," "At His Very Best" and "In a Mellotone" (among the few reissues in the Victor catalog), this set belongs in every jazz library. Even so, in terms of Ellington's total contribution, it is, to quote an Ellington tune, "Just Scratchin' the Surface." Edward Kennedy Ellington is more than a great jazz musician — he is one of the greatest musicians of our time, and the greatest American composer yet to appear. His name and his music will long outlive the tortured products of our avant-garde experimenters. Few musicians — living or dead — have worked as long and as hard as he, and he has never received a foundation grant. But his music is loved throughout the world, and no grant can buy that kind of success.

71. A. J. Bishop: "'Reminiscing in Tempo': A Landmark in Jazz Composition" (1964)

O ne of the first serious efforts to analyze *Reminiscing in Tempo* came in a 1964 article by A. J. Bishop, written nearly thirty years after the piece was recorded. As with his earlier essay on *Creole Rhapsody* (see §69), Bishop concerned himself mainly with form, proposing an overall three-part division of a composition that took up four sides of a 78-rpm recording. His emphasis on structure contrasts with the approach taken later by Gunther Schuller, who cited other features—thematic control, orchestral color, and harmonic richness—as striking in the work.[1]

Reminiscing in Tempo was written twenty-eight years ago, in 1935, and recorded in the same year. At the time, it was strongly criticised. This criticism, viewed in retrospect, was not surprising. Not only was the piece the most ambitious jazz composition, in terms of length, attempted up till that time, but it contained, as we shall see, some unconventional ideas. Unfortunately, the complete work has not been available in Britain for many years. Consequently many enthusiasts, particularly younger ones, have not been able to hear it. It is certainly time it was re-issued.[2]

The work falls into four obvious parts, corresponding to the four ten inch sides of the recording. However, I am sure that its division doesn't adequately fit the work. A concert performance would certainly throw a different light on the structure. After much listening, I have come to the conclusion that it is more accurate to divide the music into THREE sections:—

Bars 1–116. This part states, expands and varies the themes.

Bars 117–224. This part dissects and explores the themes, which are thrown together in the climax of the work.

Bars 225 to the end. The last part restates the themes in altered form, resolves to a calm conclusion.

The First Section

LAYOUT: —

$$12 + 8 + \underbrace{10 - 16 - 10}_{30} + \underbrace{16 + 4}_{30}$$

$$4 - \underbrace{10 + 10}_{20} - 8 + 8 \text{ bars.}$$

Source: A. J. Bishop, " 'Reminiscing in Tempo': A Landmark in Jazz Composition," *Jazz Journal* 17/2 (February 1964), 5–6.

[1] See Gunther Schuller, *The Swing Era: The Development of Jazz, 1930–1945* (New York: Oxford University Press, 1989), 74–83.

[2] Until recently, *Reminiscing in Tempo* has been relatively difficult to find on American reissues, as well.

The structure of this section is not only well balanced. It is far removed from conventional jazz form. The first thirty bars are, perhaps, the most successful part of the composition. Although it is conceptually possible to divide the section as I have shown above, in performance these thirty bars have a continuity, a sense of variety, growth and direction which has seldom been equalled in jazz composition. In melodic terms, we have a three note germinal motive (piano, first two bars); a theme (trumpet bars 3–9, 13–19); an expansion of the motive into an accompanying figuration (reeds bars 9–16); and a variation on the theme simultaneously with the crystallisation of the figuration into a second theme (alto and trombone in counterpoint bars 21–30). At the end of this section, other voices join the counterpoint in a very stimulating passage which leads one to hope for further contrapuntal development.

Rhythmically, the scoring of this section gives a wonderful feeling of acceleration. The opening is static, with the rhythm section marking only the first and third beats. The note values are fairly long (quarters and half notes). At the end of the first trumpet phrase the reeds enter, playing in even eighths. This figuration crosses bars twelve and thirteen, connecting the first and second sentences. A harmonic change in the second trumpet phrase preserves a feeling of forward movement. The second and third sentences are interlocked in bar twenty, where the trombone plays a linking phrase. Further impetus is added by the rhythm section, now marking four beats to the bar.

The first thirty bar section is followed by a long sixteen bar sentence, opening with a continuation of the previous contrapuntal passage, written for two trombones, trumpet and alto, with independent parts for the two basses. This interesting development ceases in bar 34. What follows is a series of variations of uneven quality. The first is by the reeds, the second by the trombone, cushioned by soft, high reed voicings, in a beautiful variation on the main theme. The third is a dialogue between muted trumpets and reeds, with a bass part for the trombones. An interlude takes us back to a subtle variation on the main theme, played on a tightly muted trumpet, in a new key. This section, in two ten-bar phrases, is beautifully harmonised, and recalls the scoring of the theme of *Blue Tune*. An interlude follows, in which Johnny Hodges' alto is heard briefly, bringing the first part of the composition to a conclusion.

The Second Section

LAYOUT: —
14 + 18 — 4 — 14 + 14 — 8 — 18 + 14 — 4

The middle section opens with a piano solo, divided into a fourteen and an eighteen bar sentence. In the first, the solo develops into a series of increasingly wide intervals, which are echoed by the brass, a few bars later in a crescendo. The second sentence, by the solo piano, is very sombre and introspective, reminding us that Ellington's mother had died a short time before. Brilliant runs of very short notes on the piano, and a rising "lead in" on the baritone sax prepares the way for a brief respite from the elegiacal mood of the previous passage. In the following ensemble section, rhythmic flexibility and brightness is achieved by the use of staccato dotted eighths and triplets of eighths (bars 153–154). The music relapses into a darker mood through a gradual de-crescendo, and a two-beat rest (bar 157) brings this short, optimistic phase to a halt. A succession of long sentences, without a pause, slowly builds up tension, as the clarinets weave continually moving lines between ominous brass chords; and the emphasis of these chords is constantly changing. The climax is reached in the fourteen bar sentence from bar 207 to bar 220, where the brass violently throws fragments of the main theme against running figures in the clarinets, figures based on the opening motive. After this tremendous climax the brass dies away, and the middle section ends calmly with a codetta borrowed from *Showboat Shuffle*.

Final Section

LAYOUT: —
32 — 6 — 32.

The conclusion is relatively calm in feeling and conventional in structure, consisting as it does, of two thirty two bar sections, divided into eight bar sentences, and separated by a six bar piano interlude. The main phrases are based on the principal theme. In its previous expositions, this was seven bars long. It is now altered to fit the new pattern. The interlude heard before in bars 101–108 is now used as a middle-eight. In the first "chorus," Rex Stewart and Harry Carney take solo parts. The second eight bars of the second "chorus" is excellently scored, with the reeds playing the melody against brass chords on the first and third beats, while a tightly muted trumpet plays distant sounding calls. The mood of the finale is passive and resigned. The reason for the use of conventional phrase-lengths in this section is obvious. They fit the calmer mood, which is present here, better than long, asymmetrical sentences would.

An analysis of *Reminiscing in Tempo* makes several points clear. From a recording point of view, it was certainly an attempt to break through the limitations of the 78-rpm record. But length is not the original thing about the composition. Four years previously, Duke had recorded the double length *Creole Rhapsody*. What was new, and revolutionary for jazz in 1935, was the structure. Improvisation, which plays such a large part in jazz, needs a simple framework; and no one has provided a better framework for it than Duke. However, there is no reason why a COMPOSITION should be tied to four bar phrases and thirty two bar AABA sections. Duke realised this much earlier. In *Creole Rhapsody*, he used five bar phrases. In *Reminiscing in Tempo*, this idea is carried much further. As we have seen, it contains sentences of seven, ten and fourteen bars. Four and eight bar phrases are used but, apart from the final section, they do not play a leading role in the structure.

Duke did not, subsequently, carry this idea as far as he might have. But he did return to it occasionally. There is a ten bar sentence in *Echoes of Harlem*, and in *Concerto for Cootie* the main theme uses ten bar sentences, and one of these has a seven bar trumpet phrase.

To return to improvisation, this plays only a small part in the composition. The only freely improvised section is the second part of the piano solo. Everything else gives the impression that it was decided on beforehand and written out. Even the solo parts for trumpet and baritone sax, in the concluding section, stick closely to the theme.

Reminiscing in Tempo is completely different from any other jazz of the middle thirties. Not only the form, but the sound, has very little in common with other jazz of the period. Duke used the orchestra with great restraint, a restraint which is emphasised by the absence of brutal timbres, and the evenness of the rhythms. The chief trumpet soloist was the late Art Whetsol, whose unique tone and subtle approach to phrasing was admirably suited to the gentler aspect of Duke's lyricism. In the last part Ellington used the more extrovert tone of Rex Stewart to underline the change of mood after the stormy middle section. The excellent playing of Lawrence Brown is worth mentioning, especially between bars 47 and 56, where his tone and vibrato are firmly controlled, for once. Duke even used the clarinets in the middle and lower register, at precisely the point where we would normally expect to hear them in the high register, at the climax! Paradoxically, this restraint gives the music a re-doubled emotional impact. Finally, amazing though it may seem, *Reminiscing in Tempo* has more in common with the "cool" jazz of ten years later than with the jazz of its own time.

72. Ellington: "Reminiscing in Tempo" (1964)

Ellington's sober and restrained tone in the following *Down Beat* article—which has nothing to do with the 1935 piece of the same title—may have resulted from his editor's request for a "philosophical utterance." Gone are the whimsical flights that characterize so many of Ellington's journalistic statements. Instead he offers a straightforward assessment of the music business over the years, reflecting on changes in the jazz press, the role of the media in disseminating jazz, and the profession of the big-band musician.

> Into each life some jazz must fall
> With afterbeat gone kickin';
> With jive alive, a ball for all,
> Let not the beat be chicken!

When we went to England for the first time in 1933, we were surprised to

Source: Duke Ellington, "Reminiscing in Tempo," *Down Beat* (2 July 1964), 8–9.

find how much people knew about us. They had had a magazine [*Melody Maker*] more or less devoted to our kind of music for several years there, and this was the first time we were really aware of the value of a musical press, as distinct from newspapers.

The first *Down Beat* came out the following year. It was what I would call conservative, but it caught on, and after about a year it began to get more daring and to defy some of the taboos of the time. There were articles by writers such as Helen Oakley, John Hammond, Marshall Stearns, Leonard Feather, Stanley Dance, Hugues Panassié, and George Frazier.

I remember that we were alternately encouraged and infuriated by the things they had to say as they fought out battles of taste among themselves. No holds were barred, the writing was inflammatory, and sometimes innocent musicians were among the victims. Though they had differing insights, those writers all had enthusiasm, and they created a great deal of public interest. Their enthusiasm wasn't a shortlived thing either, because most of them are still actively connected with the music in some way. They were pioneers who pointed out the thrills of their adventures and the joys of discovery. I think it was in 1939 that, prompted by their errors, I had the temerity to write an article criticizing the critics [see §34]. Nobody sued me. That was the kind of scene it was.

Down Beat made its appearance at the right time. I can't substantiate this, but I've always felt it significant that a few years later we found ourselves in the middle of what is now called the swing era. That was a very, very busy time, and there were probably more jazz musicians working then than ever before or since. The audience expanded overnight. Everybody wanted to be hip; nobody wanted to be square. The kids turned out in hordes to holler, scream, and dance to Benny Goodman, the way they've been doing lately to the Beatles. It was a dancing time, anyway, and there were occasions when they turned away more people from the Savoy Ballroom than they had inside.

It was strange how it all happened, how what had been so uncommercial was suddenly commercial without any compromising on the part of the musicians most responsible. I know how *Down Beat* helped, because Ned Williams, a good friend of mine, was its editor for a long time. There were certainly more big bands than ever before or since, and good ones too. Keeping pace with their activities and the comings and goings of the sidemen was one of the magazine's important functions. Of course, the musicians had their own grapevine, but now the public was allowed to see behind the scenes. (I have not always agreed that this was wise from the professional viewpoint because, as in all forms of show business, we lose too much when we lose the mystery of it.)

Out of this came, I think, a closer relationship between the listener and the player, even a degree of intimacy. That is, more people came to regard the musician on the stand as a human being rather than a uniformed figure producing agreeable sounds. A whole lot of new and valuable lines of communication were opened, and it gradually came to be accepted that many people in our field were solid citizens and not eccentrics, nor alcoholics, nor drug addicts, nor even artists starving in garrets, though hunger does have a way of persisting or recurring! And the music was always subject to attack from the unlikeliest sources. Another of my essays was concerned, I remember, with refuting some school official's accusation that swing started sex crimes [see §31]. Imagine that!

Down Beat's headlines in those days used to be much less dignified than they are today, but it was a time with pace of its own, just like the one we are in now. The annual polls, for instance, no longer have a "corn" section, but in those days the readers—who have always been very kind to us—used to elect a King of Corn with considerable zest, humor, and malice.

The changes World War II brought about stay remarkably fresh in the mind. Changes would have occurred without the war, of course, but I believe they would have been more gradual. The conditions and economic problems just hastened them along, because all kinds of irritation and frustration had to be expressed, and they found their way into the music. It was the poorest time to be leading a big band, and I have always been grateful that ours was lucky enough to survive.

The radical changes in taste didn't affect one of the mysteries that has attended the band's progress. We were puzzled for a long time because whatever we did this year was compared unfavorably with what we did last year— or 10 years before. After a while, we got used to it and decided that so long as we were still on our feet we had a future. I continue to feel, though, that criticism should be more concerned with what the artist does than with what he ought to do.

The postwar era has brought big changes in travel as well as music. We used to travel mostly by trains—big old romantic, hooting trains. Then it was all buses and automobiles, with occasional leisurely, comfortable ships as the foreign picture opened up. Today, the jets have expanded our field of action out of all recognition. In place of one-nighters in American towns and cities, we now play one-nighters in the cities of different countries. One night we may play Paris, the next Montreal.

Our tour of the Middle East last fall was a tremendous experience, and Billy Strayhorn and I are still translating it into music.[1] We flew to Bermuda for a couple of days recently, and this month we make our first trip to Japan. It's all a matter of adjusting the perspective, I suppose, and it *is* stimulating, but the pace can make it difficult to absorb the sights and sounds as thoroughly as one might wish. Maybe the musician in our field has acquired his adaptability out of necessity, but I used to marvel at the effortless way our veterans like Harry Carney, Johnny Hodges, and Russell Procope made the transitions. They are among the world's most experienced travelers; they don't ruffle easily.

We also play in a much greater variety of places than we used to. It's like being in 10 different businesses. We still play in dance halls, night-clubs, and theaters, but festivals and concert halls have assumed real importance. I am often asked about playing in concert halls, and I answer that the purpose and

---

[1] The result was the *Far East Suite,* recorded in 1966 for Victor (LSP-3782).

virtue of the concert hall is that in it people have listening isolation and do nothing but listen; whereas in a dance hall, they end up doing a lot of things people with social aspirations want to do. They want to dance and embrace the girls, and in a night-club they are probably busy drinking and smoking. Further, the concert hall is the logical place for performing extended compositions. But you cannot exist by playing there only.

We have found, though, a changing attitude on the part of today's audiences. On our last European tour, for example, we had no singer at all for the first time, and we were received as well as ever.

The old radio remotes were invaluable, but now that they've gone, it is essential that the music get more exposure on television. I know that is easier said than done, but people have every kind of entertainment in profusion on TV except music. Records and FM radio partly fill that gap, but I believe intelligent television camera work can add a great deal to music and eventually bring bigger in-person audiences.

Because the music has become an important cultural export, we mustn't be deceived into neglecting the home front. Foreign tours are a supplement to, not a substitute for, popularity at home.

Popularity cannot be forced, and the musician practicing and enjoying "freedom of expression," which is what the music is essentially about, cannot count on automatic acceptance. He couldn't 30 years ago. Things ain't what they used to be in some areas, but in others they are just the same.

Jazz is a music that came out of the United States with very deep African roots, and from the beginning—before the '20s—it represented a freedom of expression as it does today. Since that time it has taken on many complexions. It has traveled so much, and picked up influences everywhere it has gone, that, by now, I think there's a little of everybody's music in it. But it remains a very highly personalized art, and everyone says what he wants to say the way he wants to say it.

Some persons who had almost no schooling have become famous in jazz, and others with conservatory degrees have done brilliant things. I believe it is a good thing to get all the training possible, no matter what kind of music you're in, but there is always a risk, in my opinion, of original thought being modified by scholastic training, unless you know what you want to do.

The editor asked me to come up with a "philosophical utterance" of some kind. I am unpracticed in answering such requests, but I would refer you, in conclusion, to the foregoing little rhyme which recently occurred to me. It embodies my firm belief that the beat should be positive.

73. Nat Hentoff: "This Cat Needs No Pulitzer Prize" (1965)

O ne of the more notorious incidents in Ellington's career occurred in 1965 when the Pulitzer Prize committee rejected him for a special award in composition. Ellington's oft-quoted response to this rebuff—"Fate is being kind to me. Fate doesn't want me to be famous too young"—appeared in the following profile by Nat Hentoff in the *New York Times Magazine*.[1]

For the article Hentoff drew a fresh portrait of the sixty-six-year-old Ellington, partly through his success in getting band members to discuss their leader candidly. Hentoff (b. 1925) was already a veteran journalist and critic by this time, having begun contributing to *Down Beat* in the late forties. He had collaborated with Nat Shapiro on two books, *Hear Me Talkin' to Ya* (1955) and *The Jazz Makers* (1957), edited the anthology *Jazz* (1959) with Albert McCarthy, and served as co-editor of the *Jazz Review* from 1958 to 1961.

In the following edited version of the article, sections with standard biographical information have been deleted.

For Edward Kennedy (Duke) Ellington, recent months have been characteristically busy and mobile. With his orchestra, he has been constantly in motion—playing one-nighters, making climactic appearances at the major jazz festivals, and recording. Ellington the composer, moreover, has been represented this past summer in a premiere of a new suite, "The Golden Broom and the Golden Apple," with the New York Philharmonic at Lincoln Center. As composer-pianist, he has been selected along with Birgit Nilsson, Pilar Lorengar and Guiomar Novaes, to be part of the new subscription series called Great Performers at Philharmonic Hall. Mr. Ellington's date in this first recital series to be undertaken by Lincoln Center itself is Dec. 12 at 3 p.m.

Honors meanwhile, continue to be accumulated by the Duke. In August, he was presented with New York City's Bronze Medal for his contributions to music. During the course of the ceremony, the sonorous City Council President, Paul Screvane, observed that a few months before the Duke had "missed out on a prize that most people thought he deserved." Screvane was referring to the tempest that blew over this year's Pulitzer Prize in music.

Having considered no composer worthy of this year's prize, the secret three-man jury had recommended to the advisory board that a special citation be awarded Duke Ellington for the "vitality and originality of his total productivity" through nearly four decades. The recommendation was rejected. In the resultant dissonance, two members of the by then not so secret jury (Winthrop Sargeant and Robert Eyer) resigned and raucous fanfares were exchanged between the mutinous jury and the board.

Source: Nat Hentoff, "This Cat Needs No Pulitzer Prize," *New York Times Magazine* (12 September 1965), 64–66, 68, 70, 72, 74, 76.

[1] See also the section entitled "Acclaim" in *MM*, 286.

There was calm only at the center of the storm. The 66-year-old Ellington, on the road with his orchestra, reacted in his customary public manner: that of the coolly amused, persistently polite, impregnable aristocrat. "Fate," said the Duke in a now-celebrated line, "is being kind to me. Fate doesn't want me to be famous too young."

Some time later, still rolling through the land in a series of one-nighters, Ellington was reflecting on fate and prizes. It was 2 in the afternoon, and he had just awakened in his room at the Faust Hotel in Rockford, Ill. Groping for coffee, he peered at a friend. The bags under his eyes looked even more capacious than usual.

"What else *could* I have said?" the Duke asked rhetorically. "In the first place, I never do give any thought to prizes. I work and I write. And that's it. My reward is hearing what I've done, and unlike most composers, I can hear it immediately. That's why I keep these expensive gentlemen with me. And secondly, I'm hardly surprised that my kind of music is still without, let us say, official honor at home. Most Americans still take it for granted that European music—classical music, if you will—is the only really respectable kind. I remember, for example, that when Franklin Roosevelt died, practically no American music was played on the air in tribute to him. We were given a dispensation, I must admit. We did one radio program dedicated to him. But by and large, then as now, jazz was like the kind of man you wouldn't want your daughter to associate with.

"The *word* 'jazz' has been part of the problem." Ellington stretched and grimaced. "It never lost its association with those New Orleans bordellos. In the nineteen-twenties, I used to try to convince Fletcher Henderson that we ought to call what we were doing 'Negro music.' But it's too late for that now. The music has become so integrated you can't tell one part from the other so far as color is concerned. Well, I don't have time to worry about it. I've got too much music on my mind."

Two hours later, the Duke was en route to the next town, sitting in a car alongside Harry Carney, a bulky, amiable baritone saxophonist, who has been with Ellington since 1926 [*recte* 1927]. Carney drove, and Ellington leaned back, sometimes looking out the window and occasionally sketching ideas for a piece in a notebook on his lap.

The Duke has long since won what he prizes most—the freedom to devote all his time to music. His orchestra has survived the relentless decline of the big jazz band. Now only four function regularly—those of Count Basie, Woody Herman, Harry James and the Duke. Of the four, Ellington's overhead is by far the highest. In the Basie band, for example, the average sideman's salary is a little over $200 a week, with one player getting as much as $350. None of Ellington's "expensive gentlemen," however, earns less than $300 and there is a sliding scale upward for long-term members of the orchestra. Several are in the $400–$500 a week circle, and one earns $600. To meet this formidable payroll, Ellington works constantly under the booking aegis of blunt, efficient Joe Glaser, head of the Associated Booking Corporation, a major talent agency. From the dates Glaser sets, the band grosses about $700,000 a year.

The musicians earn additional income from the band's recording sessions for Reprise, a subsidiary of Warner Brothers Records. In recognition of Ellington's stature, that company—in a rare concession for record labels—permits Ellington to function as his own artists-and-repertory man on his recording dates. Ellington, therefore, has complete control over what is—and what is not—released.

While it is difficult to obtain exact figures from Ellington, it's possible to estimate his personal annual income as at least $100,000—a combination of composer royalties, record royalties, profits from his publishing firm, and his own share of the band's income from one-nighters, location dates and concerts. From time to time, there are also film and stage assignments for Ellington the composer.

In addition to his having survived economically, Ellington's musical reputation has also remained secure amid all the careening changes in jazz fashion during the past 40 years. Throughout the swing era, the ascent of modern jazz in the nineteen-forties and the current turbulence of the avant-garde, Ellington has persistently added to the single most impressive body of composition in jazz. And during all this time, he and his orchestra have been justly regarded by both other jazzmen and critics as nonpareil. Or, in the phrase he uses when silkily introducing the soloists in the band, Ellington has been judged as being "beyond category."

The act of categorization is one of the few things that visibly annoy the Duke. "The other night I heard a cat on the radio," he grumbled recently, "and he was talking about 'modern' jazz. So he played a record to illustrate his point, and there were devices in that music I heard cats using in the nineteen-twenties. Those large words like 'modern' don't *mean* anything. Everybody who's had anything to say in this music—all the way back—has been an individualist. I mean musicians like Sidney Bechet, Louis Armstrong, Coleman Hawkins. Then what happens is that hundreds of other musicians begin to be shaped by that one man. They fall in behind him and you've got what people call a category. But I don't listen in terms like 'modern' jazz. I listen for those individualists. Like Charlie Parker was."

And today's young in jazz continue to listen to Ellington as a remarkably pervasive influence on the music. Miles Davis, the astringent trumpeter, who is never profligate with praise, has said, "I think all the musicians in jazz should get together on one certain day and get down on their knees to thank Duke." Ellington's mark is also on such other bristlingly individualistic composer-instrumentalists as Thelonious Monk and Charles Mingus. And the very newest jazz revolutionaries make a point of acknowledging their debt to the Duke.

"Whenever I get in the hole for ideas," says pianist-composer Cecil Taylor, a leader of the newest wave, "one of the sources I go to is Ellington's conception of how to create colors. He's also been very important to me in another way. He showed me how it was possible to incorporate all kinds of musical and other influences as part of my life as an American Negro. Everything I've lived, I am in my music, and that's true of Duke, too." . . .

An index of the infrequency with which Ellington gets to spend time at home was his answer a couple of months ago when a friend in Des Moines asked him where he was living now. The Duke furrowed his brow, scratched his head, and finally said, "Where is it I moved to? Oh, yes, I'm in an apartment house on West End Avenue and Sixty-sixth Street."

The persistent traveling and the addiction to music leave Ellington little social life at home or on the road. Composer-arranger Billy Strayhorn, who has been Ellington's chief assistant since 1939, points out, "Duke would much rather sit up and write after work than go to a party. I'm used to his calling me at 8 or 9 in the morning to talk over a musical problem that's just developed or to tell me about a piece he's been up all night writing."

"I just don't have time to be a social cat," the Duke confirms. "If I'm not writing, I need sleep—at least eight and hopefully 10 hours—more than I need a party. And besides, I haven't been drinking for many years. I used to drink more whisky than anyone in the world, but I'd never get drunk. I finally figured that the whisky was not only not making me feel any better but it also couldn't be doing me any good physically. So I stopped. And now all my time goes into music."

What few intimates Ellington has include Strayhorn; his sister, Ruth, who is president of Ellington's publishing firm, Tempo Music; and his son, Mercer. Mercer has been a band leader and composer, owner of a record firm and a disc jockey. Currently he is road manager of his father's band, overseeing travel arrangements, taking care of other administrative details and also playing in the orchestra's trumpet section. There was a time when Mercer was not encouraged to be a continually visible member of the Ellington scene because, so Ellington's musicians said, the Duke didn't want the presence of a growing son to keep reminding him of his own advancing years. Now, however, there is a close relationship between them, and Ellington is grateful for Mercer's willingness to go on the road with him since Ellington, as a result, has more time to write.

Another intimate of the Duke is Dr. Arthur Logan, his physician and the chairman of the New York City Council Against Poverty. Ellington's chronic hypochondria first led to his association with Dr. Logan, but the professional relationship soon became a warm friendship. Ellington's acute concern with his health is not limited to any single dread. "If he stubbed his toe," says a member of the band, "he'd call his doctor. Even if he had to make the call from Egypt." On the road, for instance, when he is once settled in a room in the best hotel in the town, Ellington makes certain all the windows are closed. He is a persistent opponent of drafts.

Except for his hypochondria, Ellington tries to avoid worry. "Do you know the difference between worry and concern?" he is fond of asking. "Worry is destructive, but concern is the thinking mind solving a problem."

His determination to evade unpleasantness makes Ellington a rather permissive employer. His personal relationships with the sidemen are easy but somewhat distant. "He kids around with us," says a veteran of the band, "but if you get too close to him, he'll make a joke or put you on, and edge away."

"He doesn't keep a tight rein on us," says another sideman. "If someone's acting up, he'll say, 'I hired you because you were the best on your instrument and because I assumed you were an adult. I am going to continue on that assumption.' And that's usually it.

"Once in a while," he continued, "Ellington will briefly show displeasure in other ways, but almost always obliquely. Like, if you come in after having too much to drink, he'll call for the most difficult piece in the book featuring *you*." Another Ellington way of manifesting annoyance is to bang hard on the piano either to underline the fact that a wrong note has just been played by someone or, if a musician has been tardy returning after intermission, to advise him that his presence is required.

With one exception, no one in the Ellington band has been fired for many years. "He can't bring himself to do that," says Strayhorn. "He'll wait until it becomes obvious to the man himself that he'd be happier somewhere else. And sooner or later, the man leaves."

The exception was a hypersensitive young bass player [Charles Mingus]. Twelve years ago, he had just joined the band for an engagement at the Apollo Theatre in Harlem. Backstage, one of the elder Ellington sidemen [Juan Tizol] suggested that the youngster did not quite comprehend the rhythm patterns of a particular Ellington piece. The bass player, feeling his musicianship had been attacked, grabbed a piece of heavy steel pipe in the wings and advanced on the older musician. At that moment, the curtain rose and the bassist reluctantly dropped his weapon. The instant the performance was over, Ellington beckoned to his road manager, pointed to the bass player, and commanded, "Pay him his two weeks—*now!*"

"I'm surprised," said another sideman at the time, "Duke didn't wait until he'd split the other guy's head open."[2]

Ellington's aversion to saying or doing anything abrasive has sometimes been interpreted through the years as lack of concern about such embattled issues as civil rights. He has made no fiery statements nor has he marched on picket lines. "People who think that of me," says the Duke, "haven't been listening to our music. For the past 25 years, social protest and pride in the history of the Negro have been the most significant themes in what we've done."

A source of particular pride to Ellington in this context is the 1963 work, "My People," a fusion of music and dance which distills the past 100 years

---

[2] Mingus tells an amusing version of the story in his autobiography, *Beneath the Underdog* (New York: Alfred A. Knopf, 1971), 323–25.

of the Negro's experience in America. Included is a confrontation between Martin Luther King and Bull Connor in Birmingham:

> And when the dog saw the baby wasn't afraid,
> He turned to his Uncle Bull and said,
> "The baby looks like he don't give a damn.
> You sure we still in Alabam?"

The climax of the work is Ellington's song, "What Color Is Virtue?"

"So," says Ellington, "we've been talking about what it is to be a Negro in this country for a long time. And we've never let ourselves be put into a position of being treated with disrespect. Including in the South. From 1934 to 1936, we went touring deep into the South, without the benefit of Federal judges, and we commanded respect. We didn't travel by bus. Instead, we had two Pullman cars and a 70 foot baggage car. We parked them in each station, and lived in them. We had our own water, food, electricity and sanitary facilities. The natives would come by and say, 'What's that?' 'Well,' we'd say, 'that's the way the President travels.'

"We made our point. What else could we have done at that time? In the years since, we've done more benefits for civil-rights groups than anybody, and I don't think there's been any doubt about how we felt concerning prejudice. But still the best way for me to be effective is through music."

The creation of that music goes on at a hurtling rate. "The man," says Billy Strayhorn of Ellington, "is a constant revelation. He's continuously renewing himself through his music. He's thoroughly attuned to what's going on *now*. He not only doesn't live in the past. He rejects it, at least so far as his own past accomplishments are concerned. He hates talking about the old bands and the old pieces. He has to play some of the Ellington standards because otherwise the audiences would be disappointed. But he'd much rather play the new things."

Among current works in progress is a ballet for the Canadian Broadcasting Company, a film project in which he hopes Ella Fitzgerald will star and several plays with music. His score for "Sugar City" (a musical comedy based on "The Blue Angel") has been completed and a Broadway production is in the planning stage.

Except when he has a firm deadline for a commissioned work, Ellington does not operate on a time-conscious writing schedule. The vast majority of his pieces are self-commissioned for his own pleasure, and because of the frequency with which new projects are added to those not yet finished, the Ellington composing agenda is always in a state of multi-directional flux. "Even the unscheduled work," Strayhorn observes calmly, "is behind schedule."

"But that's the way Duke likes to live," says trumpeter Clark Terry, an alumnus of the Ellington orchestra. "He wants life and music to be always in a state of becoming. He doesn't even like to write definitive endings to a piece. He'd often ask us to come up with ideas for closings, but when he'd settled on one of them, he'd keep fooling with it. He always likes to make the end of a song sound as if it's still going somewhere."

The prospect is firm that Ellington himself will continue on the move. He scoffs at suggestions that he sharply reduce his traveling as he approaches three score and ten.

"What would I do sitting in one place?" he argues, "How would I see all my friends? And how would I get to hear the new things I write? The history of American music is filled with guys who spent their whole lives writing and who seldom got a chance to hear what they'd done. Maybe they heard a few of their pieces a few times each. But essentially, they were creating music only for themselves. They weren't communicating. I'm in contact every night with people—live people—listening to my music. What *reason* would I have to retire from the road?"

"I hope he never does," says a member of the Ellington rhythm section. "If he did, he'd be just like Dorian Gray. He'd age overnight. No, he'll be out there as long as he can move. He's found the way to stay young. Watch him some night in the wings. Those bags under his eyes are huge, and he looks beat and kind of lonely. But then we begin to play, he strides out on the stand, the audience turn their faces to him, and the cat is a new man. Pulitzer Prize? Who could *give* a musician anything to top what Duke already has?"

74. Ellington: "The Most Essential Instrument" (1965)

Writing for the British publication *Jazz Journal,* Ellington used the occasion to praise some of his favorite musicians: pianist Willie "The Lion" Smith (1897–1973), clarinetist and saxophonist Sidney Bechet (1897–1959), and trumpeter Bubber Miley (1903–1932). He also paid tribute to a number of lesser-known pianists, among them Stephen "The Beetle" Henderson, and the Washington-born songwriter Turner Layton, Jr., composer of *After You've Gone* and *Dear Old Southland.* Ellington's enthusiastic endorsements prefigured some of the short profiles of musicians he would write later for *Music Is My Mistress* (1973).

I am delighted you have recently had the opportunity to hear Willie The Lion. He has been such a very strong influence on anybody who ever listened to him. Seriously, I mean that! Art Tatum was influenced by Willie The Lion, and anyone who can influence Art Tatum has to be *really* something, for Tatum was the greatest. And I know that is right, because Oscar Peterson says so; and so too, for that matter, does Billy Strayhorn.

Yes, Willie The Lion was the foundation. He not only had his own natural

Source: Duke Ellington, "The Most Essential Instrument," *Jazz Journal* 18/12 (December 1965), 14–15.

inclinations towards piano devices, but if he thought you worthy of instruction he would demonstrate and show you the varying styles of his predecessors and their ways and means of playing the piano. To spend an evening with The Lion was really something to experience. If you troubled to hang around for a while and listen to all that was said and played (or should I say, played and saved — that doesn't quite rhyme, but you know what I mean) you'd learn something. Those beautiful tunes and melodies he wrote, they go right back, back to the school of ragtime — the real old jazz piano players. The Eastern piano players, they all played beautifully, melodically. They would swing all the time, but they also played beautiful piano — nothing ugly, grotesque, awkward, ungainly or ungraceful about anything ever played by those who were known as the ragtime piano players. What they called whore-house music was the most beautiful, full of the most lovely melodies; the *Bulldiker's Dream* and things like that. Of course, I was never in one of those places, but that is what the big boys used to tell me. Jack The Bear, Sam Gordon and Jess[e] Pickett, who wrote *The Dream* — the things they and The Lion used to play, was really beautiful music. Also it had a tremendous beat, tremendous pulse. Yes, those piano players were really on the pretty kick. Pity I wasn't around in those days, for I would probably have been a great patron of those whore-house artists' music. That music hasn't been carried on, hasn't been bettered because you can't beat pretty — when a thing is pretty, it's just pretty. It can of course get prettier, but can you develop pretty? When something is definitely pretty, just how far can it be taken? To what degree can you develop it? If something is absolutely pretty, can it be improved upon? Or is that just gilding the lily? In other words if you find a beautiful flower, it is probably better enjoyed than analysed, because in order to analyse it, you have to pull it apart, dissect it. And when you get through you have all the formulas, all the botanical information you need, and all the science of it, but you haven't got a beautiful flower anymore. And so as Mr. Strayhorn has said, "Pretty is absolute!" In other words, when something is absolutely pretty it is its own square root — having been compounded to the nth degree. Yet as Mr. Strayhorn so kindly tells us, "square root" is hardly the word for people like us to be using, tho' one part of the word almost modifies the other, if you see what I mean. We are not squares, or to bring Mr. Strayhorn's intellectual language down to the level of the man in the street, there is no such thing as a square root, for one cannot be a square and be a root — a foundation.

But back to music: Of all the musicians Bechet to me was the very epitome of jazz. He represented and executed everything that had to do with the beauty of it all, and everything he played in his whole life was completely original. No matter what he called it, even if he did a chorus on *Clap Hands Here Comes Charlie* it was like no other version of that tune — it came out as a Bechet original. He was truly a great man and no one has ever been able to play like him. He has his own ideas and nobody could execute the music from the same perspective, accomplish the same musical ends. There have been other great musicians, Louis [Armstrong] was a great trumpeter and so-and-so was a great something else (we shouldn't compare artists ever!), but Bechet was a unique representative. I honestly think he was the most unique man ever to be in this music—but don't ever try and compare because when you talk about Bechet you just don't talk about anyone else. You understand, if I were talking about Bechet, I wouldn't talk about Hodges. Hodges plays soprano too, but Hodges learnt from Bechet, and Bechet taught Hodges who used to play closer to Bechet than anyone else ever has played. They had, in fact, somewhat of the same sort of perspective, I think, at the time that Hodges was blowing soprano. It was the same when Bechet played clarinet—no one played clarinet like him—no one! No one had the same timbre—completely wood.

Now let me make this very clear, I am talking about sounds. When you ask me about musicians, you are talking about stars; I am talking about sounds, not stars. You know Guy Lombardo had it pretty rich too—he had a jazz band called The Royal Canadians, the first time I heard them, they were a jazz band, with a rich sound—and we were a jazz band too. Paul Whiteman had a jazz band, didn't he? [Vincent] Lopez, Coon-Sanders, a whole lot of cats at that time had jazz bands. But there were only a small handful of individuals who were really unique—to my mind anyway. But we are getting too close to this comparison thing again, and I don't like to discuss it that way. Because if they are artists they can't be compared, and if you compare them, then they are no longer artists, they become something that some managing outfit has built from something. The thing is that directly you say Bechet, you get a picture—in the same way you say Armstrong you get a picture, or [Dizzy] Gillespie and you get a picture, or you say Hawk [Coleman Hawkins] you get another picture.

And then, referring to the pianists, there is Tatum, Willie The Lion, Fats Waller, James P. Johnson and of course Earl Hines, yes, definitely Hines. And that cat out in New Jersey, Donald Lambert and the Beetle [Stephen Henderson]—they were in that bracket as well. It is impossible to tell you how the Beetle played, if you haven't heard him. If you say he played "good Lion" then at once he becomes not eligible, but he played wonderful piano. He never played anywhere in particular, he didn't play regularly, or in other words he didn't have good management, like some of us have been lucky enough to have. A whole lot of great talent has been channeled down the drain, you know, because of lack of management. Of course some great management has also gone down the drain for lack of talent, but that is another story. Another person you should have heard about 40 years ago was Turner Layton—he played piano in those days. Luckey Roberts was another and Dollar Bill. I never heard Dollar Bill, but I have heard The Lion's impression of what he played. Did you ever hear Strayhorn? Hardly what you'd call a jazz pianist, he is strictly from the Strayhorn school. The first and the last of that school. Have you ever heard Ben Webster play piano? No? Well you should. Ben knows The Beetle by the way. He doesn't play what you might call professionally; piano that is, of course.

A great man, Ben, a great personality. Another of the great personalities in our jazz realm was Bubber Miley. Strayhorn doesn't like that word jazz, but this was when the word was ripe. Sometime around 1926, and that was when Bechet was with us too, and played in our band. Bubber Miley and Bechet used to sit side by side, and Bechet would blow ten choruses and then Bubber would get up with his plunger and blow another ten choruses. And so every time one would get through the other would take over while the other was resting. Then he would go back and have a *taste* and then come back fresh and full of new ideas. Oh what a pity some of those things weren't recorded! The invention, the soul invention, the musical emotion ran high. Bubber was one of the great men, in fact Bubber was the first man I heard use the expression, "it don't mean a thing if it ain't got that swing." Everything, and I repeat, everything had to swing. And that was just it, those cats really had it; they had that soul. And you know you can't just play some of this music without soul. Soul is very important. And first to play this music, you have to love music. So if you love music, then it follows you love to listen to it, which makes the ear the most essential instrument, the most essential musical instrument in the world.

75. Ellington: Program Note for "A Concert of Sacred Music" (1965)

E llington's first Sacred Concert was premiered on 16 September 1965 at Grace Cathedral in San Francisco. For the program he produced a serene philosophical statement that was reprinted for performances elsewhere and later incorporated in *Music Is My Mistress* (261–63). One phrase from his text, "Every man prays in his own language," inspired a section in the third Sacred Concert of 1973.

In this world we presume many ambitions. We make many observations such as (a) everyone's aloneness (there really are no categories, you know. Everyone is so alone—the basic, essential state of humankind); (b) the paradox that is communication—the built-in answer to that feeling of aloneness.

Communication itself is what baffles the multitude. It is both so difficult and so simple. Of all man's fears, I think men are most afraid of being what they are—in direct communication with the world at large. They fear reprisals, the most personal of which is that they "won't be understood."

How can anyone expect to be understood unless he presents his thoughts with complete honesty? This situation is unfair because it asks too much of the world. In effect, we say, "I don't dare show you what I am because I don't trust you for a minute but please love me anyway because I so need you to. And, of course, if you don't love me anyway, you're a dirty dog, just as I suspected, so I was right in the first place." Yet, every time God's children have thrown away fear in pursuit of honesty—trying to communicate themselves, understood or not—miracles have happened.

Source: Duke Ellington, program note for "A Concert of Sacred Music," given at Grace Cathedral, San Francisco, 16 September 1965. In the Duke Ellington Collection, Smithsonian Institution.

As I travel from place to place by car, bus, train, plane . . . taking rhythm to the dancers, harmony to the romantic, melody to the nostalgic, gratitude to the listener . . . receiving praise, applause and handshakes, and at the same time, doing the thing I like to do, I feel that I am most fortunate because I know that God has blessed my timing, without which no thing could have happened—the right time or place or with the right people. The four must converge.[1] Thank God.

For instance, my being invited by Dean Bartlett and the Reverend John S. Yaryan to participate at Grace Cathedral.

I am not concerned with what it costs. I want the best of everything possible. I want the best musicians, the best singers and coaches—amateur or professional—and I want them to give the best they have. I want all the help I can get and to say what I hope I am good enough to say because this is the performance of all performances—God willing.

Wisdom is something that man partially enjoys—One and only One has all the wisdom. God has total understanding. There are some people who speak one language and some who speak many languages. Every man prays in his own language, and there is no language that God does not understand.

The great organ here accompanies worship—sometimes the symphony or part of the symphony—and what could seem more suitable than a harp solo? It has been said once that a man, who could not play the organ or any of the instruments of the symphony, accompanied his worship by juggling. He was not the world's greatest juggler but it was the one thing he did best. And so it was accepted by God.

I believe that no matter how highly skilled a drummer or saxophonist might be, that if this is the thing he does best, and he offers it sincerely from the heart in—or as accompaniment to—his worship, he will not be unacceptable because of lack of skill or of the instrument upon which he makes his demonstration, be it pipe or tomtom.

If a man is troubled, he moans and cries when he worships. When a man feels that that which he enjoys in this life is only because of the grace of God, he rejoices, he sings, and sometimes dances (and so it was with David in spite of his wife's prudishness).

In this program, you may hear a wide variety of statements without words, and I think you should know that if it is a phrase with six tones, it symbolizes the six syllables in the first four words of the Bible, "In the beginning God," which is our theme. We say it many times . . . many ways.

---

[1] In 1947 Ellington had set forth the same equation: "To me, [luck] means being at the right place at the right time, and doing the right thing before the right people." See §54.

76. Rex Stewart at a Recording Session for the First Sacred Concert (1966)

Sometime between the 16 September 1965 premiere of the first Sacred Concert in San Francisco and 26 December, when the work was repeated at New York's Fifth Avenue Presbyterian Church, a recording session in Los Angeles took place.[1] The cornetist and Ellington alumnus Rex Stewart (1907–1967) attended, later publishing his impressions in the British *Jazz Journal*. Notable were his comments on Ellington's use of humor to defuse tension and the bandleader's subtle techniques for inspiring musicians to do better. Over the next two years, Stewart would write a number of perceptive articles for *Down Beat* and *Evergreen Review* about his experiences with the orchestra; these were later collected and published posthumously in *Jazz Masters of the Thirties* (New York: Macmillan, 1972; rpt., New York: Da Capo, (1982)).

For more on (and by) Stewart, see §§93 and 95.

It is many years now [1945] since I was a member of the Duke Ellington band, but I still retain strong sentimental ties and old friendships with the group. So, when I heard that the band was scheduled to record here in Los Angeles one evening recently, I arrived a few minutes before starting time— just as the bus disgorged the men. Strangely enough and very different from when I was a member, they began right on schedule.

The recording studio was not set up for visitors. In the area where folding chairs are usually set up, the Herman McCoy choir of 23 men and women were ensconced. The session had been called to record the sacred music performed by Ellington and McCoy at Grace Cathedral in San Francisco last September.

I found a spare chair over near the brass section and settled down to an evening which alternated between nostalgia and appreciation as I watched the pros in action.

Duke—always the epitome of elegance even at a casual recording date— was wearing a navy blue woven shirt with collar, blue pants and the usual custom-made Italian shoes. He was in a sporty mood too. Throughout the session he clapped out rhythm, danced little jigs and generally displayed his good humour as he directed the band. Before starting one track he called out to the engineer, "Let's cut this one without rehearsing. It'll have more emotional feeling that way."

No sooner had they started on the first take when the engineer halted them, saying "Duke, somebody's humming out there." "Oh," Duke replied, "that's me. It adds to the flavour." Shortly afterwards, Cootie Williams, master of the growl trumpet and my former section mate, complained, "Hey, Duke, I

Source: Rex Stewart, "On the Sidelines: Rex Stewart Attends a Duke Ellington Recording Session," *Jazz Journal* (January 1966), 15.

[1] The LP issued for the first Sacred Concert (*Concert of Sacred Music*, RCA LSP-3582), however, used the live performance in New York on 26 December.

haven't got any music." "Ah!," Duke said gaily, "that's because you're playing a leading role—in a secondary way." That seemed to satisfy Cootie—at the conclusion of each uninterrupted take he called out in a loud voice "That's a master!"

Duke didn't seem to hear him, nor to concur, and usually ran through the number again. After the recording session had been going about an hour Duke struck A on the piano and suggested, "Let's check and see if the piano is in tune." Dutifully the fellows tuned up again. Hidden behind an unused piece of recording equipment near my seat was a paper bag containing the "bar." This consisted of a bottle of vodka and one of bourbon. My corner became very popular as various members stopped by, paper cups in hand, ready for a little taste during five minute breaks. Again the change was evident as the elder statesmen (Johnny Hodges, Cootie Williams and Harry Carney) did not join the youngsters at taste time.

After one of these breaks, the men returned to their seats and were all ready to start when Duke suddenly turned to no one in particular and asked quizzically, "Where's the other trumpet player?" The missing man was his son, Mercer, who now holds a chair in the section in addition to his chores as road manager. He was located and again they started recording, only for a big hassle to break out between the trumpet and the trombone sections. The guys in the trombone section complained that they didn't know the sequence— were they to go back to letter D or No. 6 after 16 bars? "Overtime man, overtime," I heard one of them say to the man next [to] him. "Overtime, keep it rollin'." Two of the trombonists asked Duke what the sequence was. "There's no problem, gentlemen," answered Duke—quite unperturbed, "you all ended at the same time." But this didn't satisfy the fellows. Remarks flew back and forth across the band. "You're crazy," "You don't know what you're talking about; we go back to No. 4 after 16 bars." One man suggested "Let's do it the way I said and then we can hear if it's wrong." Next the sax section started out calling instructions too and indicating to the trombones when they were supposed to come in—advice which the trombones blithely ignored. After running the selection through four or five times one of the men pleaded, "Let's take a break Duke—we're all tensed up." Duke, ever urbane, answered with a smile, "Let's not pout gentlemen. It makes bad notes."

Some time later Duke once again called a halt. "We'll have to do that one again—the piano player sounds so good." He then played an entirely different introduction and it was of course much better!

Tom Whaley,[2] who scored the arrangements for the session, had his camera and during another take started to snap a picture. There was no click as he hadn't got the band in focus but as a clinker was hit in the trumpet section Duke stopped the band. "Get a quieter camera Tom," he said, "you made a noise and messed up that take." Everyone laughed at the absurdity. Meanwhile, the band sat continuing the discussion about the sequence, while bass

---

[2] Tom Whaley (1892–1986) began working for Ellington in 1941, serving as his chief copyist and extractor (a job earlier filled by trombonist Juan Tizol), later assisting with choral conducting for the Sacred Concerts. For an interview with Whaley, see *WDE*, 44–51.

and drums played on for about nine minutes alone. Duke made a half-hearted attempt to restore order, and suggested they did number eight of the same selection. "No?" Well then finally, Duke called out, "It has obviously been decreed that we're not going to do that number tonight—and I know the *reason.*"

So, there was to be no overtime, after all. Throughout all of this, the Herman McCoy choir stood quietly in their section of the room, but when it became time for them to lend their talents to the session, they performed very capably.

Now the band pulled out the music for another number referred to as I.B.G. which turned out to have the title *In the Beginning God.* Since the choir was to do this a capella, the band had only an introduction and a tag of four chords. Johnny Hodges searched through his stack of music but couldn't find his sheet music for the tag. "Give me the notes, Duke," he called out. Duke answered, "You only have three notes to remember. Just play the blues, old man." Eventually the session came to an end. Although faced with a trip to San Francisco that evening and they had just finished a hard night's work, the band seemed to be in good spirits. Farewells were said as they piled into the bus and drove away—it was around one in the morning.

I contemplated that today, by virtue of circumstances, I find myself in the beautiful paradoxical position of being a sort of senior alumnus of a great musical organization, and at the same time its severest critic. I can't help comparing yesteryear's band with today's extension of what I believe is the most virile force in American music. Again, I marvelled at the stamina, talent and humour of the great Duke Ellington. Like your mighty river, Duke just keeps rolling along.

77. Gary Giddins on the Sacred Concerts (1975)

After the success of the first Sacred Concert, Ellington went on to produce two more: the second, premiered at New York's Cathedral of St. John the Divine in 1968, and the third in 1973 at London's Westminster Abbey. Despite Ellington's regard for these pieces—in his memoirs, for example, he called the second Sacred Concert "the most important thing I have ever done"[1]—few critics have given them serious consideration.

One admirer, though, has been the critic Gary Giddins, who surveyed all three Sacred Concerts in a review-essay published in the *Village Voice* a year after Ellington's death. Giddins pointed out highlights, weighed strengths and weaknesses, and placed the works within the context of Ellington's total output.

Giddins (b. 1948) has written extensively about jazz since 1973, when he joined the

Source: Gary Giddins, "At the Pulpit," from *Riding on a Blue Note* (New York: Oxford University Press, 1981), 159–63. Originally published, in different form, in the *Village Voice*, 19 May 1975.

[1] *MM*, 269.

376 / THE LATE YEARS (1960–1974)

staff of the *Village Voice*. His books include three volumes of criticism, *Riding on a Blue Note: Jazz and American Pop* (1981), *Rhythm-a-ning: Jazz Tradition and Innovation in the '80s* (1987), and *Faces in the Crowd: Players and Writers* (1992), and two biographical studies, *Celebrating Bird: The Triumph of Charlie Parker* (1987) and *Satchmo* (1988).

The photograph of Duke Ellington on the cover of the album from his third sacred concert, *The Majesty of God* (RCA), is uncommonly appropriate. Standing before a microphone with his hands clasped before him, he has an unself-conscious, boyish smile on his face. His eyes are closed, whether in deference to the spotlight or a prayer isn't clear. He appears to be basking in the artificial light, and the choirboy attitude is enforced by the ruffled bow under his chin, the collar of a blue satin jacket dappled with white or silver specks. His hair, carefully groomed in front, trails anarchistically over his shoulders. The picture denies the illness ravaging his tired frame. Six months later he was dead, and there can be little doubt that he attached great significance to the last edition of what he considered his most important work, the sacred concerts.

The third sacred concert is revealing, moving, and on occasion inspired. Performed at Westminster Abbey after hasty rehearsals, it is illuminating not least for showing how Ellington coped with the insoluble problem of having outlived his band. Of the major Ellington interpreters, only Harry Carney and Russell Procope were present. Cootie Williams did not make the trip, and Paul Gonsalves, who did, was taken ill at the last minute; his solos were given to Harold Ashby, the last of the saxophonists called upon to retain the Ben Webster sound in the Ellington palette. The fine Swedish singer Alice Babs was recruited, however, and the maestro predictably focused the new work on her, Carney, and the piano. The orchestra, a shadow of its predecessors, was relegated to the background. Most of the music acquits itself admirably on its own terms.

The three sacred concerts differ in several ways, so an arc in the composer's attitude can be traced from the energetic, proudly secular *Concert of Sacred Music* (RCA), created in 1965, to the more ambitious and strenuously verbal *Second Sacred Concert* (Fantasy), in 1968, to the quietly effective last work. "These concerts are not the traditional mass jazzed up," Ellington wrote. His familiar dictum "Every man prays in his own language and there is no language that God does not understand" reminds the listener that he did not attempt to apply his genius to an established idiom, but rather to bring his own music intact to the church. The difference between playing for people, whether at the Cotton Club or Westminster Abbey, and creating for the greater glory of God, was not lost on him. When Fr. Norman O'Connor commissioned a jazz mass (apparently never completed), Ellington pondered the conflict: "One may be accustomed to speaking to people, but suddenly to attempt to speak, sing, and play directly to God—that puts one in an entirely new and different position." He prayed on his own musical terms, and celebrated the talents of his collaborators accordingly; "All the members of the band played in character," he said of the first sacred concert. He did not abandon the Cotton Club; he brought the Cotton Club revue to the pulpit.

Although the sacred concerts (hereafter SC1, SC2, and SC3) are preserved on records, it's necessary to note a quality of the music lost on disc—its aural affinity for the cavernous architecture of great churches. I did not attend any of Ellington's church services, but I recall how impressive even recorded excerpts sounded echoing through St. John the Divine at Ellington's funeral. Considering the ingenuity with which he surmounted the limitations of recording studios in the late '20s (which is why Ellington records sound so vivid compared with contemporary sides by Fletcher Henderson), it seems likely that he conceived his instrumental and vocal orchestrations in terms of the church acoustics he knew so well.

SC1 was a patchwork of the new and the old. Of the new pieces, the most important was "In the Beginning God," which occupies a third of the album. Throughout the concerts, Ellington used difficult modulations and intervals, culminating in the larynx-twisting "T.G.T.T." (SC2) and "Is God a Three-Letter Word for Love" (SC3), one of his last songs. This characteristic is evident in the first six notes of "In the Beginning God," corresponding to the first six syllables in the Bible, and nobly stated by the baritone sax of Harry Carney, who also introduced SC2. When I first heard the Brock Peters vocal, I thought it mundane; I've come to admire its generosity and lack of pretension. Ellington was ambitious, but rarely pretentious, and those works for which he wrote narratives and recitatives suffer more from sugar-coated cleverness than undue extravagance. The verities Ellington held most dear are commonplaces—love, omnipotence, glory, freedom—and he honored them simply and directly. "In the Beginning God" becomes a series of climaxes: Cat Anderson playing his high notes, Louie Bellson dazzling on drums, the choir reciting the books of the New Testament over Paul Gonsalves's cumulus clouds of tenor sax. Another new piece, a rocking, offhanded new setting for "The Lord's Prayer," sung by Esther Marrow, is undistinguished.

A couple of selections were recycled from Ellington's 1963 production *My People,* but the best of the older music originated in the '40s. "New World a-Coming" was composed for one of his Carnegie Hall concerts [1943], and later rearranged as a concerto for piano with symphony orchestra. On SC1, it is a superbly played piano solo, its jaunty spirit and tricky bass figures colored by sensitive minor-key melancholy (much of the sacred concerts is in the minor key). Of equal significance is the revamped "Come Sunday," outfitted with a new introduction, definitively performed, and thoughtfully revised from the original version in *Black, Brown and Beige.* Jimmy Hamilton's clarinet beeps reminders of the Ray Nance pizzicato-violin introduction, and there is now an interlude for Cootie Williams's trumpet and sensuous reed writing before Johnny Hodges's miraculous chorus. "David Danced Before the Lord," with tap master Bunny Briggs, brings the record to an exciting conclusion; it was originally performed in *My People,* but the music is "Come Sunday" played fast.

A change of heart overtook the composer for SC2, which consists exclusively of new music. Not content with his musical message, he added long recitatives of varying success, full of outright proselytizing. Some of the choral sections are reminiscent of school pageants, and I suspect he may have had in mind just such an application. This was one of the last times the classic Ellington band of the '60s would record, and his obsession with the project is reflected in his producing and financing the tapes himself, and then selling them to Fantasy records. Some of the melodies are dim—"Something About Believing" could have been turned out by any number of Broadway tune-smiths—and Tony Watkins's gospel shouting is a good deal less invigorating than intended.

Yet there is great Ellington here. "Praise God," a wondrous vehicle for Carney, is reprised in a thunderous finale, "Praise God and Dance," with shining performances by Alice Babs and Gonsalves. "The Shepherd" is a slow blues for Cootie Williams, with stop-time passages and shifting orchestral accompaniment. Several selections have an airy, ecumenical quality. The uneven "It's Freedom" boasts a jubilant passage based on a Willie the Lion Smith lick, and an evocative song crafted from just the word "freedom." Babs is stunning in her duets with Hodges and Procope.

The winning vocalist is at the heart of SC3, where the purity of her a capella work on "Every Man Prays in His Own Language" displays an emotional serenity one associates with the singing of children. The memorable "Is God a Three-Letter Word" brings to fruition several melodic suggestions in SC2, notably "Heaven" and "Almighty God." Ellington conjures a new and poignant unaccompanied piano setting for "The Lord's Prayer," and, on "Every Man," allows for a solo by Art Baron, on the recorder—its natural, diaphanous sound echoing with quiet awe in this hushed presentation. The scrupulously crafted "The Majesty of God" is the conclusion and highlight of the concert. Ellington's spirited piano sets the stage—a reference to "Things Ain't What They Used To Be" wafts by—and the variations are lovingly spun by Carney and Babs until the full orchestra plots the resolution.

I am told that significant portions of SC3 were edited from the record, including the final section of "The Majesty of God." Clearly there was tampering with "Every Man," since the music fades up on the third syllable of the title. There are more serious problems: Tony Watkins's feature is his most palatable on record, but his recitation in the middle of "Three-Letter Word" is disconcerting to say the least; there is a trite advertisement for the United Nations, called "The Brotherhood"; and Ellington is zealous in his declaration of faith—he has Watkins sing, "If you don't believe in God / Then brother you don't exist." Considering the evident problems with space, the inclusion of a ninety-second speech by the chairman of the UN association is puzzling and annoying; the deathless message could have been printed on the liner.

Hastily, let me repeat that these complaints should not deter anyone from hearing Ellington's final testament. Despite great adversity, he was even in these last months a perceptive and unflinching artist. Indeed, the best moments of *The Majesty of God* suggest that his art was still peaking.

78. Gary Giddins on *The Afro-Eurasian Eclipse* (1976)

G ary Giddins's interest in works from Ellington's last decade has extended beyond the Sacred Concerts (see previous section). He also found much to praise in *The Afro-Eurasian Eclipse,* a suite Ellington composed for the Monterey Festival in September 1970 and recorded the following year (though issued posthumously in 1976).

The posthumous works of no major contemporary artist have inspired greater interest than Duke Ellington's, except perhaps for Hemingway's. The '60s saw a stunning rejuvenation in Ellington the composer and the result was both a series of sacred concerts and the far more ecumenical suites based on geographical motifs. Three of the most ambitious and successful works issued on record during the last decade of his life were "The Far East Suite," "Ad Lib on Nippon," and "The Latin American Suite." But there were other suites and extended works that have never appeared on record. Moreover, there were rumors of major pieces which Ellington committed to tape but never or rarely performed. It isn't generally known what was preserved and what wasn't. In the past, he had neglected to get studio time for "The Deep South Suite" and, more incredibly, the complete "Black, Brown and Beige," so how can we be sure we'll ever hear "Timon of Athens," "Murder in the Cathedral," or "The Goutelas Suite?"[1]

Well, at least we can now be reasonably sure about "The Afro-Eurasian Eclipse," recorded by Ellington in 1971 and issued this month by Fantasy (9498). I say reasonably because the record has eight parts while the list of copyrighted compositions in "Music Is My Mistress" suggests twelve. In any case, its long-awaited release should be cause for rejoicing throughout the land.

For reasons known only to himself, Ellington chose to tease the public about the "Eclipse." He would continuously perform the first part, "Chinoiserie," preceded by a mysterious spoken introduction that included several cross-cultural references and made mention of the longer work, but he generally kept the other selections under wraps. Fantasy has included that bit of verbal shadow-play on the record and I'm glad—not only for reasons of sentiment, but because behind the hocus-pocus is a clear and revealing explanation for the travel suites in general.[2] Ellington never attempted to reproduce the music

---

Source: Gary Giddins, "Duke Eclipses the Didjeridoo," *Village Voice* (5 April 1976), 104–5.

[1] The *Goutelas Suite* was issued with the *Queen's Suite* and the *Uwis Suite* in 1976 (Pablo 2310-762). As of this writing, *Timon of Athens* and *Murder in the Cathedral* have not been issued.

[2] Ellington's spoken introduction to "Chinoiserie" on the recording is as follows: "This is really the 'Chinoiserie.' Last year about this time we premiered a new suite titled *Afro-Eurasian Eclipse*. And of course the title was inspired by a statement made by Mr. Marshall McLuhan of the University of Toronto. Mr. McLuhan says that the whole world is going oriental, and that no one will be able to retain his or her identity, not even the orientals. And of course we travel around the world a lot, and in the last five or six years we, too, have noticed this thing to be

of other cultures; his impressions were ingeniously respectful but entirely idiomatic. While quoting McLuhan's observation that cultures are losing their identity, he ironically implies that his music—remember his statement on first visiting Africa: "After writing African music for 35 years, here I am at last in Africa!"—is not only broad-based enough to encompass the rhythms, melodies, and harmonies of other musics, but can retain its own identity in the process.

Just as "Latin American Suite" was melodic in motive, "Afro-Eurasian Eclipse" is about rhythm, one-chord harmonies, and chants. This one-world music reflects the ongoing jazz tradition as well: r&b, rock 'n' roll, Albert Ayler, and Cecil Taylor are all woven into the fabric. I don't mean to suggest that Ellington consulted Taylor before sitting down at the piano for "Didjeridoo"—which is virtually a piano concerto built on the premise that the piano is a percussion instrument—but I do suggest that Ellington's genius was heightened by his sensitivity to the music of his time. Borges demonstrated that Hawthorne became a prophetic writer in the post-Kafka world; in that sense, much that is indigenous to Ellington is differently perceived in a world so manifestly altered by him. Harold Ashby's solo on "Chinoiserie" is surely avant-garde.

The "Eclipse" may be Ellington's only extended work bereft of a single brass solo. It's constructed around the reeds and the rhythm section. "Chinoiserie" is the most complex piece, alternating between eight- and 10-measure themes. It is plotted thus: A(10), A(10), B(8), C(8), A1(14), A2(10). The A-theme, strongly reminiscent of Horace Silver, is rhythmically constructed on a hesitation in the fourth beat of the second bar. The rhythmic equilibrium is deliberately tenuous: The A-theme picks up from the piano vamp—based on one note—a beat late, while the 14-measure variation on A begins a beat before expected. Following the 60-measure theme is Ashby's greatest moment on records, a gallivanting, eupeptic solo using both the eight- and 10-measure patterns, aggressively supported by Ellington's piano, and culminating in a wildly exciting stuttering, shimmying stomp over static rhythm.

"Acht O'Clock Rock" begins with two blues choruses by Ashby, followed by a 32-bar theme for piano, another two blues choruses, and 32 bars for the ensemble with Norris Turney out front. It combines openhearted r&b with ominous chord substitutions. Ellington makes the piano sound like a marimba, and I do believe I hear an organ in parts, though none is listed in the notes.[3] "Hard Way" is a 16-bar blues for Turney, with a four-measure interlude sewn

---

true. So as a result, we have done a sort of a thing, a parallel or something, and we'd like to play a little piece of it for you.

"In this particular segment, ladies and gentlemen, we have adjusted our perspective to that of the kangaroo and the didjeridoo. This automatically throws us either down under and/or out back. And from that point of view it's most improbable that anyone will ever know exactly who is enjoying the shadow of whom.

"Harold Ashby has been inducted into the responsibility and the obligation of possibly scraping off a tiny bit of the charisma of his chinoiserie, immediately after our piano player has completed his rikki-tikki."

[3] I also hear organ, probably the work of William "Wild Bill" Davis (b. 1918), who was associated with Ellington's orchestra from 1969 to 1971.

in. The inexplicably titled "True" is actually an old friend, "Tell Me the Truth," from the first Sacred Concert, but this time it's been refurbished with a bright, bustling arrangement that features Paul Gonsalves, who's in high spirits. The only movement I find less than successful is "Tang," a heady concoction that begins well enough with dissonant chords and an erupting piano figure, but proves to be an exercise in redundancy, with two themes — one 12 bars, the other eight — traded between Harry Carney and the ensemble, and a rhythm riff thrown in four times along the way. "Gong" is a blues for Ellington and Carney, with a delicious flute and clarinet chorus, and "Afrique," appropriately, is both a drum feature for Rufus Jones and an exercise in the percussion value of all the other instruments.

I've only scratched at the surface. After the "Afro-Eurasian Eclipse" one has every reason to be optimistic and avaricious in awaiting the rest of the legacy Ellington reserved for posterity.

79. Stanley Dance: "The Funeral Address" (1974)

In 1972 Ellington was diagnosed with lymphatic cancer. He nevertheless kept working steadily until January 1974, thereafter alternating between periods of convalescence and sporadic performing. His last appearance onstage occurred on 22 March 1974 in Sturgis, Michigan. Two months later, on 24 May, he died in New York City.

For the funeral service, held Memorial Day at the Cathedral of St. John the Divine, Mercer Ellington asked Stanley Dance to deliver the eulogy. Dance's text follows as it appeared in *Jazz Journal*, preceded by a brief description of the funeral by then-editor Sinclair Traill.

It was a single honour for an Englishman (and a contributor to this magazine from its first issue) to be called upon to deliver the eulogy to Duke Ellington in New York's Cathedral Church of St. John the Divine, which is nearly as big as St. Peter's. That was what happened to Stanley Dance on May 27th, 1974, when Duke Ellington's funeral service took place.

By all accounts, the service was fit for a king. As conducted by the Cathedral Staff and Pastor John Gensel, it proceeded without a hitch, and with the utmost dignity. Among the priests who officiated were Fr. John Sanders from Bridgeport, Fr. Norman O'Connor and Fr. Gerry Pocock from Montreal. Bishop Wright of New York gave the final blessing. Joe Williams and Earl Hines had both flown from Nevada at their own expense, just to be there. Joe sang *Heritage* and Earl's medley of *Mood Indigo, Solitude, I Got It Bad* and *Satin Doll* was a musical tribute of the highest order. Musicians as various as Galt McDermott and Aaron Bell both commented on its tremendous force and invention. Mary Lou Williams and a bassist played Larry Gales' *Holy Ghost,* Brock Peters recited appropriate poems by a West

Source: Stanley Dance, "The Funeral Address," *Jazz Journal* 27/7 (July 1974), 14–15. Reprinted (without the introduction) in *DEP*, 215–19.

Indian poet, one with marvelous lines about 'hawks dipping their wings' and ending with these highly appropriate lines:

> A day ends,
> A way ends
> And a world ends here.

Ella Fitzgerald had cancelled a trip to Bermuda, sang *Solitude* and *Just a Closer Walk* with Billy Taylor at the piano; McHenry Boatwright sang the *Our Father* in operatic fashion to great effect, and the cathedral organist, Alec Wyton, played a magnificent version of *Lotus Blossom*. (How prophetic that number, as played by Ellington, now seems.) In between was *Onward Christian Soldiers,* with more verses than the jazz people knew, so that they were reduced to soft scatting. The last in-person musical offering was by Ray Nance on violin with [pianist] Brooks Kerr. The previous week Ray had torn everyone apart when he played *My Buddy* at Paul Gonsalves' funeral, but this time it was Johnny Hodges who broke everybody up. The recessional consisted of recordings from the second sacred concert of Alice Babs (who had flown in from Spain) singing *Heaven* and *Almighty God.* This created a very beautiful mood, but Johnny's chorus was simply too much in the circumstances, and the tears really rolled. Count Basie and his wife were in the front row opposite the family, and he wept unashamedly during a great part of the ceremony. So many musicians were present that it would be impossible to list them all, but among those recalled were many associated with the Ellington band of yesterday and today, such as Louis Bellson, Sonny Greer, Malcolm Taylor and Aaron Bell, as well as Jonah Jones, Benny Goodman, Sy Oliver, Buddy Rich, Edgar Battle, Teddy Hill, Howard Johnson, Jo Jones, Johnny Russell and Teo Macero. Even Jack Dempsey was there.

Next morning just as his father would have done, Mercer Ellington took the band off to a two-week engagement in Bermuda. Harry Carney, still under the doctor's interdict, was replaced by Earle Warren on baritone. Percy Marion was in Paul's chair, Wulf Freedman on bass, Cootie in his usual position. Russell Procope stayed behind to play at Gregory's with Brooks Kerr and Sonny Greer. Otherwise the personnel was as before.

This eulogy of Duke Ellington was delivered at the funeral service on 27 May 1974, in the Cathedral Church of St. John the Divine, New York, by Stanley Dance.

It is hard to do justice to a beloved friend, especially when the friend was a genius of the rarest kind.

So first, the basic facts of his temporal existence:

Edward Kennedy Ellington, "Duke" Ellington, born in Washington, D.C., 1899, died in New York, 1974.

Now some might claim him as a citizen of one or the other of those cities, but he was not. In the truest sense of the phrase, he was a citizen of the world. That is a cliché perhaps, but how few are those who *deserve* it as he did. He was loved throughout the whole world, at all levels of society, by Frenchmen and Germans, by English and Irish, by Arabs and Jews, by Indians and Pakistanis, by atheists and devout Catholics, and by communists and fascists alike.

So, no, not even this city in which, as he said, he paid rent and had his mailbox—not even New York can claim him exclusively for its own.

Of all the cities he conquered—more than Napoleon, and by much better methods—I remember particularly Buenos Aires when he went there the first time. He had played his final concert and sat in the car outside the theatre before going to the airport. People clutched at him through the opened windows, people who were crying, who thrust gifts on him, gifts on which they hadn't even written their names. It was one of the few times I saw him moved to tears.

As a musician, he hated categories. He didn't want to be restricted, and although he mistrusted the word "jazz," his definition of it was "freedom of expression." If he wished to write an opera, or music for a ballet, or for the symphony, or for a Broadway musical, or for a movie, he didn't want to feel confined to the idiom in which he was the unchallenged, acknowledged master.

As with musical categories, so with people categories. Categories of class, race, colour, creed and money were obnoxious to him. He made his subtle, telling contributions to the civil rights struggle in musical statements—in *Jump for Joy* in 1941, in *The Deep South Suite* in 1946, and in *My People* in 1963. Long before black was officially beautiful—in 1928, to be precise—he had written *Black Beauty* and dedicated it to a great artist, Florence Mills. And with *Black, Brown and Beige* in 1943, he proudly delineated the black contribution to American history.

His scope constantly widened, and right up to the end he remained a creative force, his imagination stimulated by experience. There was much more he had to write, and would undoubtedly have written, but a miraculous aspect of his work is not merely the quality, but the quantity of it. Music was indeed his mistress. He worked hard, did not spare himself, and virtually died in harness. Only last fall, he set out on one of the most exhausting tours of his career. He premiered his third sacred concert in Westminster Abbey for the United Nations, did one-nighters in all the European capitals, went to Abyssinia and Zambia for the State Department, and returned to London for a command performance before Queen Elizabeth. When people asked if he would ever retire he used to reply scornfully, "Retire to *what?*"

His career cannot be described in a few minutes. Where would one start? With the composer, the bandleader, the pianist, the arranger, the author, the playwright, the painter? He was a jack-of-all-trades, and master of *all* he turned his hand to. Or should one start with the complex human being—at once sophisticated, primitive, humorous, tolerant, positive, ironic, childlike (not childish), lionlike, shepherdlike, Christian . . . ? He was a natural aristocrat who never lost the common touch. He was the greatest innovator in his field and yet paradoxically a conservative, one who built new things on the best of the old and disdained ephemeral fashion.

I certainly would never pretend that I wholly knew this wonderful man, although I spent much time in his company and enjoyed his trust. The two people who knew him best were his son, Mercer, and his sister, Ruth, and their loss is the greatest of all. Otherwise, his various associates and friends knew different aspects of him, but never, as they readily admit, the whole man.

Song titles say a good deal. *Mood Indigo, Sophisticated Lady, Caravan, Solitude, Don't Get Around Much Anymore, I'm Beginning to See the Light* and *Satin Doll* are part of the fabric of twentieth-century life. But the popular song hits are only a small part of Duke Ellington's priceless legacy to mankind.

His music will be interpreted by others, but never with the significance and tonal character given it by his own band and soloists, for whom it was written. In that respect, his records are the greatest of his gifts to us. Here one can enter a unique world, filled with his dreams, emotions, fantasies, and fascinating harmonies. He brought out qualities in his musicians they did not always know they possessed. He had the knack of making good musicians sound great, and great musicians sound the greatest. As the best arranger in the business, he was able to furnish them with superb backgrounds, and as one of the most inventive—and underrated—of pianists, he gave them inspiring accompaniment. He was, in fact, more of an inspiration than an influence, and though he made no claim to being a disciplinarian, he ruled his realm with wisdom.

The importance of this realm did not go unrecognized, and he was by no means a prophet without honour in his native land. He celebrated his seventieth birthday in the White House, where President Nixon bestowed the highest civilian honour upon him, appropriately the Medal of Freedom. Presidents Johnson, Eisenhower and Truman had all recognized his achievements in different ways. No less than seventeen colleges conferred honourary degrees upon him. Other high honours came to him from the Emperor Haile Selassie, from France and from Sweden. His likeness appeared on the postage stamps of Togoland and Chad.

Withal, Duke Ellington knew that what some called genius was really the exercise of gifts which stemmed from God. These gifts were those his Maker favoured. The Son of God said, "Fear not. Go out and teach all nations. Proclaim the good news to all men." And Duke knew the good news was Love, of God and his fellow men. He proclaimed the message in his sacred concerts, grateful for an opportunity to acknowledge something of which he stood in awe, a power he considered above his human limitations. He firmly believed what the mother he worshipped also believed, that he had been blessed at birth. He reached out to people with his music and drew them to himself.

There must be many here who can testify to his assumption—conscious or unconscious—of a father's role. Those he befriended are legion. His sense of family embraced not only the members of his band throughout the years, but people from all walks of life whose paths crossed his. Wherever or whenever he could, he personally resolved for those about him problems involving doubts, anxieties, illness or grief. Loyalty was the quality he greatly esteemed in others, and it was generously reciprocated by him.

It is Memorial Day, when those who died for the free world are properly remembered. Duke Ellington never lost faith in this country, and he served it well. His music will go on serving it for years to come.

IX. Selected Commentary and Criticism (1964–1993)

Some of the most informed and perceptive writing on Ellington—as is true for jazz and popular musicians in general—can be found outside traditional scholarly publications, appearing in journalistic essays and reviews, annotations on recordings, and program notes. The following selections bear this out. They include the work of seven writers who in recent years have made significant contributions to the Ellington literature: Max Harrison, Ralph Ellison, Martin Williams, Albert Murray, Gunther Schuller, Lawrence Gushee, and Stanley Crouch. All have been chosen for their striking insights into Ellington's work and their compelling mode of presentation.

While some of these figures have had personal or professional associations,[1] the group as a whole represents no "school" of Ellington criticism. Idiosyncratic views and differences of opinion abound. What unites them, though, is a deep admiration for Ellington's music, an understanding of its history, and an ability to describe its essential qualities in language that speaks to a wide audience—from amateur music-lovers and conservatory graduates to general students of American culture.

[1] Williams and Schuller, for example, collaborated on various recording and jazz repertory projects, and Murray and Crouch are longtime friends who have worked closely together in planning the Classical Jazz series at Lincoln Center.

80. Max Harrison: "Some Reflections on Ellington's Longer Works" (1964; revised 1991)

Since the thirties many writers have debated the merits of Ellington's longer or "extended" works. This latter term derived initially from pieces like *Creole Rhapsody* (1931) and *Reminiscing in Tempo* (1935) that took up more than one side of a 78-rpm recording, thus exceeding the usual length of roughly three minutes. Later, in the microgroove era, Ellington's temporal limits expanded considerably; longer versions of old standards described as "uncut concert arrangements" appeared on the recording *Ellington Masterpieces* (1950), while *Such Sweet Thunder* (1957) and the *Far East Suite* (1966) filled entire albums.

In the following essay, the English critic Max Harrison explores Ellington's various solutions to the problem of writing longer works, focusing on three pieces from the thirties— *Creole Rhapsody, Reminiscing in Tempo, Diminuendo and Crescendo in Blue*—and viewing them as formal models that Ellington retooled (or abandoned) later in his career. Particularly valuable are Harrison's efforts to treat the subject within the broader context of jazz history and, beyond that, in relation to European art music.

The following essay first appeared in *Jazz Monthly* in 1964 and was revised and reprinted in *A Jazz Retrospect* (1976). It was substantially revised by Harrison in 1991 for inclusion in the present volume. All footnotes are the author's.

For other articles in this volume that relate to the question of Ellington's extended works, see §§28, 42, 43, 45, 46, 55, 69, and 71. For a more general discussion of the subject, see Gunther Schuller, "The Future of Form in Jazz" (1957), reprinted in *Musings: The Musical Worlds of Gunther Schuller* (New York: Oxford University Press, 1986), 18–25.

For a biographical note on Harrison, see §62.

Once Ellington's bandsmen, particularly Bubber Miley, had awakened his interest in the potentialities of jazz and he decided "to forget all about the sweet music,"* he, like a few others, was not slow to feel dissatisfaction with the cellular structure of jazz. The best of his records from the late 1920s, even when leaning heavily on Miley's thematic inspiration, sometimes reach towards an overall unity which, if as yet musically inferior to what Jelly Roll Morton had already achieved, still aimed at transcending sequences of repeating choruses to an extent that was almost certainly beyond the older man's ambitions.

Source: Max Harrison, "Some Reflections on Ellington's Longer Works," published as "Reflections on Some of Duke Ellington's Longer Works" in *A Jazz Retrospect* (Newton Abbot: David & Charles, 1976), 121–28. Originally appeared in *Jazz Monthly* (January 1964), 12–16; newly revised by the author in 1991. (Note: Quartet Books of London reprinted *A Jazz Retrospect* in 1991.)

* *Hear Me Talkin' to Ya,* edited by Nat Shapiro and Nat Hentoff (New York, 1955).

This could only lead to attempts at getting outside the cellular format altogether and to the production of works that were not only longer but organically larger. Ellington's first move, on records at least, was his 1931 *Creole Rhapsody*, which exists in two versions* of unequal merit and rather divergent character. They are also of different lengths, having originally occupied both sides of respectively 10- and 12-inch 78-rpm discs. The latter used to be subject to almost universal condemnation, seemingly at the prompting of the English composer Constant Lambert, who reckoned that the extra length was simply the result of padding.** Grateful as ever for any acknowledgement of its music by a classicist, the jazz community for several decades parroted Lambert's cursory opinion, even although the truth is something like the opposite. The earlier version consists essentially of a number of fragments which are attractive and entail a modest indulgence in unusual phrase-lengths but which, instead of being related organically, are merely strung together. This produced striking contrasts—despite the uniform tempo—but *Creole Rhapsody* is at its weakest when Ellington, having got stuck, throws in bridging piano solos, almost literally to make ends meet.

It is evident that he was aware of these failings, even if he was not yet sure what to do about them. The second recording, made six months later, shows drastic revision, this involving the excising of most of the transitional keyboard interludes and indeed of most of the second half of the first version. These are replaced with different, better, and more lyrical material that is, however, the subject of a rather too free sequence of variations. This results in there being too many disparate types of gesture in a small space of time, and the ending is inconclusive because of this. An explicit recapitulation of the *Rhapsody*'s opening idea would have yielded a more conventional but more satisfying close. This extended version represents a genuine improvement on Ellington's quite tentative first attempt, though, and not least because its several ideas are played at an apt variety of tempos. It also receives a performance considerably superior to the rather stiff reading given its predecessor. His bandsmen have been lavishly praised for a number of good reasons, but securing adequate interpretations of his more ambitious pieces was to remain a problem for Ellington.

His longer pieces in one sense arose out of the best shorter ones like *Black and Tan Fantasy* (1927) in that these were not to be sung or danced to and did not have any function at the Cotton Club but were simply meant for listening. This part of his output improved in variety and subtle richness as the 1930s wore on, yet even the most astute listener could not have anticipated Ellington's next attempt at breaking the formal boundaries of jazz. This was *Reminiscing in Tempo*, which originally took up four 10-inch 78-rpm sides. The division, though unavoidable at the time and in one way incidental, was unfortunate in that it obscured the work's actually being in three parts corresponding to an exposition, development and modified recapitulation.

* A third version, heard on the soundtrack of the 1969 American film *Change of Mind* (directed by Robert Stevens) and in which Ellington plays a Fender-Rhodes piano, will not be considered here.
** Constant Lambert, *Music Ho!—A Study of Music in Decline* (London, 1934). [See §24. For another view of *Creole Rhapsody*, see §69].

The structure is outlined by A. J. Bishop elsewhere in this volume [see §71] and his steps need not be retraced here,* though it should be noted that, as if reacting against the excessive diversity of the revised *Creole Rhapsody*'s closing minutes, Ellington shifted the balance of his new work towards repetition. In fact there is not much development of the themes but much variation of colour, texture, key, harmony. And this is done with such resource that the piece maintains a sense of forward movement over a length that was, again, exceptional for such music. Recorded in 1935, *Reminiscing in Tempo* was indeed a brave gesture made at a time when, due to the early stirrings of swing, commercial pressures were becoming especially strong. It is also to the credit of Brunswick that they were at such a time prepared to issue, in Britain as well as the USA, a piece which, *Creole Rhapsody* aside, had no real precedent in American jazz.**

One reason for the success of *Reminiscing in Tempo* as a musical structure is that Ellington forced himself to draw maximum substance from very little material—two well contrasted main themes and a few subsidiary motives. Such formal economy was seldom in evidence later, particularly in the suites. All too often when unable to extend a structure any further he would simply invent something else. The new idea might be excellent, but it would be quite unconnected with what had gone before, and the results of this procedure might be called not compositions but compilations.

At this point it might be asked whether Ellington really understood the magnitude, or even the nature, of the task he undertook in such works. During the course of some observations on *Black, Brown and Beige,* a considerably longer work dating from 1943, the American composer Robert Crowley suggested that Ellington "lacked the knowledge and experience necessary for victory. Unity in a large-scale work, organic transition, appropriate proportions, variety and strategic placement of climaxes—the skill to secure these is not congenital, as are a good ear and melodic inventiveness. This compositional skill has to be learned, by most of us through patient and wisely-directed study. Even the genius has to learn it, if only subconsciously via thorough absorption of the works which embody its principles."† These are, of course, the masterpieces of 18th- to 20th-century European orchestral and chamber music—works that were of scant interest to jazzmen of Ellington's generation, especially in their formative years.

But the musical success of *Reminiscing in Tempo* remains, and however futile such speculations may in one sense be, its status as one of the best pieces he ever wrote brings us close to what must always stand as the great unanswerable question about him as a composer. Huge advance that it was, *Reminiscing in Tempo* compels us to ask what further would have happened if he had gone all the way along the path it opened? As is common knowledge,

---

* See also the valuable further comments in Gunther Schuller, *The Swing Era: The Development of Jazz, 1930–1945* (New York, 1989).
** There were precedents in British jazz in the shape of works by Spike Hughes, Fred Elizalde and Reginald Foresythe, but Ellington and his record company are unlikely to have been aware of them.
† Robert Crowley: "*Black, Brown and Beige* After 16 Years," in *Jazz: A Quarterly of American Music* (Spring 1959). [See §45.]

hitherto the music had been worked out in conference with his band, the procedure reportedly being, at least in the early days, one of experiment, discovery and refinement, certain things being found that were quite new to music. His style seemed to depend on this relationship, and the results were inimitable apparently because they arose from the unique timbres and melodic ideas of what in the band's most fruitful years was a group of highly individual players. This is evidently why the ensemble textures had such richness and variety. But *Reminiscing in Tempo,* presumably both versions of *Creole Rhapsody,* and certainly the forthcoming *Diminuendo and Crescendo in Blue* were fully written out, with no space for improvisation.

Despite which, these and several further Ellington pieces, among them *Black, Brown and Beige* and *The Tattooed Bride* (1948), that also do without extemporised solos still preserve that least definable of entities, the spirit of jazz. A few other jazz composers have done this, for example Tadd Dameron with *Fontainebleau* (1956). In Ellington's case it is a matter of the works still in part having been prompted by the specific skills and musical personalities of his sidemen. But their subservience to their leader's drive for personal expression remains, and one has to ask what sort of creative contribution could even the most gifted of them have made to scores such as *Reminiscing in Tempo* or *Diminuendo and Crescendo in Blue.* One thinks of Jimmy Hamilton's antiseptic clarinet solo in a later piece, *The Happy-Go-Lucky Local* (1946), which destroys the special atmosphere of that score with a completeness that is almost as disconcerting as the promptness with which it is restored the moment he stops.

A main point about *Reminiscing in Tempo* is that while *Creole Rhapsody* treated the idea of repeating chorus patterns with considerable freedom, the later work abandons it altogether. Some disappointment is experienced, therefore, on finding that *Diminuendo and Crescendo in Blue* is based on a succession of blues choruses, although in all other respects this superb 1937 composition is in its original form everything that might have been hoped for from Ellington at this point. (The sensational "success," which is to say rape and murder, of this item at the 1956 Newport Jazz Festival, while a source of great pleasure to Ellington, is irrelevant because it depended on Paul Gonsalves's absurdly over-extended 27-chorus solo, not on the character and substance of the work itself.) In fact the piece is a world away from most of what we associate with the 12-bar blues, since the choruses are of unequal lengths, appear in three slightly different harmonic variants, and in the *Diminuendo* section pass through several keys.

Restless on other levels too, its ideas, melodic and otherwise, shift from one part of the band to another quickly, unpredictably—which is to say ungoverned by divisions between choruses. There are equally abrupt switches from passages in unison to others harmonised in various quite complicated ways, and the harmony is indeed of wonderful richness. It is matched by orchestral writing that merits the same description, but the themes, or rather motives, are short, simple; in fact part of the continuing drive of *Diminuendo and Crescendo in Blue* arises from the productive tension between its simple basic materials and their complex treatment. At the same time one receives a very strong impression—here and in other scores—that melody, harmony and orchestration came to him all together.*

Alas, Ellington's masterly fusion of these elements is not completely in focus because, as in their first attempt at *Creole Rhapsody,* the band performs the piece rather stiffly. And it should be acknowledged that, like *Reminiscing in Tempo* and later pieces such as *Black, Brown and Beige* and *The Tattooed Bride, Diminuendo and Crescendo in Blue* makes demands that not even top-level jazz players were normally expected to face. Relations between the few who are jazz composers in the fullest sense and their interpreters are in fact more problematic than is assumed. The music of Thelonious Monk, for instance, demands a "thematic consciousness" from those who would improvise on it, a constant awareness of the theme's melodic intervals and idiosyncratic harmonic and rhythmic vocabularies that very few of those who have undertaken these pieces, including in the recording studio with the composer, have been able to meet. Such problems lead into the open question implied earlier as to whether Ellington, having eliminated improvisation from the works just mentioned, which are among his most daring ventures as a composer, might not have reached a more complete fulfillment of his gifts if after *Reminiscing in Tempo* he had ceased bandleading altogether.

From the viewpoint of jazz orthodoxy the suggestion is plainly heretical, and it was acknowledged above that he brought most of his earlier output into being through collaboration with his musicians. To have disbanded would therefore to have been to lose his voice? Many statements by Ellington certainly emphasise that this is what he believed. Yet works such as those dealt with here do indicate a considerable, perhaps widening, gulf between him and even the most gifted of his bandsmen in terms of sheer creative drive.** *Reminiscing in Tempo* was, at least *in potentia,* the "great leap forward" in his growth as a composer, and it suggests that he could have developed quite separately from any specific group of performers. That after all is what most composers do. Contemplating, for example, the highly original chromatic harmony of *Diminuendo and Crescendo in Blue,* one almost despairs at its further scope never having been extended on the scale it deserved and with the freedom which composers in the European tradition and its equivalents in America and elsewhere take for granted.

Unless one is a supremely great composer like Haydn, perhaps having an ensemble to play immediately whatever one writes is ultimately a distraction, providing short cuts, debarring one from the uttermost heights of independent

---

* In fact the relationship between Ellington's harmony and orchestration deserves an essay to itself.

** This point is illuminated from a completely different angle by Mercer Ellington's *Stepping into Swing Society* on Affinity (E) AFF194 (an LP made up of titles from Coral (A) CRL57225 and 57293). This consists of 1958–59 performances by large ensembles packed with Ellington sidemen playing several of his best-known pieces, but led by Mercer. There is far less sensitivity to all the parameters of music than on even the most lack-lustre Ducal session, and because nearly everything is played against a heavy beat even such pieces as *Mood Indigo* or *Black and Tan Fantasy* are robbed of their true character. Nor do players like Hodges sound much like their usual selves. Such recordings suggest that Duke Ellington's proud and famous associates owed even more to him than is generally supposed.

compositional thought. At that level there can be no short cuts, and rigorous self-criticism is an absolute necessity. True musical form is a result of process, and, as just a few pieces of Ellington's demonstrate, the best works are those which discover their own form, this being different each time and arising out of the thematic material. In some other—short—pieces such as *Concerto for Cootie* (1940), with its 10-bar phrases and fairly complex ternary structure, the easy solution of repeating chorus patterns was avoided. But after such adventures, large or small, Ellington "always returned to the most fundamental forms of the music,"* this being a great comfort to conventionally-minded jazz fans.

To have disbanded in the late 1930s would have been an extraordinarily courageous act, most people would have said a foolhardy one, partly because he was a dangerously prominent member of an oppressed minority, partly because large bands were becoming so popular. . . . The hostile receptions by trade press and fans of *Reminiscing in Tempo,* of the revised *Creole Rhapsody* earlier, of *Black, Brown and Beige* later, the virtual ignoring of *Diminuendo and Crescendo in Blue* in its original guise and of *The Tattooed Bride*—which may eventually emerge as his unacknowledged masterpiece—perhaps weighed more heavily with Ellington than they should have done. However much money his band may have cost him to keep going in later years, he appeared always to be preoccupied with success in the here and now as it has been conceived by 20th-century materialist society, above all in America. And there were further distractions, the pressures, commercial and otherwise, with which he as a bandleader had to cope, and the vast amount of travel.

Probably Ellington never had the time, still less the peace or quiet, to consider whether his gifts were reaching their truest fruition, whether he was continuing to grow as great artists always must. He was the greatest jazz has produced, yet on considering some of the dreadful music concocted for the Sacred Concerts one is tempted to suggest that any thought of growth had long since been forgotten. But as their biographies repeatedly tell us, the major masters never allow anything to distract them from their mission, no matter what the cost to themselves or others. Bartók's is a representative case. He undertook a huge quantity of ethnomusicological research necessitating long journeys in primitive conditions and resulting in a vast body of publications; he was also a magnificent and original pianist, as his many recordings prove; and in the background were his several decades' work as a piano teacher in Budapest and a voluminous international correspondence. But none of this stood in the way of the complete fulfillment of his powers as one of the greatest composers of the 20th century.

Some few of Ellington's works, particularly *Black, Brown and Beige* and especially its first movement, *Black,* use the devices of thematic fragmentation, motivic development and recapitulation, while *The Tattooed Bride* goes further. Yet they are isolated, not parts of any continuing extension of his practice as a composer even if they are entirely characteristic in their energy and in

---

* Eddie Lambert in *Jazz on Record—A Critical Guide to the First 50 Years,* edited by Albert McCarthy (London, 1968).

the strongly personalised musical language they use. Perhaps his eliminating from such pieces the improvisation which many people still imagine to be the main point of jazz led to Ellington's latter-day reluctance to see his music categorised as jazz at all. But such exceptional ventures aside, he held to jazz orthodoxy, even if his own version of it.

When "large" compositions were needed his usual response became works in the suite genre, yet this was a non-solution to, or evasion of, structural questions. All he did was to bring a number of small pieces together and think of a collective title, no large form being produced. There was also the problem of maintaining stylistic unity over several deliberately contrasted movements. This might seem to offer no difficulties to anybody with as highly evolved an idiom as Ellington, until we recall the frightful effect of the electric organ in the first movement of the *New Orleans Suite* (1970) or the mere inconsequentiality of the "finale" to *Such Sweet Thunder* (1957), which sounds as if it were run up in the recording studio at the very last moment. Worse examples occur in the *Liberian Suite* (1947), starting with Dance No. 1. An out-of-tempo section, lasting about two minutes and one of the most venturesome things Ellington ever wrote, is followed by a dialogue between tenor saxophone and ensemble. Although each part makes perfect sense in itself their juxtaposition is meaningless. And Dance No. 2 is even worse. It begins with another dialogue, a series of forceful exchanges between clarinet and the rest of the band driven by Sonny Greer in exceptional form. But this is halted by the banal entry of Tyree Glenn's vibraharp in an anti-climax so extreme as to make one laugh out loud.

Equally, as the first part of Dance No. 1 indicates, these works include passages of extraordinary inspiration, *Such Sweet Thunder* having at least two. These are *Madness in Great Ones,* where Cat Anderson's high-note virtuosity is turned to acutely expressive ends with something like the power of genius, and *Sonnet for Caesar,* which has a nobility that is indeed rare in jazz and not exactly common elsewhere. The Shakespearean labellings of this particular collection, like the alleged travelogue of the *Far East Suite* (1966), were another factitious device to impose unity from outside, and Ellington's titles are routinely described as "evocative." However, if we remember that it was, for instance, at first intended to call a certain 1940 piece not *Harlem Air Shaft* but *Rumpus in Richmond* we may wonder how much evocation is going on.

Altogether more desperate as attempts at maintaining stylistic consistency over several movements were Ellington's grotesque assaults on major and minor European masters. The complaint is not about "jazzing the classics," for the originals survive intact for those who want them. Rather is the complaint that he could, in these cases, find nothing better to do with his unique powers. It is a very long way down from great adventures like *Reminiscing in Tempo* to the contemptible Tchaikovsky and Grieg manipulations of 1960, which in their worst moments anticipate the depths of Stan Kenton's Wagner LP (1964). But this lack of creative confidence was sometimes apparent elsewhere. An example is the appalling 1956 remake of *Ko-Ko,* which many would argue was in its 1940 version the greatest single Ellington record. Its essential qualities are obliterated in the later malperformance as surely as are those of Grieg or Tchaikovsky.* This is all too vivid an illustration of the penalties of trying to repeat one's past triumphs instead of outgrowing them. But no matter what his abject hagiographers say, Ellington's output is full of closely-packed specimens of good and bad, just like the production of all other highly prolific composers, great and small.

Obviously the finest of them were much better than merely "good," revealing an indisputable master of his language, in which he said many things that nobody else could have said. Yet that mastery worked consistently in the short term only. If we make a list of his longer pieces, including even the weakest, they amount to only a small body of music amidst the 2000-odd items that he is reported to have produced. Whatever their quality, the big pieces are exceptions which prove no rule.

Surely it is symbolic that several of them, including *The Happy-Go-Lucky Local, Harlem* (1951) and *The Beautiful Indians* (1946), lean back to the 19th-century European concept of the tone poem, for which Ellington's substitution was "tone-parallel." This idea surfaced elsewhere, in the character studies of John Lewis's *The Comedy* (1960–62) for the Modern Jazz Quartet, in Charles Mingus's sometimes onamatopoeic *Pithecanthropus Erectus* (1956). But in these cases organically larger, and quite different, forms were achieved. It was done in other places, on the one hand with Ornette Coleman's seamless tenor saxophone solo in *Cross Breeding* (1961), on the other with the large band version of George Russell's *Electronic Sonata for Souls Loved by Nature* (1970). It is sadly ironic that, despite the ambition which drove him to bring forth such an enormous quantity of music, these peaks were scaled in locations remote from the Ellington camp. Perhaps those who come after us will be able to decide whether this was a judgment on one who might have become one of our century's greatest composers but who instead persisted in leading a band.

81. Ralph Ellison: "Homage to Duke Ellington on His Birthday" (1969)

A special ceremony marking Ellington's seventieth birthday was held at the White House on 29 April 1969. Many musicians and dignitaries attended, and Ellington later described the event with delight, recalling how President Nixon had played "Happy Birthday" and Willie "The Lion" Smith had performed wearing his trademark derby.[1]

Two days earlier, the distinguished writer Ralph Ellison had offered the following tribute to Ellington in the *Washington Star*. Interweaving personal reflections with a probing analysis

---

* See André Hodeir's comments on this recording in "Why Did Ellington 'Remake' His Masterpiece?" [§61].

Source: Ralph Ellison: "Homage to Duke Ellington on His Birthday," *Sunday Star* (Washington, D.C.), 27 April 1969, reprinted in *Going to the Territory* (New York: Random House, 1986), 217–26.

[1] *MM*, 424–28.

of Ellington's contributions to American culture, Ellison's essay celebrated "our most important indigenous art form in the person of its most outstanding creator."

Ellison (b. 1914) received early musical training in his native Oklahoma City and at Tuskegee Institute before embarking on a literary career. His major works are the novel *Invisible Man* (1952) and two collections of essays, *Shadow and Act* (1964) and *Going to the Territory* (1986).

It is to marvel: the ageless and irrepressible Duke Ellington is seventy, and another piano player of note, President Richard M. Nixon, has ordered in his honor a state dinner to be served in the house where, years ago, Duke's father, then a butler, once instructed white guests from the provinces in the gentle art and manners proper to such places of elegance and power. It is good news in these times of general social upheaval that traces of the old American success story remain valid, for now where the parent labored the son is to be honored for his achievements. And perhaps it is inevitable that Duke Ellington should be shown the highest hospitality of the nation's First Family in its greatest house, and that through the courtesy of the chief of state all Americans may pay, symbolically, their respects to our greatest composer.

Perhaps it is also inevitable (and if not inevitable, certainly it is proper) that that which a Pulitzer Prize jury of a few years ago was too insecure, or short-sighted, to do, and that which our institutions dedicated to the recognition of artistic achievement have been too prejudiced, negligent, or concerned with European models and styles to do, is finally being done by Presidents. For it would seem that Ellington's greatness has been recognized by everyone except those charged with recognizing musical excellence at the highest levels—and even some of these have praised him privately while failing to grant him public honor.

Nevertheless, he is far from being a stranger to the White House, for during the occupancy of President and Mrs. Lyndon B. Johnson, Ellington became something of a regular guest there, and indeed, it was President Johnson who appointed him to the National Council on the Arts, thereby giving recognition to our most important indigenous art form in the person of its most outstanding creator. Certainly there is no better indication that those on the highest levels of governmental power have at last begun to recognize our arts and their creators as national treasures. Perhaps in Ellington's special case this is a proper and most fitting path to official national recognition, since for more than forty years his music has been not only superb entertainment but an important function of national morale. During the Depression whenever his theme song "East St. Louis Toodle-Oo" came on the air, our morale was lifted by something inescapably hopeful in the sound. Its style was so triumphant and the moody melody so successful in capturing the times yet so expressive of the faith which would see us through them. And when the "Black and Tan Fantasy" was played we were reminded not only of how fleeting *all* human life must be, but with its blues-based tension between content and manner, it warned us not only to look at the darker side of life but also to remember the enduring necessity for humor, technical mastery, and creative excellence. It was immensely danceable and listenable music and ever so evocative of other troubled times and other triumphs over disaster. It was also most Negro American in its mocking interpolations from Chopin's B-flat minor piano sonata to which, as Barry Ulanov has reminded us, it was once popular to sing the gallows-humored words: "Where shall we all / Be / A hundred years / From now?"

And how many generations of Americans, white and black, wooed their wives and had the ceremonial moments of their high school and college days memorialized by Ellington's tunes? And to how many thousands has he brought definitions of what it should mean to be young and alive and American? Yes, and to how many has he given a sense of personal elegance and personal style? A sense of possibility? And who, seeing and hearing Ellington and his marvelous band, hasn't been moved to wonder at the mysterious, unanalyzed character of the Negro American — and at the white American's inescapable Negro-ness?

Even though few recognized it, such artists as Ellington and Louis Armstrong were the stewards of our vaunted American optimism and guardians against the creeping irrationality which ever plagues our form of society. They created great entertainment, but for them (ironically) and for us (unconsciously) their music was a rejection of that chaos and license which characterized the so-called jazz age associated with F. Scott Fitzgerald, and which has returned once more to haunt the nation. Place Ellington with Hemingway, they are both larger than life, both masters of that which is most enduring in the human enterprise: the power of man to define himself against the ravages of time through artistic style.

I remember Ellington from my high school days in Oklahoma City, first as a strangely familiar timbre of orchestral sounds issuing from phonograph records and radio. Familiar because beneath the stylized jungle sounds (the like of which no African jungle had ever heard) there sounded the blues, and strange because the mutes, toilet plungers, and derby hats with which I was acquainted as a musician had been given a stylized elegance and extension of effect unheard of even in the music of Louis Armstrong. It was as though Ellington had taken the traditional instruments of Negro American music and modified them, extended their range, enriched their tonal possibilities. We were studying the classics then, working at harmony and the forms of symphonic music. And while we affirmed the voice of jazz and the blues despite all criticism from our teachers because they spoke to a large extent of what we felt of the life we lived most intimately, it was not until the discovery of Ellington that we had any hint that jazz possessed possibilities of a range of expressiveness comparable to that of classical European music.

And then Ellington and the great orchestra came to town; came with their uniforms, their sophistication, their skills; their golden horns, their flights of controlled and disciplined fantasy; came with their art, their special sound; came with Ivy Anderson and Ethel Waters singing and dazzling the eye with their high-brown beauty and with the richness and bright feminine flair of their costumes, their promising manners. They were news from the great wide world, an example and a goal; and I wish that all those who write so knowledgeably of Negro boys having no masculine figures with whom to identify would consider the long national and international career of Ellington and his band, the thousands of one-night stands played in the black communities of this nation. Where in the white community, in *any* white community, could there have been found images, examples such as these? Who were so worldly, who so elegant, who so mockingly creative? Who so skilled at their given trade and who treated the social limitations placed in their paths with greater disdain?

Friends of mine were already collecting Ellington records, and the more mature jazzmen were studying, without benefit of formal institutions of learning, his enigmatic style. Indeed, during the thirties and forties, when most aspiring writers of fiction were learning from the style and example of Hemingway, many jazz composers, orchestrators, and arrangers were following the example of Ellington, attempting to make something new and uniquely their own out of the traditional elements of the blues and jazz. For us, Duke was a culture hero, a musical magician who worked his powers through his mastery of form, nuance, and style, a charismatic figure whose personality influenced even those who had no immediate concern with the art of jazz.

My mother, an Afro-American Methodist Episcopalian who shouted in church but who allowed me nevertheless to leave sunrise Christmas services to attend breakfast dances, once expressed the hope that when I'd completed my musical studies I'd have a band like Ellington's. I was pleased and puzzled at the time, but now I suspect that she recognized a certain religious element in Ellington's music—an element which has now blossomed forth in compositions of his own form of liturgical music. Either that, or she accepted the sound of dedication wherever she heard it and thus was willing to see Duke as an example of the mysterious way in which God showed His face in music.

I didn't meet Ellington at the time. I was but a young boy in the crowd that stood entranced around the bandstand at Slaughter's Hall. But a few years later, when I was a student in the music department at Tuskegee, I shook his hand, talked briefly with him of my studies and of my dreams. He was kind and generous even though harassed (there had been some trouble in travel and the band had arrived hours late, with the instruments misplaced and the musicians evil as only tired, black, Northern-based musicians could be in the absurdly segregated South of the 1930s), and those of us who talked with him were renewed in our determination to make our names in music.

A few years later, a stranger in Harlem, I lived at the YMCA and spent many a homesick afternoon playing Duke's records on the jukebox in Smalls' Paradise Bar, asking myself why I was in New York and finding reassurance in the music that although the way seemed cloudy (I had little money and would soon find it necessary to sleep in the park below City College), I should remain there and take my chances.

Later, I met Langston Hughes, who took me up to Sugar Hill to visit the Duke in his apartment. Much to my delight, the great musician remembered me, was still apologetic because of the lateness of the band's arrival at Tuskegee, and asked me what he could do to aid the music department. I suggested that we were sadly deficient in our library of classical scores and recordings, and he offered to make the school a gift of as extensive a library of recordings as was needed. It was an offer which I passed on to Tuskegee with great enthusiasm, but which, for some reason, perhaps because it had not come directly from Ellington himself or perhaps because several people in the department regarded jazz as an inferior form of music, was rejected. That his was a genuine gesture, I had no doubt, for at the time I was to see a further example of his generosity when Jimmie Lunceford's orchestra, then considered an Ellington rival, came on the radio. The other musicians present kidded Ellington about the challenge of Lunceford's group, to which he responded by listening intently until the number was finished and then commenting "Those boys are interesting. They are trying, they are really trying," without a trace of condescension but with that enigmatic Ellington smile. The brief comment and the smile were enough, the kidding stopped, for we had all been listening—and not for the first time—and we knew that Duke had little to fear from the challenge of Lunceford or anyone else.

Somewhere during his childhood a friend had nicknamed Edward Kennedy Ellington "Duke," and he had proceeded to create for himself a kingdom of sound and rhythm that has remained impregnable to the fluctuations of fad and novelty, even the passing on of key members of his band.

Jazz styles have come and gone and other composer-conductors have been given the title "King of Jazz" and Duke knew the reason why, as did the world—just as he knew the value of his own creation. But he never complained, he simply smiled and made music. Now the other kings have departed, while his work endures and his creativity continues.

When the Pulitzer Prize committee refused to give him a special award for music (a decision which led certain members of that committee to resign), Ellington remarked, "Fate is being kind to me. Fate doesn't want me to be too famous too young," a quip as mocking of our double standards, hypocrisies, and pretensions as the dancing of those slaves who, looking through the windows of a plantation manor house from the yard, imitated the steps so gravely performed by the masters within and then added to them their own special flair, burlesquing the white folks and then going on to force the steps into a choreography uniquely their own. The whites, looking out at the activity in the yard, thought that they were being flattered by imitation and were amused by the incongruity of tattered blacks dancing courtly steps, while missing completely the fact that before their eyes a European cultural form was becoming Americanized, undergoing a metamorphosis through the mocking activity of a people partially sprung from Africa. So, blissfully unaware, the whites laughed while the blacks danced out their mocking reply.

In a country which began demanding the projection of its own unique experience in literature as early as the 1820s, it was ironic that American composers were expected to master the traditions, conventions, and subtleties of European music and to force their own American musical sense of life into the forms created by Europe's greatest composers. Thus the history of American classical music has been marked by a struggle to force American experience into European forms.

In other words, our most highly regarded musical standards remained those of the Europe from which the majority of Americans derived. Fortunately, however, not all Americans spring from Europe (or not only from Europe), and while these standards obtained, Negro American composers were not really held to them, since it seemed obvious that blacks had nothing to do with Europe—even though during slavery Negroes had made up comic verses about a dance to which "Miss Rose come in her mistress's clothes / But how she got them nobody knows / And long before the ball did meet / She was dancing Taglioni at the corner of the street . . ." Taglioni being a dancer who was the rage of Europe during the 1850s.

Be that as it may, the dominance of European standards did work a hardship on the Negro American composer because it meant that no matter how inventive he might become, his music would not be considered important—or even American—(1) because of his race and (2) because of the form, if he was a jazzman, in which he worked. Therefore, such a composer as Ellington was at odds with European music and its American representatives, just as he was at odds with the racial attitudes of the majority of the American population, and while primarily a creative composer, he was seen mainly in his role as entertainer. Doubtless this explains the withholding from Ellington of the nation's highest honors.

It isn't a matter of being protected, as he suggests, from being too famous too young—he is one of the world's most famous composers and recognized by the likes of Stravinsky, Stokowski, and Milhaud as one of the greatest moderns—but the fact that his creations are far too *American*. Then there is also the fact of Ellington's aura of mockery. Mockery speaks through his work and through his bearing. He is one of the most handsome of men, and to many his stage manners are so suave and gracious as to appear a put-on—which quite often they are. And his manner, like his work, serves to remind us of the inadequacies of our myths, our legends, our conduct, and our standards. However, Ellington's is a creative mockery in that it rises above itself to offer us something better, more creative and hopeful, than we've attained while seeking other standards.

During a period when groups of young English entertainers who based their creations upon the Negro American musical tradition have effected a questionable revolution of manners among American youths, perhaps it is time we paid our respects to a man who has spent his life reducing the violence and chaos of American life to artistic order. I have no idea where we shall all be a hundred years from now, but if there is a classical music in which the American experience has finally discovered the voice of its own complexity, it will owe much of its direction to the achievements of Edward Kennedy Ellington. For many years he has been telling us how marvelous, mad, violent, hopeful, nostalgic, and (perhaps) decent we are. He is one of the musical fathers of our country, and throughout all these years he has, as he tells us so mockingly, loved us madly. We are privileged to have lived during his time and to have known so great a man, so great a musician.

82. Martin Williams: "Form Beyond Form" (1970; revised 1983, 1993)

Martin Williams's *The Jazz Tradition* presents a series of chronologically arranged critical essays on major musicians, from King Oliver to Ornette Coleman. The tenth chapter, "Form Beyond Form," remains one of the best capsule introductions to Ellington's art. In it, Williams traces the composer's development from the mid-twenties through the early forties, pausing occasionally to describe pieces in detail, then moving on to show Ellington revising, borrowing from earlier works, extending techniques, and integrating new instrumental voices in his ensemble. Formal aspects are of particular interest to Williams, who points out some of the imaginative ways in which Ellington built new pieces upon older structures. Although Williams cites a few notable works from the fifties and sixties, he concentrates mainly on the period leading up to 1940—the year in which he claims Ellington brought his talent "to a fulfillment."

In the fifties and sixties Williams (1924–1992) wrote on jazz for a variety of publications, among them *Saturday Review, Evergreen Review, Down Beat,* and *The Jazz Review* (which he co-founded and co-edited with Nat Hentoff from 1958–1961). Later Williams worked at the Smithsonian Institution in Washington, D.C., where he carried out various projects relating to jazz and American music: producing concerts, reissuing recordings, publishing books and scores, and advising musicians and educators. In addition to *The Jazz Tradition,* his books on jazz include *Where's the Melody? A Listener's Introduction to Jazz, Jazz Heritage,* and *Jazz Changes.* He compiled and annotated *The Smithsonian Collection of Classic Jazz* record set and (with Gunther Schuller) *Big Band Jazz.*

Main Stem was recorded in 1942 and therefore comes from a great period for Duke Ellington as a composer, orchestrator, and leader of a large jazz ensemble. I am not sure that it is one of the masterpieces of that period, but it is at least excellent. On the face of it, *Main Stem* may seem casual enough: a blues in a relatively fast tempo. It opens with a theme played by the orchestra, followed by a succession of one-chorus solos by sidemen, and a final return to the theme. It is a big band blues, then, apparently like many another casually conceived and executed big band blues of the time.

The opening chorus of *Main Stem* is its twelve-bar theme. But the theme involves some interesting accents and phrases; it is not the usual repeated two-bar riff moved around to fit blues chords. Then there is its orchestration: a casual listening would probably not reveal which instruments and which combinations of instruments are playing what. Also, there is an interplay of accents from the brass: the phrasing and the manipulation of plunger mutes by the trumpets set up one kind of rhythm, while a more conventional accentuation of notes sets up a different pattern.

The second chorus offers Rex Stewart's cornet, apparently taking over for the band's recently departed plunger-mute soloist, Cootie Williams. However,

Source: Martin Williams, "Form Beyond Form," Chapter 10 of *The Jazz Tradition* (New York: Oxford University Press, 1970; 2nd revised ed., 1993), 94–114.

the chorus is not a solo but an antiphonal episode in which the saxophones deliver simple statements—simple, but taking off from one of the phrases in the opening theme—to which Stewart gives imitative, puzzled, plaintive, or humorous responses. Next is an alto saxophone solo by Johnny Hodges, and Hodges the melodist is left to himself with no background but the rhythm section. Then Stewart returns in his own style. He gets a background, with saxes predominating, obviously in contrast to his own brass instrument. But the background is also an imaginatively simplified version of the opening theme. Then trumpeter Ray Nance solos, and behind him the theme returns more strongly, almost exactly. The next soloist is clarinetist Barney Bigard; he juxtaposes a melodic fragment, suggested by the theme, over still another simplification of the theme, this time appropriately scored with the brass predominating. And behind Joe Nanton's plunger-muted trombone solo there is another sketch of the main melody, this one with saxes predominating.

Perhaps *Main Stem* approaches monotony at this point. What we hear next begins with a six-measure modulatory transition, almost lyric in contrast to what has preceded it. Then there are four measures by the ensemble and a fourteen-measure solo by Ben Webster, the hint of lyricism continuing in his accompaniment. We are into a second section of *Main Stem*. Webster's earnestness is followed by another four measures from the ensemble and a fourteen-measure virtuoso trombone solo by Lawrence Brown, but with a brass accompaniment that is increasingly rhythmic, preparing for what follows. And what comes next is a recapitulation of the opening theme, but not an exact one. As if to balance both sections of the piece, Ellington extends the twelve-bar theme with an eight-measure coda.

Main Stem, then, with such organization and unity, is a far from casual performance. Yet it is relatively casual for Duke Ellington.

I suppose it is the greatest tribute to Ellington's music that, from *The Duke Steps Out* and *Ring Dem Bells* on, some of his most effective pieces have basically been strings of solos by his musicians. Yet those pieces are truly Ellington works, and not just because his soloists are men whose styles we associate with Ellington. It is a high achievement to have been able to parade Rex Stewart, Johnny Hodges, Stewart again, Ray Nance, Barney Bigard, Joe Nanton, Ben Webster, and Lawrence Brown in rapid succession on *Main Stem* without overloading, and with no loss of the effect of a single, purposeful piece of music. And when one notes the details of theme-orchestration, background, and transitional scoring that contribute variety and yet help make such unity of effect possible, one also notes that these group effects are essentially simple—and very nearly perfect. And how perceptively Ellington could use, for example, the very special qualities and limitations of Nanton's trombone, Stewart's cornet, and Bigard's clarinet.

Duke Ellington lived long enough to hear himself called our greatest composer, or at least to have it acknowledged that the decision would be between his accomplishments and those of Charles Ives. Ellington left an enormous body of music: simple songwriting; theater songs; background music for dramatic films and television melodrama; solo piano works; duets for piano and bass; music for small jazz ensembles from sextet through octet; hundreds of short instrumental compositions for jazz orchestra; extended works, usually suites, for large jazz ensemble, sometimes with singers and (for the later "sacred" concerts) also with tap dancers; works for jazz ensemble and symphony orchestra combined. But Ellington's core reputation depends on his skill and art as a composer-orchestrator of instrumental miniatures for his orchestra.

Ellington is probably the largest and most challenging subject in American music for our scholars, our critics, our musicologists, our music historians. And I do not intend here to undertake a survey of his career or an evaluation of his output. But perhaps I can suggest some ways in which he moved from his rather curious beginnings on records to the masterpieces of 1939–42; that is, give an account of some aspects of his development from, say, *I'm Gonna Hang Around My Sugar* in late 1925 to *Ko-Ko* and *Dusk* in 1940—or perhaps from *Choo Choo* in 1924 all the way to that wonderful 1947 alliance of atonality and Harlem strut, *The Clothed Woman*.

Ellington's very earliest recordings may seem to preserve an inauspicious beginning for a major talent; they may make him seem a jazz musician on the wrong track, even in danger of derailment; or in some ways they may make him seem no jazz musician at all. They are stiff rhythmically and they abound in the superficial jazziness of the period. But I think we can now see that, for him, Ellington was on the right track.

If You Can't Hold the Man You Love imitates King Oliver's Creole Jazz Band, and does not do it very well. But in *Rainy Nights,* Ellington showed that he had gone to the right source to learn what would be most useful to him about orchestrated jazz. It is apparently impossible to be sure about which came first, but *Rainy Nights,* credited to "Trent, Donaldson, and Lopez" as composers, is the same piece, and has a similar arrangement, as Fletcher Henderson's *Naughty Man,* credited to "Dixon and Redman" and arranged by Don Redman.

Ellington also had several strong instrumentalists, including trumpeter Bubber Miley. And as we shall see, it was Miley particularly as the dramatic soloist and the carrier of strong, sometimes indigenous themes who affirmed for Ellington the nature of his destiny as a leader of a jazz orchestra. Although there are some few questionable moments in his playing on the early records, Miley was obviously an authentic and developed jazz musician. And through Miley we can gain insight into how much feeling and expressive depth might be retained in a developing and increasingly sophisticated instrumental music.

The earliest recorded Ellington is basically in the dance band style of the day, but a fairly sophisticated version of that style. From just such music, and from Fletcher Henderson's particularly, Ellington first absorbed the basis on which to build his own. He needed ideas of harmony, melody, orchestral color, and form, and, like all jazzmen in all periods, he readily absorbed many ideas from the music he heard around him, then sifted them, and soon learned to transmute and expand them into a musical language that became distinctly his own.

I do not mean to dismiss the Ellington of 1924 through early 1926— Ellington before *East St. Louis Toodle-Oo* and *Birmingham Breakdown.*

Besides Miley's work on several of them, there is *L'il Farina,* with its succession of solos, which compares favorably with the orchestral jazz being recorded in New York at the time. In *Choo Choo* we meet Ellington the composer and, especially in its chord pattern, meet him interestingly.

Then there is the fact that Ellington's piano (what one can hear of it on these records) reflects his upbringing in the Eastern "stride" school. The traditions of that school may possibly go back even earlier than the ragtime style of the late 1890s, but its players did learn from the great rag men, and by the middle 1920s stride piano was at a peak in New York. All of the stride men were interested in technical expansion and were busily absorbing everything they could from musical comedy scores and "light classics"—even some heavier ones. There are times when the stride men seem bent on developing a kind of Afro-American version of "proper" parlor piano. Admittedly, few of them could play with real blues feeling, and most of them were a bit stiff rhythmically compared to the New Orleans men. But each of them felt required to evolve his own style, settle on his own harmonic devices, and I think such standards tellingly influenced Ellington's ideas of music. Also, the stride style is largely orchestral; it imitates a band.

In retrospect, we can say that Ellington faced three basic problems in his first fifteen years as a band leader and composer with a potentially unique orchestral language to offer. He needed to bring his own inquisitive urbanity and relative sophistication into some kind of balance with the sometimes earthier and more robust talents of his sidemen. Ellington also needed to come to terms with the innovations of the New Orleans players, and with the brilliant elaborations of those innovations that Louis Armstrong was making. Symbolically at least, Louis Armstrong would have to be brought into the orchestra.

Also, the stride piano style held limitations for Ellington as an orchestrator by its very nature. As it imitated a band, so Ellington's early orchestrations imitated the piano keyboard virtually finger by finger. Gunther Schuller points out that Ellington's early approach to orchestration is succinctly revealed if we compare the piano and orchestra versions of *Black Beauty* from 1928. Ellington's third problem, then, was to learn to write directly for his horns without taking the route through his keyboard.

In late 1926 Ellington began recording Bubber Miley's pieces—*East St. Louis Toodle-Oo* was the first. He was also still acquiring other outstanding instrumentalists: Nanton was present and baritone saxophonist Harry Carney [by 1927], and two years later, Johnny Hodges and Barney Bigard.

Late 1927 saw a crucial event in Ellington's career. King Oliver turned down an offer from a swank Harlem night club, the Cotton Club, and Ellington took the job. It meant steady work and keeping the orchestra together. It also meant national fame through nightly broadcasts. Most important, it meant playing the Club's shows, its miniature revues. In working on these shows; in preparing overtures, chorus dances, accompaniments to specialty dances, "production" numbers; in working with featured singers and contributing some of their songs; in preparing musical transitions and "filler," Ellington began to discover what kind of music he was to make, and he began his singular expansion of the orchestral language. Ellington took the idiom that Miley represented, took what he had learned from Redman and Henderson, took his own innate urbanity, and in effect started all over again with a new approach to the large ensemble. King Oliver had tried a big band style that basically substituted a reed section (saxophones frequently doubling on clarinets), with written parts, for the single improvising clarinet of his earlier New Orleans group. And Redman and Henderson had converted the American dance band, with its compartmentalized reed, brass, and rhythm sections, into a jazz band. Ellington now made his big band over by making it also a show band, a theater orchestra.

Some of the sketches and production numbers in the Cotton Club shows were lurid affairs, with "jungle" nonsense, or sheiks kidnapping fair maidens, etc., and the music occasionally had to be bizarre and always immediate in its effect. Ellington approached his tasks with his own kind of urbane but optimistic irony, and he could use preposterous titles like *Jungle Nights in Harlem* for the benefit of the "slumming" white crowds at the club at the same time that he was expanding the sonorities, the color, the orchestrational resources of his ensemble and creating a memorable and durable music. The superficially sensational and quasi-primitive effects actually had a deeper role: they were kept quite musical and compositionally intrinsic, and they were a means of exploration and growth for the orchestrator and the orchestra.

Stanley Dance reminded us in his eulogy at the composer's death that Edward Kennedy Ellington retained his youthful nickname because he was a natural aristocrat. He was also a democratic aristocrat. Much as the great dramatists have worked with the talents of their lead actors and the resources of their companies, and the great dance directors have learned to work with the accomplishments and potential of their dancers, the great European composers with specific instrumentalists and singers, each learning from the other, so Ellington worked with his sidemen.

Ellington not only learned to cut across the compartmentalized trumpet, trombone, and reed sections of other jazz orchestras but he came to know he was scoring for the individuals in his ensemble and their sounds. He thereby became the jazz composer *par excellence*. He knew that Harry Carney's baritone sound was crucial to the sound of his saxophones and to the sound of his orchestra. But what genius was it that told Ellington not to score Carney's sound always as the *bottom* of his harmonies, where it might seem to belong, but move it from one position to another for its strongest effect? Indeed Ellington was so attuned to the sounds of his men that the very originality of his textures and the daring of his harmonic language were determined not in the abstract but in his inquisitiveness about, let us say, how this reed player's low A-flat might sound when juxtaposed with that brassman's cup-muted G.

Ellington's works were produced in an atmosphere of improvisation and experiment. The solos usually came from the soloists, and, as alternate "takes" and the surviving broadcast versions confirm, the players were free to stick to them from one performance to the next. They were also free to reinterpret and ornament them, and—depending on the context and if so moved—to reject them and come up with new solos.

All the great Ellington works depend on a relationship between soloist and group, between what is written (or perhaps merely memorized) and what may be extemporized, between the individual part and the total effect, and a relationship among beginning, middle, and end. A great Ellington performance is not a series of brilliant episodes but a whole greater than the sum of its parts. He learned how to discipline improvisation and extend orchestration—to the enhancement of both.

Ellington was coaxing a temperamental and brilliant group of soloists and players into discovering and developing their own best resources, into contributing constantly to the act of mutual composition, orchestration, and performance, and paradoxically into integrating their own talents into a total effect.

There is a moment in *Shout 'Em Aunt Tillie* that I think is a small but succinct revelation of Ellington's role. It is his striking and original piano accompaniment to Cootie Williams's solo. His left hand is not striding, and in rhythm, sound, melody, and harmonic relationship to the soloist, the piano becomes an effective piece of contrasting orchestration. The maturing Ellington learned to think directly as an orchestrator—a jazz orchestrator—even when playing piano.

As Gunther Schuller has pointed out, there was an imbalance in the earlier works with Miley, as exciting and important as they are. The first important Ellington-Miley collaboration, *East St. Louis Toodle-Oo,* is impressive, but Miley's anguished *wa-wa* horn dominates it, as it does the second important joint work, *Black and Tan Fantasy.* Ellington's orchestral effects and secondary themes seem weak, out of place, and perhaps affected by comparison. *Creole Love Call,* another early collaboration, is better balanced perhaps because Ellington did not contribute any thematic material.

In their later versions, both *East St. Louis Toodle-Oo* and *Black and Tan Fantasy* are improved works, less dominated by the themes and the interpretations of a single musician, more balanced and appropriate in the contributions of their orchestrator-leader.

Miley's contribution to *East St. Louis Toodle-Oo* is a dramatic combination of themes in AABA song form. Ellington surely added the piece's third theme, a melody intended for contrast. But it seems a rather inappropriate melody, and it employs almost archaic ragtime-like accents—indeed, it suggests one of the themes in Scott Joplin's *Heliotrope Bouquet.* In the 1937 "new" *East St. Louis Toodle-Oo,* featuring Cootie Williams, that theme is gone, the whole is much better orchestrated, the juxtaposition of the featured soloist against the orchestration and against the other soloists is balanced and proportioned. And to cite one detail, the plunger response executed by the full trumpet section on the first entrance of the bridge is startlingly effective.

Similarly with the new *Black and Tan Fantasy* of 1938. Ellington's secondary theme does not appear in the main section but is now the basis of an effective *Prologue to Black and Tan Fantasy.* The piece is played more slowly, which gives an introspection to Miley's broader proclamations. And the *Fantasy* itself becomes a beautifully played and scored exploration of Miley's blues theme climaxed by Cootie Williams's solo. *En route,* it is enhanced by a middle chorus which juxtaposes Nanton's plaintive trombone, Ellington's piano, and Barney Bigard's superb glissando, which moves from an upper register D-flat through D and into F, and from a whisper to *forte*.

Thus Ellington's sophistication, sometimes inappropriate in its early manifestations, held the greatest promise.

I do not suppose that one could overestimate Cootie Williams's importance to Ellington, much as one could not overestimate Miley's. Not a great improviser, Williams was nevertheless a great player, and it was he who brought the Armstrong style and spirit into the Ellington orchestra. He also brought a sound brass technique and the ability not only to take over the plunger trumpet role that Miley had created but to expand it, in flexibility, in varieties of sonority, and in emotional range. It is fitting that one of the durable successes of early Ellington should be Williams's contribution *Echoes of the Jungle* (1931). It is also fitting that his work on that piece is in a sense a pastiche of the work of his predecessors, the plunger-muted trumpeters, Miley and Arthur Whetsol. And it is most fitting of all that one of Ellington's later masterpieces should have been his *Concerto for Cootie*.

The years 1930–32 were important for Ellington, a first flowering of his genius. With only twelve musicians in 1930 he produced the astonishing *Old Man Blues,* a masterpiece of orchestration and dense sonorities in AABA song form. And in the same year there was *Mood Indigo.* The first version is exceptionally well composed and orchestrated, but not very well played, and it is prophetic in its singular juxtaposition of muted trumpet, trombone, and lower-register clarinet.

The haunting opening chorus of *The Mystery Song* from the following year is one of the unique moments in Ellington, and is probably undecipherable for even the keenest ear in its instrumentation and its voicings. It is an early confirmation of André Previn's famous tribute that Duke Ellington could lower one finger, some musicians would play something, and every composer and orchestrator in the house would respond with "What was *that?*"

By 1932 a rhythmic turning point had been reached in *It Don't Mean a Thing,* with its prophetic subtitle, *If It Ain't Got That Swing.* The piece was obviously conceived as an instrumental, although it was first recorded with a vocal by Ivie Anderson, taking over (it seems clear) passages first designed for Cootie Williams's plunger and Johnny Hodges's alto. *It Don't Mean a Thing* is an orchestral and not a pianistic piece, and it is composed and performed with an Armstrong-inspired, swing phrasing throughout.

I should also mention the astonishing *Daybreak Express* from 1933, a part of a series of virtuoso pieces for the orchestra which would include *Hot and Bothered* (1928), *Braggin' in Brass* (1938), *The Flaming Sword* (1940), and the *Giddybug Gallop* (1941) — all except the last, by the way, *Tiger Rag* derivatives.

The accomplishments of 1937–39 provided a prologue to the sustained accomplishments of 1940. From 1937 there is *Azure,* a small masterpiece, and a part of the by-then-established tradition of outstanding Ellington instrumental ballads — or "mood" pieces, as they were called. Otherwise, it became clear in these years (if it had not been clear already) that Ellington was capable of seeming to do one thing while doing quite another, and on occasion of injecting something quite unexpected by anyone. In 1938, while offering what could pass for more medium and fast "swing band" instrumentals like *Hip Chic* or *Slap Happy,* he could also offer *Blue Light* and *A Gypsy Without a Song.*

Blue Light is a beautifully self-contained slow blues for only seven [*recte* eight] instruments. Again, it may seem largely a succession of solos but *Blue Light* is structured in contrasts. Ellington himself sets the mood with a piano introduction, provides mobile but unifying comments throughout, and a kind of summary in his own final solo. Barney Bigard's opening clarinet solo provides a series of thoughtful, liquid ascending-descending phrases. The twelve-measure passage which follows uses the *Mood Indigo* alliance of a muted trumpet and trombone and lower register clarinet in a simple succession of half and whole notes, beautifully voiced for the three horns, compellingly effective, but without strong melodic content. Lawrence Brown's trombone chorus which follows is a robust, climactic melody. (It was Brown's own, and an improvisation, by the way, and so strong that Ellington later used it as the basis of *Transblucency* in 1946.)

A Gypsy Without a Song is in no way typical of the big band music of the times, nor is it typical of its composer except in its excellence. *A Gypsy Without a Song* in AABA song form has its compositional elements so perfectly in balance that one is brought up short by the realization that Juan Tizol's and Lawrence Brown's trombones are both heard in solo, as are Cootie Williams and Johnny Hodges — Tizol twice and Williams thrice.

In 1939, Ellington had the daring to transform the obvious, sure-fire effectiveness of the *Bugle Call Rag* into *The Sergeant Was Shy,* an array of subtle — even elusive — effects. He offered what passed for big band riff tunes *(A Portrait of the Lion)* and big band boogie woogie *(Bouncing Buoyancy),* but, as we have come to expect, each was more than what it seemed to be. And Ellington recorded another slow blues, *Subtle Lament,* with five choruses, again virtually theme-less in the orchestrated sections. The opening ensemble is a series of descending half and whole notes in fascinating voicings for the saxophones, but with one of the tenors doubled by Joe Nanton's plunger-muted horn. And in the second chorus Ellington uses the typical touch of introducing new thematic material on his piano while having the brass respond with allusive, carry-over phrases in a faint echo of the opening ensemble.

Both *Blue Light* and *Subtle Lament* are blues with ensemble writing that is almost theme-less, and with a burden of melody falling to some of the soloists. It is an idea Ellington would return to.

There is nothing extrinsic, nothing out of place, in either *Blue Light* or *Subtle Lament,* but until he wrote them, there was, I think, a still-lingering tendency in Ellington to introduce inappropriate secondary themes in otherwise successful works. *Bundle of Blues* from 1933 brilliantly juxtaposes Cootie Williams's resilient growls against keenly timed responses from the orchestra. But Ellington has Lawrence Brown state a second theme whose lyricism seems to interrupt *Bundle of Blues.* Similarly, *Echoes of Harlem* from 1936 begins robustly and memorably but has a secondary theme for the saxophones (borrowed from the earlier *Blue Mood*) that seems jarringly out of place—but which does take on life when Williams interprets it later in the performance.

In *Blue Light* and *Subtle Lament* and *Gypsy Without a Song*, Ellington prepared for the consistency of 1940–42, for *Ko-Ko, Conga Brava, Concerto for Cootie, Dusk, Sepia Panorama, Blue Serge, Moon Mist*. And for the shining satellites that gather around their brilliance, *Cotton Tail, Never No Lament, Harlem Air Shaft, Warm Valley, Across the Track Blues, Sherman Shuffle*, and the rest.

The *Concerto for Cootie* is in a sense the ultimate refinement of the influence of ragtime structures on later jazz composition. It opens, after its eight-bar introduction, with an AABA in song form, but the A theme is ten bars rather than eight, and each use of that A theme in the *Concerto* is a variation on its first appearance for both the soloist and the ensemble. The second section of the *Concerto* is its sixteen-measure C theme. And the performance ends with a brief variation of A, limited to six bars, followed by a beautifully sustained ten-measure coda.

Such comments may of course make the piece sound like an exercise in breaking down four- and eight-bar phrases—something which Ellington had worked on since *Creole Rhapsody* in 1931. In the *Concerto* the two-bar extensions of the A phrase, which are there functionally to allow the soloist to change his mutes, flow naturally. Williams and the orchestra share ten-bar segments, not eight-bar phrases with an extra two bars tacked on. Cootie Williams is balanced against the orchestra; he does not dominate it, and once again he plays beautifully. He uses all his sonorous resources: a tightly cup-muted sound; the *wa-wa* of a plunger mute in motion; the plunger held close; the hard "growl" with the plunger held partly open over a straight mute; and open horn on the C theme. The scoring is simple harmonically but constantly varied, and the settings and transitions, dominated by the saxophones, are beautifully conceived and beautifully played.

Portions of the *Concerto* had been previously tested. The forceful B melody is an adaptation of one of Cootie's blues phrases, one which introduces the 1938 *Mobile Blues*. The coda is an adaptation of one Ellington used on *Moonglow* in 1935 [*recte* 1934].* The new portions are the lyric themes, A and C, and they are the work of Ellington the composer in 1940.

Ko-Ko could be called the *Concerto*'s opposite. Its point of departure is simple, a succession of twelve-bar blues choruses in minor, using two main themes or sections; however, its orchestration is far from simple, particularly in its harmonic voicings. The *Concerto* undertakes a variety of material in a brief performance; *Ko-Ko* undertakes a simplicity of material without letting the results seem monotonous.

Ko-Ko begins with a brooding, eight-measure introduction. The main twelve-measure section or theme is then given antiphonally by the ensemble and Juan Tizol's valve trombone. The piece moves immediately to its second

---

* What of the Will Hudson–Eddie Delange *Moonglow*, incidentally? Its structure obviously owes a great deal to the 1932 Ellington piece *Lazy Rhapsody* and its melody to *Lazy Rhapsody* and an interlude in *It Don't Mean a Thing*.

section, and in contrast to Tizol's fluid instrumental sound, offers Joe Nanton's slide trombone in a continuous twenty-four-measure exposition. And Nanton's accompaniment includes saxophone figures which derive from *Ko-Ko*'s main section, thus linking the two sections and the performance's first three choruses.

The main section then returns as Ellington provides an increasingly bold obbligato to relatively basic antiphonal ensemble figures. A simple ensemble variation on the main section follows, but with carry-over brass figures from the previous chorus.

We then return to the second section for a call-and-response chorus between the ensemble and breaks for Jimmy Blanton's solo bass statements. A full, richly orchestrated almost optimistic variation on *Ko-Ko*'s opening theme follows. The piece then ends with an approximate recapitulation of the introduction completed by a four-measure coda.

In *Ko-Ko*, Ellington's talent reaches a full expression. The piece provides evocative primary and secondary material, all of it derived from elementary, even primitive, blues phrases. He handles these with appropriate robustness, continuity, and contrast, with the composer's sophistication used to enhance the themes and enhance the work of his soloists. And the final variation, before *Ko-Ko*'s ending, is one of the most richly orchestrated moments in all of Ellington and all of jazz.

Ko-Ko might be sketched as follows:

Introduction (eight measures)
A   Ensemble and Tizol (twelve measures)
B AND B1   Nanton and the ensemble (twenty-four measures)
A1   Ensemble and Ellington (twelve measures)
A2   Ensemble (twelve measures)
B2   Ensemble and Blanton (twelve measures)
A   Ensemble variation (twelve measures)
ENDING   Recap of the introduction plus a coda (eight plus four measures)

Ko-Ko again returns to the idea, heard in *Blue Light* and *Subtle Lament,* of an instrumental blues without a strong written melody in the conventional sense, without even a conventional riff theme. *Ko-Ko* has, in basic terms, nothing we would come away whistling or humming, even in its solos. But *Ko-Ko* has a singular and memorable character as an instrumental entity, and it succeeds in an area of "pure" music as perhaps no other previous Ellington work.

The stature of the Ellington orchestra at this period reveals itself in details as well as in full performances. There is the original, contrasting saxophone line behind the simple trumpet riffing that opens *Harlem Air Shaft;* the band's playing on *Never No Lament,* especially behind Cootie Williams's solo; the beautiful saxophone ensembles on *Rumpus in Richmond,* especially as they move upward through the piece's chordal steps behind Cootie Williams's second solo; or the polyphonic opening choruses of *I Don't Know What Kind of Blues I've Got,* a small marvel in the Ellington repertory.

For *Blue Serge,* Ellington turned to the most challengingly simple and potentially monotonous of forms, the eight-bar blues. He and the orchestra meet the challenge with an ingenious variety of techniques, including unobtrusive modulations, always with a probing sustained emotion.

The introduction to *Blue Serge* is six measures, but for good reason it is broken into four measures plus two. The opening four give the main theme, by clarinet and brass, but only for its basic melodic figure. This exposition is interrupted for a brooding, two-bar transition, a sort of vamp by the trombones, that sets the mood for the performance. It also sets up the idea of a "floating" two bars which ingeniously reappears several times, extending one chorus to ten measures, or breaking another into six plus two.

In the first chorus of *Blue Serge* Ray Nance's trumpet restates the theme in a full exposition, and in a full realization of its introspective character. The second chorus is a thematic variation scored for reeds and muted brass, a thing of marvelous color and one of the hundreds of examples in Ellington where only the closest listening will reveal what combinations of what instruments with what mutes are playing what, to produce this shifting sonority. This chorus also offers the first extension of the eight-bar chorus; it is unobtrusively and quite effectively eight plus two.

The next two choruses are tied. The first is a non-thematic plunger solo by Joe Nanton. As is usual with Ellington's settings for Nanton's dramatic simplicity, the chorus is excellently accompanied. By a slight harmonic manipulation, this chorus is joined to the next, which is a written (but non-thematic) variation, with plunger trumpets predominating. This episode, however, ends after six bars, leaving two bars for the piano. This "premature" introduction of the piano ties the fourth chorus to the fifth, which is a thematic piano variation for a full eight bars. The next chorus is a secondary theme, a twelve-bar solo by Ben Webster played over the trombones. (But is it actually four bars plus eight bars?) The record concludes with a return to a beautifully orchestrated variation, just barely thematic but strong enough to leave the performance with a feeling of resolution and with no lingering need for a recapitulation.

The successes of 1938 to 1942 obviously have to do with a coming together of specific talents: the leader in maturity, and the sidemen with whom he had worked for years, like Williams, Stewart, Brown, Nanton, Tizol, Hodges, Bigard, Carney, and so on. Tempering the more sophisticated talents in the orchestra in 1940 were those of the musically robust midwesterners who joined at about the same time, Jimmy Blanton and Ben Webster. Then there is the presence of the orchestra's second composer-arranger, Billy Strayhorn, who joined in late 1939. Strayhorn's was a talent compatible with Ellington's in several ways, and perhaps we shall never know in detail who has contributed what to the Ellington book from the day Strayhorn joined him. Strayhorn had his moments of chic sophistication as his early songs *Lush Life* and *Something To Live For* will reveal. But he could alter the chords of *Exactly Like You* perceptively for *Take the "A" Train,* and he was soon producing *Johnny Come Lately, Day Dream, Chelsea Bridge,* and *Rain Check*.

Inevitably the less imaginative arrangers of the 'thirties and 'forties borrowed from Ellington's themes, effects, and backgrounds, two and four bars at a time, sometimes to turn them into simple, repeated riffs. Pieces like *Slap Happy* and *The Jeep Is Jumping,* for example, are ahead of their time in that they use a variety of riffs to form continuous melodies. The more perceptive students of Ellington did not undertake to grasp the subtler aspects of his orchestral language until the late 'thirties, and at first such efforts were likely to go on in orchestras, like those of Charlie Barnet and Erskine Hawkins, that were frankly engaged in tributes to his talent.

Some commentators have seen Ellington as an impressionist. Surely we are invited to do so by his own descriptive and programmatic titles — *Daybreak Express, Misty Morning, Harlem Air Shaft* — and also by the manner in which he has coached his soloists, almost as though they were a group of actors, into evoking specific emotions appropriate to specific situations. Perhaps impressionism is his means on occasion, but his highest ends include *Concerto for Cootie, Ko-Ko,* and *Blue Serge,* which are pure instrumental music.

I have neglected here the question of Ellington the distinguished composer of instrumental ballads *(Sophisticated Lady, In a Sentimental Mood, Lost in Meditation, Prelude to a Kiss, I Let a Song Go Out of My Heart, Warm Valley)* and the subject of Ellington the songwriter *(I Got It Bad, I'm Beginning To See the Light).* But since those two subjects are often (too often?) the same subject, the question is obviously not a simple one.

As I say, by 1940 he had dealt with the nature of his talent and brought it to a fulfillment. During the early 'thirties, he learned to orchestrate less as a pianist and more as the leader of a group of instrumentalists, individually and collectively. He had also absorbed the challenging rhythmic and melodic idiom of Louis Armstrong. And by 1938 he was using the possibilities of his own sophistication in orchestration in balance with the statements of his sidemen. Ellington refined jazz beyond the achievements of anyone else. He orchestrated and enriched its message without taking away its spontaneity, its essential passion and life.

One problem in Ellington's later career was that he sometimes ceased to work quite as closely with the specific talents of his players. Often he could not because of the departures of some of his key musicians. Choosing to maintain a continuity of his basic style, he was required to get new players to take over what Cootie Williams had done earlier, what Joe Nanton had done, etc. Carney remained, however. And fortunately, Ellington lost Johnny Hodges only briefly, and the combination of communal earthiness, rhythmic drive, and sophisticated lyricism which Hodges possessed made him perhaps the perfect Ellington sideman.

However, there is the related example of Ellington's willingness to return to his own standards and try to discover something new or something still challenging in them. He could succeed superbly. His 1950 "concert" version of *Mood Indigo,* with one section a waltz, is (its vocal aside) his best version, and one of his best recordings.

Particularly since his death, the question of Ellington's longer works has been raised anew. It seems to me that it might best center first on *Reminiscing in Tempo* (1935); *Diminuendo and Crescendo in Blue* (1937); *Suite Thursday* (1960), a pun after John Steinbeck and an integrated blues suite in which all parts are ingenious variants of the simple riff which opens the first section; and perhaps *The Queen's Suite* (1959, for Elizabeth II). Ellington's most ambitious long work, and perhaps his most challenging, remains *Black, Brown and Beige* from 1943, and it may be the best. In view of the often subtle relationships of some of its themes and motives (the second section's "Emancipation Celebration" is, appropriately, a variant of the sacred "Come Sunday" theme of the opening section, for example) and the fine ingenuity of the blues section, Ellington's own evident dissatisfaction with the work—and particularly the last two movements, which he changed several times and finally dropped— seems puzzling.

Ellington remained the major leader of a large jazz ensemble, and there are excellencies from every period of his career. True, he sometimes misjudged his audiences in his later years. He sometimes offered a medley of Ellington "hits," or a facile and banal use of saxophonist Paul Gonsalves's fine talent, or of trumpeter Cat Anderson's phenomenally high "screamers" to audiences who would rather have heard his *Such Sweet Thunder* suite, or a full version of his exceptional score for the film, *Anatomy of a Murder*, or for the *Asphalt Jungle* television series.

Nevertheless, Ellington remained on the surface the supreme popular artist. His audience still had at its core couples who danced to his *Sophisticated Lady* on their honeymoons, and he knew it. And if it interested him to provide a program of popular dance band ballads, he would provide one, and very possibly do so with brilliance.

Throughout his career, Ellington met audience after audience on its own level and transported it up to his own. He made his music, guided his sidemen, and reached his listeners with a perceptive sense of the realities of his situation. He made his music out of a positive optimism, a capacity for seeking the best and making the best of any situation and any individual. But he also made a music that denied nothing in the American experience. He embraced it all.

83. Albert Murray: From
The Hero and the Blues (1973)

I n a lecture entitled "The Blues and the Fable in the Flesh," delivered at the University of Missouri in 1972, the novelist and critic Albert Murray (b. 1916) compared Ellington's working methods to those of Elizabethan playwrights and ranked his artistic achievements with those of great American writers. His discussion of Ellington arose during a far-ranging exploration of André Malraux's concept of "stylization"— the process by which "the raw material of human experience becomes style."

Murray's lecture was published in *The Hero and the Blues*, and the statement on Elling-

Source: Albert Murray, from *The Hero and the Blues* (Columbia: University of Missouri Press, 1973), 84–87. Reprinted and slightly revised for the liner notes for *Duke Ellington 1939* (The Smithsonian Collection, R010).

ton appeared slightly edited with the notes for *Duke Ellington 1939,* a Smithsonian recording issued in 1977. The latter is the source for the version below.

A longtime resident of New York, Murray was born in Alabama and graduated from Tuskegee Institute. He is the author of two novels, *Train Whistle Guitar* (1974) and *The Spyglass Tree* (1991), also *The Omni-Americans* (1970), *Stomping the Blues* (1976), and (with Count Basie) *Good Morning Blues: The Autobiography of Count Basie* (1985).

I don't think anybody has achieved a higher aesthetic synthesis of the American experience than Duke Ellington expressed in his music. Anybody who achieved a literary equivalent of that would be beyond Melville, Henry James and Faulkner.

Duke Ellington, the most masterful of all blues idiom arranger-composers, was the embodiment of the contemporary artist at work. The Ellington orchestra was frequently booked for recitals in the great concert halls of the world, much the same as if it were a 15-piece innovation of the symphony orchestra, which in a sense it is.

Nevertheless, by original design and by typical employment as well, Ellington was still an itinerant song and dance man. Moreover, his repertory clearly reflects the fact that, over the years, most of his performances have been in night clubs, theaters, dance halls, and at popular music festivals.

Show business motivation underlies Ellington's construction of numbers for the special solo talents of, say, Cootie Williams, Johnny Hodges, and Ben Webster, no more and no less than it underlies Shakespeare's composition of soliloquies for the actor Burbage.

This similarity is perhaps at least as important to the understanding of Ellington's aesthetics as are existing psycho-political theories about black experience, by which is usually meant black misery.

But what is perhaps even more significant is that the arranger-composer's sense of structure and movement is in large measure derived from the small informal combo and the jam sessions which proceed in terms of a tradition of improvisation which is fundamentally the same as that which Elizabethans inherited from the commedia dell'arte. And when, as often happened, the arranger-composer works from existing tunes, as the typical Elizabethan playmaker often employed existing story lines, improvisation becomes in actuality the same process of stylization in terms of which Malraux defines all art.

When Ellington creates blues-extension concertos, in which the solo instrument states, asserts, alleges, quests, requests, or only implies, while the trumpets in the background sometimes concur, as the woodwinds moan or groan in the agony and ecstasy of sensual ambivalence and the trombones chant concurrence or signify misgivings and even suspicions, with the rhythm section attesting and affirming, he is quite obviously engaged in a process of transforming the raw experience of American Negroes into what Malraux calls style.

He is also stylizing his sense of the actual texture of all human existence, not only in the United States or even the contemporary world at large, but also in all places throughout the ages.

Such is the nature as well as the scope, authority and implication of art, and it should be just as obvious that Ellington, who is not only a genius but who after all is no less dedicated to music (and no less accomplished at it) than a Herman Melville or Mark Twain or even a Henry James was to fiction, is likewise no less involved with what T. S. Eliot referred to as the objective correlative or the objective equivalent, to feeling.

Also obvious is that he is concerned as Suzanne K. Langer's "Problems of Art" points out, that all artists are concerned with the life of human feeling (which is to say, how it feels to be human) beyond everything else.

But what should be, if anything, most immediately obvious, was that for Duke Ellington himself, and that for members of his orchestra, textures of human feeling exist in terms of arrangements and compositions which were always related to other arrangements and compositions.

Accordingly, the performance of an Ellington composition was not nearly so dependent upon the personal feelings of his musicians as upon their attitude toward music and the styles of other musicians. The performer's personal feelings did count for something, of course, but only insofar as he could relate them to his musical imagination and his musical technique.

84. Gunther Schuller: "Ellington in the Pantheon" (1974)

Few have written so extensively and knowledgeably about Ellington's music as Gunther Schuller (b. 1925). In articles, liner notes, and especially the lengthy chapters in *Early Jazz* (1968) and *The Swing Era* (1989), Schuller has demonstrated a rare ability to explain the inner workings of Ellington's compositions. The authority behind Schuller's commentary derives from several sources: his insights as a composer and arranger; his practical experience as a performer and conductor, both in the classical and jazz fields; his clarity as a writer; and, not least, his expertise as a transcriber which allows him to comment directly on Ellington's musical language.

Schuller contributed the following article to a commemorative issue of *High Fidelity* published in November 1974, following Ellington's death that May. In it he reflected on Ellington's position within the "pantheon of musical greats"; at the same time he searched for the special ingredients that set Ellington's music apart from the work of other composers.

What is there left to say about the art of Duke Ellington after a lifetime of successes caressed in superlatives and now, since his death, after months of I-knew-him-too tributes by musicians and fans alike?

Very little, I suppose—except that as usual, and perhaps understandably,

Source: Gunther Schuller, "Ellington in the Pantheon," in *Musings: The Musical Worlds of Gunther Schuller* (New York: Oxford University Press, 1986), 47–50. First published in *High Fidelity* (November 1974), 63–64.

much more attention has been given to the man, the charismatic Ellington personality, the inveterate traveler of thousands of one-night stands, Ellington the tune writer, than to his compositions. Admittedly, it is hard to talk about music in words: Music, especially Duke's music, speaks better for itself, and talk *about* music is often necessarily subjective and impressionistic. On the other hand, there are some things to be said about all great music that are more objective and factual than we sometimes care to admit. For greatness is not altogether accidental, altogether intuitive or mysterious. Much of it results from simple hard work, selflessly applied energy, and a fierce determination to learn and apply what has been learned.

If I dare to include Ellington in the pantheon of musical greats—the Beethovens, the Monteverdis, the Schoenbergs, the prime movers, the inspired innovators—it is precisely because Ellington had in common with them not only musical genius and talent, but an unquenchable thirst, an unrequitable passion for translating the raw materials of musical sounds into his own splendid visions. But that is still too general, something that can be said even of minor composers.

What distinguishes Ellington's best creations from those of other composers, jazz and otherwise, are their moments of total uniqueness and originality. There are many such flashes in his *oeuvre,* and it is a pity that they are virtually unknown to most non-jazz composer colleagues. Perhaps this is due to the fact that you cannot go into the nearest music store or library and obtain the orchestral scores of Duke Ellington. There is no Ellington *Gesamtausgabe,* alas, although this is something that should become someone's life work. However, even if such scores existed, they still would not readily disclose the uniqueness of which I speak. For Ellington's imagination was most fertile in the realm of harmony and timbre, usually in combination. And as played by some of the finest musicians jazz has ever known, the specific effect produced in performance and on records is such that no notation has yet been devised to capture it on paper.

Nevertheless they exist—alas *only* on records, and they are none the less real for that and no less significant. The opening measures of "Subtle Lament" (1939) (ex. 1), and the second chorus of "Blue Light" (1939) (ex. 2)—both wondrous harmonic transformations of the blues; the muted brass opening of "Mystery Song" (1931); the last chorus of "Azure" (1937) (ex. 3a, 3b) with its remarkable chromatic alterations; or the total orchestral effect of the first bridge of "Jack the Bear" (1940) (ex. 4), not to mention the uniquely pungent

Ex. 1

Ex. 2

Ex. 3a

Ex. 3b

Ex. 4

harmonies of "Clothed Woman" (1947): These are all moments that can literally not be found in anyone else's music. They are as special and original in their way as the incredible D minor–D-sharp minor mixture and instrumentation that opens the second part of the *Rite of Spring* or the final measures of Schoenberg's *Erwartung*.

Citing musical examples can give only a severely limited impression of the total effect in performance. For finally it is the unique sound of a "Tricky Sam" Nanton, a Cootie Williams, a low-register Barney Bigard that transmutes those harmonies into an experience that even master colorist/harmonists like Debussy and Ravel could not call upon from their orchestras.

It was part of Ellington's genius — what I called earlier his fierce determination and unquenchable thirst — to assemble and maintain for over forty years his own private orchestra, comprising musicians more remarkable in their *individuality* than those of any symphony orchestra I know. Not since Esterhazy had there been such a private orchestra — and Esterhazy was not a composer. But like Haydn, who practiced daily on that band of Austrian/Hungarian musicians to develop the symphonic forms we now cherish, so Ellington practiced on his "instrument." This is a luxury we other composers simply do not know, and the whole experience of writing consistently for a certain group of musicians is a phenomenon we have never savored.

In Ellington's case, collaboration of such intimacy and durability was bound to produce unique musical results. These can be heard on literally hundreds of Ellington orchestra recordings in varying degrees of "uniqueness." When that alchemy worked at its best, the result was such as cannot be heard anywhere else in the realm of music.

A large statement? Preposterous? Check it out for yourself. The originality of Ellington's harmonic language, with its special voicings and timbres, gives the lie to the often-stated suggestion that he learned all this from Delius and Ravel. Rubbish! This is no more tenable than it is to say that Debussy and Ravel sound alike, even if they both use ninth chords. Like these masters, and others such as Scriabin and Delius, Ellington always found a special way of positioning that chord, of spreading or concentrating it, of giving it a unique sonority that cannot be mistaken for any other's.

Like Webern, he limited himself to small forms — a few notable exceptions notwithstanding. In fact it was not entirely by choice in Ellington's case, but the three-minute ten-inch-disc duration was simply imposed on jazz musicians for a variety of technical/practical/commercial/social/racial reasons. What matters is that he took this restriction and turned it into a virtue. He became the master in our time of the small form, the miniature, the vignette, the cameo portrait. What Chopin's nocturnes and ballades are to mid-nineteenth-century European music, Ellington's "Mood Indigo" and "Cotton Tail" are to mid-twentieth-century Afro-American music.

In his inimitable way the Duke towered over all his contemporaries in the jazz field and equaled much of what is considered sacred on the non-jazz side.

He is gone now, alas. Yet his music lives on and is still with us — at least on recordings. I believe that is not enough.

85. Gunther Schuller: "The Case for Ellington's Music as Living Repertory" (1974)

I n the same November 1974 issue of *High Fidelity* that included "Ellington in the Pantheon" (see the preceding section), Schuller argued persuasively for the continued performance of Ellington's works by modern jazz orchestras. As a prime instigator of the "jazz repertory" movement—in which ensembles recreate older styles preserved on recordings—Schuller wrote from personal experience, especially in transcribing and conducting the music of Ellington.[1] Today his article seems prophetic. In the intervening years many Ellington works have been performed by repertory ensembles in the United States and Europe, a few transcriptions and editions have been published, and plans are afoot to make major Ellington compositions available in volumes issued in the Smithsonian Institution's Jazz Masterworks series.

Is it possible—and is it right—that Ellington's music should be relegated to perpetuation solely by mechanical reproductive means? Is this remarkable musical output not to survive in live performances or perhaps only in transmutations and improvisations by others, based on the Duke's tunes?

Since Ellington's death, the factions have formed, in most cases rigidly affirming previously conceived notions. And curiously, much of the argumentation directly or indirectly opposes the perpetuation of his music as a living repertory.

The arguments run something like this. 1) Jazz is a spontaneously created, largely improvised music that cannot be recaptured for repetition. Some even say "should not." Therefore, jazz has no re-creatable repertory, as classical music does. It is constantly renewable but only in terms of improvisation, i.e., other "spontaneously created" versions of the original. It is not a music ever to be fixed.

2) Should one play Ellington's work while some of his musicians for whom the music was originally created are still alive? Indeed, his orchestra continues under his son Mercer's leadership, presumably obviating the need for others to concern themselves about the preservation of Ellington's music.

3) Since it is "impossible" to imitate the great soloists/personalities of the Ellington ensemble—Johnny Hodges, Lawrence Brown, Rex Stewart—this whole body of music is relegated to survival only in archival form, in the "museum" of recordings.

In addition there are always certain obsessively possessive jazz critics who believe that jazz is some kind of exclusive area of music belonging to them, and that treating it as repertory and thus making it available to other musicians and audiences will automatically dilute and desecrate its purity.

Source: Gunther Schuller, "The Case for Ellington's Music as Living Repertory," *Musings: The Musical Worlds of Gunther Schuller* (New York: Oxford University Press, 1986), 47–50. First published under the title, "Are the Recordings Enough?," in *High Fidelity* (November 1974), 87–88.

[1] See, for example, his recordings *Homage to Ellington in Concert* (Columbia XM 33513, 1975) and *Duke Ellington: "Symphony in Black"* (Smithsonian Collection N1024, 1981).

I cannot believe that a music as profoundly important as Ellington's (and Billy Strayhorn's) should meet such an uncertain fate. And indeed there is no reason why this music—or at least some of it—cannot continue to be played close to how it was originally conceived. The qualifying words here are "some of it" and "close."

There is, obviously, some jazz literature that could, in fact, never be re-created. One would not think of duplicating one of John Coltrane's thirty-five-minute improvisations or Eric Dolphy's amazing solos on "Stormy Weather" or indeed Hodges's "Warm Valley" performance. But Ellington's music is not limited to that kind of improvised jazz. It is well known that the Duke rejected the narrowing stigmatization of the term "jazz" for his music. And in truth much, perhaps the greater part, of his output consists of *orchestral compositions*—for a "jazz" orchestra perhaps, but an orchestra nevertheless—very often fully notated or fixed in some permanent way by himself or his musicians or both in combination. In many of these works the "improvised" solos are brief, incidental, and surprisingly "fixed" as a permanent feature of that performance. Certain "solos" were even handed down from player to player through the decades, as witness Bubber Miley's contributions from the late 1920s being played virtually the same way by his successors Cootie Williams, Ray Nance, Cat Anderson, Clark Terry, and several others. Such solos were never pure off-the-top-of-the-head improvisations to begin with. They were well-thought-out, prepared, and integrated into the total piece, and *because* this was so they were generally not tampered with by later incumbents of that chair.

This is not very far removed, if at all, from the instance of a classical composer writing a solo or a concerto, perhaps with a certain musician in mind (think of the Brahms concerto written for Joachim), which is then played by others with a slightly different style, tone, interpretation, and character.

Apart from the "solo" question in such orchestral jazz pieces, the orchestral frame is, of course, even more specifically fixed, notated, rehearsed, and played more or less the same way in each performance. It seems to me that such pieces—and Ellington created hundreds of them—are eminently suitable to performance by others if sensitively and conscientiously approached.

In answer to the second point, even when Duke was still alive a huge number of his most famous compositions were not in the band's repertory. So there were no live performances by him of such masterpieces as "Ko-Ko" or "Blue Serge" or "Azure" or "Reminiscing in Tempo" or "Dusk."[2] Duke undoubtedly had his reasons for not maintaining much of the old material, apart from the fact that it is simply not possible to keep over a thousand pieces in a single band's repertory. I think his reasons were mostly personal. For example, when Hodges died, virtually all the recent pieces associated with him were eliminated from the then repertory of the band, because, I think, Hodges's loss was such for Ellington that he could not bear to have anyone else play them—even if there had been someone in the band who *could* play them.

---

[2] With the exception of *Dusk,* live versions of all these pieces (i.e., air checks from public performances) have surfaced. See the index to *ERMDE.*

With all respect for Duke's feelings, one must say that once a composer creates a work it cannot remain the exclusive property of its creator or the person(s) for whom it was created. It belongs, in the broadest (non-copyright) sense, to the world. One simply comes back to the point that pieces as original, as perfect, as imaginative, as beautiful as Ellington's best cannot just be buried in the past. They must survive; they must be heard.

And something must be done about it before more of Ellington's music, scores and parts, disappear. Perhaps more exists than one can ascertain at this time, so soon after his death. I do know that in trying to obtain the parts for a half-dozen Ellington scores a few years ago, several days of diligent search on the part of Tom Whaley and Joe Benjamin produced nothing. Perhaps they'll turn up, but one shudders to think of the possibility that they may not.[3]

Some will say it is enough to take some of Ellington's pieces—like "Satin Doll" or "Sophisticated Lady"—and use them as a basis for improvisations and arrangements. Unfortunately that preserves very little of Ellington. Miles Davis improvising on "Satin Doll" will come out much more Miles Davis than Duke Ellington. Furthermore most jazz musicians perform their own tunes, largely for financial reasons (like record royalties), and very few improvise on compositions by others. Beyond that, it is a fact that the majority of Ellington's music does not lend itself to that kind of improvisation. His pieces are always more than tunes, a set of changes, or a line. They are true fully thought-out compositions written for orchestra, often very complex in structure and form. Should these perish simply because they do not conform to the norm of tunes on which musicians like to blow choruses?

The remarkable fact is that a great deal of Ellington's music is *not* dependent upon performance by his own orchestra or by the Browns, Carneys, and Hodgeses. It transcends those personal qualities. It turns out that it ultimately doesn't matter whether an eight-bar "solo" by Brown, for example, in the middle of a mostly arranged composition has *exactly* Brown's tone or vibrato or slide technique. What is important is to preserve the essence and character and as much of the specifics of that "solo" as possible, because it would be difficult to conceive of anyone doing anything better in its place. Whether Brown or Ellington or both chose the notes, the result that was finally approved by Duke and performed or recorded in that form is without question the best possible realization of that musical idea or moment. *That* is what is important to preserve: the music as it was *originally* conceived, either singly by Duke or jointly by him and his musicians.

There can be little doubt that the original creative impulses and the conditions under which they occurred constitute the most complete and perfect realization. These conditions include the inspiration Ellington received from his players to create certain pieces and musical ideas for them. But it does not necessarily follow that those musical creations are limited to performance by those who first inspired them. That is obviously not true in classical music and need not be in jazz either.

[3] In fact, the acquisition of Ellington's music library by the Smithsonian Institution in 1988 unearthed a huge cache of scores and parts—much more material than Schuller, writing in 1974, knew existed.

In truth, Ellington's compositions are, *as* compositions, so durable that they can be played by others sensitively re-creating the original notes, pitches, rhythms, timbres, etc. But what is most astonishing is that they can, in performances by fine musicians with fine ears, not only re-create the original, but bring to it an excitement and drive that has its own validity, even though it may not be precisely the excitement that Ellington and his men got.

This is, of course, an exact parallel to classical repertory, where no two interpretations of a Brahms or Tchaikovsky symphony are the same, despite the fact that conductors and performers will be playing from the same notated parts and score. It is in that same sense that much of Ellington's music can be preserved—and *must* be. It is too important a part of our American musical legacy.

Ellington, who was always *sui generis* and conceptually ten years ahead of his contemporaries, produced an *oeuvre* that transcends the parochial views of most jazz purists. Indeed many of them did not accept or understand his musical innovations when they first appeared. It would be most inappropriate if they now would kill the growing movement toward the preservation of the jazz repertory, not only Ellington's.

86. Lawrence Gushee: "Duke Ellington 1940" (1978)

I n the late seventies Martin Williams initiated a series of Ellington reissues through the Smithsonian Collection of Recordings. Each album focused on music from a single year and included annotations by a distinguished writer on jazz: Gunther Schuller for 1938 (released in 1976); James Patrick, 1939 (1977); Lawrence Gushee, 1940 (1978); and Gary Giddins, 1941 (1981). In addition to making material available that was either out of print or obtainable only on imports, these sets helped promote a critical stance held by Williams, Schuller, and others: that the period between 1938 and 1942 represented a high ridge in Ellington's career, with 1940 forming the summit.

In his provocative essay and inspired annotations for the 1940 set, Lawrence Gushee provides ample evidence to support this view, although not endorsing it explicitly. He does contend that Ellington in 1940–41 produced "the best performed, most adventurously crafted, and finally most emotionally serious works to come from the U.S. 'dance band.'" But ultimately Gushee is less interested in rating Ellington's achievement than in finding ways to describe its character and dimensions. He goes about the task with a refreshing blend of scholarship and enthusiasm, reflecting his collective experience as musicologist, critic, and performer (on clarinet).

Gushee (b. 1931) began writing on jazz while a graduate student at Yale University in the late fifties and early sixties, contributing to the *American Record Guide, The Jazz Review,* and Ralph J. Gleason's *Jazz: A Quarterly of American Music.* A specialist in medieval music and a faculty member at the University of Illinois since 1976, he is best

Source: Lawrence Gushee, liner essay for *Duke Ellington 1940* (Smithsonian Collection R013, 1978).

known in jazz for his work on the Creole Band, Jelly Roll Morton, King Oliver, and Lester Young.

Note: the two-record set for which Gushee wrote the following notes contained most, but not all, of Ellington's commercial recordings for Victor in 1940. Between Gushee's annotations for pieces below, I have inserted session dates and locations in brackets. Personnel for the orchestra is as follows: Wallace Jones, Cootie Williams, trumpets; Rex Stewart, cornet; Joe Nanton, Lawrence Brown, trombones; Juan Tizol, valve trombone; Barney Bigard, clarinet, tenor saxophone; Johnny Hodges, alto and soprano saxophone; Otto Hardwick, alto saxophone; Ben Webster, tenor saxophone; Harry Carney, baritone and alto saxophone, clarinet; Duke Ellington, piano; Fred Guy, guitar; Jimmy Blanton, bass; Sonny Greer, drums; Ivie Anderson, vocals.

The entry for Duke Ellington in a reputable children's encyclopedia, copyright 1972, reads: "Ellington, Duke (1899–) is an American jazz composer, band leader, and pianist. He is generally considered the most important figure in the history of jazz. . . ." Half truths continue through the rest of the article. Although there is a small photograph, nowhere is one told that he was either Afro-American, or Negro, much less an Afro-American of a particular background or socio-economic group. And despite Duke's very explicit ambivalence about such musical categories as "improvisation" and "jazz," something he shares with many another Afro-American musician, he is firmly placed in the jazz box. Of course, Duke was a ragtime player, a jazz band, then a swing band, leader, and eventually became a much honored jazz composer. But as much as his career and work belongs to the history of jazz, it also belongs to the larger history of Afro-Americans who were simultaneously performers, song-writers, band leaders and conductors, and finally composers. Such men go well back into the nineteenth century, but we are only beginning to know the careers of the more recent figures, like Scott Joplin, James Reese Europe, "Jelly Roll" Morton, Will Marion Cook, Will Vodery, and James P. Johnson, the last three of whom had something important to do with the concept of music and the place within it that Duke Ellington developed.

The careers of such men unfolded against a backdrop of peculiarly American 19th-century assumptions: First, that—barring replicas or survivals of European idioms—our nation had little or no folk music of its own, except possibly that of the black tenth of the population; second, that Afro-American entertainers were especially gifted at certain kinds of entertainment, dancing, comedy, and some sports. In music they were also widely understood to possess a natural expressiveness and sincerity (because uncorrupted by civilization), as well as naturally beautiful voices. All of this together with other more general attitudes of contempt, fear, sexual and economic anxiety, and so on.

The bread offered to musicians by one hand of the white community was matched by a stone in the other. The black American performer, as a representative of his "folk" was tolerated, even esteemed. But the passage from acceptance as a folk musician to musician, pure and simple, from stereotyped entertainer to independent artist, was extremely difficult. The Afro-American who considered himself (and *was*) a civilized musician almost necessarily survived by working in show or dance music as leader, arranger, or musical director, often with a seriousness or dignity that seems out of place. His higher aspirations often found their outlet in a world of black opera companies, church choirs, symphony orchestras and musical clubs. This was not Duke Ellington's fate.

It was Ellington's good fortune to come from Washington, D.C., which during Ellington's youth had a very high proportion (as documented by occupational censuses) of Afro-American musicians and teachers of music. Many of these Washingtonians left this large, urban, diversified, cultivated, and yet still black community for New York, searching for an exciting and somewhat risqué good time. Thus, when Ellington came to New York, he brought with him a keen awareness of an Afro-American heritage as perceived through the eyes of a predominantly black community in a very white environment.

Ellington had little formal musical education apart from his high-school contact with Henry Grant and possibly others, the details of which are not known. But it seems that he learned something from men he came to know in New York, such as Cook and Vodery, although once again the details are not known. In any event, by 1926 or 1927 he had discovered that he could make music that was both entertaining to audiences and rewarding to his imagination and feelings by doing two things: piecing works together from odd combinations and variations of the conventional forms and harmonies of popular music; and assigning musical (or perhaps musico-dramatic) roles to his players which were compatible with their personalities as well as with what white listeners expected of black musicians (the exotic, primitive, naively soulful or unrestrained).

Through a combination of good management, radio exposure, an extended engagement at the Cotton Club in conjunction with what are often judged to have been revues of extraordinary vigor and polish, a great deal of recording, and the beginnings of thoughtful critical attention (mostly from abroad), Ellington and his band had by the mid-thirties achieved great popular acceptance. This was not so much as a dance band, although they could and did function that way, but as a glamorous show band which could produce records with unforgettable tunes and settings. In the first years of the swing craze (1936–39), Ellington's recording career was unfocused: a mixture of humdrum pop songs, continued exploitation of previously mined veins, awkward and perplexing extended compositions, mini-concertos for some soloists, and the occasional work with intimations of things to come. After an extended stay with the Brunswick label and its corporate successor, Columbia, Ellington returned as a recording artist to RCA Victor in 1940 and, over the course of the next two years, produced a large number of works which were the best performed, most adventurously crafted, and finally most emotionally serious works to come from the U.S. "dance band"—for which we need a new name.

Ellington was working as a composer in something of a peculiar environment, however, an environment characterized by the multitude of musical languages available to him, along with the exigencies of an aggressively commercial recording industry.

To be a contemporary American, Afro-American, "serious" composer puts one in the midst of a field of three (at least) polarities. First of all, *classical* and *popular*—that is to say, enduring and ephemeral, inspirational and industrial, idealistic and functional. The second is that of *Old Europe,* from which some of "our" forefathers came, and *New America.* (The cries of despair, from the plaintive to the outraged, of the American composer have sounded for over a century.) Finally, the quintessentially simplistic American polarity of black (even brown and beige) and pink.

What it means to be important or successful in this minefield of ideology is not easy to say. Perhaps it does not matter much to the musician post mortem, whether he joins the angelic oratorio society or attains blissful non-existence.

In the special case of jazz or jazz-related music, there has existed for nearly two generations a small group of writers, critics, musicians, and listeners who understand their music to mediate these extreme poles, a music basically not for financial profit, yet not co-opted by institutions, neither absolutely contemporary nor traditional, partly "functional" and entertaining, partly not, and finally, neither completely black or pink, American or European.

Against such views are ranged the practical realities of the recording industry and the various ways in which musical traditions are carried on in writing and in teaching. The rapidity with which great achievements are discarded without ever having been understood is spectacular and saddening. In the long run, accolades and freely-bestowed titles of greatness or artistic genius count for very little if the work is not available. Propaganda can whet the appetite and direct the attention, but the work itself must make its own case for survival.

With "jazz" or music categorized as such, there are problems peculiar to the nature of the music and to the nature of the phonograph record industry. Obviously, much of the strength of the music lies in spontaneities of performance or individual nuance for which we have no notation and thus no easy road to re-creation. If jazz had a more stable and orderly system of apprenticeship, perhaps that would alleviate the problem. Ultimately, however, the phonograph recording can be seen as the best means of preserving these ephemeral heights of human expression. But as matters worked out, the recording, red or black label notwithstanding, was primarily a means of entertaining, and at the same time making money for an industry which reflected to perfection all the polarities mentioned above, with a new one: that of the wiggly groove which could be experienced but not read, as against the written score.

My earliest experience of Ellington's music, over thirty years ago, was twofold: first, there were available in neighborhood record stores a certain number of reissued recordings from RCA Victor's holdings, mostly works of the late 20s or early 30s, such as *The Mooche* or *East St. Louis Toodle-Oo;* second, the sequined band itself, lit in shifting colors, in Saturday matinees at the Earle Theatre. These were two very different kinds of experiences, but in any event, as nearly as I can recall, the works of 1940–41 were either not available at all, or not publicized. Early in the LP era, however, there appeared a 10″ recording both here and in Europe (RCA Victor LPT 3107/HMV DLP 1034 etc.), which included some of the recordings discussed and reissued here. This was most illuminating and artistically rewarding to a great many people for whom the living experience of the "big band era" was tenuous at best, or who did not much care for the Ellington band of the day. In the course of the 50s, through the French critic André Hodeir, some British writers, and in the pages of *The Jazz Review*, analysis and interpretation of these works began—and stalled. The reissues from this period disappeared, to reappear unpredictably and sporadically in a confusing series of repackagings, only to disappear again in their turn.

Meanwhile, Ellington and his band continued to compose and perform, and bit by bit during the 60s he was accorded the wide public attention and honor that would have been appropriate twenty years earlier. Better late than never, of course, but whether the new respect went to the Ellington of the Newport Festival 1956, of *Satin Doll*, or of the sacred concerts, it did not result in any dramatic new attention or even availability of the works of 1940–41. This neglect was neither the judgment of history nor of an elite of musicians, arrangers, teachers and critics, but a reflection of the realities of selling phonograph records (i.e., jazz doesn't sell), and our perhaps ingrained national slovenliness in favoring tearing down or allowing the old place to fall into decay rather than keeping it in good repair.

The Band

In its instrumentation, the Ellington band was like hundreds of others active in the late 30s, with some very significant differences. First, he carried three trombones from the early part of the decade, all of them idiosyncratic, and one of them a tonally contrasting and more agile—especially in the low register—valve trombone, Juan Tizol. Many otherwise adventurous arrangers of the time did little with their available two trombones, except in quintet scoring with the trumpets.

Second, Ellington was early in moving to four saxes from the standard trio of the 20s; but instead of a second tenor, he added Harry Carney's baritone, scored in a wide variety of ways. Ellington's addition of a fifth sax—and not incidentally his first major tenor sax soloist, Ben Webster—was not unique for the time, but had a somewhat different effect with Ellington than with, say, Lunceford or Goodman. This was partly because Duke's frequent use of Bigard's clarinet, sometimes with the brass, often reduced the saxes to a quartet. In addition, certain other doublings define the Ellington sound, e.g., Carney on bass clarinet, Hodges on soprano sax. (Can someone tell me when Hardwick stopped playing bass sax?)

It is difficult to know the details of how the sections were scored, but indications are that the allocation of the lead to one player (or to two in the trumpets) was more common in other bands, producing more homogeneity, but also a certain monotony of phrasing. It is useful to remember that, throughout the 30s, black bands, especially their saxes, were problematic for white reviewers, who often decried carelessness of attack and intonation in section work, while granting virtues of hotness, swing, and richness of color. I can't imagine that Ellington was ever bothered.

I've chosen to discuss all the works in the order recorded. This locks me into a marked repetitiveness of form only compensated for by the startlingly broad range of musical techniques and structures mastered by Ellington. In the designation of solos I've sometimes been remiss or, no doubt, incorrect. But all truly major contributions are cited and should be sufficient guide to those who are unacquainted with the musical personalities of Ellington's sidemen.

My remarks sometimes pick out brief passages in the interior of a work and frequently refer to overall symmetries of form. Ellington's practice of using more than one chord progression or song form in the same piece does not make reference to these matters easy, so I must ask the reader to listen for the main points of division, and to count measures in twos, fours, and eights. In giving the overall plan for a work, I use capital letters, sticking with one letter so long as the basic harmony and form remain the same, but with the option of writing A′, A″, etc. for variations to which I wish to draw analytical attention. The letters I, X, M, and T indicate Introduction, Transition, Modulation, and Tag, respectively. Lowercase letters serve, then, to refer to the subdivisions of a chorus. With all letters numerical subscripts can be used to show the number of measures contained. Two choruses of a conventional song form with bridge could then be shown as: $I_6 \; A_{32} \; (a_8 a_8 b_8 a_8) \; X_4 \; A_{32} \; T$

(Chicago, 6 March 1940)

Jack the Bear
$I_8 \; A_{12} \; X_4 \; B_{32} \; (aaba) \; X \; C_{12} \; C'_{12} \; C''_{12} \; D_8 \; X \; A_{12} \; T_4$

The formal plan is not obvious on first listening. Discounting the introduction and the tag, the first and last choruses, featuring piano and bass, respectively, with orchestral responses, are the same twelve-measure quasi-blues. There follows an aaba section, 32 measures long, with Bigard and Williams soloing, then three unmodified blues choruses for Carney, Nanton, and the whole band. These four sections (counting the three straight blues choruses as one) are set off with an identical four-measure unison sax figure. D_8 is a truncated blues chorus. The piece has the effect of a showcase for Blanton, who is strongly recorded even when not explicitly playing solo, but is also a small masterpiece of formal play and sleight-of-hand (it all sounds like blues), use of motivic cross-reference and scoring across the seams between choruses. For the former, compare the Introduction with the C chorus for the full band, for the latter the bridging sax figures in C and C′. *Jack the Bear* was a Harlem piano player *circa* 1900.

Ko-Ko
$I_8 \; A_{12} \; B_{24} \; A'_{12} A''_{12} \; B'_8 \; A'''_{12} \; A_{12} \; T \; [I_8 + 4]$

It's odd that two quite distinct major landmarks in jazz—this along with Charlie Parker's reworking of *Cherokee*—should have the same title. Here the emotional vein exploited is that of primitivism and savagery, and it does not surprise to learn (via Barry Ulanov) that *Ko-Ko* is an excerpt from a projected opera on an African theme, *Boola*. The work is mostly minor blues, but that says nothing about the symmetry of form (once again) or the climactic plan. After the first chorus mixing Tizol with the reeds, the second is a gangly 24 measures consisting to my ears of an initial four bars and seemingly endless extensions for Nanton and the brass. Matters are brought to a preliminary peak in A′, with the saxes in G-flat major against the basic e-flat minor and Duke splattering chords and runs all over the keyboard. A″ retreats to convention, and then is followed with a compressed restatement of the alternating harmonies of B, and finally the climactic fourth blues chorus with a concentration of dissonant brass writing such as had never been heard in any "dance" band.

Morning Glory
$$I_4 \ A_{32} \ X_2 \ A_{32} \ T_6$$

This is Rex Stewart's place in the sun in these performances. I find neither the tune—which seems to me unrepresentative of Duke's song style in 1940—nor Stewart's playing particularly attractive, and think the flashy sax writing in the second chorus poorly coordinated with the rest of the band. Discographies sometimes list Stewart as playing cornet only with Duke. Although that is true here (into a hat for the first chorus, then open), I believe he is often playing trumpet, except on occasions when Duke wanted the constricted and grayish sound that Rex could produce, almost in defiance of the model which he followed to a degree in phrasing and line, Bix Beiderbecke.

(Chicago, 15 March 1940)

Conga Brava
$$I_4 \ A_{54} \ (a_{20} \ a_{20} \ b_8 \ c_6) \ A'_{40} \ b_8 \ A''_{20} \ B_{16} \ c_6 \ I_4 \ A_{54}$$

I have a friend who will always remember me as the person who introduced him to this work. But not because of the letter plan printed above, which is merely this month's idea of how the work goes. *Conga Brava*'s vamp and the basic tune are first cousins to *Caravan*—another, more famous, work credited partly to Tizol. The tune is an odd twenty measures in length, subdivided 8, 4, and 4, with 4 to fill in at the end. Its harmony is prolonged F-7th with ornaments, so the square-cut and harmonically active bridge—which also breaks the Latin rhythm—comes as a large surprise, as also the abbreviated six-measure show band ending. I believe it possible that Ben Webster is lost, brilliantly lost, during A′. Duke plays subdominant and dominant chords in Webster's 15th and 16th, 35th and 36th bars, clearly marking the cadence points in Tizol's 2 × 20 bar structure. Webster, however, is playing 12, 8, and 4 measure phrases having nothing to do with the tune. After he ends *in medias res,* the strangely old-timey bridge returns, to be followed by a reed statement of the tune larded with Rex Stewart's superb counter-melody. I have labelled as B the coruscating brass quintet subdivided 10, 6, and 6, with the last phrase taking us back to c, and a literal restatement of the opening. Did the dancers simply gape open-mouthed at this headlong tour through conflicting rhythms?

Concerto for Cootie
$$I_8 \ A_{36} \ (a_{10} \ a_{10} \ b_8 \ a_8) \ X_2 \ B_{16} \ a'_8 \ T_8$$

This work was the basis of an analytical *tour de force* by André Hodeir [see §57]. His discussion alerts us to many important subtleties: the small variations in the endings of the phrases of the first theme, the differing colors used by Cootie Williams, the daring of the modulation into D-flat for the bravura climax for open horn (B in the scheme above), the delectable dissonances in the sax voicings behind the various repetitions of a, and more. His parsing of the overall form: Introduction; Exposition (F major, 40 mm.); Central part (D-flat major, 18 mm.); Recapitulation and Coda (F major, 16 mm.), does not make much sense to me—the proportions are crazy and the reference to "classical" structure unhelpful. It is nonetheless interesting and revealing that such a brief piece can present problems for analysis.

Part of the problem lies in a possible misunderstanding of the "theme": its memorable part is a long up-beat *plus* the indispensable trombone trio response. Next, I doubt that we should count as "exposition" any more than the first 10 measure phrase, with subsequent repetitions considered orchestral variations. Linking all the sections are flowing sax figures and colors first heard in the Introduction.

Me and You
$$I_8 \ A_{32} \ (a_8 \ b_8 \ a_8 \ c_8) \ X_4 \ A_{32} \ A_{32} \ A_{32} \ T_4$$

After Duke's fancy three against four phrasing and implied establishment of d minor in the Introduction, this performance is an uncomplicated setting of a 2 × 16 pop song. The scoring at the outset is attractive, with trombones in whole notes and a unison sax figure backing Cootie Williams. Sonny Greer is pretty obtrusive here, along with the usually unnoticed Freddy Guy. The latter uses a hackneyed dotted rhythm in the first chorus that seems half a dozen years past its prime. Otherwise, the listener might pay attention to the tenuous brass duet (again with unison saxes) behind Ivie Anderson's serene voice. The trading of fours and twos by Lawrence Brown and Johnny Hodges is remarkable only by the rarity of the device in this series of works. Barney Bigard over a crisp tutti and Greer on the edge of rushing the time close an unremarkable performance . . . Except that in defiance of logic and the usual norms of jazz performance (particularly a flowing, propulsive rhythm section à la Basie), the band swings very hard. There was of course Jimmy Blanton counteracting the choppiness of the drumming, but also Duke's firecracker accents. And I suppose it must help to have played together for a decade.

(Hollywood, 4 May 1940)

Cotton Tail
A_{32} A_{32} A_{32} A_{32} A_{32} A_{32}

Who wouldn't have been knocked on their ears in 1940 by this incredible version of *I Got Rhythm?* (There are a few minor changes in section lengths and chords.) The tempo nowadays seems less ferocious than right, at an exceptional 250 quarter-notes per minute. The new tune written over the old harmonies is already exciting enough, with its accented ninth at the beginning and its flatted fifth shortly thereafter, but the one deployed in the fifth chorus for the saxes is one of the landmarks of the pre-war band era. To turn to the less obvious: the scoring of the first ensemble chorus merits rehearing, e.g., the trombones generally, the ingenious counterpoint of the saxes to the brass lead in the last four measures, and the way in which intensity and spaciousness are conveyed simultaneously by the simple device of doubling the sax lead with Cootie Williams' trumpet.

Although I often fall prey to the received adverse opinion of Sonny Greer as a drummer, I forgive him all for his constantly varied and energizing work here. A listening or two just for Blanton and Greer on this performance is worth the time.

Ellington had not to this date ever made such a wide-open and driving piece, and this is undoubtedly the major exhibit showing the new fertilization of the band from the West (namely, Blanton and Ben Webster). Two things perhaps might be mentioned: Duke had never had a hot tenor, and was also a bit stand-offish about "improvisation" and "jam sessions," preferring a balance of planning—though not necessarily written planning—with calculated doses of short solos, and the occasional showpiece for one player. Many treasure these 1940 recordings just because Webster managed to lay claim to such large tracts of Ellington's turf, showing him that you could think on your feet and still play fine music.

Never No Lament
I_{16} (a_8 a_8) A_{32} A_{32} T_8 (a_8)

Another of Ellington's tunes with an unforgettable upbeat measure. It is similar to *Concerto for Cootie* in that and in having the answering orchestral phrase an indispensable part of the tune. It was "commercialized" by the addition of lyrics and widely popular as *Don't Get Around Much Anymore*. The major formal surprise here is framing the two aaba choruses with two a's as an introduction and one as a coda, thus something of a simple variation form. Johnny Hodges is the nimble and witty star here, with Lawrence Brown at the beginning and near the end a perfect foil. The climax lies in the second eight of the second chorus, with admirable sax and trombone counterpoint behind Cootie Williams. I also find the elegance of phrasing, individually and collectively, notable here.

(Chicago, 28 May 1940)

Dusk
I_4 A_{16} (a_4 a_4 b_4 a_4) A_{16} A_{16} X_2 A_8' (b a)

Never underestimate the power of the chord of the flatted sixth (here G-flat 7th in B-flat). The other harmony which makes this floating piece in *Mood Indigo* voicing go to the heart is a quite simple—in the description—turn to the relative minor via a C diminished chord in measures nine and ten. Formally there are no games being played, but the alterations of harmony behind Rex Stewart in the second chorus defy simple description. More changes are rung on the elementary harmonies in the ensuing third chorus for trombone trio and bubbly saxes, with "out of key" piano chords *passim* that no one else at the time would or could have added. I know of no other work for jazz orchestra that conveys such an impression of tranquility on the verge of tears.

Bojangles
I_8 A_{16} (a_8 a_8) A_{16} A_{16} B_{16} (2×8) A_{16} A_{16} B_{16} T_8

Music historians have learned from experience that even the titles given to works by their composers are often added after the fact, but surely no one will object to hearing this happy-go-lucky hop as a "portrait" of dancer Bill Robinson. It is Duke's major achievement here to get us to listen to the Dixielandish chord progression for ten eight-measure sections, with only four sections of the same length as relief. The overall plan thus corresponds to no standard song form. Barney Bigard is used here, as he often was, to represent manic high spirits or comedy. The orchestral mix of clarinet and brass in the fifth A section is characteristic, and its éclat leads effectively into the second pseudo-bridge (B; actually the climax of the work). All ears should be on the linear sense of the bass, here quite prominently recorded.

A Portrait of Bert Williams
I_5 A_{16} (a_4 a_4 b_4 a_4) B_{16} A_{16} B_8' [a_4 T_8 or a_2 T_{10}]

Bert Williams, active in U.S. vaudeville and musical comedy for nearly 25 years until his death in 1922, made many records featuring his lazy and sometimes pathetic baritone, and in the case of his all-time hit, *Nobody,* a talking trombone.

Make of this what you will. This is also a piece with an elaborate and interesting structure which eludes first hearing and even rehearing. Part of the problem is that the 4×4 aaba first chorus (A) is separated from its repetition by another 4×4 section to different harmonies (B). But Joe Nanton's solo in the last four-measure section of B makes the ear believe a new large section has begun, in turn seemingly concluded by four measures of a Bigard solo which are actually the beginning of the second A. Such deviousness is consistent with the brilliant five measure mosaic of the introduction and the structural ambiguities of the last twelve measures. Rex Stewart begins what seems to be the final statement of the subject (a), but it lasts only two, not four bars. Nanton then plays what seems to be the beginning of the tag but comes to a very definite cadence after two bars, with eight more bars to run.

Blue Goose
$I_6 \ A_{32} \ (a_8 \ a_8 \ b_8 \ a_8) \ X_4 \ A_{32} \ T_4$

If you think this sounds like *Stardust,* it's because of the harmony of the first eight measures of this aaba tune (*Stardust* is abab'). With Johnny Hodges playing solo soprano sax first and last, and elsewhere in ensemble, the sax voicings are often wide open. The bridge of the second chorus has some complex interaction between brass and reeds, but generally the work is designed for solo interest. Lawrence Brown's sixteen bars I find wholly admirable, despite my usual dislike for his idiosyncratic sound in the central trombone register.

(New York, 22 July 1940)

Harlem Airshaft
$I_{12} \ (3 \times 4) \ A_{32} \ (a_8 \ a_8 \ b_8 \ a_8) \ A_{32} \ A_{32} \ A_{32} \ T_2$

There is a well-known description by Duke describing this as a portrayal of raunchy, ebullient urban apartment living. Duke also believed as an alert performer that if a piece sounded good it was good. What's left for the annotator to say?

Not too much in this case perhaps, except to single out the players who are already structurally singled out, Williams and Bigard, both of them at the top of their form. One might also mention the tripartite introduction, a gem of unconnected connectedness. Then follow four choruses of pseudo-blues in A-flat: blues in the nature of the riffs, the break structure of the second chorus, and the characteristic I–IV progression, but pseudo in formal outline (aaba) and the overall harmony. The fine rhythmic dovetailing of the trombones, clarinet, and saxes in the second chorus is less audible than it should be, due to under-recording of the saxes. This seems to be no problem in the final chorus, remarkable in the concerted creation of climax in a short space: first, by the tried-and-true technique of taut understatement by a tightly-muted Williams, then by the surging lift of the bridge with Bigard soaring, and finally in the basic brass against reed riffing of the final eight. I don't find the last four completely successful, but can live with it. As a postscript, I hear some connection between the Introduction and some of the sounds of Charlie Barnet's very successful *Skyliner* of 1945, particularly the sax timbre.

At a Dixie Roadside Diner
$I_8 \ A_{32} \ (a_8 \ a_8 \ b_8 \ a_8) \ X_4 \ A_{32} \ X_4 \ A_{32}$

Ellington's pen as a lyricist was decidedly not golden, and his Swanee River piano introduction is more clever than musically relevant. We have here three straight-forward choruses, one of them in support of Ivie Anderson's rah-ther academic singing. She was a much better singer than she seems on these recordings—or better, she was always a good singer who often delivered second-rate material—the plight, in a word, of the girl band singer—even Ellington's. Jimmy Blanton's bass is wonderful, though, and Harry Carney bounces along with good swing at the start of the third chorus, unfortunately losing the thread in his seventh and subsequent measures. A muted Rex Stewart plays quietly at the beginning, then takes the last chorus out with good high B-flats (and one strong C). Actually, getting back to the lyrics, I reckon the song was supposed to be pretty amusing (some of the rhymes, and "with the slot machine playing," etc.). Maybe you had to be there.

All Too Soon
$I_6 \ A_{32} \ (a_8 \ a_8 \ b_8 \ a_8) \ A_{32}$

Two choruses of a structurally typical aaba pop tune don't add up to much, right? Wrong: I doubt that Lawrence Brown's slithering mellowness was ever more tasteful. I wish I could figure out who plays the prominent high countermelody behind him. I suppose Otto Hardwick, but how like a violin! A special point of interest in the first chorus is Duke's reuse of the chromatic flutters of the introduction before the bridge and at the very end. The mood changes drastically for Ben Webster's second chorus, first via the abrupt key-change from C to D-flat, then through the eerie mixture of cup and straight muted trumpets which obsessively accompanies him.

Rumpus in Richmond
$I \ I_4' \ A_{32} \ (a_8 \ a_8 \ b_8 \ a_8) \ A_{32} \ X_4 \ A_{32} \ T_4$

Surely the most conventionally (and superbly) hot player in the band was Cootie Williams—something that was more in evidence in some small Ellington units (cf. the small combo version of *Caravan*) and, a few months after this recording, with Benny Goodman. The abstract chord progression, rising by semitones from G-7th and never quite sure whether it wants to end in C major or e minor, fills our ears for most of the three choruses. There is additional shape given by Williams' climactic third chorus, by a short patch of brilliant writing in the first half of the bridge, using Barney Bigard prominently, and by a key change to E-flat from C. A note on the limitations of letter diagrams: the passages marked X and T above are in fact close kin to I', something which is frequently the case in other works.

I have often found it instructive to play only a second or two of an Ellington ensemble passage, thus bringing out a great adventurousness in fine detail. Try it here with the tag, or even the last two chords plus piano suffix, and figure out how many different pitches are in the clusters. Such throwaways must have been arrangers' despair in those days.

(New York, 24 July 1940)

Sepia Panorama
$$A_{12} \; B_{16} \; C_8 \; D_{12} \; D_{12} \; C_8 \; B_8' \; A_{12}$$

Ellington here exhibits the most rigorous arch form of all the 1940 works, with the four initial sections repeated in inverse order. Or you can understand the plan as two central blues choruses framed by three sections. The key plan is F major for the first two sections, then B-flat major, then back to F. The elimination of half of the B section on its second appearance seems to me unsatisfactory and perhaps the result of recording time limits. The harmonies of this section — altered ninth chords — form their own arch, rising by whole steps and falling chromatically. Unusual as the general plan is by any standards of the time — including Duke's — it might be considered primitive. Musical fun and games aside, is there a musical structure that goes a little deeper?

My affirmative answer hinges on two things. First, the side arches created by the dissonant and tonally innovative reed chorus (B), and the basic blues style of the solos (D). Duke's backing of Jimmy Blanton's agile triplets is totally common property, and Ben Webster almost blows the sophisticated plan wide open with his Kansas City (and environs) tenor. Another kind of conflict is in the use of blues clichés and formulas in unusual places or juxtapositions. Where the famous *Diminuendo and Crescendo in Blue* of a few years before did this in an almost manic or surreal conglomeration (which I hear as an extreme example of musical wit), *Sepia Panorama* succeeds in the mode of sobriety and order with just enough discord to make perfect harmony.

I think the first take — the one issued — has a slight edge in balance and steadiness of tempo, yet some of Duke's interpolations on the second take, Webster's more tentative solo, and Blanton's riskier double timing seem to me to amply merit preservation.

(Chicago, 5 September 1940)

In a Mellotone
$$I_8 \; A_{32} \; (a_8 b_8 a_8 c_8) \; X_2 \; A_{32} \; A_{32}$$

. . . is a medium tempo chestnut, *Rose Room*, in its chords. Duke's riffish tune preserves the character of the original in putting non-triadic pitches in stressed position. The arrangement is conceived for the most part as a dialogue, with much in the scoring and in the solo work that seems to me old-fashioned (e.g., the sixteenth-note flashiness of the saxes in the second chorus and Hodges' final brilliant solo). Why not, though: *Rose Room* was written in 1917. I find the second chorus generally amusing, but particularly in the exchanges between Cootie Williams and the saxes in the second sixteen, in which one or the other seems deliberately to misunderstand the other's message. For an example of how one player's sound could count, listen to what Harry Carney's grittiness does to the low unison sax statement of the lead during the first chorus.

Warm Valley
$I_4 \ A_{32} \ (a_8a_8b_8) \ A'_{24}(b_8a_8a_8)$

Sing over quickly to yourself *Sweet and Lovely*. The chords are different, but the phrasing is very similar and the idea of a bridge in a distant key (B-natural to the tune's B-flat) is preserved. No matter: the emotional implications of a descending chromatic progression have been with us for centuries. And it is well known that it was one of Johnny Hodges' roles in the Ellington troupe to talk of love, usually in a detumescent, floating phrase, although the more idealistic may prefer to think of yearning and dreaming before the fact. The title has been said to be an anatomical reference.

There may have been some rearrangement of sections to make *Warm Valley* fit on the record, chiefly the elimination of the first eight of the second chorus, but the work does not seem badly proportioned to me as it stands. The trombone writing (sometimes combined with high trumpet) interests my ear here, especially from the modulating phrase leading into the second bridge and then behind Hodges. Note also, along with some characteristic filigree from Duke in the first chorus, some nearly polytonal chords in the next to last eight measure section of the second. This passage is drastically replaced on the third take, made six weeks later and the one issued, by a much less interesting but safer passage for the saxes. I also prefer Hodges on the first take: his chops seem fresher and his handling of the last bridge better in keeping with the mood.

The Duets

Practically every piano passage in the 1940 recordings is duet-like, and even in orchestral passages Jimmy Blanton is often so strongly recorded that he seems in conversation with the band. Everyone in the band must have reveled in Blanton's inspired bass parts. His career has often been compared to Charlie Christian's, both revolutionaries on their instruments, both quite young, both using St. Louis as their springboard to national prominence, and both soon tragically extinguished by tuberculosis. But one can find precedent for the guitar as a solo instrument, both in its acoustic and electrical form. But apart from buffoonery like *Slappin' the Bass* and *Big Noise from Winnetka,* and a few breaks here and there, the bass was still recovering from its 1920s and early 30s eclipse by the tuba, and the excellent New Orleanians who still remembered how to use a bow and play something other than two or four in a bar were not much in evidence—though of course Duke had had one in his band for an important period, Wellman Braud. In any event, I wonder whether Blanton would have received so much exposure and been given so many opportunities to display his genius in another band, one in which propulsive time-keeping and section playing was more of a fetish.

(Chicago, 1 October 1940)

Pitter Panther Patter
$I_8 \ A_{32} \ (a_8a_8b_8a_8) \ A_{32} \ B_{32} \ (a_8a_8b_8b_8) \ A_{32}$

Light-hearted, playful, even *cute* are inevitable adjectives for this New York-jivey, Wallerish bit of verbal and musical wit. To this day it is difficult to believe that the double bass could have undergone such a character change from the solemn thumping workhorse of the big band to a light-footed and rapid dancer for whom no tempo held terrors. There is not the slightest lagging behind when Blanton plays in rhythmic unison with Duke; indeed it seems as though he pulls him along. Be aware also of the resonance and clarity of the eighth notes, and the excellent intonation when playing in the second octave of the highest string. Both this and the other up-tempo duet are in a key which is advantageous for the player (G major). If one needs convincing that classic virtuoso statements remain classic statements, even when made at dawn, he can compare the original version with that done in 1973 by Duke and the excellent Ray Brown (Pablo 2310-721: "This One's for Blanton").

Body and Soul
$I_4 \ A_{32} \ (a_8a_8b_8a_8) \ X_4 \ A_{16} \ (b_8a_8)$

. . . was already canonized by Hawkins' masterpiece of about a year earlier. Blanton takes it in the standard key, although somewhat slower than Hawkins. Even so, the daring in playing bowed 16th notes even at this sedate pace is again unparalleled in recorded jazz. I don't think that his execution was quite up to the task at first, but there are no time problems when he hangs up his bow for the second chorus. Execution aside, Blanton astounds because he can think at this speed, though mostly in chromatically descending sequences on each quarter note beat—which, since Hawkins anyway, were becoming part of the tune.

Sophisticated Lady
$I_4 \ A_{32} \ (a_8a_8b_8a_8) \ X_2 \ A'_{16} \ (b_8a_8)$

. . . at an only slightly faster tempo, follows the same plan and is also in the "correct" instrumental key of A-flat. Where *Body and Soul* is a first-rate recording, this is, in my opinion, absolutely superb. No sluggishness of bowing is in evidence and the entire chorus, from the opening melodic statement to the climactic double stops at the end, unfaltering. I get a little weary of the descending chromatic sevenths after a good meal of them in *Body and Soul,* but the lady wouldn't be very sophisticated without them. Listeners interested in links between Duke and Thelonious Monk will note the brief piano introduction . . .

Mr. J. B. Blues
I_{16} A_{12} A_{12} B_{16} A_{12} A_{12} A_{12} A_{12} A_{12} [first take]

. . . as they will also note the fourth chorus of this work, a kind of polytonal parody which Monk learned very well. The first of the two takes was the one issued, and I have no quarrel with the choice. Taking it out with the last three choruses *arco* is more effective, and the slightly brighter tempo and extra chorus on the second take do little to compensate for less coherence in Mr. J. B.'s playing and—could it be?—boredom on Duke's part. I can find nothing to say in favor of the oddly repetitious extended introduction or the B chorus. Many of Ellington's permutations or variations of blues structure are very attractive, but on something which is otherwise a straight-ahead blues, why bother?

(Chicago, 17 October 1940)

The Flaming Sword
I_8 A_{64} $(a_{16}a_{16}b_{16}a_{16})$ A_{64} A_{64} T

I have some notion that Marcus Garvey is in the wings—but would also want to include this work in an anthology of versions of the jazz standard *Panama*. The overall shape strikes me as less successful than many other works of the period: the counterpoint of the first bridge is more intricate than what follows, and with the modulation to the subdominant (A-flat) for the third chorus, the work smacks of various flagwavers of a decade earlier (*Tiger Rag* and sundry clones) with their endless trumpet and clarinet trios. The use of contrasting trombone color in the first two "a" sections of the second chorus (Juan Tizol and Joe Nanton, respectively) is a good example of how what some band leaders might well consider a flaw could be put to effective artistic use. Returning to the matter of shape: these lengthy Latin specialties without easily memorable tunes, e.g., *Conga Brava*, need special treatment. With the kind of inverted plan followed here, it is one of the few works in this series that seems not to fit its time-frame.

(Chicago, 28 October 1940)

Across the Track Blues
I_4 A_{12} A_{12} A_{12} A_{12} A_{12} T_2

Finally, a more stellar role for Barney Bigard, who while he is practically always in evidence, and as much as Duke always loved his hollow, woody sound, is rather in eclipse as a focal point in the 1940 recordings. Although not shown in my letter diagram, since all sections are 12 bar blues, the plan is roughly an arch, with clarinet solo in opening and closing choruses, preaching cornet (Stewart) and trombone (Brown) with congregational responses from trombones and saxes, respectively in the second and fourth, and a central moment of sophisticated harmony for clarinet and saxes together. Bigard's final solo is compressed, seemingly anchored at the beginning to the lowest note on his instrument (and also the tonic), then up three octaves for a nonpareil gliss.

Chloe (Song of the Swamp)
A_{32} ($a_8b_8a_8c_8$) X_4 B_{16} A_{32} T_4

The arrangement has been accredited to Billy Strayhorn. This classic hit of 1927 (by Neil Moret and Gus Kahn) is intractable as a jazz "vehicle," being so highly-colored and distinctive as it stands that it just needs to be played. With its lyrics it teeters on the edge of the ludicrous, and indeed was brilliantly done to death by Spike Jones in 1945.

There is little, if any, formal interest here, but rather an exploration of highly-colored voicing, with a few odd polytonal excursions (listen particularly to the brief bass figure in the second sixteen bar section). The use of both wa-wa and strangled trombone, together with a Mood Indigoesque background is pretty sinister. I thought for a moment Harry Carney was being used on bass clarinet, but finally doubt it. The second A shows Ben Webster playing with a paradoxical mixture of intensity and restraint and then modulates for the third time—more in the manner of a stock arrangement—for the conclusion by the whole band. The scale figures introduced here for the saxes and also used in the tag are mocked by Duke with a final piano run in B-natural after a close in B-flat.

I Never Felt This Way Before
I_4 A_{32} ($a_8b_8a_8c_8$) X_4 A_{32} c_8

Help! I have *Mood Indigo* on the brain, but Duke here does after all use its key and voicing at the start. However, this 2×16 abac tune uses four distinct mixtures in the first chorus, with an especially effective eight bars for high trombone lead over closely-written low saxes. Even after the key change to G for Herb Jeffries' urbane vocal, brass and saxes are kept low, making good contrast for Lawrence Brown to take it out in his extremely well-controlled high range.

(Chicago, 28 December 1940)

Sidewalks of New York
I_{16} A_{32} ($a_8b_8c_8d_8$) X_2 A_{32} A_{32} d_8

". . . and now featuring Tricky Sam Nanton and our saxophones." Although there is something to be heard in phrasing, harmony, and background figures, that overworked adjective "pedestrian" seems to me to apply punningly here. My ear is unhappy with X, Duke's two-measure modulation to D-flat for Nanton's bluesy solo, and the second sax soloist—I suppose Otto

Hardwick—in the last chorus is present only in body. Jimmy Blanton is stalwart throughout, but the rest of the rhythm section seems to be following a different drummer.

Although these annotations are not designed to state the general case for the importance or interest of the works presented here, we can draw some general conclusions:

- Much of the merit of the 1940 recordings resides in their brevity, compression, and economy. On contemporary non-commercial recordings (mostly of radio broadcasts) of the Ellington band as well as of others, we often hear more and longer solos, and works of up to five minutes in length. These are effective and refreshing to hear for different reasons than the commercial studio recordings. (Note: I'd like to know a lot more about the specific conditions under which these recordings were conducted, particularly whether there was some deliberate choice by Victor—which had just captured Ellington from Columbia—to record such challenging material, or whether Ellington himself had free or nearly free choice.)
- Such brevity emphasizes the aspect of formal play, variety of orchestration and avoidance of repetition in these works: a lot happens in very little time.
- These recordings are landmarks neither of jazz improvisation nor of electrifying dance music. But it seems that Sonny Greer especially is a much more swinging drummer on jobs for which we have non-commercial recordings, when soloists often were given freer rein.
- There is a strain of craziness in Ellington that is never pervasive, yet can often be heard in his piano accompaniment, in odd trombone phrases ending in mid-air, and in brief passages of polytonal or extremely dissonant harmony. They are there for the very attentive, but the ordinary listener can and does pass them by. The avant-garde calls this hedging; the successful performer, prudence.

In many of these works, Ellington realized a kind of balance between sentiment and structure, mannerism and naturalism, program and absolute music, which renders both formalist and "impressionistic" criticism inadequate. A lot of the latter has been done, and people will always make too much of titles, so I have perhaps erred in the direction of formalism.

- The ear will always be struck by two properties of the Ellington band: great richness of color in the sections deriving from a mixture of highly distinctive individual sounds (not so much in the trumpets), and extraordinary collective agreement on the dynamic and accentual curve of a melody. Neither one of these could have been achieved by other ensembles of the time. Some of this has to do with being Afro-American, some with maturity and length of experience together, some with the fact that leader, composer, arranger, and sideman were the same person (a unique case).

- These properties, coupled with Ellington's conscious intent to release, yet focus the individuality, even the eccentricity, of his players, creates a music which is heard as expressive because (ideally) every member of the band is expressive, even when there is no particularly obvious "message," or when formal games are being played.
- In none of these works did Duke face the problem of how, given the ability to sustain ferocity, gaiety, tenderness, gloom or what have you over three or four minutes, one can work on a broader time scale. But *we* can, by combining triads of works, say *Sepia Panorama, Dusk*, and *Cotton Tail*, construct longer works which are as "deep" or "musically interesting" as much European or U.S. concert music of the time (and perhaps, time will tell, even more so).
- Neither the conventional categories of jazz nor those of classical music provide a comfortable niche for these works. On the former, see above. On the latter, there is the matter of falling between the two chairs of chamber music and symphonic music, and perhaps more important, that of being very difficult or impossible to recreate.

It's my hope that this collection of the greater part of the recordings made by Ellington in 1940 for RCA Victor will speak for itself to a large degree. Naturally, a wider knowledge of Ellington's earlier and later work, as well as that of contemporary bands, will make them more interesting and significant in terms of historical context. It will also confirm the notion that neither Ellington himself, nor any other band, had ever before produced so rich a variety of works which still interest the ear and refresh the spirit after repeated listening.

87. Stanley Crouch on *Such Sweet Thunder,* *Suite Thursday,* and *Anatomy of a Murder* (1988)

C hallenging the received notion that Ellington's greatest compositional achievements clustered around the year 1940, the writer and critic Stanley Crouch (b. 1945) has long championed works from the composer's later years. In the following program notes for a concert at Lincoln Center in 1988, he called the period from 1957 to 1967 the most remarkable in Ellington's career. Support for the position derived from three works composed by Ellington and Strayhorn between 1957 and 1960: *Such Sweet Thunder* (1957), the Shakespearian suite premiered at Town Hall in New York City;

Source: Stanley Crouch, excerpt from program notes for a concert in the Classical Jazz series, held on 10 August 1988 at Alice Tully Hall, Lincoln Center of the Performing Arts, New York.

Anatomy of a Murder (1959), from the soundtrack of the film by Otto Preminger; and *Suite Thursday* (1960), based on John Steinbeck's novel *Sweet Thursday* and premiered at the Monterey Jazz Festival.

The concert for which Crouch wrote these notes was part of the Classical Jazz series, begun in 1987 with Wynton Marsalis as artistic advisor and Crouch as artistic consultant. Since its inception the series has been devoted to reviving outstanding works in the jazz repertory, many of which—as on this particular occasion—have rarely received performances in the concert hall.

Crouch has written on music, politics, race, and culture for the *Village Voice* and other publications since the seventies. Some of these writings are collected in *Notes of a Hanging Judge: Essays and Reviews, 1979–1989* (1990). Currently he is completing a novel, *First Snow in Kokomo,* and working on a biography of Charlie Parker.

Even though every aesthetic idiom produces an inevitable caboose of critical commentary, some are more burdened by that last car than others. Of all the new arts that have come forward in this century, jazz has suffered the most from lightweight analysis, and Duke Ellington, whose output was of such size and variety that its very massiveness functioned as a deterrent to detailed evaluation, never received the level of informed commentary that his position in twentieth-century music both deserves and demands. More than any other musician in the history of jazz, and perhaps in the history of twentieth-century music itself, Ellington sustained his development, ever extending his style and his expressiveness, creating a body of composition so rich in contrasts and self-imposed challenges that he maintained his position at the head of the pack for nearly forty years. That is why the performance this evening of *Such Sweet Thunder, Suite Thursday,* and selections from the film score for *Anatomy of a Murder* has a special significance; it points up the longest reigning misconception in jazz criticism, which is that Ellington's greatest period was the four-year streak of three-minute masterpieces he and his orchestra produced between 1939 and 1942.

Though one cannot deny the quality of the material that was immortalized through recording technology during those four years, the truly serious listener will find Ellington did more than periodically meet the standards of his so-called golden period. Between 1942 and the end of his life at seventy-five in 1974, Ellington went on to deepen the clarity and conception of his craft, very nearly creating something every decade that was superior to all high points in his previous work. In fact what has been too often referred to as the pinnacle of his career was more accurately the last phase of the completion of an aesthetic language that he had been working on successfully since 1927, when Ellington first issued recordings now considered masterworks. Consequently, the fifteen-year period that culminated in 1942 provided the maestro with the scope of emotional, technical, compositional, and conceptual material upon which he would make, to use Albert Murray's phrase, "extensions, elaborations, and refinements" until the very end.

The works featured this evening are from what was probably Ellington's most remarkable decade, 1957 to 1967, though the two suites and the selections from the film score were all written between 1957 and 1960. During that decade, Ellington produced so many pieces of such enduring value, extending himself and dialoguing with his own past successes, that the density and the quality of the output form an almost overwhelming achievement. In some works, one hears Ellington consciously turning almost back to the beginning of his style by using Russell Procope's New Orleans-inspired clarinet at the top of the orchestra as he often had through the thirties and the early forties when he had Barney Bigard, or adding to the lyric pinnacles Johnny Hodges had provided on his alto saxophone, or allowing Paul Gonsalves to remake the tenor as harmonic power-forward in the Ellingtonian context, or taking a timbral and harmonic tour through the possibilities of the trumpet as inspired by the stretch from Armstrong to Gillespie, and so on. Those approaches are all deftly orchestrated in these pieces this evening.

Such Sweet Thunder [1957] was inspired by characters in Shakespeare and is one of the peaks in late Ellington. Billy Strayhorn, Ellington's co-composer for nearly thirty years, said that he and Ellington worked on the piece for six months, and talked to a number of people about it as they toured the country. This suggests that they availed themselves of the various scholars who might have known a good amount about the Bard and might also have been devoted Ellington fans. Though some might have considered the subjects beyond jazz, no musician was better suited to transfer his impressions of Shakespeare into music than Ellington, who had performed for and had known the high and low all of his career—powerful politicians, royalty, and gangsters; soldiers, servants, and thieves; murderers, dancers, and romantics; businessmen, poets, and buffoons. They had come in all classes, all races, all religions, all sizes, shapes, and features. Given his gift for luminous detail, Ellington was well prepared and the resulting work is distinctively original and imposingly mature.

Of the thirteen pieces that comprise *Such Sweet Thunder,* the four "sonnets" are different in mood, orchestration, and rhythm, but have in common, as Ellington scholar Bill Dobbins points out,[1] fourteen phrases of ten notes each, musically mirroring the fourteen lines of iambic pentameter (ten syllables) that make up the literary sonnet Shakespeare favored. Throughout, there are witty and dramatic, melancholy and romantic sections, some combining aspects of various works for poetic fusions of material, such as "The Telecasters," which combines the three witches (the trombones) from *Macbeth* with Iago from *Othello* (the baritone), or the concluding section, "Circle of Fourths," "inspired," as Irving Townsend wrote in the original notes for the album, "by Shakespeare himself and the four major parts of his artistic contribution: tragedy, comedy, history, and the sonnets."

Suite Thursday was composed for and performed first at the 1960 Monterey Jazz Festival. Inspired by John Steinbeck's novel *Sweet Thursday* [1954], it is made up of four parts, "Misfit Blues," "Schwiphti," "Zweet Zursday," and "Lay-By." The variety and the power Ellington and Strayhorn were capable

---

[1] Dobbins, on the faculty at the Eastman School of Music, had transcribed with David Berger the version of *Such Sweet Thunder* played on the program.

of is heard in the lyric themes and the love of the permutations possible within the blues, all growing from a minor sixth interval, which is indicative of how sophisticated the composing for the organization had become. By this point Ellington knew well the fundamental components of music and could build upon any one of them: intervals (from which come melody and harmony), timbre (from which comes color), and rhythm.

Anatomy of a Murder [1959] is one of Ellington's grandest accomplishments. In a recent and devastating review of James Lincoln Collier's insipid, sloppy, and irresponsible biography *Duke Ellington,* writer and former jazz pianist Tom Piazza called the recording of the film score "the closest thing we have to a vernacular American symphony."[2] Coming twenty years after what was supposed to have been the beginning of Ellington's all too brief golden period, the film score not only detailed extraordinary development but showed just how far Ellington and Strayhorn had stretched the language of jazz and just how far they were beyond all contenders. In a period when one jazz composer after another was floundering around trying to fuse jazz and European concert music, Ellington and his musicians went right on using blues, swing, idiomatic polyphony, plungers, dance rhythms, and a grasp of the majestic that was as old as the Negro spiritual.

Building his variations on three themes, Ellington created a work that brought forward much of what he had been refining for over three decades. The reeds that Ellington might turn into a huge orchestration of the feeling of one, woody New Orleans clarinet wailing with multiple powers could also double as blues voices, as expansions of Sidney Bechet, as descendents of the harmonic victories of Coleman Hawkins, emulate the serpentine lyricism of Charlie Parker, or purvey refined approaches to texture that could as easily be percussive as vocal. The lessons of Louis Armstrong and the range of colors brought into the Ellington orchestra by a long list of exceptional trumpet players worked with or in contrast to the equally resilient tonal manipulations heard from the trombone section. All told, Ellington had a magnificent instrument that he could stretch, bend, or twist any way he wanted. The result was work that dwarfed most efforts and gave exceptional lessons to those, such as Charles Mingus, who were capable of understanding just what the true challenges facing an American composer were. Ellington had addressed them all of his life, and at this point in the maestro's career, the view from the mountain top was as clear and as precise as that of an extraordinary hunting bird who continued to amaze as he swooped down into the valley, got what he needed, then started moving up higher, and higher, leaving an indelible image in the sky.

Born in 1899, Ellington grew up with jazz and understood what made it so different from all other music. It was his grasp of the essences of the idiom that allowed him to maintain superb aesthetic focus throughout his life, no matter how much he developed as a musician and developed the very art itself through his own inventions. Ellington was the truest and most complete innovator: he so thoroughly remade the fundamentals that they took on new life

[2] Tom Piazza, "Black and Tan Fantasy," *The New Republic* (11 July 1988), 39.

while maintaining the vitality that gave the music its specific distinction. His orchestration was the result of how much he was taken by the polyphony of the New Orleans jazz band, with the cornet carrying the melody as *obbligatti* were played above and below it by the clarinet and the trombone. Ellington took the growl effects of the plunger mutes imitating the timbres, inflections, and speech patterns of the Afro-American voice and developed them into rich compositional resources for his brass section. Compositions such as Jelly Roll Morton's "Black Bottom Stomp" taught Ellington tension and release lessons about thematic variety, modulation, changes of rhythm and pulse that at first inspired progressively profound short pieces with fanfares, interludes, and so on. But Ellington went on to use those lessons for longer works that eventually opened the way for the best composing and arranging that came in his wake.

In order to do what his creative appetite, his ambition, and his artistic demon asked of him, Ellington had to maintain an orchestra for composing purposes longer than any other, almost fifty years. The only precedent in the entire history of Western music was the orchestra Esterházy provided for Haydn; the only difference, however, is that Ellington was artist *and* sponsor, using the royalties from his many hit recordings to meet his payroll and make it ever possible to hear new music as soon as he wrote it. That orchestra was, as Albert Murray observed in *The Hero and the Blues*, "booked for recitals in the great concert halls of the world, much the same as if it were a fifteen-piece innovation of the symphony orchestra—which in a sense it is."[3] One of the most startling aspects of that idiomatic American orchestra was the way in which Ellington learned over the years to create the textures of instruments he *didn't* have. The reeds sometimes emulated the textures of strings, the baritone saxophone could stand in for a bassoon, two clarinets might be voiced in a way that created the illusion of an oboe in the ensemble, and, as far back as "Rude Interlude" in 1933, we can hear the trombone used for French horn effects.

Beginning in 1927, Ellington had distinctively used the clarinet at the top of his orchestra in "Creole Love Call," and had also introduced the wordless voice into his reservoir of timbral resources, an idea that he extended a number of ways, for both secular and religious music. From pieces such as "Creole Love Call," which is a blues, Ellington went on to write in that form with astonishing invention, but he also probably introduced the blue *mood*, as Gunther Schuller pointed out. "Rude Interlude," is a good example, and one in which Ellington not only expanded upon the feeling of blues but also found another way to use the wordless voice, this time Louis Bacon pulling Louis Armstrong's color into the ensemble. In 1946, Ellington pushed the idea further, using the wonderful soprano of Kay Davis for the extraordinary "Transbluescency," a piece on which the clarinet and the voice meet again but for far more sophisticated purposes than they first did. "Come Sunday," from Ellington's *Black, Brown and Beige* of 1943, first showed his command of religious music, a skill that was given even greater presence when the piece

---

[3] Albert Murray, *The Hero and the Blues* (Columbia: University of Missouri Press, 1973), 84. [See §83.]

was recorded again in 1958 with the addition of the peerless Mahalia Jackson: her wordless humming after she sang the lyrics brought together Ellingtonian timbres, religious emotion, and the voice as a sound, a purely instrumental color. An overwhelming masterpiece with Jackson is "The Twenty-third Psalm," a composition so remarkable it truly explains what Ellington meant when he described something as "beyond category." There Ellington brings this beacon of gospel majesty into a context of modern sound far more harmonically complex and thick with dissonance than any she had ever encountered before or would ever be a part of again. By 1973, Ellington had the splendid Swedish soprano Alice Babs winging her wordless pitches over the choir during the title selection and conclusion of his last sacred concert, *The Majesty of God*.

With pieces like "Pyramid" from 1938, Ellington worked out variations on the Afro-Hispanic, Latin, or "Spanish tinge" seminal composer Jelly Roll Morton said was essential to jazz. Collaborating with trombonist Juan Tizol or Billy Strayhorn, or doing all the work himself, Ellington produced quite a good number of works, preceding by a decade the fascination with Latin rhythms heard in the big bands of Dizzy Gillespie and Stan Kenton. Probably his most famous pieces in that direction are "Caravan" and "Perdido," but far more significant work with exotic moods and colors is contained in three albums from the sixties: *Afro Bossa* (compare, as David Berger points out,[4] the version of "Pyramid" contained here with the original), *The Far East Suite*, and *The Latin American Suite*, where "The Sleeping Lady and the Giant Who Watches Over Her" reveals just how far Ellington had come in thirty years. In fact, it is pretty evident that Ellington addressed more different kinds of rhythms in his material than any other composer of this century, especially when one considers the fact that he evolved through the twenties, the thirties, the forties, the fifties, the sixties, and part of the seventies. Ellington's attentiveness and imagination allowed him to make much of the dance rhythms, the musical arrivals from the third world, and the developments of jazz.

The concerti he began writing in the 1930s, and that were probably a response to the format Louis Armstrong was then using in his big band, remained throughout. Over the years, many features especially crafted to exhibit the virtues—or to challenge them!—of a specific player were written. It didn't matter what the instrumentalist played; Ellington wrote for them all, everyone from the clarinetist to the baritone saxophonist, from the trumpet to the trombone, for the string bass or the trap drums. And as the language of jazz broadened, the various harmonic devices and rhythmic ideas that entered the music were added to what was already the largest and most consistently developing body of sonorities, thematic conceptions, harmonies, and rhythms in the music. All of them were brought to bear in the concerti, which called upon Ellington's players to express perhaps the broadest range of engagement with human life contained in the music of any twentieth-century composer. Such demands were the result of Ellington's will to produce music

---

[4] David Berger, conductor for the concert, had transcribed much of the music performed that evening. He is on the faculty of the Manhattan School of Music.

that was good if not excellent, excellent if not classic. Those demands came in the form of his responses to the numberless nights in dance halls, bars, barns, state parks, amusement centers, private parties—everything from the lairs of the aristocrats to the hang-outs of the well-heeled or the worn-down night creatures who held tenuous bearings between the street and the penitentiary. Those many nights and matinees provided Ellington with inspiration, and made his orchestra so accurate at wedding human meaning and musical technique that its powers of expression came to seem infinite.

X. Ellingtonians

During a career that stretched more than half a century, from his first professional jobs in 1917–1918 to his death in 1974, Ellington performed with hundreds of musicians. Some of these associations were brief—guests with the band, or members for only a short time—while others lasted for many years. From the long and illustrious roster of Ellingtonians, fourteen have been singled out for special consideration.

An attempt has been made to spotlight some of the most original and important members of the Ellington organization, also to include writings of historic significance (Roger Pryor Dodge's 1940 article on Bubber Miley), musical interest (Al Sears's comments on learning Ellington arrangements), and literary distinction (Stanley Crouch's rhapsodic tribute to Ben Webster). For the most part these pieces appear in chronological order, save for the two on Billy Strayhorn which close this volume.

Readers in search of more information on Ellingtonians should consult Jeff Aldam's "The Ellington Sidemen," in Peter Gammond, ed., *Duke Ellington: His Life and Music* (1958); Ellington's sketches in *Music Is My Mistress* (1973); and the excellent profiles in Stanley Dance's *The World of Duke Ellington* (1970) and Rex Stewart's *Jazz Masters of the Thirties* (1972). Suggestions for additional reading appear in the introductions for some of the following figures.

88. Helen Oakley (Dance): "Impressions of Johnny Hodges" (1936)

Alto saxophonist Johnny Hodges (1907–1970) joined Ellington's orchestra at the Cotton Club in 1928, staying with him nearly continuously—except for a brief hiatus in the fifties—for the next forty years. Although "never the world's most highly animated showman or greatest stage personality," as Ellington wrote in a eulogy for the saxophonist,[1] Hodges was an outstanding soloist, a leading voice in the reed section, and one of the primary tone colors in Ellington's orchestral pallette.

Helen Oakley's portrait of the twenty-nine-year-old Hodges was one of the first articles to celebrate his musicianship and describe his character. Oakley had first met Ellington and members of his band in 1933, when she heard a performance at the Fox Theater in Detroit. In December 1936 she began producing a series of Ellington small-group sessions for Irving Mills's Variety label.[2]

For a biographical note on Oakley, see §29.

It is amazing that there are many people in the music business to whom the name Johnny Hodges means less than nothing and yet he is one of the outstanding instrumentalists to be heard today. Johnny plays second alto in Duke Ellington's saxophone section, and he is the soloist heard with him so often on recordings and over the air.

The alto saxophone is reputed to be an instrument with limitations so far as modern solo-style is concerned. Its tone does not lend itself easily to hot intonation. Nevertheless, the instrument as played by Johnny Hodges knows very few limitations. Hodges is without peer on his instrument and has proven himself to be, from the point of view of other qualifications, the equal of any musician known today.

He has an unlimited musical imagination, the manner in which he employs his knowledge of harmonic structure is amazing, his every phrase swings, and his intonation is superb. These are sweeping statements and may well cause the reader some doubt, but when employed in qualifying Hodges' musicianship, they are not too strong. It would be difficult to find a legitimate criticism of his work.

He employs a tone on his instrument which defies classification. The only musician who achieves a tone at all similar is Toots Mondello, who formerly

Source: Helen Oakley, "Impressions of Johnny Hodges," *Tempo* (November 1936), 10, 12.

[1] *MM*, 119.
[2] For an account of Helen Oakley's early association with Mills, see her notes to *The Duke's Men: Small Groups, Vol. 1* (Columbia/Legacy C2K 46995).

played first saxophone with Benny Goodman. Incidentally, Toots is Johnny's greatest admirer.

Johnny's phrasing in a section is delicately shaded, and is in the best of taste; he supplies a fullness and body to Duke's section, and is most important support for Oto [Otto] Hardwick, lead saxophone. It is in improvisation that one may best become aware of the supreme ease with which he plays. His ideas have great fluency, and he never appears at a loss. His choruses, always constructed spontaneously, hang together magnificently. Each phrase has a distinct relationship to the other, and the whole builds up invariably to a fitting climax. There is nothing indefinite about his work.

It seems incredible that any one musician can play so much and consistently maintain such a strong conception of a whole. He never begins a chorus which starts off in one vein and finishes in another, or starts off in a powerful manner to wind up ineffectively, and the same may be said of him whether speaking of merely one chorus or several choruses—each one is based upon the other and the whole, and each and every phrase is complete, both individually and collectively.

Johnny is an unsurpassable impressionistic musician. In some of the Ellington opuses, in which harmonies are unusually weird and suggest a breath from another and less prosaic world, Johnny's tone supplies a key note. At times, it has a decidedly "unearthly" quality. At other times, it is positive and there is a push and strength to it, that one would be more liable to expect from the tenor saxophone.

Still, Johnny's true medium can be found with the blues. Here I do not mean merely the average "blues," an eternal story invariably interpreted, though of course with certain modifications, according to the instrument employed and according to the degree of immersion sustained by the soloist. The "blues" as interpreted by Johnny Hodges might serve as a symbol of the eternal and all-powerful cry of the race. It has something more to it than merely swing, it has in it something of religion, something not to be caught in words, something of the supernatural. Underlying everything, there is the strain of melancholy, of elusiveness, of the indefinable, and those qualities remain even when the phrases become shorter, more forceful, less delicate.

Even though the intonation loses something of its purity, and the conception becomes deliberately rude, still those qualities linger, and Johnny Hodges is singing to himself what is to him the most powerful of all music, "alley music."

Johnny has so many admirers that it would be senseless to attempt to list them, but suffice it to say that Teddy Wilson invariably wishes him to record with him, and does so whenever possible; Benny Goodman believes him to be without peer on his instrument; and Mildred Bailey, ever most particular about her accompaniment, is most insistent about his presence on her recording dates.[3]

Johnny is a source of amazement to other saxophone players in the fact that he never exerts himself on his instrument, his expression never changes, and he plays his most beautiful choruses with no exterior indication what-

[3] Between 1935 and 1938 Hodges made a number of recordings with Teddy Wilson's orchestra and a handful of sides with Mildred Bailey (1935–1936).

soever. He is very slight and gives the impression of extreme nonchalance. He never wastes words, though he is an energetic thinker. He has an extremely quick sense of humor and when he does speak, his remarks are most apt and may quite possibly prove extremely disconcerting to whomsoever his remark is addressed. Like Duke, he is one of the finest "jive artists" to be encountered. He has plenty of character, and would be enraged were he to believe he had been tricked or taken advantage of in any manner.

In closing, it will suffice to say that Johnny Hodges is an engaging personality and above all, a truly inspired musician.

89. "The Duke Ellingtons—Cotton Clubbers En Masse" (1937)

An entertaining group portrait of the personalities in Ellington's band emerges from sixteen biographical sketches published in *Metronome* in 1937 during an engagement at the downtown Cotton Club in New York. Irving Mills's publicity team may have assembled the descriptions, which contain their share of exaggerations and slight distortions—as in the statement, for example, that trombonist Juan Tizol left Puerto Rico for the United States "to play symphony" (in fact he joined the Howard Theater pit orchestra in Washington, D.C.). Despite such factual blemishes, the collective profile gives a sense of the characteristic diversity within the Ellington organization at any point in its history.

All ellipses appeared in the original source.

For an earlier annotated roster of Ellingtonians, see the series of "Blue Notes" columns by Chester Nerges in the local edition (only) of the *Chicago Defender,* which appeared in five weekly installments, beginning 1 August 1931. (Thanks to Steven Lasker for calling this to my attention.)

Duke Ellington (leader and piano)—God's greatest gift to jazz . . . tremendously popular and exceedingly modest . . . world's greatest jive artist and protagonist of Ellingtonian chivalry . . . hates peanuts on pianos, whistling on stage, three on a match, dangling buttons . . . consequently the inventor of wrap-around coats . . . rabid bridge player . . . calls his slight, slender wife "Tubby"[1] . . . always orders last so that the stuff he swipes from other people's plates will agree with what he's eating . . . deadly serious only about his music . . . his colossal feats in that department are too well known to bear repetition.

Otto Hardwick (1st sax)—bald at 19 . . . now 32 . . . looks older . . . used to fiddle bass in Washington . . . dad carried it to work for him . . . got his first

Source: "The Duke Ellingtons—Cotton Clubbers En Masse," *Metronome* (April 1937), 19.

[1] "Tubby" was not Edna Ellington, from whom Duke had been separated since the late twenties, but his companion Mildred Dixon.

sax job from Duke . . . very amiable and exceedingly sociable with drinkers
. . . biggest ambition is to beat Duke "pulling those two-a-day gags."

Barney Bigard (2nd sax and featured clarinet) hates playing tenor but dotes
on clarinet . . . wants Duke to get a straight tenor man . . . a Noo Ohlins
Creole who used to play with King Oliver and who's blessed with thousands
of French relatives who drag him off all trains to kiss him . . . unlimited hot,
cold, sweet or bitter coffee drinker . . . a bridge fanatic who's devoted to his
wife and three kids too . . . described as a yard wide and a yard and one inch
tall in stature.

Johnny Hodges (3rd sax and featured alto)—one of those small men who
loves his night life and the wing of any chicken . . . always has a box of food
that's quickly devoured by the sea-gullic Ellingtonians . . . perpetual gambler
who always stays the full limit . . . spends his winnings on lamb chops and
peas.

Harry Carney (4th sax and featured baritone)—a big, bashful Bostonian who
used to play with Toots Mondello . . . very easy-going . . . partner with Hardwick in Amateur Photography Co. . . . has two trunkloads full of all kinds of
stuff . . . one of those very lovable guys . . . charter member of the new vocal
trio.

Artie Whetsol (1st trumpet)—went to Howard University to become a doctor
but the call of the wild, in the form of Ellington, got him . . . very loyal . . .
always on job even when not well . . . intellectual . . . tender personality . . .
a press agent's pet love . . . a bridge fanatic . . . a press agent's pet hate.

Cootie Williams (trumpet)—a statuesque figure with great esprit de corps who
just gives and gives in whoops . . . terrific over-eater and chronic gambler . . .
but a smart one . . . good adviser on both music and commercialism . . .
another bridge fiend . . . always borrowing somebody's trombone to emit the
best gut-bucket slide choruses in the band.

Rex Stewart (trumpet)—round guy: sort of a five-cent scoop of ice cream on
top of a ten-cent figure . . . a graduate of Wilberforce University . . . loves his
horn best of all . . . tries all different styles . . . can hit E above C above high
C . . . another gambler and trio man.

Freddy Jenkins (trumpet)—back in the band after two years' absence due to
illness . . . nicknamed "Posey" because of his posing ways . . . showman all
the time . . . a solid jive man, maladjusted New Jersey real estate agent and
another Wilberforce grad . . . always writing letters in the world's fanciest
hand.

Joe Nanton (trombone)—strictly gut bucket . . . a fine story-teller . . . used to carry tricks around in his pocket (thus nicknamed "Tricky") . . . now always carries *Time* magazine in his pocket and an almanac in his berth to answer all arguments he bets on . . . a fine connoisseur of liquors.

Lawrence Brown (trombone)—a crooner at heart . . . has played symphony . . . his dad, a Topeka minister, taught him every instrument except trombone . . . excellent ideas on arrangements . . . disagrees in all arguments but in a gentlemanly way . . . used to be a policeman in Los Angeles . . . husband of famed dramatic actress, Freddie Washington . . . always explains the straight and narrow path idea to all young girls.

Juan Tizol (trombone)—musically the most thoroughly educated man in the band . . . arrived from Porto Rico to play symphony . . . still plays valve trombone . . . goes into raptures over Spanish music . . . dances a plenty solid rhumba.

Freddy Guy (guitar)—close pal of Duke's who's been with him since 1923 when he joined as a "fly banjo" player . . . in bed most of the day . . . one of the bridge players . . . claims to have the most perfect watch in the world upon which the sun depends entirely.

Bill Taylor (bass)—a real family man . . . three kids . . . world's greatest five and ten shopper . . . always sending novelties and electric stuff home . . . famous for putting dimmers in Pullman car lights . . . very sincere sort of chap . . . conservative too.

Hayes Alvis (bass)—a Chicagoan who used to play with Jelly Roll Morton . . . mystery man when it comes to age . . . outstanding amateur photographer . . . has passed his first aviator's test . . . a member of the new trio . . . used to have charge of Mills Blue Rhythm bunch . . . possesses some sort of a mysterious office in California.

Sonny Greer (drums)—with Duke since 1920 . . . oldest but youngest looking man in band . . . spends all his money buying drums and all his time making sure they're shined . . . a great belly-laugh provoker . . . two drinks and he's knocked out "thereby," in the words of Duke, "saving the wear and tear on the body" . . . loves to look at high buildings and to be two hours early for every show . . . has friends everywhere . . . leads a heavy night-life . . . a grand-father at the age of 37!

90. Roger Pryor Dodge on Bubber Miley (1940)

The writer and dancer Roger Pryor Dodge (1898–1974) worked briefly with trumpeter Bubber Miley (1903–1932) in the 1931 revue *Sweet and Low,* later publishing two articles on this important but somewhat elusive Ellingtonian. The first of these appears below. Published in the Hot Record Society's *H.R.S. Rag,* it presented new biographical information on Miley and discussed salient features of his style.[1] In observing that Miley's artistry derived in large part from the actual *notes* played—not just from tone and muting techniques—Dodge set forth a critical view developed more fully by Gunther Schuller in his writings for *The Jazz Review* (1959–1960) and *Early Jazz* (1968). As for Dodge's assertion that Miley was the first brass player to use a rubber plunger mute, the examples of King Oliver and Johnny Dunn, among others, prove otherwise.

For a biographical note on Dodge, see §23.

Bubber Miley died of tuberculosis in 1932. He held a unique position among the jazz musicians of the late twenties, and in time I hope to write an extended story of his life including a thorough review of his recordings. Let this short sketch outline his musical life and emphasize his importance as a jazz musician.

Bubber was born in Aiken, South Carolina, in the year 1903. At the age of six he was brought to New York. As a child he used to sing on the streets, sometimes bringing home as much as five dollars. By the time he was a school boy of fourteen he was already taking music lessons from a German professor—first on the trombone and then on the cornet. At fifteen he joined the navy. Eighteen months later he was honorably discharged and joined a small band known as the Carolina Five. This band included Johnny Welch, soprano sax; Wesley, piano; English, violin; and Cecil Benjamin, clarinet.[2] They played gig dates and boat rides and moved through those places familiar to every small outfit in the early twenties. They played at Purdy's and they played at Dupres' Cabaret at 53rd Street and finally landed, in the winter of '22 at Connor's Cabaret on 135th Street off Lenox Avenue. They remained here well through the year 1923. Following this Bubber went on an extended tour through the South with a show called *The Sunny South.* When the tour closed he joined Mamie Smith's Jazz Hounds, along with Coleman Hawkins. From there he went into Duke Ellington's Band [1923] with whom for the next four years or so, he toured, composed, made records and played steady engagements. The Ellington span roughly covers the early days of the Kentucky Club through their famous days of the Cotton Club in Harlem. In May 1929 he

---

Source: Roger Pryor Dodge, "Bubber," *H.R.S. Rag* (15 October 1940), 10–14.

[1] Dodge's second article on Miley appeared in *Jazz Monthly* (May 1958), 2–7, 32. Prolix in style, it recapped much of the information presented earlier in "Bubber."

[2] This listing may contain both printer's errors and incomplete information. In Dodge's *Jazz Monthly* article on Miley, the same personnel appeared as follows: "Trumpet, Bubber Miley; Clarinet, Cecil Benjamine; Soprano Sax, Johnny Wesley; Violin, English; Piano, ———— [left blank]."

went to Paris with Noble Sissle for a month's engagement. When he returned to New York he joined Zutty Singleton's band at the Lafayette Theater in Harlem, along with the late Charlie Green, trombonist. From here he went into Connie's Inn with Allie Ross's band and a floor show featuring Earl "Snake Hips" Tucker and Bessie Dudley.

At this time, in 1930, I had an act in Billy Rose's revue, *Sweet and Low,* in which we danced to the Ellington-Miley *East St. Louis Toodle-O.* In January, 1931, I had the great luck to find Bubber dissatisfied at Connie's Inn and very willing to come with me. He played his own *East St. Louis Toodle-O,* spotted on a high stool on the stage, and stayed with me until the close of the show in late spring. He often played with Leo Reisman for recordings and broadcasts, and for one week, when working for me, doubled at the Paramount movie house, specially featured by Reisman's stage band. Dressed as a Paramount usher he would rise out of a front row seat, play a hot *St. Louis Blues* as he stood in the aisle, and then streak his way out through a side exit to growl the *East St. Louis* for us. That summer, backed by Irving Mills, Bubber was enabled to build up his own orchestra. He secured the services of Gene Anderson, piano, and Zutty Singleton, drums. The band was placed in a show called the *Harlem Scandals.* They opened at the Lincoln Theatre in Philadelphia and subsequently came to New York and played at the Lafayette. But in Philadelphia Bubber had been running a high fever and at the Lafayette he was an obviously ill man. It wasn't long after this that I got a letter from his mother, telling me he was sick. I went to meet him at her house. He had dwindled to seventy-six pounds—a little shrivelled old man. It seems that he had had tuberculosis for some time. Later I got another letter telling me to come to Bellevue. Now he was James Wesley Miley and only his relatives remembered him. His mother told me he was to be taken to Welfare Island. I missed the visitors' hour when I went to see him there, and a few days later I heard he was dead. He was twenty-nine years old.

My wife and I went to his funeral. It was held in a bare whitewashed parlor. Apparently no musicians were there although there was a large wreath of flowers from Duke Ellington. The mourners were out of his mother's life. Was this the funeral of one of the greatest artists of our time? The place Bubber had made for himself in music history was completely ignored. Not knowing who Bubber was, one would have thought it was a service for some good little colored boy. The congregation sang *Rock of Ages,* and all through it we heard Bubber's horn, playing the *Black and Tan* [*Fantasy*].

Bubber was co-author of many of Duke's most famous pieces. Miley told me that the inspiration for the *East St. Louis Toodle-O* came one night in Boston as he was returning home from work. He kept noticing the electric sign of the dry-cleaning store Lewando's. The name struck him as exceedingly funny and it ran through his head and fashioned itself into

Subsequently this piece became Duke Ellington's radio signature. The *Black and Tan Fantasy* was suggested to Bubber by his mother's constant humming of the *Holy City*.

Among the many great records made by the Duke with Bubber Miley are *Got Everything But You, Flaming Youth, Yellow Dog Blues, Jubilee Stomp,* etc. A disconcerting feature of the early Duke recordings made with Bubber, is the fact that Bubber would usually take the first chorus with such charged intensity that the record as a whole would suffer through shooting its bolt at the offset. Once, to record the tune *Rockin' Chair,* Hoagy Carmichael got together a rare combination including Bix Beiderbecke, Bubber, Benny Goodman, Krupa, Bud Freeman, Venuti, Tommy Dorsey and Eddie Lang and although as so often happens, they cut but fairly indifferent music for such a master band, nevertheless Bubber took three-quarters of the first chorus and did the best work of the side [recorded 21 May 1930 for Victor]. Bix is hardly used and barely recognizable. Bubber's is the rhythmic, boyish, half-talking half-singing counter voice to Carmichael's deep-toned pappy!

Miley made six sides under the label, Bubber Miley's Mileage Makers [May–September 1930]. They were exasperating recordings of commercial tunes. On one or two of them, he did not even play and the few solos he condescended to take were over before they began. To my knowledge, he made but two records with Leo Reisman; one, *What Is This Thing Called Love,* where he plays the first chorus straight and only employs his regular style as obbligato to the vocal, and a very good chorus on *Puttin' on the Ritz.*[3] The latter resembles somewhat his chorus on *Diga Diga Doo* made for Duke Ellington. It is not quite certain whether Bubber is playing on the old Perfect recording of *Down in the Mouth Blues* and *Lenox Avenue Shuffle* (composed by Ray-Miley and played by the Texas Blues Destroyers).[4]

To Bubber Miley is attributed the first use of a rubber plunger as mute. Bubber would often tell of the time he went to the ten cent store looking around for something new to mute his horn and how he suddenly came upon the rubber plunger used by plumbers. He said right there he took his trumpet out of its case and tried it to his own and everybody else's high amusement.

Bubber's melodic originality is hidden within his growl style. He fixed his notes into a beautiful melodic entity regardless of whether one likes this style of delivery or not. Listeners must judge growl music not only in terms of intonation but in terms of good or bad *actual* musical line. In the hands of Miley, Jabbo Smith and Tricky Sam [Nanton], growl music can be more musical than open brass playing. Equally, a great style minus significant musical content, can be a disconcerting experience. It is quite noticeable that facility on the open trumpet, even with such a great musician as Armstrong, leads into a florid style—an over-crowded virtuosity. Whereas the mute, in competent hands, coaxes out a closely knit jazz with plenty of invention. The mute, besides introducing noises ordinarily foreign to the instrument, can

[3] In *Jazz Records, 1897–1942,* 5th ed. (New Rochelle, N.Y.: Arlington House, 1983), Brian Rust lists Miley as participating in a half-dozen other sides made by Reisman's orchestra in 1930 and 1931.

[4] Standard personnel is given as Miley, trumpet, and Arthur Ray, organ.

inspire the player to subtle melodic invention. Perhaps the tightly squeezed-out notes demand more respectful attention than the easy array which roll out of an open trumpet.

Bubber rehearsed many numbers with me. Among other things he played the *King of the Zulus,* composed by Louis Armstrong, and played from notation his own forgotten improvisations on the *Yellow Dog Blues.* When I first showed him notations of his solos, taken off records, he was quite confused—doubted he ever created them! But we soon discovered that when *reading* notes he used the correct valve, whereas when improvising he reached for them with his lip, sometimes reaching as much as a whole tone. I found through rehearsing with him that he was very conscious of what was important to jazz. He never had to warm up to play hot; he could play with immediate hot emphasis—even when his lips were still cold. He also *thought* in terms of musical invention and was never blandly satisfied with jungle intonation for its own sake. When he improvised a melodic turn that was inventive, he tried to remember it. Often before going on stage, he thought of new complicated little breaks to introduce. He was a musician packed with half-formed ideas for written composition. He was very slow in fully materializing them. Unless he was supervised by a Duke Ellington, who would see to it that any good idea was completed, he would leave it hanging in his mind or just play about with it in the dressing-room.

Miley was a player who, sometimes more sometimes less, *set* his solos. In other words, after he had played a piece many times he was not entirely improvising from then on. What he did was to play a developed version of an earlier improvisation. Unless we are really familiar with an instrumentalist's attitude towards certain hot choruses it is over-confident to judge them as completely spontaneous improvisation. What is known as improvised music is not always *strictly* improvised. However, when a solo is remembered from one time to the next, the tendency is for the solo to be much clearer in outline the second time. For if the kernel of the improvised idea is apparent in the early example, very often the surrounding matter does not stand out firmly on its own. In the recording field, a good example is Miley's solo on the *Black and Tan Fantasy* recorded by him on Brunswick, as compared to his later version recorded on Victor. On the Victor recording his sudden dynamic burst of notes following the first long sustained note covering four bars, has far more definiteness of form than the similar passage on Brunswick. Every part of the Victor solo stands out in high relief by comparison. The same is true of the Victor *East St. Louis Toodle-O* as compared to earlier versions on Columbia and Vocalion. Bubber was a musician who could musically so crystallize an improvisation that the improvisation did not die after the impeccable white-heat delivery of its first presentation; his new outline had such backbone that it, in turn, could be used to take off from. In other words another musician without playing the actual notes of the original improvisation, perhaps not even in the same style, could simply keep the general outline of Bubber's solo in the back of his head as you would a song, and improvise a new solo, not on the original tune or chordal foundation, but on Bubber's already improvised solo.

Now, my greatest regret is that I did not have records made of all the material we rehearsed. Once, we did go to a very poor recording studio, and under unfavorable conditions Bubber was kind enough to make a new *Black and Tan* solo and a chorus or so of the *King of the Zulus*. But this is all we ever recorded. Nobody will ever know what he got out of *Sister Kate;* his countless variations on *East St. Louis Toodle-O* and *Black and Tan Fantasy*; his poignant preoccupation with the *largo* from the *New World Symphony*.

Bubber's personal appearance was extremely natty. His manner was quiet but always on the verge of laughter. When walking down the street he possessed an endearing swagger and he could generally wheedle whatever he wanted from anybody. His speech was intense with the color of both his race and his profession and he was about as careless with his money as he was with his horn—which was pretty careless. He left it everywhere. He sported a flashy Auburn car and had absolute credit at Big John's.[5] Mention his name to any musician who played with him and you'll hear, "Now that boy. There was nobody like him. And I mean it."

(I am greatly indebted for much of my information to Zutty Singleton, Freddie Jenkins, Graff Zepplin, and Mrs. Eva Miley, Bubber's mother.)

91. Ivie Anderson (1942)

 lthough various singers performed with Ellington's band in clubs and theaters during the twenties, the first to become a full-time member was Ivie Anderson (1905–1949), who joined in 1931. The following *Down Beat* profile by Paul Eduard Miller, while hardly distinguished journalism, provided useful background on the singer and included excerpts from an interview with her. The article was accompanied by two sidebars, one listing Anderson's favorite vocalists (Ella Fitzgerald, Mildred Bailey, Connee Boswell, The Smoothies), the other giving her "tips" to young singers.

In August 1942, a month after this piece appeared, Anderson left Ellington. She made occasional appearances in Los Angeles and managed a restaurant, Ivie's Chicken Shack, that had opened there on 13 June 1941.

When Duke Ellington hired Ivie Anderson the engagement was for four weeks. She stayed on the job 12 years—and hasn't finished the run yet. Ivie now holds the record as the name-band vocalist with the longest service record in the business.

On February 13, 1931, Ivie had just finished a 20-week stand at the Grand Terrace in Chicago when she was asked by the Balaban and Katz organization to join Duke during a four-week tour of B & K theaters. January 23, 1942,

---

[5] A popular Harlem bar for musicians, located on Seventh Avenue between 131st and 132nd streets.

Source: Paul Eduard Miller, "Ivie Joined the Duke for Four Weeks, Stays with Band for Twelve Years," *Down Beat* (15 July 1942), 31.

Ivie was back at the Oriental again for the twenty-third one-week stand at that theater since her initial opening there!

It was anniversary week for Ivie. She never left Ellington, and during those years she had built up for herself an estimable reputation, but what is more, she had become one of the best showwomen in the dance-band business. It was no accident. Ivie's personality—spirited, vivacious, earnest—is a natural asset.

Born in Gilroy, California, she studied voice at St. Mary's Convent from the ages of nine to 13. Then she went to Washington, D.C., to study two more years under the tutelage of Sara Ritt. At school she sang in the glee club and the choral society. By 1923 she was ready for her first job—at Tait's in Los Angeles. There she also worked at The Tent owned and operated by Mike Lyman, bandleader Abe's brother. She became a line girl in a Fanchon & Marco revue featuring Mamie Smith. When the soubrette of the show fell ill, Ivie got her chance, and she stepped in to fill the spot on an hour's notice. This led to her work as a soubrette with the *Shuffle Along* musicale, to work at Sebastian's Cotton Club, to a five months' tour of Australia with a Fanchon & Marco unit, and finally to heading her own revue on the West Coast for a 20-week stretch. She even sang with Anson Weeks' band at the Mark Hopkins Hotel in San Francisco.

And so, by 1930, when she began her engagement at the Grand Terrace, she already was a seasoned performer. But it was the unique combination of Ellington and Anderson which was to bring Ivie recognition and acclaim, not only of the profession, but of the public as well. She was the first singer ever to join a colored band as part of the regular organization, missing by only a year the record established by Fritzi White, who will be remembered as the vocalist who joined George Hall late in 1929. Veteran singer Mildred Bailey joined Paul Whiteman in 1930.

Ivie frankly admits her indebtedness to Ellington.

"For example, when I first started with Duke," she recalls, "I used to wear colored dresses. When he suggested I wear only white, I tried it out and found it so effective that I've been doing it ever since. And for another thing, Duke helped me tremendously in molding my style of singing. When I joined his band I was just an ordinary singer of popular songs. Duke suggested I find a 'character' and maintain it. What's more, he's a leader who believes in taking a lot of time and trouble to find the right background for his singer. He's always supplied me with ideal accompaniment, one which suited the 'character' which I adopted. The combination of these two things resulted in the type of songs I'm still doing today.

"The first one I sang that way was *Minnie the Moocher,* when the boys in the band worked out the idea of talking back to me while I was singing. *I Want a Man [Like That]* is another of this type. And I'll never forget the first record I made—*It Don't Mean a Thing If It Ain't Got That Swing*—one of Duke's own hit tunes and one which helped greatly to identify me in the character of my songs to this very day. Duke knows how to write arranged accompaniments that fit my voice perfectly, and I think that's why I'm more contented now than I've ever been."

We all know the "character" in which Ivie sings. When she walks out on a stage her appearance is serene dignity. Poised, with an almost serious expression on her diminutive face, she confronts her audience with a deceptive demeanor. A seasoned and judicious showman, she knows just how to make the most of the marked contrast between her appearance and the abandoned, low-down quality of her vocalisms.

Singing for the Duke of Windsor and appearances in movies have been milestones in Ivie's career. She's made innumerable records. Those she liked best include *Cotton, Love Is Like a Cigaret[te], I've Got It Bad, All God's Chillun Got Rhythm, My Old Flame, Troubled Waters,* and *I Want [recte I've Got] To Be a Rug Cutter.*

Ivie may well be proud of her record and reputation. During her 12 years with the band she has maintained the same spirited quality in her singing. A trouper who takes her job seriously, never can it be said of her that she did not put her utmost into every song that she sang. And she'll continue to as long as she's with Duke and the boys. Of that I'm sure.

92. Reactions of a Newcomer: Al Sears Interviewed by George T. Simon (1944)

Various musicians have told wry stories of playing with the Ellington orchestra for the first time—discovering, for example, that no parts existed for certain pieces, that an arrangement was to be performed differently from how it was written, or that they were expected to solo in the style of some previous member, now departed.

One of them was tenor saxophonist Al Sears (1910–1990), who joined Ellington in May of 1944, filling the chair vacated by Ben Webster the previous year. (Skippy Williams had held the post briefly in between.) Discussing the experience with journalist George T. Simon, Sears conveyed both the excitement and frustration of learning Ellington's repertory on the job. His comments illuminate the way pieces were edited and revised during performance and describe the informal apprenticeship system in which the band's veterans helped out newcomers. At the time of Sears's interview, the Ellington orchestra was appearing at the Hurricane Club, at Broadway and 51st Street.

George T. Simon (b. 1912), who interviewed Sears, wrote regularly for the *Metronome* and served as its editor-in-chief from 1939 to 1955. His books include *The Big Bands* (1967; 4th ed., 1981), *Simon Says: The Sights and Sounds of the Swing Era, 1935–1955* (1971), and *Glenn Miller and His Orchestra* (1974).

The tenorman in the band came over and sat himself down next to me. Al Sears was both beaming and bewildered. Apparently, the initial shock of working in Duke Ellington's band still hadn't worn off.

Sears, who's as intelligent as he looks (he was graduated from the University

Source: George T. Simon, "It's Like Nothing Else!," from the column "Simon Says," *Metronome* (July 1944), 34.

of Illinois, by the way), readily admitted that he couldn't get over and couldn't get used to playing with the greatest of all bands.

"It's like nothing else!" he exclaimed. "Really, you've got no idea of what it's like till you've actually tried playing in the band!"

It being my turn to admit readily, I readily admitted I had no idea of what it was like, except that it sounded wonderful to me, as always, and that went for Al's blowing, too.

"Naw," Sears came back, "I'm not playing right—yet. It's going to take me more time to get used to it—more than just a few weeks."

He grinned. The Sears grin is abnormally broad. "It's not like any other band. In another band you just sit down and read the parts. Here you can sit down and read the parts and suddenly you find you're playing something entirely different from what the rest of the band's playing."

That didn't seem quite logical to me. I said so.

"That's just it—it's not logical," retorted Al. "You start at letter 'A' and go to 'B' and then suddenly, for no reason at all, when *you* go to 'C' the rest of the band's playing something else which you find out later on isn't what's written at 'C' but what's written at 'J' instead. And then on the next number, instead of starting at the top, the entire band starts at 'H'—that is, everybody except me. See, I'm the newest man in the band and I just haven't caught on to the system yet."

Al explained what he considered the solution, or, to be more explicit, what he thought was the reason. It seems that the band, whenever it does write out its music, plays through it a few times and then one or two men come up with ideas for changes, and before *you* know it (*they* know it all along, of course), the whole routine is altered and the brass is playing a different figure behind the sax chorus and that part where the trombone is blowing isn't in at all anymore because the baritone's playing a part that wasn't written in the first place for the trumpet from whom it was taken away.

"And if it weren't for Johnny," went on Al, pointing to Hodges, who was at least sitting where he was supposed to be sitting, "I'd be completely lost. He cues me. Sometimes it's a couple of bars before I realize it's my solo. He's wonderful, the way he helps. Why, the other night on a broadcast he practically pushed me into the mike to make sure I'd come in right on my chorus, and then, when it was all over, he actually yanked me back by my coat to make sure I'd stop! I did."

Such are the trials and tribulations of playing with the greatest band in the world. A guy gets pushed into a mike and yanked into his seat by his coattails. But, from the way Duke sounded on his last night at the Hurricane, it should easily be worth it—and more. The band was immense, as immense as ever, and that goes all the way from its oldest members, Messrs. Ellington, Greer and Hardwicke right down to its newest member, who, besides being confused by cues, isn't always certain what tune's up next. Seems nobody says anything; Duke just plays an undetermined number of measures, in which are hidden a few thematic fragments, and then—boom—you're off.

So far Sears hasn't gone into *Perdido* while the rest of the band fell into *Harlem Airshaft*. But maybe that's because Hodges keeps sitting next to him.

93. Inez M. Cavanaugh: Three Interviews (1945)

I n 1945 a remarkable series of interviews with Ellingtonians by the African-American journalist Inez M. Cavanaugh appeared in *Metronome*. Two of them featured veterans from the twenties: saxophonist Otto Hardwick (or Hardwicke, 1904–1970) and trombonist Joseph "Tricky Sam" Nanton (1904–1946). Both shared memories about Bubber Miley, while Nanton offered instructive commentary on using the plunger mute, a specialty of Ellington brass players.

Cornetist Rex Stewart (1907–1967), by contrast, provided Cavanaugh with a more straightforward autobiographical account, discussing his youth and experiences with the orchestras of Fletcher and Horace Henderson before joining Ellington in 1934. (For more on Stewart, see his memoirs edited by Claire Gordon, *Boy Meets Horn* (Ann Arbor: University of Michigan Press, 1991)).

Raised in Detroit, Cavanaugh worked in Harlem for the *Amsterdam News* and later ran night clubs in Paris, Monte Carlo, London, and Copenhagen. She was also a singer and close friend of the Danish writer and promoter Baron Timme Rosenkrantz. Cavanaugh wrote the liner notes for Ellington's 1944 Victor recording of *Black, Brown and Beige*.

All ellipses appeared in the original articles.

Otto Hardwick

"Du sublime au ridicule il n'y a qu'un pas. . . ."

Just as surely as there is but one step from the sublime to the ridiculous, so there is but one nuance, one well-turned phrase necessary, in the music we like to listen to today, to turn our thoughts to performers of yesterday. Personal and enduring are trade marks they've left on this lusty, living art.

Otto Hardwicke, perfectionist and sturdy perennial of the all-time, all-star Ellington sax section was head reminiscer. We listened. Open-mouthed.

Dancing on limpid air, the dulcet tones of Johnny Hodges' saxophone tugged at the strings of Otto's memory as he half-thought, half-said: "Sidney Bechet . . . you can hear Bechet in there . . . Hodges always thought a lot of him. . . ."

This was perfect! So you WILL talk!

"Tell us something about the old days, Otto, about Bubber Miley, for instance. Bubber's been just a legend . . . deep, blue-black feeling flung into your being from a spinning, well-worn blue-black disc . . . but, what kind of a guy was he . . . you know . . . what was *his* story?"

"Bubber was unpredictable. Do you know we had to shanghai him into

---

Source: Inez M. Cavanaugh, "Reminiscing in Tempo: Toby Hardwick Thinks Back Through the Years with Ellington: The Lion, Lippy, Bubber . . . ," *Metronome* (November 1944), 17, 26; "Reminiscing in Tempo: Tricky Sam Goes Over the Great Times He Had with Duke, Bubber, Freddie Jenkins," *Metronome* (February 1945), 17, 26; "Reminiscing in Tempo: Vexatious Rexatious Recalls the Balls with and without Duke," *Metronome* (November 1945), 19, 48.

the band. Whetsel went back to Howard University and we needed a good man. We wanted Miley. Even then, we had a reputation of sticking together and Bubber knew this. He was playing at a little place uptown and was happy there, so he stalled us off, thinking that if and when Whetsel came back, we'd let him go.

"One night after we finished work, we went up to Harlem, got Bubber stiff, and when he came to he was in a tuxedo growling at the Hollywood, on Broadway!

"The Hollywood was quite a spot. Jimmy and Tommy Dorsey, Bing, Whiteman, Joan Crawford, well, today's headliners crowded the place. We wanted to add a few more pieces, but the bandstand was so small, we had no room for a bass fiddle, that's how Bass Edwards came to play with us. We had to find a man with an instrument to fit the stand, and Bass played an upright recording tuba . . . so he got the job. We also added a trombone . . . Charlie Irvis. He was strictly a gutbucket trombonist and when we got him he was playing with Willie 'The Lion' Smith at the Capitol Palace. I think *Good Housekeeping* got the "seal of approval" idea from The Lion. In those days, before you could CARRY an instrument around Harlem, much less play one, you had to get the Lion's okay.

"The word gutbucket must have stemmed directly from Irvis's style and his use of a real bucket for a mute. He was a growler, too, but not like Miley. However, he and Bubber got together on duets after growling at each other for a few days, and thus set the style of the band.

"Willie The Lion has never been recognized for his tremendous influence on the music of today. This I cannot understand, unless it's because indifferent persons have been doing the recognizing. Duke, Fats, James P., every pianist of that glorious era has borrowed copiously from the Lion. That is, his influence is strong in all of them.

"There was a mad procession of pianists . . . the peak of the parlor social era . . . the days when the great left hands were developed. Know why? Well . . . everybody wanted to treat the piano player. Drinks were lined up ten deep all night long . . . and to keep the ball rolling, the box-beater had to reach for a drink with his right hand and keep the melody going with his left. That's how left-hands were born! Did you ever hear of 'One Leg' Willie [Joseph]? James P. Johnson can tell you about him. Willie would park his crutch on the piano and take charge of any session. Anyone seeking to dethrone him would wind up wearing a crutch for a collar! Then there was Kid Griffin, who wore wide-leg pants, a number four shoe and weighed 250 pounds; the King of the harmony players, Willie Bryant, from Brooklyn; Sam Gordon, from Jersey, had the fastest right hand in the business; Alberta Simmons, from down in the Jungles, could beat the average man 'striding'; Harold 'Bon Bon' Gardner; Freddie Tunstell [Tunstall]; 'Egg Head' Willie Sewell of Baltimore; The Beetle [Stephen Henderson]; Ralph 'Zwieback' Ross; Bob Hawkins. . . .

"Willie 'The Lion' Smith, Jack 'The Bear' (no one ever knew his right name), Raymond 'Lippy' Boyd, Willie 'Leopard' Gant, James P. 'The Brute' Johnson, the late Thomas 'Fats' Waller, Cliff Jackson, Russell Brooks and Corky Williams were the greats of those rip-snorting days.

"Eddie Heywood, Sr., played with my Lafayette Theatre pit band, during one of my vacations from the Ellington crew. He was an excellent arranger and I know where his brilliant son got his inspiration. . . ."

"But . . . Otto . . . you've gotten away from Bubber . . . and how about Coney Island . . . ?"

"I'll bet you didn't know that Fats Waller was supposed to play with us when we came to New York with Elmer Snowden! Yep . . . but Fats wouldn't stoop to play with greenhorns and didn't even show up.

"Then Duke was persuaded to join us and the first thing we wanted to do when he got here was to see Coney Island. With a couple of bucks between us, Sonny, Duke, Whetsel and I subwayed out there and spent our dough on hot dogs and just watched the fun. We came upon a fortune teller, and stood on the fringe of the crowd to listen. Suddenly, he called to us. We shook our heads in unison, moving back a step. He shouted: 'I know you haven't any money, but I want to tell you something, anyway. You're thinking of going back home . . . don't do it . . . something's going to break for you in three days and you fellows will work together the rest of your lives and never have to look for a job again . . . !' I could use his telephone number, right now!

"To get back to Bubber . . . he was a character. A happy-go-lucky, moon-faced, slim, brown boy with laughing eyes and a mouth full of gold teeth. Bubber loved to play. He went to church to get musical ideas *from the music*. That's how he got his ideas for *Black and Tan Fantasy*. A master showman . . . completely uninhibited . . . irrepressible. Nothing at all for him to stop in the middle of a chorus, remembering some nonsense, double up in hysterics . . . nothing coming out of his horn but wind! We'll never forget the job we lost because of him. We were working at Ciro's, a swank spot, and the manager wasn't for any hot licks. Just the melody . . . play the melody, boys . . . make it sweet . . . play those show tunes . . . never mind the hot stuff . . . but Bubber couldn't be held down.

"He'd slide through the first three or four sets and suddenly tear out! We'd have a helluva time quieting him down.

"One night, Bubber was bubbling over and wanted to play his horn. It was touch and go. Next evening, the manager came up in the elevator, bespatted, with gloves, cane and hat in hand. Right behind him . . . fifteen minutes late . . . marched Bubber . . . bespatted, with gloves, cane and hat in hand. All eyes avoided us, the air was spotty, a nervous feeling ran through the bunch of us, but we went in and changed. Just as we came out of the dressing-room to go on the stand another band struck up their music and we realized we were fired! Bubber couldn't out-growl that gang that night.

"You should have seen him in his miniature Oakland with his chauffeur up front. The car cost $50. There was Bubber, gloved hands resting on his cane, sitting in the back seat . . . his knees bumping the driver's neck!

"I'm almost sure that Bubber was the first Negro musician featured with a white band. He had the job all musicians dream about with Leo Reisman. Bubber entered the pit . . . smiled into the spotlight . . . lifted his horn . . . growled out the *St. Louis Blues* for the three minutes . . . and went home!

East St. Louis Toodle-Oo, with which he had a lot to do, was the first record-ing with us and to this day one of the greatest.[1]

"Bubber taught Tricky his growling technique and was constantly besieged by valve men. The only answer they could get out of him as to 'how' he did it was: 'I don't know how I do it. I'm just crazy.' Bubber often said he wasn't going to teach anybody how to take his job from him. That's why there's a dearth of growl trumpet players today. Cootie Williams, who followed Bub-ber, got his schooling from Tricky and that's all, brother!"

"Tricky Sam" Nanton

Once aboard the California Limited transporting the greatest band in the world to the *Esquire* All-Star Jazz Concert, in Hollywood, I had a notion that the problem of loosening the tongue of the gravel-toned growler, "Tricky Sam" Nanton, would be simplified. However, I was traveling with the Elling-ton band for the first time, and had not reckoned with the tenacity with which most musicians apply the seat of their pants to the seat of a chair at a card table, once they've boarded a train.

Club car! That's the ruse to cut him loose! Needless to say it worked . . . and in no more time than was required to down a few bourbons, we were peeping over our glasses and a great shining bulge of perfect understanding was hanging there between us. The guard was down . . . communication lines were wide open and out it poured:

"I first met Bubber Miley at the Waltz Dream Dance Hall on 53d Street. Bubber had just left Mamie Smith's Jazz Hounds and he used to drop in and play a number or so with us whenever we played there with our four-piece combination. This was about 1921, when I met him and we struck up a beautiful friendship. Bubber soon went to work at Reisenweber's, but no matter where he worked he always came where we were playing. I met Charlie Irvis the same way. I went into a place where he was playing and I didn't think he was playing a number the way I thought it should be played and I said so. . . . Charlie understood and we began to exchange ideas. He was really and truly a gut-bucket trombonist. And as Otto said, he actually used a bucket for a mute. He was a jolly fellow on Sonny Greer's order and could bend an elbow with the best of 'em. We practically started out together and he was good for me, because where I was timid and reluctant to extend myself, Charlie was aggressive and certainly not afraid to try any ideas that popped into his mind. When I was shy about playing some place, perhaps because of some certain musician who'd be playing there, Charlie would push me on and grum-ble: 'Oh, that guy's nothing' . . . he's just full of tricks . . . you can play better than him any day! He really sent me out and made me play!

"When Duke came and asked me to play in the band I didn't want to go

---

[1] Miley's earliest recordings with Ellington were *Choo Choo* and *Rainy Nights* in 1924; the first version of *East St. Louis Toodle-O* (or *Toodle-Oo*), which Miley co-wrote with Ellington, dates from 29 November 1926.

because he was offering me my friend's job. 'He'll be back next week,' I said. Duke insisted. I promised to join him, but I didn't show up. The following night Duke came by and asked why I didn't come in. This time he waited until I got dressed and he TOOK me with him. He was playing at the Plantation then, at Fiftieth and Broadway. The first week I had to wait two days for my pay and the second week there wasn't any pay. So the place closed and we went to New England. I had drawn about $30 security on the week and had to give some of that back on the pro-rata basis. Somehow the band was booked for Huntington, West Virginia, and that sounded like the South . . . so we said 'Nay! Nay!' and came back to the Kentucky Club. I guess everyone knows that story—well, when we went into the Cotton Club we only had one trumpet, Bubber; then we added Louis Metcalf and [Arthur] Whetsel returned from school in Washington. Metcalf quit because he felt he wasn't getting enough solo parts and that's when Freddy Jenkins came into the band.

"Freddy Jenkins grew up in the 'Jungles' in West 62nd St. with Bubber, and like the rest of the young fellows down there, he looked up to Bubber because he was the oldest of them. Benny Carter and Bobby Stark were two more great musicians whom Bubber inspired to play music.

"Bubber was an idea man. For instance, we'd have a printed orchestration . . . Bubber'd always have some stuff of his own and soon we'd have a trio or quartet on the part and if one of us didn't know the chorus the others would tell us what to play. Soon we had it down so pat we'd take the whole brass section out and sit in with other bands and jam. We'd just tell the brass section to lay out and we'd take over and play the parts we'd worked out . . . have a drink . . . tear out and go to another place. Our pet spots then were Charlie Johnson's and Smalls' Paradise.

"After several planned battles of music at the Rockland Palace they decided we were all right and left us alone. This was pretty rough going as we were playing our own tunes which nobody dug then . . . everyone was playing pop stuff in those days . . . but later on they decided we had some pretty good tunes, I guess . . . we're still playing them!

"A lot of people have asked me how I acquired and formulated my style. Well, around 1921 I heard Johnny Dunn playing a trumpet with a plunger, so I decided the plunger should be good on trombone. I was working on a little job in Newark at the time. . . . I got the plunger, all right, but it sounded so terrible, everybody howled: Throw that thing away! I told them to go jump in the lake and kept on trying until I got it to sound in tune. After a couple of months they began to see the light when I finally came up with something in tune. Today, trombonists try the plunger and discover it's way out of tune . . . they don't understand that it takes a helluva lot of experimentation and above all the *ears* have to be in tune. They have to violate all the principles of trombone playing to use the plunger properly, therefore it is not advisable to use a plunger and try to be a good trombone player unless the musician is going to use that style exclusively. You have to play about a quarter tone flatter . . . when they see the kind of mute I use and get one, they find they're sharp. It's not all slide . . . you have to use your lip, too, and work it out until the desired effect is obtained. After doing this over a period of years, that's all you're good for. . . .

"Let's see . . . where were we? . . . Oh, yes, around 1929. Harry White came into the band for four or five weeks . . . you remember 'Father' White, of the famous White Brothers Orchestra of Washington . . . well, don't let anybody tell you differently . . . Father White originated the word 'jitterbug'! He had a pet name for all his musician pals . . . used to call them 'my bug.' Whenever Father White had a solo to play, he always stepped off the stand or into the wings and took himself a big snort of what he called 'jitter sauce' . . . and believe me, he really had 'em every day. One day, however, some practical joker hid Father's bottle, and in his agitation to get it back and into the spot for his solo, he hollered: 'Whoinhell took my jitterbug?' And somehow it floated around and finally got fastened onto the lindy-hoppers . . . but he's the guy who first said it.

"Well, Father's jitters got everyone jittery and he was replaced by Juan Tizol. By this time Tizol had almost put music aside. He was playing valve trombone and nobody wanted a valve trombone and, too, he was a legit man. I don't have to go into his work with the Ellington band here . . . that's history . . . well known.

"I may be veering a bit . . . but there's more I'd like to tell about Bubber. . . . He was a very funny guy . . . scared of his shadow. Bubber and I roomed together. One night I went out of the room and left the light on . . . to sit in a card game with the boys . . . and Bubber awakened . . . remembered that he'd put the light out when he went to sleep . . . and dashed into the room with us and swore someone was after him . . . That's the night he decided to learn to play poker. It was a pretty expensive lesson and price to pay for company because we won his whole week's salary from him. . . . What a lovable guy . . . even rival trumpet players loved him. He was loaded with personal magnetism and dominated any situation. His ideas were more or less the backbone of the band. His ideas and the tunes he wrote helped set the band's style . . . *East St. Louis Toodle-Oo* and certain parts of *Black and Tan Fantasy* (except my contribution) . . . some parts of which we used to play when we were running around together before he joined the band, were the most important.

"I came along playing his style and we worked together in perfect harmony and understanding always. Then, when he passed on, I had to keep the same idea going until Cootie Williams caught on. Cootie took his pages out of my book and carried it on. After Cootie left, the weight of the style (the growling) was on my shoulders.

"Whetsel was a truly great trumpet player. When Bubber left, Whetsel could play most of his parts . . . not exactly as Miley played them . . . but almost. Whetsel had a brilliant mind and was extremely adaptable . . . complete master of his horn . . . his ideas for obbligato were astounding . . . had lots of soul.

"Now, Freddy Jenkins was a great showman. Ray Nance's showmanship emanates from a close study of Freddy Jenkins . . . he's just a carbon copy of Freddy, that's all there is to it. We used to call Freddy 'Posey.' *Little Posey* was written by him and inspired by the nickname we'd given him. When Freddy came in the band, Bubber regarded him as a youngster. Jenkins used to sit in the middle and Bubber was always scolding him for 'posturing and posing' so much. Miley switched him to the end chair so he couldn't be seen as well. But it didn't work . . . Freddy pulled more tricks than ever . . . so we all gave up. We found, though, that the public had caught on and liked his antics, so we put him on his own. Freddy'd do anything to attract attention . . . got himself some tiny cymbals which he crashed together . . . and soon was the spark plug of the band with his comedy routines. After all of the years since he's been out of the band, people still ask for Freddy Jenkins . . . and he left the band back in 1934 . . . well, they still ask for the 'left-handed trumpet player'!"

Rex Stewart

He's a shy guy, this vexatious Rexatious, who finds it intolerably difficult to relax—until he puts his lips to his horn and b-l-o-w-s! After more than ten years, Rex The Inscrutable is a puzzle to the men with whom he has produced some of the greatest jazz of our times. On and off the bandstand, Rex sort of enshrouds himself in the mystery of his impenetrable thoughts and looks more like a bronzed bas-relief of a booted Buddha than anything else. However, this introversion takes flight like a shooting star when boy meets horn and Rex comes alive and the notes start swinging, zinging, prancing, dancing through the bell of his horn and one suddenly envisions a frisky little puppy happily wagging its tail.

Prior to winning acclaim as one of the greatest trumpeters in the world with the Duke Ellington orchestra, Rex William Stewart, Jr., had to go through the usual process of getting himself born. Thus, on February 22, 1907, at Philadelphia, Pa., without too much activity on his part, he found himself the proud possessor of a mother who sometimes took time out as pianist in the neighborhood movie; a father, whose melodious violin lulled him to sleep; a grandfather, proficient as an organist, and a poetess-grandmother.

At about ten, his vexatiousness began to sprout when he proved his gratitude for this unusually aesthetic heritage by wanting to play ball! Two years of violin scratching left him cold, just as cold and unrelenting as the two previous years his mother labored to interest him in piano. Somewhere between the piano and the violin interlude the family moved to Georgetown, near Washington, D.C. Matters had just about reached an impasse when Rex proceeded to tear up the bridge of his violin to make a ukelele, finally tuning it to sound like a uke; that's when he got one of the roundest, soundest spankings of his life. In desperation his mother got a cop! She enlisted the aid of a policeman who organized a boys' band in the neighborhood. This particular keeper of the peace had the kids "marching to his music" long before the band idea took shape. The fact that they all "respected" Officer Johnson probably explains Stewart's sudden interest in alto, his first assigned instrument with the band.

Rex flashed one of his quick smiles and added: "S-o-o-o, I had to play 'peck horn' for almost two years, whether I liked it or not! Finally, I switched to fifth trumpet, which I still play. . . ."

We may safely assume that the direction of thirty-boys-in-brass proved too much for the stout heart of disciplinarian Johnson, who passed away to a more quiet realm after two years. For three months thereafter, Rex refused to toot a toot! Then along came Daniel O'Doy, who had tall tales to tell about his gigging with Duke Ellington. . . .

Let's let Rex take it from here:

"O'Doy decided to organize a band in our neighborhood, and I'll never know why he chose me to play cornet. Up to that time, I'd only played polkas, mazurkas, schottisches and other high-flying dance music. Our boys' band music had been confined to church activities, community songfests and parades. After about a year with O'Doy—*he died.* I was about 12 years old then, and feeling like a veteran musician. Ollie Blackwell, pianist, took the band over and damn near ended my career. Ollie lived in southwest Washington and I lived in Georgetown. Mother began to balk at my coming in so late from rehearsals. She left the theatre at 10:30 every evening and insisted that I meet her at the door. Some fast talking was indicated and I must have convinced her of my interest in music at last, anyway, I stayed with the band. It was pretty corny. We wore funny hats and sat on pianos.

"I was pretty excited when I heard about Duke Ellington, Otto Hardwick and the late Art Whetsol going ALL THE WAY OUT TO WISCONSIN and making good money in the summertime, consequently when Ollie Blackwell and His Jazz Clowns had an offer to leave town with the Mason-Henderson musical comedy revue *Go Get It,* I wanted to go get it. I knew what I'd get if mother got wind of my plans, so I took a little bundle of clothing and my horn and climbed out the bathroom window onto the back porch and was off to get it. I sent her a card about a week later (I had left a note on the kitchen table) *without* a return address. After six weeks on the road the show closed in Philadelphia and I was back home and broke. We ate hot dogs for a week and tried to hold the band together. Well, it finally fell apart and I was faced with the problem of finding that next nickel for that next hot dog. Too proud to let my family know, I kept writing cheerful letters.

"The Musical Spillers caught our act before *Go Get It* got it. Luckily, they needed a trumpet player. They took me to New York (I was fifteen) and the job was all right. I was being taught music and playing xylophone, tenor and cornet, not too much on any of them, but I was *supposed* to be playing all of them. The glamour of night life bedazzled me. Curfew was 10:30, so Willie Lewis (later to become a celebrated bandleader in Europe) sneaked me out and allowed me to stay up 'til midnight! The Garden of Joy and Connor's were our favorite haunts. At 16, I quit the Spillers and worked at Smalls' on Fifth Avenue with the late Jimmy Harrison, trombone, and 'Crip' the drummer.

"In those days, I didn't stay on one job over a month, played every cabaret in town, there must have been a hundred. I broke my own record by remaining with Billy Pa[i]ge's Broadway Syncopaters at the Capitol Palace for three months!

"A summer in Asbury Park resulted in my meeting up with a pianist noted for his white dungarees and his tremendous capacity to imbibe . . . plus a lot of great piano, even that far back . . . Count Basie! And he was right across the street from my job, playing exactly the same as he does to-day.

"Returning to New York, the late Jimmy Harrison got me a job with Elmer Snowden's band, where I remained for two years, just to play with Jimmy and Prince Robinson. Later I joined the Cotton Pickers 'cause Prince was with them. Things rolled along amazingly well, in spite of the fact that I was fired every other Sunday night and re-hired Monday morning. Then Louis Armstrong hit town! I went mad with the rest of the town. I tried to walk like him, talk like him, eat like him, sleep like him. I even bought a pair of big policeman shoes like he used to wear and stood outside his apartment waiting for him to come out so I could look at him. Finally I got to shake hands and talk with him.

"There's one night I'll never forget: Fletcher Henderson, Louis Armstrong and the late Big [Charlie] Green came down to the Nest Club where I was working with Snowden, and we played our fool heads off! I was the most surprised person in the world when Louis called me a couple of months later and offered me his job! I thanked him and told him I didn't think I was qualified to sit in the great Louis's seat. When he left, at least twice a week someone would ask why I didn't join Fletcher at Roseland. After two months of this I gave in. I took a fling at it for three months, then one night I hung up my uniform and let my father send me back to school. I completely abandoned the idea of playing music, disgusted with the whole business. Years later Fletcher told me he had waited one month for me to return before he hired the late Tommy Ladnier."

Rex arrived at Wilberforce University firmly resolved to cram his cranium with things intellectual, only to be met at the train by Horace Henderson, Fletcher's brother, who took one look at Rex's bag and shouted: "Where's your horn!"

"I gave it up!"

"Oh, no, you didn't. We've gotta have your horn in our band!"

Several drinks later the two arm-in-armed it to town and Rex came back to school with a new horn under his arm.

Rex added, "All of which meant that I didn't study anything, after all. I was constantly away from school with the band."

When Joe Smith left to join the Cotton Pickers, Fletcher wired Rex to rejoin the band, which he did in 1927.

"I was surprised and delighted to find my old horn, which Fletcher had thoughtfully kept for me. Hawk [Coleman Hawkins], Jimmy Harrison and [Russell] Procope were still there and it was a real homecoming."

Stewart stayed with Fletcher four years and along came the Cotton Pickers with an attractive bid and Prince Robinson, and though Rex felt Fletcher had the best band, he thought he could sacrifice the music for the money; but it didn't work. Rex stayed with the Cotton Pickers nine months and went back "home" to Fletcher, to remain until 1933 when he got the leader bug and went into the Empire Ballroom opposite Roseland and after a year gave that up. During this engagement, he recorded with a small group for Brunswick, the first under his own name. *Stingaree, Baby Ain't You Satisfied* (Rex on vocal, ex-umph!).

Luis Russell wooed the restless Rex on some one-nighters and during a stop-over in New York Stewart bumped into Ellington in the Mills office one day in December 1934, and Rex's roving days were over.

At this point Rex veered: "Let me tell you about the eating contest between Benny Carter, Coleman Hawkins and Jimmy Harrison and me! Hawk had three steaks, two orders of ham and eggs, a platter of fried potatoes and two slices of pie. We were neck and neck until we got to the pie. Benny had one piece and nosed Jimmy and me out, but when Hawk ordered the second slice Benny folded up!

"To get back to Ellington, on our first trip to Europe, a certain member of the band absolutely refused to go to bed at night aboard ship. We were playing poker in the smoking room of the S.S. *Champlain* and the game dwindled down to just the two of us with about $400 in chips on the table and buckets of champagne close by. There was a glorious glow upon us and between us. About three a.m. this friend decided to write a tune. He did. Then back to the game. Then things got foggy. My next conscious moment found me sprawled in my berth. Busted! Also wondering how my head got through the door it was that much larger! Moral: Don't sit under the apple tree with ANYBODY!

"When Hugues Panassié left America I promised to do a recording date for him in Paris, as I couldn't find the time while he was here. When we finally got to Paris we had so little time we had to do five sides in one hour! Only four were released: *Low Cotton, Finesse, I Know That You Know,* and *Django's Jump,* on Hot Club of France labels and later on H.R.S. in America. *Solid Rock* the fifth side will be released in a month or so by H.R.S.

"When I was introduced to Django [Reinhardt], I turned to Panassié and asked how Django was going to play with us, as nothing had been written and we had no pianist on the date.

"Panassié murmured: 'Don't worry, just play them, he will follow.' He did. In my opinion, out of the ten great guitarists in the world, Django is five of them!"

94. Double Play: Harry Carney and Johnny Hodges Interviewed by Don DeMichael (1962)

By 1962, when the following article by Don DeMichael appeared in *Down Beat,* saxophonists Harry Carney (1910–1974) and Johnny Hodges (1907–1970) had been key figures with Ellington for three and a half decades. Carney officially joined Ellington's band in 1927 (though he may have played in it occasionally the preceding year in New England), while Hodges became a full-time member in 1928.

As DeMichael's piece revealed, Carney and Hodges shared more than their long expe-

Source: Don DeMichael, "Double Play: Carney to Hodges to Ellington," *Down Beat* (7 June 1962), 20–21, 44.

rience together in the Ellington reed section. Both hailed from Massachusetts (Carney from Boston, Hodges from Cambridge), came under the influence of Sidney Bechet early on, and spoke of their experience as Ellingtonians with a mixture of cool professionalism, obvious pride, and unabashed awe for their leader's abilities.

For a later look at Carney see Johnny Simmen, "Harry Carney: An Encounter," *Cadence* (July 1987), 14–17.

It's hard to keep track of some jazzmen. One week they're with so-and-so's band, the next week with a different group. It seems they change jobs as easily as they change clothes—and sometimes as often. But when a man joins the Ellington band, he usually stays.

Take the two senior members of the band. Harry Carney has been with the band since he was 17, and that was 36 years ago. Johnny Hodges, except from 1951–55, has been an Ellingtonian since 1928. So strong has been the association of men and band that Hodges' flowing, sensuous alto and Carney's full-blooded baritone are as much a part of the "Ellington sound" as are plunger-muted brass and Duke's piano.

But the Hodges-Carney relationship extends beyond their careers in the Ellington band. Both are from the Boston, Mass., area, and though Hodges is four years older than Carney, they were boyhood chums.

"Johnny and I lived a few doors apart," Carney said recently. "We used to get together and listen to records. And, of course, I've always been a great admirer of Johnny. I was trying to play alto in the same vein, and I stuck as close to him as he would allow me. It did me an awful lot of good."

Carney, a large man, sat quietly on the edge of a hotel-room bed. Hodges, a small man, sprawled on the bed, watching the flickering picture of a silent television set. He chuckled occasionally. It was difficult to tell if he was amused by the TV show or by Carney's reminiscences of far-away days.

Carney continued: "Hodges was in New York before I came there. He was instrumental in getting me my first job in New York. That was in 1927.

"He was with Chick Webb at the Savoy Ballroom. They were having what they called a Masquerade Ball Night, an all-day, all-night affair. Instead of the regular two bands playing, there were four bands. Johnny got me a job in one of the relief bands. In the band was a fellow, Henry Saytoe [Henri Saparo], who had a job coming up in a couple of weeks at the Bamboo Inn, a Chinese-American restaurant. I got permission from my folks to stay, and I took that job. I was 17."

Hodges chuckled again.

While Carney was at the Bamboo Inn, Ellington often came in on his nights off to dine and listen to the band. After Carney had been at the restaurant for about three months, the place burned down.

But he evidently had made an impression on Ellington.

"One day I bumped into Duke on the street," Carney said. "He inquired as to what I was doing. I told him I was jobbing around, gigging. That's when he made me the offer to join him. He was taking a band up to New England, which was my stomping ground. I'd been away from home long enough to be homesick, and it didn't take much for him to influence me to go back."

Still an altoist, Carney added baritone saxophone to his doubles during his first week with the band.

"There were quite a few good baritone players in those days," he said. "Sonny Adams. Willie Grant. Joe Garland. Foots Thomas with the Missourians. As a matter of fact, all the bands used baritone if the band was above a certain number of pieces. The average nine- or 10-piece band would have baritone or someone who doubled baritone. I continued with alto, though, to about '32 or maybe later than that."

Hodges, who speaks much the same way he plays, stirred when asked how he joined the band.

"I'd been with Chick Webb," he said, "You see, Duke started Chick, gave Chick his first band. Duke was working at the Kentucky Club, six pieces. Another club opened up on 50th St. and Seventh Ave. I don't remember the name of it. But it wanted a band just like Duke's. So he asked me to have a band, and I didn't want any part of having a band. He asked Chick. (Chick would stand on a corner and sing whole arrangements.) We got together with six pieces and tried to make it sound like Duke. We did pretty good until we had a fire. During that time fire was common in clubs. We went up to the Savoy for two weeks. Stayed about six months.

"I left and started gigging with a fellow named Luckey Roberts. The bread was good. Thought it would last forever. So I kept gigging and gigging and gigging.

"Meanwhile, Otto Hardwicke [who was playing alto with Ellington] had an accident, went through the windshield of a taxicab. Had his face all cut up, and I had to go to work for him. Duke offered me a job. I still wouldn't take the job, kept putting it off and putting it off. Everybody was trying to talk me into taking it. So I finally took it. And here I am."

Hodges would have it that nothing much happened between then and now. He fails to mention that in those years he became one of the important alto saxophonists, that his manner of playing influenced countless musicians. He will mention in an off-hand manner the small band he led from 1951–55 ("a little experience of my own, a few knocks, a few headaches").

But Hodges comments freely when the topic of discussion turns to Sidney Bechet (pronounced "Bash-shay" by those who knew the late soprano saxophonist well).

"I went to hear him at a theater in Boston," Hodges said. "My sister knew him very well. Made myself known, had a little soprano under my arm. He asked me to play. I caught the show two, three times to catch as much as I could. And then I started buying records. Him and Louis Armstrong. The Clarence Williams Blue Five.

"The best thing that ever happened to me was when I went to New York and was playing at a little cabaret on 135th St. He came after me. He had a club of his own called Club Bechet on 145th St. He came after me and offered me a job. He would tell me to learn this and learn that. 'The old man won't be here long,' he'd say. I didn't know what he was talking about then, but he would go away and get lost, and I was supposed to play his part. At the same time, I was learning, getting an education.

"They used to have midnight shows at the Lafayette Theater every Friday. All the clubs used to put on their shows free. Fantastic. We put on our show, and that's how I got to be known, through him. We played *I Found a New Baby* in duet form. So I was a big guy from then on, playing a duet with Bechet.

"That was way before Carney. I was 17. I used to come to New York and stay a week and run back. I'd take a job in a dancing school that would pay about $40 a week and only draw $8 or $10, just enough to go home. Day before payday, I'd go home, and we'd sit down and compare notes. Me, him [Carney], and Charlie Holmes [a saxophonist prominent in the late '20s and '30s, especially during his stay with the Luis Russell Band when it was fronted by Louis Armstrong]. Go back next week and do the same thing."

Carney, too, came under Bechet's influence.

"It was through Johnny that I became Bechet-conscious," he said. "That was before I left Boston. After I got with Duke, I heard so many fabulous stories about Bechet. Finally I met him and found he was a wonderful guy, very humorous, dry."

But it was Hodges who absorbed Bechet into his playing. For example, Hodges' alto solo on his small-band recording of *Dream Blues,* made in 1939 and reissued last year on an Epic LP, if played at 45 rpm instead of 33⅓ sounds like Bechet's soprano.

"I had quite a few of his riffs," Hodges said, smiling. "Quite a few of his pets. My pets too. Used to nurse him."

Hodges turned to Carney, the conversation about Ellington small-unit recordings seemingly having reminded him of something.

"You know those test records they used to give us?" he asked Carney. "I got all those. *Jeep's Blues.* You remember when you, me, and Cootie were getting it together?"

Carney nodded.

"I got all those," Hodges said. "They'd do four or five takes and keep one or two. And one or two of what they didn't use would be better than what they put out."

The mention of trumpeter Cootie Williams, who was a mainstay of the Ellington band from 1929 to 1940 when he left to go with Benny Goodman, brought to mind the Ellington band of the late '30s and early '40s, considered by many to be the golden era of the band.

But Carney would have none of this the-1940-band-was-the-best-band.

"A lot of people come up and start talking about the 1940 band and say, 'Gee, that was *the* band.' For the most part, they've stopped going where the band's playing. Then they come out one night and say, 'Oh, this band is nothing like the band of 1940.' And they actually haven't heard enough or absorbed enough of the current band's playing to say that. In 1940 there was something that did something to them, and that's all they remember."

Carney's point was well taken. Ellington, through both his music and the band, has evolved. For example, the band's library has several arrangements of Ellington tunes that have become standard.

"Take *It Don't Mean a Thing*," Hodges said. "I used to play the verse. You never heard the verse, didcha? That's the original. Then Ivie Anderson came in, and there was another arrangement. Then they had one for Ben Webster. And one for the brass section. Had one for Ray Nance. Then another one for Ray Nance, a different one."

"Rosemary Clooney did one," Carney added.

"We got all those," Hodges said. "We got a million of 'em. And they're all in the book."

"The book is jammed," Carney said. "We just carry them all over the country."

"And don't even mention the arrangements for *Caravan*," Hodges sputtered.

Nor is the library numbered, which, to say the least, makes finding a seldom-played arrangement difficult.

"He's very unpredictable," Carney said, referring to Ellington. "If someone comes up and asks for something, he'll have everyone digging through the book looking for it. Sometimes we find it, sometimes we don't."

In addition to carrying a large library filled with yesterday, the band carries a spirit and tradition that began the day before yesterday. Spirit and tradition are strong.

One of these traditions, an Ellington sound, is the plunger-growl trumpet, a tradition that started with Bubber Miley, was inherited by Cootie Williams, and continues, to a great extent, in the playing of Ray Nance.

"If Duke finds an individual who can do it," Carney commented, "he gives him the work to do. It must be gratifying to a player to know he plays enough to satisfy the Duke in this particular style.

"I can say the same thing about Russell Procope playing clarinet. When he plays clarinet, he plays Barney so well."

Commenting on the spirit of the band, Carney said, "There're a lot of nights when . . . everybody can't feel well all the time. But if the band gets something going, the spirit just comes up."

The tradition of the band members adding to, making suggestions about, arrangements is well known. It also is indicative of the band's spirit.

"For instance," Carney began, "when you go into a recording studio, you might have an arrangement all made, yet it'll probably be changed. Guys come up with ideas of injecting something. That still goes on."

"Everybody pitches in—all the time," Hodges interjected. "Somebody might have ideas to make it a little better."

"In other words," Carney said, "everybody is still conscious of making a good record."

Spirit. Tradition. Both are contagious. Both are magnets, drawing new blood into the band but blood that is Ellington blood. For the band has always been made up of musicians best described as "Ellington people." When they leave the band, if they ever do, that special sheen of Ellington usually remains.

It is made up, in part, of suavity, urbanity, self-confidence. It is something no other band imparts to its members. It is a unique attractive-force.

Perhaps Carney said it best: "You still hear musicians say the height of their ambition is to play in the Ellington band."

95. Rex Stewart: "Illustrious Barney Bigard" (1966)

The cornetist Rex Stewart brought an insider's knowledge and an ebullient prose style to his writings on jazz and its players. Both qualities characterize the series of profiles that he wrote about Ellingtonians for *Down Beat* in the sixties and which were later collected in his *Jazz Masters of the Thirties* (1972).

One of the outstanding band members profiled by Stewart was the clarinetist and tenor saxophonist Barney Bigard (1906–1980). As in his other memoirs of musicians, Stewart painted a vivid portrait of his subject by swirling together personal history, anecdotes, character analysis, and musical commentary.

For Bigard's story in his own words, see *With Louis and the Duke,* edited by Barry Martyn (New York: Oxford University Press, 1986).

Albany Leon Bigard is one of the illustrious sons of New Orleans. He is also one of the clarinetists taught by the Tio family, Papa Tio and his nephew, Lorenzo. Evidently, there was unusual rapport between this musical Mexican clan and fledgling clarinetists, for the Tios sent out an impressive list of artists to dazzle the worlds of jazz and classical music.

Among the Tio jazz scholars were Albert Nicholas, Jimmie Noone, Omer Simeon, and, of course, Barney Bigard. But in the beginning, Bigard's tone on the clarinet was not something of which the Tios would have approved. It was quite a while after Bigard started playing that he became accepted as a professional by fellow musicians.

Barney describes his tone then as something horrible, resulting in his being nicknamed the Snake Charmer. Barney enjoyed the nickname at first, feeling he was now one of the gang. Then one night he overheard a drummer (who later became big in the business) tell a friend: "Guess who's on clarinet tonight—that g.d. Snake Charmer!" The remark made him feel like going through the pavement, Barney says. It also had a positive effect—Bigard decided that he was going to become one of the best clarinet players that New Orleans had ever known. He started woodshedding at home, in addition to taking lessons from Lorenzo Tio.

With one of those hearty bursts of laughter for which he is known, Bigard relived the scene of his brothers, Alexander and Sidney, going through the

Source: Rex Stewart, "Illustrious Barney Bigard," *Jazz Masters of the Thirties* (New York: Macmillan, 1972; rpt., New York: Da Capo, (1982)), 113–20. Originally published in *Down Beat,* 8 September 1966.

house with their fingers in their ears. And even Papa Bigard, who was a music lover, found things to do outside the house when Barney started practicing.

Barney was about twelve when Johnny Dodds (who played in the band of Emile Bigard, Barney's uncle) lent him an E-flat clarinet, an instrument chosen because Barney's small fingers could not cover the wider key span on a B-flat clarinet.

It wasn't too long before the men who had put him down began competing with each other for his services. In those days, as Barney tells it, every musician had a little book in which to write down data concerning his dates—time, place, pay. The money was of paramount importance; it would run from seventy-five cents to $1.50 for a dance or funeral. All the musicians would accept several gigs for the same night and then, at the last minute, choose the one that suited them the most, judging this either by the pay or by whom they would be playing with. Thus the ex-Snake Charmer was in a position to snub some of the cats who formerly had derided him.

Bigard is a fine fusion of French, Spanish, Indian, and Negro, with a coloration that is almost white. He is Creole, of an imposing, dignified appearance that belies his occupation. His patrician profile is a facsimile of an old Roman's, with prominent nose, deep-set eyes, and an expression of benign tolerance. Barney is the second of three sons born to Emanuella and Alexander Bigard. He was born in 1906. One brother, Sidney, is dead. Alexander Jr. still plays drums in New Orleans.

The Bigards are one of the oldest families in New Orleans, dating back to the middle 1700s. Through the lineage, there have always been musicians. Most of them played only as a hobby, however, and earned their living in fields such as cabinet-making (they were considered the most talented in the city) and cigar manufacturing. Barney's father was in the insurance business, far removed from the remote ancestor who buccaneered with Jean Lafitte.

Trumpeter Buddy Petite led the first big-time New Orleans band in which Barney played. He soon achieved mastery of the clarinet. About that time, the saxophone was becoming a favored instrument among musicians and audiences, and Barney switched to tenor. Again, he showed such promise that the word spread to Chicago and cornetist Joe (King) Oliver.

When Oliver got a contract to open at the Royal Garden in Chicago (formerly the Lincoln Gardens), he started looking for new sidemen. His original men had been snapped up by other bandleaders like Erskine Tate, Dave Peyton, and Charlie Cook, who could pay more than Joe.

Oliver, going back to the source, wrote friends in New Orleans to recommend young, talented musicians who would play for less than the Chicago fellows. Barney was high on the list of recommendations, and in the fall of 1924, he went off to Chicago to play with Oliver. He was hired as a tenor saxophonist, but when Albert Nicholas and Omer Simeon left, Oliver remembered that Barney played clarinet and bought him an instrument. From then on, Barney doubled on tenor and clarinet.

When Bigard and the other young New Orleanians arrived in Chicago from the South, considerable resentment arose among local musicians over the imported competition. This attitude may or may not have been responsible for the mysterious fire that burned the Royal Garden to the ground. In any case, the new musicians were left in a rough spot, looking for work in the strange city.

At this point Barney credits fate. Omer Simeon, then working mostly with Jelly Roll Morton, left Morton for Charlie Elgar. So Barney started playing with Jelly Roll on record dates and one-nighters, earning a living until Oliver could get started again.

When Oliver opened at the Plantation Club, Bigard was with him and, as he tells it, had his first close-up of the gangster scene. One Saturday night, the place was crowded with the usual throng—shipping clerks and their girls from the north side, pimps and race-track hustlers, fresh-faced housewives and spouses from suburban Oak Park. Then, as if by magic, the dance floor cleared, and four men slow-walked through an aisle of people. Barney says he didn't realize that the men in front were being herded out of the place at gun point—until they passed the bandstand. Then, he says, he got so frightened he grabbed his horns and ran home, where he stayed until Luis Russell, Oliver's pianist, came and got him. Later, he saw newspaper pictures of the people he had seen being ushered from the club. They were quite dead.

During those Chicago days, Barney also recalls a place called Dreamland. This was a huge ballroom that boasted three bands. The featured orchestra was that of the illustrious Doc Cook. He led an eighteen-piece group, then the largest Negro dance band in the world. There were sixteen instrumentalists held together by two drummers, one of whom was the famed Jimmy Bertrand. Cook offered Barney a job with this band, but Bigard refused, explaining that he felt more at home with Joe Oliver. There were obviously strong rapport and great mutual admiration between the two New Orleans musicians. And when Joe headed east in 1927, Barney was with him. On the way to New York City, the band, as Barney vividly remembers, became stranded in St. Louis after leaving Chicago. They were bailed out by the management of New York's Savoy Ballroom so they could open there as scheduled.

Oliver's 1927 Savoy band consisted of Red Allen, Oliver, trumpets; Jimmy Archey, trombone; Albert Nicholas, reeds; Luis Russell, piano; Pops Foster, bass; Paul Barbarin, drums; and Bigard.

After the Savoy engagement, pianist Russell took the group into the Nest Club, where Barney remained until bassist Wellman Braud induced him to join Duke Ellington in 1928. Barney did not want to leave Russell because the tips in the Nest Club were so good, but Braud painted a great musical future for the Ellington band and persuaded Barney to make the change.

When Barney became part of the Ellington organization, there were lots of excellent clarinet players around New York. Buster Bailey was with Fletcher Henderson; Prince Robinson held down both the clarinet and tenor saxophone solo posts with Elmer Snowden at the Nest Club; William Thornton Blue, with an inimitable buzz style, was featured with the Missourians (which later became Cab Calloway's orchestra); Jerry Blake was with Chick Webb; and a Cuban wizard with the improbable name of Carmelito Jejo dazzled audiences at Smalls' Sugar Cane Club.

At the time, Duke's band was an unknown quantity for Harlem's musicians because the crime syndicate, which operated the Cotton Club where Duke played, made no exceptions in its lily-white customer policy. A black man was forbidden to darken the Cotton Club door. Therefore, we musicians heard the Washingtonians only on records—not that we habitués of the Rhythm Club cared. As a matter of fact, Ellington at that period meant little to us, and the newspaper ads proclaiming all that "jungle jazz" show stuff irritated Harlem so much that the public and the tooters alike ignored the existence of the club—and the Duke.

This was the attitude until Duke came out with a record of his tune *Jig Walk*. It was his first recorded effort and a hit in Harlem, though lots of folks took exception to the title. They used the word jig in a fraternal sense among themselves and were offended when it was employed as a song title. But the musicians loved the record. It wasn't too much later that Barney made his first record with Ellington, which, he recalls, was *Bugle Call Rag*.

When the clarinet players found out that Bigard had come out with an unorthodox way of swinging on the instrument, they all wanted to get him in a session to see if they could cut him (or steal what they could). This was easier desired than accomplished since, with the exception of trombonist Joe (Tricky Sam) Nanton and trumpeter Bubber Miley, the Ellingtonians were rarely caught sitting in at a jam session. Drummer Sonny Greer and his side-kick, altoist Otto (The Baron) Hardwick, were at the bars nightly, but no jamming ever interfered with their relaxation periods—that was for peasants, according to Toby Hardwick.

Finally, one night we were all standing at the bar in Big John's Saloon, where most cats congregated, when Jonesy, a Cotton Club waiter who doubled as Ellington's band valet, came in. He proclaimed that Ellington had the greatest band in the world and was the King of Harlem. All the musicians stopped talking and listened with amusement as Jonesy continued that there were no trumpet players in town to compare with Bubber Miley. Several heads nodded acknowledgement while grins grew broader.

Jonesy went down the list of fellows in Duke's band until everybody in the place became bored. We knew the capabilities of the Washingtonians. But when Barney Bigard's name was mentioned, everyone looked blank. Bigard? Nobody seemed to know him. But it happened that Happy Caldwell, the Chicago tenor saxophonist, popped in then and told us that, in his opinion, Barney played great clarinet.

William Thornton Blue spoke up, saying to Jonesy, "Well, if your man is so great, you tell him to be in the Rhythm Club with his horn, and I'll show him how to play it."

Such public challenges were rare, but sure enough, the next night the Rhythm Club was packed. Blue told Bobby Henderson, an up-and-coming piano man, to play *The World Is Waiting for the Sunrise* in a very fast tempo. Then Blue proceeded to play the devil out of the song, swinging with his familiar growl (a vibration emanating from the throat that Benny Goodman learned from Blue during Harlem jam sessions).

On this night, old Blue was blowing in extra fine form. He took over the house until. . . . It was Barney's turn. He damn near split our eardrums, opening his chorus with a wild, screaming high note, which he held all through the first chorus. Then he played the second chorus with lots of what Ellington later called "waterfalls," which I can only describe as sounding like chromatics, except that when one analyzes the passages, they prove not to be true chromatics at all.

Barney glissed, swooped, soared, making his clarinet smoke to the point that Blue packed up his horn and said, "Well, Barney, I guess Jonesy was telling the truth. I'll be in Big John's, and the drinks are on me."

Barney's Ellington days started at a time when all the guys were young and full of animal spirits, which came out not only in their music but also in the form of pranks they played on each other.

There was the time the arrangement called for Wellman Braud to make a quick switch from his string bass to tuba. At the crucial moment, Braud, unaware that Barney had filled the upright bass to the brim with water, blew a cascade of H_2O down on the sax section, with Barney catching most of the deluge.

There was the stink-bomb episode, contributed by a brother who shall remain nameless. This, according to Bigard, happened on the stage of the Pearl Theater in Philadelphia.

With rapt attention, they were accompanying a famous female singer when, as she reached her shining moment at the end of the song, a faint aroma of something quite unpleasant was detected onstage. As it grew stronger, guys started looking accusingly at each other, trying hard to preserve a dignified appearance. But the tension increased as the odor mounted, until there was no containing the mirth. Then, noticing a vacant chair, they had the answer, for the absent musician was noted for his stink-bomb jokes. Revenge was in order, so later on, the culprit's tuxedo was doused with itching powder. The combination of those oldtime klieg lights onstage and the powder soon had the guy in agony. And the air was clear from then on.

In addition to joining in the jollity, Barney also was inspired to create melodies during those Ellington days. Among the credits he claims are *Mood Indigo, Saratoga Swing, Minuet in Blue, Saturday Night Function, Stompy Jones, Clouds in My Heart, Rockin' in Rhythm.* There are many others, too, that he sold or gave away.

In 1942 he left the Ellington band to join pianist Freddy Slack. He stayed with Slack's band a year or two, then played a while with Kid Ory, and in 1946 joined Louis Armstrong, working with him off and on for some fifteen years. While with Satchmo, he toured the world and made many observations. He recalled playing theaters in the southern United States where Negroes were afraid to show appreciation until the white audiences indicated it was good. Later, he found a similar situation in Africa, where the tribal chief's approval apparently was as necessary as the white people's in the South.

Today, Bigard is semiretired because he's tired of travel. However, he always enjoys playing at sessions and college dates, if they are not too far from his home in Los Angeles. He and his wife Dorothe are frequently visited by the children of his earlier marriage—Barney Jr., Wini, Patricia, and Marlene, plus eleven grandchildren.

Jazz of today is Barney's pet peeve. He says it does not employ melody and sacrifices rhythm just to be different. He also says he feels that if this continues, jazz will continue to die.

Barney's playing differs from any other clarinetist's in that he does not play orthodox harmonic lines. His tone ranges from a keening wail in the upper register down to a somber, rich, dark-hued tone. Bigard is an artist of tremendous facility. He is a virile, creative instrumentalist. To an acute listener, clarinet by Bigard creates a broad expanse of melodic excitement, a departure that soars fresh and warm from his soul.

96. Guitarist Freddy Guy Interviewed by John McDonough (1969)

Although he was one of the original Washingtonians who went on to play with Ellington for nearly twenty-five years, from 1925 to 1949, guitarist Freddy Guy (1897–1971) remained one of the more obscure Ellingtonians. Partly this resulted from his self-effacing musical identity: whether on banjo in the twenties or guitar in the thirties and forties, Guy always seemed to play a secondary role in the proceedings. He was rarely featured in solo spots, and unlike Freddie Green with the Count Basie orchestra, his presence in the rhythm section—on recordings, at least—often went unnoticed.

In contrast to his receding musical personality, Guy spoke out forcefully in the following 1969 interview with John McDonough, especially on the subject of Irving Mills and on life with Ellington's band in the twenties. Two years later, in a state of depression, Guy took his own life.

Two or three years ago there appeared a jazz piece in *Jet* magazine in which the author named his choice for three of the most important rhythm guitarists in jazz history: "Charlie Christian, Freddie Green, and the late Freddy Guy."

Every time Fred Guy recalls that story these days, he chuckles and a twinkle lights his eye. Though the guitarist, who played Ellingtonian rhythms with Sonny Greer and assorted bassists for 26 years, today enjoys the best of health, marking his 69th [*recte* 71st?] birthday last May, perhaps there is little fault in having lost track of someone who has not drawn a paycheck as a musician for 19 years, even if he is a Duke Ellington alumnus.

Since Guy left Ellington in 1949, he has worked for Chicago's Parkway Amusement Corp., managing a local ballroom and arranging private parties. Though he still keeps his guitar gleaming and ready, his job has never seemed to offer him time to sit in with former colleagues during their swings through town. Today he lives with his second wife, a charming lady, in an 11th-floor apartment overlooking Lake Michigan.

Source: John McDonough, "Reminiscing in Tempo: Guitarist Freddy Guy's Ellington Memories," *Down Beat* (17 April 1969), 16–17.

A man of moderate height with a full head of graying hair, Guy looks somewhat younger than his years because he carries no extra weight on his lean figure.

He's had few regrets about leaving the band, he said, partly because he keeps in close contact with his old friends. He was compelled to leave early in 1949 because his first wife, who died a year later, was seriously ill. But there were other reasons too. Life on the bus had little appeal to him.

"The only sleep the driver ever got was when we were onstage," he said. "We'd pull in after driving 400 miles, unload, and get a bite to eat. Then we'd work four hours. Afterwards, the driver would be up again to help load, and we'd be on our way. I could never be completely comfortable roaring down some turnpike at 65 miles an hour and knowing that the driver had only three hours' sleep."

Perhaps the buses seemed bad because Guy remembered too well the elegant style in which the band traveled during a good part of the 1930s. In those days, two chartered sleeping cars carried the men across the United States like royalty—and nobody ever had to take an upper.

There was a third car for baggage, so as not to cramp the living quarters. And that was just what they were, since during southern tours accommodations were often limited either to a run-down black hotel or the local preacher's house.

"So we'd just pull over on a side track," Guy said, "plug into the local power lines, and set up housekeeping. Even our laundry would be taken care of."

Guy went to New York from Georgia in the early 1920s, when jazz was still young. His AFM Local 802 union card bears the number 987; today the 802 scroll is up to 5,305, and that's just for the initial G. He made a decent living jobbing with various groups. Each job gave him a connection to another, so it wasn't long before he was making more money gigging than he could with steady work.

It was Fats Waller who provided the connection to Ellington. "Fats was in a little band I was playing banjo with," Guy recalled, "and one night Duke and the boys came in to hear us. Everybody heard everybody else in those days. Fats looked over his shoulder, pointed Duke out to me, and asked if I knew him. I said I didn't. As the night went on, Duke asked if I'd play a number or two with his men. He said he didn't have any music but would call the chords. I said that was fine. We had a pretty good session that night."

That was in the summer of 1923, just prior to the Washingtonians' three months at Barron Wilkins' Exclusive Club, a celebrated Harlem pleasure dome. When Elmer Snowden left the group and the leadership passed to Ellington, Guy was asked to join.

"I was working with a fellow called John Smith, who was just coming to his peak period of bookings. I told Duke that I couldn't leave at this point, so he said he could wait a little while. I finally went with the band in February, 1924, just in time for the downtown opening at the Kentucky Club on 49th St. and Broadway.[1] I even took a cut in pay to join."

---

[1] Actually the Washingtonians had opened there on 1 September 1923.

The Kentucky Club was a cramped basement cafe seating some 130 people. The bandstand was so small that there was no room for a bass fiddle. Any visiting musician with a yen to sit in had to do it from his table. Typical clientele on a given night included a variety of assorted thugs and underworld big-shots, bejeweled dowagers and debutantes from the social galaxy, and the usual run of show people and tourists ogling the show people.

"Duke always avoided a steady diet of one-nighters and theater dates because the right people were never there," Guy said—the right people being bookers and the smart writers. But they flocked to the Kentucky Club. Moreover, Paul Whiteman was playing around the corner at the Palais Royal (which today houses the Latin Quarter), and this brought Bix Beiderbecke, the Dorsey brothers, Miff Mole, and the rest of the Whiteman jazz contingent into contact with the band.

"The style of music that began to develop was different from anyone else's," Guy said. "Duke worked largely from head arrangements then, and he insisted that everyone memorize their parts. He thought you really couldn't get inside a piece of music if you were busy trying to keep up with the charts. When we first came to Chicago, no one could figure out how we could play so much music without music stands."

It was during the Kentucky Club period that the band picked up Harry Carney, who was then "about the size of this cigarette," said Guy, holding up his half-smoked king-size. He was so young, in fact, that, as is well known, his mother's permission was needed before he could be hired full time. In 1926 [probably 1927], Guy went to Boston, Mass., to negotiate for his services and recalls the following dialog:

"Mrs. Carney," he pleaded, "we wish you'd let Harry stay with the band and travel with us this summer on a New England tour."

"Well, I don't know—I don't think so," Mrs. Carney replied. "He's got to finish school, and he's still my baby boy, you know."

"But don't you think it's going to be pretty hard to keep him in school after he's been making the kind of money he has with the band? Anyway, he'll be graduating this June, just in time to make the tour."

"Well, who would live with him? I don't want him getting in with any bad people. He's still a baby, you know."

Guy, who was planning to get married, told her Harry could live with him. This set her mind at ease.

"'Well, I don't know,' she said, hemming and hawing. 'I guess if he really wants to go, it might be all right. But I want you to look after him personally.'"

Guy recalled that the next two years brought Barney Bigard and Johnny Hodges, the latter "a sickly kid who'd smoke cigars to make himself feel more grown up," into the Ellington orbit. It also landed the band in the Cotton Club for another celebrated long run.

Herman Stark, manager of the club, and Dan Healy, the silent partner, were looking for a band to replace the Andy Preer group, whose leader had died in 1927. At the urging of songwriter Jimmy McHugh, the bosses heard the band at the Lafayette Theater. "Right next to the theater there was a tavern," Guy said, "and the contract was signed right there. I was with Duke all night that night. The next day we had to leave for a date in Philadelphia for a week, which gave us no time between our return and our opening. When we got back, we had to rehearse the entire show routines all afternoon and night—literally right up until showtime."

There was some reluctance to take the Cotton Club offer until it became apparent that it was more than an "offer"; it was "take the job or else." That was the word from the bosses, despite any other contracts the band might have.

By now Irving Mills had taken over the management of the band. During the long life of the Ellington orchestra there have been occasional feuds and bickerings between various men. But perhaps the most protracted and bitter episode of antipathy was between Guy and Mills. Guy spoke at length about it:

"Mills did his best to isolate Duke from the band—even made him sleep in a separate railroad car when we were traveling by train. I don't know why he did this for sure, but I think it was because he was afraid someone would wise Duke up."

Many times Guy would try to be that someone.

"Listen, let me tell you something," he said he would tell Ellington. "Don't let no one take away the personal touch you've got with the men. These men came along with you and helped you build the kind of outfit where you'd need managers and the rest. If you lose that touch, all you have is a bunch of musicians waiting for payday."

But Mills had other ideas, Guy said, explaining, "He wanted Duke to be the star, not the band. The men were just the rank and file. But I could see through him, man, and he hated me for it. He even tried to get Duke to fire me. Mills could have done a lot more for the band than he did, but he never learned that if you sacrifice something now, you may pick up a million dollars later on. He wanted everybody's right arm."

Guy recalled an incident attendant to a Ziegfeld booking as characteristic of Mills' manner:

"I heard this rumor over my old Stromberg-Carlson radio one night that the Cotton Club Orchestra was to be featured with Ruby Keeler in a new Ziegfeld show, which was then considered, like the Palace Theater, to be the top work in the business. But when I mentioned it to the men, nobody knew anything about it, not even Duke. The next day Duke told Irving what I'd said. Mills told him that I was crazy, that they weren't going to have a Negro band in the Follies, and that he wouldn't make the attempt."

Mills' attitude made Guy mad and so did Ellington's, for that matter, because Guy thought he listened to Mills too much. So he went to Ellington's apartment one night, he said, and told him how things were.

"Listen," Guy recalled telling Ellington with some annoyance, "did it ever dawn on you that this band is my living as well as yours? Have I ever sent you on a wild goose chase in my life? It won't cost a thing to walk into Stanley Sharp's office (Sharp was Ziegfeld's front man) and say, 'How are you, Mr. Sharp?'"

Ellington was persuaded, Guy said, and the next day took a cab to Sharp's Seventh Ave. office. In Guy's words the meeting went thusly:

"Well, gee, Duke, how have you been?" Sharp said. "We've been thinking about you lately."

After a minute or two of small talk about the bull market and the weather, Sharp reached into the top drawer of his desk, pulled out a contract, and pushed it across to Ellington with a pen. The Ziegfeld job was his.

"But what really broke Mills' heart about this thing," Guy chuckled, "was that when the show opened, the billing was 'Florenz Ziegfeld Presents Duke Ellington,' not 'Irving Mills Presents.'. . . . When we saw him during a rehearsal at the club, mind you, he was crying real tears. Duke had gone over his head, and Mills wanted to fire him and get a new piano player. Can you imagine that?"

In 1939, Ellington broke with Mills and associated with the William Morris agency.

Guy's memories of most of his former colleagues are more pleasant. Of trombonist Juan Tizol, the practical joker, for example, Guy said, "He'd go to these trick stores and buy a lot of stuff. I guess itching powder was a favorite. He'd stick it in the fellows' pants before a show, and they'd get out under those lights and scratch like a s.o.b. We fixed him once, though. We poured a bunch of it in his shirt and shoes. When it came time for his solo, he stood up on the stand and was red as a beet. When he came off, man, did he fly for that shower."

The mere mention of drummer Sonny Greer's name triggers a cascade of images in Guy's memory that produces a hearty laugh and a walloping slap on his knee.

"The Great Greer!" he exclaimed. "He kept you dying laughing all the time, and what a drummer, at least when he was not loaded. I could always tell before the first chorus if he'd had too much. His foot would be slow.

"But Sonny's always had such terrific flair. When he was in the band he was always cleaning his cymbals so they sparkled in the lights. And when times got good, he'd hire someone to do it. When his skins got a little dirty— what the hell!—he'd get a whole new set of heads. He was always finicky about his drums—'my stuff,' he used to call them. What a man!"

Guy reached over his shoulder to a table and produced a yellowed photo in a wood frame of the Ellington rhythm section during the '20s.

"There's Sonny," he said. "He looks like a high school kid. He hasn't changed that much—just a little more dried up."

Sadly, there are only a few records that come to mind on which Guy can be heard in anything approximating a solo role. *Red Hot Band* (1927) and *Echoes of the Jungle* (1931) both have prominent banjo spots, and he takes a guitar break on *The Sergeant Was Shy* (1939).

The Ellington era of the guitar began, as it did with most bands, during 1931; the move went a long way toward rounding off the square rhythmic wheels on which the band had thumped along since the beginning. Guy received much encouragement and advice from Eddie Lang and often sought out local guitarists for tips.

"When we played a place that had a regular house band," he said, "I'd get the guitarist off somewhere and have him play teacher for a while. Once I picked up a book on six-string harmony for guitar in a State St. music shop in Chicago, and that's where I really learned most of the basics."

He pointed to a magazine rack near a large console phonograph where a rather dog-eared instruction book on six-string harmony sat. It was the one he picked up in Chicago.

Today, despite Guy's long absence from the music world, he is still close friends with his boss of many years, who visits frequently in his apartment when he's in town. Much of the planning for Ellington's *My People* show of 1963 was carried out over the coffee table in Guy's living room.

The last time the band was in Chicago for a concert, Guy's phone rang at about 6:30 a.m.

"Love you madly and sorry for waking you," the voice at the other end said, "but I'm going to sleep and I wanted to tell you that there will be tickets waiting for you at the box office tonight."

"He's a hell of a man," Guy said, "and I'm proud to have known him all these years."

97. Sonny Greer Interviewed by Whitney Balliett (1974)

O ne of the most gregarious Ellingtonians, drummer William Alexander "Sonny" Greer (1902–1982) was also one of its longtime veterans. He began playing in groups with Ellington in Washington, D.C., in 1920 and remained the orchestra's drummer until 1951. "Sonny Greer is an endless story," Ellington wrote in *Music Is My Mistress,* "full of sparkles, *double entendres,* and belly laughs."[1] Greer's impish wit and love of language were captured in this profile by Whitney Balliett from 1974, when the drummer was seventy-two.

Chief writer on jazz for *The New Yorker* since 1957, Balliett (b. 1926) has published many volumes of criticism and musician profiles, most recently *Goodbyes and Other Messages: A Journal of Jazz, 1981–1990* (1991) and *Barney, Bradley and Max: Sixteen Portraits in Jazz* (1989). The following piece, together with many other essays in Ellingtonia, will appear in Balliett's forthcoming book, *On Ellington.*

Sonny Greer is an elegant pipestem, with a narrow, handsome face and flat black hair. His eyes are lustrous, and his fingers are long and spidery. He was with Duke Ellington for almost thirty years, and sat godlike above and behind

Source: Whitney Balliett, *American Musicians: Fifty-six Portraits in Jazz* (New York: Oxford University Press, 1986), 54–59. Originally published in *The New Yorker,* 23 December 1974.

[1] *MM,* 53.

the band, surrounded by a huge, white, blazing set of drums. He played with vigor and snap. He switched his head from side to side to accent beats and, his trunk a post, windmilled his arms. His cymbals dipped and reflected his sudden smiles. His playing was homemade and unique, and he isn't sure himself where it came from. He used timpani and tomtoms a lot, filling cracks and cheering the soloists. He used deceptive, easy arrays of afterbeat rimshots that drove the band while remaining signals of cool. He flicked cowbells to launch a soloist, and he showered everyone with cymbals. He sparkled and exploded, but his taste never faltered. He and Ellington set the streamlined, dicty tone of the band; after Greer left, the band never fully recovered. Ellington didn't care for drum solos, but Greer takes a lot of two-bar breaks on "Jumpin' Punkins," and during a soundie [*Jam Session*, 1941, released 1942] (a three-minute film made to be shown on a jukebox equipped with a small screen) Greer takes a crackling, expert double-timing twelve-bar solo on "C Jam Blues" which matches his idol, Sid Catlett. Greer lives in a new building on Central Park West with his wife, Millicent, who was a Cotton Club dancer when he married her in the late twenties. They have one daughter, and a granddaughter who is a vice-president of a bank in Omaha. Greer's life has been distilled in his mind into a collection of tales that are elastic, embroidered, interchangeable. He likes to tell them in the same way he plays the drums— with poppings of his eyes and quick, geometric gestures. His voice is low and hoarse, his speech legato. He often sits at his dining-room table and talks, his back to a window, his face alternately smiling and straight. He remembers his own dictum "When you're getting ready to lie, don't smile." He talked one afternoon:

"I first met Duke Ellington and Toby Hardwicke on a corner in front of a restaurant near the Howard Theatre in Washington, D.C., and they asked me what New York was like, and I painted a beautiful picture for them. I liked Duke and Toby right away, and we were inseparable the next thirty years. I first took them to New York on March 10, 1921—Toby, Duke, Artie Whetsol, and Elmer Snowden—and when we got there the booker said he wanted names, so the job collapsed. I introduced them around—to James P. Johnson and Luckey Roberts and so forth—and if I didn't know somebody I introduced them anyway. New York amazed them—all the music you could desire, and much more. We got jobs playing house-rent parties—one dollar plus eats. We ran into Bricktop on Seventh Avenue. She was the chanteuse at Barron Wilkins', and she helped us out. We played a lot of pool. We survived. We ended up back in Washington, but when we returned to New York, in 1923, we went into the Kentucky Club, at Forty-ninth and Broadway, and we were there three or four years. It was a basement club, and if a revenue agent came around the doorman stepped on a foot buzzer and the place turned into a church. Johnny Hudgins, who did pantomime, was in the show, and so was the trumpeter Joe Smith, who made talking sounds on his horn with his hands. Fats Waller was in the show, along with singers and dancers. People like Texas Guinan and Polly Adler came in. Duke and I played a party for Polly Adler once. Fats would sit at a little piano in the middle of the floor, and I'd sing risqué songs with him. When Leo Bernstein, who was one of the owners, got plastered, he'd ask me for 'My Buddy.' I'd sing a long version, and he'd start crying and tell me he wanted to give me the joint and everything else he had. We went from there into the Cotton Club, where Duke and the band began to be world famous.

"I made a deal back then with the Leedy drum people, in Elkhart, Indiana. In return for my posing for publicity shots and giving testimonials, they gave me a drum set that was the most beautiful in the world. Drummers would come up to me and say, 'Sonny, where did you get those drums? You must be rich, man,' and I'd nod. I had two timpani, chimes, three tomtoms, a bass drum, a snare—the initials S.G. painted on every drum—five or six cymbals, temple blocks, a cowbell, wood blocks, gongs of several sizes, and a vibraphone. The cymbals were from the Zildjian factory. I'd go out to Quincy when we were working in the Boston area, and one of the Zildjians would take me around. He'd tell me to choose cymbals with flat cups—that's the raised portion at the center—and instead of hitting a cymbal to show me how it sounded he'd pinch the edge with his fingers, and you could tell just by the ring. I learned how to keep my drums crisp, to tune them so they had an even, clear sound. I knew about showmanship, about how audiences eat it up— that it ain't what you do but how you do it. Things like hitting three rimshots and opening and closing one side of my jacket in time. I always strove for delicacy. I always tried to shade and make everything sound beautiful. It was my job to keep the band in level time, to keep slow tempos from going down and fast tempos from going up. Those things meant more to me than solos, which I rarely took.

"My parents taught me that way of caring. I was born December 13, 1902, in Long Branch, New Jersey, which is just this side of Asbury Park. My mother was a modiste. She copied original gowns for wealthy white people. She was tall and had a charming personality. My father was about the same height and he was a master electrician with the Pennsylvania Railroad, and his greatest ambition was for me to follow in his footsteps. There were four children— Saretta, who was the oldest, then me, and Madeline, and my brother Eddie. I was named after my father—William Alexander Greer, Jr. I was interested in the affection our parents showed us, but beyond that our life was an everyday occasion, except that we never went hungry a day. I always had an ambition to make an honest dollar, to make money and not have money make me, and that's the way it's been. When I was twelve, I'd take my homemade wagon and load up at the fish place after school for fifty cents—cod, blowfish, blues, bass. My customers would wait for me on corners, and some of those fish were so big you had to bake them. I also had a paper route, and I delivered groceries. My first love was playing pool, ten cents a game. I practiced pool like other kids practice violin or piano. I'd practice two hours a day. I'd hide a pair of long pants, and after school put them on and go to the poolroom. I had a natural knack for it. Nobody in my family was musically inclined, including me, so my becoming a drummer was an accident—a hidden talent. We had Keith vaudeville in Long Branch, and when J. Rosamond Johnson brought his company through he had a drummer named Peggy Holland— Eugene Holland. He was tall and thin and immaculate—the picture of sartorial splendor. He could sing and dance and play, and he had great delicacy. He fascinated me. The company was in town two weeks, and every time he came into the poolroom I'd beat him. I told him I admired his playing, and he said, 'Kid, teach me to play pool like you play, and I'll do the same for you.' I bought him a box of cigars just to put an edge on it, and he gave me six or seven lessons, and some of the things he showed me I still use. I went to the Chattle High School, where they had a twenty-five-piece band. Mme. Briskie was in charge of it. She also taught languages, at which I was very good. I didn't think the drummer was too hot, so I told Mme. Briskie, 'I can beat that guy playing.' I gave her a light taste, then I poured a march on her, and all the kids watching were prancing. I got the job. I could sing, too—like a mockingbird. We put together a small band, and it had six white boys, two white girl singers, and me, the Indian. Jersey was like Georgia then, it was so prejudiced, and I was learning how to look trouble in the face. Along with my other money-making enterprises, I was a first-class caddie, and for a year I'd been the personal caddie to one of the daughters of Krueger Beer. One day, she sliced a ball into a water hazard, and when I got there I laid the bag of clubs down and started into the water. Then I saw that a snake had that ball in his mouth, and I said, 'Oh, no.' She got mad and I quit and walked away and left her there, bag and all. Later that summer, our little band played a dance at the country club where she played golf, and she was sitting at ringside. She kept looking at me—she could hardly help it, because I was the sore thumb—and asking who I was. Finally, she asked me, 'Don't I know you? Didn't you used to caddie for me?' I told her, 'No'm. Not me. That was my twin brother.' She didn't find out the truth until I met her backstage years later at Carnegie Hall after an Ellington concert.

"I left high school the year before graduation, and that broke my parents' hearts. But my soul was set on the music. Sundays, I used to go up to New York for rehearsals at the Clef Club with Will Marion Cook, who had a lot of Lester Lanin-type bands. My mother asked me what we were rehearsing for, and I said, 'A trip to Russia.' She said, 'A trip to *what?* That's it! No more rehearsing!' When I was around nineteen, I played in the Plaza Hotel on the boardwalk at Asbury Park. Fats Waller was on piano and Shrimp Jones on violin. A string ensemble called the Conaway Brothers worked there, too, and I became friendly with them. They were from Washington, D.C., and they invited me down for three days, and I stayed several years. Marie Lucas had a band at the Howard Theatre, and one morning the manager came into the poolroom next door and said Marie Lucas needed a drummer, since hers had run off to Canada with the alimony agents after him. That was my first Washington engagement. The bootleggers had the habit of stacking money on a table for the entertainers who worked at the Dreamland Café, around the corner from the Howard. Soon I was doubling there with Claude Hopkins and Harry White from midnight until six in the morning, and after we collected our money from that table we had so much in our pockets it was a sin.

"Duke Ellington was like my brother, and I was like his. He was once-in-a-lifetime, and I wish I had a third of his personality. It overshadowed everybody else. He was sharp as a Gillette blade. His mother and father drilled that into him—Uncle Ed and Aunt Daisy, we used to call them. His father was a fine-looking man, and *polished*. Duke learned his way of talking from Uncle Ed. Fact, his father taught him everything he knew. Duke would never let a guy associated with the band down, no matter what hour of the day or night the trouble might be. He couldn't tolerate dissension in the band, or trouble from a new guy. He could sense right away when a guy wasn't right. But he never had a mean streak in his life. Duke was sort of a dreamer. Even when he'd play cards with us on the train, he'd have a song or a piece of music going through his head. *That* was his life. Every tick of the clock, somebody in the world is playing an Ellington tune.

"We first went to Europe in 1933—right from the Cotton Club. We went directly to London, where we played the Palladium. After, we did a party for Lord Beaverbrook—champagne and brandy in front of every one of us. I poured a glass of each to get my nerves together. Anna May Wong was a guest, and Jeannette MacDonald, and the future King George. He sat in on piano, and he and Duke played duets. Then I noticed this skinny little guy squatting near the drums and watching me, and pretty soon he asks can we play 'The Charleston.' We did, and he danced like crazy. Then he asked me could he sit in on drums, and I said, 'Of course, my man.' Somebody told me who he was: the Prince of Wales. I christened him the Whale, and it stuck. After I'd left the Duke, in the fifties, he came across the street from El Morocco to the Embers, where I was working, and I called him the Whale, and we sat and talked and told a few lies.

"By the early forties, the band was a bunch of admired stars, each with a different style. Johnny Hodges was very even-mannered. He was a thoroughbred. Whenever you'd wake Toby Hardwicke up, he was ready to go. But Ben Webster was the *king* of the playboys. We called him Frog, or the Brute, even though he was most congenial. Cootie Williams liked to gamble, but he didn't drink much. Lawrence Brown didn't drink, either, but he loved the ladies. Tricky Sam Nanton—he and Ben Webster and Toby were all in the same category: curiosity always got the better of them. Jimmy Blanton was a lovely boy, and he was crazy about his instrument. He'd stay up with us all night just to hear other people play. Ben was his umbrella and watched out for him. Ray Nance was a cocky kid, and we called him the Captain. He was always ready when asked—'Just a minute, I'll be right with you.' Barney Bigard was the best, and here is how he got his nickname—Creole. Once, when we were down South and in a bus on our way back to our Pullman car after a job, we stopped at a greasy spoon to get something to eat. Duke sent Bigard and Wellman Braud in, because they looked practically white. They were in there a long time before the door banged open and Barney came out shouting, 'I'm Creole! I'm Creole!' The owner of the place was right behind him, waving and shouting back, 'I don't care how old you are, you can't eat in here!' We travelled by Pullman before the war—one car to sleep and eat in, and one car for our instruments and baggage. That way, we didn't have to face the enmity of looking for a place to stay. No other band travelled as well or looked as well. If we did six shows a day in a theatre, we changed our clothes six times.

"I feel good, and I can still play. Lazy people retire. As long as you feel active, *be* active. Retired people lie under a tree and play checkers, and first thing you know they're gone. Last time I saw Duke in the hospital, he said, 'I want you to go out and play again, Nasty.' He called me that because I had always defended him against all comers through the years. I guess the Man isn't ready for me yet. The only regret I have is that my parents and my sisters never saw me play with the Duke Ellington band. My brother Eddie did, but somehow they didn't, and I'm still sorry about that."

98. Gary Giddins on Paul Gonsalves (1985)

T enor saxophonist Paul Gonsalves (1920–1974) was one of Ellington's outstanding soloists in the later years, joining the orchestra in 1950 and remaining with it until the end of his life. In reviewing a newly released album featuring Gonsalves that had been recorded more than twenty years earlier, during the sixties, Gary Giddins deftly assessed the saxophonist's style and mused on the general subject of unissued Ellingtonia.

For a biographical note on Giddins, see §77.

Duke Ellington wrote of Paul Gonsalves that his refusal to make demands on himself evinced the purity of mind worthy of a good priest. "His punch line, of course, is 'Jack Daniels,'" Ellington continued, "but that is just a kind of façade."[1] The image of Father Gonsalves must have amused his many friends, but none could have failed to understand what Ellington was getting at. The key tenor saxophonist of the Ellington orchestra for 24 years went Jesus one better. He could walk on sour mash, an ability that may have been either a consequence or a cause of his remarkable diffidence. Gonsalves, known to colleagues as Mex and to Ellington's audiences as the Hero of the Newport Jazz Festival (or Strolling Violins—he was known to hop off the stand to serenade a member of the audience) abjured power in any guise, including self-promotion. That he had a reputation at all was entirely due to his lavish talent and the existence of a few people who could appreciate same. To them, the name Gonsalves was almost synonymous with *underrated:* not even his conquest of Newport in 1956—when he galvanized the audience with a 27-chorus blues solo that put Ellington on the cover of *Time* and his orchestra back on top after five years of neglect—secured him much individual attention.

I don't think he cared in the least; he and the people close to him knew who he was and besides, to sit in the Ellington band was all he ever wanted from life. By all accounts, Ellington was his biggest fan, which helps to explain

Source: Gary Giddins, "Paul Gonsalves, Featuring Duke Ellington," *Village Voice* (26 February 1985), 72, 74.

[1] *MM*, 221.

why he tolerated Gonsalves's unrigorous approach to discipline—unlike Basie, with whom Gonsalves had previously worked. Yet until the release this month of *Featuring Paul Gonsalves* (Fantasy F-9636), hardly anyone knew about the extraordinary bouquet the maestro tossed him in 1962. As was his habit, Ellington had secured a few hours of studio time to record music for his private cache. But as he hadn't written any new music—according to Stanley Dance's liner notes—he announced, on the spot, an entirely novel course of action: an album that featured Gonsalves and only Gonsalves. Except for a few measures of clarinet on "C-Jam Blues," no one else—including the leader—gets to solo. There's never been a Duke Ellington record like it.

Gonsalves's music probably seemed too effortless for his own good. He didn't do knee-bends or look pained while he played, and he could produce a marathon solo with a near-marathon cadenza at the drop of anybody's downbeat. Though his style had its obvious influences—chiefly Ben Webster and Webster's mentor, Johnny Hodges—he didn't sound like anyone else. Whereas Webster was elliptical and gruff, Gonsalves was all liquid rhapsody. The notes poured forth in cascades; somewhere in the mist, the melody invariably renewed itself. Half of *Featuring Paul Gonsalves* is blues and all the pieces are familiar, but all the treatments are new and the energy dazzles.

In fact, it may not be quite accurate to say that Ellington wrote no new music, since most of the pieces are revised and some of the revisions are too intricate to be head arrangements. Consider the bebop figures the band plays behind Gonsalves toward the climax of "C-Jam," or the locomotive harmonies on "Happy Go Lucky Local," or the waltzy transitional passage on "Take the 'A' Train." Hodges was taking it easy that day, but Harry Carney's edgy baritone powers the reed section; Sam Woodyard and Aaron Bell make for a steadfast rhythm section; and Ellington, as always, commands from the piano. On "Caravan," he states the changes with single bass notes while Gonsalves works up a sandstorm, and then vamps a clever change in tempo.

Gonsalves's quicksilver improvisations resonate with passion and wit, and though he hesitates momentarily, he never loses his footing—a remarkable feat, considering that he probably didn't have a clue what would happen when he walked into the studio. The present version of the blues "Ready, Go" is just as dynamic as the one on 1959's *Ellington Jazz Party,* and I prefer its slightly breathless cadenza. The present version of "Paris Blues" easily outclasses all the others. The theme from the 1961 movie for which Gonsalves dubbed Paul Newman's tenor sax started life as a piano theme, but was arranged for Hodges and Lawrence Brown on the disappointing soundtrack album; Gonsalves was given a chorus on subsequent versions. Here he takes it at a much faster tempo, lagging behind the beat in the first chorus, interpolating two transitions, and expanding his embellishments through each of five choruses. "Just a-Settin' and a-Rockin'," which he inherited from Webster and made his own, has a passage for tenor and rhythm that illuminates his impact on David Murray, who often mentions him, and "Take the 'A' Train" is thoroughly refreshed with two tempo changes and a flag-waving climax. Dance writes that after playing it (I suspect that most if not all of these performances are first takes), Gonsalves "turned to Ray Nance, whose show-case it usually was, and gave his familiar, self-deprecating Stan Laurel grin."

The question arises: Why wasn't this session issued 23 years ago? Ellington's 1962 recordings consisted of small-group encounters with Hawkins, Coltrane, and Mingus and Roach, and a couple of relatively undistinguished orchestral projects, such as his salvaging of a forgettable and forgotten Strouse and Adams musical, *All American,* the highlight of which was Gonsalves's interpretation of "I've Just Seen Her." The tenor saxophonist was between contracts—a year later he signed with Impulse—and might have benefited greatly from its release. Although maybe not. One recalls the general level of Ellington criticism and can easily imagine the most likely responses: "Not a single Johnny Hodges solo!" "We've heard these pieces before!" "Another instance of Ellington's decline!" Another question arises: How much more hidden Ellington is there? New Ellington music has seen the light of day virtually every year since his death, some of it—*The Queen's Suite, Afro-Eurasian Eclipse*—major, all of it worthy. Pablo has just issued *The Stockholm Concert 1966* (2308-242), a likable Ella Fitzgerald recital with the Ellington orchestra that doesn't add much to their known collaborations from the period (*Cote D'Azur* and the recently reissued *Ella at Duke's Place* (Verve UMJ 8236)); it has the best version I've heard of "Imagine My Frustration," Ellington's whimsical attempt at rock and roll, but Fitzgerald is elsewhere a bit manic, and songs like "Wives and Lovers" don't sound any better now than they did then. *Featuring Paul Gonsalves,* though, is a triumph—the definitive Gonsalves album, and evidence of yet another ace up Ellington's capacious sleeve. I don't expect we'll see many new tenor albums this year that can touch it.

99. Stanley Crouch on Ben Webster (1986)

Compared with other major Ellington reed players—Johnny Hodges, Harry Carney, Russell Procope, Barney Bigard, Jimmy Hamilton—tenor saxophonist Ben Webster (1909–1973) spent a relatively brief period with the Ellington orchestra: a few stints in 1935–36, and full-time from 1940 to 1943 and again from 1948 to 1949. Yet with his robust sound and formidable improvising skills he made a great impact on Ellington's music, launching a tradition of hard-blowing tenors later carried on by such Ellingtonians as Al Sears and Paul Gonsalves.

In a special 1986 jazz supplement to the *Village Voice,* the critic Stanley Crouch gave an overview of Webster's career, capturing in expressive prose the sound, style, and soul of the saxophonist both during his tenure with Ellington and after.

Two pieces on Webster by Whitney Balliett are also recommended: "Big Ben," *The*

Source: Stanley Crouch, "Rooster Ben: King of Romance," *Village Voice* Jazz Supplement (June 1986), 6–7.

New Yorker (19 January 1963), 70–75, and "Fauntleroy and the Brute," The New Yorker (15 August 1983), 70–72.
    For a biographical note on Crouch, see §87.

During the late '40s, Duke Ellington gave a college concert in which one segment featured Kansas City's Ben Webster as tenor saxophone soloist par excellence.[1] The piece was an arrangement of "How High the Moon," which opened with an eight-bar up-tempo shout of brass and reed bebop figures intended to rattle. Then Webster, his tone a sensuous burr, entered and dissolved the tempo into a romantic flotation of a cappella swing, as surprising a break as any in the history of jazz (though Louis Armstrong had Johnny Dodds use the same dramatic de-escalation 20 years earlier). As the rhythm section joined him, Webster maintained the dream mood at a seductive tempo through which he shaped each note with such richly colored emotional characterization that the individual pitch had the effect of a song in itself. Next, the tempo went up to a nice medium velocity and Webster stated the theme he had been so abstractly implying in belly rub rhythms, swells of assent rising from the band as he danced the melody along. Then the brass took a break that roared in a swift third tempo and Webster transformed his sound into a gravelly howl as determined as the controlled scorch of a great lover nearing the consummation of ardor. In fact, those three tempos and the sultry coda that Webster performed, climaxing with a cry both raucous and sensual seem not an onomatopoeia of the bare facts of sex but of love-making, from the tender to the mellow to the flaring and tempestuous. The difference is spiritual, and the tenor saxophonist knew it well.

By presenting Webster in a concerto arrangement that moved through three moods and tempos, Ellington provided as good an introduction to the art of Ben Webster as any novice listener would need. One heard the translucent tone so smooth and so powerful in every register; the crooner's skills that would decimate almost any actual singer; the boody-butt ease of absolute swing; and the giant-killing power that never gave way to hysteria when Webster had to slash through a song on an express schedule. At that point, with his broad shoulders, the bags beginning beneath his pugnacious eyes, the handsomeness that seemed part Indian, and the reputation for being intolerant of jive (whether or not he was in his cups), Webster had completed an apprenticeship that made for one of the most lyrical and muscular styles in the history of jazz.

When Webster joined Ellington in 1940, he was 31 years old and had come a long ways from Kansas City and the distaste for the violin his family wanted him to play. He preferred the piano early on and performed in a honky-tonk style that perfectly mirrored one aspect of the latter-day Dodge that was Kansas City, where everything was wide open and fun was rarely corralled. Prohibition was ignored, hustlers and loose women were everywhere, people par-

---

[1] Recorded on 10 December 1948 at Cornell University, Ithaca, New York, and released on World Record Club (T-160).

tied the night away, and there was such a large audience for music that it ranged from square-dance tunes to blues to jazz to hoity-toity society bands. Webster's great ambition at the time was to tickle the ivories in a stride style and he led one of his first bands from the keyboard, Rooster Ben and His Little Red Hens. He was playing piano in Amarillo, Texas, in 1929 when Budd Johnson showed him scales on the saxophone, an instrument that began to entrance Webster. Saxophone-fascinated but lacking a horn, Webster joined the Young Family, a traveling ensemble of parents and children who played musical instruments. Through the soon-to-loom innovator Lester Young, who was one of the children and five months Webster's junior, Rooster Ben fell for the tenor and was soon blowing like hell.

Near the end of 1932 Webster was already so good that he was recording with the Bennie Moten Orchestra, helping announce the new feeling of Kansas City swing, and flying over the instrument with brusque authority. Of that Webster, who was also to measure and develop his talent in many other bands, Rex Stewart wrote, "During his early period, he blew with unrestrained savagery, buzzing and growling through chord changes like a prehistoric monster challenging a foe."[2] Webster played the instrument hard and with an heroic tone that Stewart says was the talk of the tenors when Rooster Ben arrived in New York, a big man whose eyes radiated the dark moods of a willing scrapper. In 1936, he recorded with Teddy Wilson and Billie Holiday, exhibiting a style that was part Coleman Hawkins and part Benny Carter, tied together with traces of Chu Berry. But I think that Holiday's phrasing on "The Way You Look Tonight," where her voice arches itself up over the chunk-chunk-chunk-chunk of the rhythm guitar in lyrical phrases much like romantic smoke signals, struck Webster as he stood there listening just as Lester Young's gifts had seeped into the emerging saxophonist. Those two influences were not to surface in Rooster Ben's own work for a few years, and then they would be so transmogrified that their impact wasn't even noticed. (There were already Young-like rhythms in the last part of Webster's "Toby" improvisation in 1932.)

During his tenure with Ellington from 1940 to 1943, Webster established a role for the tenor in that most magnificent of jazz orchestras. Sculpting his emblematic passion through ballads and blues or serving as heavy artillery on stomping, swinging numbers, Webster's roar of triumph, terror, and rage celebrated existence, revealed the shocks of life, and declaimed a bubbling disgust for all limitations. His performances on "Cotton Tail," "Conga Brava," "All Too Soon," and various others set precedents; his successive replacements suffered the outrage of fans who couldn't get Rooster Ben's sound out of their ears and weren't above asking the other tenor players how dare they sit in Ben Webster's seat. Those fans relaxed when Webster rejoined Ellington from 1948 to 1949, and they calmed down a few years later when Paul Gonsalves began to develop his extension of Rooster Ben's approach.

In maturity, Webster crafted a style that embodied the rich stretch from

[2] Rex Stewart, *Jazz Masters of the Thirties* (New York: Macmillan, 1972; rpt., New York: Da Capo, 1982), 128.

the meditative to the violence inherent in blues—the whisper followed by the cry, the cry contrasted by a choked display of tenderness, and so on. But his greatest victory stemmed from a rejection of the European-derived idea of the virtuoso as a spokesman for velocity. Like Basie, Ellington, and Monk, he chose to strip his materials down to elemental Negro techniques. He became a virtuoso of nuance. In the process, Webster appropriated the entire vocabulary of Negro vocal and instrumental timbres into his saxophone. In a given performance, he could sound like the entire Ellington tonal arsenal compressed into a gold-plated, curved, and multi-keyed vessel of effortless expression. But there was a point larger than tonal variety as an end unto itself. Rooster Ben realized that the subtle to dramatic use of timbre could result in extensions of harmony and rhythm, even melody, a personalization of Ellington's idea that men with distinct sounds could make a chord as much an assemblage of colors as pitches. Webster not only reminded one of a wispy singer or a growling trombone or a cup-muted or plunger-muted trumpet, but his control of color also had the same melodic implications of timbre found in Lester Young, whose alternate fingerings could make a repeated single note successively sound like a different entity, given the lightness or the weight of it on the ear. Yet Webster took that control of texture beyond what Young, or anyone else, had done with it. More than any other saxophonist in jazz, Rooster Ben rivaled the flexibility of the human voice and brought together a synthesis of phrasing rooted in Armstrong, Young, Holiday, Carter, Hodges, and Parker. His was a sense of rhythm as acute as that of Thelonious Monk; it disavowed prolixity in favor of the essences of delay, anticipation, and superbly placed accent, giving the individual phrase a feeling of suspense and victory.

However much he disliked the instrument when he was young, Webster later said of the violin that nothing could rival its sound for purity and sweetness. I think Webster was mistaken and that the irony of his contribution in that regard is that he was one of the central figures who made it clear that the solo and ensemble powers of the saxophone formed the American parallel to the function of strings in European music. Obviously Webster's concern with capturing the timbres of Negro speech, song, instrumental techniques, and the percussive rhythms of Negro dance were beyond the roles of the strings in Europe, but his clarity and variety of sound and subtle expression rival that of any instrumentalist and surpass the purity of all but the greatest players, regardless of idiom.

Though Webster had composing and arranging gifts that might have rivaled those of Benny Carter if he had chosen to focus on them, once Rooster Ben absorbed the work of his Ellington section mate, Johnny Hodges, he settled for writing that never rose again to the height of the harmonized saxophone section in "Cotton Tail." He was content to become a drifter with a tenor. Though he might tour with Jazz at the Philharmonic or sit in with Ellington, Webster moved around making beauty or railing through his horn at the shortcomings of the world when and where he felt like it. (In 1964, he moved to Europe, where he remained, working with pickup rhythm sections until his death nine years later.) In a sense, he telescoped his arranging skills through his own lines, riffs, and gestures, setting timbres against one another with such detail he could make a single performance sound as though it were the work of more than one horn player. Rooster Ben woodshedded a style of such inclusive expressiveness that he could follow a dramatic contrast in inflection with a dissolving note that went past pitch into pure air. It was sort of a toneless white noise, as much like the breath Armstrong let float past a sung note as it was a first cousin of brushes on a snare drum.

As the recorded work shows, he was invincible after a point. From 1943 until his death 30 years later, Webster made music as remarkable for its content as it was for its consistency. One could play a more innovative style than his or one could play something absolutely different from what Webster did, but it was impossible to sound *better* than Rooster Ben. Though the Ellington classics are rightfully made much of, I think there are a number of performances away from the Maestro that deserve mention, though they are so many I will only scoop out a few for this list. His overwhelming improvisation on "Funky Blues" (*Norman Granz Jam Sessions/The Charlie Parker Sides,* Verve) is a timelessly contemporary gathering of sandpaper tones that buzz forward in a superb cleanup feature to the work of Johnny Hodges, Charlie Parker, Benny Carter, and Flip Phillips. There is the peerless satisfaction and excruciation of his singing tenor on *Ballads* (Verve); the work with Billie Holiday on *Songs for Distingué Lovers* that might just settle a score with Lester Young; the nearly terrifying intensity of his "Fine and Mellow" work on the 1957 television show *The Sound of Jazz;* his own *King of the Tenors* (Verve), which includes astonishing versions of "Danny Boy" and "Tenderly"; the sessions with Coleman Hawkins and with all-star masters of his era that are in the two-record set, *Tenor Giants* (Verve); and the deftly expressive ballads and blues of *Soulville* (Verve).

But what impresses me most about Webster's continued dedication is his ability to create swing or cloudlike flotation even when held down by willing but unswinging European rhythm sections. Ten months before his death, Rooster Ben recorded *Did You Call?* Though the performances are slightly marred by the mannered piano of Tete Montoliu, Webster was in classic form. His expression was absolute. The precision of timbre, the variety of rhythmic ideas, the melodic gifts, the brusque to humorous swing, and the spiritual resonance of his lyricism were displayed to perfection. There, as ever, one is amazed that such a sound could come out of an instrument made of brass and sonically manipulated by breath pushing across a cane reed. The notes seem to radiate straight from the man, and this is a man whose understanding of human desire and intimacy makes nearly every romantic lead of stage and screen seem like a beginner. I also like one of his last recordings from the year of his death, *My Man* (Inner City). Rooster Ben Webster, staring into the face of eternity, lets loose the lion's call of combat for all comers on "I Got Rhythm" especially. It is the sound of an uncrushable courage, the sort he probably found necessary to protect his devotion to the aesthetic revelations of romance.

100. Billy Strayhorn Interviewed by Bill Coss (1962)

No one was so intimately involved with Ellington's creative process as Billy Strayhorn (1915–1967). For nearly thirty years he served as Ellington's closest associate, especially by writing new pieces—among them *Johnny Come Lately, Daydream, Chelsea Bridge, Passion Flower,* and the band's theme, *Take the "A" Train.* He also helped with arranging chores and took the Maestro's place at the keyboard from time to time.

The nature and extent of Strayhorn's contributions to the musical world of Ellington still await detailed investigation. In the following interview from 1962 with *Down Beat*'s Bill Coss, however, some clues to this fascinating musical relationship can be gleaned.

One of Strayhorn's most surprising remarks to Coss, in light of prevailing critical opinion, is how different he believes his composing and piano styles to be from Ellington's. Yet what they share, according to Strayhorn, is "the fact we're both looking for a certain character, a certain way of presenting a composition, [which] makes us write to the whole, toward the same feeling."

For an earlier biographical profile, see Leonard Feather, "Billy Strayhorn—The Young Duke," *Jazz* 1/5 (1943), 13–14, 31.

For nearly everyone interested in jazz, the names Duke Ellington and Billy Strayhorn are, if not synonymous, at least inextricably connected. But the connection is not as close, though it is unique, as might be assumed. This is no parallel of Damon and Pythias, though the loyalty of one to the other is strong. Nor is this an example of Abbott and Costello, with only one straight man, or Edgar Bergen and Charlie McCarthy.

This connection is a corporation, really a co-operation, that has, except when the members are working singly, produced some of the finest music and offered one of the greatest orchestras available in jazz, or, for that matter, American music.

But for most, even for those closely associated with jazz, the relationship has not been clear. Who did, does, will do, what? Or, more precisely, how does Strayhorn fit into the Ellington dukedom?

Recently, *Down Beat*'s associate editor Bill Coss spent an afternoon talking with Strayhorn in his apartment. The conversation ranged from the particular to the general and the inconsequential. Strayhorn, as charming as Ellington, never was at a loss for words. Following is a transcription of the pertinent parts of the conversation.

COSS: How did you and Ellington first get together?

STRAYHORN: By the time my family got to Pittsburgh, I had a piano teacher, and I was playing classics in the high-school orchestra. Each year in the school, each class would put on some kind of show. Different groups would get together and present sketches. I wrote the music and lyrics for our sketch and

Source: [Bill Coss], "Ellington & Strayhorn, Inc.," *Down Beat* (7 June 1962), 22–23, 40.

played too. It was successful enough so that one of the guys suggested doing a whole show. So I did. It was called *Fantastic Rhythm*. I was out of high school by then, and we put it on independently. We made $55.

At that time, I was working in a drugstore. I started out as a delivery boy, and, when I would deliver packages, people would ask me to "sit down and play us one of your songs."

It's funny—I never thought about a musical career. I just kind of drifted along in music. But people kept telling me that I should do something with it. By the time I had graduated to being a clerk in the drugstore, people really began to badger me about being a professional musician.

Then, one time [in 1938] Duke Ellington came to Pittsburgh, and a friend got me an appointment with him. I went to see him and played some of my songs for him. He told me he liked my music and he'd like to have me join the band, but he'd have to go back to New York and find out how he could add me to the organization. You see, I wasn't specifically anything. I could play piano, of course, and I could write songs. But I wasn't an arranger. I couldn't really do anything in the band. So he went off, and I went back to the drugstore.

Several months went by; I didn't hear anything, but people kept badgering me. Finally, I wrote his office asking them where the band was going to be in three weeks. They wrote back that the band would be in Philadelphia.

At the time I had a friend, an arranger, by the name of Bill Esch. At the time he was doing some arrangements for Ina Ray Hutton. He was a fine arranger, and I learned a good deal from him.

Anyway, right then he had to go to New York to do some things for Ina Ray, so he suggested that we go together. He had relatives in Brooklyn, and I had an aunt and uncle in Newark, so we figured at least we would have a place to stay.

By the time I got to Newark, Duke was playing there at the Adams [*recte* Paramount] Theater. I went backstage. I was frightened, but Duke was very gracious. He said he had just called his office to find my address. He was about to send for me.

The very first thing he did was to hand me two pieces and tell me to arrange them. They were both for Johnny Hodges: *Like a Ship in the Night* and *Savoy Strut*, I think. I couldn't really arrange, but that didn't make any difference to him. He inspires you with confidence. That's the only way I can explain how I managed to do those arrangements. They both turned out quite well. He took them just the way they were.

From then on, Duke did very little of the arranging for the small groups. Oh, he did a little, but he turned almost all of them over to me. You could say I had inherited a phase of Duke's organization.

Then he took the band to Europe only a month after I joined the band in 1939. I stayed home and wrote a few things like *Day Dream*. When he came back, the band went to the Ritz Carlton Roof in Boston. Ivie Anderson had joined the band, and he asked me to do some new material for her.[1]

After that, I inherited all the writing for vocalists, though not for those

[1] This was near the end of Anderson's tenure with Ellington, which lasted from 1931 to 1942.

vocalese things he wrote for Kay Davis. I think what really clinched the vocal chores for me was when Herb Jeffries came with the band [in 1939]. He was singing in a high tenor range, and I asked him whether he liked singing up there. He said he didn't, so I wrote some things for him that pulled his voice down to the natural baritone he became after *Flamingo*.

COSS: How do you and Duke work together? Do you have a particular manner of doing an arrangement or a composition? How do you decide who will do the arranging?

STRAYHORN: It depends. There's no set way. Actually, it boils down to what the requirements of the music might be. Sometimes we both do the arranging on either his or my composition because maybe one of us can't think of the right treatment for it and the other one can. Sometimes neither of us can.

Sometimes we work over the telephone. If he's out on the road somewhere, he'll call me up and say, "I have a thing here," and, if he's at a piano, he'll play it and say, "Send me something." I do, and eventually we get it to work out when we get together.

That's surprising, you know, because we actually write very differently. It's hard to put into words. . . . The difference is made up of so many technical things. He uses different approaches—the way he voices the brass section, the saxophone section. He does those things differently than I do. That's as much as I can say. I'm sure that's as clear as mud.

Still, I'm sure the fact we're both looking for a certain character, a certain way of presenting a composition, makes us write to the whole, toward the same feeling. That's why it comes together—for that reason.

The same thing goes for the way we play piano. I play very differently than Edward. You take *Drawing Room Blues*. We both played and recorded it at a concert. Then I didn't hear it for about a year. I must admit I had to listen a few times myself to tell which was which. But that's strange in itself, because we don't really play alike. I reflect more my early influences, Teddy Wilson and Art Tatum, whereas Ellington isn't in that kind of thing at all.

It's probably like the writing. It isn't that we play alike; it's just that what we're doing, the whole thing, comes together, because we both know what we're aiming for—a kind of wholeness. You know, if you really analyze our playing, you could immediately tell the difference, because he has a different touch, just to begin with. Still, I have imitated him. Not consciously, really. It's just that, say at a rehearsal or something, he'll tell me to play, and I'll do something, knowing this is what he would do in this particular place. It would fit, and it sounds like him, just as if I were imitating him. . . .

I can give you a good example of something we did over the phone. We were supposed to be playing the Great South Bay Jazz Festival about three years ago. Duke had promised a new composition to the people who ran it. He was on the road someplace. So he called me up and told me he had written some parts of a suite [*Great South Bay Suite*, a.k.a. *Toot Suite* and *Jazz Festival Suite*]. This was maybe two or three days before he was due back in New York, and that very day he was supposed to be at the festival.

He told me some of the things he was thinking of. We discussed the keys and the relationships of the parts, things like that. And he said write this and that.

The day of the festival, I brought my part of the suite out to the festival grounds. There was no place and no time to rehearse it, but I told Duke that it shouldn't be hard for the guys to sight-read. So they stood around backstage and read their parts, without playing, you understand.

Then they played it. My part was inserted in the middle. You remember I hadn't heard any of it. I was sitting in the audience with some other people who knew what had happened, and, when they got to my part, then went into Ellington's part, we burst out laughing. I looked up on the stage and Ellington was laughing too. Without really knowing, I had written a theme that was a kind of development of a similar theme he had written. So when he played my portion and went into his, it was as though we had really worked together—or one person had done it. It was an uncanny feeling, like witchcraft, like looking into someone else's mind.[2]

COSS: How about the larger pieces—what's the extent of your work on them?

STRAYHORN: I've had very little to do with any of them. I've worked on a couple of the suites, like *Perfume Suite* and this one. I've forgotten the name of it. That day, it was called *Great South Bay Festival Suite*.

The larger things like *Harlem* or *Black, Brown and Beige* I had very little to do with other than maybe discussing them with him. That's because the larger works are such a personal expression of him. He knows what he wants. It wouldn't make any sense for me to be involved there.

COSS: You have differentiated between arranging and writing. That can be confusing. As you know, writing can simply be a matter of a melody line; the majority of the work could be the arranger's.

STRAYHORN: Not in our case because we do it both ways. We both naturally orchestrate as we write. Still, sometimes you're just involved with a tune. You sit at the piano and write what represents a lead sheet.

It all depends on how the tune comes. Sometimes you get the idea of the tune and the instrument that should play it at the same time. It might happen that you know Johnny Hodges or Harry Carney or Lawrence Brown needs a piece. Or you think of a piece that needs Johnny or Harry or Lawrence to make it sound wonderful. Then you sit down and write it.

After it's done, Duke and I decide who's going to orchestrate—arrange— it. Sometimes we both do it, and he uses whatever version is best.

We have many versions of the same thing. You remember *Warm Valley?* It was less than three minutes long. But we wrote reams and reams and reams of music on that, and he threw it all out except what you hear. He didn't use any of mine. Now, that's arranging. The tune was written, but we had to find the right way to present it.

I have a general rule about all that. Rimski-Korsakov is the one who said it: all parts should lie easily under the fingers. That's my first rule: to write

---

[2] Ellington tells a similar story in *MM* (156), in which he and Strayhorn independently arrived at a similar opening theme for *In the Beginning God* from the first Sacred Concert.

something a guy can play. Otherwise, it will never be as natural, or as wonderful, as something that does lie easily under his fingers.

We approach everything for what it is. It all depends on what you're doing. You have the instruments. You have to find the right thing—not too little, not too much. It's like getting the right color. That's it! Color is what it is, and you know when you get it. Also, you use whatever part or parts of the orchestra you need to get it.

For example, you have to deal with individual characteristics. Like, Shorty Baker, who has a certain trumpet sound. If you're writing for a brass section and you want his sound, you give him the lead part. The rest follow him. Or if you want Johnny Hodges' color or Russell Procope's color in the reeds, you write the lead parts for either of them.

For a soloist, you just have to look at the whole thing, just like looking at a suit. Will this fit him? Will he be happy with this? If it's right for him, you don't have to tell him how to play it. He just plays it, and it comes out him, the way he wants. If you have to tell him too much how to play it, it isn't right for him.

Here's a good example of writing for characteristic soloists. Duke wrote *Mr. Gentle and Mr. Cool.* He started off thinking of two people: Shorty Baker *(Gentle)* and Ray Nance *(Cool).* The tune wrote itself from his conception of these two people.

We write that way much of the time. Sometimes it doesn't happen right away. A new guy will come in the band. You have to become acquainted with him, observe him. Then you write something.

In Ellington's band a man more or less owns his solos until he leaves. Sometimes we shift solos, but usually they're too individual to shift. You never replace a man; you get another man. When you have a new man, you write him a new thing. It's certainly one of the reasons why the music is so distinctive. It's based on characteristics.

For example, when Johnny was out of the band, we played very few of his solo pieces—well, the blues-type things and *Warm Valley,* but Paul Gonsalves played that solo. You see we wouldn't give it to another alto to play. We changed the instrument; otherwise, except for things you have to play, we just avoided those songs. Otherwise, you'd spoil the song itself. It was written for him—maybe even about him.

Coss: So many people suggest a question which, I suppose, is the kind you expect when someone gets into a position as important as is Duke's. What it comes down to is that Duke doesn't really write much. What he does is listen to his soloists, take things they play, and fashion them into songs. Thus, the songs belong to the soloists, you do the arrangements, and Duke takes the credit.

Strayhorn: They used to say that about Irving Berlin too.

But how do you explain the constant flow of songs? Guys come in and out of the band, but the songs keep getting written, and you can always tell an Ellington song.

Anyway, something like a solo, perhaps only a few notes, is hardly a composition. It may be the inspiration, but what do they say about 10 percent inspiration and 90 percent perspiration? Composing is work.

So this guy says you and he wrote it, but he thinks he wrote it. He thinks you just put it down on paper. But what you did was put it down on paper, harmonized it, straightened out the bad phrases, and added things to it, so you could hear the finished product. Now, really, who wrote it?

It was ever thus.

But the proof is that these people don't go somewhere else and write beautiful music. You don't hear anything else from them. You do from Ellington.

Coss: How about those people who say Duke should stay home? They say, look, he's getting older, he has enough money coming in; why does he waste all his energy on the road when he could be at home writing?

Strayhorn: He says his main reason for having a band is so he can hear his own music. He says there's nothing else like it, and he's right. There's nothing like writing something in the morning and hearing it in the afternoon.

How else can you do it? Working with a studio band isn't the same thing. You have to be out there in the world. Otherwise you can't feel the heat and the blood. And from that comes music, comes feeling. If he sat at home, it would be retreating. He'll never do it. He'd be the most unhappy man in the world. The other is such a stimulus.

On the road, you find out what is going on in the world. You're *au courant* musically and otherwise. It keeps you alert and alive. That's why people in this business stay young. Just because they are so alive—so much seeing things going on all over the world.

Coss: Duke is often criticized for playing the same music over and over.

Strayhorn: What else can you expect? Even though that's not a fair criticism, some part of it has to be true merely because he is the talent he is.

Have you any idea how many requests he gets? After he's through playing all of them, the concert or the dance is all over, and he's hardly started with other requests. . . . That's why he does the medley that some writers criticize.

Actually, there's a great deal of new music all the time. The thing I'm concerned about is that some of that will get to be requested. Then what will happen? What it really comes down to is that there is never enough time to hear an excess of talent.

101. Ellington: "Eulogy for Swee' Pea" (1967)

B illy Strayhorn's death on 31 May 1967 affected Ellington profoundly. Soon after receiving the news he wrote a brief tribute to his friend and alter-ego; it was later included with other reflections on Strayhorn in *Music Is My Mistress*.[1]

A musical response followed in the form of *And His Mother Called Him Bill*,[2] an all-Strayhorn album by the Ellington orchestra recorded in August and September of 1967. At the end of the last recording session Ellington played Strayhorn's *Lotus Blossom* unaccompanied at the piano, in a gesture at once elegiac and affirming.

Poor little Swee' Pea, Billy Strayhorn, William Thomas Strayhorn, the biggest human being who ever lived, a man with the greatest courage, the most majestic artistic stature, a highly skilled musician whose impeccable taste commanded the respect of all musicians and the admiration of all listeners.

His audiences at home and abroad marveled at the grandeur of his talent and the mantle of tonal supremacy that he wore only with grace. He was a beautiful human being, adored by a wide range of friends, rich, poor, famous, and unknown. Great artists pay homage to Billy Strayhorn's God-given ability and mastery of his craft.

Because he had a rare sensitivity and applied himself to his gifts, Billy Strayhorn successfully married melody, words, and harmony, equating the fitting with happiness. His greatest virtue, I think, was his honesty, not only to others but to himself. His listening-hearing self was totally intolerant of his writing-playing self when or if any compromise was expected, or considered expedient.

He spoke English perfectly and French very well, but condescension did not enter into his mind. He demanded freedom of expression and lived in what we consider the most important and moral of freedoms: freedom from hate, unconditionally; freedom from self-pity (even throughout all the pain and bad news); freedom from fear of possibly doing something that might help another more than it might help himself; and freedom from the kind of pride that could make a man feel he was better than his brother or neighbor.

His patience was incomparable and unlimited. He had no aspirations to enter into any kind of competition, yet the legacy he leaves, his *oeuvre*, will never be less than the ultimate on the highest plateau of culture (whether by comparison or not).

God bless Billy Strayhorn.

Source: Duke Ellington, "Eulogy for Swee' Pea," written 31 May or 1 June 1967, published in *Down Beat* (13 July 1967), 11. Reprinted in *MM*, 159–60.

[1] *MM*, 156–62.
[2] RCA LSP-3906, reissued on the Bluebird CD 6287-2-RB13.

Topical Index of Selections

General Commentary and Criticism

12. A Landmark in Ellington Criticism: R. D. Darrell's "Black Beauty" (1932) 57
21. The "Secret" of the Ellington Orchestra (1933) 98
24. Constant Lambert on Ellington (1934) 110
27. John Hammond: "The Tragedy of Duke Ellington" (1935) 118
32. Aaron Copland on Ellington (1938) 130
36. Wilder Hobson on Ellington, from *Jazzmen* (1939) 141
43. The Debate in *Jazz* (1943): John Hammond, Leonard Feather, and Bob Thiele 170
44. *Black, Brown and Beige* in a List of "Classical Records" (1946) 178
55. Alec Wilder on Ellington (1948) 258
56. Ellington's Silver Jubilee in *Down Beat* (1952) 265
57. André Hodeir: "A Masterpiece: *Concerto for Cootie*" (1954) 276
58. An African View of Ellington (1955) 289
61. André Hodeir: "Why Did Ellington 'Remake' His Masterpiece?" (1958) 297
63. Irving Townsend: "When Duke Records" (1960) 319
77. Gary Giddins on the Sacred Concerts (1975) 375
80. Max Harrison: "Some Reflections on Ellington's Longer Works" (1964; revised 1991) 387
81. Ralph Ellison: "Homage to Duke Ellington on His Birthday" (1969) 394
82. Martin Williams: "Form Beyond Form" (1970; revised 1983, 1993) 400
83. Albert Murray: From *The Hero and the Blues* (1973) 412
84. Gunther Schuller: "Ellington in the Pantheon" (1974) 414
85. Gunther Schuller: "The Case for Ellington's Music as Living Repertory" (1974) 418
86. Lawrence Gushee: "Duke Ellington 1940" (1978) 421
87. Stanley Crouch on *Such Sweet Thunder, Suite Thursday,* and *Anatomy of a Murder* (1988) 439

Musical Analysis

23. Roger Pryor Dodge on *Black and Tan Fantasy,* from "Harpsichords and Jazz Trumpets" (1934) 105
28. Enzo Archetti: "In Defense of Ellington and His 'Reminiscing in Tempo'" (1936) 121
45. Robert D. Crowley: "*Black, Brown and Beige* After 16 Years" (1959) 179
46. Brian Priestley and Alan Cohen: "Black, Brown & Beige" (1974–1975) 185
52. An Ellington Solo Piano Transcription in *Down Beat* (1944) 250
57. André Hodeir: "A Masterpiece: *Concerto for Cootie*" (1954) 276
62. Selections from *The Jazz Review* (1959): Mimi Clar, Quincy Jones, and Max Harrison 302
69. A. J. Bishop: "Duke's *Creole Rhapsody*" (1963) 347
71. A. J. Bishop: " 'Reminiscing in Tempo': A Landmark in Jazz Composition" (1964) 355
86. Lawrence Gushee: "Duke Ellington 1940" (1978) 421

Interviews with Ellington

8. Two Early Interviews (1930): Janet Mabie and Florence Zunser 41
10. The Ellington Orchestra in Cleveland (1931) 50
17. Ellington Defends His Music (1933) 80
25. Ellington's Response to Lambert (1935) 112
26. Ellington on Gershwin's *Porgy and Bess*—and a Response from the Office of Irving Mills (1935/1936) 114
31. "Ellington Refutes Cry That Swing Started Sex Crimes!" (1937) 128
37. A Celebrity Interview (1941) 143
39. Interview in Los Angeles: On *Jump for Joy,* Opera, and Dissonance as a "Way of Life" (1941) 148
49. Richard O. Boyer: "The Hot Bach" (1944) 214
53. "Why Duke Ellington Avoided Music Schools" (1945) 252
54. "Interpretations in Jazz: A Conference with Duke Ellington" (1947) 255
66. Ellington with Stanley Dance: "The Art Is in the Cooking" (1962) 332
67. Ellington on the Air in Vancouver (1962) 338

Profiles of Ellington's Musicians (Including Interviews)

18. Hugues Panassié: "Duke Ellington at the Salle Pleyel" (1946) 81
88. Helen Oakley (Dance): "Impressions of Johnny Hodges" (1936) 449
89. "The Duke Ellingtons—Cotton Clubbers En Masse" (1937) 451

90. Roger Pryor Dodge on Bubber Miley (1940) 454
91. Ivie Anderson (1942) 458
92. Reactions of a Newcomer: Al Sears Interviewed by George T. Simon (1944) 460
93. Inez M. Cavanaugh: Three Interviews (1945): Otto Hardwick, "Tricky Sam" Nanton, and Rex Stewart 462
94. Double Play: Harry Carney and Johnny Hodges Interviewed by Don DeMichael (1962) 471
95. Rex Stewart: "Illustrious Barney Bigard" (1966) 476
96. Guitarist Freddy Guy Interviewed by John McDonough (1969) 481
97. Sonny Greer Interviewed by Whitney Balliett (1974) 486
98. Gary Giddins on Paul Gonsalves (1985) 491
99. Stanley Crouch on Ben Webster (1986) 493
100. Billy Strayhorn Interviewed by Bill Coss (1962) 498
101. Ellington: "Eulogy for Swee' Pea" (1967) 504

Reviews of Performances and Recordings

2. The Washingtonians: First New York Review (1923) 21
3. Reviews from the Kentucky Club (1925) 22
5. First Cotton Club Review (1927) 31
6. R. D. Darrell: Criticism in the Phonograph Monthly Review (1927–1931) 33
7. Abbé Niles on Ellington (1929) 40
10. The Ellington Orchestra in Cleveland (1931) 50
15. Ellington at the Palladium (1933) 75
16. On the Air in London (1933) 78
29. Helen Oakley (Dance): The Ellington Orchestra at the Apollo (1936) 125
42. Two Reviews (1943): Paul Bowles in the New York Herald-Tribune, Mike Levin in Down Beat (1943) 165
48. Carnegie Revisited (1943/1944) 209
59. George Avakian: Ellington at Newport (1956) 290
62. Selections from The Jazz Review (1959): Mimi Clar, Quincy Jones, and Max Harrison 302
70. Dan Morgenstern on The Ellington Era (1963) 350
76. Rex Stewart at a Recording Session for the First Sacred Concert (1966) 373
78. Gary Giddins on The Afro-Eurasian Eclipse (1976) 379

Biographical Profiles

11. Ellington Crowned "King of Jazz" by the Pittsburgh Courier (1931) 54
13. Spike Hughes: Impressions of Ellington in New York (1933) 69

22. Warren W. Scholl: Profile of Ellington in the *Music Lovers' Guide* (1934) 102
30. R. D. Darrell: Ellington in an Encyclopedia (1936) 127
49. Richard O. Boyer: "The Hot Bach" (1944) 214
73. Nat Hentoff: "This Cat Needs No Pulitzer Prize" (1965) 362

Writings by Ellington

1. On Washington, D.C. (1973) 5
9. First Article: "The Duke Steps Out" (1931) 46
19. "My Hunt for Song Titles" (1933) 87
33. "From Where I Lie" (1938) 131
34. In *Down Beat:* On Swing and Its Critics (1939) 132
38. "We, Too, Sing 'America'" (1941) 146
47. "Defense of Jazz" (1943/1944) 207
50. "Certainly It's Music!" (1944) 246
51. "Swing Is My Beat!" (1944) 248
60. "The Race for Space" (*ca.* late 1957) 293
64. "Where Is Jazz Going?" (1962) 324
72. "Reminiscing in Tempo" (1964) 358
74. "The Most Essential Instrument" (1965) 368
75. Program Note for "A Concert of Sacred Music" (1965) 371
101. "Eulogy for Swee' Pea" (1967) 504

Feature Pieces

4. The Washingtonians "Set New England Dance Crazy" (1927) 24
10. The Ellington Orchestra in Cleveland (1931) 50
14. Spike Hughes: "Meet the Duke!" (1933) 72
20. Wilder Hobson: "Introducing Duke Ellington" (1933) 93
22. Warren W. Scholl: Profile of Ellington in the *Music Lovers' Guide* (1934) 102
40. Previews of the First Carnegie Hall Concert (1943): Helen Oakley (Dance) and Howard Taubman 155
65. Pete Welding: "On the Road with the Duke Ellington Orchestra" (1962) 326
68. Eddie Lambert: "Duke Ellington—1963" (1963) 342
73. Nat Hentoff: "This Cat Needs No Pulitzer Prize" (1965) 362

Miscellaneous

35. The Parting of Ellington and Irving Mills (1939) 140
41. Program for the First Carnegie Hall Concert (23 January 1943) 160
79. Stanley Dance: "The Funeral Address" (1974) 381

General Index

Acht O'Clock Rock, 380
Across the Track Blues, 408, 436–37
Adams, Sonny, 473
Ad Lib on Nippon, 379
Admiration, 37
Africa, 43, 45, 53, 98, 186, 188, 289–90, 380
African-American history, 10, 44, 45, 49, 116, 145, 150, 160, 217–18, 237–38, 366–67. See also *Black, Brown and Beige*; *Boola*; *My People*
African-American life/music: and Basie, 496; and classical music, 398–99, 423–24; Crouch on, 443, 496; and dance, 49; Darrell on, 58–65; Ellington as distancing himself from, 120; Ellington on, 41, 42–45, 48–50, 53–54, 59–60, 60n3, 73, 80, 81, 87–89, 131, 135, 144–50, 156, 159, 210–11, 218, 238, 254, 325, 363, 423; and the Ellington orchestra, 438; Ellison on, 396; as folk music, 74, 80–81, 422; and Gershwin, 114–17; Giddins on, 496; Gushee on, 422–24, 425, 438; Hughes on, 73–74; and jazz, 49, 53–54, 73, 74, 108, 135, 145, 177, 178, 208, 218, 238, 257, 361, 363; and *Jump for Joy*, 148, 149; Larkin on, 144–45; and Monk, 496; Murray on, 413; and *New World A-Comin'*, 210–11; and patriotism, 150; and race pride, 59–60n3, 73–74, 112, 113–14; and race relations, 149–50, 184, 237, 422–23, 464, 480; and rock 'n' roll, 325; Sargeant on, 207, 208, 209; and song titles, 87, 88–89; as a source for comparing Ellington's work, 131; and swing, 145; Thiele on, 177, 178; and Webster, 496. See also *Black, Brown and Beige*; *Symphony in Black* (film)
African Americans, as musicians, 184, 207, 208, 209, 237, 398–99, 423–24, 425, 464, 480
Afro Bossa (album), 444
The Afro-Eurasian Eclipse, 317, 379–81, 493
Afrique, 381

Ailey, Alvin, 317
Ain't But the One, 317
Air Mail Special, 284
Alexander, Willard, 141
All American (album/musical), 493
Allen, Red, 478
All God's Chillun Got Rhythm, 460
All of Me, 345
All Too Soon, 269, 432, 495
Almighty God, 378, 382
Almost Cried, 314
Alvis, Hayes, 126, 453
Amen, 193
American Lullaby, 156, 157
American Society of Composers and Publishers (ASCAP), 92
Amos 'n' Andy, 37n4, 55, 89, 94, 265
Anatomy of a Murder, 263, 313–15, 321, 412, 439–41, 442
Anderson, Gene, 455
Anderson, Ivie/Ivy, 51, 52, 104, 125–26, 354, 396, 406, 475; biographical sketch of, 458–60; and the Ellington orchestra of 1940, 422, 428, 431–32; and Ellington's popularity, 95; Ellington's relationship with, 459; and the European tour (1933), 67, 76, 77, 78, 79, 85; favorite recordings of, 460; favorite vocalists of, 458; joins the Ellington orchestra, 50; leaves the Ellington orchestra, 50, 177, 458; milestones in career of, 460; as a restaurant owner, 234, 458; Strayhorn's arrangements for, 499
Anderson, John, 22
Anderson, Marian, 267
Anderson, William "Cat," 214, 303, 311–12, 377, 393, 412, 419; and the European tour (1963), 343, 344; health of, 328–29; joins the Ellington orchestra, 205; and the Newport Jazz Festival (1956), 292
And His Mother Called Him Bill (album), 503
Ansermet, Ernest, 110, 285
Apollo Theatre (New York City), 125–27, 366
Archetti, Enzo, 121–25

Arlen, Harold, 29, 272
Armstrong, Louis, 71, 95, 102, 334, 350, 396; Archetti on, 121; and Bechet, 473; and Bigard, 480; Crouch on, 442, 443, 444, 494; Dodge on, 456, 457; Ellington on, 87, 140, 364, 369, 370; Ellington's recordings with, 317; Giddins on, 496, 497; Hodeir on, 277, 287, 297, 299, 301n*; imitations of, 79, 98, 99, 178, 336, 470; influence on Ellington of, 411; Lambert on, 110, 344; and the Luis Russell band, 474; Overstreet on, 98, 99; Stewart on, 470; Thiele on, 177, 178; transcription of a solo by, 250; Webster compared with, 496, 497; and the Welles–Ellington film project, 149; Williams (Cootie) compared with, 344; Williams (Martin) on, 403, 411
Asbury Park, New Jersey, 10–11, 19, 469–70, 489
Ash, Paul, 55
Ashby, Harold, 317, 376, 380, 380n2
Askland, Gunnar, 255–58
The Asphalt Jungle Theme, 329, 344, 412
At a Dixie Roadside Diner, 431–32
At His Very Best (album), 354
Avakian, George, 290–92
Awful Sad, 36, 60, 61, 65, 128, 226, 226n2, 233, 242
Ayler, Albert, 380
Azure, 91, 406, 415, 419

Babs, Alice, 317, 376, 378, 382, 444
Baby Ain't You Satisfied, 470
Baby, When You Ain't There, 67, 71
Bach, Johann Sebastian: Ellington compared with, 64, 103, 109, 110, 112, 246, 307; Ellington on, 42, 45, 215–16, 246; Hobson on, 95; Hodeir on, 288
Bacon, Louis, 443
Bailey, Bill, 67, 77, 78, 85
Bailey, Buster, 85, 478
Bailey, Mildred, 450, 458, 459
Bailey, Ozzie, 312
Baker, Harold "Shorty," 211, 219, 245, 312, 314, 322; and Black, Brown and Beige, 169, 181, 190, 193, 200–201; characteristics/personality of, 502; and the European tour (1963), 344; influences on, 220; joins the Ellington orchestra, 153; and relationships among band members, 245; self-criticism of, 220; on trumpet playing, 220; and World War II, 92
Bakiff, 150n5, 173
Balliett, Whitney, 486–91
Bal Masque (album), 322
Barbarin, Paul, 478

Barnes, Mae, 335
Barnet, Charlie, 140, 254, 254n2, 411, 431
Barris, Harry, 339
Barron's (New York City), 20, 21, 172, 240, 482, 487
Barrymore, Lionel, 267
Bartlett, Dean, 372
Bartók, Béla, 298, 392
Barzallai-Lou, 218n1
Basie, Count, 141, 144, 311–12, 363; and African-American life/music, 496; Ellington on, 139; and Ellington's funeral, 382; and Ellington Week, 267; Hammond's relationship with, 174; imitation of, 428; popularity of, 211, 263; Stewart on, 469–70
Battle, Edgar, 382
Battle of Swing, 91
BBC, 67, 78–79, 103, 273
Beasley, Bill, 14
Beatles, 317, 359, 370–71
The Beautiful Indians, 394
Bechet, Sidney, 110, 337, 364, 368, 369–70, 442, 462, 472, 473–74
The Beetle (Stephen Henderson), 20, 368, 370, 463
Beiderbecke, Bix, 85n3, 102, 126, 236, 427, 456, 483
Beige (from Black, Brown and Beige), 169, 170, 181, 188, 199–204
Bell, Aaron, 327, 381, 382, 492
Bell, Archie, 50–54
Bell, Clive, 59, 59n3
Belle of the Nineties (film), 91, 266
Bellson, Louie, 269, 377, 382
Benjamin, Cecil, 454, 454n1
Benjamin, Joe, 420
Berger, David, 441n2, 444, 444n4
Berlin, Irving, 71, 502
Bermuda tour, 360, 382
Bernstein, Leo, 487–88
Bernstein, Leonard, 179
Berry, Bill, 327, 329
Berry, Chu, 495
Berry Brothers, 32
Berton, Vic, 24
Bertrand, Jimmy, 478
Best Wishes, 79, 89, 89n4
Bethlehem Records, 263, 297–302, 313
The Bethlehem Years, Vol. 1 (album), 297
Bigard, Barney: and Armstrong, 480; biographical sketch by Stewart of, 476–81; Bishop on, 347, 349; and Black, Brown and Beige, 171, 172, 173, 177, 182; Carney on, 475; characteristics/personality of, 85, 452, 476–77, 480, 490; as a

clarinet player, 479–80, 481; as a composer/arranger, 480; Crouch on, 441; Crowley on, 182; "Detector" on, 79; and the early Ellington orchestras, 38n5, 39n6, 96, 242, 422, 425, 426, 428, 430, 431, 432, 436–37; Ellington on, 48, 96, 160, 172, 233; and the European tours, 76, 77, 79, 81, 83, 84, 85–86, 346; favorite clarinetists of, 85–86; favorite instruments of, 85; favorite recording of, 85; first recordings of, 479; Greer on, 490; Gushee on, 425, 426, 428, 430, 431, 432, 436–37; Guy on, 483; Hammond on, 172, 173; Hobson on, 142–43; Hodeir on, 283, 284; Hughes on, 70; interviewed by Panassié, 81, 83, 84, 85–86; joins the Ellington orchestra, 29, 48, 96, 96n4, 242, 403, 478, 483; Lambert on, 346; leaves the Ellington orchestra, 153, 171, 176–77, 352, 480; and the *Metronome* profiles, 452; Morgenstern on, 352, 353, 354; musical development of, 476–78; nicknames for, 476, 490; Oakley on, 126; and race relations, 480; role in orchestra of, 97; Schuller on, 417; Stewart on, 476–81; on swing, 86; Thiele on, 177; Trussell on, 171; Williams (Martin) on, 401, 403, 405–6, 407, 410; Williams (Ned) on, 271
Bigard, Emile, 477
Big House Blues, 38
Big John's Saloon (New York City), 458, 479, 480
Big Noise from Winnetka, 434
Billy Paige's Broadway Syncopaters, 469
Birmingham Breakdown, 34, 36, 48, 61, 88, 128, 241, 259, 268, 402
Bishop, A. J., 347–49, 355–58, 389
Bitches' Ball, 200, 200n
Black (from *Black, Brown and Beige*), 167, 168, 169–70, 181, 187–95, 199, 200, 392–93
Black and Tan Fantasy: and African-American life/music, 108; Bell (Archie) on, 51; and the *Black, Brown and Beige* premiere, 160, 172; and celebrities' favorite Ellington recordings, 269; Clar on, 308; classical music compared with, 105, 108, 109; composing of, 241, 456, 464; Darrell on, 33, 34, 36, 59, 65, 128; Davis on, 143; as distinctively Ellington, 3; Dodge on, 105–10, 457, 458; Ellington on, 230, 339–40; and Ellington's "best" compositions, 103; Ellison on, 395–96; and the European tour (1933), 77; Hammond on, 172; Hardwick on, 464; Harrison on, 388; Hughes on, 71; and the Mercer Ellington

orchestra, 391n*; at Miley's funeral, 455; Mills on, 274; Morgenstern on, 354; Nanton on, 467; Niles on, 41; Overstreet on, 103; recordings of, 33–34, 36, 41, 65, 457; as a regular feature in Ellington's shows, 126; as a title, 89; Ulanov on, 212, 396; Williams (Martin) on, 405; Zunser on, 45
"Black Beauty" (Darrell essay), 29, 33, 57–65, 93, 102, 125n3
Black Beauty (piece): and *Black, Brown and Beige*, 155, 166; Bowles on, 166; composing of, 241; Darrell on, 35, 36, 60, 63, 128; dedication to Mills (Florence) of, 383; and the European tour (1933), 67; Niles on, 41; Overstreet on, 103; recordings of, 35, 41, 65; Schuller on, 403; Williams (Martin) on, 403; Zunser on, 45
Blackbirds Medley, 96–97
Blackbirds of 1928, 79
Black Bottom Stomp, 443
Black, Brown and Beige: and African-American life/music, 146, 156, 182, 186, 199, 218, 218n1, 249; analyzed by Priestley and Cohen, 153, 185–204; audience for, 267; Boston performance of, 158, 178, 185; Bowles on, 165–66, 167, 179, 180, 182, 199; as a career highlight, 266–67; Cavanaugh's liner notes for, 462; Chase on, 180, 180–81n1; Chicago performance of, 181; and classical music, 165, 166, 170, 178–79, 248; Cleveland performance of, 158; Cohen on, 153, 185–204; Crowley on, 153, 179–85, 389; dance in, 158, 166, 195–96; and Dance's eulogy, 383; debate about, 170–78; development of, 44, 49–50, 93, 98, 153, 160, 169, 180, 186, 193, 198n, 202; Ellington on, 156, 186, 199, 209, 249, 257, 266–67; and the Ellington orchestra, 153, 165, 168, 182, 201–2; and the Ellington–Strayhorn relationship, 501; as an extended work, 91; Feather on, 155n1, 171, 173–75; Giddins on, 377, 379; Green on, 167; Hammond on, 119, 171–75; Harrison on, 389, 390, 391, 392–93; Hobson on, 93, 98; influences on writing of, 241; length of, 167, 178, 180, 186, 193; Levin on, 165, 166–70, 174, 180; List on, 178–79; Oakley on, 155–58; and patriotism, 157, 157n4, 170, 199, 201–2; portraitures in, 155, 158, 173; premiere of, 44, 153, 160–70, 165n1, 170–78, 180, 181, 182–83, 185, 186, 192, 196, 198, 199, 201–2, 258–59, 266–67, 290; previews of, 155–60; program for premiere of, 160–65; recordings of, 165n1, 168,

Black, Brown and Beige (*continued*)
178, 179, 181–82, 183, 185, 186, 189,
190, 191, 191n4, 192, 193, 195, 196, 197,
199, 199n, 201, 266, 462; rehearsals for,
168, 169, 201–2; reviews of, 165–204;
Schubart on, 214; second Carnegie Hall
performance of, 195, 209, 210, 211, 212,
214; social significance of, 157, 182, 195–
96; story line of, 44, 156–57, 160, 169–
70, 181, 187, 202, 257; and *Symphony in
Black* (film), 186–87, 187n*; Taubman on,
155, 158–60; tentative titles for, 98; Thiele
on, 171, 175–78; Trussell on, 171; Ulanov
on, 180, 186, 195, 199, 200, 201–2, 210,
211, 212; Wilder on, 180, 259, 260;
Williams (Martin) on, 412
Blackwell, Ollie, 469
Blanton, Jimmy: characteristics/personality of,
490; Clar on, 303, 309; death of, 309,
434; and the Ellington orchestra of 1940,
422, 426, 428, 429, 432, 433, 434, 435,
438; and Greer, 182, 490; Gushee on, 426,
428, 429, 432, 433, 434, 435, 438; Hodeir
on, 283, 284, 300; joins the Ellington
orchestra, 91; leaves the Ellington
orchestra, 171, 176–77; Morgenstern on,
354; and *This One's for Blanton*, 435;
Trussell on, 171; Williams (Martin) on,
409, 410
Blind Johnny, 14, 20
Block, Harry, 32
Blue, William Thornton, 478, 479–80
Blue Belles of Harlem, 156, 157, 169, 173,
211
Blue Bubbles, 65
Blue Goose, 182, 431
Blue Light, 91, 407, 408, 409, 415
Blue Mood, 407–8
Blue Moon, 289
Blue Ramble, 67, 71, 77, 103
Blues: Avakian on the, 290–91; Crouch on
the, 443; Darrell on the, 58; Ellington on
the, 45, 209; Ellison on the, 396; Gushee
on the, 436; Hammond on the, 172;
Hodeir on the, 280; influence of the, 44–
45; Oakley on the, 450; patterns in the,
209; Schuller on the, 443; Williams
(Martin) on, 412. *See also specific
composition*
The Blues (from *Black, Brown and Beige*),
153, 157, 169, 178–79, 196, 197–98,
198n, 202
Blue Serge, 160, 408, 409–10, 411, 419
Blues I Love to Sing, 37, 65, 128, 241
Blues in Orbit, 321
Blue Tune, 70, 71, 77, 96, 103, 353, 356
Boatwright, McHenry, 382

Boatwright, Ruth Ellington. *See* Ellington,
Ruth Dorothea
Body and Soul, 129, 280, 435
Bojangles, 430
Bolden, Buddy, 216, 236, 238
Boo-Dah, 309
Boola (unproduced opera), 116, 116n3, 160,
169, 180, 186, 218, 249, 427
Bouncing Buoyancy, 407
Bowles, Paul, 130, 165–66, 167, 170, 179,
180, 182, 199, 209–10
Bowser, Clarence, 14, 15, 239
Boyd, Bobby, 323, 327, 329, 330
Boyd, Jack, 214, 215, 217, 219, 221–22,
224, 231, 233, 272
Boyd, Raymond "Lippy," 463
Boyer, Richard O., 205, 214–45
Braggin' in Brass, 91, 406
Braud, Wellman: and Bigard, 478;
characteristics/personality of, 490; and the
early Ellington orchestras, 38n5, 39n6, 48,
242, 434; Ellington on, 48, 354; and the
European tour (1933), 77, 82–83; joins the
Ellington orchestra, 242; and race
relations, 490; role in orchestra of, 354;
Stewart on, 480
Brauner/Bronner, Shrimp, 12, 14
Bricktop (chanteuse), 487
Bricktop's (Paris), 82n1, 87
Briggs, Arthur, 82n1, 87
Briggs, Bunny, 377
Britton, Jimmy, 153, 157, 157n4, 201–2
Brooks, Harvey, 11, 11n5
Brown (from *Black, Brown and Beige*),
169, 170, 181, 188, 195–99, 200, 209,
211
Brown, Chauncey, 18
Brown, Lawrence: biographical sketch of,
223; Bishop on, 358; and *Black, Brown
and Beige*, 173, 182, 194, 200–201; Boyer
on, 219, 223, 229; characteristics/
personality of, 223, 453, 490; Clar on,
303; Crowley on, 182; "Detector" on, 79;
and the Ellington orchestra of 1940, 422,
428, 429, 431, 432, 436, 437; Ellington's
relationship with, 226, 229, 343; and the
European tours, 67, 76, 77, 79, 343–44;
Giddins on, 492; Greer on, 490; Gushee
on, 428, 429, 431, 432, 436, 437;
Hammond on, 173; Hobson on, 142–43;
Hodeir on, 283; Hughes on, 69, 70–71;
imitation of, 418; joins the Ellington
orchestra, 67; Lambert on, 343–44; leaves
the Ellington orchestra, 263; McPhee on,
213; and the *Metronome* profiles, 453;
Morgenstern on, 353, 354; Oakley on,
125; Priestley and Cohen on, 194, 200–

201; rejoins the Ellington orchestra, 263; Schuller on, 418; Ulanov on, 211, 212; Welding on, 327, 328; Williams (Martin) on, 401, 407, 410

Brown, Louis, 5, 14, 15, 16, 239

Brown, Ray, 435

The Brownskin Gal, 268

Brunswick Records, 27, 43, 64–65, 104, 423, 470. *See also specific composition*

Bryant, Marie, 266

Bryant, Willie, 463

Bugle Call Rag, 77, 85n2, 104, 407, 479

Bulldiker's Dream, 369

Bundle of Blues, 407

Burrows, Roy, 327, 328–29, 344

But I'm a Long Ways from Home, 58

Cabin in the Sky (film), 211

Caldwell, Happy, 479

Calloway, Cab, 46, 88n1, 96, 102, 140, 141, 273–74, 478

Canadian Broadcasting Company, 367

Capitol Records, 263

Caravan, 211–12, 269, 309, 353, 383, 427, 432, 444, 475, 492

Carmichael, Hoagy, 456

Carnegie Blues, 198

Carnegie Hall: and the classical music–jazz debate, 205, 209–14, 247; Ellington on, 229–30; Ellington's performances at, 200n, 205, 209–14, 250; Hobson predicts Ellington will play at, 98; jazz musicians at, 153, 156, 156n2, 158, 267; *Night Creature* premiere at, 325; Philadelphia Orchestra at, 268; and race relations, 182. See also *Black, Brown and Beige*, premiere of

Carney, Harry: and Bechet, 472, 474; biographical sketch of, 472; Bishop on, 347, 357; and *Black, Brown and Beige*, 169, 173, 181–82, 189–90, 192, 196, 197, 201, 203; characteristics/personality of, 360, 452, 472; Clar on, 303; Crowley on, 181–82; "Detector" on, 79; early career of, 472–73; and the early Ellington orchestras, 39n6, 48, 242, 422, 425, 426, 432, 433, 437; on Ellington, 475; Ellington on, 48, 226, 227, 254n1, 326, 328, 360, 363, 404; and the European tours, 77, 79, 83, 84, 342, 344, 345, 346; favorite saxophone players of, 473; Giddins on, 376, 377, 378, 381, 492; Gushee on, 425, 426, 432, 433, 437; and Guy, 483; Hammond on, 173; Harrison on, 315; health of, 382; Hobson on, 142–43; Hodeir on, 283; and Hodges, 472–76; Hughes on, 70; interviewed by DeMichael, 471–76; joins the Ellington

orchestra, 242, 471, 472–73, 483; Jones (Quincy) on, 312; Lambert on, 342, 344, 345, 346; Levin on, 169; and the *Metronome* profiles, 452; Morgenstern on, 353–54; Oakley on, 126; Panassié on, 83, 84; Priestley and Cohen on, 189–90, 192, 196, 197, 201, 203; and race relations, 232; Stewart on, 374; Ulanov on, 212; Welding on, 327, 328; Williams (Martin) on, 403, 404, 410, 411

Carolina Shout, 18–19, 19n10, 239

Carroll, Earl, 26

Carter, Benny, 69, 96, 466, 471, 495, 496, 497

Categorization of music, 424, 439; Ellington on, 324, 326, 332–38, 364, 371, 383, 419, 422, 444

Catlett, Sid, 487

Cavanaugh, Inez M., 183n2, 462–71

CBS, 339

Celley, Al, 327, 330, 331

Century of Negro Progress Exposition (1963), 317

Chant of the Weed, 139

Chase, Gilbert, 180, 180–81n1

Check and Double Check (film), 37n4, 41, 55, 67, 94, 265, 266, 339

Chelsea Bridge, 91, 269, 305, 410, 498

Cherokee, 426

Chevalier, Maurice, 41, 55, 94, 256

Chicago, Illinois, 126, 212, 234; Bigard in, 32, 477–48; and Chicago style jazz, 208; Ellington performances in, 181, 205, 224, 340, 426, 427, 430, 433, 435, 436–38, 483, 486

Chinoiserie, 379–80, 380n2

Chloe, 309, 437

Chocolate Kiddies (musical revue), 259n2, 339

Choo-Choo, 402, 403, 465n1

Chopin, Frederic, 58, 396, 417

Christian, Charlie, 434, 481

Circle of Fourths, 441

Ciro's (New York City), 464

Civic Opera House (Chicago), 205

Civil rights, 366–67, 383. *See also* Race relations

C Jam Blues, 211, 213, 307, 487, 492

Clap Hands Here Comes Charlie, 369

Clar, Mimi, 302, 303–11

Clarinet Lament, 130, 233, 284, 353

Classical Jazz series (Lincoln Center, New York City), 385n1, 439–45

Classical music: and African-American life/music, 398–99; and African-American musicians, 423–24; Bell (Archie) on, 51;

Classical music (continued)
and the Black and Tan Fantasy, 105, 108,
109; and Black, Brown and Beige, 160,
165, 166, 170–79, 183–85, 248; and
Carnegie Hall jazz performances, 205,
207–9, 213, 247; Crouch on, 442, 443;
Crowley on, 183, 184–85; Darrell on, 38,
39, 40, 58, 60, 61, 62, 63, 64, 97, 127,
131; Dodge on, 104, 105, 108, 109;
Ellington on, 45, 110–14, 115, 134–35,
135n2, 160, 207–9, 246–48, 253, 256,
257–58, 326; Ellington's favorite works of,
268–69; and Ellington as "The Hot Bach,"
205; Feather on, 171, 173–75; Grainger
on, 103; Gushee on, 423–24, 439;
Hammond on, 120, 170, 171–75; Harrison
on, 389, 393–94; Hentoff on, 363; Hibbs
on, 122; Hobson on, 93, 95; Hodeir on,
284–88; and the inferiority of jazz
musicians, 183–84; as an influence on
Ellington, 42, 124–25, 246–48; and the
Jazz debate, 170–78; Lambert on, 110–14;
Levin on, 170; List on, 178–79; and the
Modern Jazz Quartet, 184–85; and the
Naumberg lecture-recital series, 134–35,
135n2; Panassié on, 178; and Porgy and
Bess, 115–16; Sargeant on, 207–9;
Schubart on, 213, 253; Schuller on, 415,
417–18, 419, 420, 421; Taubman on, 158;
Thiele on, 171, 175–78. See also specific
composer
Clef Club Orchestra, 153
Clinkscales, Marietta, 6, 16, 54, 56, 95, 238
Clooney, Rosemary, 475
The Clothed Woman, 402, 415, 417
Clouds in My Heart, 480
Club Bechet (New York City), 473–74
Club Richman (New York City), 23, 31,
31n1
Club Zanzibar (New York City), 205, 255n3
Cock o' the World (musical), 146
Cohen, Alan, 153, 185–204
Coleman, Ornette, 311, 324, 394
Collier, James Lincoln, 442
Coloratura, 214
Coltrane, John, 317, 324, 419, 493
Columbia Records, 65, 103; Ellington's
relationship with, 33, 104, 205, 261, 263,
423; Townsend on Ellington's recording
sessions with, 319–24. See also specific
composition
The Comedy, 394
Come Sunday (from Black, Brown and
Beige): Crouch on, 443–44; Crowley on,
181; Feather on, 175; Giddins on, 377;
List on, 178–79; Priestley and Cohen on,

187, 191, 192, 194–95, 196, 201, 202;
Townsend on, 320; Williams (Martin) on,
412
Composers/arrangers: definition of, 297;
Ellington on, 237, 294; jazz musicians as,
420. See also specific person
Concerto for Cootie, 91, 276–88, 283n1,
358, 392, 406, 408, 411, 428, 429
Concerto for Klinkers, 198n
Condon, Eddie, 158
Confrey, Zez, 60
Conga Brava, 150n5, 408, 427–28, 436,
495
Connie's Inn (New York City), 20, 455
Connors, Chuck, 327, 343
Connor's Cabaret (New York City), 20, 454,
469
Conway/Conaway, Ewell, 17, 489
Conway/Conaway, Sterling, 20, 489
Cook, Charlie, 477
Cook, Doc, 478
Cook, Mercer, 289
Cook, Will Marion, 241, 289, 422, 489
Coon-Sanders orchestra, 25, 35, 370
Cooper, Buster, 343
Copland, Aaron, 57, 60, 111, 130, 267
Copout, 321, 345
Coss, Bill, 498–503
Cote D'Azur (album), 493
Cotton, 460
Cotton Club (Los Angeles), 94, 459
Cotton Club (New York City): African-
Americans barred from the, 70, 478–79;
Boyer on the, 241–42; dress of Ellington's
orchestra at the, 142; Ellington as central
to the, 98; Ellington's debut at the, 24, 31,
45, 96, 142, 172, 241–42, 265, 320, 403,
484; and Ellington's popularity, 24, 45, 48,
55, 56, 96, 98, 100, 142, 172, 242, 488;
Ellington's return engagements at the, 69–
72, 91, 129, 266, 268, 272–73, 341;
Ellington on the, 339; environment of the,
29; Green on the, 32; Greer on the, 488;
Gushee on the, 423; Guy on the, 483–84;
Hobson on the, 98; Hughes on the, 69–72;
location of the, 29, 70n2, 91, 341;
longevity of Ellington's band at the, 48,
266; and the Mills–Ellington relationship,
274–75; Morgenstern on the, 352; Nanton
on the, 466; popularity of the, 29; radio
broadcasts from the, 29, 42, 78, 78n1, 96,
266, 273, 339; reminiscing about the, 466,
478–79, 483–84, 488; and the Sacred
Concerts, 376; Snelson on the, 55; staff of
the, 32; Stewart on the, 478–79; Williams
(Martin) on the, 403–4; Williams (Ned)

on the, 271, 272–73. *See also* Harlem
Footwarmers; Harlem Music Masters;
Jungle Band
Cotton Club Stomp, 242
Cotton Tail, 173, 212, 307, 408, 417, 496;
and celebrities' favorite Ellington
recordings, 269; and the Ellington
orchestra of 1940, 429, 439; as a
masterpiece, 91
Country Gal, 268
Coward, Noël, 70
Cox, Leon, 327, 328, 329
Crazy Rhythm, 48
Creager, Willie, 24
The Creeper, 241
Creole Love Call: composing of, 241; Crouch
on, 443; Darrell on, 36, 37, 63, 65, 128;
as distinctively Ellington, 3; Ellington on,
339; and the European tour (1933), 67,
79; Hodeir on, 297; Overstreet on, 103,
104; recordings of, 36, 65, 104; Scholl on,
102; Williams (Martin) on, 405
Creole Rhapsody: analyzed by Bishop, 347–
49, 357; Crowley on, 180; Darrell on, 40,
63, 65, 128; and Ellington's favorite
records, 268; and the European tour
(1933), 75, 77; as an extended work, 118,
387; Harrison on, 387, 388, 390, 391,
392; Lambert on, 111, 388; Overstreet on,
104; recordings of, 40, 63, 65, 104, 111,
268, 347–49; Scholl on, 102; Schuller on,
347; Williams (Martin) on, 408
Crescendo in Blue. See *Diminuendo and
Crescendo in Blue*
Critics: of African-American musicians, 425;
and the commercialization of swing, 132;
Ellington on, 132, 135, 136–37, 253; and
extended works, 392; and the
intellectualization of Ellington's music,
260; lightweight analysis of jazz by, 440;
and the repertory movement, 418. *See also
specific person or composition*
Crosby, Bing, 94, 250, 339, 463
Crosby, Bob, 139
Crouch, Stanley, 385, 385n1, 439–45, 447,
493–97
Crowley, Robert D., 153, 179–85,
389
Cuban music, 53, 150, 150n5
Cullen, Countee, 49
Cullen, Jack, 338–41
Cy Runs Rock Waltz, 199n

Dakar, Senegal, 289
Dameron, Tadd, 390
Dance, Helen. *See* Oakley (Dance), Helen M.

Dance, Stanley, 82, 125, 326, 332–38, 351,
359, 381–84, 404, 492
Dance: and African-American life/music, 49;
and *Black, Brown and Beige*, 158, 166,
195–96
Dance jobs, theater playing versus, 52–53
Dance music: and African-American life/
music, 60; and commercialism, 64, 208,
361, 412, 438; as cyclical, 159; effect on
people of, 45, 53; Ellington on, 45, 53, 88,
159, 361; in Ellington performances/shows,
69; and Ellington's Carnegie Hall
performances, 208, 209, 210, 212;
Ellington's drift away from, 172, 173, 175,
176, 210, 212; and Ellington's musical
development, 352, 402, 423; and
Ellington's popularity, 210, 412, 423; and
Ellington's uniqueness, 61, 421, 427; and
experimentation, 60, 171, 172, 261; and
extended works, 172, 173, 175, 176, 209,
210, 212, 352, 361; and jazz, 176, 208,
352; as listening music, 261; and primitive
instincts, 53; social aspects of, 361; and
swing, 88; as a type of Ellington music,
61
Dance of the Flying Saucers, 293
Dancers in Love, 214
Dandridge, Dorothy, 266
Daphnis and Chloe (Ravel), 268
Darrell, R. D., 121, 127–28; biographical
sketch of, 33; "Black Beauty" by, 29, 32,
33, 57–65, 93, 102, 125n3; and Ellington's
"most important" works, 128; and
Ellington's originality, 97; and Ellington's
reputation as a composer/arranger, 72,
131; favorite Ellington recordings of, 65;
Phonograph Monthly Review article of,
33–40, 57
David Danced Before the Lord, 317, 377
Davis, Almena, 143–46
Davis, Kay, 205, 339, 443, 499–500
Davis, Meyer, 17
Davis, Miles, 297, 364, 420
Davis, Pike, 20
Davis, William "Wild Bill," 380n3
Daybreak Express, 119, 128, 227, 259, 406,
411
Day Dream, 160, 165, 169, 173, 410, 498,
499
Dear Old Southland, 265
Debussy, Claude, 61, 113, 120, 124–25, 131,
268–69, 417
Decca Records, 67
Deep South Suite, 205, 379, 383
Delius, Frederick, 58, 110, 120, 165;
Ellington compared with, 61, 64, 417;

Delius, Frederick (*continued*)
  Ellington on, 95; and Ellington's favorite
    works, 268–69; as an influence on
    Ellington, 124–25, 125*n3*; as a source for
    comparing Ellington's work, 131
DeMichael, Don, 471–76
Dempsey, Jack, 382
DeRose, Peter, 157
Dicty Glide, 88, 96
Didjeridoo, 380
Diga Diga Doo, 79, 456
Diminuendo and Crescendo in Blue: Avakian
    on, 290–92; Chase on, 180, 180–81*n1*;
    Copland on, 130; Crowley on, 180; and
    the Ellington orchestra of 1940, 433; as an
    extended work, 91; Gushee on, 433;
    Harrison on, 387, 390–91, 392;
    Morgenstern on, 351, 353; and the
    Newport Jazz Festival (1956), 290–92;
    recordings of, 129, 130; Williams (Martin)
    on, 411
Dinah's in a Jam, 273
Dirge, 155
Dishman, Lester, 14, 15, 16, 239
Dissonance, Ellington on, 150–51
Dixie, 79
Dixon, Dean, 267
Dixon, Ike, 20
Dixon, Mildred, 92, 451*n1*
Django's Jump, 471
Dobbins, Bill, 441, 441*n2*
Dodds, Johnny, 477, 494
Dodge, Roger Pryor, 105–10, 141, 302, 447,
    454–58
Doin' the Frog, 32, 32*n4*, 35
Doin' the New Low Down, 48, 79
Doin' the Voom Voom, 36, 242
Dolphy, Eric, 324, 419
Do Nothin' Till You Hear from Me, 212,
    278, 278*n**, 279, 280, 344
Don't Get Around Much Any More, 166,
    169, 211, 383, 429
Dorsey, Cliff, 20
Dorsey, Jimmy, 463, 483
Dorsey, Tommy, 138, 260*n3*, 456, 463, 483
Double Check Stomp, 37, 71
Down in Our Alley Blues, 34, 241
Down in the Mouth Blues, 456
Drawing Room Blues, 500
Dream Blues, 474
Dreamy Blues, 38–39. See also *Mood Indigo*
Drew, Charles, 14
Drop Me Off at Harlem, 71–72, 72*n3*, 103,
    128, 254*n2*
A Drum Is a Woman, 149*n4*, 263, 314, 320,
    321

Duchin, Eddie, 272
Ducky Wucky, 83, 84, 89, 96
Dudley, Bessie, 67, 76, 77, 78, 455
Duke Ellington's Serenaders, 3, 23
Duke of Windsor, 268, 460
The Duke Steps Out, 65, 71, 401
Dunn, Johnny, 20, 454, 466
Dusk, 315, 402, 408, 419, 419*n2*, 430, 439
Dvořák, Antonín, 44

East St. Louis Toodle-O: and celebrities'
    favorite Ellington recordings, 269;
    composing of, 109–10, 241, 335, 338–39,
    455–56; Darrell on, 33, 34, 35, 36, 37*n4*,
    61, 63, 65, 128; as distinctively Ellington,
    3; Dodge on, 109–10, 455–56, 457;
    Ellington on, 338–39; Ellison on, 395; and
    the European tour (1933), 79; Gushee on,
    424; Hardwick on, 465; Hodeir on, 297;
    Hughes on, 71; meaning of title, 36*n3*, 88,
    338–39; Morgenstern on, 354; Nanton on,
    467; Niles on, 41; Priestley and Cohen on,
    190, 191–92; radio broadcasts of, 395;
    recordings of, 24, 33, 34, 36, 41, 65, 424,
    457, 465*n1*; as a theme song, 88, 125,
    456; as a type of composition, 61; Wilder
    on, 259; Williams (Martin) on, 402, 403,
    405
Echoes of Harlem, 91, 126, 277, 287, 342,
    357–58, 407–8
Echoes of the Jungle, 40, 65, 71, 406, 485
Echo in the Valley, 71, 104
Edwards, E. Burley, 119*n4*
Edwards, Henry "Bass," 24, 463
Eerie Moan, 233
The Eighth Veil, 343
Eisenhower, Dwight D., 295, 295*n2*, 384
Eldridge, Roy, 178, 344
Elgar, Charlie, 478
El Gato, 311, 312
Elizabeth (Queen of England), 383, 412
Ella at Duke's Place (album), 493
Ellington, Daisy Kennedy (mother): death of,
    91–92, 118, 244, 356–57; and Ellington's
    musical development, 6, 11, 56, 238;
    Ellington's relationship with, 5–6, 7, 8–9,
    10, 56, 240, 340, 384; Greer on, 489–90;
    musical talents of, 11, 42; and religion, 6,
    8
Ellington, Edna (wife): marriage to Ellington
    of, 3, 92; separation from Ellington of, 56,
    217, 245, 451*n1*
Ellington, Edward Kennedy "Duke":
    biographical sketch of, 3–21, 55–56, 95–
    96, 217–18, 237–44, 245, 423; birthdays/
    anniversaries of, 3, 95, 265–76; career

highlights of, 265–68; on concert music, 360–61; death/funeral of, 317, 377, 381–84, 414; defends his music, 80–81; depression of, 367; education of, 6, 6*n*, 9–10, 10*n*, 12, 42, 55–56, 129, 237, 239; favorite music of, 268–69; on freedom of expression, 295–96, 301*n**, 333, 361, 383, 503; guitar playing by, 17; health of, 5–6, 131, 186, 217, 365, 367, 376; image of, 54–55, 96, 237–38, 245, 274, 275; income of, 245, 340, 364; inspiration for, 48–49, 172, 254, 335, 420; intimates of, 365; *Metronome* profile of, 451; on modern jazz, 364; on music, 44, 45, 87–88, 218, 232–36, 248–50, 294–95, 326, 333–38, 371; musical aspirations of, 88, 113–14, 131, 132, 135; musical development of, 6, 9, 11, 14–15, 16, 18–19, 24, 42, 53, 56, 73, 95, 172, 184, 238, 253, 255–56, 301*n**, 352, 387, 400–412, 422, 423; nicknames for, 11–12, 42, 56, 73, 96, 238, 252, 272, 398, 404, 491; on popular music, 44, 45, 49; on retirement, 368, 383, 503; as a role model, 45, 54, 64, 97, 104, 179, 184, 185, 364–65, 397, 410–11; stage fright of, 266–67; utopian views of, 236; as a vocalist, 53
— **characteristics/personality of:** artistic talents of, 9–10, 15, 17, 42, 56, 95, 239; athletic interests of, 6, 7, 9, 53, 56, 95; as a bandleader, 238; charm/disposition of, 114, 119, 120, 132; and composing/arranging, 145, 149, 159, 187, 215, 219, 221–22, 233, 242–43, 244, 252, 365, 414; and criticism, 117; and deadlines, 367; as a dresser, 81, 149, 217, 222, 238, 252, 255, 373; and Ellington's versatility, 103; and food, 7, 9, 10–11, 21, 150, 215–16, 219, 224–25, 228, 234–35, 240, 252, 255, 319; and friendships, 271–72; and lateness, 320; and money, 13, 119, 245; and negativism/unpleasantness, 119, 120, 132; pet aversions of, 117–18; physical characteristics, 59, 76, 222, 255; as a public person, 114; and reading habits, 9; and sleep habits, 149, 159, 215, 219, 221–22, 233, 252, 365; and social life, 365; as a stage personality, 217–18; and superstitions, 271, 272–73, 320; and trains, 216, 218–19, 220–21, 232–34; and women, 12, 13, 92, 217, 224, 272, 323
— **as a composer/arranger:** and African-American life/music, 53–54, 413, 443; aims/aspirations of, 88; and the ASCAP-radio broadcasters' dispute, 92; and audiences, 303; bandleading as a benefit to,

227, 229, 297–98, 391, 417, 438–39, 443, 503; and collaboration with band members, 48, 59, 97, 100–101, 158, 225–27, 229, 233, 249, 259, 277, 309, 319–24, 353, 367–68, 390–92, 404, 411, 417, 444, 460, 466, 467, 475; and composing/arranging for individual band members, 101, 148, 158, 160, 177, 254, 303, 330, 439, 444, 499, 501, 502; and deadlines, 367; and the durability of Ellington's music, 110–11, 421; Elizabethan playwrights compared with, 412–14; and Ellington as the "first genuine composer" of jazz, 72, 73; and Ellington as a great modern composer, 216, 228, 399; Ellington on, 42, 43, 48, 53, 116, 116*n3*, 145, 218, 228–29, 232–34, 254; and Ellington as one of the three greatest composers in history, 110; and Ellington's popularity, 172; and the Ellington–Strayhorn relationship, 220–21, 224–25, 229, 498–503; and endings for pieces, 367–68; and income, 340; and length of compositions, 91; and mental pictures, 233, 335, 338–39; and the Mills–Ellington parting, 141; and the musicians' strike, 92; and on-the-spot composing/arranging, 321–24, 339–41, 461, 475, 492; and originality, 48–49; and "ownership," 420; and personal characteristics/personality, 145, 149, 159, 187, 222, 242–43, 244, 365, 414; and the piano's role, 254; and playing an individual's piece after he leaves, 502; and publication of compositions/arrangements, 101–2, 141, 141*n2*, 145–46, 146*n4*; and the Pulitzer Prize, 362–63; and quantity of compositions/arrangements, 29, 103, 158, 216, 241, 394, 441; and race pride, 44; reasons for, 42; and recording sessions, 319–24; and rehearsals, 97; rules in, 48, 50, 53, 305, 333; and sight/color, 218; Strayhorn on, 367; and study/training, 73, 183, 239, 241; and style, 35, 38, 40, 61, 61*n*, 62–63, 302, 303–11; types of Ellington's compositions/arrangements, 61; and the "working from scratch" method, 259, 259*n1*; as a youth, 11, 12, 12*n8*, 18, 239. *See also* Classical music; Extended works; *specific composition*
— **influences on:** of Armstrong, 411; of Brooks, 11, 11*n5*; of classical composers, 124–25, 246–48; of Cook (Will Marion), 241; of Europe (Jim), 95–96; of Grainger (Percy), 125*n3*; of Grant, 42; of Henderson, 139, 402, 404; of Johnson (James P.), 18–19; of modern composers,

Ellington, Edward Kennedy "Duke" (*continued*)
176; of Morton, 443; of Perry, 14–15, 18, 42, 239; of ragtime piano players, 14–16, 253; of Smith (Leroy), 20; of Smith (Willie "The Lion"), 463; of Sweatman, 20–21; of Waller, 200*n*. *See also* African-American life/music
—as a pianist, 39, 40, 84, 309, 312, 323, 346, 356–57, 362, 403; early jobs as a, 12, 13, 16–17; and early training, 6, 16, 54, 56, 95, 238; influences on, 11, 14–16, 18–19; Strayhorn on, 500; transcription of a piano solo of, 250–52. *See also* Study/ training; *specific composition*
Ellington, James Edward "J.E." (father): characteristics/personality of, 7, 8; death of, 91–92, 244; Ellington's relationship with, 7, 8, 9, 10, 238, 240, 490; employment of, 7, 56, 95, 395; Greer on, 489–90; musical talents of, 11, 42; as "Uncle Ed," 5, 238, 489–90
Ellington, Mercer (son): as bandleader, 382, 391, 391*n**, 418; as a band member, 365; birth of, 3; as a composer, 145–46, 160, 245; and Dance, 332; and Ellington's funeral, 381; Ellington's relationship with, 56, 95, 114, 145, 365, 383; and Mercer Records, 263; professional background of, 365; as road manager, 365; Stewart on, 374
Ellington, Ruth Dorothea (sister), 5, 56, 95, 145–46, 238, 365, 383
Ellington at Newport (album), 290
The Ellington Era, Volume 1 (album), 350, 351–54
Ellington Jazz Party (album), 492
Ellington Masterpieces (album), 387
Ellington orchestra: and African-American life/music, 438; and alcohol, 374; Carney on the, 472–76; and concert music, 360–61; dress of the, 22, 76, 142; drivers for road trips of the, 330; Ellington's relationship with members of the, 217, 222–23, 225–27, 230, 238, 245, 254, 303, 309, 311, 326, 332, 366, 484; Ellington on the, 48, 132, 159, 337–38, 339, 360; enlargement of the, 29, 45, 96, 153, 172, 274; fines of members in the, 87; Greer on the, 490; Guy on the, 483; Hardwick on the, 464; hiring/firing of members of the, 296, 366; image of the, 142; imitators of the, 352–53; income of the, 55, 93, 94, 94*n*3, 103, 119, 141, 240, 242, 244–45, 363–64; as an inspiration for Ellington, 254, 420, 445; inspirations for the, 135; intensity of the, 222; lateness of

the, 327; as a legend, 216–17; memorization of pieces by the, 97, 99, 101, 104, 265, 483; and Mercer Ellington as bandleader, 382, 391, 391*n**, 418; musical aspirations of the, 135; Nanton on the, 465–68; of 1940, 421–39, 474–75; personnel changes in the, 22, 153, 171, 176–77, 182, 201–2, 205, 240, 263, 317, 327, 344, 352; and playing an individual's piece after he leaves, 502; problems of the, 224; pseudonyms for the, 29, 38–39, 38*n*5, 65, 104; and race relations, 221, 231–32, 245, 397, 490; recording sessions of the, 319–24; relationships among members of the, 97, 135, 145, 158, 160, 214, 219–20, 245, 327–32, 374, 460, 464, 465, 467, 480, 484; reminiscing about the, 230–31, 240, 245, 462–71, 472–76, 478–80, 482–86, 490; salaries of members of the, 93*n*3, 245, 363, 482; "secret" of the, 98–102; size of the, 97; spirit/tradition of the, 475; Stewart on the, 373–75, 478–80; Strayhorn on the, 270; strikes by members of the, 120; style of the, 62, 98–102, 302, 303–11, 463, 467, 483; theme songs of the, 88, 91, 125, 456; typical itinerary for the, 227–28; typical program/performance of the, 222–24, 329–30, 342–43; uniqueness of the, 61, 97, 98, 104, 145, 303–11, 352–53, 391, 391*n**, 421, 427, 438; working habits of members of the, 100. *See also* Ellington, Edward Kennedy "Duke"—**as a composer/arranger**, and collaboration with band members; Ellington, Edward Kennedy "Duke"—**as a composer/arranger**, and composing/ arranging for individual band members; Harlem Footwarmers; Harlem Music Masters; Jungle Band; *specific composition*
"Ellington Study Group" conferences, 342
Ellington Week (17–23 January 1943), 153, 180, 267
Ellis, Beatrice "Evie," 92
Ellison, Ralph, 385, 394–99
Emancipation Celebration (from *Black, Brown and Beige*), 178–79, 197, 203, 412
Endorsements, 75, 488
England: Ellington's reception in, 72–78, 94, 112, 113, 216, 243–44, 358–59; and the European tour (1933), 67, 72–79, 82, 94, 99–102, 104, 112, 113, 172, 243–44, 358–59; and the European tour (1963), 342–46; jazz in, 389*n***; race relations in, 237; restaurants in, 235; *Sacred Concert* performance in, 375; special radio broadcasts to, 273
Estrelita, 219, 230

Europe, 94, 133, 216, 234–35, 237, 244; audiences in, 155–56; Ellington on, 155–56; Ellington's reception in, 67, 72–78, 172, 216, 243–44; as an emotional restorative for Ellington, 243–44. *See also* Tours of the Ellington orchestra, Europe; *specific country*
Europe, James Reese, 20, 95, 153, 422
Evans, Gil, 297
Every Man Prays in His Own Language, 371, 372, 376, 378
Ev'ry Tub, 71–72, 72n3, 88
Exactly Like You, 410
Experimentation, 51, 63, 96, 97, 142, 303, 324, 349, 404, 466; and dance music, 60, 171, 172, 261. *See also* Ellington, Edward Kennedy "Duke" — **as a composer/arranger**, and collaboration with band members
Extended works: and the Carnegie Hall performances, 205; Crowley on, 180, 182–84; and dance music, 172, 173, 175, 176, 209, 210, 212, 352, 361; Ellington on, 116, 116n3, 159, 250, 361; and the Ellington–Strayhorn relationship, 501; in the fifties, 263; Giddins on, 380; Hammond on, 118–20; Harrison on, 387–94; Mills on, 275–76; Murray on, 413; Overstreet on, 104; Thiele on, 176; Whiteman as a pioneer in, 159; Wilder on, 258; Williams (Martin) on, 411–12. *See also specific composition*

Fantastic Rhythm (musical), 499
Fantasy Records, 376, 378, 379, 492–93
The Far East Suite, 317, 360n1, 379, 387, 393, 444
Fargo, North Dakota, 1940 performance in, 145n3
Feather, Leonard, 99, 155n1, 170, 171, 173–75, 176, 250, 263, 351, 359
Featuring Paul Gonsalves (album), 492–93
Ferguson, Otis, 141
Festival Session (album), 322
Fields, Dorothy, 29, 31
Fields, Herb, 31
Fields, Lew, 31
Film, Ellington on music in, 314. *See also specific film*
Fine and Mellow, 497
Finesse, 471
Finkelstein, Sidney, 353
Fitzgerald, Ella, 317, 367, 382, 458, 493
Flamingo, 182, 268, 268n2, 269, 500
The Flaming Sword, 150n5, 160, 406, 436, 456
Flaming Youth, 36, 109–10, 242

Flirtibird, 314
Folk music, 58, 172; and African-American life/music, 74, 80–81, 422; Ellington on, 44, 80–81, 218, 249; and jazz, 171, 177, 207, 207n1, 208, 218, 324–25; and rock 'n' roll, 324–25; and swing, 249
Fontainebleau, 390
Fontessa, 184
Foster, Pops, 478
Four Step Brothers, 125
France, 234–35, 384; Ellington's reception in, 94, 215, 243; race relations in, 237; tours in, 67, 81–87, 243, 244, 299, 326, 342. *See also* Paris, France
Frankie and Johnny, 250–52
Frazier, George, 138, 359
Frazier, Mal, 20
Freedman, Wulf, 382
Freeman, Bud, 456
Fulton Theater (New York City), 41, 256
Funeral March (Chopin), 34, 58

Gales, Larry, 381
Galli-Curci, Amelita, 43–44
Gammond, Peter, 214
Gangsters, 224, 241–42, 337, 478
Garland, Joe, 473
A Gathering in a Clearing, 343
Gensel, John, 381
George (King of England), 216, 243–44, 268, 490
Georgia Grind, 65
Gershwin, George: Bishop on, 349; Darrell on, 39, 40, 57, 58, 60, 62–63, 127; Ellington on, 44, 114–18, 250; Hughes on, 74; List on, 179; *Porgy and Bess* by, 114–18; *Rhapsody in Blue*, 44, 74, 115–16, 349; *Sam and Delilah*, 39, 40; Schillinger's influence on, 260n3; technique of, 261; Wilder on, 180, 261
Gershwin, Ira, 62
Giddins, Gary, 297, 375–78, 379–81, 421, 491–93
Giddybug Gallop, 406
Gilbert, Gama, 112–14
Gillespie, Dizzy, 322, 334, 370, 444
Gilman, Lawrence, 57, 57n1
The Girl I Left Behind Me, 196
Giuffre, Jimmy, 179, 184
Glaser, Joe, 363–64
Gleason, Ralph J., 180, 303n3
Glenn, Tyree, 205, 263, 336, 393
God Save the King, 243
Goffin, Robert, 94, 236
Goin' Home, 44
Goin' Up, 169, 211

The Golden Broom and the Golden Apple, 362

Golden Cress, 259

Gong, 381

Gonsalves, Paul: Avakian on, 291, 292; and *Black, Brown and Beige*, 192; characteristics/personality of, 331, 491–93; Clar on, 303; Crouch on, 441; Dance on, 492–93; Ellington on, 336, 491–92; and the European tour (1963), 345; funeral of, 382; Giddins on, 376, 377, 378, 381, 491–93; Hamilton compared with, 345; Harrison on, 315, 390; and Hodges's solos, 502; image of, 491; influence of, 493; influences on, 492, 495; joins the Ellington orchestra, 263; Jones (Quincy) on, 312; Lambert on, 345; and the Newport Jazz Festival (1956), 290, 291–92; Priestley and Cohen on, 192; recordings of, 492, 493; Webster compared with, 336; Welding on, 327, 329, 331; Williams (Martin) on, 412

Goodman, Benny: autobiography of, 165; as a bandleader, 138; Bigard on, 85; at Carnegie Hall, 153, 156, 156*n2*, 158, 247; and classical music, 135, 135*n2*; discography of, 102; Ellington on, 134, 135, 138–39; and the Ellington orchestra of 1940, 428, 429; and Ellington's funeral, 382; and Ellington Week, 267; and Hodges, 449–50; imitations of, 134, 177; and the Naumberg lecture-recital series, 135, 135*n2*; and the *Philadelphia Inquirer* Music Festival, 267; popularity of, 359; recordings of, 456; Stewart on, 479; and Webster, 425; and the William Morris Agency, 141; and Williams (Cootie), 145, 231, 432, 474

Gordon, Sam, 369, 463

I've Got Everything But You, 36, 65, 109–10, 456

Gould, Morton, 267

Goutelas Suite, 317, 379, 379*n1*

Grace Cathedral (San Francisco), 371–72

Graceful Awkwardness, 209

Grace Valse, 315

Grainger, Percy, 95, 103, 110, 112, 125*n3*, 131, 216

Grainger, Porter, 20, 60*n5*

Grand Terrace (Chicago), 458, 459

Grant, Henry, 5, 16, 18, 42, 54, 56, 95

Grayson, Milt, 327, 343, 344, 346

Great Performers at Philharmonic Hall series, 362

Great South Bay Jazz Festival, 500–501

Great South Bay Suite. See *Toot Suite*

Green, Abel, 21–22, 31–32, 167

Green, Charlie, 455, 470

Green, Freddie, 481

Greer, William Alexander "Sonny": biographical sketch of, 487, 488–89; and *Black, Brown and Beige*, 169, 173, 181, 182, 191, 196; and Blanton, 182; Boyer on, 219, 222, 223, 239–40, 241, 244, 245; characteristics/personality of, 98, 223, 339, 453, 479, 485, 486, 487; Crowley on, 181, 182; Darrell on, 39; "Detector" on, 79; as a drummer, 46*n1*, 486–87; early career of, 20–21, 487; and the early Ellington orchestras, 20, 21, 22, 24, 27, 38*n5*, 39*n6*, 48, 96, 239, 422, 428, 429, 438; Ellington on, 18, 19–20, 21, 48, 96, 97, 239–40, 254*n1*, 337, 339, 453, 486–87, 491; and Ellington's funeral, 382; and the European tour (1933), 76, 77, 79, 244, 490; fire destroys drums of, 241; Gushee on, 428, 429, 438; Guy on, 485; Hammond on, 173; Hardwick on, 464; Harrison on, 393; Hobson on, 97, 98; Hodeir on, 283; Hughes on, 71; influences on, 465, 487; intensity of, 222; interviewed by Balliett, 486–91; joins the Ellington orchestra, 486; leaves the Ellington orchestra, 263, 486, 487, 490; Levin on, 169; and the Mercer Ellington orchestra, 382; and the *Metronome* profiles, 453; Morgenstern on, 354; musical development of, 488–89; Nanton on, 465; nickname of, 245; Oakley on, 126; popularity of, 21, 54; Priestley and Cohen on, 191, 196; Prince of Wales/Duke of Windsor plays with, 67, 243–44, 268, 490; and rhythm, 48; role in orchestra of, 98, 487, 488; Simon on, 461; as a singer, 339, 487–88, 489; Snelson on, 54; and Sonny Greer's Memphis Men, 65, 104; Stewart on, 479

Grofe, Ferde, 103, 157, 272

Guitar Amour, 343, 345

Gushee, Lawrence, 91*n1*, 385, 421–39

Guy, Fred, 77, 283; biographical sketch of, 481; and Carney, 483; characteristics/personality of, 453, 481, 482; death of, 481; and the early Ellington orchestras, 24, 38*n5*, 39*n6*, 48, 422, 428; Ellington on, 48, 231, 254*n1*, 453, 484, 486; interviewed by McDonough, 481–86; joins the Ellington orchestra, 241, 482; leaves the Ellington orchestra, 481, 482; and Mills, 481, 484–85; musical development of, 485–86; recordings of, 485; and Waller, 482

Gypsy Sweetheart, 322

A Gypsy Without a Song, 407, 408

Hackett, Bobby, 140

Hall, Adelaide, 51, 339

Hall, Henry, 79

Hallett, Mal, 24, 25, 54, 337

Hamilton, Jimmy: Boyer on, 230; and the European tour (1963), 345; favorite instrument of, 245; Giddins on, 377; Gonsalves compared with, 345; Harrison on, 315, 390; joins the Ellington orchestra, 153; Lambert on, 345; leaves the Ellington orchestra, 317; McPhee on, 213; Priestley and Cohen on, 192; Thiele on, 177; Townsend on, 322; Ulanov on, 211; Welding on, 327, 328, 329, 330

Hammerstein, Oscar II, 101n1

Hammond, John Henry, Jr., 69, 319, 359; Archetti on, 121; characteristics/personality of, 137; Ellington on, 119, 132, 137–38, 174; and Ellington's 1933 European tour, 86, 87; and Ellington's self-image, 112; Feather on, 171, 171n1, 173–75; financial interests of, 173–74; "Is the Duke Deserting Jazz" article by, 170, 171–75; and jazz at Carnegie Hall, 153; musical to be produced by, 93, 98, 105; and social issues, 137, 137n3, 174; Thiele's comments about, 176; "The Tragedy of Duke Ellington" essay by, 118–20, 132; Trussell on, 171; Ulanov on, 209, 210

Hampton, Lionel, 284, 330–31

Handy, W. C. (William Christopher), 20, 40, 44–45

Happy Anatomy, 315

The Happy-Go-Lucky Local, 390, 394, 492

Happy Reunion, 312

Hard Way, 380–81

Hardwick, Otto "Toby": and *Black, Brown and Beige*, 182, 203; Boyer on, 239, 240, 245; characteristics/personality of, 20, 451–52, 479, 490; Crowley on, 182; "Detector" on, 79; early career of, 487; and the early Ellington orchestras, 18, 19, 21, 22, 24, 96, 239, 422, 425, 432, 437–38; Ellington on, 18, 19, 20, 96, 240, 254n1, 337; and the European tour (1933), 67, 77, 79, 83, 84; Green on, 22; Greer on, 490; Gushee on, 425, 432, 437–38; Hodeir on, 283; and Hodges, 450, 473; Hughes on, 70; interviewed by Cavanaugh, 462–65; leaves the Ellington orchestra, 176–77, 205, 254n1; and the *Metronome* profiles, 451–52; Morgenstern on, 353; nickname of, 245; Oakley on, 450; Panassié on, 83, 84; Priestley and Cohen on, 203; rejoins the Ellington orchestra, 67; reminiscing of, 240, 462–65; Simon

on, 461; Stewart on, 469, 479; Ulanov on, 212

Harlem (New York City), 70, 75, 98; Ellington on, 49, 87–89, 160, 170, 235, 257; Ellington's desire to go to, 20; and Ellington's titles, 87–89. *See also specific club*

Harlem, 263, 267, 394, 501

Harlem Air Shaft, 91, 187, 235, 306–7, 393, 408, 409, 411, 431

Harlem Footwarmers, 38–39, 38n5, 64–65, 104

Harlem Music Masters, 39, 39n6, 64–65

Harlem River Quiver, 31, 31n1, 31n2, 35

Harlem Speaks, 125, 254n2, 353

Harman, Carter, 263n1

Harmony in Harlem, 268

Harper, Leonard, 22, 22n1

Harrison, Jimmy, 469, 470, 471

Harrison, Max, 185, 313–15, 385, 387–94

Haughton, Chauncey, 92, 153, 160, 173, 196, 201

Haunted Nights, 65

Haupé, 315

Hawkins, Bob, 463

Hawkins, Coleman, 69, 71, 280, 435; and the blues, 337; Ellington on, 337, 364, 370; Ellington's recordings with, 317, 493; Ellington's similarity to, 442; imitations of, 337, 495; and Miley, 454; Stewart on, 470, 471; and Webster, 497

Hawkins, Erskine, 411

The Hawk Talks, 269

Haydn, Franz Joseph, 103, 417, 443

Hayes, Roland, 49, 58, 59, 64

Healy, Dan, 31, 271, 483

Heaven, 378, 382

Heliotrope Bouquet, 405

Henderson, Fletcher, 95, 141, 142, 178, 298, 353, 377, 478; Ellington on, 139, 363; as an influence on Ellington, 139, 402, 404; pre-eminence of, 24; and Procope, 470; and Stewart, 462, 470

Henderson, Horace, 462

Henderson, Stephen. *See* Beetle

Hentoff, Nat, 269n3, 302, 362–68, 400

Heritage, 381

Herman, Woody, 263, 363

Herman McCoy Choir, 373, 375

Hero to Zero, 314–15

Heyward, Dorothy, 114

Heywood, Eddie, Sr., 464

Hibbler, Albert, 181, 212, 219, 222, 278n*, 312

Hibbs, Leonard, 121, 122–25

Hi Fi Fo Fum, 313
High Life, 36
Hill, Teddy, 382
Hines, Earl, 38, 95, 267, 370, 381
Hip Chic/Hip Chick, 273, 407
Historically Speaking (album), 297–302
Hite, Les, 11*n*5
Hobson, Wilder, 93–98, 141–43, 153, 153*n*1
Hodeir, André, 276–88, 297–302, 425, 428
Hodes, Art, 173
Hodges, Johnny: Avakian on, 292; band of,
    473; and Bechet, 337, 370, 462, 472, 473–
    74; biographical sketch of, 472–73; Bishop
    on, 347, 349, 356; and *Black, Brown and
    Beige*, 155, 158, 166, 169, 173, 175,
    187*n**, 192, 194, 201, 203; Bowles on,
    166; Boyer on, 223, 226, 231, 237, 242;
    and Carney, 472–76; characteristics/
    personality of, 292, 360, 451, 452, 472,
    490; Clar on, 303; Crouch on, 441; death
    of, 317, 419; early career of, 472–73; and
    the early Ellington orchestras, 29, 39*n*6,
    48, 242, 422, 425, 428, 429, 431, 433,
    434; Ellington on, 48, 172, 226, 272, 337,
    360, 370, 419, 449; and Ellington's
    funeral, 382; and the Ellington–Strayhorn
    relationship, 160, 499; and European
    tours, 76, 77, 83, 84, 87, 344–45; fans of,
    223; Giddins on, 377, 378, 492, 496, 497;
    and Goodman, 449–50; Greer on, 490;
    Gushee on, 425, 428, 429, 431, 433, 434;
    Guy on, 483; Hammond on, 172, 173; and
    Hardwick, 450, 462; Harrison on, 313,
    314, 315; Hobson on, 142–43; Hodeir on,
    283; Hughes on, 70, 71; imitators of, 337,
    418; influence of, 473, 492, 496; influences
    on, 472; interviewed by DeMichael, 471–
    76; joins/rejoins the Ellington orchestra,
    29, 242, 263, 403, 471, 472, 473, 483;
    Jones (Quincy) on, 312; Lambert on, 344–
    45; leaves the Ellington orchestra, 263;
    Levin on, 169; McPhee on, 213; and the
    Mercer Ellington orchestra, 391*n**; and the
    Metronome profiles, 452; Morgenstern on,
    353; musical development of, 473–74; and
    the Newport Jazz Festival (1956), 292;
    nickname for, 245, 272; Oakley on, 126,
    155, 158, 449–51; Panassié on, 83, 84, 87;
    Priestley and Cohen on, 187*n**, 192, 194,
    201, 203; and race relations, 237;
    recordings of, 145*n*2; role in orchestra of,
    461; Schubart on, 213; Schuller on, 418,
    419; Stewart on, 175, 374, 375; and
    Tempo Music, 146*n*4; Tizol compared
    with, 231; Townsend on, 322; Ulanov on,
    211, 212; Welding on, 327, 328; Williams

(Martin) on, 401, 403, 406, 407, 410, 411;
    Williams (Ned) on, 272
Hoefer, George, 265
Holiday, Billie, 91, 177, 186–87, 495, 496,
    497
Holland, Eugene, 488–89
Holland/Netherlands, 67, 82, 234, 244
Holliday, Frank, 10, 13–14, 16
Hollywood Club (New York City). *See*
    Kentucky Club
Holmes, Charlie, 474
Holy Ghost, 381
Homage to Ellington in Concert (album),
    418*n*1
Home Again Blues, 39
Homzy, Andrew, 198*n*
Honeysuckle Rose, 211
Hop Head, 33, 241
Hopkins, Claude, 12, 14, 20, 489
Horne, Lena, 267
Hot and Bothered, 35–36, 41, 65, 95, 111,
    112–13, 128, 406
Hot Club of France, 81, 82, 471
Hot jazz/music, 94, 141, 237
Howard, Paul, 11*n*5
Howard Theater (Washington), 13, 14, 16,
    19, 239, 289, 451, 487, 489
How High the Moon, 494
Hughes, Langston, 117, 120, 146, 147, 397
Hughes, Patrick "Spike," 67, 69–75, 93, 112,
    118, 172, 389*n***
Hurricane Club (New York City), 205, 236,
    245, 460, 461
Husing, Ted, 266
Hy'a Sue, 260
Hyde Park. See *Ev'ry Tub*
Hylton, Jack, 67, 73, 75, 76, 80, 82, 87
Hymn of Sorrow, 116*n*3

I Can't Give You Anything But Love, 79
Idiom '59, 263
I Don't Know What Kind of Blues I've Got,
    305–6, 409
I Found a New Baby, 474
If You Can't Hold the Man You Love, 402
I Got It Bad, 269, 381, 411, 460
I Got Rhythm, 429, 497
I Know That You Know, 471
I Let a Song Go Out of My Heart, 211–12,
    268, 273, 341, 353, 411
I Love You, 26
Imagine My Frustration, 493
I'm a Good Gal, 58
*I'm a Little Blackbird Looking for a
    Bluebird*, 32*n*3
I'm Beginning to See the Light, 383, 411

I'm Coming, Virginia, 337
I'm Going to Get Even with You, 51
I'm Gonna Hang Around My Sugar, 402
Imitation, 335–39, 418. *See also specific person*
Immigration Blues, 3
Improvisation: Archetti on, 123; Bishop on, 357, 358; Boyer on, 218; as a characteristic of jazz, 177; disciplining of, 405; Dodge on, 105, 108, 109, 457; and the Elizabethan playwrights, 413; Ellington on, 325–26, 422; Giddins on, 492; Gushee on, 422, 429, 438; Harrison (Max) on, 315, 391, 393; Hobson on, 97, 142–43; Hodeir on, 277, 284; and Miley, 457; Murray on, 413; Oakley on, 450; Overstreet on, 98, 99–102; and the repertory movement, 418, 419; Schubart on, 213; Schuller on, 418, 419, 420; Thiele on, 176–78; Williams (Martin) on, 404, 405. *See also* Soloists; *specific composition*
Impulse Records, 493
I'm So in Love with You, 45, 60
I Must Have That Man, 79
In a Jam, 353
In a Mellotone, 298, 300, 307–8, 354, 433
In a Sentimental Mood, 126, 128, 143, 211–12, 233, 341, 411
Income: of Ellington, 245, 340, 364; of the Ellington orchestra, 55, 93, 94, 94n3, 103, 119, 141, 240, 242, 244–45, 363–64; from radio broadcasts, 103; from recordings, 244, 341, 364; and salaries of members of the Ellington orchestra, 93n3, 245, 363, 482
India tour (1963), 80n1, 317
The Indispensable Duke Ellington (album), 354
I Need You to Drive My Blues Away, 58
I Never Felt This Way Before, 437
Instruments, 75, 443–44; Ellington expands conventional ranges of, 100–101
International Duke Ellington Conference (1991), 198n
In the Beginning God, 375, 377, 501
In the Shade of the Old Apple Tree, 67
Irvis, Charlie, 24, 239, 335, 463, 465
Is God a Three-Letter Word for Love?, 378
"It don't mean a thing," Miley as the first to use the expression, 371
It Don't Mean a Thing If It Ain't Got That Swing: arrangements of, 475; Clar on, 307, 308, 309; Darrell on, 65, 128; Davis on, 143; and Ellington's "best" compositions, 103; and the European tour (1933), 79;

Hobson on, 95; Hodges on, 475; Morgenstern on, 353; Overstreet on, 103; and the popularity of swing, 159; recordings of, 65, 459; as a regular feature in Ellington shows, 125; as a title, 89; Williams (Martin) on, 406, 408n*
It's a Glory, 83, 96, 287
It's All True (Welles–Ellington film project), 149–50, 149n4
It's Freedom, 378
I've Got the World on a String, 79
I've Just Seen Her, 493
Ives, Charles, 401
I Want a Man Like That, 77, 459
I Want To Be a Rug Cutter, 460
I Was Made to Love You, 37

Jackson, Cliff, 463
Jackson, Edgar, 121, 121n1
Jackson, Mahalia, 181, 185, 320, 443–44
Jackson, Milt, 185
Jackson, Quentin "Butter," 181, 205, 300, 301, 336, 343
Jackson, Rudy, 25
Jack the Bear (person), 369, 426, 463
Jack the Bear (piece), 91, 212, 259, 269, 297, 309, 415, 426
James, Burnett, 125n3
James, Danny, 168
James, Harry, 140, 363
Jam Session (film), 487
Jam with Sam, 344, 345
Japan tour (1964), 317, 360
Jazz: as American music, 134–35, 236, 254, 257; as an art form, 165, 210, 350; as a concert form, 176, 209–10; and dance music, 176, 208, 352; as dangerous to American youth, 128–29; definition of, 248, 334, 383; development of, 177, 255, 257, 297, 389; Ellington as the "first genuine composer" of, 72, 73; and Ellington as the "King of Jazz," 54–56; Ellington on, 41, 43, 45, 49, 87–88, 132–35, 145, 159, 207–9, 218, 255, 256–57, 293–96, 324–26, 332–38, 361, 363, 383, 419, 422; emotional vocabulary of, 207–8, 209; etymology of, 93; in Europe, 94, 133, 216, 389n**; and folk music, 171, 177, 207, 207n1, 208, 218, 324–25; functions of, 352; future of, 324–26; growth of popularity of, 133–34, 238; and lyrics, 181; and musicianship, 134; polarities in, 424; progressive theory of, 350; and rock 'n' roll, 324–25; as serious music, 87–88; subsidization of, 324; and swing, 132–35, 159, 248–50; and syncopation, 52, 170,

Jazz: as American music (*continued*) 179; terms for, 332–33; validation of, 110. *See also* Categorization of music; Classical music; Symphonic jazz

Jazz at the Philharmonic, 496

Jazz Convulsions, 37

Jazz Festival Jazz, 312

Jazz Festival Suite. See Toot Suite

Jazz Lips, 37

Jazz musicians, 183–84, 216, 236, 240, 260, 420

Jazz Party (album), 322

Jazz repertory, 418–21, 440

The Jeep Is Jumping, 411

Jeep's Blues, 474

Jeffries, Herb, 171, 201–2, 266, 305, 306, 437

Jejo, Carmelita, 478

Jenkins, Freddy, 70, 347; characteristics/ personality of, 452; and the early Ellington orchestras, 29, 39n6, 48; Ellington on, 48, 272; and the European tour (1933), 77, 82–83, 84; joins the Ellington orchestra, 466; leaves the Ellington orchestra, 468; and Miley, 458, 468; Nanton on, 466, 467–68; nickname for, 272, 452, 467–68; popularity of, 468; role in orchestra of, 97

Jig Walk, 259, 259n2, 479

Jitterbug, 467

Jive Stomp, 71–72, 72n3, 88

Joe Turner's Memphis Men, 65, 104

Johnny Come Lately, 155, 410, 498

Johnson, Axel, 102, 121

Johnson, Budd, 495

Johnson, Fred, 82, 82n1, 86–87

Johnson, Howard, 382

Johnson, James P., 18–19, 19n10, 21, 60, 235–36, 239, 370, 422, 463, 487

Johnson, J. Rosamond, 20, 488

Johnson, Lyndon B., 384, 395

Johnson, Percy "Brushes," 18–19

Jolly Wog, 37

Jolson, Al, 271

Jones, Bill, 14

Jones, Jimmy, 322

Jones, Jo, 290, 291–92, 382

Jones, Jonah, 382

Jones, Nat, 177n2

Jones, Quincy, 311–14

Jones, Richard Bowden "Jonesy," 214, 224, 231, 272, 479, 480

Jones, Rufus, 381

Jones, Shrimp, 489

Jones, Spike, 437

Jones, Wallace, 92n2, 219–20, 283, 422

Joplin, Scott, 405, 422

Jordan, Taft, 211, 212

Joseph, "One Leg" Willie, 463

Jubilee Stomp, 34, 61, 241, 456

Juilliard School of Music, 253, 255

Jump for Joy (revue), 91, 146, 149, 149n4, 198n, 266, 383; run of, 148

Jumpin' Punkins, 173, 487

The Jungle Band, 29, 37, 38, 39, 40, 64, 104

Jungle music, 55, 73, 240–41, 304, 396, 404, 479

Jungle Nights in Harlem, 39, 60, 65, 404

Juniflip, 312

Just a Closer Walk, 382

Just A-Settin' and A-Rockin', 342, 492

Kay, Brad, 118n1

Keeler, Ruby, 271, 484

Keep a Song in Your Soul, 39–40

Kemp, Hal, 139

Kennedy, Alice (grandmother), 3, 5

Kennedy, James William (grandfather), 3, 5

Kennedy, John (uncle), 10

Kenton, Stan, 303, 393, 444

Kentucky Club (New York City): Ellington debuts at the, 96, 240, 482; and Ellington's popularity, 3, 26–27, 56, 172; fire destroys the, 26, 241, 473; Greer on the, 487; Guy on the, 482–83; Hodges on the, 473; Mills first sees Ellington at the, 45, 274; Nanton on the, 466; radio broadcasts from the, 240; reminiscing about the, 240–41, 463, 466, 473, 482–83, 487; reviews about Ellington at the, 21–28

Kern, Jerome, 16n9, 58, 71, 101n1

Kerr, Brooks, 11n6, 382

Kicking the Gong Around, 96

Kinda Dukish, 342–43, 346

King, Martin Luther, Jr., 367

King of Spades, 71–72, 72n3

King of the Tenors (album), 497

King of the Zulus, 457, 458

Kirby, John, 158

Knauer, Wolfram, 186

Koehler, Ted, 29, 89, 272

Ko-Ko: Bowles on, 166; and the Carnegie Hall debut program (1943), 160; Clar on, 302n2, 309; and the Ellington orchestra of 1940, 426–27; Gushee on, 426–27; Hammond on, 173; Harrison on, 393–94; Hodeir on, 277, 280, 288, 297, 298–301; Jones (Quincy) on, 311, 313; Levin on, 169; as a masterpiece, 91; Priestley and Cohen on, 186, 193, 200; recordings of, 297–302, 299n*, 313; Schuller on, 419; Ulanov on, 427; Williams (Martin) on, 402, 408–9, 411

Kolodin, Irving, 158, 165, 167, 170
Krupa, Gene, 456
Kuller, Sid, 266

Ladnier, Tommy, 470
Lady of the Lavender Mist, 259
Lafayette Theater (New York City), 455,
    464, 474, 483
Lambert, Constant, 110–11, 112–14, 119,
    172, 388
Lambert, Donald, 370
Lambert, Eddie, 342–46, 392n**
Lang, Eddie, 60, 456, 485
Larkin, R. L., 144–45
Lasker, Steven, 451
The Latin American Suite, 317, 379, 380,
    444
Latin America tour (1968), 317, 326, 382–83
La Virgen de la Macarena, 343
Lawrence, Marjorie, 267
Lay-By, 441
Layton, Turner, Jr., 368, 370
Lazy Rhapsody, 67, 70, 71, 95, 408n*
Leave It to Jane (musical), 16n9
Lederman, Minna, 130
Lee, Roscoe, 12, 14, 15
Lenox Avenue Shuffle, 456
Le Sacre du Printemps (Stravinsky). See *Rite
    of Spring*
Levesque, Jacques-Henri, 215
Levin, Mike, 165, 166–70, 174, 180
Lewis, Bert, 23
Lewis, John, 179, 184, 185, 394
Lewis, Ted, 85n3, 102
Lewis, Willie, 469
Liberian Suite, 205, 288, 393
Light (from *Black, Brown and Beige*), 193,
    195, 201
The Lighter Attitude (from *Black, Brown and
    Beige*), 195, 211
Lightnin', 79, 96, 103
Like a Ship in the Night, 145n2, 499
L'il Farina, 403
Limehouse Blues, 40, 65, 71, 79, 96–97, 104
Lincoln Center (New York City), 362, 385n1,
    439–45
Lincoln Gardens (Chicago), 477
Lincoln Theatre (Philadelphia), 455
List, Kurt, 178–79
Live sessions, vs. recordings, 84
Locke, Alain, 60n4
Loeffler, Charles Martin, 51, 57, 57n1
Logan, Arthur, 266, 317, 323, 365
Lombardo, Guy, 54, 94, 132, 139, 370
Lopez, Vincent, 25, 26, 55, 370
The Lord's Prayer, 377, 378

Los Angeles Philharmonic Orchestra, 157
Lost In Meditation, 411
Lotus Blossom, 382, 503
Louisiana, 36, 65
Love Is Like a Cigarette, 460
Low Cotton, 471
Low Key Lightly, 315
Lucas, Marie, 19, 489
Lunceford, Jimmie, 139, 144, 283, 301n*,
    398, 425
Lush Life, 410
Lyman, Abe, 54, 459
Lyrics, 60, 74, 181

Mabie, Janet, 41, 42–44, 112
McCarthy, Albert, 362
McDonough, John, 481–86
MacDowell, Edward, 57n1
McEntree, Edgar, 11–12
Macero, Teo, 382
McHugh, Jimmy, 29, 31, 48, 241, 242, 483
Mack, Richard, 114, 117–18
Mack, Sticky, 14, 15, 16
McKinney's Cotton Pickers, 470
McLuhan, Marshall, 379–80n2, 380
McPhee, Colin, 130, 209–10, 213
Madden, Owney, 29
Madness in Great Ones, 343, 393
Mad Scene from Woolworth's (Hughes and
    Leonard), 146
Main Stem, 91, 345, 400–401
The Majesty of God, 376–78, 444
Mallard, Sax, 177n2
Malraux, André, 412, 413
Mamoulian, Rouben, 117
The Man I Love, 62–63
Manning, Willie, 254, 255
Maori, 37
Margie, 301n*
Marion, Percy, 382
Marrow, Esther, 377
Marsalis, Wynton, 440
Martin, Sara, 335n1
Mason, Daniel Gregory, 207n2
Mauve. See *The Blues*
Me and You, 428
Meditation, 11, 11n6
The Melody Maker Concert, 78, 78n3, 99–
    102
Mercer Ellington orchestra, 382, 391, 391n*,
    418
Mercer Records, 263
Merry-Go-Round. See *King of Spades*
Metcalf, Louis, 466
Metropolitan Opera House (New York City),
    267

Mexico tour (1968), 317

Mezzrow, Mezz, 85–86, 299

Middle East tour (1963), 80*n1*, 317, 360

Midnight Indigo, 315

Miley, James "Bubber": as an influence, 466; biographical profile of, 454–55; Boyer on, 216, 230–31, 233, 240; Carney on, 475; characteristics/personality of, 216, 240, 455, 457, 458, 462–63, 464–65, 467, 468; death of, 110, 216, 354, 454, 455; Dodge on, 105, 108–10, 447, 454–58; and the early Ellington orchestras, 24, 27; Ellington on, 109–10, 172, 230–31, 233, 240, 337, 368, 370–71, 387, 405, 455–56, 457; as the first to use the expression "It don't mean a thing if it ain't got that swing," 371; Green on, 22; and Greer, 465; Hammond on, 172; Hardwick on, 462–63, 464–65; Harrison on, 387; imitations of, 335, 419; influence of, 465, 467, 475; and Jenkins, 468; joins the Ellington orchestra, 240, 454; leaves the Ellington orchestra, 354; as a legend, 216; and the Mileage Makers, 455, 456; Morgenstern on, 354; musical development of, 454–55; and Nanton, 465, 467, 468; in Paris, 454–55; Priestley and Cohen on, 190; recordings of, 456, 456*n4*, 457, 458, 465*n1*; reminiscing about, 462–63, 464–65, 467, 468, 475, 479; role in orchestra of, 240; Schuller on, 405, 419; Stewart on, 479; transcribed solos of, 106–7; trumpet style analyzed, 105–10; Williams (Cootie) compared with, 336; Williams (Martin) on, 402, 403, 404, 406. See also *Black and Tan Fantasy*

Miley, Josie, 335*n1*

Milhaud, Darius, 216, 228, 399

Miller, Bill, 17, 18, 19

Miller, Brother, 18, 19

Miller, Felix, 18, 19

Miller, Glenn, 260*n3*

Miller, Max, 76, 76*n1*

Miller, Paul Eduard, 458–60

Mills, Florence, 20, 31, 32, 32*n3*, 131, 155, 158, 173, 383

Mills, Irving: accomplishments of, 140, 142, 273, 274; and Calloway, 96; characteristics/personality of, 82, 140; and the Cotton Club engagement, 100; and the *Down Beat* Silver Jubilee issue, 269, 269*n3*, 273–76; Ellington compares Hammond to, 174; and Ellington as a composer/arranger, 97, 98; and Ellington, Inc., 141; Ellington on, 140, 273, 274–76; and Ellington's image, 54; Ellington's parting from, 92, 140–41, 273–74, 485;

and the enlargement of the Ellington orchestra, 45, 96, 274; and the European tour (1933), 76, 82, 243; as exploiting Ellington, 118–20; first sees Ellington at the Kentucky Club, 45, 274; functions of, 24; Guy on, 481, 484–85; Hammond on, 118–20; Hobson on, 93, 96, 142; and Miley, 455; Oakley works for, 125; and publications/recordings of Ellington, 141; as road manager, 241; Williams (Ned) as an employee of, 270; Zunser on, 45

Mills Blue Rhythm Band, 453

Mills Ten Blackberries, 29

Mingus, Charles, 179, 184, 317, 324, 364, 366, 366*n2*, 394, 442, 493

Minnie the Moocher, 88*n1*, 96, 140, 459

Minuet in Blue, 480

Misfit Blues, 441

Missourians, 473, 478

Mr. Gentle and Mr. Cool, 312, 502

Mr. J. B. Blues, 436

Misty Morning, 347, 411

Mittler, William, 245

Mobile Blues, 408

Modern Jazz Quartet, 184–85, 394

Mole, Miff, 483

Mondello, Toots, 449–50, 452

Monk, Thelonious, 297, 364, 391, 435, 436, 496

Monologue, 267

Monterey Jazz Festival, 379, 439–40, 441–42

Montoliu, Tete, 497

The Mooche, 45, 71, 103, 128, 307, 309; and celebrities' favorite Ellington recordings, 269; and the Cotton Club performances, 242; and the European audiences, 67; recordings of, 35–36, 41, 65, 424; as a regular feature in Ellington shows, 126; as a title, 88

Mood Ellington (album), 259

Mood Indigo: BBC broadcast of, 103; and the *Black, Brown and Beige* premiere, 169; and celebrities' favorite Ellington recordings, 269; Clar on, 304; Copland on, 130; and the Cotton Club performances, 242; Darrell on, 38–39, 61, 63, 65, 128; Davis on, 143; as an Ellington legacy, 383; Ellington on, 230, 339–40; and the Ellington orchestra of 1940, 430, 437; and Ellington's "best" compositions, 103; and Ellington's funeral, 381; and the European tour (1933), 67, 77, 79, 84; Gushee on, 430, 437; Hobson on, 96; Hughes on, 71; and the influence of classical music on Ellington, 246–47; Lambert on, 111, 113; Levin on, 169; lyrics for, 340; Mabie on,

43; and the Mercer Ellington orchestra, 391*n**; Morgenstern on, 353; and the New York Philharmonic Symphonic Society concert, 103; Overstreet on, 103, 104; Panassié on, 84; recordings of, 38–39, 41, 65, 96, 104, 113; Schuller on, 417; Stewart on, 480; story line of, 230; as a title, 89; as a type of composition, 61; Ulanov on, 211–12; Williams (Martin) on, 406, 407, 411; Williams (Ned) on, 271; Zunser on, 45

Moonglow, 279, 287, 408, 408*n**
Moon Mist, 160, 211, 213, 408
Moon Over Cuba, 150*n*5
Moon River, 328
Moore, Monette, 20, 335*n*1
Morgen, Joe, 323
Morgenstern, Dan, 350–54
Morning Glory, 427
Morrow, Edward, 114–18
Morton, Benny, 178
Morton, Jelly Roll, 40, 387, 422, 443, 444, 453, 478
Moten, Bennie, 495
Mozart, Wolfgang Amadeus, 63, 135, 282
Mullens, Eddie, 327, 330
Mulligan, Gerry, 312
Multicolored Blue, 312
Murder at the Vanities (film), 91, 266
Murder in the Cathedral, 379, 379*n*1
Murray, Albert, 385, 385*n*1, 412–14, 440, 443
Murray, David, 492
Murray, Don, 85, 85*n*3
Music: definition of, 207*n*1, 208; Ellington on, 44, 45, 87–88, 218, 232–36, 248–50, 294–95, 326, 333–38, 371; Schuller on, 415. *See also type of music*
Musical Spillers, 469
Musicians: African Americans as, 184, 207, 208, 209, 237, 398–99, 423–24, 425, 464, 480; audience's relationship to, 359–60; as critics, 137; and critics' role/function, 136–37; Ellington on, 136–37, 359–60; jazz, 183–84, 216, 236, 240, 260, 420; jealousy among, 477–78; management of, 370; personal feelings of, 414; popular views of, 359–60; reaction to *Black, Brown and Beige* by, 167; strikes by, 92, 120, 181
Music Is My Mistress (Ellington autobiography): biographical sketch in, 5–21; copyrighted compositions in, 379; and Dance (Stanley), 332; Ellington on, 114; Ellington's views about Jo Jones in, 290; as the "Good Book," 114; and the Newport Jazz Festival (1956), 290; and the

Palladium performance, 75; philosophical statements in, 371–72; profiles of musicians in, 368; tributes in, 317
Musicraft Records, 205, 341
My Buddy, 382, 487–88
My Gal Is Good for Nothing But Love, 37
My Heart Sings, 181
My Man, 497
My Old Flame, 126, 460
My People, 146, 195, 317, 366–67, 377, 383, 486
The Mystery Song, 37*n*4, 61, 61*n**, 63, 65, 71, 96, 128, 406, 415

Nance, Ray: arrangements for, 145; and *Black, Brown and Beige*, 173, 181, 191–92, 196; Carney on, 475; characteristics/personality of, 330, 490, 502; Clar on, 303, 309; Crowley on, 181; and Ellington's funeral, 382; Ellington's relationship with, 226, 272; and the European tour (1963), 342, 343, 344; Giddins on, 377; Greer on, 490; Hammond on, 173; Harrison on, 314, 315; Hodges on, 475; influences on, 475; joins the Ellington orchestra, 145, 145*n*3; Jones (Quincy) on, 312; Lambert on, 342, 343, 344; McPhee on, 213; Nanton on, 467; nickname for, 490; Priestley and Cohen on, 191–92, 196; Schubart on, 213; Schuller on, 419; Ulanov on, 211, 212; Welding on, 327, 329, 330; Williams (Martin) on, 401, 410; Williams (Ned) on, 272
Nanton, Joseph "Tricky Sam": Bell (Archie) on, 51; and *Black and Tan Fantasy*, 108, 108*n*2, 109; and *Black, Brown and Beige*, 166, 169, 172, 181, 190, 191, 196, 197; Bowles on, 166; Boyer on, 223–24, 226, 227, 229, 242, 245; characteristics/personality of, 84–85, 223, 453, 465–68, 490; Clar on, 303; Crowley on, 181; death of, 205; "Detector" on, 79; Dodge on, 456; and the early Ellington orchestras, 38*n*5, 39*n*6, 48, 242, 422, 426, 427, 430, 431, 436, 437; and Ellington as a genius, 215; Ellington on, 48, 172, 226, 227, 229, 336, 337; and the European tour (1933), 77, 79, 83, 84–85; Glenn compared with, 336; Greer on, 490; Gushee on, 426, 427, 430, 431, 436, 437; Hammond on, 172; Hardwick on, 465; Hobson on, 142–43; Hodeir on, 283, 300, 301; Hughes on, 70; imitations of, 335; influences on, 466; interviewed by Cavanaugh, 465–68; joins the Ellington orchestra, 242, 465–66; Levin on, 169; and the *Metronome* profiles, 453;

Nanton, Joseph "Tricky Sam" (*continued*)
and Miley, 465; Morgenstern on, 353;
nickname for, 453; Panassié on, 83, 84–85;
Priestley and Cohen on, 190, 191, 196,
197; reminiscing by, 245, 465–68;
Schubart on, 213; Schuller on, 417;
Stewart on, 479; style of, 466–67; on
trombone playing, 466–67; Ulanov on,
211, 212; and Williams (Cootie), 465;
Williams (Martin) on, 401, 403, 405–6,
407, 408–9, 410, 411; Williams (Ned) on,
271
Naughty Man, 402
Naumberg, Walter W., 134–35, 135n2
NBC, 29, 55
NBC Symphony Orchestra, 267
Negro. *See* African-American history;
African-American life/music; African
Americans
Nemo, Henry, 272–73, 341
Nest Club (New York City), 470, 478
Never No Lament, 408, 409, 429
New England, tours in, 3, 24, 26–28, 337–
38, 466, 471, 472–73, 483
Newman, Ernest, 172
"New Negro," 59–60, 60n4
New Orleans jazz, 95, 176, 208, 337, 403,
443. *See also specific person*
New Orleans Low Down, 34, 36, 61, 65
New Orleans Rhythm Kings, 85n3
New Orleans Suite, 393
Newport Jazz Festival (1956), 263, 290–92,
390, 425, 491
New World A-Comin', 209, 210–11, 213,
219, 245, 377
New World Symphony (Dvořák), 44, 458
New York City Blues, 260
New York Philharmonic Orchestra, 57n1,
362
New York Philharmonic Symphonic Society
concert, 103
Nicholas, Albert, 476, 477, 478
Nichols, Red, 34, 35, 39, 40, 41n1, 62
Night Creature, 263, 325
Niles, Edward Abbé, 40–41, 72
Nine Little Miles from Ten-Ten-Tennessee,
39, 61
Nixon, Richard M., 384, 394, 395
Nocturne, 155, 160
Noone, Jimmie, 85, 299, 476
*Norman Granz Jam Sessions/The Charlie
Parker Sides* (album), 497
Norvo, Red, 134, 140, 169

Oakley (Dance), Helen M., 119n4, 125–27,
138, 155–58, 359, 449–51
O'Connor, Norman, 376, 381

O'Doy, Daniel, 469
OKeh Records, 34, 35–36, 38–39, 41, 64–
65, 85n2, 104
Old Man Blues, 37n4, 45, 61, 67, 79, 128,
353, 406; and Ellington's favorite records,
268; inspiration for composing, 335;
recordings of, 39, 41, 65, 268
Old Man River, 101, 101n1
Oliver, Joe "King," 36, 216, 402, 403, 404,
452, 454, 477, 478
Oliver, Sy, 298, 382
Olsen, George, 25
On a Turquoise Cloud, 259
One More Time, 345
One O'Clock Jump, 211
Onward Christian Soldiers, 382
Opera, 43–44, 114–17. *See also Boola*
Oriental Theater (Chicago), 55, 271, 459
Original Dixieland Jazz Band, 95
Ory, Kid, 11n5, 480
Ottley, Roi, 210
Our Father, 382
Overstreet, H. A., 98–102

Pablo Records, 379n1, 435, 493
Palace Theater (New York City), 255n3, 265,
484
Palestrina, 109
Palladium (London), 67, 75–78, 99, 159,
216, 243, 266, 290, 490
Panama, 436
Panassié, Hugues, 81–87, 138, 178, 236,
359, 471
Paramount Theater (New York City), 55, 455
Paris, France, 81–87, 289–90, 299, 311,
454–55, 471
Paris Blues, 329, 492
Parish, Mitchell "Mike," 340
Parker, Charlie, 277, 297, 299, 337, 364,
426, 442, 496, 497
Parlor Social Stomp, 34, 34n2, 36, 60, 65,
89
Passion Flower, 305, 307, 498
Patrick, James, 421
Patriotism, 146–48, 150, 157, 157n4, 170,
199, 201–2, 384
Payne, Bennie, 39n7
Perdido, 343, 344, 345, 444
Perfect Records, 35, 65, 456
Perfume Suite, 205, 214, 501
Perry, Oliver "Doc," 5, 14–15, 16, 18, 42,
239
Peters, Brock, 377, 381–82
Peterson, Oscar, 368
Petite, Buddy, 477
Petkere, Bernice, 23
Peyton, Dave, 24, 477

Philadelphia Inquirer Music Festival, 267
Philadelphia Orchestra, 57*n1*, 268
Philharmonic Auditorium (Los Angeles), 267
Phillips, Flip, 497
Piano Improvisations Part IV, 200*n*
Piano/pianists: and composing/arranging, 254; Ellington on, 46–48, 370; Hardwick on, 463; ragtime, 14–16, 403; Willie "The Lion" Smith as an influence on, 463. *See also* Ellington, Edward Kennedy "Duke" — **as a pianist**
Piazza, Tom, 442, 442*n2*
Pickett, Jesse, 369
Pithecanthropus Erectus, 394
Pitter Panther Patter, 435
Pittman, John, 148–51
Pocock, Gerry, 381
Poor Butterfly, 322
Popular music, 44, 45, 49, 61–62, 64, 103–4
Porgy and Bess (Gershwin), 79, 114–18
A Portrait of Bert Williams, 430–31
A Portrait of the Lion, 353, 407
Powell, Mel, 184
Praise God, 378
Praise God and Dance, 378
Preer, Andy, 483
Prelude to a Kiss, 307, 411
Presser, Theodore, 255
Prestige Records, 155*n1*, 185, 191, 191*n4*
Pretty and the Wolf, 342–43
Previn, André, 303, 406
Priestley, Brian, 153, 185–204
Prima Bara Dubla, 312
Prince of Wales, 52, 67, 243–44, 268, 490
Procope, Russell: Carney on, 475; characteristics/personality of, 360; Crouch on, 441; Ellington on, 360; and the European tour (1963), 342, 345–46; Giddins on, 376, 378; Harrison on, 314; and the Henderson band, 470; influences on, 475; joins the Ellington orchestra, 205; Lambert on, 342, 345–46; and the Mercer Ellington orchestra, 382; Stewart on, 470; Townsend on, 322; Welding on, 327, 328, 329–30
Progressive Gavotte, 259–60
Pulitzer Prize, 362–63, 395, 398
Puttin' on the Ritz, 456
Pyramid, 344, 345, 444

The Queen's Suite, 379*n1*, 412, 493

Race pride: and African-American music, 59–60*n3*, 73–74, 112, 113–14; and *Black, Brown and Beige*, 156; and composition, 44; Ellington on, 49, 73, 112, 113–14, 135, 146–48, 160, 199, 271, 366–67; and Ellington's education, 10; and Ellington's popularity, 55; and patriotism, 146–48, 199
Race relations, 70, 74, 174, 396–97, 398; and African-American life/music, 149–50, 184; and African-American musicians, 237, 422–23, 464, 480; and Carnegie Hall performances, 182; Ellington on, 10, 41, 43, 120, 147–48, 149–50, 218, 232, 294, 295–96, 366–67; and the Ellington orchestra, 221, 231–32, 245, 397, 490; in Europe, 237, 244; Greer on, 490; Guy on, 482; Hardwick on, 464; in New York City, 118–19; and patriotism, 147–48; in the South, 480, 482; and tours, 221, 231–32, 245
Radio broadcasters–ASCAP dispute, 92
Radio broadcasts, 70, 71, 423, 438; and censorship, 92, 273; and the classical music–jazz debate, 247; from the Club Zanzibar, 205, 255*n3*; from the Cotton Club, 29, 42, 78, 78*n1*, 96, 266, 273, 339; and Cullen's interview of Ellington, 338–41; dedicated to Roosevelt (FDR), 363; of *East St. Louis Toodle-O*, 395; Ellington on, 361; and Ellington's popularity, 55, 56, 94, 96, 142; from and to England, 78–79, 273; and the European tour (1933), 67, 75, 78–79; from the Hurricane Club, 205; income from, 103; from the Kentucky Club, 22, 240
Raglin, Junior, 173, 177, 197, 212, 219, 223, 227, 245
Ragtime, 200, 200*n*. *See also* Piano/pianists
Ragtime pianists, 14–16, 403
Rain Check, 91, 410
Rainy Nights, 402, 465*n1*
Ramsey, Frederic, Jr., 105, 141
Rappolo, Leon, 236
Ravel, Maurice, 38, 40, 111, 112–13, 131, 211, 246, 268–69, 417
Ray, Arthur, 456, 456*n4*
RCA Victor Records. *See* Victor Records
Ready, Go, 492
Recording industry, Gushee on the, 424
Recordings, 61*n**, 65, 261, 275, 384, 403, 440; availability of, 424–25; ban on, 92, 92*n3*, 205; celebrities' favorites of Ellington, 269; from the Cotton Club, 29; and Ellington as an a&r man, 353; Ellington on, 320, 323, 341, 361; Ellington's control over, 364, 438; and Ellington's popularity, 24, 27; importance of, 100; income from, 244, 341, 364; from the Kentucky Club, 29; live sessions vs.,

Recordings (*continued*)
84; and the Mills–Ellington parting, 141;
and the preservation of works, 424;
quantity of, 29, 158, 423; sales of, 102–3,
215, 244; and the "secret" of the Ellington
orchestra, 99; Smithsonian Collection
reissues of, 421; takes on, 320;
unsuccessful, 104. *See also specific
recording or record company*
Recording sessions, 319–24, 340, 373–75, 475
Red Hot Band, 35, 485
Redman, Don, 95, 102, 139, 298, 402, 404
Reflections in Ellington (album), 118*n*1
Rehearsals, 22, 98–100, 105, 303; for the
Black, Brown and Beige premiere, 168, 169,
201–2; and composing/arranging, 97, 149;
Ellington's dress for, 238; and the practice-
vs.-theory debate in jazz, 237; time of, 97
Reinhardt, Django, 13, 471
Reisenweber's (New York City), 465
Reisman, Leo, 455, 456, 456*n*4, 464
Religion: and Daisy Ellington (mother), 6, 8;
and Ellington, 8–9, 217, 225, 237, 244,
254, 294–95, 317, 384, 397. See also
Come Sunday; *Sacred Concerts*
Reminiscing in Tempo: analyzed by Bishop,
349, 355–58, 389; Archetti's defense of,
121–25; and the *Black, Brown and Beige*
premiere, 156, 169, 171; Chase on, 180,
180–81*n*1; Crowley on, 180; Darrell on,
128; and Ellington's favorite records, 268;
as an extended work, 91, 118, 387;
Hammond on, 118–20, 121, 171; Harrison
on, 387, 388–90, 391, 392, 393; Hughes
on, 118; inspirations for, 244; Jackson on,
121–22; Levin on, 169; Mills on, 275; and
mother's death, 244; Oakley on, 156;
recordings of, 119, 121, 268, 389; Schuller
on, 355, 419; Williams (Martin) on, 411
Rent parties, 89, 235, 238–39, 487
Rent Party Blues, 60, 89
Reprise Records, 364
Rhapsody in Blue, 44, 73, 74, 115–16, 349
Rhythm, 62, 63, 290, 307; Ellington on, 46–
48, 49–50; and swing, 249; of trains, 227
Rhythm Boys, 339
Rich, Buddy, 382
Rimsky-Korsakov, Nicolai, 39, 63, 127, 247,
501
Ring Dem Bells, 45, 98, 211, 401; and
celebrities' favorite Ellington recordings,
269; in *Check and Double Check* (film),
265; and the Cotton Club performances,
242; and the European tour (1933), 77;
recordings of, 37–38, 39, 41
Rinker, Al, 339

Rite of Spring (Stravinsky), 38, 63, 125*n*3,
129, 417
The River (ballet), 317
The River and Me, 39–40
Roach, Max, 317, 493
Robbins, Jack, 92, 141*n*2
Roberts, Luckey, 16, 370, 473, 487
Robertson, Dick, 39
Robeson, Paul, 43, 49, 58, 59, 70, 95
Robinson, Bill "Bojangles," 20, 155, 158,
173, 430
Robinson, Clarence, 21
Robinson, Prince, 470, 478
Roché, Betty, 153, 169, 175, 177, 198, 211,
219
Rochester, Joe, 15, 20
Rockin' Chair, 456
Rockin' in Rhythm: and the *Black, Brown
and Beige* premiere, 166, 172- 73; Bowles
on, 166; Darrell on, 39, 61, 65, 128; and
the European tour (1933), 67, 77;
Hammond on, 172–73; Lambert on, 342–
44; McPhee on, 213; recordings of, 39, 65;
as a regular feature in Ellington shows,
125; Stewart on, 480; Ulanov on, 212
Rock 'n' roll, 324–25
Rocky Mountain Blues, 38
Rodgers and Hart, 71, 289
Roger Wolfe Kahn Orchestra, 24
Roosevelt, Franklin Delano, 185, 363
Rose, Billy, 105, 455
Rose of the Rio Grande, 165, 173
Rose Room, 65, 77, 79, 96–97, 433
Ross, Allie, 20, 455
Rude Interlude, 103, 119, 128, 443
Rumpus in Richmond, 409, 432
Runnin' Wild, 38, 65
Rushing, Jimmy, 322
Russell, George, 394
Russell, Johnny, 382
Russell, Luis, 141, 471, 474, 478
Russell, Pee Wee, 85
Russell, William, 141
Rust, Brian, 57, 187, 456*n*4

Sacred Concerts: and *Black, Brown and
Beige*, 195; Crouch on, 444; and Dance's
eulogy, 384; Ellington on, 375, 376;
Ellington's program note for, 371–72; First
(1965), 185–86, 192, 317, 371–72, 373–
75, 376–78, 381, 501; Giddins evaluation
of, 375–78; Gushee on, 425; Harrison on,
392; Second (1968), 317, 375, 376–78,
382; Stewart attends record session for,
373–75; Third (1973), 317, 371, 375–78,
383, 444

Saddest Tale, 128

Sad Night in Harlem, 126

St. John the Divine, Cathedral of (New York City), 375, 377, 381

St. Louis Blues, 44–45, 71, 95, 102, 104, 126, 455, 464

St. Matthew Passion (Bach), 288

Salle Pleyel (Paris), 81–87, 289–90

Sam and Delilah, 39, 40, 104

Sanders, John, 181, 343, 381

Saparo, Henri, 472

Saratoga Swing, 480

Sargeant, Winthrop, 207–9, 207n1, 207n2, 246, 362

Satin Doll, 263, 381, 383, 420, 425

Saturday Night Function, 36, 60, 89, 235, 480

Savoy Ballroom (New York City), 472, 473, 478

Savoy Strut, 145n2, 499

Schillinger, Joseph, 260, 260n3

Schoenberg, Arnold, 286, 288, 298, 417

Scholl, Warren W., 102–5

Schubart, Mark, 210, 213–14, 252–53

Schubert, Franz, 63

Schuller, Gunther: and the blues, 443; "The Case for Ellington's Music as Living Repertory" by, 418–21; and *Creole Rhapsody*, 347; "Early Duke" by, 302; on Ellington as orchestrator, 403; "Ellington in the Pantheon" by, 414–17; on extended works, 385, 385n1, 387; Hodeir's influence on, 276; on Miley, 405, 454; recordings by, 418n1; on *Reminiscing in Tempo*, 121, 335; and the Smithsonian Collection of Recordings, 421; *The Swing Era* by, 121, 414

Schwiphti, 441

Scotland tour, 80–81

Scott, Raymond, 231

Sears, Al, 447, 493; interviewed by Simon, 460–61

Second Sacred Concert (album), 376

Selassie, Haile, 384

Seldes, Gilbert, 38, 94

Selmer instruments, 75

Send Me, 88

Senegal, 289

Sentimental Lady, 212, 213

Sepia Panorama, 259, 408, 433, 439

Serenaders, Duke Ellington's, 3, 23

Serenade to Sweden, 174

The Sergeant Was Shy, 91, 254n2, 353, 407, 485

Sewell, Willie "Egg Head," 463

Shakespeare, William, 413. See also *Such Sweet Thunder*

Shapiro, Nat, 269n3, 362

Sharp, Stanley, 484–85

Shaw, Artie, 139, 267

Shaw, Mack, 337

Shearing, George, 184–85

The Sheik of Araby, 96–97, 104, 142

Shepard, Ernie, 346

The Shepherd, 378

Sherman Shuffle, 408

Shout 'Em, Aunt Tillie, 242, 405

Show Boat (musical), 101, 101n1

Showboat Medley, 101n1

Showboat Shuffle, 268, 357

Show Girl (Ziegfeld show), 56, 94, 266

Shribman, Charles, 26, 27, 337

Sibelius, Jean, 63, 115, 122, 170

Sidewalks of New York, 437–38

Siesta, 72, 72n4

Silk Lace, 345

Silver, Horace, 380

Silverman, Sime, 274

Silver Slipper (New York City), 31, 271

Simeon, Omer, 476, 477, 478

Simmons, Alberta, 463

Simon, George T., 460–61

Sinatra, Frank, 263

Singleton, Zutty, 455, 458

The Siren's Song, 16, 16n9

Sirocco, 72, 72n4

Sissle, Noble, 454–55

Sissle and Blake, 20

Sister Kate, 458

The Skrontch, 273

Skyliner, 431

Slack, Freddy, 480

Slap Happy, 407, 411

Slappin' the Bass, 434

The Sleeping Lady and the Giant Who Watches Over Her, 444

A Slip of the Lip, 92

Slippery Horn, 71–72, 72n3, 103

Smalls' Paradise (New York City), 20, 240, 397, 466, 469

Smalls' Sugar Cane Club (New York City), 478

Smith, Bessie, 20

Smith, Charles Edward, 105, 141

Smith, Jabbo, 108n2, 109, 456

Smith, Joe, 20, 178, 220, 470, 487

Smith, Leroy, 20

Smith, Mamie, 11n5, 20, 454, 459, 465

Smith, Roland, 22

Smith, William Overton "Bill," 184

Smith, Willie "The Lion," 21, 98, 353, 368–69, 370, 378, 394, 463
Smith, Wonderful, 266
Smithsonian Institution, 101*n1*, 149*n4*, 418, 420*n3*
Snelson, Floyd G., 54–56
Snowden, Elmer, 19, 20, 21, 22, 172, 239, 464, 470, 478, 482, 487
Socé, Ousmane, 289–90
Social issues, 116–17, 157, 294–96. See also *Black, Brown and Beige*, social significance of; Civil rights; Race relations
Soda Fountain Rag, 11, 11*n7*, 239
Solid Rock, 471
Soliloquy, 33–34
Solitude, 124, 128, 143, 156, 211–12, 353; and celebrities' favorite Ellington recordings, 269; as an Ellington legacy, 383; Ellington on, 233, 340; and Ellington's funeral, 381, 382; and the influence of classical music on Ellington, 246–47; as a regular feature in Ellington shows, 125
Soloists: Avakian on, 292; Darrell on, 61, 62; Dodge on, 457; and the Ellington–Strayhorn relationship, 502–3; Gushee on, 438; Hobson on, 97; Hodeir on, 277, 281–82, 284–86; and the Newport Jazz Festival (1956), 292; and the orchestra, 281–82; Panassié on, 83–84; Schuller on, 419, 420; Williams (Martin) on, 401, 404–5. *See also specific person or composition*
Some of These Days, 67, 77, 126
Something About Believing, 378
Something Else!!!!, 311
Something to Live For, 145*n2*, 268, 268*n2*, 410
Song of the Cotton Field, 34, 60, 60*n5*, 65
Songs for Distingué Lovers (album), 497
Song titles, 87–89, 273, 321, 393
Sonnet for Caesar, 393
Sonny Greer's Memphis Men, 65, 104
Sophisticated Lady: and African-American life/music, 325; and celebrities' favorite Ellington recordings, 269; Clar on, 308; and the Cotton Club performances, 242; Darrell on, 128; Davis on, 143; as an Ellington legacy, 383; Ellington on, 325, 340; and the Ellington orchestra of 1940, 435; and Ellington's "best" compositions, 103; and the European tour (1933), 79; Gushee on, 435; Hughes on, 71; Morgenstern on, 353; Oakley on, 156; Overstreet on, 103; as a regular feature in Ellington shows, 125; Schuller on, 420; as a title, 89; Ulanov on, 211–12; Williams (Martin) on, 411, 412

Soulville (album), 497
South: race relations in the, 480, 482; tours in the, 367, 482
Soviet Union tour (1971), 317
Spaeth, Sigmund, 324
Spirituals, 59
"Spirituals to Swing" concerts (1938, 1939), 153
Stack O'Lee Blues, 85*n2*
Star-Crossed Lovers, 345
Stardust, 211, 249, 431
Stark, Bobby, 466
Stark, Herman, 483
Stearns, Jean, 88*n2*
Stearns, Marshall, 88*n2*, 138, 359
Steinbeck, John, 411–12, 439–40, 441
Stephens, Bob, 341
Stepping into Swing Society, 391*n**
Stevedore Stomp, 61
Stewart, Rex: on Bigard, 476–81; Bishop on, 357, 358; and *Black, Brown and Beige*, 160, 165, 166, 169, 173, 175, 192, 193, 196, 197; Bowles on, 166; Boyer on, 219–20, 223, 226, 232, 244, 245; characteristics/personality of, 223, 452, 468; Clar on, 303; and the Ellington orchestra of 1940, 422, 427–28, 430–31, 432, 436; and Ellington's compositional methods, 160; Ellington's relationship with, 226; and the European tours, 244, 471; Gushee on, 427–28, 430–31, 432, 436; Hammond on, 173, 175; and Henderson, 462, 470; Hobson on, 142–43; Hodeir on, 277, 283; and the image of the Ellington orchestra, 142; imitation of, 418; influences on, 470; interviewed by Cavanaugh, 468–71; and the *Jig Walk* recording, 259*n2*; joins the Ellington orchestra, 91, 471; leaves the Ellington orchestra, 176–77, 205; Levin on, 169; and the *Metronome* profiles, 452; nickname of, 245; Oakley on, 126–27; Priestley and Cohen on, 192, 193, 196, 197; and race relations, 232, 244; recordings of, 142, 470, 471; on *Sacred Concert* record sessions, 373–75; Schuller on, 418; self-criticism of, 220; Thiele on, 177; Ulanov on, 211, 212; on Webster, 495; Williams (Martin) on, 400–401, 410; writings of, 92*n2*, 373–75, 476–81
Still, William Grant, 103, 267
Stingaree, 470
The Stockholm Concert 1966 (album), 493
Stokowski, Leopold, 216, 228, 268, 399
Stompy Jones, 197, 480
Stormy Weather, 77, 89, 272, 309, 419
Strauss, Johann, 113, 114

Strauss, Richard, 63, 127
Stravinsky, Igor, 58, 111, 298, 417; Ellington
  compared with, 38, 40, 63, 112–14, 169,
  246; Ellington on, 113–14, 160; and
  Ellington as one of the greatest modern
  composers, 216, 228, 399; as an influence
  on Ellington, 124–25, 125n3; and music as
  a cause of crime, 129; as a source for
  comparing Ellington's work, 131
Strayhorn, William (Billy): and *Black,
  Brown and Beige*, 155, 158, 173, 175;
  Boyer on, 214, 220–21, 224–25, 229, 230;
  characteristics/personality of, 498; Clar on,
  305, 309; Crouch on, 441, 444; death of,
  91, 317, 503; and the *Down Beat* Silver
  Jubilee issue, 265, 269–70, 269n3; and the
  Duke Ellington Piano Method for Blues,
  250; on Ellington, 269–70, 365, 366, 367;
  and the Ellington orchestra of 1940, 437;
  and Ellington's favorite pieces, 268n2; and
  the Ellington–Strayhorn relationship, 91,
  145, 220–21, 224–25, 229, 269–70, 305,
  309, 321, 360, 365, 370, 410, 441–42,
  444, 498–503; and the *Esquire* jazz
  awards, 267; eulogy for, 503; and the
  European tour (1939), 499; Gushee on,
  437; Hammond on, 173; influences on,
  500; interviewed by Coss, 498–503; on
  "jazz" (term), 370; joins the Ellington
  orchestra, 91, 145n2, 410, 498–99; Jones
  (Quincy) on, 312; musical development of,
  498–99; nickname for, 220; Oakley on,
  155; as a pianist, 370, 500; on "pretty"
  (term), 369; Schubart on, 213; Schuller on,
  419; and Tempo Music, 146n4; thesis of,
  148; Ulanov on, 211; Wilder on, 259;
  Williams (Martin) on, 410; on Willie "The
  Lion" Smith, 368
"Stride" piano, 403, 463. *See also* Piano/
  pianists; Ragtime; Ragtime pianists
Study/training, 184, 307; Ellington on, 14–
  15, 42, 53, 56, 73, 208–9, 253–54, 255,
  256, 257, 296, 324, 361; and Ellington's
  youth, 14–16, 18–19; and the ragtime
  pianists, 14
Sublett, John "Bubbles," 116
Subtle Lament, 353, 407, 408, 409, 415
Such Sweet Thunder, 263, 313–14, 321, 343,
  352, 387, 393, 412, 439–42
Sugar Hill Penthouse (from *Black, Brown
  and Beige*), 178–79, 199, 199n, 201
Suite Thursday, 352, 411–12, 439–42
Summertime, 212
Sunswept Sunday, 315
Swampy River, 60, 67, 243, 268
Swanee Rhapsody, 103, 128
Swanee River, 197, 431

Sweatman, Wilbur C., 20, 21, 43, 95–96
Sweden, 244, 266, 384, 493
Sweet and Lovely, 434
Sweet and Low (revue), 105, 454, 455
Sweet Chariot, 38–39
Sweet Dreams of Love, 65
Sweet Jazz O' Mine, 65
Sweet Mama, 37, 85n2
Sweet Thursday (Steinbeck novel), 342, 440,
  441
Swing: and African-American life/music, 145;
  Bigard on, 81, 86; commercialization of,
  132; Count Basie orchestra as greatest
  exponent of, 139; as dance music, 88;
  definition of, 87, 89, 248–49; Ellington on,
  87, 89, 132–35, 359, 360; and folk music,
  249; future of, 249–50; Gushee on the,
  423; and jazz, 132–35, 159, 248–50; and
  musicianship, 134; and rhythm, 249; and
  sex crimes, 128–29, 360
Swing Low, Sweet Chariot, 191
Symphonic jazz, 111, 159, 248–50, 263. *See
  also* Classical music; Extended works
Symphony Hall (Boston), 158, 178, 185
Symphony in Black (film), 91, 116n3, 186–
  87, 187n*
Symphony of the Air, 325
Syncopation, 52, 170, 179, 307

Take It Easy, 34, 35, 41, 61, 63, 85, 85n2,
  128
Take the "A" Train, 91, 210, 211, 213, 269,
  312, 410, 492–93, 498
Tang, 381
Tate, Erskine, 477
The Tattooed Bride, 203, 205, 390, 391,
  392–93
Tatum, Art, 98, 178, 368, 370
Taubman, Howard, 155, 158–60
Taylor, Bill, 126, 382, 453
Taylor, Cecil, 324, 364–65, 380
Taylor, Deems, 267
Tchaikovsky, Peter I., 170, 317, 393–94
Tea for Two, 211
Teagarden, Jack, 140, 178
The Telecasters, 441
Tell Me the Truth, 381
Tempo Music, 141n2, 146n4, 185, 365
Tenderly, 328, 497
Tenor Giants (album), 497
Terry, Clark, 311, 312, 315, 344, 367–68,
  419
Teschemacher, Frank, 85–86
Texas Blues Destroyers, 456
Theater, versus dance jobs, 52–53
Theory, music, 53, 150–51, 237. *See also*
  Study/training

Thiele, Bob, 170, 175–78
Things Ain't What They Used To Be, 210, 212, 308, 345, 378
Thomas, Foots, 473
Thomas, John Charles, 267
Thomas, Louis, 14, 15, 16, 17, 43, 56, 95, 239
Thomson, Virgil, 130
Thornton, Caroline, 15
Three-Cent Stomp, 259
Three Dances, 178–79
Three Little Words, 37–38, 61, 77, 96–97, 104, 265, 273, 339
Tiger Rag, 45, 71, 77, 118n1, 129, 406, 436
Timon of Athens, 379, 379n1
Tizol, Juan: biographical sketch of, 451; and *Black, Brown and Beige*, 173, 191; Boyer on, 219–20, 226, 227, 231, 242; characteristics/personality of, 453, 485; and composing/arranging, 226, 227; and *Conga Brava*, 150n5; as copyist, 100, 101n1, 374n2; Crouch on, 444; and the early Ellington orchestras, 19, 29, 39n6, 48, 242, 422, 425, 427, 436; Ellington on, 48, 150n5, 160, 231, 444; and the European tour (1933), 77; Gushee on, 425, 427, 436; Guy on, 485; Hammond on, 173; Hodeir on, 283; Hodges compared with, 231; joins/rejoins the Ellington orchestra, 242, 263, 467; leaves the Ellington orchestra, 153, 205; and the *Metronome* profiles, 451, 453; Mingus's attack on, 366; Morgenstern on, 353; Nanton on, 467; Priestley and Cohen on, 191; recordings of, 150n5; role in orchestra of, 100, 101n1; Stewart on, 374n2; as a trombonist, 231; Williams (Martin) on, 407, 408–9, 410
Toledano, Ralph de, 93n2, 105
A Tone Parallel. See Black, Brown and Beige
Toot Suite, 263, 321, 322, 500–501
Tours of the Ellington orchestra: Africa, 380; Bermuda, 360, 382; and Ellington's popularity, 55; Europe (1933), 8, 67–87, 94, 99–102, 112, 113, 155, 172, 237, 243–44, 266, 358–59, 490; Europe (1939), 132, 140–41, 155, 215, 244, 266, 499; Europe (1950), 263, 299; Europe (1958), 263, 342, 343; Europe (1959), 263; Europe (1963), 342–46, 361; France, 67, 81–87, 243, 244, 299, 326, 342; India (1963), 80n1, 317; Japan (1964), 317, 360; Latin America (1968), 317, 326, 382–83; Mexico (1968), 317; Middle East (1963), 317, 360; Midwest (1962), 326–32; New England, 3, 24–25, 26–28, 337–38, 466, 471, 472–73, 483; and race

relations, 221, 231–32; Scotland, 80–81; in the South, 118, 367, 482; Soviet Union (1971), 317; and working habits of band members, 100
Townsend, Irving, 137n3, 319–24, 441
Training of musicians. *See* Study/training
Transblucency, 407, 443
Transcription, 105–10, 250–52, 302–11, 418
Trees, 67
Trent, Jo, 259n2
Trocadero Theatre (London), 78n3, 99
Troubled Waters, 460
True, 381
Truman, Harry S, 267–68, 384
Trumbauer, Frankie, 40
Trumpet in Spades, 160, 165, 212, 277
Trussell, Jake, Jr., 171, 176
T.T. on Toast, 273
Tucker, Earl "Snake Hips," 95, 455
Tucker, Mark, 200n
Tunstall, Freddie, 463
Turner, Joe, 104, 266
Turney, Norris, 380
Twelfth Street Rag, 39, 65, 104, 231
The Twenty-Third Psalm, 444

Ulanov, Barry: and the *Black and Tan Fantasy*, 396; and *Black, Brown and Beige*, 180, 186, 187, 195, 199, 200, 201–2; as editor of *Metronome*, 99; Ellington collaboration with, 271; on Ellington's second Carnegie Hall performance, 209, 210–12; and *Ko-Ko* as an excerpt from *Boola*, 427; and the Mills–Ellington parting, 140; on the Williams (Ned)–Ellington relationship, 270
Upper and Outest, 315
Uwis Suite, 379n1

Vallee, Rudy, 54, 55, 93–94
Van Norman, Horace, 121–22
Van Vechten, Carl, 94
Variety Records, 125, 449
Vaudeville, 52–53, 75, 76
Venuti, Joe, 40, 60, 456
Verve Records, 493, 497
Victor Records: Darrell's favorites of Ellington's works for, 64–65; and Ellington's popularity, 55; Ellington's relationship with, 104, 205, 423, 438; Gushee on the, 421–39; as a major recording studio for Ellington, 29, 43; Race Series of, 35, 37; and record sales, 103. *See also specific composition or album*
Vocalion Records, 24, 27, 32n4, 34, 35, 65, 457

Vocalists. *See specific person*
Vocal music, 60, 104–5. *See also specific vocalist*
Vodery, Will, 422

Wagner, Richard, 45, 63, 247, 393
Walker, George, 32
Walker, T-Bone, 125
Waller, Thomas "Fats": Ellington on, 370; and Ellington's early years in New York City, 21, 23–24; and Greer, 19, 487, 489; and Guy, 482; Hardwick on, 463, 464; Hodeir on, 297; influence on Ellington of, 200*n*; influences on, 463; as a pianist, 370; Taubman on, 158
Wang Wang Blues, 19, 21, 23–24, 39, 158, 200*n*
Ward, Aida, 31–32
Waring, Fred, 35, 54, 139
Warm Valley, 269, 273, 408, 411, 419, 434, 501, 502
Warren, Earle, 382
Washingtonians: Darrell on the, 58–65; early New York reviews of the, 21–28; and Ellington's musical development, 172; formation of the, 96; New England tour of the, 24–28; Niles on the, 41; organization of the, 56, 96; personnel of the, 21–22, 27; recordings of the, 24, 27; twentieth anniversary of the, 160. *See also* Cotton Club; Kentucky Club
Washington Wabble, 35
Waters, Ethel, 20, 51, 70, 272, 396
Watkins, Tony, 378
Way Early Subtone, 314
Way Low, 198
The Way You Look Tonight, 495
Weaver, Jim, 171
Webb, Chick, 472, 473, 478
Webster, Ben: and African-American life/music, 496; and *Black, Brown and Beige*, 173, 196, 198, 200, 201, 203; characteristics/personality of, 490; Clar on, 303; as a composer/arranger, 496; Crouch on, 447, 493–97; Crowley on, 182; death of, 496; Ellington on, 336, 370; and the Ellington orchestra of 1940, 422, 425, 427–28, 429, 432, 433, 437; Giddins on, 376, 492; Gonsalves compared with, 336; Greer on, 490; Gushee on, 425, 427–28, 429, 432, 433, 437; Hammond on, 173; Hodeir on, 283; Hodges on, 475; influence of, 492, 493, 495; influences on, 493, 495, 496; joins/rejoins the Ellington orchestra, 91, 171, 494, 495; leaves the Ellington orchestra, 205, 460; musical development

of, 494–95; nicknames for, 490; as a pianist, 370; Priestley and Cohen on, 196, 198, 200, 201, 203; recordings of, 497; as a saxophonist, 494–97; Stewart on, 495; Trussell on, 171; Williams (Martin) on, 401, 410
Webster, Paul Francis, 266
Weill, Kurt, 267
Wein, George, 291
Welburn, Ronald G., 33
Welding, Pete, 326–32
Welles, Orson, 149–50, 149*n4*
Wells, Dickie, 115, 115*n2*
Wells, Gertie, 12, 15
West, Mae, 266
West End Blues, 36, 250
West Indian Dance/Influence (from *Black, Brown and Beige*), 156, 178–79, 195, 196, 197, 209, 211
Westminster Abbey (London), 375, 383
Whaley, Tom, 153, 312, 374, 374*n2*, 420
What Can a Poor Fellow Do?, 34, 65
What Color Is Virtue?, 367
What Good Am I Without You?, 39
What Is This Thing Called Love?, 456
What You Gonna Do When the Bed Breaks Down?, 12, 12*n8*, 18
When a Black Man's Blue, 39
When You're Smiling, 37, 273
Where Has My Easy Rider Gone?, 115–16
Whetsol, Arthur, 70, 271, 349, 358, 406; and *Black, Brown and Beige*, 181; characteristics/personality of, 452; death of, 354; early career of, 487; and the early Ellington orchestras, 19, 21, 29, 38*n5*, 39*n6*, 48, 96, 239; Ellington on, 48, 96, 230, 233; and the European tour (1933), 77, 79; Hardwick on, 464; joins/rejoins the Ellington orchestra, 29, 466; leaves the Ellington orchestra, 29, 240, 463; and the *Metronome* profiles, 452; Nanton on, 466, 467; Stewart on, 469
The Whispering Tiger. See Tiger Rag
White, Harry "Father," 467, 489
White, Paul, 266
Whiteman, Paul, 40, 58–59, 62, 69, 95, 183, 459; *Blue Belles of Harlem* commissioned by, 157, 158; at Carnegie Hall, 157, 158; and commercialization, 139; Ellington on, 132, 139, 159, 370; Ellington's impact on, 26, 27, 272, 463, 483; and Ellington Week, 267; and extended works, 159; on Greer, 27; imitators of, 339; popularity of, 55, 259; and symphonic jazz, 103, 159; tours of, 25, 102, 337
The Whoopee Makers, 29, 40

Who Struck John?, 267

Wilder, Alec, 180, 258–61

Wilkins, Barron. *See* Barron's

Wilkins, Ernie, 297, 297*n1*

Willard, Patricia, 149*n4*

William Morris Agency, 92, 141, 170, 245, 485

Williams, Bert, 20, 32, 88*n2*, 131, 155, 158, 173, 430–31

Williams, Charles "Cootie": Armstrong compared with, 344; Bishop on, 347; and *Black, Brown and Beige*, 175; Carney on, 475; characteristics/personality of, 83, 85, 452, 490; Clar on, 303; Crowley on, 182; Davis on, 145; and the early Ellington orchestras, 29, 39*n6*, 48, 242, 422, 426, 428, 429, 431, 432, 433; Eldridge compared with, 344; Ellington on, 48, 145, 231, 272, 336, 373–74; and European tours, 77, 81, 83, 84, 85, 86, 342, 344; Giddins on, 376, 377, 378; and the Goodman band, 145, 231, 432, 474; Greer on, 490; Gushee on, 426, 428, 429, 431, 432, 433; Hardwick on, 465; Hobson on, 142–43; Hodeir on, 283*n2*; Hodges on, 474; Hughes on, 70, 71; influences on, 467, 475; interviewed/described by Panassié, 81, 83–85; joins/rejoins the Ellington orchestra, 242, 317, 342, 344, 352; Lambert on, 342, 344; leaves the Ellington orchestra, 171, 176–77, 352, 474; and the Mercer Ellington orchestra, 382; and the *Metronome* profiles, 452; Miley compared with, 336; Morgenstern on, 352, 353; and Nanton, 465, 467; nickname for, 272; Oakley on, 126; *Old Man River* recording of, 101*n1*; Schuller on, 417, 419; Stewart on, 373–74; Thiele on, 177; Trussell on, 171; Williams (Martin) on, 405, 406, 407–8, 409, 410, 411; Williams (Ned) on, 272. *See also* *Concerto for Cootie*

Williams, Clarence, 20, 40, 473

Williams, Corky, 463

Williams, Joe, 381

Williams, Martin, 276, 302, 385, 385*n1*, 400–412, 421

Williams, Mary Lou, 211, 381

Williams, Ned, 269, 269*n3*, 270–73, 359

Williams, Skippy, 211, 212, 460

Williams, Spencer, 20, 200*n*

Willow Weep for Me, 322

Will You Be There?, 317

Wilson, Derby, 67

Wilson, Edith, 20, 32, 58*n2*

Wilson, Lena, 58, 58*n2*

Wilson, Meredith, 157

Wilson, Teddy, 291, 450, 495, 500

Winter Garden (New York City), 21, 26

Wives and Lovers, 493

Wodehouse, P. G., 16*n9*

Wood, Booty, 336

Woode, Jimmy, 292, 312

Wooding, Russell, 16

Wooding, Sam, 82*n1*, 259*n2*

Woodman, Britt, 263, 343

Woodyard, Sam: Avakian on, 292; and *Black, Brown and Beige*, 182; characteristics/personality of, 328, 331; Crowley on, 182; and the European tour (1963), 343, 346; Giddins on, 492; Jones (Quincy) on, 312; Lambert on, 343, 346; and the Newport Jazz Festival (1956), 292; Welding on, 327, 328, 329, 331; writing ambitions of, 331

Work Song (from *Black, Brown and Beige*), 178–79, 186, 187, 188–89, 191, 193, 200, 201, 203

World Festival of Negro Arts (1966), 289

The World Is Waiting for the Sunrise, 479

Wright, Bishop, 381

Wyton, Alec, 382

Yankee Doodle, 197

Yaryan, John S., 372

Yellow Dog Blues, 109–10, 456, 457

Youmans, Vincent, 71, 211

Young, Lester, 337, 495, 496, 497

Young, Trummy, 301*n**

Your Socks Don't Match, 249

Your Time Now, 200*n*

Ziegfeld, Florenz, 20, 56, 94, 266, 484–85

Zunser, Florence, 44–46

Zweet Zursday, 441